THE HISTORIAN'S GUIDE

TO

LOUDOUN COUNTY, VIRGINIA

VOLUME I

COLONIAL LAWS OF VIRGINIA

AND COUNTY COURT ORDERS,

1757-1766

JOHN T. PHILLIPS, II

First Edition

Direct inquiries and comments to:

Colonial Laws Project
Goose Creek Productions
P. O. Box # 776
Leesburg, VA 20178 -0776

Cover page illustration, a rendition of the first Loudoun County Courthouse built in Leesburg circa 1759, by Caroline Phelps Phillips.

This work is dedicated to the Memory of

Commander William Henry Phillips

and the thousands of other Sons and Daughters

of Loudoun County

who devoted their lives

to the service of our Nation

and the pursuit of knowledge.

From all the facts assembled

arises a certain grandeur.

Aristotle

CONTENTS

Appendices

Maps and Illustrations

Title page and dust jacket art:
Pen and ink of the first Loudoun County Courthouse in Leesburg, circa November 1760, by Caroline Phelps Phillips, Virginia Beach.

Detail art work on the various maps:
Pen and ink, by Wade C. Snyder, Chicago.

Foreword

The central motivation for this work is the premise that we, as a community, cannot truly appreciate where we are going until we understand where we have been. The history of European settlement in our country is a relatively short one: for Loudoun County, Virginia, dating from the early eighteenth century and spanning barely three centuries. It is, therefore, somewhat surprising how little we understand today of our colonial past.

In this book, I attempt to revive a decade of colonial Virginia, 1757-1766, when day-to-day living was carried on in a very different manner than today. Colonials spoke, acted, and often thought quite differently from the way modern Virginians do. Colonial Loudoun County was suffused with a sense of community, genial sociability, a love of outdoor life, generous and open-handed hospitality, a taste for speculation, and a habit of civility. Perhaps, with a clearer understanding of those who came before us, we can better appreciate what we are all about today.

Several years ago I began a study of my Phillips ancestor who had served in Virginia's Ninth Continental Line during the American Revolution. As it happens, Elijah Phillips grew up in Loudoun County. In trying to put my ancestor's life into the perspective of his own time, I quickly realized that there was a large void where I was searching for background information on the colonial history of Loudoun County. How did Loudoun's colonial residents go about their business? Previous experience in old court records led me directly to the Loudoun County Court Order Books, which fortunately contain one of the finest sets of preserved colonial records in the Commonwealth of Virginia.

The study of my family was instructive in several respects. During the 1757-1766 decade, there were at least ten different Phillips family groups in Loudoun County. Their migrations into and through Loudoun reflected the larger migration patterns of the colonial population. Some of the families moved west up the Potomac and Occoquan rivers from their plantations in the tidewater, bringing with them nearly a century of heritage and connections in Richmond and Accomac counties. One family migrated into Loudoun from the Shenandoah during the French and Indian Wars; others moved across the Potomac river from

Maryland, or came down the Carolina Road from the Welsh and Quaker settlements in the Pennsylvania and Delaware colonies.

Several worthy books have been written about Virginia's colonial history, Loudoun's early years, and the colonial period on the Potomac. I encourage the reader to spend time with the following: *Colonial Virginia*, by Richard Morton; *A Hornbook of Virginia History*, edited by Emily J. Salmon; *The Potomac*, by Frederick Gutheim; *The Fairfax Proprietary*, by Josiah Look Dickinson; *Virginia 1705-1786; Democracy or Aristocracy?* by Robert and B. Katherine Brown; *Landmarks of Old Prince William*, by Fairfax Harrison; *Fairfax County, Virginia: A History*, by Nan Netherton, and others; *Legends of Loudoun*, by Harrison Williams; *Cameron Parish in Colonial Virginia*, by Margaret Lail Hopkins; and *From Frontier to Suburbia*, by Prof. Charles Preston Poland, Jr. Loyalty to legend and precedent, while an endearing human quality, too often limits our rational inquiry into the most entertaining events and circumstances of our existence. I have chosen, with trepidation and only after extensive research, to disagree with most of the foregoing authorities on one occasion or another. Regardless, these writers and their works, collectively, provide a good starting point for anyone who is studying the origin of early European settlement in northern Virginia.

My book is actually two books in one: both a review of the development of colonial laws and a record of county court Orders. Virginia's laws both shaped and reflected the colonial experience. Colonial Burgesses discussed their thoughts, aspirations, and politics, and confronted their prejudices, in their laws. Colonial attorneys noted their exasperation at the difficulty of trying to determine which laws were in effect, and when. This was due to long delays in communications with British Kings, who frequently rejected colonial statutes. Accordingly, the first section in each chapter presents topical reviews of colonial laws in combination with a running discourse on the context of various local events. I hope that in this way, the long, dense legal fog will lift a little.

The second section of each chapter contains an original set of abstracts of the Orders of the colonial Loudoun County Court. These records are supplemented with historical and genealogical information identified in colonial correspondence, wills, deeds, marriage records, Clerk's fee books, and other period resources.

Before the creation of Stafford County in the 1660s, there were no white settlements in what we now know as Loudoun County. Archival county records for the European experience in Loudoun, from 1662 to 1757, are located as follows:

1662 - 1731 Stafford County, Stafford, Virginia
1731 - 1742 Prince William County, Manassas Courthouse
1742 - 1757 Fairfax County, Fairfax Courthouse

Loudoun Court records, from 1757 to 1766, are maintained by the Clerk of the Circuit Court in the archives in Leesburg:

July 1757 to June 1762	Order Book A
July 1762 to July 1765	Order Book B
August 1765 to September 1767	Order Book C

These Loudoun County Court Orders are also available through the Virginia State Library, Richmond, Virginia, on microfiche series 1000, reels 70 and 71. Citations in "The Record" of each chapter, when found in the Loudoun County Court Order Books, are given in abbreviated form; for example "Book A, p. 107."

Wherever possible, I have retained the spelling of colonial names exactly as found in the original source documents. I have also retained the earliest identifiable place names and spellings, supplemented by references to modern place names when use of the colonial name alone would create confusion. Where alternative names were in use, I rely on the apparently predominant colonial spelling in my commentaries and indexes.

Before Europe's Gregorian New Style calendar was adopted in 1752, March 25th was New Year's Day on the English calendar. In an attempt to reduce confusion in this work, dates in January, February or March, prior to 1752, are given in the New Style form. For example, I would refer to March 24, 1750 as March 24, 1751.

I have also included two useful appendices: a Chronology for Colonial Virginia and a Glossary of Colonial Terms. I suggest that the reader become familiar with both of these before plunging into the text.

This work was never intended to be another *Seven Pillars*. Nonetheless, the industrious reader should find the four corners of a firm foundation, and an occasional brick of wisdom, within. Over the years, my thirst for a better appreciation of Loudoun County's colonial and Revolutionary past has evolved into a quest. I invite you now to join me on the journey.

Acknowledgements

Editorial support:

Shalla Young of Lincoln, Nebraska
Mary Henry of Nashville, Tennessee
Cheryl Vazzana of Middleburg, Virginia

Conceptual design and primary research support:

Jane Sullivan, Thomas Balch Library, Leesburg

Proofreading:

Lynn Brazinski
Heather Lovell
John Ranck-Christman, Esq.
Liane Cooper
Joyce Williams
Julie Cornelius
Steve Harms

Research assistance:

E.J. Hemenway
Tracy J. Gillespie
Don Wilson
Beth Hinckle
Laura Dutton
Marty Hiatt
Gerry Gawalt
Sara Collins
Theresa Dye
Sandy Florence
Louisa Hutchison
Mary Fishback
Karen A. Titus
Anthony Tartaro
Dieter Deleeuw

Graphics and design assistance:

Wade Snyder
James Hambleton
Library of Congress Staff

Conceptual design and marketing:

Karen Ackermann
Richard Lobb

Other authors and historians; discussion and advice:

John Gott
Dr. Charles P. Poland, Jr.
Eugene M. Scheel
Craig Roberts Scott
Ned Douglass
Nan Netherton
Dr. Marvin W. Lee
Margaret Lail Hopkins
Sam Sparacio
James Dewey O'Brien

Encouragement, insights and support:

Commander and Mrs. John T. Phillips

Abbreviations for the Primary Sources Cited Throughout the Text

Assembly - *Journals of the House of Burgesses of Virginia*
Balch/Lewis - Lewis MS, Thomas Balch Library, Leesburg
Baron - *Virginia Baron, The Story of Thomas 6th Lord Fairfax*
Black - *Black's Law Dictionary*
Boone - *Daniel Boone*
Braddock - *Braddock at the Monongahela*
Browne - "With Braddock's Army; Mrs. Browne's Diary ..."
C & O - *The Chesapeake & Ohio Canal ...*
Calendar - *Calendar of Virginia State Papers*
Cameron - *Cameron Parish in Colonial Virginia*
Cartography - *The Cartography of Northern Virginia*
Church - *The Colonial Church in Virginia*
Colport - *Colchester, Colonial Port on the Potomac*
ColVa - *Colonial Virginia*
Council - *Executive Journals, Council of Colonial Virginia*
Courthouse - "A History of Loudoun County Courthouses"
Cresswell - *The Journal of Nicholas Cresswell, 1774-1777*
Customs - *Colonial Virginia; Its People and Customs*
DALD - *Deed Abstracts of Loudoun County, 1757-1789*
Democracy - *Virginia 1705-1786; Democracy or Aristocracy?*
Fairfax - *Fairfax County, Virginia, A History*
Fauquier Papers - *The Official Papers of Francis Fauquier*
Ferry - "A Phantom Ferry"
Frontier - *From Frontier To Suburbia*
FXCOCO; FXCODB; FXCOWIL - Fairfax County Court, Order Books; Deed Books; Will Books
FXCOSUR - Fairfax County Court Surveys
Grants - The Land Grant Books of the Proprietor ...
GW Papers - *The Papers of George Washington*
GW Writings - *The Writings of George Washington*
HDC - Hambleton Document Collection
Hening - *Hening's Statutes [of Virginia] at Large*
Heritage - *Northern Virginia Heritage*
Home - *Virginians at Home; Family Life ...*
Hornbook - *A Hornbook of Virginia History*
Independence - *The War of American Independence*

Abbreviations for the Primary Sources Cited Throughout the Text

Indian - *The Conspiracy of Pontiac and the Indian War*
Jamestown - *Jamestown, 1544-1699*
Justice - *Justice in Colonial Virginia*
Land - *Land Records of Long Standing, Fairfax County ...*
Landmarks - *Landmarks of Old Prince William*
LDCH - *Loudoun County Chancery Suits, 1754-1874*
LDCOCO; LDCODB; LDCOWIL - Loudoun County Court, Order Books; Deed Books; Will Books
LDTX/# - *Tithables, Loudoun County Virginia, 1758-1781*
Lee - *Lee of Virginia, 1642-1892*
Legends - *Legends of Loudoun*
Letterbook - *The Letter Book of James Abercromby ...*
Lord Loudoun - "Campbell, John, fourth Earl of Loudoun"
Maps - *A Description of the Country, Virginia's ...*
MdGaz. - *Maryland Gazette*
Middleburg - *The History of Middleburg and Vicinity*
Mills - "Loudoun County Water Mills"
MRLD - *Marriages of Loudoun County, Virginia, 1757-1853*
MRLD1 - *Loudoun County Virginia Marriage Records to 1891*
NorNeck - *Virginia, Northern Neck Land Grants, (1694-1770)*
NorNeck WS - *Abstracts of Northern Neck Warrants ...*
Patents - Map entitled "Patents and Northern Neck Grants ..."
Potomac - *The Potomac*
PRWMCOA - "Prince William County, Virginia; Order Book ..."
Proprietary - *The Fairfax Proprietary*
Radicalism - *The Radicalism of the American Revolution*
Soldiers - *Virginia's Colonial Soldiers*
Truro - *Minutes of the Vestry, Truro Parish Virginia, 1732-1785*
VaGaz. - *Virginia Gazette*
Virginia - *Virginia; A Bicentennial History*
WAFX - *Abstracts of Wills & Inventories, Fairfax County ...*
WALD - *Abstracts of Wills and Administrations in Loudoun ...*
WAPRWM - *Prince William County, Virginia Will Book C ...*
Waters - *Legal Rights in Potomac Waters*
White Oak - *Beginning at a White Oak ...*

[full citations in "Bibliography of Primary Sources" Appendix.]

Indians and the Land

Perhaps 15,000 years ago, nomadic bands of American Indians began to migrate into the lands of northern Virginia that comprise modern Loudoun County, traversing eastwardly across the several small mountain ranges we now know as the Alleghenys and the Blue Ridge. Following in pursuit of the herds of large game animals that roamed the valley and across the piedmont of Virginia, these peoples were descendants of the waves of migrants who had crossed the Asian land bridge thousands of years before. By the time of Christ, Indian bands had formed into tribes which, in turn, grouped together with others utilizing similar root languages and methods of subsistence. Tribal groups were arrayed in numerous rival geographic confederations. An interlocking network of trade routes along rivers, and through valleys and the mountains, linked tribes that were a thousand or more miles apart.

Indian groups that followed the Potomac River valley east out of the mountains eventually pushed their settlements to the shores of the Chesapeake Bay. Inspired by the massive migrating flocks of geese and duck that stopped to forage and rest on the shores above the falls, the Iroquois named the Potomac River Cohongaroton, or "Goose River." Small nomadic Sioux-language tribes (Manahoac) roamed Virginia's upper piedmont, including Loudoun, in the centuries preceding the arrival of Europeans, following the herds that amply sustained them. In the eastern Potomac tidewater, interspersed on the islands and the shores of the peninsulas, Anacostan, Piscataway, Nanticoke tribes and their friendly neighbors, the Algonquian of northern Virginia called the Doeg, used slash and burn farming to raise corn and squash to supplement their seafood and fowl diet. To the south and east, on Virginia's middle and southern peninsulas and further south into the Carolina tidewater, the Powhatan confederacy (a group of Algonquian-language tribes) held sway. For generations, tribes on the Cohongaroton had warred against and traded with Algonquian in southern Virginia when, in the late 1500s, they and the Sioux living on Virginia's piedmont began to feel the influence of the Iroquois League of New York, who "made warre with all the world," and the equally martial Susquehannock of Pennsylvania.

In response, Algonquian tribes on the Cohongaroton maneuvered diplomatically to maintain their distance from the Powhatans. This was, essentially, the state of affairs observed by the first European explorers when they arrived in Virginia in the 1500s.

The Indian's frequent use of brush fire to drive game had resulted in a deforestation of the eastern piedmont and created a prized grassland that sustained large herds of bison and deer east of the Blue Ridge. And records of the first English explorers on the Potomac suggest that the "Sturgeon River" would have been an appropriate designation for the Potomac River below the falls. Potowomek Indians frequently harvested large quantities of corn, fish and fowl, openly sought protection from their Indian neighbors, and had adopted the English as a political counterweight against the Powhatans. Discord among the various Indian tribes contributed to the survival of the Virginia Colony during the first two decades of settlement. When food supplies ran low, as they often did in Jamestown in the early 1600s, colonists found that the Indians on the upper Cohongaroton were more reliable trading partners than the Powhatans. But, as the Virginia colony stabilized, the focus of English trade on the Potomac rapidly progressed from the acquisition of foodstuffs to the procurement of beaver, deer and buffalo skins and other trade goods.

Early in the 1600s, north and northeast of Virginia's piedmont, the warrior-hunter communities of Susquehannock and Delaware Indians embraced in a death grip with their eventual conquerors and compatriots, the Iroquois League. Perpetual Iroquois raiding forced the Manahoac on the piedmont to remove from Virginia altogether, relocating first south and then across the mountains to the west. After evicting the Sioux, the Iroquois claimed the hunting grounds on the Virginia piedmont as their exclusive preserve. Fifty years after the Sioux removed, deforested areas were still evident on the Loudoun piedmont and generally referred to as the "poison fields" by English hunters and explorers who arrived in force after 1690. The northern Indians travelled hundreds of miles to "visit" their Loudoun hunting grounds, and trade with or raid the Virginia Algonquian tribes and the Tuscarora, Catawba and Cherokee Indians in the Carolinas. In the process, well-worn foot paths through the forests were established following the line of the lowest fords, along the base of the broken hills, down the Shenandoah valley, and through the mountain gaps. The first white explorers who recorded their journeys into the Blue Ridge usually referred to existing pathways as "Indian thoroughfares." Eventually, the English colonists would take these land routes for their own, calling the Shenandoah valley path the "Philadelphia Wagon road," while the more easterly route under the broken hills below the Blue Ridge, roughly traced by the course of modern Rte. 15 through Loudoun, was named the "Carolina Road." The old Indian trail down Virginia's Northern Neck, connecting the first inland fords on the tributaries of the Potomac, would be known as the "Ridge Road" or "Potomac Path" in colonial times and in modern times as Rte. 7.

After seven decades of intermittent Indian warfare in the Virginia tidewater, Bacon's Rebellion provided the expedient for English colonists to subjugate the entire Powhatan confederacy. In 1677, the chief of the Pamunkey tribe was accepted as head of the surviving Powhatan confederates, tidewater Algonquian tribes retired to the squalor of protected reservations, and all Algonquian were thereafter considered "tributaries" of the King of England. Virginia's tributary Indians were exempt from colonial taxation - one treaty provision that Virginians continued to honor in the following centuries. By 1690 the aggressive Iroquois League, armed with Dutch and French weaponry, had overwhelmed their Susquehannock opponents in Pennsylvania. The resolution of these two separate conflicts for the first time placed the English colonists on the expanding Virginia frontier in increasingly direct contact with the martially organized Iroquois League, which now included the remnants of the Susquehannock tribes.

Encounters in the Potomac valley with Iroquois (Seneca and Mohawk) hunting parties increased dramatically as Virginia's back settlements extended north and west above the Occoquan. The fortification of an Indian hunting camp at the falls of the Potomac in 1689 caused quite a stir among the frontier Virginians. Constant political pressure from the Iroquois, and the proximity of colonial settlements on both sides of the river, occasioned the removal of the Piscataway (Anacostan and Doeg) villagers from their traditional lands along the upper Potomac. The Piscataways resettled, first on the west side of the Bull Run mountains near The Plains in modern Fauquier County and then, two years later, at the northern-most extremity of the Virginia piedmont, on Conoy Island in the middle of the Cohongaroton. The Piscataway tribe erected a fortified settlement on the west end of Conoy Island, technically within the bounds of the Maryland colony, about a mile upriver from the primary Iroquois river crossing that later became the "Carolina Road" crossing. Despite constant prodding from Virginia officials, the Piscataways lived at Conoy for two decades, tending fish traps and growing their crops in relative isolation.

In 1711 the Tuscaroras, a group of Iroquois-language tribes that had lived for over a century in eastern Carolina, blundered into a total war by massacring a budding settlement of Swiss at what is today New Bern, North Carolina. Carolina colonists and their Catawba Indian allies crushed the Tuscaroras in 1713. The tattered survivors of the Tuscarora fled north and reunited on the Virginia piedmont before eventually finding sanctuary on Iroquois lands in New York. In Loudoun County, a mile south of the town branch of Tuscarora Run, Indian mounds along the old Carolina Road probably mark the site where the Tuscaroras paused on the Iroquois hunting grounds to recover their strength and bury their dead the following winter. Was it here, on the Loudoun piedmont, that the relentless Catawba warriors caught up with the Tuscarora and inflicted "numberless" additional casualties? [contra see, Landmarks, p. 90, and Legends, p. 64].

Virginians grew increasingly anxious over the constant stream of Indian parties traversing near their frontier settlements, and eventually acted to eliminate the threat. In 1721, responding to an invitation from Virginia Governor Spotswood, the Iroquois League sent representatives to Williamsburg for a parlay. Most of the Iroquois died under mysterious circumstances shortly after their arrival in the Virginia capital but the survivors concluded an agreement with Spotswood that was enrolled the following year at Albany, New York. In the Treaty of Albany, Iroquois and their "dependent" tribes agreed to abandon their claims to the Virginia piedmont, and to obtain a passport from English colonial officials before venturing south of the Potomac River and east of the Blue Ridge. The status of the Piscataways, as dependents of the Iroquois League, was also clarified and they promptly left Conoy Island and remigrated to the Maryland and Pennsylvania tidewater. But the Iroquois continued to traverse the valley of Virginia in the course of their ancient war with the Cherokees, occasionally committing minor outrages against the Virginia settlements. Their regular passage served to unnerve the colonists and was a constant reminder to Williamsburg that Indians were still positioned to disrupt Virginia's frontiers. A generation after the Treaty of Albany, the Iroquois, Delaware and Shawnee tribes entered into a new treaty with Virginia, Maryland and Pennsylvania. In the Treaty of Lancaster (Pennsylvania), enrolled on July 7, 1744, the Iroquois and their dependents relinquished their rights of passage through the Shenandoah valley, finally giving Virginians the expectation of a free hand in the settlement of the western areas of the Northern Neck. A little less than a decade later, bloodied and battered settlers in northern Virginia would learn to their horror that the Canadian French and their Indian allies had no regard for the Treaty of Lancaster. In the ensuing French War, and then in Pontiac's War which followed on the heels of the Treaty of Paris in 1763, the Virginia colony, for the last time, won the right to settle the western lands of the Northern Neck without further molestation from the native Indian tribes.

Europeans and the Virginia Colony

Spaniards and Englishmen, and probably the Dutch, had briefly explored the Potomac River during the 1500s, but continuous European contact was initiated when the Virginia colony sent its representatives into the Potomac in 1608. Captain John Smith's exploration party charted the river up to the Little Falls that summer, coming in contact with the Nanticoke, Manahoac and northern Algonquian tribes. Smith named the river after the Potowomek Indian town that was situated on the main western stretch of the river, near the modern town of Stafford. The name, in Algonquian, meant "where something is brought in," or "trading place," and for decades Virginians found that the upper Potomac River was indeed a great trading place, where abundant supplies of corn and game were obtained from the Algonquian of Maryland and Virginia, and the Manahoac, Iroquois (from New York) and Shawnee (from the Ohio River valley) brought their pelts for barter. Despite their location on the periphery of the colony, the Potowomek tribe was involved in several momentous events in Virginia history. In 1612, they conspired with Captain Samuel Argall to effectuate the kidnapping of the Powhatan princess Pocahontas. This event led to a truce between the English and the Powhatans, which in turn facilitated the cultivation of tobacco and its development as an export crop. In 1619, the

Potowomeks' bumper harvests probably filled the tables at the first American Thanksgiving celebration held at Berkeley Hundred on the James River that December. During the 1620s and 1630s, a number of Captains from the Virginia colony, notably, Henry Spelman, William Claiborne, John Utey and Henry Fleet, explored and expanded the Indian trade on the Potomac River. Capt. Fleet was on the Potomac in 1634 when the first Maryland colonists arrived, assisting them in locating their capital (St. Marys) at his old landing and warehouse site. For the next thirty years, trade and exploration on the upper Potomac River was dominated by Maryland colonists, while Virginia's Northern Neck settlements gradually extended northwestward from the lower peninsula.

In 1649 when Parliament beheaded Charles I, his 18 year old son, in exile in Paris, became Charles II, the English sovereign. At the time, the Virginia colony was one of the young King's few domains to maintain unswerving loyalty to his crown. Despite Parliament's military victory in the civil war, the Virginia colony persisted in its loyalty to Charles II for several years, and became a haven of exile for royalists who had become targets of the increasingly radical and vindictive Puritans. In September of 1649, seven months after his father's death, while living in exile at St. Germains on Ley, Charles II made a grant of the entire northern region of Virginia to seven men who had been among his father's most loyal supporters. This grant became known as Virginia's Northern Neck Proprietary. A century later, surveys would show that the Proprietary contained nearly five million acres, but the first grant was limited to the tidewater lands "within the head," below the falls, of the "Quiriough" [sic - intending Potomac] and Rappahannock Rivers. At the time of the first Northern Neck grant English settlement of the Loudoun piedmont, which was an open Indian hunting grounds, was still beyond contemplation.

King Charles I had carved another Proprietary (Maryland) out of northern Virginia in 1632, granting Cecil Calvert, Lord Baltimore, all the land in Virginia lying north of the southern shore of the Potomac River. Calvert claimed that all the land in the Northern Neck above Aquia Creek (including Loudoun) was his, relying on the errors of early map makers who misunderstood Capt. John Smith to have identified "Quiriough," ie. Aquia, as the primary course of the upper Potomac River. Lord Baltimore dropped his claims on the Northern Neck when one of his map makers, Augustine Herrman, confirmed the true course of the upper Potomac in 1670. The grant to Lord Baltimore preset the northern boundary and served as a prototype for the first Northern Neck grant, but the political consequences, whereby Maryland had ascended to the status of an autonomous colony and then pursued claims for additional Virginia territory, caused no small discomfort to the administrators of the Virginia colony. The resulting distrust of the Northern Neck Proprietors, and the attendant political distance between the Proprietors and Virginia's colonial officials, led to a sectionalism that is still felt in twentieth century Virginia, at this writing nearly 350 years after the first Northern Neck grant.

Virginians finally submitted to Parliament's power in 1652 after a battle fleet and an army were dispatched to America for the purpose, but Charles II never forgot their loyalty. Recognizing his distant colony as a last redoubt of loyal supporters, Charles II awarded Virginia the status of "Commonwealth" and after his Restoration in 1660 the King was known to refer to the Virginia colony as his "Old Dominion." Members of the King's party in the English civil war had been called "Cavaliers," and the Virginia colonists proudly adopted both the title and nickname for their colony, and the appellation for themselves. Fortunately, the Restoration of Charles II brought other changes to Virginia. Under the terms of the Restoration, most of the Cavalier families had been disenfranchised of their English holdings. The entire Northern Neck was revitalized as increasing numbers of martially capable Cavaliers settled in the Proprietary and delighted in finding themselves in exile among friends. Royalists who came to Virginia at the time of the Restoration and rapidly advanced to positions of prominence included William Fitzhugh, a Governor's Councilor and the founder of that substantial Northern Neck family, and Philip Ludwell, a Secretary of the colony. By the turn of the century, it was observed that the Virginia "gentlemen called Cavaliers are greatly esteemed and respected and are very courteous and honorable. They hold most of the offices ... sit[ting] in judgment with girded swords." [Jamestown, p. 88].

In the decades following the Restoration of Charles II, North Carolina, New York, New Jersey, Delaware, South Carolina and Pennsylvania were all constituted as British colonies. Among colonial promoters there was a remarkable increase in competition for English, Scots, Irish and German migrants who were essential to colonial development. As a direct result, the pace of expansion on Virginia's northwestern frontier slowed in the last four decades of the 1600s. The Northern Neck was also under a great deal of pressure from Indian raiders in the decades after the Restoration. Virginians in the Northern Neck had known forty years of unhappy experiences with, alternately, the Anacostan, Doeg, Susquehannock and Iroquois. In 1675 an uneven Indian trade on the Northern Neck frontier created a misunderstanding that flashed into an indiscriminate colony-wide Indian war, which became known as Virginia's "Bacon's Rebellion." A number of the "rebels" who were hung or imprisoned were men from the back settlements of the Proprietary who had taken up arms against their neighbors, but the treaty that marked the end of hostilities in 1677 also signalled the final taming of the tidewater Indians in Virginia.

During the interregnum of Parliament's rule, the Council and Assembly in Virginia, over the protestations of the grantees, ignored the legal effect of the King's Northern Neck grant and continued the patenting of Proprietary lands on the basis of Virginia's "headrights" scheme. After Charles II's Restoration, conflicting claims to jurisdiction over the Proprietary set off a political tug-of-war, clouding title to the entire Northern Neck. One resolution was obtained in 1688, when James II renewed the grant. Fortunately for the Proprietors, the Crown and colonial leaders were looking beyond the fall line for potential areas of settlement. The 1688 grant extended the Northern Neck to "the first heads or springs" of the boundary rivers, unquestionably placing the Loudoun piedmont within the Proprietary. By the 1680s, the Northern Neck Proprietary was consolidated in the family of Lord John Culpeper. Lord Culpeper had served as Chancellor of the Exchequer for Charles I in the 1640s, was a trusted councillor to the Prince of Wales (Charles II) in the final stages of the civil war, and was serving as a member of the court in exile when Charles II made the Proprietary grant. As a precondition to the 1688 grant, the Culpepers abandoned all claims to land that had been patented under Virginia's headrights, and agreed to maintain the political organization of the Northern Neck under the Virginia county system. In 1689, Lady Catherine Culpeper Fairfax, the only daughter and heiress of Thomas, the 2nd Lord Culpeper, and the wife of Thomas, the 5th Lord Fairfax, inherited all but one of the shares of the Proprietary.

After the demise of the Powhatans, Virginia's frontier settlements rapidly pushed westward, reaching the southern Blue Ridge in the early 1700s. Westward expansion in the Northern Neck was stunted by the uncertainty of title to the lands, the Proprietors' indifference and the unrelenting threat of Indian incursions. With James II's 1688 grant the matter of title, at least on the Loudoun piedmont, was no longer an issue. The second barrier was hurdled in 1703 when Robert Carter was appointed as the Proprietary agent. And the Treaty of Albany eliminated the immediacy of the Indian threat on the piedmont in 1722, opening Loudoun for essentially unmolested settlement by the English.

The Piscataways on Conoy Island found themselves playing host with increasing frequency after 1700. Swiss explorer Louis Michel, followed by the Swiss promoter Baron de Graffenried, surveyed the upper Potomac and the Loudoun piedmont, but their development plans for the area went unfulfilled. The patenting of land on the upper Potomac, above the falls, began tentatively when Daniel McCarty (soon to be Thomas Lee's brother-in-law) took up a tract at Sugarland Island in 1709. In 1711, Thomas Lee was appointed as the new land agent for the Proprietary, replacing Robert Carter for his ostensibly poor performance in generating Proprietary revenues although prospective purchasers had probably been put off by the continued Indian presence on the piedmont.

In 1713 at the Treaty of Utrecht, which marked the end of the War of Spanish Succession, Europeans recognized the Iroquois League as British subjects (ie. Iroquois lands were considered British territory), even though the French continued to subvert the English-Iroquois alliance with their seduction of the Seneca tribe. Virginia's Governor Spotswood, aware of the new legal status of the Iroquois lands and with one eye on the valley and mountains beyond the Blue Ridge, took an active role in colonial expansion into the northern piedmont. In 1716, Spotswood led his Knights of the Golden Horseshoe from Germanna on the Rapidan across the piedmont to Swifts Run gap in the Blue Ridge. The following year, perhaps having viewed some of the proverbial handwriting on the wall, Thomas Lee and the scions of several other prominent Virginia families began patenting lands on and above Goose Creek in the Loudoun piedmont. Shortly thereafter, Gov. Spotswood initiated a series of official communications with the Iroquois that led to the conclusion of the 1722 Treaty of Albany.

In an ironic twist of fate, when Lady Catherine Culpeper Fairfax died in 1719 the Northern Neck devolved into the sole possession of Thomas, the 6th Lord Fairfax, whose ancestors had opposed Charles I seventy years before. His great grandfather, Ferdinando, the 3rd Lord Fairfax, organized Yorkshire in support of the Covenanting Scots and against King Charles I. During the English civil war Lord Fairfax and his son, Sir Thomas, were active combatants at the head of Parliament's armies. Sir Thomas (later 4th Lord Fairfax), became Commander-in-Chief of Parliament's New Model Army in 1645, and his military leadership and political unobtrusiveness were ultimately critical elements in Parliament's victory in the war. Scholars to this day debate whether Oliver Cromwell merely misled and manipulated a pliant Thomas Fairfax, or had in Fairfax a knowing conspirator, when Cromwell's party engineered the execution of King Charles I.

After the 6th Lord Fairfax began to assert his control over the Proprietary and the Treaty of Albany effected the removal of the Indians from the Northern Neck east of the Blue Ridge, interest in Virginia's piedmont increased rapidly. During the 1720s the first white settlements appeared on the Loudoun Potomac, inspired by the Nolands at Broad Run, the McCartys at Sugarland, the Hallings at the Lost Corner, and the Lees above the falls and around Goose Creek. Robert "King" Carter resumed his duties as land agent for the Proprietary in 1723, promptly taking up 90,000 acres of an eventual 300,000 acres that he would patent in the Northern Neck before his death in 1732. During the final six years of his second agency, "King" Carter masked his acquisitions by leasing the entire Northern Neck from Lord Fairfax for £450 in annual rent, farming the quitrents of the Proprietary for a tidy profit. The Carter family acquired substantial acreage in Loudoun, including large tracts all along the western side of upper Goose Creek, at Frying Pan in what is now a part of Fairfax County and on both sides of Bull Run at Sudley. The seating of the Loudoun piedmont began in earnest during Robert Carter's second agency. Cheap labor in the form of convict servants began to arrive around 1720. Coincidentally, at the same time, Scots-Irish were leaving their leaseholds in Ireland and migrating to the upper Chesapeake, and German families were arriving in the Pennsylvania colony in large numbers. These Germans, finding that the best arable land in Pennsylvania was occupied, soon joined the Welsh and Quaker families who were beginning the migration to Loudoun and the southern colonies along the Carolina Road.

In 1724 the Duke of Newcastle, Thomas Pelham-Holles, was appointed British secretary for the southern department in "Prime Minister" Walpole's Whig government. Under Newcastle, the British Crown embarked on an American colonial policy of "salutary neglect" and Virginia entered a twenty-two year period of expanded local rule. Flexing of the colonial political muscle contributed to a renewal of the dispute between Virginia officials and the Proprietor over the western and southwestern boundaries of the Northern Neck. Virginia Governor Gooch quickly adopted a policy of open confrontation, issuing grants for over 300,000 acres of Northern Neck land (most of it in the Shenandoah valley) between 1727 and 1735. To his credit, Proprietary agent Carter constantly protested against the Virginia grants, and vigorously promoted the Northern Neck for Lord Fairfax. As a result, large sections of Loudoun's open piedmont were patented and rendered available for settlement during this period. When Robert "King" Carter died in 1732, Lord Fairfax arranged for his cousin, William Fairfax, to take over as the Proprietary's resident agent, a position he would hold, off and on, for most of the next fifteen years.

Lord Fairfax responded to the challenge from Virginia's colonial government by visiting the Northern Neck in 1735. For two years Lord Fairfax weighed his opposition and his allies, issued land patents, and commissioned exhaustive surveys of his domain. One result was placement of the "Fairfax Stone" at the headwaters of the Potomac. Riding over his immense Proprietary with a train of surveyors, Lord Fairfax set aside 150,000 acres (Leeds Manor in honor of his Leeds Castle home in Yorkshire), from Williams Gap in Loudoun, spanning the Blue Ridge, south to Manassas Gap - and 12,500 acres on the Potomac in "Loudoun" called the Great Falls Manor. At the same time, William Fairfax established two substantial manors, on either side of the Short Hill in Loudoun - Piedmont Manor on 17,000 acres on the east and Shannondale Manor on 29,000 acres to the west. A decade later, Lord Fairfax built his Virginia plantation home, Greenway Court, on yet another manor that he would create on the west side of the Shenandoah River. In 1737 Lord Fairfax closed his land office and returned to England, with his surveys, for an audience in the King's Privy Council where he successfully argued his case for the boundaries of the Northern Neck Proprietary. During his cousin's absence, William Fairfax proceeded with the construction of his Belvoir plantation home on the upper reaches of the Potomac and continued his rise on the Governor's Council.

The first edifices of permanent European settlement had been erected above Goose Creek in Loudoun in 1732 and 1733 when construction was begun on two water mills on Kitoctin Creek and an Episcopal chapel at Big Spring. But the Proprietary land office closed for two years upon the death of Robert Carter and the first great migration into Loudoun ebbed. Following the official surveys of the Northern Neck, by 1737 it was common knowledge throughout the colonies that title to Virginia's northern piedmont was not in question. That fact, combined with the enthusiasm for his Proprietary that Lord Fairfax had displayed, brought a renewal of the migratory tide. Traffic along the Carolina Road increased enough to justify Francis Awbrey's licensing of a Potomac ferry, and congregations of "dissenters" formed in several places on the Loudoun piedmont. Although the Privy Council had delayed a ruling on the Proprietary boundaries for several years, Lord Fairfax authorized his cousin to reopen the Northern Neck land office in 1739, and a second great wave of land patents promptly patented the balance of the large tracts in Loudoun. A potato famine in Ireland brought more indentured servants to the upper Potomac in 1741, and both Fairfax County with its Springfield Courthouse, and a second Potomac ferry on the Carolina Road, were founded in 1742. Shortly thereafter, the King's Council confirmed the Proprietary boundaries of the Northern Neck and a great land rush developed in the upper Shenandoah valley, prompting colonial officials to confirm the peace with the "western" Indians in the Treaty of Lancaster. The Privy Council decision also led the Virginia Assembly to confirm the Governors' Northern Neck land patents, clarifying the title to lands everywhere in the Proprietary. [Hening, VI/198-199].

In 1745 the Right Honorable Thomas, 6th Lord Fairfax, Baron of Cameron, Proprietor of the Northern Neck, moved his residence to Virginia. Initially, he conducted the land office for the Proprietary at Belvoir, but construction on Shenandoah Manor was hastened and around 1752 Lord Fairfax moved to Greenway Court in Frederick County. Despite the savagery of the frontier Indians in both the French (Seven Years) War and Pontiac's War, and the harsh confiscations of British property in Virginia in 1779, Lord Fairfax continued in residence at Greenway Court for three decades. His residency in the Northern Neck spanned the years leading up to the creation of Loudoun County, as well as the American Revolution. Until his death in 1781, Lord Fairfax lived the fairy tale existence of America's only true resident English Baron, amidst retainers and supplicants, the Lord and master of a tract of land that was eventually surveyed at over 5 million acres.

In the wake of the "Rising" of the Highland Scots and the continental wars that had preoccupied the British Crown for years, John Russell, the Duke of Bedford, ushered in a sea change in colonial policy when he advocated an increase in the exercise of the "Royal Prerogative" in 1746. Thereafter, up to the time of the Revolution, communications between colonial officials and the Crown became increasingly strained. Meanwhile, throughout the 1740s, Scots merchants on the Potomac were busy extending their trading activities westward from bases at Quantico and Belhaven. In 1747 Thomas Lee banded together with a select group of Northern Neck planters and several influential London merchants to form the Ohio Company - with the intent of opening up the lands west of the Proprietary for Virginia's eventual expansion. The organization of this powerful partnership for investment in frontier real estate was a momentous event in the history of the American colonies. The Ohio Company was in essence a natural extension of the Scots' mercantile efforts on the Potomac, and the acquisition of real estate was on the mind of every colonist who had two coins to rub together. But the exertions of the Ohio Company, relentless surveying and road making into the Ohio River basin, soon alarmed the "western" Indians and led to, first, direct confrontation and then open warfare between the English and the French on Virginia's new northwestern frontier.

Loudoun County was born during a time of great military activity in the Northern Neck. The decade before incorporation was filled with the parry and thrust of the Indian traders on the Ohio, Indian massacres on the frontiers and the whir and clash of empires that colonists would call the French War. Virginians were shocked by the incompetence of British troops in frontier fighting, and were repeatedly offended by the high-handed dealing of the British officers and Crown policies that seemed to impose new constraints on colonists without providing commensurate benefits.

Despite the several military disasters suffered by Washington and Braddock, colonists learned to trust in their own martial abilities. The Loudoun piedmont, as a way-point to the Ohio frontier, was for a shimmering moment the focus of British imperial interest. Shortly after Lord Loudoun arrived in New York in 1756, he instituted reforms that improved the military organization and coordination among the colonies. But Lord Loudoun never set foot in Virginia, and his imperious attitude toward colonials was a legacy remembered long after his achievements were forgotten.

Loudoun County

When the Virginia county system of political organization was inaugurated in 1634, the Northern Neck was incorporated in a district called Chicacoan. Many of the early Chicacoan settlers were exiles from the Maryland colony, and their presence inspired Lord Baltimore to agitate for a new survey of the Potomac, which he believed would establish Aquia Creek as his southern boundary. The Virginia Assembly responded to the Maryland land-grab by reorganizing the northern region of the Virginia colony in 1649. Their enactment that October asserted that "the inhabitants ... seated on the south side of the Petomecke River [sic] shall be included ... within the [Virginia] County of Northumberland." Other political subdivisions of the Northern Neck followed, and as English settlements spread westward and Virginians reasserted themselves on the upper Potomac, the new counties were erected, one after another, in the western regions. In 1653, the frontier of the Northern Neck was organized as Westmoreland County, but the Westmoreland County Court was temporarily merged back into the Northumberland County Court in March of 1662 "on account of disturbances with the Potomack [meaning the Doeg, not the Pamunkey] Indians." The influx of Cavaliers following the English Civil War and Restoration, and a corresponding westward surge of English settlements in the Proprietary, sparked the resurrection of the temporarily defunct Westmoreland County, and in short order led to the creation of Stafford County above it. [Hening, I/362, I/381 and II/151; and see, infra, p. 7].

Although Virginia records for the period are sketchy, Stafford County was created after the Restoration of Charles II, probably in 1664. The Virginia statute incorporating Stafford was lost somehow; the first reference to Stafford County in Virginia law, in October of 1666, was an exemption of the "new" counties of Westmoreland and Stafford from the immediate implementation of an act requiring Virginia counties to obtain and provide for a public weaver. The new Virginia county echoed the name of the heavily wooded Staffordshire in England, apparently with the intent of honoring the Duke of Buckingham. Buckingham was the hereditary noble of Staffordshire, a son of King James I's court favorite and, in his own right, a favorite at the court of Charles II. Stafford County initially contained all the western lands of the Northern Neck above Westmoreland (including Loudoun) and, as such, was home to the northwestern-most "frontier" settlements of Virginia and the Proprietary for six decades before Prince William County was created. The Assembly was cognizant of the influx of transported convicts on the Potomac River in the 1720s, and openly discussed proposals for the creation of a county named Hartford, where all transported convicts could be segregated. One of the Hartford county proposals, in 1726, called for a new county above Aquia Creek in Stafford, but the Northern Neck Burgesses voiced their considerable opposition and the proposal was defeated in Assembly. [Hening, II/239 and II/406; Landmarks, p. 311].

Later petitions for a division of Stafford County, inspired by the Carters and Masons, were successful and Prince William County was erected in 1731, coterminous with a new parish named Hamilton, containing the entire Northern Neck northwest of Chopawansick Creek. From 1731 to 1742, when Loudoun was part of Prince William, the county court was conducted at Woodbridge plantation on the south bluff above George Mason's Occoquan ferry. Proposals to subdivide Prince William were put forward almost immediately, and in 1732 Truro parish was erected in the northern half of the county on lands that would subsequently comprise Fairfax and Loudoun. Truro was named for a mining district in Cornwall in keeping with the hopes that "King" Carter had for the region, and incorporated all of the lands that became Fairfax County a decade later. In 1734, Prince William's western boundary was established at the Blue Ridge when Orange County was incorporated with the lands to the west of that range. Subsequent petitions for another northern county were caught in the snarl of colonial politics in 1736, 1738 and 1740, but finally met with success when Councilor and Northern Neck agent William Fairfax moved to Belvoir plantation and became the County Lieutenant for Prince William in 1741. [Hening, IV/303].

Fairfax County (including Loudoun) was formed out of northern Prince William in 1742, incorporating all the land east of the Blue Ridge and north of the Occoquan, Bull Run and Ashby's Gap. During its first decade, until May of 1752, the Fairfax County seat was at colonial "Springfield" on the Potomac Path - Freedom Hill at modern Tyson's Corner. This original location of the Fairfax Courthouse was suspiciously convenient to the growing areas of new settlement all along Goose and Kitoctin Creeks and the new Fairfax family manors of Shannondale and Piedmont in Loudoun, and we need look no farther than the Proprietor's family for the reason. William Fairfax donated the Courthouse site at Springfield, along with enough land for a jail and an ordinary or two, under restrictive covenants. In 1752, Scots merchants and influential Belhaven residents agitated for the removal of the Fairfax Courthouse fifteen miles east, to Alexandria. Relocation of the Courthouse to Alexandria, with its attendant inconvenience, prompted residents of Cameron parish to petition for the creation of their own county, which had been anticipated for some time. The Assembly passed a Bill to divide Fairfax County in the spring of 1755, but political uncertainties resulting from the French War prejudiced the effort and the Governor's Council did not concur.

On April 20, 1757, tidewater interests in the Assembly referred yet another "Petition of sundry Inhabitants of Fairfax County, praying a Division of the said County ... to the Consideration of the next Session of Assembly." But Lt. Governor Dinwiddie and William Fairfax, who had advanced to become the President of the Council and was still the Prince William County Lieutenant, must have exerted their considerable influence on behalf of Loudoun's residents. In May that year, the Governor, in Council, issued a new Dedimus and Commissions of the Peace for both Fairfax and (as yet unfounded) Loudoun County. Petitions from the "back inhabitants" of Fairfax were then reintroduced to the Burgesses and the Assembly reversed itself and enacted the law establishing Loudoun County early in June. This sudden sense of urgency may have been yet another result of the impact that the French War was having on the Virginia frontier. With Indian parties raging throughout the Shenandoah during the preceding two years, many settlers from western Virginia had relocated to the Loudoun piedmont, swelling its population. For fifty years the Assembly had followed a general rule that new counties had to have at least 800 tithables and, by the end of 1756, Loudoun contained in excess of 1,050 resident tithables, with a population of perhaps 3,300. The inconvenience of Fairfax's Alexandria Courthouse and population growth on the piedmont were probably only two of three factors that contributed to the success of the Loudoun petitions. Another explanation may be rooted in the intricacies of colonial politics. When Lord Loudoun arrived in America, with the rank of both the Commander-in-Chief of the British colonial forces and the Governor of Virginia, he demanded funding and other military measures that Virginia's colonial Assembly was reluctant to enact. It would certainly have been "good politics" for the Virginia Assembly to honor Lord Loudoun by naming a new county after him as a conciliatory gesture to show that no personal affront was intended in their resistance to his legislative package. In any event, the urgency that worked to create Loudoun County in 1757 was narrowly defined - petitions that year from Lunenburg and on behalf of Fauquier were denied and deferred to the 1759 Assembly. [Assembly, (1756) p. 425].

Lines on the Ground

Loudoun County's most obvious natural boundary is also its oldest political limit. The water line on the south bank of the Potomac was first designated as a political boundary when the Maryland Proprietary was granted to Lord Baltimore back in 1632. Exactly one century later, in 1732, Loudoun's southern boundary line was fixed when Truro parish was erected above "Bull Run ... from thence to the Indian Thoroughfare [Ashby's Gap] of the Blue Ridge." This parish boundary was maintained as the political boundary line first between Fairfax and Prince William Counties, and subsequently between Loudoun, Prince William and Fauquier. Loudoun's southern boundary line as defined in 1732 has never been altered but, over time, surveys have changed the view of where various property owners pay their taxes. Between 1688 and 1734, the western boundary for Stafford and Prince William (including Loudoun) was, arguably, the western-most branch of the Potomac river, ie., the western boundary of the Proprietary. Since the Northern Neck boundaries were in dispute during this period, the Virginia Assemblies consistently avoided a specific definition of the western bounds. Orange County was nominally granted jurisdiction west of the Blue Ridge when it was created in 1734 but, in the aftermath of the Northern Neck surveys, the Blue Ridge boundary was firmly fixed in 1738 when Frederick County (named for Frederick, Prince of Wales and father of George III) was organized to incorporate the Proprietary lands lying northwest of the crest of the Blue Ridge. [Hening, IV/367].

A substantial segment of the original eastern boundary of colonial Loudoun County was defined in October of 1748, when Truro parish was divided at Difficult Run and Popes Head Run, with the western half organized as Cameron parish. When Loudoun County was established in 1757, Fairfax County was divided along the Cameron-Truro line running south from the Potomac up Difficult Run, but then southwest from the head spring of Difficult to the mouth of Rocky Run on Bull Run. For the first five years of its existence, colonial Loudoun County contained roughly 98% of Cameron parish but after 1762, when the southeastern section of Cameron parish between Rocky Run and Popes Head was returned to Truro parish, Loudoun County and Cameron parish were geographically identical. This situation continued until 1770 when Shelburne parish was created in western Loudoun County, incorporating the lands between Goose Creek, Little River and the Blue Ridge, but Loudoun's eastern county line was not affected in the parish reorganization.

The modern eastern boundary line of Loudoun County was finally established in 1798, when the lands between Sugarland Run and Difficult Run were returned to Fairfax County in a political reorganization of northern Virginia that also took into account the founding of Washington D.C.. Thus, the colonial, Revolutionary and Continental experiences of Loudoun County provide four decades of history for a large area that is now in Fairfax County. The western Fairfax neighborhoods of Riverbend, Great Falls, Herndon, Reston, Dulles, Chantilly, Centreville and Bull Run were all in Loudoun County between 1757 and 1798.

And more ...

For more details regarding the history of Virginia and the Northern Neck Proprietary, events leading up to the French (and Indian) War and the careers of the Lord Fairfax and the Earl of Loudoun, refer to the Chapter on the Loudoun County Militia, infra, and the Appendix titled Chronology for Colonial Virginia.

Courtesy of the Loudoun Museum, Leesburg, Virginia.

VIRGINIA, ſc.

By the Hon. *FRANCIS FAUQUIER*, Eſq;
His Majeſty's LIEUTENANT GOVERNOUR, and COMMANDER in CHIEF of the ſaid Colony and Dominion:

A PROCLAMATION,

For the MEETING *of the* GENERAL ASSEMBLY

WHEREAS the General Aſſembly ſtands prorogued to the 1ſt THURSDAY in NOVEMBER next, and his Majeſty's ſervice, and the general intereſt of this colony, render it neceſſary that the ſaid ASSEMBLY meet as ſoon as poſſible, I have therefore thought fit, by and with the advice of his Majeſty's Council, to iſſue this PROCLAMATION, in his Majeſty's name, requiring their attendance at the CAPITOL, in WILLIAMSBURG, on the day above-mentioned, for the deſpatch of publick buſineſs.

GIVEN under my Hand, and the Seal of the Colony, at Williamſburg, *this 8th day of* October, 1766, *and in the 6th Year of his Majeſty's Reign.*

FRANCIS FAUQUIER.

GOD ſave the KING.

This notice in the *Virginia Gazette* on October 24, 1766 is a Proclamation of Gov. Fauquier, on behalf of King George III, calling the Virginia Assembly into session. It is exemplary of the notices issued "in his Majesty's name" by Virginia's colonial Governors, but displays the coat of arms of King George II, who had died in 1760. 'Dieu Et Mon Droit', the motto on the royal arms, ("God and my Right"), was first assumed by King Richard I.

The House of Burgesses of the Virginia Colony, also known and referred to as the Virginia Assembly, was initially composed of representatives of the colonial townships along the James River. The townships were alternately referred to as boroughs, and they gave their representatives the title of "Burgess." The Assembly was created pursuant to the Great Charter of 1618, which terminated the operation of the Virginia Company's military government in the colony. After elections the following spring, the first meeting of the Assembly was held July 30, 1619 in the choir loft at the church in Jamestown. The original Assemblymen acted in much the manner as the county courts of the 1700s - they were responsible for the compilation of lists of tithables in their townships, they established roads and they appropriated funds to meet local needs. The Assembly met in Jamestown throughout the 1600s, but removed to a newly constructed capitol at Middle Plantation (Williamsburg) after the third statehouse in Jamestown burned down in 1698. [Hening, I/121 and I/143].

Expansion of the area of colonial settlement resulted in a corresponding increase in the Assembly's administrative duties and led the Assembly to create the first eight county courts in 1634. In the process the Assembly reorganized itself along the new county lines, with two Burgesses from each shire. The disruptions of the English Civil War were barely felt in the colony, and as the number of Burgesses grew in proportion with the total number of counties, by 1643 the Assembly had become unwieldy in both size and function. The Governor's Council, the "upper house" of the Assembly, which was composed of men appointed by the King, separated itself from the Assembly that year and began conducting separate business meetings. The Council acted as a conduit for laws proposed by the King, and reviewed, revised and occasionally vetoed legislation enacted by the Assembly. Colonial Governors, together with their Councils, acted as the executive body of the colony and appointed the county justices of the peace, sheriffs, coroners and the tobacco inspectors, while at the same time sitting as the colony's resident supreme court. The first Councils were composed largely of men fresh "off the boat," but by the 1750s Councilmen were normally native Virginia colonists who had been selected from among the leadership of the General Assembly.

Initially, the Council conducted trials once each quarter when felony charges were referred to Jamestown from the county courts, leading to their adoption of the title "Quarter Court." In 1634 the Council assumed the name of "General Court" while acting in its judicial capacity. In addition to trying all felonies and treasons, the General Court sat as a trial court for cases involving substantial money damages, was the exclusive colonial probate court for large estates (over £200), and served as the colonial court of appeals for the review of rulings of the county courts when at least £5 was in controversy. During the 1700s Virginia Councilors frequently advanced to become the acting Governor of Virginia due to an anomaly in the appointive process. Hanoverian Royal Governors viewed the Virginia colony as little more than their personal fiefdom, and the practice rapidly developed whereby an administrative subordinate was contracted for and designated as Lt. Governor of the colony. From 1706 to 1768, Lt. Governors were, in fact, the resident Governors of Virginia, and when they died or returned to England the President of the Virginia Council would become the acting Governor of the colony. Just such a circumstance propelled Thomas Lee, the colonial visionary of the Northern Neck who was subsequently honored when Leesburg was named, to the status of acting Governor in 1749. Lord Loudoun, nominally Governor of Virginia when Loudoun County was formed in 1757, never set foot in Virginia and when his Lt. Governor, Robert Dinwiddie, returned to England in January of 1758 the President of the Council, John Blair, advanced to become the acting Governor. In this way, Virginians in the councils of government were drawn further into a swirling debate over the appropriate methods of managing the British King's empire.

Around 1746, a British colonial policy of "salutary neglect" was replaced by an increase in the exercise of the Crown's "royal prerogative." In practical terms, this meant that the King, his Governors and the English ministries adopted a combative stance when the Virginia colonists acted to exercise what their experience had taught them to consider to be their "rights as Englishmen." Colonial attempts to increase the responsiveness of the Virginia Assembly were openly opposed by Royal Governors, and laws of the Assembly were rejected in London in a seemingly random and arbitrary fashion. Lord Loudoun was not the only Tory known to openly urge an increase in the exercise of the Royal prerogative in order to subdue the "excessive" power of the Virginia Assembly. At one point, the Crown delayed a ruling for several years before rejecting a revision of the procedures in Virginia's General Court, while accepting a companion law that revised the county court procedures. The two laws were so intertwined that confusion reigned in Virginia's colonial courts for years, much to the consternation of both the Virginia Assemblymen and their electors. Increasingly, after 1750, intellectual efforts of the colonial Assembly were held in contempt by British ministers who seemed to be concerned more with maintaining the arbitrary power of the Crown than they were with the practical management of a remote and increasingly self-sufficient colony. Most Virginia colonists labored under the false assumption that heavy-handed colonial administration was the fault of the British government in power rather than a manifestation of the wishes of the Hanoverian Kings. When the truth was eventually realized, American Independence became a foregone conclusion. [Independence, p. 19].

While members of the Virginia Council were appointed by the King or his Governor, Assemblymen were elected directly by the colonists living in each county. It has been fairly demonstrated that the growing middle class of small land owners held and wielded the decisive power in Virginia Assembly elections in the years leading up to the Revolution. Accordingly, Burgesses were demonstrably responsive to their constituents. By the 1750s the members of the Virginia Assembly had come to share the general view that they, like Parliament, were the guardians of English liberty, even though colonial customs had expanded the traditional English forms beyond the bounds of what was still comfortably accepted in London. Only three positions of authority in Virginia were elected posts - Burgesses in the Assembly, lesser officers of the county militias, and the vestrymen for the parishes. Parish vestries and county militias were essentially self-perpetuating once they were constituted. In order to force a public election of a new vestry, a finding of impropriety and then an Act of the Assembly was required. Accordingly, only the men in the Virginia Assembly stood for reelection on a regular basis. In the early years when mere existence was problematic, colonial voting practices departed from the traditions of the mother country and all free colonists "of known integrity and good conversation" were encouraged to exercise their voice in elections. Voting status in Virginia in the early 1600s was determined as much by an ability to stay alive as it was by the ownership of property. The vote was extended to "any person [who] shall pay equal taxes" in Virginia during Parliament's reign in the 1650s, and briefly during Bacon's Rebellion to "all freemen." These colonial experiments in democracy were, however, aberrations from the more traditional English approach - expressed, in the extreme, in the political postulations of Adam Smith - which imposed standards requiring that voters have a personal interest in the society their vote was going to affect. For wont of a better measure, personal interest was viewed in terms of the ancient concepts of English property rights. Thus, for five decades in the mid-1600s, the "householders" of the Virginia colony (meaning the heads of households), the same individuals voting in vestry elections, were entitled to vote in the Virginia Assembly elections. [see generally, Democracy; Independence, p. 20; Hening, I/403, I/475, II/82, II/280, II/356 and II/425; and infra, Chapter on Cameron Parish].

When Governor Berkeley returned in 1676 at the end of Bacon's Rebellion, the Crown instructed the imposition of a new legal standard for voting in the colony. Thereafter, and until a decade after the American Revolution, only "freeholder"s were entitled to vote in the Virginia Assembly elections. The term was generally understood, and legislated as early as 1684, to indicate an individual who had a perpetual, a reversionary or a life interest in real estate (land). A key provision of the 1705 voting law eliminated the requirement of residency, enabling land owners to vote in every county where they owned an appropriate amount of land. This practice was continued until well beyond the American Revolution. Another provision, suggested in 1705 but not adopted until 1736, required that freeholds contain either 100 acres of unimproved land or 25 acres of land with a house. In the Loudoun piedmont, tenants normally rented manor lands under a "lease for lives," which was legally considered to be a freehold. The 1736 law also included owners of a town lot with a house as freeholders, which eventually worked to the benefit of a number of Leesburg residents. Similar to the residency requirements in vestry elections, freeholders were not eligible to vote unless they had held their property for one year before an election. In 1756, the year before Loudoun County was created, Governor Dinwiddie remarked that "most of the people are freeholders, in course have votes for choosing assembly men, on which [event] they strenuously insist on their privileges." But a fruitful balance had been struck - the breadth and functionality of colonial democracy proved "strong enough to moderate the autocratic tendencies in the gentry" - and Virginia prospered. The Assemblies of 1762 and 1769, asserting that frequent elections "tend greatly to the happiness and good government of this colony," attempted to broaden the definition of a freeholder, reducing the requirement of undeveloped land to 50 acres and the ownership period to six months, while imposing new requirements that houses on town lots had to be at least 12 feet square. But both the 1762 and 1769 voting laws, endorsed by the Governor, were rejected by the King in another exercise of the royal prerogative. Most Loudoun properties, including 95% of the leaseholds, were larger than 100 acres. And Leesburg's restrictive covenants on town lots required larger houses than those called for in the revisions. So the "vetoed" laws would have resulted in little change in the Loudoun County electorate, in any event. [Hening, II/425, III/26, III/172 and VII/517; Democracy, pp. 125-127, 132-133, 137 and 147; Glossary; Virginia, p. 36].

Age, sex, race and religion, as well as property, were all taken into account in the voting laws. The vote was restricted to free men over the age of 21. All women, criminals, slaves and recusants were specifically barred from voting. Virginia's laws were adapted in 1699 to account for Parliament's Acts of Religious Toleration and the Assembly allowed for Quakers, who could give an affirmation instead of the voter's Oath. While recusants technically were not eligible to vote, as a practice catholics and other non-Episcopals were not prosecuted in Virginia under the recusant statutes. The custom developed, particularly in Loudoun, whereby every adult man in the community, regardless of religion, was allowed a vote if he was otherwise qualified as a freeholder. Henry Peyton, an owner of property in colonial Loudoun and a losing candidate for Burgess in 1761 in Prince William County, challenged George Brent's vote because Brent was Catholic but the Assembly rejected the challenge when it was established that Brent met the property qualifications and otherwise was of good character. In 1723, relying on allegations of the complicity of free Negroes in an aborted slave insurrection, the Assembly extended voter prohibitions to bar all free Negroes, mulattoes and Indians from the voting franchise. [Hening, III/172, III/236 and IV/133; Glossary; Democracy, p. 131; Assembly (1761) pp. 126-130].

At various times the Assembly intervened to confirm the right to vote: in one instance for a minister claiming a vote based solely on the parish glebe lands; and, in another for a man who moved a lean-to shack onto his small town lot just before an election. The vote was reinstated to "householders" in Norfolk, Jamestown and Williamsburg in the unincorporated town Acts of the 1700s. Eventually, the vote was also extended to anyone who served a five-year apprenticeship in a trade in one of the King's boroughs. Servants in Norfolk were specifically excluded from the vote, but indentured workers in Loudoun who met the other voting requirements were not similarly disabled. [Democracy, p. 132; Hening, III/53, III/404, IV/475, V/204 and VI/261].

Participation in colonial elections was an affirmative responsibility, not an option. As early as 1646, "every freeholder actually resident within his county," was required to personally appear and, after reciting an exacting oath to the Sheriff, give his vote for the Burgesses. Only free contract servants were exempt from the fine of 100 lbs. of tobacco imposed for not voting. The penalty for not voting was increased to 200 lbs. of tobacco in 1662; the same penalty that applied in the 1750s. Storms and harvesting often kept colonial voters away from the polls, but there is no evidence that the penalty for not voting was enforced in colonial Loudoun County. [Hening, I/333-334, II/82 and VII/517].

The colonial Sheriffs, assisted by their deputies, were responsible for conducting elections and certifying results to the Clerk of the Assembly for enrollment. Loudoun Sheriffs would receive a notice from the Secretary of the colony, on behalf of the Governor, at least thirty days before the date set for the seating of every new Assembly, and "within three days [of receipt ... the Sheriff was obligated to] cause a copy thereof to be delivered to the minister and reader[s of the local] parish," designating the Courthouse as the site for an election of Burgesses to take place at least ten days before the next Assembly. Every time the Secretary of the Colony issued a writ calling for the election of Burgesses, he charged the county 350 lbs. of tobacco, which was thereupon supposed to be "levied on the inhabitants" in the annual county budgeting. Virginia Sheriffs frequently manipulated Assembly elections by selecting an election day that was advantageous to their own candidate, but this practice was not a significant factor in Loudoun elections. Shortly after sunrise on election day, the Sheriff would arrange a row of tables on the lawn of the Courthouse, or inside the Courtroom if the weather was inclement. The Sheriff, often with the assistance of the County Clerk, would administer the voter's oath to each voter in his turn. Candidates would personally greet voters in line or from a position behind the election tables. Either the candidate or a prominent member of the community, representing him, would be seated at the election tables and would record the name of each of the voters as they stated their preferences for Burgess. The Sheriff had the authority to adjourn an election, continuing voting until the following day, if he determined that bad weather or some other exceptional situation had caused the absence of a significant number of voters. Otherwise, the Sheriff would usually close the polls at sunset after loudly announcing his intention several times. The law designated "the hours of one and three of the clock in the afternoon" on election day as the "time appointed for a [session of the county] court to be held for receiving the propositions and grievances, and the publick claims," all of which would be certified to the new Assembly. If the election was conducted inside the Courthouse due to bad weather, the Sheriff would have to adjourn election activities while the county court convened for the session of public claims. This method of certifying petitions and claims to the Assembly insured that newly elected Burgesses were aware of the concerns of their constituents and that, aside from campaign posturing, Burgesses were charged with an agenda by their county court. [Hening, III/172, V/330 and VII/517-530; and, Assembly, (1770) p. 57; infra, Chapter on the County Militia].

In the 1700s the Virginia Assembly grew increasingly concerned with various untoward and coercive activities that candidates employed. It had become a standard practice, in fact a Virginia election day ritual, for candidates and their supporters to "treat" voters after they had cast their vote, serving dozens of gallons of intoxicating punch, hams and sides of beef at a location convenient to the election tables. But treating voters before they cast their ballots was considered improper, so candidates side-stepped this prohibition simply by arranging for supporters to advance the cost of the treating. Nonetheless, the Assembly's Committee of Privileges and Elections occasionally refused to seat

Northern Neck Burgesses who had crossed the line. John Awbrey (first known resident on the "Leesburg" site) probably went too far when he used his position as tobacco inspector to sway the Prince William County election of 1736 for the benefit of fellow inspector Thomas Osborne, in the process ruining his own political future. "Enormous misdemeanors" in that election resulted in the adoption of a new Virginia law that basically barred all tobacco inspectors from participation in future campaigns. Loudoun's colonial Burgesses never experienced the censure of their peers in the Assembly, but then again they never sank a ferry or destroyed a bridge to obstruct the passage of opposing voters, nor is there any record of drunken rioters with drawn swords interfering with the peaceful conduct of balloting in colonial Leesburg. The modern reader will be surprised to learn that candidates in colonial times were not supposed to make promises during election campaigns - and quite often, when a winning candidate was found to have promised his vote for a particular purpose, the other members of the Assembly would refuse to seat him and order a new election. The idea, discarded in the 1770s as pre-Revolutionary frictions increased, was that Burgesses were elected to lead, not follow, and accordingly were under a primary obligation to use their personal judgment in matters deliberated in the Assembly. The Burgesses went to great lengths in codifying additional election rules in the ill-fated 1762 election law and, despite the Crown's disapproval of the law, the Assembly adopted most of the new rules in their internal ethical processes. [Hening, III/173, III/243 and VII/517; Assembly, (1736) p. 264, (1745) p. 292-293, (1756) p. 456, (1758) p. 83, and (1761) pp. 17 and 269; Democracy, pp. 152-159].

In September of 1758, Loudoun Sheriff Aeneas Campbell suffered the supreme indignity of having the Assembly summon him to appear in Williamsburg in person to amend his faulty election return. Campbell arrived two weeks later and, under arrest, tendered amendments to his Writ of return of Loudoun's election and paid the cost of his summons. A Loudoun election return was again found defective in form in 1761, but the Assembly accepted Sheriff Nicholas Minor's Writ anyway. And the irregular form of Loudoun's return was still drawing attention when Sheriff Charles Tyler's Writ was reviewed by the Assembly in 1766 before it was found to have been "made in the Form prescribed by Law." [see infra, The Record, pp. 34, 35 and 37].

There were few "privileges" allowed to Burgesses, but only members of the Assembly while they were actually in session (and Virginia militiamen in active service), were immune from the civil process of the county and General Courts. Wages for the Virginia Burgesses were first authorized by the Assembly in 1636. In 1642 counties were instructed to pay the wages of their Burgesses directly from the annual county levy. In 1660, noting "excessive expenses of the Burgesses causing diverse misunderstandings between them and the people," the Assembly first limited Burgesses' wages to a specific per diem amount. The wage rates and travel expense limits set in 1699 and reenacted in 1705 would remain essentially unchanged for 70 years, and were still in effect when Loudoun County was created in 1757. The county courts were responsible for the wages of the Burgesses until 1723, when Burgesses began drawing their salaries and expenses directly from the public Treasurer of the colony. [Hening, I/229, I/267, III/172, IV/136, IV/279, VII/115 and VII/249].

Between 1757 and 1762, Loudoun Burgesses were allowed 10 shillings in wages for each day in attendance (valued in Loudoun County at 80 lbs. of tobacco), eight days of travel time at the same rate, and travel expenses limited to 1,040 lbs. of tobacco, all paid by the public Treasurer of the colony rather than the county court. The 1762 Assembly briefly changed the pay rate to "fifteen shillings a day for coming to, attending at, and returning from every session ... and ... to every burgess for ... Loudoun, five days coming and five days returning" for a travel allowance. But the same Assembly reinstated the 10 shilling rate after the public expressed outrage at the increases. While the counties were again instructed to pay their Burgesses' wages directly, as Loudoun did in 1760 and 1764, members of the Assembly generally drew their wages and expenses directly from the Treasurer of Virginia, in cash, whenever they could. Burgesses relied on the excuse that it was "a great ease to the poorer sort of people, by lessening the levy by the poll" that was imposed annually by each of the county courts, but an unstated, additional benefit was that this procedure also limited the public scrutiny of the Assembly's wages and expenses. This practice continued even, as in 1762, when there was "not money sufficient in the Treasurer's hands to pay the Burgesses wages." [Hening, VII/249, VII/440, VII/508, VII/527, VII/ 596, VII/658, VIII/181 and VIII/293; see infra, pp. 35, 36].

The Governor's Council was almost universally comprised of members of the colonial Assembly who had been promoted, but some local functionaries were not allowed to advance to the Assembly. The Assembly disqualified every "sheriff or under sheriff of any county, or inspector of tobacco at any of the publick warehouses ... for two years next after he shall be out of office." Sheriffs conducted the Assembly elections and were responsible, at least on paper, for the collection and disbursement of the Burgesses' wages, so the Assembly considered it unseemly to have anyone serve in both capacities simultaneously. The tobacco inspectors, colonial functionaries who derived a substantial franchise income while collecting the King's tobacco duties, generally obtained appointment by the recommendation of their Burgesses, and as such were essentially employees of the Assembly. The principle of separation of the executive and legislative powers was thus applied in a limited manner in colonial Virginia before the Revolution. On the other hand, county court justices and clerks were not barred from service in the Assembly, and Loudoun County was not exceptional in having two senior Justices of the Peace, members "of the Quorum" of the colonial county court, as its representatives in the Virginia Assembly. [Hening, VI/185, VII/529 and VIII/95; Landmarks, p. 327; Frontier, pp. 18-21; infra, Chapter on the County Court].

The first election of Burgesses for Loudoun County took place on July 20, 1758. The permanent location for the County Courthouse had been established by the Governor in Council the previous month, so Loudoun Sheriff Aeneas Campbell should have selected Nicholas Minor's plantation house at Fruitlands, near the future site of Leesburg, as the location of the first election. Francis Lightfoot Lee, the youthful County Lieutenant who had inherited a large estate in eastern Loudoun, and James Hamilton, a senior Justice of the county court and a respected Captain of the militia living in western Loudoun, were elected as Burgesses. Anthony Russell and Fielding Turner probably ran unsuccessfully in the first election. They were militia Captains and senior Justices of the county court who both lived east of Goose Creek in the Broad Run area and had asked to be passed over in the appointment of the first Loudoun Sheriff in order to maintain their eligibility for election. A contemporary political pundit remarked that an election that was to be held the same day in Fairfax

County would "weaken Colo. [Francis] Lee's interest and it is thought occasion him to be Dropt" from consideration in Loudoun. Col. Lee knew better, maintained his candidacy, and was elected ahead of James Hamilton. Lee's supporters undoubtedly made a point of voting early in Alexandria and riding out to Loudoun to cast a second set of votes before sunset, or vice-versa. Lee and Hamilton were reelected when colony-wide elections were conducted in 1761, and again in 1766 on the strength of their staunch opposition to the Stamp Act. A second loss in the 1761 election probably prompted Anthony Russell's retirement from public life that year. Colonel Lee continued to represent Loudoun in the Assembly until he lost a contested election early in 1769, while James Hamilton served in the Assembly through 1771. Together, they gave Loudoun the most stable county delegation in the Virginia Assembly in the decade before the Revolution.

In the 1758 elections, Colonel George Mason of Gunston Hall and George Johnston of Belvale defeated Charles Broadwater of Difficult Run, replacing George William Fairfax and John West ("Junr." of Alexandria) as Fairfax County Burgesses. Broadwater's electoral loss should be attributed to the creation of Loudoun, and a corresponding loss of support from his immediate neighbors in the theretofore western reaches of Fairfax. Elsewhere in the Northern Neck, Thomas Ludwell Lee was elected from Stafford County along with Thomson Mason (subsequently the owner of Raspberry Plain and a Burgess for Loudoun). Richard Henry Lee, another of Francis Lightfoot Lee's brothers, was elected in Westmoreland County along with cousin "Squire" Richard Lee of Lee Hall. There were 51 new members among the 106 Burgesses when the Assembly convened in Williamsburg on September 14th, and the Burgesses from the Northern Neck included three of the Lee brothers and their Lee cousin, the two Mason brothers, and George Washington, who had won election in Frederick County. [GW Papers, V, pp. 265 and 288; Hening, VIII/9].

Before the end of the 1760s, Francis Lightfoot Lee was appointed to three standing committees in the Assembly and was widely considered to be among nine Virginians, including George Washington and Patrick Henry, who were ranked just below the Speaker and Treasurer in their influence in the Assembly. The advance of Francis Lee and his peers was a manifestation of the sea-change then taking place in the power structure of the colony.

During the 1760s and 1770s, the concentration of political power in the Virginia Assembly shifted gradually from the tidewater to the piedmont, and as the Revolution approached, the "firebrands" were often representatives elected in either the piedmont or the Northern Neck. On February 27, 1766, a host of modest planters joined "Loudoun," or "Frank," Lee (as his family called him), and other tidewater leaders, at Leedstown on the Rappahannock river, expressing opposition to the Stamp Act. Shortly after losing in the 1769 election in Loudoun, Francis Lightfoot Lee found solace in a marriage to his third cousin Rebecca Tayloe, a daughter of John Tayloe II. The couple settled at Lee's Menokin plantation in Richmond County, but Governors continued to appoint Francis Lee as a Loudoun Justice. Promptly upon his change of residence, "Loudoun" Lee was elected to the Assembly in the fall of 1769 in Richmond County. Lee resumed his advance in the leadership of the Assembly, culminating in his selection as one of Virginia's representatives in the Continental Congress from 1775 to 1779. In that capacity, Francis Lightfoot "Loudoun" Lee joined his brother Richard Henry Lee in signing the Declaration of Independence in 1776. [Assembly, (1761) p. Lxxiii; Lee, p. 217; Landmarks, p. 344; Legends, p. 104; infra, Chapter on the Militia].

James Hamilton appears to have been the son of John Hamilton, Fairfax County's first Deputy King's Attorney, who had served "Loudoun" in that capacity from 1742 until his death late in 1751. In June of 1754, James Hamilton began an active role in the business affairs of western Fairfax, lending financial support to William West by agreeing to act as security on West's ordinary bond. Shortly thereafter, the first petitions were advanced to the Virginia Assembly requesting the formation of Loudoun County. James Hamilton resigned his seat on the vestry of Truro parish in 1755, and he and his wife, despite the severe disruptions of the western frontier caused by the renewal of Indian warfare, moved from Truro parish in eastern Fairfax to the western reaches of Cameron parish. James Hamilton timed his westward move with political providence. In September of 1755 Hamilton accepted an appointment as a Justice of the Fairfax County Court, receiving his copy of the "Body of Laws" from recently retired Fairfax Justice Stephen Lewis. That month, Hamilton was also commissioned as a Captain of the Fairfax County militia. In these dual capacities, just months after Gen. Braddock's disaster in the woods, James

Hamilton became the most senior resident public official in, and assumed the mantle of leadership for, Fairfax County west of the Kitoctin/Bull Run mountains. It seems that James Hamilton's reputation as a leader was forged in the crucible of that precarious time on Loudoun's upper piedmont - when the concern for public safety was very real and men of distinction rose to meet the challenge. In 1756, when William Dodd opened his ordinary near Clark's Gap, James Hamilton supported the venture by acting as a security on the ordinary bond. In this way, and perhaps as a silent partner in Dodd's ordinary, Hamilton strengthened his acquaintances with the yeomen who lived between Goose Creek and the Short Hill. [FXCOCO (1754) pp. 100, 404, 418 and 448; and see infra, Chapter on the County Militia].

Early in 1758, James Hamilton purchased the westernmost town lot on Loudoun Street in Leesburg, and Hamilton took an active role in the founding of the new town. He accepted a position as one of the town Managers prior to incorporation, and subsequently was appointed one of the first town Directors by the Virginia Assembly. That spring, before Loudoun's first election, Capt. Hamilton led draftees of the Loudoun militia to Winchester for service in the frontier forts. Promptly after his election as a Burgess, Hamilton moved westward, up the Shenandoah Road, renting out his Leesburg townhouse to William West's son-in-law Craven Peyton. Hamilton was commissioned as the Major of the Loudoun County militia in December of 1758, and as such he was one of George Washington's hosts on the later's travels along the great road to Winchester during the French War. James Hamilton spent his entire career in the Virginia Assembly on the Committee of Public Claims, where his experience with militia and financial matters was undoubtedly viewed as an asset. In 1762, Hamilton participated in the Fredericktown meetings, where the theme was the expansion of mercantile interests in the upper Potomac. In June of 1765, when William Fitzhugh was removed from the Loudoun militia colonelcy, the Governor commissioned James Hamilton as the Lt.Col. of the Loudoun militia. If the large number of colonial Loudoun residents who registered tithables with him every year is any evidence, James Hamilton enjoyed a comfortable reputation in the community. [infra, Chapter on Leesburg and Chapter on the Militia; GW Writings, p. 181; Landmarks, p. 579; generally, see LDTX/1].

September 18, 1758 - In the Assembly at Williamsburg, "the Returns of the Writs for electing Burgesses for the Count[y] of ... Loudoun ... are [found to be] not made in the Form prescribed by Law." Refusing amendment of the Writ at the Clerk's table, the Assembly "Ordered that the Sheriff of Loudoun [Aeneas Campbell], be sent for ... to amend his Return." Assembly, (1758) p. 11.

September 22, 1758 - Apparently after seating the Burgesses from Loudoun County despite the rejection of the Loudoun County election Return, the Assembly appoints Francis Lightfoot Lee to the first of his many special committee assignments. This assignment involved a review of the conduct of the military expedition against the Shawnee in 1756. Assembly, (1758) p. 21.

October 2, 1758 - "The House [of Burgesses] being informed, that the Sheriff of Loudoun attended at the Door in Custody of the Serjeant at Arms. Ordered that he amend his Return of the Writ for electing Burgesses for the said County in the Office, and that he be discharged out of Custody [of the Serjeant at Arms after] paying Fees." Assembly, (1758) p. 33.

October 4, 1758 - Francis Lightfoot Lee is appointed to a second special committee in the Assembly, to review a Petition concerning military equipment supplied to Fort Cumberland on the frontier. Assembly, (1758) p. 37.

October 12, 1758 - Lt. Governor Fauquier prorogues the Assembly.

November 9-12, 1758 - The Assembly meets in an emergency session to consider military developments in the French War. ColVa, p. 722.

February 23, 1759 - Burgesses Francis Lightfoot Lee representing Loudoun County, and George Washington who is representing Frederick County, are appointed to serve on the Virginia Assembly's prestigious Committee on Propositions and Grievances. Assembly (1758) p. 57.

February 28, 1759 - The leaders of the Virginia Assembly finally give James Hamilton a committee assignment, appointing "Mr. Hambleton" [sic] to serve on the Committee of Claims. Assembly, (1758) p. 70.

March 13, 1759 - The Virginia Assembly, in session in Williamsburg, hears a Petition from "sundry Inhabitants" of Loudoun County seeking a Bill to authorize the payment of levies and fees in money rather than tobacco. Assembly, (1758) p. 88.

March 14, 1759 - After a second reading in Assembly, the Loudoun "money fee" Bill is referred to a special committee composed of Francis Lightfoot Lee, James Hamilton, and "Mr. Walker," for the drafting of final amendments. Assembly, (1758) p. 93; see infra, Chapter on Agriculture and Economics.

March 17, 1759 - Francis Lightfoot Lee is appointed to another special committee of the Virginia Assembly, this time to review the Petition presented by Lt. Col. Adam Stephens on behalf of the Virginia militia who survived Major Grant's expedition against the French at Pittsburgh. Assembly, (1758) p. 97.

March 19, 1759 - In an event marking his ascension into the ranks of the leadership of the Virginia Assembly, after the Bill allowing Loudoun residents to pay public levys and officers fees in money rather than tobacco is passed on a third reading, Francis Lightfoot Lee is instructed to "carry up the said Bill to the Council for their concurrence." Assembly, (1758) p. 100.

March 26, 1759 - Francis Lightfoot Lee is appointed to yet another special committee of the Virginia Assembly, for final amendment of "A Bill for encouraging Arts and Manufactures" in the colony. Assembly, (1758) p. 109.

November 9, 1759 - Francis Lightfoot Lee and George Washington are appointed as a special committee of the Virginia Assembly to review a Petition from a militiaman who fought against the Indians while at "Fort Ligonier" (in Pennsylvania) in November of 1758. Assembly, (1758) p. 142.

November 12, 1760 - In the itemization of the annual County Levy debits are listed for: "James Hamilton for Burgesses Wages [and expenses] ... 2,052 [lbs. tobacco, valued at £12, 16 shillings, 6 pence] ... [and] Francis Lightfoot Lee for Burgesses Wages [and expenses] ... 3,460 [lbs. tobacco]." Book A, p. 404.

November 12, 1760 - "Ordered that Nicholas Minor Gent. pay unto James Hamilton Gent. [£7], three Shillings and four pence [?!?] (for his Burgesses Wages in May 1760) out of the [County's] Money in his Hands." Book A, p. 405.

March 16, 1761 - The leadership of the Assembly, for some reason, reiterates the appointment of Francis Lightfoot Lee to the powerful Committee for Propositions and Grievances. Assembly, (1758) p. 215; but see supra, p. 34.

Tuesday, May 26, 1761 - In the first year of the reign of George III, a newly elected Virginia Assembly convenes in Williamsburg. Hening, VII/ 639.

November of 1761 - A new Virginia Assembly convenes. Francis Lightfoot Lee and James Hamilton are returned from Loudoun County. Thomas Harrison and Thomas Marshall are seated from Fauquier, John Baylis and Henry Lee from Prince William, George Johnston and John West from Fairfax, and George Washington and George Mercer from Frederick County. These ten Burgesses continue to serve their respective Counties for the next three years - the duration of the 1761 Assembly. Assembly, (1761) pp. 2, 169, 201 and 313.

November 10, 1761 - While in session in Williamsburg, the Virginia Assembly determines that "the Return of the Writ ... for electing Burgesses for ... Loudoun [County was] not made in the Form prescribed by Law ... Ordered that the Return ... be amended by the Clerk at the Table."

January of 1762 - Burgesses reconvene in Williamsburg.

November 4, 1762 - The Virginia Assembly once again reconvenes and reconstitutes its Committees, with Francis Lightfoot Lee advancing on the Committee of Propositions and Grievances, and James Hamilton named to the Committee of Trade. Assembly, (1761) p. 69-70.

December 11, 1762 - Francis Lightfoot Lee and James Hamilton, with the Burgesses from Fairfax, Fauquier and Prince William Counties, are appointed to another special committee of the Assembly. Assembly, (1761) p. 145.

October 31, 1764 - Committees of the General Assembly are reconstituted, with Francis Lightfoot Lee advancing on the Committee of Propositions and Grievances, and James Hamilton on the Committee of Public Claims. Assembly (1764) p. 230-231.

November 13, 1764 - In the itemization of the Loudoun County Levy, a debit is listed for "James Hamilton for Burgesses Wages and Expenses ... 2,736 [lbs. tobacco]." Book B, p. 495.

November 14, 1764 - In the itemization of the County Levy, a debit is listed "To ... Francis Lightfoot Lee, Esqr., for Burgesses Wages and Expenses as Per Account ... 2,633 [lbs. tobacco - about £16, 9 shillings]." Book B, p. 497.

May 6, 1765 - Francis Lightfoot Lee is appointed to a special committee of the Assembly that is charged with the consideration of a petition from Frederick County seeking higher bounties for killing wolves. Assembly, (1764) p. 325.

May 11, 1765 - Finally advancing in seniority in the Virginia Assembly, James Hamilton is appointed to a special committee charged with "amend[ing] an Act for raising a Public Levy." Assembly, (1764) p. 335.

December 27, 1765 - Francis Lightfoot Lee is included on the special committee of the Assembly appointed to consider the petition of Peter Pelham, who claims that the church organ in Williamsburg is "almost unfit for use." Assembly, (1764) p. 355.

January 1, 1766 - Believing that an increasingly vocal and radical element in the Assembly (who oppose the Stamp Act and other manifestations of the Royal Prerogative) will be eliminated in new elections, the Governor dissolves the Virginia Assembly of 1764. Assembly, (1764) p. 364.

November of 1766 - A newly elected Virginia Assembly reconstitutes itself in Williamsburg. Francis Lightfoot Lee and James Hamilton are returned from Loudoun County, as are Thomas Harrison and Thomas Marshall from Fauquier, Henry Lee from Prince William, and John West from Fairfax. George Washington, formerly representing Frederick, is elected from Fairfax, Foushee Tebbs is a new Burgess from Prince William, and James Wood and Robert Rutherford are initially returned from Frederick County. The Writs for the Elections in Frederick and Hampshire Counties, however, had been miscarried and new elections were ordered for those seats. Assembly, (1766) pp. 3-4.

November 7, 1766 - Francis Lightfoot Lee is appointed to a select committee of the Virginia Assembly, and instructed to examine the allegations of irregularities in the Office of former Virginia Treasurer John Robinson. Assembly, (1766) p. xxi.

November 7, 1766 - The Virginia Assembly, in session in Williamsburg, reconstitutes its committees. Francis Lightfoot Lee, in keeping with his increasing stature in the House, is added to the Committee of Privileges and Elections for the first time, along with George Washington, and is again returned to the Committee of Propositions and Grievances. James Hamilton is returned to the Committee of Public Claims. Assembly, (1766) pp. 14-15.

November 7, 1766 - The Virginia Assembly receives "A Petition of the Justices of the County of Loudoun, praying to be reimbursed a Sum of money which they have paid for the revised Laws. [It is] Ordered That the said Petition be referred to the Committee of Claims that they do examine ... and report the same, with their Opinion." Assembly, (1766) p. 19; see infra, Chapter on the County Court in Colonial Times.

November 21, 1766 - The Virginia Assembly heard "An Account of William Mead, for Sundries ... and referred to the Consideration of the Committee of Claims." One William Mead at this time is a maltster in Loudoun. Could this account "for sundries" actually be the Virginia Assembly's beer tab? Assembly, (1766) p. 35; and see infra, Chapter on Apprentices and Tradesmen.

November 25, 1766 - The Assembly, after scrutiny of the Loudoun County election procedures, resolves that "The Return of the Writ for electing [Francis Lightfoot Lee and James Hamilton] Burgesses to serve in this present General Assembly for ... Loudoun County ... [was deemed as] made in the Form prescribed by Law." Assembly, (1766) p. 38.

December 4, 1766 - Francis Lightfoot Lee is appointed to a select committee of the Assembly that is instructed "to prepare Inscriptions for the Obelisk intended to be raised to express the Gratitude of this Colony to the several noble and worthy Patriots who distinguished themselves, in both Houses of the Parliament of Great Britain in procuring the Repeal of the Stamp Act." To minimize any offense to the Crown, a new "Statue of his Most Excellent Majesty" King George III is also proposed. Assembly, (1766) pp. 38 and 53.

December 4, 1766 - Francis Lightfoot Lee and James Hamilton are appointed to a special committee of the Assembly charged with consideration of the Petition of Ralph Wormeley, Esqr., who had petitioned to have entails docked on some of his land. Assembly, (1766) p. 54; infra, Chapter on Lands.

December 8, 1766 - The Virginia Assembly resolves: "That the Petition of the Justices of the County of Loudoun [presented a month earlier] is reasonable and that they ought to be allowed the sum of £18. 19 [shillings]. 4 [pence] Halfpenny to reimburse them the Judgment and Costs of Suit obtained by the surviving Executors of William Hunter, deceased, against Charles Binns, Clerk of the Court of the said County of Loudoun, for the Copies of the Laws in their Petition mentioned." Assembly, (1766) p. 57; supra, The Record, p. 37; see infra, Chapter on the Courthouse, Clerk of Court and Attorneys.

December 12, 1766 - A select committee of the Virginia Assembly, with our "Mr. Francis Lee" as a member, reports its findings: that "many Errors and Omissions having been discovered ... at the Death of John Robinson ... there remains due from the late Treasurer [of Virginia] ... a Balance due to the Publick of £100,761.7.5." Assembly, (1766) pp. xxi-xxii.

December 18, 1766 - "On Tuesday last the Hon. House of Burgesses adjourned themselves to the 12th of March next, when they will meet and go through the business of this session." VAGAZ/PD, p. 2, col. 3.

The summer after the "Great Charter" of Virginia ended the military government of the colony in 1618, the administration of justice in the Virginia colony began four decades of evolution. At first, commanders of the various plantations replaced the colony's military leaders as local judicial functionaries. Monthly courts were installed at three plantations in 1622. However, when barely a thousand colonists survived the Indian massacres of 1623, with most of them huddled in fortified settlements along the James River, the judicial system regressed. As the population grew and the area of settlement again expanded into the interior of the tidewater, the need for accessible local courts became evident. The "Monthly Courts" were reestablished in 1634 as part of the scheme of county organization, and county courts replaced them in 1643. Plantation commanders were replaced in their judicial capacities by the commissioners of the monthly, and then county, courts. The number of commissioners (Justices) in each county varied with the number of men available to serve and the pleasure of the Governor. A rise in partisan politics came along with the growing number of county court commissioners, until the Assembly found it necessary, to "preserve the peace of the people ... that the commissioners in each county be restrained to the number of eight ... being at present [in 1658] the eight first in each commission." This limit included the Sheriffs, who did not sit on the bench of the courts, so the practical effect was to limit sitting county courts to seven Justices. In 1662, the commissioner of the county court was retitled as "Justice of the Peace," the title for a county court judge that was still in use in Virginia at the time of the American Revolution. "For the better dispatch of all buiseness [sic]," the Council directed Governor Berkeley to resume the appointment of supernumerary county Justices in 1672. [Jamestown, p. 110; Hening, I/224, I/273 and II/21; Justices, pp. 50-53; Lee, p. 68].

Governors appointed county court Justices as the need occasioned, naming the members of the court and charging them with the King's commission in a document titled "Dedimus and Commission of the Peace." Justices were always listed in the Dedimus in their order of seniority, although occasionally there were inadvertent omissions, mis-orderings and misspellings. By the

1750s, it was common practice for the sitting county Justices to recommend a slate of additional nominees from their county for the Governor's consideration. Justices, after all, had personal experience with the nominees and were in the best position to weigh the fitness and merits of candidates for the county court. Virginia's Governors learned to rely on the slates when preparing new county commissions although, occasionally, they appointed political favorites or men who had produced introductions from London. When the Secretary of the Colony issued "a commission of the peace, and Dedimus, to administer the oaths and recording the same," he assessed a charge of 160 lbs. of tobacco, with a fee of 100 lbs. of tobacco for "a commission of Oyer and Terminer, and Dedimus [for a felony trial ... each] to be repaid the county by the public." Charges were assessed on the particular county, and then "by the Justices levied on the inhabitants thereof" in the annual county levy. [Hening, I/125, I/132, I/273, I/372, I/402, I/480, II/69-70 and V/330; Glossary; infra, pp. 56-62].

The practice of appointing supernumerary Justices to the county courts was ultimately codified in Virginia law in 1710. The Governor was to appoint "eight or more justices of the peace" for each county court. Reenacted in 1748, this law provided the procedural governance for Virginia's county courts during Loudoun County's first decade. Restating an administrative rule that was first instituted by the 1661 Assembly, the law stipulated that "any four [Justices], one being of the quorum, shall be sufficient to hear and determine all causes depending in the said county courts." [Hening, III/504 and V/489; Justices, p. 51; Lee, p. 68].

"Quorum" had a special legal meaning in colonial Virginia. "According to the ancient custom" of England a county Justice who was referred to as "of the Quorum" was a senior judge who was considered experienced enough to preside over court. If no Justices "of the Quorum" were in attendance on court day the county court could not convene, regardless of the number of junior Justices on hand. Courts in the small, older tidewater counties had difficulty convening when several senior Justices would die in unison. Addressing this problem, and resolving the proprieties when a commission occasionally failed to designate which Justices were of the Quorum, in 1742 the Governor's Council resolved that the senior "one half and one more" of the Justices of a county court were to be considered of the Quorum in the absence of a commission to the contrary. This "formula" was often ignored by the Governor in his issuance of county commissions. In Fairfax County, over half of the Justices were of the Quorum in 1764, while less than half were so designated in 1767. It was not unusual when only 7 of the first 16 Justices appointed in Loudoun County were of the Quorum in 1757, and when 9 out of a total of 18 Loudoun Justices were identified as of the Quorum in the 1766 Dedimus. Every time a county court adjourned, the "first justice in commission then sitting," always a member of the Quorum, had the duty and honor of signing the minute book. [Hening, V/489 and V/497; Glossary; Council V, p. 93; Justices, pp. 64 and 84].

The number of Justices on any colonial county court varied with the size and projected growth of the county. Augusta County at times had as many as three dozen Justices. Fairfax and Stafford usually had two dozen justices while, during its first decade, Loudoun County had an average of sixteen men serving. The first Loudoun County Court consisted of thirteen Justices, with only the first six designated as of the Quorum. Three more Justices were appointed in December of 1757, including Francis Lightfoot Lee who was then named "First Justice." Lee, who was also the County Lieutenant, brought to seven the total number of Justices of the Quorum. In 1762 and 1766 there were 18 Justices, and in 1764 there were 21 Justices appointed to the Loudoun County Court. But the number of appointees did not necessarily indicate the number of Justices available for county court sessions. The Loudoun Sheriff, always a senior Justice, never sat on the bench at a county court. And deaths, moves and refusals to qualify often shortened the list of available Justices, as in 1765 when only 16 of 21 appointees were able to serve. During Loudoun's first decade, the March 1759 court days were the best attended, when ten Justices were present. On three other occasions before 1767, nine Justices attended Loudoun County Court sessions, but there were many, many more instances when the bare minimum of four Justices were on the court bench. On the average, seven Justices, including the Sheriff, were in attendance at Loudoun County Court days, with only four or five normally on the bench at any one time. If the Loudoun County Court appointments are any indication, the Governor gave some thought to geographic balance in his appointments to the county courts. For example, the first commission for Loudoun included seven men from above Goose Creek and six from below, with the Justices of the Quorum well distributed. Additional appointments to the Loudoun Court appear to reflect patterns of population growth in the county, and to "fill in" from neighborhoods where no Justice had been in residence. [infra, pp. 55, 59 and 61].

County court Justices gave a number of Oaths when they took office: an oath appointed by act of Parliament; an oath of abjuration; the "test"; and Oaths of a Justice of the Peace and Justice of the County Court for Chancery. [see infra, Glossary]. The Oath of a Justice of the Peace was:

> *"[I will] do equal right to the poor and to the rich, after [my] cunning, wit, and power and according to the law; ... [I will] not be of counsel of any quarrel hanging [pending] before [me] ... and truly do [my] office of a Justice of the Peace, as well within [the] county court as [individually] without and ... [that I will] direct [all warrants] to the Sheriff or bailiffs [constables] ... So Help [me] God."*

In the Oath of a Justice in Chancery, the Justice would:

> *"[promise to] serve our sovereign lord the King and his people ... do equal right to all manner of people, great and small, high and low, rich and poor, according to equity and good conscience, and the laws and usages of this colony and dominion of Virginia, without favour, affection, or partiality ... So Help [me] God."* [Hening, V/489-491].

The colonial gentry viewed service on a county court as a responsibility and the embodiment of their obligation to lead the community, as well as a suitable opportunity to enhance their personal stature by fostering and encouraging dependents through their patronage. Appointment to a colonial county court was also an indication of an individual's overall level of business success and reputation, not to mention political influence. The Justices, aside from the Sheriff, were not paid a salary, nor were they reimbursed for the expenses normally incurred in fulfilling the obligations of their office. But the inconveniences involved in the constant conduct of the public's business were surely outweighed by the intangible benefits deriving from the influence that accrued to men who were recognized as the leaders of their community.

In their administration of justice, colonial county courts functioned as a combination of orphans, probate and claims courts. County courts had jurisdiction "to hear and determine all causes ... except such criminal causes where the judgment upon conviction shall be for the loss of life or member [limb] ... outlawry against any person ... [or cases] of less value than [25] shillings." Every county court Justice, alone, had jurisdiction to hear and resolve any dispute involving less than 25 shillings. Acting individually or in pairs, Justices of the Peace could issue warrants at any time for the apprehension of traitors, rioters, pirates, anyone breaking the peace, or for anyone accused of committing a crime. After a local "arraignment," all felony trials were conducted in Williamsburg in the General Court unless the Governor issued a Special Dedimus of Oyer and Terminer. Sitting together in session as the county court, Justices were empowered to hear all civil cases involving more than 25 shillings in controversy, appeals of the rulings of individual Justices, and cases where a misdemeanor was alleged.

Before 1767 county commissions did not automatically authorize Oyer and Terminer trials in the county courts. Any white colonist who was accused of murder, treason or any other felony was tried in Williamsburg. The only capital cases that were heard at a county court were the felony trials of slaves. In those instances the county court set forth the circumstances of the case in a petition to the Governor, who would issue a Special Dedimus of Oyer and Terminer for the conduct of the trial in the county court. A Special Dedimus invariably named the sitting Justices in the county and the process came to be widely viewed (except by the accused) as an unnecessary expense and a waste of time and energy. Colonial amendments of the law in 1765 put it within the discretion of the Governor whether or not to include an Oyer and Terminer authorization in a county's General Dedimus, which Gov. Fauquier instituted as a regular practice in 1767. While the Stamp Act crisis may have been a catalyst for streamlining procedures for the local trial of slaves, the change in the law did not result in any real or perceived increase in the power of Virginia's colonial county courts. [infra, Chapter on Crimes and Punishment; Hening, VI/104 and VIII/138; Justices, p. 53].

Colonial county courts appointed new county Constables annually. Grand juries and trial juries, like the deputy Sheriffs, were selected by the Sheriff but became officers of the county court once they were sworn in. The Sheriff, Constables and grand juries have full and separate treatment in other chapters, but we pause here to discuss petit (ie., trial) juries.

"For the more regular inquiry into the breaches of penal laws, and trials of matters of fact," the Sheriff was obliged to "summon a sufficient number of the bystanders ... to attend the court" every day that the colonial county court was seated, so "that out of them may be impanelled sufficient juries, for the trial of causes depending in such court." In order to be eligible for service on a petit jury, a colonist was to "be possessed of a visible estate, real or personal," valued at not less than £50. This was a lesser financial standard than that exacted of grand jurors but may not have been applied carefully because, unlike the grand juries, once a trial jury was sworn in no exception to judgment in the case was allowed on the basis of an individual juror's financial eligibility. Any prospective juror who did not attend the county court when he was summoned was fined 400 lbs. of tobacco, or 50 shillings, just as John Davis and Robert Watson were in April of 1765.

> *"For the more speedy recovery of small debts, it [was] lawful for the justices of any county court to hear and determine all suits ... not exceeding [£5] ... or [1,000 lbs.] of tobacco, by petition, without the solemnity of a jury ... [provided that] the petition shall express whether the debt arises by judgment, obligation or other specialty, or by account."*

Misdemeanor charges originating under the warrant of a Justice, debts, contract disputes and grand jury presentments involving more than £5, matters affecting the title to real estate, and other cases requiring the determination of equity, were all subject to the right of trial by petit jury. When a colonial defendant requested a jury trial in a county court, the county Clerk would note that the defendant had "Put himself upon the Country." A large number of petit juries were impanelled in Loudoun County during its first decade - so many, in fact, that we have omitted the listings of the individual jurors from The Record herein. [Hening, V/498 and V/523-526; infra, The Record, p. 61; infra, Chapter on the Grand Jury, and Chapter on Crimes and Punishment; Glossary].

Various functions of the colonial county courts directly affected property rights. The county courts: took proofs of the transfer of title to land and personal property; established the routes for new county roads (in essence condemning the land in their county that was to be used for roadways); dedicated riverfront lands for use as public landings; condemned lands that were to be flooded or otherwise used in the operation of a water mill; and individual County Justices ordered the punishment of captured runaway servants and slaves (a unique form of "property") and arranged their return to an owner.

The colonial county court functioned as the sole executive body of local government. Justices were responsible for: annual identification and listing of the "tithable" (taxable) residents; establishing the annual county budget and assessing taxes in the annual "levy" on tithables; contracting for and overseeing construction of the county's public buildings and other public improvements like bridges over streams; maintaining and improving the "King's Highways" through the appointment and supervision of "surveyors," overseers of the roads and their "hands"; licensing new grist mills in their county and the ferries across interior rivers; regulating the inspection of flour, beef, pork, tar and turpentine that was intended for export; licensing and authorizing the establishment of all inns and taverns (ordinaries); and establishing the retail prices that the local ordinaries were permitted to charge for liquors, meals and provender.

County courts were also charged with the organization of new Episcopal parishes in their county. Sheriffs certified the results of parish vestry elections to the county court and new colonial Vestrymen were required by law to give the Oaths of their office to the County Justices in open court. Justices coordinated with parish vestries to provide for the maintenance of the poor, sick and disabled, and frequently arranged with local tradesmen for the apprenticing of impoverished youth and orphans. If a servant or apprentice was abused by his/her master, or a cripple or aged individual was unable to pay the county levy, and the matter came to the attention of the Loudoun County Court, it usually acted to remedy the situation without hesitation. Colonial county courts also had quasi-legislative functions, most notably the review and certification of Petitions and Public Claims that were intended for the Governor or the House of Burgesses.

Among the judicial responsibilities that the new Loudoun County Court did not take lightly was the maintenance of the dignity and decorum of the court, as evidenced by the contempt citations that were issued in open court in 1758 and 1759. It is most curious that these citations were issued against four men, Cornelius Donnehue [sic], Dennis Dallis, Alexander Farrow and Ferdinando O'Neale, who were all overseers of slaves and, after a graduated increase in the penalty that was meted out, there were no more citations issued for cursing in court for a number of years. [infra, pp. 55 and 56; see infra, the Chapter on Attorneys].

Appeals were allowed in common law and chancery cases involving county court judgments over £10 or 2,000 lbs. of tobacco, or in cases affecting the title to land regardless of the monetary amount involved. Since only about one of every twenty contested matters in a county court involved a judgment of this magnitude, the Loudoun County Court was generally viewed as a court of last resort. The appeal of a county court ruling was taken first to the General Court in the Williamsburg. After the General Court, the King's Privy Council in London was a court of final appeal that was seldom frequented by Virginians due to the incredible expense of trans-Atlantic litigation. [Hening, II/65, V/489 and V/491].

When Prince William County was created in 1730, the court days were set "upon the third Wednesday in every month." After several reconfigurations, the 1748 "Lawyers Session" of the Virginia Assembly changed the monthly Fairfax County Court to a quarterly schedule, with sessions held in March, June, September and December. That year the Fairfax County Court days were also changed, to the 3rd Tuesday of the month, while Prince William was to meet every 4th Monday and Frederick County on the 1st Tuesday. The act calling for quarterly courts in Fairfax County expired in 1752 and Fairfax resumed a monthly court schedule when the Courthouse was relocated to Alexandria that spring. [Hening, IV/303, V/265, V/490, VI/201 and VI/231-232].

From the time of its creation in 1757 until March of 1765, the Loudoun County Court began each session of court on the second Tuesday of the month, in the week following the Frederick County Court and the week preceding the Fairfax County Court. On November 29, 1764, the Virginia Assembly was advised that the "court days are inconvenient" and acting on a Motion, probably introduced by Loudoun County's senior Burgess Francis Lightfoot Lee, amended the county court schedules in and around Loudoun. Court days for the Loudoun County Court were changed to the second Monday of each month, court days for Fairfax County were changed to the third Monday, and Court days for Fauquier County were set to begin on the fourth Monday of the month. The Act of Assembly was given a first reading on December 6th, and a third reading, engrossed and passed all on December 13th. The Council "Agreed to the Bill" on the 15th and the Governor gave "his Assent" on December 21, 1764. The new county court days took effect and were observed on schedule the following March. Virginia law provided that, "if the business of any of the [county] courts cannot be determined on the court day, the justices may adjourn from day to day, until all causes and controversies, then depending before them shall be heard and determined or otherwise continued." As a matter of course, colonial county courts were extremely reluctant to hold session for more than one week at a time. In this regard, the colonial Loudoun County Court was exemplary. [Hening, VII/148 and VIII/47; Assembly, (1764) pp. 278-284, 292, 295 and 308; generally, LDCOCO].

Thomas, Lord Fairfax, held a Commission from the King that directed all county courts in the Northern Neck Proprietary to admit him as their "Chief Justice." In this capacity, Lord Fairfax frequently presided over the Frederick County Court sessions in colonial Frederick Town (Winchester), and occasionally he would take the bench along with the Fairfax County Court at colonial Springfield (Freedom Hill at Tyson's) and in Alexandria. But there is no evidence that Lord Fairfax ever exercised his Commission as Chief Justice to sit with the Loudoun County Court in Leesburg. [see, FXCOCO, 1749 Book, p. 45].

Before Loudoun County was created, a number of notable men served the area as county justices. Perhaps the most distinguished, and almost certainly the first "Loudoun" resident Justice, was Francis Awbrey who was one of the initial Justices of the Quorum in Prince William County when that County was created in 1731. Before 1735, Awbrey moved up the Potomac from the area now known as Rosslyn in modern Arlington County to the Big Spring area in "Loudoun," where he resided until his death in 1741. Awbrey was followed by Jeremiah Bronaugh and Richard Osbourne, justices first in Prince William and then Fairfax who may have lived in southeastern "Loudoun" before their deaths in 1749 and 1750, respectively. John Gregg, who lived near the Prince William line, was a Fairfax Justice for two years before his death in 1743. Amos Sinclair, a resident Justice of the Clarks Run section, served in the Fairfax Court for two years before his death in 1744. Andrew Hutchison, who lived near the Mountain road on the Salisbury Plain and was appointed to the Fairfax Court in 1745, had certainly retired from the court before 1749, the year of the earliest surviving records for colonial Fairfax. Unfortunately, the only surviving colonial record of his service as a county justice is the distinction that was accorded him when he was referred to as a "Gentleman," the standard honorific applied to county justices. Captain John Middleton, who owned lands above Little River, was also appointed to the Fairfax Court in 1745, but was dropped from the commission by 1748. Three other "Loudoun" residents of Fairfax, Moses Linton, Joseph Watkins and Francis Hague, were appointed in 1749. Moses Linton served the County as a Justice as well as Cameron parish as a Vestryman until his death in 1752. Fairfax Justice Joseph Watkins was responsible for taking the lists of tithables "up Cameron" parish in 1749, but was dropped from the commission by 1751. Francis Hague, a Quaker preacher at the Fairfax Meeting at Waterford, apparently refused to take the Oaths required of a county justice. There is no record of Hague's service on the bench of the Fairfax Court even though he was an active litigant and continued to be selected for and serve on juries. Hague was still so well respected in 1758 that he would be named as one of the first Trustees of Leesburg. Sampson Turley was appointed to the Fairfax County Court in 1755. Turley was a member of one of the oldest landowning families in Virginia's Northern Neck and was allowed the choice of association when Loudoun County was formed. The 1757 survey of the Fairfax-Loudoun line revealed that Turley's plantation house was west of the boundary and in Loudoun, but he continued to serve as a Justice on the Fairfax County Court. Upon his election to the vestry of Cameron parish in 1759 Sampson Turley retired from the Fairfax Court. Turley never sought nomination to the Loudoun County Court although he took an active role in Loudoun affairs. In 1766 Sampson Turley acted as a Security on Loudoun Sheriff Francis Peyton's bond, and he continued to serve as a Vestryman for Cameron parish until the 1771 vestry elections. [see infra, Chapter on Leesburg; Council, IV/239, V/103, V/122, V/179 and V/279; infra, Chapter on Surveys; see generally, FXCOCO].

The Fairfax County Court of the 1750s was the proving ground for most of the "Loudoun" residents who were appointed to the first Loudoun County Court as Justices "of the Quorum." For five months before Francis Lightfoot Lee was appointed in December of 1757, Anthony Russell was Loudoun's first "First Justice." Russell had purchased land on the upper reaches of Broad Run in 1729, and was well settled there by the time he was first appointed as a Justice for Fairfax in 1748. It appears that his older brother, William Russell (who settled in Fauquier), served as one of the rangers on Governor Spotswood's Golden Horseshoe expedition in 1716, and Anthony continued the family's martial traditions - he held a militia Captain's commission for the Loudoun section of Fairfax County during the French War. When Loudoun County was created in 1757, Russell was initially named as the senior Justice in the new county. Anthony Russell retired from active duty on the Loudoun Court around 1761, perhaps after losing a second campaign for Burgess. In May of 1775, as Loudoun braced for the coming Revolution, Anthony Russell was resurrected politically and elected to serve on the Loudoun Committee of Correspondence. Fielding Turner, who had settled above Cub Run on the Mountain Road in the 1740s and served as the Fairfax County Constable for his precinct in 1748 and 1749, joined Anthony Russell on the Fairfax Court in August of 1752. When Turner took his seat on the bench of the Fairfax County Court, he was taking the place of Lawrence Washington, who had died the previous month. Both Turner and Russell were dedicated jurists, and the pair continued to serve on the Fairfax County Court at Alexandria through June of 1757 - a month after the Governor had removed them from the Fairfax County commission. Turner was commissioned Major of the Loudoun County militia in 1765, about the same time that he began providing room and board to Rev. John Andrews of Cameron parish, but Turner was dropped from the Loudoun County commission in 1768. Upon the creation of Shelburne parish in 1771, both Anthony Russell and Fielding Turner were elected to the reconstituted Cameron parish vestry. James Hamilton and Aeneas Campbell joined the Fairfax County Court in 1755. We have previously discussed James Hamilton in the Chapter on Loudoun County's Burgesses. He served on the Loudoun Court as a Justice of the Quorum, without interruption, from 1757 until his death in 1775. Aeneas Campbell migrated up the Potomac from the Virginia tidewater to settle at Raspberry Plain around 1754. Justice Campbell was responsible for listing the tithables between Broad Run and Kitoctin in 1756, became Loudoun's first Sheriff in 1757, and began construction of the first Loudoun Courthouse in Leesburg in 1758. Official life was not always easy for Aeneas Campbell - in 1758 the General Assembly had him arrested and brought to Williamsburg for giving a faulty election return, and in 1765 the other Justices of the Loudoun Court prosecuted him for non-performance on the Loudoun Courthouse construction bond. Around 1765 Campbell entered a brief partnership with Fairfax merchant and Justice Robert Adams, but when the Loudoun Court continued to prosecute on the Courthouse construction bond in 1768, Campbell left Loudoun County and moved to Frederick County, Maryland. Campbell later distinguished himself, serving as a Colonel of the Maryland militia during the Revolution. [Landmarks, p. 204; Legends, p. 102; Council, V/279, V/400 and VI/51; FXCOCO, (1749) pp. 15, 222, 242 and 265, (1754) pp. 202, 338, 404, 418 and 501, and (1756) pp. 100 and 135; LDCOCO, Book D pp. 30 and 76, and Book E pp. 89 and 137; LDCOWIL, Book A, p. 252; supra, Chapter on Burgesses; infra, Chapter on Cameron Parish].

The other two original Loudoun Justices of the Quorum were William West and Nicholas Minor. While neither had prior personal experience on a county court, both were related to a host of colonial jurists. The brothers, fathers and grandfathers of both William West and Nicholas Minor served as Justices elsewhere in the Northern Neck, and William West's nephews, Hugh West and (Loudoun Justice) George West, were the Deputy King's Attorney and Surveyor, respectively, of both Fairfax and Loudoun County. [Council, V pp. 103, 179 and 330; Landmarks, pp. 138 and 344].

Occasionally news of the death of a County Justice would not reach the Governor's Council prior to the issuance of a new Dedimus. The instance of Loudoun Justice Richard Coleman's death around February of 1764 affords an example. The Governor reappointed Justice Coleman to the Loudoun Court in October of 1764, a good nine months after his demise. Similarly, an appointment for the Fairfax County Court had been offered up to the spirit of Lawrence Washington in 1753. [infra, The Record, p. 61; infra, Chapter on Coroners and Deaths; Council, V/400].

Francis Lightfoot Lee was commissioned as Loudoun's second "First Justice" in December of 1757 and was elected as a Loudoun Burgess in 1758. Francis "Loudoun" Lee was a Burgess for Loudoun's entire first decade, and the Governor continued to appoint him to the Loudoun County Court as Second Justice even after he moved to Richmond County in 1769. He and his brother Richard Henry Lee were two of the Virginia representatives who signed the Declaration of Independence in 1776. [supra, Chapter on Loudoun Burgesses; infra, Chapter on the Militia].

The reader should beware of the confusion surrounding Benjamin Grayson. There were three men with the name who rose to prominence in "Loudoun" in the late colonial period. One Benjamin Grayson [\1] was a Glasgow merchant who settled at Dumfries, purchased considerable tracts of Loudoun land in the 1730s, served as a Justice in Prince William for three decades, fathered (Loudoun's second King's Attorney) William Grayson, (Loudoun Justice) Spence Grayson and Benjamin Grayson\2, and died in the mid-1750s. Benjamin\2, served as a Fairfax County Justice from 1759 until his death in 1768, was in a commercial partnership with (King's Attorney) Hugh West (Junr.) and was a frequent litigant at the Loudoun County Court. Benjamin Grayson\3, a Loudoun County Justice, was probably a nephew of the first. He apparently tied his fortune to the Colchester tobacco trade, and John Ballendine's wheat mills and bread ovens at Occoquan, and as a consequence suffered considerable financial embarrassment before his death in the spring of 1763. [Council, V pp. 103, 238 and 394; Justices, pp. 64-65; Fairfax, p. 65; infra, Chapter on Familial Relations, and Chapter on Deaths and Estates; generally, see Landmarks, FXCOCO, and Colport].

One distinguishing characteristic of county justices in the late colonial period is that, almost to the man, they owned slaves. And the Gentlemen Justices of the Loudoun County Court were a good example. In the 1750s, less than 100 residents in Loudoun County owned slaves - about 15% of white heads of households. All, save one, of the "Loudoun" resident Justices who served between 1735 and 1766 owned slaves when he was appointed to his county court. Even Francis Hague, the Quaker appointee for the Fairfax Court in 1749, was a slave owner. Among the first forty "Loudoun" Justices, only John McIlhaney did not own slaves when he was appointed to the court (in 1757), and even he acquired slaves before he advanced to the status of Justice of the Quorum. McIlhaney probably settled at the Gap of the Short Hill in order to act as manager for John Tayloe's tract, which would explain the preferment accorded him in Loudoun County's first Dedimus since John Tayloe was on the Governor's Council at the time. [see infra, Chapter on Slaves; generally, LDTX/1].

The reader might be surprised to learn that no fewer than seven of the first dozen Justices of the Loudoun County Court, James Hamilton, Aeneas Campbell, William West, Richard Coleman, George West, Charles Tyler and John Moss Senr., at one time either owned, operated or financially backed an ordinary (tavern) prior to their appointment as a county justice. At least eight others with a hand in the Loudoun ordinary business in the 1757-1766 decade, James Lane, Craven Peyton, John Moss Junr., Philip Noland, Leven Powell, John Minor, James Coleman and Charles West, also eventually advanced to the Loudoun County Court. Thus, one can readily deduce that the operation of a tavern in Virginia's colonial piedmont frequently served as a convenient springboard to a career in colonial politics.

Another surprising connection exists between the county courts of Loudoun and Fairfax and their Episcopal parish vestries. Of the first thirty men elected to the vestry of Cameron parish before 1765, no less than nineteen were also member Justices of their county court. Other commentators have noted the existence of this Court-vestry correlation in the Virginia tidewater, but the story here lies in the relative prominence of a healthy minority of the vestry who were not members of the county court. An even more remarkable connection bears witness to the development of an increasingly mature Loudoun-Fairfax community shortly before the Revolution, and is worthy of a small digression.

Early in the summer of 1755 the Fairfax County Court admitted a youthful member of a prominent tidewater family to practice as an attorney. His name was Lee Massey. When the Loudoun County Court organized in 1757, Lee Massey was promptly authorized to practice law there as well. Young Mr. Massey so impressed the Justices in both Fairfax and Loudoun that something of a bidding war must have developed, and the next thing you know Lee Massey was Commissioned a Justice in Fairfax in 1759, and recommended for Justice in Loudoun the following spring and again in December of 1761. In the spring of 1760, Massey, with a servant and several slaves, seated himself in Loudoun on Clarks Run. Meanwhile, he continued to serve as a Justice of the Fairfax County Court in Alexandria throughout the winter of 1761-1762. In the spring of 1762, Massey was finally appointed a Justice in Loudoun County, and he promptly took his seat on the bench of the county court in Leesburg.

Whether Lee Massey's venture above Limestone Run had proven unsuccessful, his industry and personality had come to the attention of the Mason family who were his neighbors in Loudoun, or he had begun to miss the relative urbanity of life below the falls, when the Rev. Charles Green of Truro parish died in 1764 Massey promptly moved back to southern Fairfax County where he was warmly received. The Fairfax Court wasted no time, again recommending Massey's appointment as a Justice and noting that his previous position in seniority on the Court should be restored. But some of Massey's friends seem to have had other plans and Justice Massey did not rejoin the Fairfax Court. The creation of Fairfax parish from the northern half of Truro parish in 1765 had resulted in two vacant Episcopal Rectories in Fairfax County, and Massey's friend and a former fellow Justice on the Fairfax County Court, Townshend Dade, left the Court and was confirmed as the Rector of the new parish. This still left the Truro parish Rectory vacant. In February of 1766, the vestry of Truro resolved that:

> *"... Mr. Lee Massey an Inhabitant of this Parish ... offered to supply the place of a minister herein, and the Vestry being of opinion that he is a Person well Qualified for the Sacred Function, have agreed to recommend him to the Favour of his Grace the Bishop of London & of the Governor of this Colony, for an Introduction to this said Parish, and to Receive him upon his return properly Qualified."*

Governor Fauquier and the Bishop of London both complied and Lee Massey, the former Justice for Fairfax and Loudoun Counties, established a residence at his 'Bradley' plantation near Pohick Church and became the Rector of Truro parish.

The example set by Massey and Dade was not lost on a scion of another tidewater family, Spence Grayson. Spence joined the Loudoun County Court as a Justice in 1766, but shortly thereafter answered the call of the cloth and left for theology studies and ordination in England. In 1771, Spence Grayson, former Loudoun County Justice, returned home and was advanced to the Rectory of Cameron parish, which he served until 1777. So, at the time of the American Revolution, all three Episcopal parishes that encompassed the lands of Loudoun and Fairfax east of Goose Creek had as their Minister a native of the Northern Neck who had previously served in his community as either a Loudoun County or Fairfax County Justice. This connection between the Court and the Cloth, at a critical time in our colonial history, is truly remarkable! [see infra, Chapter on Attorneys; FXCOCO, 1754 Book p. 304, 1756 Book p. 369, and 1763 Book p. 60; Church, p. 325; Truro, pp. 98 and 102; Landmarks, p. 421; infra, pp. 56, 58, 61 and 62; infra, Chapter on Cameron Parish].

The Loudoun County Court was active in opposing the Stamp Act and, like most of the county courts in Virginia, simply refused to convene during the winter of 1765-1766. Josias Clapham, John Peake and John Minor refused to qualify as Justices at about that time and may have done so as an additional measure of protest since both Clapham and Minor rejoined the county court following the repeal of that odious Act. John Peake, whose older brother William Peake Junr. was a Justice in Fairfax County, apparently never joined the bench of the Loudoun County Court and, of the 28 men who were appointed as a Justice of the Peace in Loudoun County before 1767, John Peake was the only one who never took office. The political career of Leven Powell, who was appointed as a Loudoun County Court Justice in 1764, eventually included service as a Virginia Representative in the U.S. Congress when he succeeded the Revolutionary War hero Gen. Daniel Morgan in 1799. [infra, The Record, pp. 61-62].

Summaries of the judicial careers of the twenty-eight men who were appointed as colonial Justices of the Peace for Loudoun County during the 1757-1766 decade are presented for the reader at the end of this chapter, on pages 63 and 64.

The Loudoun Record

July 12, 1757 - The first Dedimus and Commission of the Peace for Loudoun County is read in open court: "Anthony Russell, Fielding Turner, James Hamilton, Aneas Campbell [sic], Nicholas Minor, William West [those six, as Justices] of the Quorum; Richard Coleman, Josias Clapham, George West, Charles Tyler, John Moss, Francis Peyton and John Mucklehany [sic]" are named County Justices in the Dedimus. On May 24, 1757, the Governor and his Council approved and ordered issuance of the Commission at a Council meeting in Williamsburg. Book A, p. 1; Council, VI/51; Legends, p. 327; Glossary.

December 14, 1757 - Francis Lightfoot Lee as "First Justice," James Lane Junr. and Benjamin Grayson, in a second Dedimus and Commission of the Peace, are named as additional Justices for the Loudoun County Court. William Fairfax, Philip Ludwell Lee, a brother of Francis Lightfoot Lee, and John Tayloe, who would eventually become father-in-law to Francis Lightfoot Lee, were three members of the Governor's Council. Book A, pp. 59-60; and, Council VI/51.

March 14, 1758 - William West, George West, "John Mucklehaney" and Benjamin Grayson renew their Oaths as County Justices. Book A, p. 67.

March 15, 1758 - Francis Lightfoot Lee, William West, Nicholas Minor, George West and Benjamin Grayson are the sitting Justices at the Loudoun County Court. Book A, p. 68.

April 11, 1758 - Francis Lightfoot Lee, Fielding Turner, Nicholas Minor, William West, Richard Coleman, Josias Clapham and Benjamin Grayson are the sitting Justices at the Loudoun County Court. Book A, p. 80.

April 11, 1758 - "Cornelius Donnehue ... fined twenty shillings for swearing four Oaths [in the presence of the Court, is to] ... give sufficient Security ... [and pay his fine] at the next Parish Levy or receive on his Bare back ten Lashes." Book A, p. 87.

May 9, 1758 - James Hamilton and Francis Peyton renew their Oaths as Justices and join Nicholas Minor, William West, Richard Coleman, George West, "John Mucklehany" and Benjamin Grayson on the bench. Book A, p. 99.

June 14, 1758 - James Hamilton, Nicholas Minor, William West and James Lane Junr. are the sitting Justices at the county court. Book A, p. 115.

July 11, 1758 - Francis Lightfoot Lee, Anthony Russell, James Hamilton, Nicholas Minor, Charles Tyler and George West are sitting Justices at the Loudoun Court. DALD, (1758) p. 17.

August 10, 1758 - Fielding Turner, Nicholas Minor, William West, Richard Coleman, George West and Francis Peyton are the sitting Justices at the Loudoun County Court. Book A, p. 145.

September 13, 1758 - Nicholas Minor, William West, James Lane Junr. and Benjamin Grayson are the sitting Justices at the Loudoun County Court sessions. Book A, p. 163.

November 14, 1758 - Dennis Dallis is fined twenty shillings (ie., £1) for swearing, apparently in the presence of the county court. Book A, p. 177.

December 12, 1758 - James Hamilton, Nicholas Minor, William West, Charles Tyler, Francis Peyton and John McIlhaney are sitting Justices at the Loudoun Court. DALD, (1758) p. 23.

February 13, 1759 - "Alexander Farrow ... to answer a Contempt offered to the said Court ... [Farrow is fined] twenty shillings" and required to enter a Peace Bond. Book A, p. 191.

March 13, 1759 - Fielding Turner, Nicholas Minor, William West, Richard Coleman, George West, Charles Tyler, Francis Peyton, James Lane Junr.

and Benjamin Grayson are all sitting as Justices at the best-attended county court session during Loudoun's first decade. Book A, p. 207.

May 8, 1759 - Nicholas Minor, Fielding Turner, Richard Coleman and Francis Peyton are sitting Justices at the county court. DALD, (1759) p. 27.

May 9, 1759 - Ferdinando O'Neale is fined 20 shillings for "prophane Swearing," apparently in the presence of the county court. Book A, p. 244.

June 14, 1759 - "Ordered that the Court be adjourned till the second Tuesday in July next." Book A, p. 263.

July of 1759 - No Loudoun County Court session is convened.

August 14, 1759 - Fielding Turner, James Hamilton, Nicholas Minor, Richard Coleman, George West, Francis Peyton and John Mucklehaney [sic] are the sitting Justices at the Loudoun County Court. Book A, pp. 264 and 265.

September 11, 1759 - Nicholas Minor steps down from the bench and accepts his Commission as the Loudoun Sheriff. Loudoun's first Sheriff, Aneas Campbell then renews his Oaths as a County Justice and joins Richard Coleman, Josias Clapham and George West as a sitting Justice of the county court. Book A, pp. 283, 284 and 285.

November 13, 1759 - Fielding Turner, James Hamilton, William West, Richard Coleman, Aeneas Campbell, Benjamin Grayson and George West are the sitting Justices at the Loudoun County Court. DALD, (1759) p. 31.

December 12, 1759 - "Ordered that Court be adjourn'd till the second Tuesday in January next." Book A, p. 321.

January of 1760 - No regular county court is convened.

January 14, 1760 - Fielding Turner, James Hamilton, Aneas Campbell [sic], Josias Clapham, John Mucklehaney and James Lane are the sitting Justices convening a special criminal session of the county court. Book A, p. 321.

March 12, 1760 - Fielding Turner, Aneas Campbell [sic], Richard Coleman, John Mucklehaney and Benjamin Grayson are the sitting Justices at the Loudoun County Court. Book A, p. 327.

May 13, 1760 - James Hamilton, Richard Coleman, George West and John McIlhaney are sitting Justices at the Loudoun Court. DALD, (1760) p. 36.

May 14, 1760 - Fielding Turner, James Hamilton, Richard Coleman, Josias Clapham, George West and James Lane are the sitting Justices at the Loudoun County Court. Book A, p. 345; and see, DALD, (1760) p. 40.

May 14, 1760 - Lee Massey, Craven Peyton, John Gerrard, William Jett [Junr.] and Philip Noland are recommended as "proper Persons to be added to the Commission of the Peace." [It appears that John Gerrard was never appointed as a Loudoun Justice, and the others were not added to the Commission of the Peace for Loudoun County until 1762.] Book A, p. 348.

June 28, 1760 - Occasioned by the first trial of a slave in Loudoun County, a Special Dedimus [naming the entire Loudoun County Court, except for Nicholas Minor who was serving as Sheriff] was addressed to "Francis Lightfoot Lee, Anthony Russell, Fielding Turner, James Hamilton, Aneas Campbell, William West, Richard Coleman, Josias Clapham [of the Quorum], George West, Charles Tyler, John Moss, Francis Peyton, John Mucklehaney, James Lane Junr.

and Benjamin Grayson Gent. ... to Determine all Treasons ... or Misprisions ... perpetrated within ... Loudoun by James a Negro Man Slave belonging to Thomas Gant of ... [Prince Georges County] Maryland." Book A, p. 382.

August 12, 1760 - Fielding Turner, James Hamilton, William West, Richard Coleman and John Mucklehaney [sic] are the sitting Justices at Court. Book A, pp. 384 and 385.

November 11, 1760 - Fielding Turner, James Hamilton, Josias Clapham and John Mucklehaney are the sitting Justices who convene the Loudoun County Court. "George West Gent." and "William West Gent." join their fellow Loudoun Justices on the bench and are noted in the Court Order Book as "Prest." [ie., present]. Book A, pp. 401 and 402.

December 11, 1760 - James Hamilton, Aneas Campbell, William West, Richard Coleman, Josias Clapham, George West and James Lane are the sitting Justices at the Loudoun County Court. Book A, pp. 316 and 317.

February 10, 1761 - James Hamilton, Richard Coleman, Josias Clapham, George West, John Mucklehany and Francis Peyton are the sitting Justices at Court. Book A, p. 409.

February 13, 1761 - John Carlyle, John Hunter and Robert Adam are three of the Justices on the Fairfax County Court. LDCODB, Book B, p. 170.

March 10, 1761 - A new Dedimus and Commission of the Peace for Loudoun County names all of the Justices of the Peace: Francis Lightfoot Lee, Anthony Russell, Fielding Turner, James Hamilton, Aneas Campbell, Nicholas Minor, William West, Richard Coleman, Josias Clapham [of the Quorum], George West, Charles Tyler, John Moss, Francis Peyton, John Mucklehaney, James Lane Junr. and Benjamin Grayson, Gent. are all reappointed to the county court. Sheriff Nicholas Minor, omitted from the Special Dedimus in 1760, is again listed as a member of the Quorum of the Court. Book A, p. 426.

March of 1761 - "Ordered that the Court be adjourned till the Second Tuesday in April next." Book A, p. 449.

April of 1761 - No Loudoun County Court session is convened.

June 9, 1761 - Charles Tyler and Benjamin Grayson renew their Oaths as Justices of the Peace and join Fielding Turner, James Hamilton, George West, John Mucklehaney and Francis Peyton on the bench of the Loudoun County Court. Book A, p. 449.

July 20, 1761 - A special Dedimus issued from the Loudoun County Court identifies a number of the Justices in Prince William County: Henry Lee, Bertrand Ewell, John Baylis, Allan Macrae, George Brett, William Tebbs, Thomas Lawson and John Linton. LDCODB, Book C, p. 42; and see, Glossary.

August 12, 1761 - James Hamilton, Aneas Campbell [sic], Richard Coleman, Josias Clapham, Charles Tyler, and Benjamin Grayson are the sitting Justices at Court. Book A, p. 486.

September 10, 1761 - James Hamilton, Aneas Campbell [sic], Nicholas Minor, Josias Clapham and George West are the sitting Justices at the Loudoun County Court. Book A, p. 504.

Tuesday, October 13, 1761 - At the last Court held in "the First Year of the Reign of King George the Third," Justices convening the Loudoun Court are Nicholas Minor, Charles Tyler, John Mucklehaney and Benjamin Grayson. Book A, p. 525.

November 11, 1761 - Fielding Turner, Aneas Campbell, Nicholas Minor, Richard Coleman and Francis Peyton are the sitting Justices at the Loudoun Court. Book A, p. 531.

December 9, 1761 - Henry Lee, Bertrand Ewell, Allan Macrae, William Tebbs, William Carr, Thomas Lawson and John Linton are some of the Justices of the Prince William County Court. LDCODB, Book C, p. 171.

December 8, 1761 - "Ordered that James Rogers be committed to the Stocks for a Misbehavior there to remain for the space of four Minutes." Book A, p. 547.

December 9, 1761 - James Hamilton, Aneas Campbell [sic], Nicholas Minor, Josias Clapham and James Lane Junr. are the sitting Justices at the Loudoun County Court. Book A, p. 548.

December 9, 1761 - The sitting Justices of the Loudoun County Court, "Absent Josias Clapham Gent.," recommend Lee Massey, William Jett Junr., Craven Peyton, John Moss Junr. and Philip Noland "... as proper Persons to be added to the Commission of the Peace for this County." Book A, p. 549.

February 9, 1762 - James Hamilton, Aneas Campbell [sic], Nicholas Minor, Richard Coleman, Francis Peyton and Benjamin Grayson are the sitting Justices at the Loudoun County Court. Book A, pp. 552-553.

March 10, 1762 - Nicholas Minor, Richard Coleman, Francis Peyton and John Mucklehaney are the sitting Justices at the county court. This is the last monthly county court session that Richard Coleman attends. Book A, p. 562.

March 12, 1762 - "Ordered that the Court be adjourned till the second Tuesday in April next." Book A, p. 581.

April of 1762 - No Loudoun County Court session is convened.

May 11, 1762 - A new Commission of the Peace and Dedimus names the Loudoun County Justices: Francis Lightfoot Lee, James Hamilton, Aneas Campbell, Nicholas Minor, William West, Richard Coleman, Josias Clapham, George West, Charles Tyler, Francis Peyton [of the Quorum], John Mucklehaney, James Lane, Benjamin Grayson, Lee Massey, William Jett Junr., Craven Peyton, John Moss Junr. and Philip Noland, Gent.. [Note that the five men nominated at the end of 1761 are all appointed to the Loudoun County Court, while Anthony Russell and John Moss Senr. are removed from the list and Fielding Turner is omitted.] Book A, p. 582.

May 11, 1762 - James Hamilton, Nicholas Minor, George West, Charles Tyler, John Mucklehaney, Lee Massey and James Lane Junr. are sitting Justices at the Loudoun County Court. Book A, p. 583; DALD, (1762) p. 98.

Friday, May 14, 1762 - Nicholas Minor, James Lane, Lee Massey and John Moss Junr., Gent. are the sitting Loudoun County Justices. Book A, p. 607.

May 14, 1762 - Thomas Fields, "being before the Court and Misbehaving in being Drunk & Cursing and Abusing the Court while sitting ... fin'd five Pounds [£] to be paid down immediately and [the Court ordered that

Fields] give Security for his good Behavior." Book A, p. 622.

June 9, 1762 - Sitting Judges at the Loudoun County Court are James Hamilton, Aneas Campbell, Nicholas Minor, George West, John Moss Junr., and Philip Noland. Book A, p. 630.

July 13, 1762 - James Hamilton, Aneas Campbell [sic], Nicholas Minor, Josias Clapham, James Lane, Lee Massey and John Moss Junr. are sitting Justices at the Loudoun County Court. Book B, pp. 1, 2 and 3.

July 13, 1762 - Lee Massey returns a list of tithables for Loudoun "given in to me since the 9.th of June ... as also my own." LDTX/1, p. 25.

August 11, 1762 - James Hamilton, Aeneas Campbell, Nicholas Minor, Josias Clapham, George West, James Lane and John Moss Junr. are sitting Justices at the Loudoun County Court. Book B, pp. 32-33; DALD, (1762) p. 112.

September 14, 1762 - "At Loudoun County Courthouse ... A new Commission of the Peace and Dedimus for this County bearing Date the seventh Day of May last past, Directed to Francis Lightfoot Lee, Fielding Turner, James Hamilton, Aneas Campbell, Nicholas Minor, Richard Coleman, Josias Clapham, George West, Charles Tyler, Francis Peyton [of the Quorum], John Mucklehany [sic], James Lane, Benjamin Grayson, Lee Massey, William Jett Junr., Craven Peyton, John Moss Junr. and Philip Noland Gentlemen Justices of the said County [18 total] were presented and Openly Read and pursuant to the said Dedimus the said Aneas Campbell took the Oaths appointed by Act of Parliament ... and repeated and Subscribed the Test also took the Oaths appointed by a late Act of Assembly to be taken by Justices of the Peace all which Oaths were Administered to him by the sd. Charles Tyler and Francis Peyton and then the said Aneas Campbell Administered all the aforesaid Oaths to the said Nicholas Minor, Josias Clapham, George West, Charles Tyler, Francis Peyton, Lee Massey and John Moss Junr. who took the same and repeated and Subscribed the Test." [In the only change, Fielding Turner is returned to the Quorum of the court, replacing William West.] Book B, p. 53; see Glossary.

October 25, 1762 - The records of the Truro parish vestry, in Fairfax County, include the payment of 1200 lbs. of tobacco to "Hugh West, Deputy Kings Attorney." It appears that Hugh West continued serving as the King's Attorney (prosecutor) for Fairfax County after Loudoun was organized. Truro, p. 85.

November 9, 1762 - Aneas Campbell, Nicholas Minor, Francis Peyton, John Moss Junr. and Philip Noland are the sitting Justices at the Loudoun County Court. Book B, p. 69.

December 14, 1762, (second Tuesday) - Aneas Campbell, Nicholas Minor, George West, Charles Tyler and Philip Noland are the sitting Justices at the Loudoun County Court. Book B, p. 76.

December 15, 1762 - It is "Ordered that the Court be adjourned till the second Tuesday in January next." Book B, p. 83.

January of 1763 - No Loudoun County Court session is convened.

March 14, 1763 - Nicholas Minor, George West, Charles Tyler, Francis Peyton, Lee Massey and Philip Noland convene a special criminal session of the Loudoun County Court. Book B, p. 84.

April 15, 1763 - Fielding Turner, Aneas Campbell [sic], Nicholas Minor, George West, Charles Tyler, Francis Peyton and Philip Noland are sitting Justices at the Loudoun County Court. Book B, pp. 112 and 114.

May 10, 1763 - Fielding Turner, James Hamilton, Aeneas Campbell, Nicholas Minor, George West, James Lane, Lee Massey and Philip Noland are sitting Justices at the Loudoun Court. Book B, pp. 121 and 124.

June 14, 1763 - Fielding Turner, James Hamilton, Nicholas Minor and Philip Noland are the sitting Justices at the county court. Book B, p. 159.

July 12, 1763 - Fielding Turner, James Hamilton, Aneas Campbell, Nicholas Minor and Lee Massey are the sitting Justices at the Loudoun County Court. Book B, p. 191.

August 10, 1763 - William Carr Lane, Leven Powell, John Peak, John Pearce and John Minor, Gent., are recommended to the Governor by the sitting Justices of the Loudoun County Court "as proper Persons to be added to the Commission of the Peace for [Loudoun] County." Book B, p. 201.

August 11, 1763 - Justices James Hamilton, Nicholas Minor, Aneas Campbell, George West, Charles Tyler and John McIlhaney preside at the Loudoun County Court sessions. Book B, p. 207.

September 13, 1763 - Fielding Turner, James Hamilton, Aneas Campbell, Nicholas Minor, George West and Philip Noland are the sitting Justices at the Loudoun County Court. Book B, p. 230.

September 15, 1763 - Virginia Burgess Francis Lightfoot Lee renews his Oaths as the "First" (chief) Justice of the Loudoun County Court, and joins Fielding Turner, James Hamilton, Aneas Campbell [sic] and James Lane on the bench as a sitting Justice at the Loudoun County Court. Book B, pp. 243-254.

October 11, 1763 - James Hamilton, Aneas Campbell, Nicholas Minor, John Mucklehaney [sic] and Lee Massey are the sitting Justices at the Loudoun County Court. Book B, p. 258.

December 13, 1763 - James Hamilton, Aneas Campbell, Charles Tyler and Philip Noland are the sitting Justices at the county court. Book B, p. 268.

February 14, 1764 - A new Commission of the Peace and Dedimus for Loudoun County is "Directed to Francis Lightfoot Lee, Fielding Turner, James Hamilton, Aneas Campbell, Nicholas Minor, Richard Coleman, Josias Clapham, George West, Charles Tyler, Francis Peyton, John Micklehany [sic] [of the Quorum], James Lane, Lee Massey, Craven Peyton, John Moss Junr., Philip Noland, William Carr Lane, Leven Powell, John Peak, John Pearce and John Minor, Gentlemen Justices" of the County [in all, a total of 21] is received and recorded. James Hamilton, Aneas Campbell, Nicholas Minor, John Micklehaney [sic] and John Pearce give their Oaths of office and take a seat on the bench of the Court. This Commission adds all of the 1763 nominees, replacing William Jett Junr. and Benjamin Grayson, who appear to have died in the summer of 1762 and spring of 1763, respectively. Book B, p. 269; and see infra, Chapter on Coroners, Deaths and Estates.

February 15, 1764 - James Lane and William Carr Lane Gent. "took the usual Oaths ... of a Justice of the Peace and of the County Court in Chancery" and joined Justices James Hamilton, Nicholas Minor, Aneas Campbell and John Pearce on the bench of the Loudoun County Court. Book B, p. 273.

April 10, 1764 - James Hamilton, Aneas Campbell, Nicholas Minor, James Lane, John Pearce and William Carr Lane are the sitting Justices at the Loudoun County Court. Book B, p. 314.

May 8, 1764 - James Hamilton, Aneas Campbell, Nicholas Minor, George West and John McIlhaney are the sitting Justices at the Loudoun County Court sessions. Book B, p. 353.

June 12, 1764 - Fielding Turner, James Hamilton, George West, Charles Tyler, John McIlhaney, Philip Noland and William Carr Lane are the sitting Justices at the Loudoun County Court. Book B, pp. 358, 359 and 360; LDCODB, Book D, pp. 224 and 231; and, DALD, (1764) pp. 51 and 52.

June 13, 1764 - Francis Lightfoot Lee, Gent., again renews the Oaths of his several Offices. Book B, p. 367.

August 14, 1764 - Fielding Turner, James Hamilton, Nicholas Minor and Philip Noland are sitting Justices at the Loudoun County Court. LDCODB, Book D, p. 256.

September 11, 1764 - James Hamilton, George West, Philip Noland and John Pearce are the sitting Justices at the county court. Book B, p. 432.

October 23, 1764 - At the Capitol in Williamsburg, the Secretary of the Governor's Council is instructed to issue a new Commission of the Peace for the Loudoun County Court appointing: "Francis Lightfoot Lee, Fielding Turner, James Hamilton, Oeneas Campbell [sic- Aeneas Campbell], Nicholas Minor, Richard Coleman [sic- marked "dead"], Charles Tyler, George West, Josiah Clapham [sic- Sheriff Josias Clapham; sic- marked "refuses to Qualify"], Francis Peyton, John McIlhaney, of the Quorum; James Lane [Junr.], Lee Massey [marked "removed"], Craven Peyton, John Moss Junr., Philip Nowland [sic- Philip Noland], William Carr Lane, Leven Powell, John Peake [marked "refuses," ie., refuses to qualify], John Pearce & John Minor [also marked "refuses"] Gent." The notations appear to have been taken from a return of the 1764 Commission and used in preparation of the Commission issued in 1766. Josias Clapham "refused" to qualify while he was Sheriff in 1764, but was again sitting on the Court by October of 1765. Justices, p. 57; supra, this page; and infra, p. 62.

November 15, 1764 - Aneas Campbell, Nicholas Minor, George West, Charles Tyler, Philip Noland and William Carr Lane are the sitting Justices at Court. Book B, pp. 501, 504 and 507.

February 12, 1765 - James Hamilton, Aneas Campbell, Nicholas Minor and George West are the sitting Justices at the county court. Book B, p. 517.

February 12, 1765 - Charles Tyler steps down from the bench of the Court to become Loudoun Sheriff. Book B, p. 518.

April 8, 1765 - James Hamilton, Aneas Campbell, Nicholas Minor and George West are the sitting Justices at the county court. Book B, p. 536.

April 9, 1765 - "John Davis and Robert Watson being summoned as Jurors and not appearing altho' Solemnly called, It is Ordered that they be fined each of them [400 lbs.] of Tobacco for such their contempt." Book B, p. 548.

May 14, 1765 - Fielding Turner, Aneas Campbell, Nicholas Minor, James Lane, Philip Noland and Leven Powell are the sitting Justices at the Loudoun County Court. Book B, p. 578.

June 10, 1765 - Fielding Turner, James Hamilton, Nicholas Minor and John McIlhaney are the sitting Justices at the county court. Book B, p. 617.

July 8, 1765 - Fielding Turner, James Hamilton, Nicholas Minor, Francis Peyton, John McIlhaney, William Carr Lane and Leven Powell are Justices sitting at Court. Book B, pp. 673-674.

August 13, 1765 - Fielding Turner, Aeneas Campbell, Nicholas Minor and Philip Noland are sitting Justices at the Loudoun County Court. LDCODB, Book D, p. 573.

August 13, 1765 - William Douglass and Spence Grayson, Gent., are recommended for addition to the Commission of the Peace as new Loudoun County Justices. Book C, p. 21.

October 14, 1765 - James Hamilton, Aeneas Campbell, Josias Clapham, Nicholas Minor and John McIlhaney are sitting Justices at the Loudoun County Court. LDCODB, Book D, p.635.

November and December of 1765 - No general sessions of the Loudoun County Court are held, as a measure of civil disobedience adopted by Justices of the county courts throughout the Virginia Colony, in response to the British Parliament's imposition of the Stamp Act. Book C, p. 73.

June 12, 1766 - John Minor, apparently still named in the Commission of the Peace for the County, takes the Oaths of a Justice of the Loudoun Court. Book C, pp. 120-121.

October 13, 1766 - Fielding Turner, James Hamilton, Philip Noland and John Pearce are the sitting Justices at the Loudoun County Court. LDCODB, Book E, p. 219.

November 6, 1766 - The Governor and his Council, meeting in Williamsburg, order the issuance of a "New Commission of Peace ... for Loudoun" County. The Secretary of the Governor's Council issues a new Commission of the Peace for the Loudoun County Court appointing: "Francis Lightfoot Lee, Fielding Turner, James Hamilton, Eneas Campbell [sic- Aeneas Campbell], Nicholas Minor, George West, Charles Tyler [marked "dead"], Francis Peyton [noted as "Sh:" ie., Sheriff], John McIlhaney, of the Quorum; James Lane [Junr.], Craven Peyton, John Moss Junr., Philip Noland, William Carr Lane, Leven Powell, John Pearce, William Douglas & Spence Grayson, Gentlemen." The notations appear to have been made by the Governor's secretary in 1767 when a new Commission was in preparation. Council, VI/683; and, Justices, pp. 71-72.

November 13, 1766 - Josias Clapham, Gent., renews his Oaths as a County Justice. Book C, p. 229.

December 9, 1766 - Charles Tyler renews his Oaths as a Loudoun County Justice. Book C, p. 232.

LOUDOUN COUNTY JUSTICES, 1757-1766

ANTHONY RUSSELL *, [not listed, 1762] died @ January 1779
(1st, 1757Q; 2nd, 1757Q-1761Q) (rec.1769 ...
[previously, Fairfax County Justice, 1749-1757]

FIELDING TURNER *, [not listed, 1768]
(1757Q-1761Q; as 2nd Justice: 1762Q-1768Q)
[previously, Fairfax County Justice, 1752-1757]

JAMES HAMILTON *, [Burgess] died @ April 1775
(1757Q-1768Q; as 2nd, 1768Q-1771Q; 1771Q- ...
[previously, Fairfax County Justice, 1755-1757]

AENEAS CAMPBELL *, [not listed, 1768] moved to Maryland
(1757Q-1766Q-1768Q, moved)
[previously, Fairfax County Justice, 1755-1757]

NICHOLAS MINOR *, [militia Colonel] died @ July 1782
(1757Q-1766Q-1771Q- ...

WILLIAM WEST *, [innkeeper] died @ October 1769
(1757Q-1763Q, retired)
[retired from Court when he became Sheriff, 1762]

RICHARD COLEMAN *, [innkeeper] died @ January 1764
(1757-1760; 1760Q-1764Q, died)

JOSIAS CLAPHAM *, [refused to qualify @ 1765]
(1757-1760; 1760Q-1765Q; 1766Q-1772Q ...

GEORGE WEST *, [militia Colonel] died April 1786
(1757-1762; 1762Q-1771Q- ...
Loudoun County Surveyor, 1757-@1786

CHARLES TYLER *, died @ February 1767
(1757-1762; 1762Q-1767Q, died)

JOHN MOSS SENR. *, [not listed, 1762] died @ March 1768
(1757-1761, retired)

FRANCIS PEYTON *,
(1757-1762; 1762Q-1771Q- ...

JOHN MCILHANEY *, died @ April 1773
(1757-1764; 1764Q-1771Q- ...

----

* - "original" Justice; Q - Member "Of the Quorum"
rec. - recommended; .../@ - date uncertain; app. - appointed

LOUDOUN COUNTY JUSTICES, 1757-1766

FRANCIS LIGHTFOOT LEE, moved to Richmond County Va., 1769
(1st Justice, Dec.1757Q-1766Q-1771Q, moved)
(maintained as 2nd Justice, 1771Q- ...

JAMES LANE [JUNR.],
(Dec.1757-1768; 1768Q-1773Q- ...

BENJAMIN GRAYSON, died spring of 1763
(Dec.1757-1763, died)

LEE MASSEY, moved to Fairfax County
(1762-1764, moved)
[previously, Fairfax County Justice, 1759-1762]
Rector of Truro parish, 1767-1777

WILLIAM JETT JUNR., died summer of 1762
(app.1762, died)

CRAVEN PEYTON, [innkeeper] died @ August 1781
(1762-1768; 1768Q-1771Q- ...

JOHN MOSS JUNR., [omitted from list after Senr.'s death]
(1762-1768, retired)

PHILIP NOLAND [JUNR./2ND], [Potomac ferry owner]
(1762-1768; 1768Q-1771Q- ...

WILLIAM CARR LANE, died @ November 1770
(1764-1768; 1768Q-1770Q, died)

LEVEN POWELL,
(1764-1771; 1771Q- ...

JOHN PEAKE, [refused to qualify @ 1765]
(rec.1763) (app.1764, refused)

JOHN PEARCE, ["deaf and infirm"] died early in 1778
(1764-1767, resigned)

JOHN MINOR, [refused to qualify @ 1765]
(app.1764, refused) (1766) (1771-1772- ...

WILLIAM DOUGLASS,
(rec.1765-1766; 1766-1772- ...

SPENCE GRAYSON, [omitted from the list, 1768]
(rec.1765; 1766-1768, withdrew)
Rector of Cameron parish, 1771-1776

----

* - "original" Justice; Q - Member "Of the Quorum"
rec. - recommended; .../@ - date uncertain; app. - appointed

Militia - the Officers and Supplies

From the first days of the founding of the Virginia colony, provision for adequate self-defense was an overriding concern of the colonial government. Indian "massacres" of large numbers of white settlers in 1622-23, 1644, and again in 1686, strengthened the resolve of Burgesses and Governors in their provision for an active local colonial militia that would be capable of rapid response when events required. Significant colonial innovations - the first use of paper money anywhere in the British empire and the structural development of forms of self-reliant local government (both of which would ultimately facilitate the colonial Revolutionary movement) - were born of military necessity. Security of the Virginia frontier was still a concern when Loudoun County was formed in 1757; the new county was even named for the British commander-in-chief in the American colonies. Colonial Loudoun was chock full of martially experienced men, a tradition that continued for decades. By the end of the American Revolution, despite the presence of several large resident Quaker communities, Loudoun County fielded and armed two full battalions, nearly 1,750 men, the largest force of county militia anywhere in the Commonwealth of Virginia. [Hening, I/349; Legends, p. 123].

The citizen soldiers of the Virginia militia were organized county by county, and served under their own local officers. The senior local officer was addressed as "Colonel" but was actually titled the "County Lieutenant." A Colonel, Captains, Lieutenants and Ensigns, and in the large counties a Lt. Colonel, Major and Quartermaster, rounded out the officer corps. Senior officers were appointed by the Governor with the advice of County Lieutenants, and usually had previous command experience. Officers of lesser ranks, particularly Ensigns and Lieutenants, were frequently elected by their companies. Commissioned officers were to "be an inhabitant of, and resident in the county," but the local "residence" of Loudoun's first militia Colonel, William Fitzhugh of Stafford, probably consisted of nothing more than his slaves' quarters.

The County Lieutenant, or in his absence the Colonel, had the authority to "depute" and commission lesser officers. Captains would often appoint the "Serjeants, corporals or drummers" for their companies. Before taking command under a commission, officers were directed to appear in their county court and "take the oaths appointed by law ... [as well as] the abjuration oath, and subscribe the same with the test." Loudoun's commissioned officers, for the 1757-1766 decade, are identified in The Record hereinafter and in the Table at pp. 90-91. The size of a militia company determined both the rank and number of officers that could be commissioned. For every 50 soldiers in the company, "not more than one captain, one lieutenant, one ensign, three serjeants [sic] or corporals, and one drummer" were to be commissioned; "for every company consisting of thirty men, not more than one lieutenant, one ensign, and two serjeants; and for every company not exceeding fifteen men, not more than one ensign, and one serjeant." Farmers and artisans occasionally advanced to become officers in the militia but, as elsewhere in Virginia, militia officers in Loudoun County were invariably the leading planters, merchants and ordinary keepers in the community. The vast majority were, in fact, respected member Justices of the County Court. General Forbes, commander of the expedition against Ft. Duquesne in 1758, was a caricature of British aristocracy when he sneered that the Virginia militia officers in his command were a "bad Collection of broken Innkeepers, Horse Jockeys & Indian traders," and that the militiamen "under them, are a direct copy of their Officers." While discipline was never a strong suit of the colonial militias, British army officers, to the great discomfort of their own troops, would consistently undervalue the character and abilities of American militia units long into the 19th century. [Hening, VII/93-102 and VII/114; ColVa, p. 712; Independence, pp. 12 and 21; supra, Chapter on the County Court; infra, Chapter on Ordinaries].

The Virginia militia was structured to meet the "invasions of foreign enemies by sea ... incursions of Indians at land, and great dangers ... by the insurrections of negroes ... for all which the militia settled by law is the most ready defence ... [and] by the divine assistance ... able to suppress and repel such insurrections and invasions." The colonial Assembly mimicked Parliament in its deep suspicion of permanent standing armies and insisted on its right to regulate the Virginia military establishment, providing both detailed direction and a statement of purpose to the Governor and the county officers. Every officer of the Virginia militia who had knowledge or notice of an impending invasion or insurrection was directed to "raise the militia under his command ... send intelligence to the [his] county lieutenant ... and ... immediately proceed to oppose the enemy ... until further orders arrive." As well as directing the militia forces under his immediate command, every County Lieutenant was to:

> *"give immediate notice to the officers of the militia of the next adjacent counties ... and the situation and circumstances of the enemy according to the best of his information and judgment ... [and] dispatch an express to the Governor ... notifying [him of] the danger ... the strength and motions of the enemy."*

Upon the receipt of such a notice, it was then incumbent on the commanding militia officer in each adjacent county to:

> *"summon and hold ... a council of his field-officers and captains ... immediately raise the militia of his county and march part thereof, not exceeding two-thirds, against such enemy ... the remaining part of his militia not so marched to remain in arms in the[ir] county for the defence and protection thereof."*

The Assembly also provided that the Governor:

> *"shall have full power and authority to levy, raise, arm and muster ... the militia of this colony ... to be led, conducted, marched, transported and employed ... in this dominion ... suppressing and repelling of all such invasions and insurrections, and such forces again to discharge and disband as the cause of danger ceases."*

The militia, when mobilized, was simply Virginia's home defense force. [Hening, VI/112-113 and VII/107].

Virginia county militias patrolled their communities to suppress "dangerous combinations" of the slaves as early as 1726 but, beginning in 1757, militias took over some of the duties of constables. Thereafter, small monthly patrols, consisting of an officer and four militiamen, were to police slave quarters, arrest "strollers," idlers and disorderly persons, and return runaway slaves and servants to their masters. Militia patrols were not instituted in Loudoun until 1764. At first, patrollers were exempt from paying county levies, but in 1766 their pay was increased and the levy exemption eliminated. If a County Lieutenant anticipated trouble he was authorized to order any company or his entire compliment of militia to "go **armed** to their respective parish churches." This provision was made with slave uprisings in mind - those sad events usually occurred on Sundays, when blacks were at liberty to visit other plantations and the whites generally went about their business unarmed. [Hening, IV/202, VII/96, VII/104 and VIII/195; see infra, Chapter on Slaves].

The entire county militia turned out, fully armed, once a year at a "general muster" that was conducted in either March or April, usually during the county court days. The rolls were called, the eligibility status of every resident reviewed, and the companies drilled at the direction of their County Lieutenant. In 1757, the same Assembly that created Loudoun County determined that the exigencies of the French War required more frequent musters, and "every Captain ... [was instructed] once in three months, and oftner [sic] if required ... to muster, train and exercise his company." Additionally, all county militias were to have a second annual "general muster and exercise" in September or October. By November of 1762 the crisis on Virginia's frontiers had eased. "General muster[s] of the several companies of [the] militia [were again to be held] once only in every year ... in the months of March or April," and the company-sized quarterly, (ie., "private"), musters were discontinued. Thereafter, up to the time of the American Revolution, general musters of the county militia were conducted in every county in Virginia, including Loudoun, each spring. [Hening, VII/95-96, VII/537 and VIII/244].

The day after a general muster, the County Lieutenant met with his Captains at the county courthouse and conducted a "court martial." Before 1757 and beginning again after 1762, courts martial were held after the general musters in March or April. In 1757 courts martial were required in both the spring and the fall, and from 1758 through 1762, they were held only after general musters in the fall. The officers' court martial was supposed to:

> *"enquire of the age and abilities of all persons inlisted [sic], and to exempt such [men] as they shall adjudge incapable of service, and [sit in judgment] of all delinquents returned ... for [their] absence from musters or appearing without arms, powder, or ball."*

[Hening, VII/96-97, VII/537-538 and VIII/244].

By the mid-1750s, every male in the Virginia colony, regardless of marital status, between the ages of 18 and 60, except only "imported servants," was enrolled in the command of a county militia officer. A few skills and occupations were so important to the welfare of the colony that they were exempted as a class from mustering. As early as 1723, millers, founders, mine workers and overseers of slaves were exempted from the general musters of the county militias. In 1748, the men who operated Virginia's public ferries were also declared "free of ... public services of musters." At the height of the French and Indian War, when the 1757 Assembly instituted a draft to increase the number of militiamen in service in the Virginia Regiments, militia exemptions were extended to all Councilmen, clerks, ministers, the professors and students at William & Mary, public jailers, and overseers of "four servants or slaves." The normal daily exertions of the millers and overseers of slaves were deemed to be so vital to the colonial war effort that these individuals were to be summarily fined 20 shillings if they even "presume[d] to appear at any muster." [Hening, IV/119, V/17, VI/22, VII/93-103 and VII/274].

As the French War wound down, the 1762 Virginia Assembly exempted county Justices who were not commissioned officers, all "persons bred to and actually practising physick [sic] or surgery, and all inspectors at the publick [tobacco] warehouses" from "appearing or mustering ... at the private or general musters." The 1762 class of exempts were, however, required to "appear with their arms and ammunition ... and be incorporated with ... the other militia" in times of invasion or insurrection. Late in 1766, an exemption from militia musters was finally extended to Quakers who could produce a "testimonial or certificate from the[ir] monthly meeting." Even then, Quakers were still subject to the draft during an invasion and in those emergencies were required to "provide an able and sufficient substitute" or summarily forfeit and pay a £10 penalty. Despite the fact that Quakers found this law objectionable and constantly lobbied for revision, similar provisions were actively enforced during the Revolution and resulted in the summary seizure of Quaker properties. [Hening, VII/534-537 and VIII/241-245; Independence, p. 275].

Officers of the militia were required to:

> *"appear well armed ... every county lieutenant, colonel, lieutenant colonel, major with a sword; ... every captain and lieutenant with a firelock and a sword, and every ensign with a cutting-sword; every corporal and serjeant with a cutting-sword and halbert."*

The Virginia Assembly established "a firelock well fixed, a bayonet fitted to the same, a double cartouch-box, and three charges of powder" as the standard set of arms and ammunition for every militiaman. Every mustering Virginian was instructed to:

> *"constantly appear with the same at the time and place appointed for muster and exercise, and shall also keep at his place of abode one pound of powder and four pounds of ball, and bring the same with him into the field when he shall be required."*

Colonists had one year from the date of their eligibility to obtain a full and proper set of arms commensurate with their rank. Anyone who failed to supply arms was subject to a £5 penalty, but County Lieutenants were authorized to purchase a set of arms on behalf of militiamen who were "so poor as not to be able to purchase the arms" for themselves. In those circumstances, county courts charged the cost in the annual county levy - but there is no record of such an instance in Loudoun prior to 1766. County Justices, doctors, inspectors at the tobacco warehouses and the various counsellors, clerks and aldermen who were exempt from militia musters were all required to supply one or more full sets of arms and ammunition for the use of their county militia. A militiaman's arms and ammunition was exempt from forfeiture or the claims of creditors under any action in debt. Quakers were not exempted from the requirements of owning or furnishing a set of arms and ammunition until late in 1766. Virginia's colonial laws also directed that free mulattos, Negroes and Indians who volunteered to enlist were not to be armed, but to "be employed as drummers, trumpeters, or pioneers, or in such other servile labor." [Hening, VII/93-103, VII/534-538 and VIII/241-245].

The colonial Assembly occasionally instituted a draft of the militia in order to man the "Virginia Regiment," either for defense of the frontier or to "feed" auxiliary units into service when British regulars campaigned in the Americas. When the regiment was intended for service outside of the colony, as in the Cartagena campaign of 1741, Virginia's military drafts targeted idlers, vagrants and the unemployed. A 1756 colonial draft, providing for an active force of 1,500 militia serving under the Governor and colonial officers, for the defense of Virginia's frontiers, was a departure from the norm. Shortly after enactment of the draft, public notices were posted at "places of public resort" throughout

Virginia calling on volunteers who were to be rewarded with an enlistment bonus of £10. All able-bodied single militiamen were then required to muster and draw lots until a force equal to 1/20th of the total of eligible men was fielded. Anyone who drew a lot was "taken to be an inlisted soldier" unless he could "immediately procure some other able-bodied person to serve as a soldier in his stead," or pay the penal sum of £10 for release from his obligation. A second law, passed in the 1756 session, suspended the draft in Fairfax (Loudoun) and other counties where the militia had been activated by the Governor. [Hening, VII/9-25 and VII/31-32].

The 1756 draft was not a success - another draft was necessary just to bring the colony's active force level up to 1,270 men in 1757. County Justices were summoned to join the militia's field officers and Captains in a court martial, to "enquire into the occupation and employment of the several inhabitants .... between the age of eighteen and fifty years." The Assembly returned to traditional drafting methods, ordering summary enlistment of "all ... able-bodied persons ... found loitering and neglecting to labor for reasonable wages; all who run from their habitations, leaving wives or children ... and all other idle, vagrant, or dissolute persons." A new quota was established at "one man for every forty effective soldiers in the militia of each county." Freeholders and householders (in towns) who were qualified to vote at an election of Burgesses were exempt. Volunteers were paid a £5 bonus, and draftees £3, no later than "three days after ... arrival at the place of general rendezvous." In an effort to insure the cooperation of draftees, the Assembly provided that anyone who used a firearm, sword or other weapon while resisting an enlisting officer was to "suffer death as in cases of felony." [Hening, VII/70-73].

The authorized strength of the Virginia Regiments was increased to 2,000 in 1758 in preparation for General Forbes' campaign against Ft. Duquesne. The £10 enlistment bonus was reinstated; about 800 new enlisted soldiers were "formed into a regiment, consisting of ten companies," commanded by a Colonel, Lieutenant Colonel, Major, seven Captains, twenty Lieutenants, and ten Ensigns. A large number of colonial regiments of the Continental Army would be organized in much the same manner during the Revolution. Anticipating that troops in the Virginia Regiments "should be marched upon an expedition," provision was made for the Governor and County Lieutenants:

"to cause and direct ... so many men to be draughted out of the militia as ... shall appear necessary to garison [sic] the forts built for the protection of this colony, during the absence of the soldiers ... [but] not continued in garison [past] December [20, 1758]."

The Virginia Regiments were to be discharged on December 1, 1758, but continued in service on the frontiers through April of 1759. Drafted militia garrison troops were required to remain at their duty stations until they were relieved by new militia drafts or the soldiers of the regiment. We have no evidence to suggest that Loudoun militiamen were drafted for duty in the Shenandoah forts in 1758, perhaps because of their active service in previous campaigns. [Hening, VII/163-169 and VII/172-178; Chronology].

The militia draft law of 1757 was reactivated and revised again in January of 1764, when the Virginia Assembly established a £2 bounty for "every person who will voluntarily engage in the service ... for one year." Pontiac's Indian War ended the following fall, eliminating most of the risk of active service, and the 1765 Assembly repealed all militia service and enlistment bonuses after determining that the "bounties hath occasioned a great expense to the colony." [Hening, VIII/10-11 and VIII/151; Chronology].

At the onset of the French War, surgeons and all officers above the rank of Captain "drawn out into actual service" were paid ten shillings per day, troopers of the horse and foot soldiers were all paid one shilling per day, and officers of the intermediate ranks in proportion. Blacksmiths were paid five shilling a day, the same pay as a Lieutenant or the clerk of the county militia; wheelwrights and carpenters were paid three shillings a day, more than double a sergeant's pay; and "a look-out, after the rate of twenty shillings per month." Express riders were allowed 4 pence for every mile and 5 shillings for each day while in the service of the colony. [Hening, VI/22 and VII/27-30].

The 1757 Assembly revised the daily pay for active duty militia: a Major to eight shillings, a Captain to six shillings, blacksmiths to four shillings, Lieutenants to three shillings, and Ensigns to two shillings. In recognition of their rediscovered importance, a look-out's pay was raised to thirty shillings a month, while the daily pay grades for Colonels, surgeons, wheelwrights, carpenters, serjeants and corporals (16 pence), drummers (14 pence) and soldiers (12 pence) remained unchanged. Apparently beginning to feel the financial pinch of intermittent, recurring militia activity, the Assembly proscribed that there would be "no pay or allowance" for any active service period of less than three days. Another provision, the predecessor of a modern law called the Soldiers and Sailors Act, suspended law suits of creditors while militiamen were "drawn out" into the active service of the colony. By September of 1758, Virginia's soldiers were owed "considerable arrears," but disbanding the Virginia Regiments was considered a "dangerous consequence to the safety and welfare of this colony," and they were continued in service, with a reduced compliment of officers, "ranging" on the frontiers through April of 1759. This reduction of the Regiment, and elimination of the Colonel's allowance "for the expences of his table," led George Washington to resign his commission and return to Mt. Vernon in December of 1758. Supplemental pay was adopted in 1764, authorizing an additional 6 pence per day for all ranks below Captain through the end of December, 1764. A new pay grade, "of five shillings a day to such person employed as a scout by direction of the Governor," was instituted. [Hening, VII/112-115, VII/171-172 and VIII/10-11; infra, Appendix titled Chronology for Colonial Virginia].

Petitions to the Assembly for militia salaries, like those recited and discussed hereinafter, were necessary only where a special circumstance required dispensation from the Assembly for full payment of the claim. For example: if an officer's company was under-strength for his rank; or if unusual expenditures for provisions were incurred. [ColVa, p. 712; infra, pp. 81 and 88].

In 1755, the Virginia Assembly adopted a measure to exact some revenge for the depredations taking place in the frontier settlements, offering a £10 reward for each hostile Indian killed or captured in the colony. As the French War lingered and the horrors of atrocities on the frontier became more well known, this reward was supplemented in 1758 with an additional £30 bounty paid "for every Indian enemy so taken prisoner, killed or destroyed" within Virginia. King George III's "Proclamation of 1763" confirmed a grant of 200,000 acres of land near Pittsburgh to the soldiers and officers who had enlisted in response to Governor Robert Dinwiddie's "Proclamation of 1754." Ultimately, most of the Ohio Proclamation lands would be obtained by the officers of the regiment and a few land speculators who bought up soldier warrants. The Loudoun County Court did not experience a flood of activity for certificates in proof of service in the regiment. [Hening, VI/530, VII/163-170 and VII/661-669].

The regular discipline of the Virginia militia centered around participation in general musters. An extensive schedule of fines was instituted for delinquent behavior, ranging from 1 shilling "for appearing at muster without a double cartouch-box," or 3 shillings for "every soldier ... without a firelock well fixed," up to 10 shillings for a soldier "failing to appear at muster." Militia field officers who failed to muster, and Captains who did not list and report the delinquents in their companies, were all subject to a £10 fine. Should a militiaman "refuse to perform the command of his officer, or behave himself refractorily or mutinously, or misbehave himself" at a muster, the commanding officer could order the offender "tied neck and heels, for any time not exceeding five minutes" or whipped with up to 20 lashes. In 1762, the Virginia Assembly replaced the option of 20 lashes (which was typically imposed in criminal offenses) with authority for militia court martials to impose a 40 shilling fine. Thereafter, the only corporal punishment allowed in militia muster offenses was when an offender was tied neck and heels for five minutes. Sheriffs were authorized to seize and sell the goods of any delinquent militiaman who did not pay court martials' muster fines by April 10th each year. The proceeds from militia muster fines were supposed to be used by County Lieutenants "for buying drums and trophies for the use of the militia of the county." All of this was in sharp contrast to corporal punishment meted out in the regular British Army - where it was not uncommon for 500 or 800 lashes to be ordered for fighting in the ranks, insubordination or petty theft. Are we the least bit surprised that Virginia militiamen were reluctant to enroll in the regiments of the King's regular army? [Hening, VII/96-99, schedule of fines @ VII/99, VII/538 and VIII/244].

During the extremis of an invasion or insurrection, when Virginia militiamen were called into service "amongst the forces ... of this colony," fines and discipline imposed on the militia was much more severe. Soldiers "guilty of prophane swearing, drunkenness, or any other like offense" were to pay a 5 shilling fine or have 5 lashes "on the bare back well laid on." Any soldier who "disobey[ed] the lawful commands of his superior officer" was fined £5, and had to either "pay down such fine immediately" or receive 39 lashes on the bare back. Mutiny and desertion were punishable by death in court martials, and county courts were allowed to summarily impose any fine or corporal punishment, short of death or dismemberment, on deserters that were brought before them. Militia fines in these circumstances, when collected by a county Sheriff, were split evenly, half to the "informer" and half for supplying arms and ammunition for the county's militia. [Hening, VII/96-99, VII/108-115 and VII/364; GW Papers, IV].

As discussed in the initial chapter, the French War had a profound influence on the development of the section of northern piedmont that became Virginia's Loudoun County. For additional background information, the reader is referred to the Appendix, entitled "A Chronology for Colonial Virginia," infra.

General Braddock's campaign against Pittsburgh in the spring of 1755 was a definitive event in the maturation of the colonial Loudoun community. In mid-March, Sir Peter Halkett's 44th Regiment and Col. Thomas Dunbar's 48th Regiment went into camp around Alexandria, where Braddock had established his headquarters. On April 12th the 48th Regiment, Gen. Braddock, his aides, and a number of colonial volunteers (including George Washington) crossed into Maryland at what is now Georgetown and marched through Frederick County to a fort at Cumberland, Maryland on the upper Potomac. Halkett's crack 44th Regiment left Alexandria, in sections, between the 9th and 26th of April, and marched through "Loudoun" along the Potomac Ridge road and the Shenandoah road before crossing over the Blue Ridge at Keys' (Vestal's) Gap. Their first marching camp was established at the old Fairfax County "Springfield" courthouse (Freedom Hill); the second camp was at Richard Coleman's Sugarland run ordinary; a third day's march brought the regiment to Nicholas Minor's plantation near a crossroads that is now Leesburg; the last "Loudoun" station on Halkett's march was Edward Thompson's home at the Gap of Short Hill. On July 9th, after three months of marching and road making, advance units of Braddock's army, a column of 1,000 British regulars and about 400 Virginia militia and volunteers, neared the objective. French and their Indian allies ambushed the column, inflicting an incredible 65% casualty rate. Aside from George Washington, only a handful of Virginians distinguished themselves and survived to share their experience: militia Captain Adam Stephen, Loudoun's Francis Peyton (Colonel Burton's volunteer adjutant) and wagoners Daniel Morgan, Daniel

Boone, and Joshua Gore from Loudoun. One of the few surviving Maryland volunteers, Joseph Hopkins, moved to Loudoun after the expedition. [generally see, Browne; Braddock, pp. 216-222].

Gen. Braddock's disaster had several positive effects in Loudoun. A panic ensued in Virginia's western frontier counties, spurring a reverse migration, and a number of Shenandoah valley families resettled on the Loudoun piedmont. At the same time, many tidewater families halted their westward migration in Loudoun rather than crossing the Blue Ridge into harms way. And north-south migration from Pennsylvania to the lower Shenandoah and the Carolinas shifted eastward to the Carolina Road, a route that brought the migrants through Loudoun. All three factors contributed to a rapid population growth in western Fairfax County at the time that Petitions for the creation of Loudoun County were pending before the Virginia Assembly. The shock of Braddock's defeat also stirred the British administration to finally think in terms of eliminating the French altogether from the western boundaries of the Atlantic colonies, a policy long advocated by Virginia colonists. And the utter failure of the British army, combined with the relative success of the colonial militia, reinforced the growing sense of colonial independence that would have far-reaching consequences for the British empire.

In the aftermath of the defeat of General Braddock's army in 1755, the Virginia Assembly convened in Williamsburg to deal with the "incursions and depredations of our cruel and savage enemies, who are daily destroying the lives and estates of the inhabitants" of frontier settlements. On March 25, 1756, an Act "for the better protection of the Inhabitants on the Frontiers of this Colony" was passed. This law instituted the compulsory military draft of 1756 and authorized Virginia's Treasurer to issue treasury notes, "convenient for their circulating in payment," of up to £25,000 for "raising, maintaining, arming and providing" for 1,500 men for the Virginia regiments. This force was not to be "marched out of this colony," but since the charter for Virginia extended westward to modern California, this restriction can only be interpreted as an effort of the Assembly to retain Virginia militiamen in service in defense of their home soil. The Assembly also authorized £2,000 for the construction of a chain of frontier forts - several of which were later garrisoned by Fairfax/Loudoun militiamen. Another £1,000 was authorized for the construction of a fort, soon to become known as Fort Loudoun, at Winchester, Virginia. [Hening, VII/9-25 and VII/33; ColVa, p. 690].

The 1756 militia law also included a schedule of payments for "divers companies of the militia of Fairfax ... lately drawn out into actual service [in 1755] for the defence and protection of the frontiers of this colony, against the incursions and depredations of the French and their Indian allies." Officers and soldiers were paid in Virginia colony treasury notes at the rate of 10 shillings for every 100 lbs. of tobacco claimed, while contractors were paid 8½ shillings for every 100 lbs. of tobacco in their accounts. This amounted to an official devaluation of militia claims, since 12½ shillings was the established value of 100 lbs. of tobacco in the Northern Neck at the time. Among the men in companies of the Fairfax Horse were a number of individuals we can identify as having an association with or living in Loudoun County: Captain Lewis Ellzey; Lieutenant Sampson Turley; corporals Jeremiah Hutchinson, Joseph Stephens and Philip Grymes; troopers Daniel Thomas, Benjamin Hutchison, Robert Watson (Lewis Ellzey's servant), William Pickett, Jesse Martin, Thomas West, David Thomas Junr., Edward Davis, William Peake Junr., William Trammell, Gilbert Simson Junr., William Musgrove, Thomas Triplett, William Morris, William Smith, John Stephens, Thomas Osborn, George Saunders, Daniel Shoemaker, Joseph Burson, Simon Shoemaker, Edward Hardin, Nicholas Grymes, Michael Regan Junr., William Owsley, Joseph Jones, Joseph Martin, and John Sinclare. John Williams, Charles Broadwater, Henry Taylor, John Summers, Daniel French, John Hough, John Pultney [sic - John Poultney] and Jacob Morris were paid for impressed horses; Richard Moxley and John Gladin "for necessaries for the soldiers"; William West "for necessaries and expresses"; and the Alexandria mercantile firm of "Carlyle and Dalton, for powder, lead, flints, and for an express [rider]." All of the merchants and suppliers of provisions were apparently aware of the advantage gained by rendering their accounts in "current money," while the value of the service of officers and militiamen were accounted for in pounds of tobacco. It also appears that Benjamin Edwards, Leesburg's first ordinary keeper, was a trooper in the Prince William Horse in 1755. Note that the Fairfax County schedule may identify other colonials that the reader would recognize as inhabitants of the "Loudoun" section of western Fairfax. [Hening, VII/9-25].

Shortly after Lord Loudoun's arrival in the colonies in 1756, he instructed the Virginia Assembly to adopt two measures that he deemed essential to the military prosecution of the war with the French and Indians. The first measure, passed during a brief session of the Assembly early in 1758, increased the authorized troop strength of the active Virginia regiments to 2,000 men, funded their pay, and authorized "the commanding officer of his majesty's forces in North America," (no longer Lord Loudoun), to use the active regiments of the Virginia militia anywhere in the Americas when he deemed it appropriate "to annoy or attack the enemy." The Assembly activated three companies of "rangers" for duty on Virginia's southwest frontier, authorized the "import into this colony, [of] a quantity of goods, such as may best answer the wants and occasions of the Indians ... coming to our assistance," and provided for drafts of militia to supplement the garrisons in the forts in the northern Shenandoah valley. All together, financing for these measures required the issuance of £32,000 in new Virginia treasury notes. The second, more controversial, measure that Lord Loudoun continually insisted upon was destined to serve America as his permanent reminder. His demand for the quartering (housing) of British troops in private homes inspired prohibitive clauses in both the Virginia and U.S. Constitutions. The Virginia Assembly waited until his Lordship had been recalled to England before responding in an amendment to the "Act for preventing mutiny and desertion." Following the lead of the Pennsylvania Assembly, the Virginians authorized county Justices of the Peace to billet "the soldiers in his majesty's service [only] in ordinaries and licensed taverns, and in no private houses whatsoever." Inn keepers were to provide soldiers "with vinegar, salt and the use of fire to dress their victuals without demanding any reward or satisfaction for the same." This approach had proven to be marginally acceptable in Philadelphia that winter, but the Virginia Assembly knew that there were not enough ordinaries in Virginia to meet the billeting requirements of the King's army. [Hening, VII/163-170; see infra, in the Chronology Appendix for March 10, 1757 entry; and see Hening, IX/113].

Detractors have referred to Lord Loudoun as a short, ill-tempered and unimaginative man who accomplished little during his military career. Regardless, it is generally acknowledged that Lord Loudoun was responsible for expanding the use of rangers in the British colonial corps and that the first semblance of military unity among the American colonies was obtained during his watch. Loudoun introduced innovations in the recruitment and training of the Royal American regiment that ultimately lead to British victory in the French War. One of Lord Loudoun's directives instructed that "to qualify them for the Service of the Woods ... [members of the American Regiments] are to be taught to load and fire, **lyeing on the Ground and kneeling"** [my emphasis]. Loudoun valued the painful lessons of General Braddock's experience, and instituted tactical changes including a new army command, "Tree all," to effect a dispersal when ambushed. Lord Loudoun was a first rate military recruiter and organizer, but he lacked the calculated fearlessness that was essential for success in battle, and he displayed a callousness and high-handed disregard for the King's colonial subjects whom he had been sent to protect. [Wars, pp. 135, 153 and 160; Braddock, pp. 126 and 287 n.14].

The 1758 Assembly passed another "Act for the defence of the Frontiers," paying for provisions and militia salaries incurred in campaigns against the French "and their Indian allies." The 1758 schedules for Fairfax County militiamen identify a number of men who were residents in the "Loudoun" section of the county. Captain Nicholas Minor and his entire company of 5 officers and 45 men were paid for 52 days of active duty during 1756 and 1757, and £10, 4 shillings and 1 pence was paid to Captain James Hamilton for "his pay and guards subsistence carrying [draftee] soldiers to Winchester." Assuming a slow, six day round trip to Winchester, and knowing that the pay rate for conveying enlistees and draftees to their duty stations was 15 pence per man per day, we can estimate that Capt. Hamilton's detail consisted of 20 or 30 "Loudoun" militia draftees. The schedule for Captain Minor's company included listings for: Lieutenant Josias Clapham; Ensign William Trammell; "Serjeants" Charles Martin, Francis Summers and Jesse Martin; and £2, 12 shillings to every trooper in Minor's company, including Edward Hardin, John Donaldson, Samuel Philips, James Thomas, Samuel Jenkins, Samuel More [sic], Philip Merchant, George Valendingham, Benjamin Williams, John Davis, Thomas Jenkins, Francis Awbrey [Junr.], Joshua Claypole, Thomas Saunders, Simon Shoemaker, Joseph Martin, William Jackson, William Massey, Franklin Perry, and George Shoemaker. [Hening, VII/73 and VII/171-225, schedules @ VII/217-218].

Militiamen in Nicholas Minor's company were away from their homes, serving in Col. George Washington's command on the frontier, when Loudoun County was created. On June 20, 1757, an order of the Governor's Council instructed the "Officers of Militia in ... Fairfax [which then still included Loudoun] ... to march one third part of their militia to Fort Loudoun [near Winchester] immediately." At the time the "Loudoun" militiamen must have already been in motion, crossing the Blue Ridge, because they were on duty at Winchester before the Governor's order arrived in Fairfax. Letters written by George Washington on June 24th and June 25th, 1757, while his frontier command was headquartered at Ft. Loudoun, reveal the activities of the "Loudoun" militia. Washington's letter of the 24th gave orders for the campaign operations of Capt. Minor's company and included the defense of "Neallys" fort within Minor's area of responsibility. The second letter was addressed to Col. William Fairfax, the County Lieutenant of the Fairfax militia, and advised him:

> *"D[ea]r. Sir: ... [Fairfax County] Captains [Bryan] Fairfax and [Nicholas] Minor arrived here with their companies on tuesday last [June 21, 1757] ... I have sent [Capt. Minor] to Pattersons and Mendenhalls; small forts lying under the North-mountain and much exposed to the incursions of the Enemy."*

On July 8, 1757, Col. Washington requested £18 in bounties for some of the Fairfax volunteers and draftees, who were then paid £5 and £3, respectively. This was merely a supplemental expenditure. Two days later, in a letter to Virginia Governor Robert Dinwiddie, Col. Washington confirmed that: "We have at this time about 50 of the Militia from Fairfax ... at different posts employed in scouting, and assisting the inhabitants in harvesting." Nicholas Minor apparently left his company on the frontier under the command of either Lieutenant Clapham or Ensign Trammell, because Minor was back in Loudoun County by July 12, 1757 when he, Lt. Aeneas Campbell, and fellow Fairfax militia Captains James Hamilton, Fielding Turner and Anthony Russell were all sworn in as five of the new Loudoun County Justices. Three weeks later, on August 3, 1757, the Loudoun militiamen were relieved of their garrison duty in Mendenhall's fort, at Maidstone on the upper Potomac. The reader can find great entertainment in Col. Washington's correspondence regarding the missions of the companies of Fairfax and Loudoun County militiamen during the frontier campaign of 1757. [Council, VI/58; GW Writings, pp. 72-155, @ 72-75, 78 and 88; GW Papers, IV/253, 260, 267, 290, 291 and 362; see supra, p. 71; re forts generally, infra, p. 90].

The 1758 schedules of the Assembly provide an accounting of the Public Claims that were certified by the Loudoun County Court in July of 1758, clearly for militia services rendered during the preceding year, after Loudoun had been incorporated:

"... [for]	*LOUDOUN COUNTY.*	*£*	*s.*	*p.*
To	*captain Nicholas Minor,*	*1*	*00*	*00*
	AEneas Campbell, lieutenant	*-*	*7*	*6*
	Francis Wilks,	*1*	*17*	*-*
	James Willock [sic- James Wheelock],	*1*	*15*	*-*
To	*John Owsley, and William Stephens, 15 s. [shillings] each,*	*1*	*10*	*-*
To	*Robert Thomas*	*-*	*10*	*-*
	John Moss Junr.	*-*	*4*	*-*
	John Thomas, for provisions,	*-*	*5*	*-*
	John Moss, do. [provisions]	*-*	*2*	*8*
	William Ross, do. [provisions]	*-*	*2*	*-*
	£	*7.*	*13.*	*2*

..." [Hening, VII/217-225, @ /222; and see infra, p. 86].

After "Pittsburgh" was retaken in 1758, Col. Washington marched the Virginia Regiment back to Winchester for garrison and "ranging" duty in the northern Shenandoah. The battlefronts of the French War shifted further north and south, until only isolated incidents were reported from frontier settlements in 1762. When the western Indians, inspired by Pontiac, renewed their attacks on the frontier in 1763, the Virginia militias were activated once again. The most junior Captain of the Loudoun militia, John Moss Junr., left his father in charge of their Leesburg ordinary and led a militia company west to defend Winchester. At least one of the officers, Lieutenant Joshua Gore Junr., was elected by the company. Lt. Gore probably received his Commission on a blank form that the Governor would have signed and supplied to County Lieutenant Francis Lightfoot Lee in anticipation of just such an event. An interesting account of the service of Capt. Moss and his undersized company of Loudoun militia, responding to the Indian raids of 1763, is presented herein. [infra, below and @ p. 88].

The October 1765 session of the Virginia Assembly authorized supplemental payments of militia expenses and salaries incurred during the military campaigns against the French and Indians in 1757 and 1763. The several individuals from Loudoun and Prince William, (who do not appear to be listed elsewhere), with the reason for and amount of payment, are given as follows:

		£	s.	p.
"...	*LOUDOUN*			
1757. To	*Robert Adams*, assignee of Stephen Thatcher, for his pay,*	*5*	*12*	*6*
	Do. do. [meaning Adams, assignee] of Thomas Bond, for do. [his pay]*	*4*	*10*	*-*
	Thomas Gore for a rifle gun impressed	*4*	*10*	*-*
	Stephen Emorie, dressing guns for militia,	*-*	*13*	*-*
	James Clemons for a gun impressed,	*4*	*10*	*-*
1763.	*Captain Moss, for 60 days pay at 6s.*	*18*	*-*	*-*
	Lieutenant Gore for do. at 2[sic-3]s. 6d.	*10*	*10*	*-*
...	*PRINCE WILLIAM*			
1763. To	*William Baylis and company per roll,*	*35*	*10*	*6*

..." * - Robert Adams was a Leesburg merchant and a Fairfax Justice. [Hening, VIII, 132-133; infra, Chapter on Trades].

When Loudoun County was incorporated in 1757, not more than 600 men were eligible for militia service. At the time, the effective fighting force of the county was perhaps only 300 or 400 men. Three different analyses lead us to these conclusions. Roughly 50% of the tithables in Loudoun, 500 of perhaps 1,000, were either slaves or whites in exempt professions like millers, ferrymen, overseers and "imported servants." This would leave about 500 men eligible for militia service, 600 if one starts with an estimate of 1,200 tithables in the county. The size of Captain Hamilton's troop, 20 or 30 men, who were transported to Winchester indicates that 800 to 1,200 men from Fairfax were eligible for the 1757 draft (and "Loudoun" would have accounted for about half). It seems likely that the four commissioned Captains who were resident in the new county at the time of incorporation in 1757 would not have commanded more than 350 militia. The command structure of the Loudoun militia a decade later, in 1766, supports the notion that eight to ten active militia companies were then composed of 600 or 750 effectives, with perhaps 1,100 eligibles county-wide. As already noted, a total of about 1,750 Loudoun militiamen were activated for service during the Revolution. Thus, the Loudoun County militia doubled in size during its first decade, and the pace of growth was sustained for at least another decade or two thereafter. [supra, pp. 65 and 79].

In 1757, militiamen in Loudoun County were organized under four resident Captains, Nicholas Minor and James Hamilton west of Goose Creek, and Fielding Turner and Anthony Russell in the east. There were no field officers living in the county until Francis Lightfoot Lee arrived with his commission in December of 1757, so the first musters of the Loudoun militia were probably conducted by the four commissioned Captains. Lee's assumption of command of the militia, seating as First Justice on the County Court, and subsequent election to the Assembly all worked to the disadvantage of Anthony Russell. Capt. Russell was Loudoun's first First Justice and the eldest resident militia Captain in 1757, and must have had hard feelings over being surpassed by a youthful newcomer to Loudoun County - Francis Lightfoot Lee was only 23 years old in 1757. Anthony Russell apparently refused to serve under Lee's command, and after an early retirement from the County Court in 1761, Russell did not resume a leadership role in Loudoun until 1771. Then, two years after Col. Lee had left the County, Russell accepted a position on the reconstituted Cameron parish vestry. The other three original Captains, Nicholas Minor, James Hamilton and Fielding Turner, advanced to become the ranking field officers of the Loudoun County militia under Col. Lee in 1765. [supra, pp. 49, 63-64 and 66].

Colonel Lee would have first given the order calling out the Loudoun militia for a general muster in the spring of 1758, when dozens of lots had already been subscribed in Leesburg and Nicholas Minor's house might have already been put in use as the county courthouse. As a consequence, we could speculate that all of the general musters of Loudoun's colonial militia, beginning in 1758, were held on the "poison fields" to the northeast of colonial Leesburg, in an area subsequently known as "Brown's meadow." The formal commissions for the inferior field officers of the militia did not arrive until December of 1758. The delay leads us to speculate that the Loudoun militia officer corps was not fully organized until the general muster in September of 1758, with the commissions from the Governor confirming the results of company elections that had taken place three months before. Additional companies were apparently formed up at the general muster in the spring of 1759. [supra, Chapter on the Courthouse].

The officer corps of the Loudoun County militia was reorganized again in 1765-1766 and a third time when Francis Lightfoot Lee left Loudoun in 1769. The seemingly regular arrival of officer commissions during the summer months, several months after each of the spring general musters between 1761 and 1766, suggests that Loudoun County's militia officers were all elected by the rank and file during this period.

The second reorganization of Loudoun County's militia corps took place at the conclusion of the French and Indian War, when William Fitzhugh was removed from his absentee Colonelcy. The "old guard" - Nicholas Minor, James Hamilton and Fielding Turner - all advanced in rank, and a host of new company officers were elected and commissioned. Among the "new guard" was Sheriff/Captain Francis Peyton, who had first proven himself a decade earlier while serving as a volunteer on Gen. Braddock's campaign. As previously suggested, most of the Loudoun militia officers were also member Justices of the County Court; before 1766, all but one of the Loudoun officers commissioned above the rank of Ensign (the exception was Joshua Gore) either already were or would become County Court Justices. The "new guard" of militia officers included scions of some of the leading families in colonial Loudoun; many of them actively served the cause of independence during the Revolution. By 1766, the Lane, Eskridge, Summers, Lewis, Minor, Tyler and Noland families were all represented in the junior officer corps of the Loudoun County militia. Aeneas Campbell (embroiled in the dispute over his failure to complete construction of the first Loudoun Courthouse), John Moss (in the process of relocating to Fairfax County), and William Grayson, Leven Powell, George West and Charles West (each of whom would distinguish himself at the head of a colonial regiment during the Revolution), were all notably absent from Loudoun County's militia command structure in 1766.

And More ...

The reader is encouraged to peruse the additional background information about Lord Loudoun's military career, colonial and Indian warfare, activities of the county militias and the campaigns of the Virginia Regiments that has been included, infra, in the Appendix titled "A Chronology for Colonial Virginia."

FRANCIS LIGHTFOOT LEE

Francis Lightfoot Lee was the first County Lieutenant commissioned for the Loudoun militia. The sixth son of former Virginia Governor Thomas Lee, Francis Lightfoot Lee first took his Oaths of office as the County Lieutenant and as the "First Justice" of the County Court in December of 1757, when he moved to Loudoun County. Francis "Loudoun" Lee and James Hamilton were the first Burgesses elected in 1758 to represent Loudoun County in the Virginia Assembly. In these several capacities, Lee served as the most senior officer and representative of the King's government in Loudoun County until he married and moved to Richmond County in 1769. [supra, p. 86; see Lee, p. 170].

Courtesy of the Loudoun Museum, Leesburg, Virginia.

August 28, 1757 - In a "Size Roll" for the company of the Virginia regiment serving directly under George Washington, the only soldier listed from Loudoun County is a David McGennett [sic- David McGinnis?], aged 40. The roll indicates that McGennett enlisted in March of 1756, was a "sawyer" by trade, 5'6" in height, born in Ireland, with "brown complextion, hair brown & strait a very dirty Lubberly Look." Several soldiers were enrolled from Fairfax County: William Bagent, aged 31; Francis Farmer, 22; William Stephens, 20; William Baylis, 35; William Gerram, 24; and Edward Brown, aged 29. [GW Papers, IV].

December 13, 1757 - "Francis Lightfoot Lee, Esqr., County Lieutenant for [Loudoun] took the usual Oaths to his Majesty's Person and Government and subscribed the Abjuration Oath and the Test." Book A, p. 56.

July 21, 1758 - "The Act concerning Public Claims was read ... James Hamilton Gent. exhibited ... a Claim for the Allowance and expence of a Draught [draft] of the Militia to Fort Loudoun [at Winchester]"; "Nicholas Minor Gent. exhibited ... an Account ... for Provisions and Stores for the Company of Militia under his Command and likewise the several Claims of the said Militia"; "John Moss and John Thomas exhibited ... Accounts ... for Provisions & services in the Militia for Men under their command"; "Robert Thomas exhibited ... an Account for services in the Militia"; "William Ross ... a Claim for services and expences in conducting the militia to the County Goal"; "Nicholas Minor & Aneas Campbell Gent., John Moss Junr., James Wheelock, Francis Wilks, William Stephens and John Owsley severally exhibited ... Claims for services in the Militia"; and a "Petition of sundry of the Inhabitants ... for Regulating Officers fees was produced ... No Propositions were Offered." Book A, pp. 133 and 134.

July 22, 1758 - The Fairfax County Court, acting on presentments of other Public Claims, certifies an "account from Captains Nicholas Minor & James Hamilton for provisions found for the [Fairfax] Militia by John McCormack," [who apparently is a resident of Fairfax]. FXCOCO, 1756 Book, p. 272.

November 25, 1758 - Col. George Washington and several companies of the Virginia militia participate in the taking of Ft. Duquesne. ColVa, p. 722.

December 12, 1758 - "Francis Lightfoot Lee, County Lieutenant, Nicholas Minor, Lieutenant Colonel, and James Hamilton, Major in the Militia ... [each take] the usual Oaths to his Majesty's Person and Government ..."; and, William West, Richard Coleman, and Josias Clapham, Captains in the militia, take their Oaths of office in the Loudoun County Court. Book A, p. 185.

February 13, 1759 - Benjamin Grayson, Lieutenant of the Loudoun County militia, takes the appropriate Oaths. Book A, p. 190.

March 14, 1759 - William Fitzhugh as Colonell [sic], Fielding Turner as Captain, and Francis Summers as Lieutenant, each take the Oaths as Officers of the militia. Book A, p. 216.

April 10, 1759 - William Starks takes the Oaths of an Ensign of the County militia. Book A, p. 231.

November 12, 1759 - "William Norris and Thomas Owsley exhibit ... Claims for Services in the Militia [while they were] under the Command of Capt. Anthony Russel [sic - Loudoun Justice Anthony Russell]." Book A, p. 296.

March 17, 1761 - The Virginia Assembly, in session in Williamsburg, receives a Petition from Thomas Green [probably of Loudoun County], praying to be compensated for "two Horses impressed into his Majesty's service, one of which was killed, and the other never returned to him." Assembly, (1758) p. 215.

August 11, 1761 - William Jett Junr. as Quarter Master, James Lane Junr. as Captain, and Charles Eskridge as Ensign, take their Oaths as Officers of the militia. Book A, p. 484.

May 11, 1762 - Charles Eskridge takes the Oaths of a Lieutenant in the militia. Book A, p. 588.

May 14, 1762 - John Moss Junr., takes the Oaths of a Captain in the militia. Book A, p. 622.

November 25, 1762 - The Virginia Assembly, in session is Williamsburg, rejects three claims of: "John Ross for provisions at Pearsall's Fort in the year 1756 ...; Gersham Keys for provisions furnished the Militia of Fairfax County ...; [and] John Palmer, to be allowed for a horse and bridle impressed for the use of the Fairfax Militia." Assembly, (1761) p. 114.

April 15, 1763 - Charles Binns, "Quarter Master in the Militia," takes the appropriate Oaths to the King. Book B, p. 119.

July 12, 1763 - Fielding Turner, a Captain of the County militia, takes the Oaths of an Officer. Book B, p. 192.

August 1, 1763 - The Governor and Council, including William Byrd, Philip Ludwell Lee and John Tayloe, meeting in Williamsburg, note their receipt of "many Letters ... giving a Relation of the further Incursions of the Indians and more Depredations and Murders. [F]or the better Protection of the Frontiers the Council ... advis'd his Honour [the Governor] to order Colo. Stephen [in Frederick County] to draught [draft] five hundred [500] Men ... to protect the Frontier from Potowmack to Lord Fairfax's lines, out of Hampshire and Frederick and ... Culpeper, Fauquier and Loudoun, in proportion to the number of Militia in each County." This resulted in the muster of one full company of the Loudoun County militia for service on the frontier. Lead by Capt. John Moss Junr. and Lt. Joshua Gore Junr., they spent two months on duty. Council, VI/267; schedule of payments, supra, p. 82; see infra, Assembly record, p. 88.

August 9, 1763 - Francis Summers, George Summers and Joshua Gore Junr., Lieutenants, and Vincent Lewis and James Lane Senr., Ensigns, all takc the Oaths of "Officers in the Militia of this County." Book B, p. 196.

October 11, 1763 - Aneas Campbell, a Captain of the militia, takes the Oaths. Book B, p. 258.

October 26, 1763 - William West submits "an Account of the Receipts for Provisions of the Company of Militia under his Command and likewise the several Claims of the said Militia."; John Herryford and Fleming Patterson each gives an account of his "Expenses for Provisions for the Militia."; and, Stephen Emrey [a blacksmith] and Christopher Perfect [at one time a Leesburg constable] give "Accounts for services done the Militia." Book B, p. 260.

August 14, 1764 - Francis Summers takes the Oaths of a Captain of the County militia. Book B, p. 403.

November 2, 1764 - A report of "the Accounts of Pay, Provisions, Arms, and Necessaries of the Militia of ... Loudoun ... was presented to the House ... [and] referred to the Consideration of the Committee of Claims." Assembly, (1764) p. 235.

November 9, 1764 - At a Virginia Assembly session, Frederick County Burgess "Mr. George Washington laid before the House a Report" from the Commissioners of Militia Claims giving, among others, an account of the military activities of a small company of the Loudoun County militia that served on the Virginia frontier from August to October in 1763: "Capt. John Moss [Junr]., with Lieutenant [Joshua] Gore [Junr.], an Ensign [Vincent Lewis ?], and 24 private Men, were ordered by Colonel [Nicholas] Minor ... to march to Winchester, there to take Orders from Col. Stephen ... at the same Time telling Capt. Moss that he [Col. Minor] would complete the Company, and send the Number then wanting immediately up to Winchester, under the Command of an Officer ... after Capt. Moss's Arrival at Winchester he was ordered by Col. Stephen to proceed to one of the Forts on the Frontiers, and an Express [rider] was sent [by Stephen] ... to inform Col. Minor that he need not send up any more Men ... which Express met the Men sent by Col. Minor ... on the Blue Ridge, whereupon they returned [to their homes in Loudoun County], and Capt. Moss remained in the Service, with the aforesaid [undersized] Company, 60 Days." The Commissioners authorized militia pay for "the Ensign, two Sergeants, and the private Men ... referring the [question of pay for] the Captain [Moss] and Lieutenant [Gore] to the Consideration of the House." Subsequently, the House of Burgesses authorized full pay for those two Loudoun County militia officers. Assembly, (1764) pp. 247-248; supra, schedule of payments for service rendered in 1763, at p. 82.

June 13, 1765 - "James Hamilton ... Lieutenant Colonel in the Militia of this County [takes] the usual Oaths to his Majesties Person & Government and ... Subscribed the Abjuration Oath & the Test." Book B, p. 671.

July 8, 1765 - "Nicholas Minor, Esqr., Colonel, and Fielding Turner, Esqr., Major, in the Militia of this County ..." each take the Oaths of Officers. Book B, p. 673.

June 10, 1766 - Philip Noland, William Carr Lane, John Minor and Charles Tyler as Captains, and Lieutenants John Tyler and Philip Noland Junr.

all take their "Oaths to His Majesty's Person and Government" as militia Officers for Loudoun County. Book C, p. 97.

June 12, 1766 - Thomas Lewis takes the Oaths of an Ensign of the Loudoun County militia. Book C, p. 122.

August 11, 1766 - Richard Eskridge takes the Oaths of Lieutenant of the militia. Book C, p. 147.

August 13, 1766 - Francis Peyton as Captain, and Stephen Donaldson and Joshua Gore as Lieutenants, take their Oaths as Officers of the Loudoun County militia. Book C, p. 165.

December 15, 1766 - The Virginia Assembly "Resolved, That the Several Commissioners appointed for Settling the Accounts of the Militia be allowed [paid] ... for their respective services ... James Hamilton, Gentleman [Lt.Col. of the Loudoun militia], for 20 days Attendance at, and 1 Day for going to, and 1 Day for returning from Winchester, the Sum of £22 ..." The other Commissioners at Winchester were Burgesses William Green, Thomas Marshall [from Fauquier County] and Richard ["Squire"] Lee [from Westmoreland County]. Assembly, (1766) p. 71.

March 28, 1767 - The House of Burgesses is presented with the Petition of Mr. Job Pearsall of Hampshire County. A large fort was erected on his land under the orders of Col. Washington in 1756; "Fort Pearsall" was in use until shortly after the conclusion of General Forbes' campaign against Ft. Dusquesne [Pittsburg Landing] late in the winter of 1758. The fort was reactivated and garrisoned once more during the Indian war of 1763, now known as "Pontiac's War," through the winter of 1764. Pearsall was requesting reimbursement for the loss of timber and use or loss of his land. His Petition described the typical founding and use for the several forts that were manned by companies of Fairfax and Loudoun militia during the French and Indian Wars. Assembly, Vol. 11 (1766) pp. 100-101; and, regarding the Loudoun militiamen serving in the valley forts, see supra, @ pp. 80-81 and 88.

Militia Officer Commissions for Loudoun County

Date Sworn In	Name	Rank
June 10, 1749	Moses Linton	Captain ?, Fairfax
Dec. 19, 1752	Fielding Turner	Lieutenant, Fairfax
June 19, 1753	Nicholas Minor	Captain ?, Fairfax
July 17, 1753	Richard Coleman	Lieutenant ?, Fairfax
Mar. 20, 1754	Francis Summers	Ensign ?, Fairfax
Sept. 18, 1755	James Hamilton	Captain, Fairfax
"	Sampson Turley	Lieutenant, Fairfax
Dec. 15, 1755	John Carlyle	Colonel, Fairfax
c..., 1756-7	Fielding Turner	Captain, Fairfax
unknown	Josias Clapham	Lieutenant, Fairfax
"	William Trammell	Ensign, Fairfax
unknown-Fairfax	John Moss [Senr.?]	[Captain ?]
"	Robert Thomas	[Lieutenant ?]
"	John Moss Junr.	[Ensign ?]
"	John Thomas	[Ensign ?]
"	James Wheelock	[Ensign ?]
"	Francis Wilks	[Ensign ?]
"	William Stephens	[Ensign ?]
"	John Owsley	[Ensign ?]
"	Anthony Russell	Captain
"	William Norris	[Lieutenant ?]
"	Thomas Owsley	[Ensign ?]
Dec. 13, 1757	Francis Lightfoot Lee	County Lieut.
c..., 1757-8	Aeneas Campbell	Lieutenant
Dec. 12, 1758	Francis Lightfoot Lee	County Lieut.
"	Nicholas Minor	Lieut. Colonel
"	James Hamilton	Major
"	William West	Captain
"	Richard Coleman	Captain
"	Josias Clapham	Captain
Feb. 13, 1759	Benjamin Grayson	Lieutenant
Mar. 14, 1759	William Fitzhugh	Colonel
"	Fielding Turner	Captain
"	Francis Summers	Lieutenant

Militia Officer Commissions for Loudoun County

Date Sworn In	Name	Rank
Apr. 10, 1759	William Starks	Ensign
Aug. 11, 1761	William Jett Junr.	Quarter Master
"	James Lane Junr.	Captain
"	Charles Eskridge	Ensign
May 11, 1762	Charles Eskridge	Lieutenant
May 14, 1762	John Moss Junr.	Captain
Apr. 15, 1763	Charles Binns	Quarter Master
July 12, 1763	Fielding Turner	Captain
Aug. 9, 1763	Francis Summers	Lieutenant
"	George Summers	Lieutenant
"	Joshua Gore Junr.	Lieutenant
"	Vincent Lewis	Ensign
"	James Lane Senr.	Ensign
Oct. 11, 1763	Aeneas Campbell	Captain
Aug. 14, 1764	Francis Summers	Captain
June 13, 1765	James Hamilton	Lieut. Colonel
July 8, 1765	Nicholas Minor	Colonel
"	Fielding Turner	Major
June 10, 1766	Philip Noland [Senr./2nd]	Captain
"	William Carr Lane	Captain
"	John Minor	Captain
"	Charles Tyler	Captain
"	John Tyler	Lieutenant
"	Philip Noland Junr. [3rd]	Lieutenant
June 12, 1766	Thomas Lewis	Ensign
Aug. 11, 1766	Richard Eskridge	Lieutenant
Aug. 13, 1766	Francis Peyton	Captain
"	Stephen Donaldson	Lieutenant
"	Joshua Gore [Junr. ?]	Lieutenant

Charles Binns Senr. was the first Clerk of the Loudoun County Court. He served in that capacity continuously until 1796, when he was succeeded by his son Charles Binns Junr. The Binns family plantation home, Rokeby, was on the Carolina Road south of Leesburg and was the site of the County Clerk's office for several decades. *Courtesy of the Loudoun Museum, Leesburg.*

The Courthouse, Clerk of Court and Attorneys

Controversy continues to this day over the actual location of the first "courthouse," where the organizational meetings and the initial County Court sessions were conducted in 1757. The Fruitlands plantation home of Nicholas Minor, just east of what is now downtown Leesburg, was rented for the use of the County Court in 1759 and 1760, while construction of the first Courthouse in Leesburg was underway, but the 1757 site of the County Court sessions remains a matter of conjecture. This writer is of the opinion that, in July of 1757, the Loudoun County organizational meetings were held at William West's ordinary at Fruit Hill and not at Fruitlands. West's plantation and ordinary were situated at the intersection of the Carolina and Mountain Roads, probably the busiest crossroads in Loudoun County in mid-1757.

Around 1743, William West leased land from G.W. Fairfax and established an ordinary at the Springfield (Freedom Hill at Tyson's Corner) site of the Fairfax County Courthouse, where his older brothers Hugh and John served as County Justices. West's ordinary was situated within the Fairfax prison bounds at the Springfield Courthouse when a plat was made in March of 1746. Sometime before the Fairfax Courthouse was moved to Alexandria in the spring of 1752, West moved his ordinary business to his plantation home at Fruit Hill. William West had come to the attention of Virginia's Governors as early as 1753, dispatching couriers to the colonial government with appraisals of the severity of Indian incursions in the Northern Neck. When the Loudoun County Court met to organize the administration of the County in July of 1757, it must have seemed natural to the individuals assembling for a County Court to do so in familiar surroundings, albeit at a new location. Additional ammunition is provided by the presence of Charles Binns, the first Loudoun County Clerk who, according to Loudoun tithable lists, was in residence at West's ordinary at Fruit Hill in 1757 and the spring of 1758. Charles Binns' wife was one of the Alexanders, of the family that William West's brother had flattered and then allied with to found Alexandria in 1748-49. Other ordinaries in operation in 1757 (Dodd's and the ordinary at the Goose Creek ferry), were more convenient to Fruitlands than was West's, and land records show that Binns acquired his Rokeby plantation lands, just south of Leesburg, rapidly after the permanent site of the Courthouse was established. So why was the new County Clerk living at West's ordinary if not for its proximity to or status as the site of the earliest County Court sessions? As tempting as this puzzle is, for the time being we will leave its resolution to an uncertain future, but at least one avenue of academic inquiry remains open. The petitions from Loudoun residents in 1757 and 1758, submitted to the Assembly and the Governor's Council seeking a determination of the site for the County Courthouse (if they still exist somewhere in the Virginia Archives), could provide the missing clues to help solve the puzzle. There is one indication that Loudoun County Court sessions were held at a site near Leesburg as early as June of 1758. Colonial courts awarded non-resident witnesses their travel costs based on the number of miles they travelled from their residence, and Rodolphus Ellinger, a witness from Maryland, apparently travelled only four miles to reach the Loudoun "Courthouse" for that session of the Loudoun County Court. [FXCODB, Book B, p. 233; LDTX/1, p. 1; Council, V, p. 428; infra, Chapter on Ordinaries; infra, text @ p. 513].

On November 1, 1757 the Governor's Council considered establishing a seat for the Loudoun County government, resolving:

> *"to examine the most convenient Place for holding Courts in the County of Loudoun [and] ... Ordered that the [Council's] Clerk write to the Sheriff of the said County to signify to those Gentlemen [meaning the County Court], and all others concerned ... and require their Appearance ... at the Capitol."*

It seems that there was some competition for the placement of the Courthouse, possibly pitting the Potomac and up-country settlers against the Prince William plantation families. On May 3, 1758 the Council "continued" consideration for one month, and once again instructed their clerk to "write to the Sheriff requiring him to give notice to the Parties concerned, to Attend." On June 15, 1758, four months before the Assembly incorporated the town of Leesburg, the Council apparently ratified the consensus of local opinion and fixed the site for the Loudoun County Courthouse "on the lands of Nicholas Minor," meaning the site that would become Leesburg. On September 13, 1758, for £365, Loudoun Justice Aeneas Campbell undertook the construction of Loudoun's first

Courthouse, to be situated on Leesburg town Lots #27 and #28. Completion was scheduled for August of 1760, but County Court sessions were probably not held in the unfinished building until November of 1760. Finishing work continued throughout the first decade, but in 1765 and 1768, Loudoun's King's Attorneys were instructed to sue Justice Campbell for non-performance on his construction bond. [Council, VI, pp. 70, 89 and 103; infra, The Record, pp. 103 and 108; Landmarks, pp. 326-328].

A depiction of the first Loudoun County Courthouse as it must have appeared in 1760 is presented on the dust cover and title page of this tome. No contemporary rendition of the original Courthouse is known to have survived into the Twentieth century, but the dimensions and detail work for Loudoun's first Courthouse were specified by the colonial Loudoun Court in their Orders of August 9, 1758. Georgian architecture was the near-universal style of construction in Virginia's Northern Neck at the time. The original brick Courthouse structure measured only 40'x28', with an attached 16'x16' jury room. Inside, County Court Justices sat at a raised, semi-circular bench. Juries sat in two elevated galleries on the side walls, above the Sheriff's boxes. Litigants presented their case to the Court from a bannistered, railed area known as the "Lawyers Bar." [supra, p. i; infra, The Record, p. 103].

Construction of a wooden bell tower on the Courthouse was authorized in October of 1769, but the bell did not arrive until late in 1772, and the belfry on the original structure was not completed until 1773 or 1774. Prior to the addition of the bell and belfry, Loudoun Court sessions were probably heralded by the Sheriff or a deputy Clerk clanging an iron triangle on the front lawn. The first Courthouse served Loudoun for over 50 years but was replaced around 1811 by a larger brick structure that was built either on or immediately adjacent to the original site. The cornerstone of the Courthouse which stands today, in 1994, above the site of the 1811 structure, was laid in a Masonic Ceremony on April 24, 1894. [LDCOCO, Book D, pp. 247 and 278].

Charles Binns Senr. was the first Clerk of the Loudoun County Court. He served in that capacity continuously from 1757 until 1796, when he was succeeded by his son Charles Binns Junr. The colonial County Clerk scheduled and managed the County Court sessions and, due to the extensive responsibilities of the County Courts, the County Clerk's office probably served as the political and business hub of every County. In June of 1676, the Virginia Assembly had granted the county courts the power to "nominate, appoint, place and displace their clerks as they see cause," but by the mid-1700s, the right to appoint the county court clerks had returned to the colonial capitol and settled squarely on the Secretary of the Virginia Colony. Accordingly, Charles Binns Senr. received his Commission as Loudoun County's first Clerk from "Thomas Nelson, Esqr., Deputy Secretary of this Colony." [Hening, II/355; see infra, The Record, p. 102].

The Binns' Rokeby plantation home, built before 1760 south of Leesburg and near the Carolina Road, was the site of the County Clerk's office during the entire colonial and Revolutionary period. A 1745 law called for "the Justices of [every] ... county court ... [to] annually, appoint two or more fit persons of their number to inspect the Clerk's office ... to report ... the condition in which they find the papers and records." Ignored, for the most part, by the Loudoun County Court, this provision of Virginia law was complied with only twice in Loudoun's first decade, first in 1760, again 1763, and only sporadically thereafter. The first of these inspection orders may have signified the completion of the Clerk's office at Rokeby. Inferential evidence suggests that the original Courthouse may have been refurbished and converted for use as the County Clerk's office when the second Courthouse completed and put in use around 1811. [Hening, V/344].

The normal duties of the Loudoun County Clerk were spelled out in the law that established his annual salary, with cask, at 1248 lbs. of tobacco, or just under £8. The Clerk's annual salary was intended as the sole compensation for his public services:

> *"... viz. entering and issuing copies of orders for appointing surveyors of high ways, appointing constables, grand juries, taking the list of tithables, entering guardian accounts ... binding out poor orphans and appointing guardians, entering the levy ... and of the list of tithables for the collector[s]; ... issuing the orders for recommending Sherifs and Justices, and for processioning, and all other public services for which no particular fee is allowed."*

From this recitation, it is clear that the "public services" expected of a colonial County Clerk extended far beyond the administration of the local court, and included a great deal of list making.

However, a County Clerk's duties in the administration of justice constituted the real source of his income, as can best be understood by examining the schedule of Clerks' fees that were charged for various services, rated by value in tobacco:

"To the County Court Clerks.	*Pounds of Tobacco.*
For recording deeds of lease and release for ... settling of lands, [with] bond to perform covenants; certificate of ... acknowledgement ... and all matters relating thereto,	*150*
... ... [making] a copy thereof ...	*55*
... recording every deed of feoffment, or bargain and sale, or other single deed ... and all matters relating ...	*100*
... issuing and recording a commission to take the ... privy examination of a feme covert ...	*40*
... recording a deed of land [emphasis added:] <u>from the proprietors of the Northern Neck</u> ...	*50*
... recording a deed concerning slaves, or any personal matter or thing only ...	*40*
... recording a letter of attorney,	*30*
... a certificate of the proof or acknowledgment thereof,	*10*
... a copy of a letter of attorney, with such certificate,	*25*
... recording a bond with condition, other than for performance of covenants in deeds of conveyance ...	*20*
... a copy of any other obligation or promissory note,	*10*
... the probation of any will or testament and recording same ... [or] commission of administration of [an] intestate ...	*40*
... recording an inventory ... [valued under] £10,	*10*
... Where the [inventory] appraisement [sic] ... is under £50,	*50*
... a copy of a will or inventory ... within one sheet,	*30*
... a copy of a will ... for every such sheet besides the first,	*20*
... a copy of an act of Assembly,	*40*
... recording an age of a servant or slave, adjudged in court,	*10*
... a certificate of any person's departure out of the country,	*15*
... attending a court for examination of criminals ...	*200*
... a copy of a list of tithables taken by a justice in his precinct,	*20*
... the whole fee for an ordinary license and bond,	*50*
... a copy of the rates of liquors,	*15*
... a marriage license, certificate and bond,	*50*
... proving rights for land ... belonging to one person ...	*18*
... every search for any thing, above a year's standing,	*5*
...	*[con't.] ...*

"To the County Court Clerks. [con't.] Pounds of Tobacco.

... every writ, other than such ... particularly mentioned,	*10*
... a copy of such writ,	*5*
... every writ of execution ... [or] writ of attachment ...	*15*
... an attachment, granted by a Justice of the Peace, returnable to the Court ... and putting the same on the docket,	*20*
... every summons, to summon a garnishee on [an] attachment,	*10*
... docketing every cause, except by petition, to be paid but once,	*5*
... entering special bail ... [or] security for costs ...	*10*
... entering the appearance of the defendant ... [or] entering [the appearance of] attornies [sic] for each party,	*5*
... every trial, swearing the jury and witnesses, filing all papers, and recording a general verdict,	*40*
... swearing the witnesses in every other cause except by petition,	*10*
... entering every judgment, or for a copy thereof,	*10*
... filing a bill, answer, replication ... in chancery, for each,	*10*
... a copy thereof, for every thirty words,	*1*
... recording the report of a jury, in the county ...	*20*
... taxing costs ... where costs are recovered, or for a copy ...	*11*
... entering an appeal, and taking bond to prosecute it,	*20*
... entering each order, for a witness's [sic] attendance ...	*10*
... the whole fee chargeable, for every petition, for debt, detinue, assumpsit, or trover, and all the proceedings therein, including a copy of the judgment, and taxing costs,	*50*
... entering an attorney in such petitions ... not to be taxed ...	*5*
... [and] recording any thing not herein particularly mentioned, or for a copy thereof, for every thirty words,	*1*

..." The Loudoun Clerk's fees were discounted 20% from the above schedule under a provision in the Loudoun County incorporating statute and, after Loudoun was officially put on a "cash" basis in 1759, fees were payable in either tobacco or money, at the exchange rate of "twelve shillings and six pence per hundred" pounds of tobacco due, or 3 pence for every 2 lbs. of tobacco. Loudoun County Clerk Charles Binns claimed that the calculations of the fee discounts were a great inconvenience, but his petition to the Assembly in 1762, requesting modification of the discount schedule, was rejected. Ultimately, abuses of some County Clerks led the Assembly to enact a law disallowing any charge "for the search for any thing in [their] respective offices

where a copy is taken or made." [Hening, V/331-336, VII/292, VII/385 and VIII/267; infra, The Record, p. 106].

Deputy King's Attorneys were the colonial equivalent of a Commonwealth's Attorney and a County Attorney, combined. In other words, King's Attorneys served as both the Prosecutor for the King in criminal cases and as the lawyer for the colonial County "government," embodied by the County Court. Loudoun's first Deputy King's Attorney, Hugh West Junr., was a son of Hugh West Senr., the founder of Alexandria, and apparently began his law practice in mercurial fashion in 1751 when he replaced John Hamilton as the King's Attorney for Fairfax County. His rapid political advance culminated with election in Frederick County as a Burgess in December of 1755 (he lost to George Washington in the next election, on July 24, 1758). He was promptly confirmed as the King's Attorney for Loudoun County in 1757, while his brother George West became Loudoun's first Surveyor and his uncle William West was appointed as a Loudoun Justice of the Quorum. Hugh West Junr. married Elizabeth Minor, the niece of Leesburg founder Nicholas Minor, and they made their home in Alexandria on a town lot that Hugh had inherited in 1754. For the sixteen years before his death in 1767, Hugh West Junr. served the Loudoun community as the King's Attorney of, first, Fairfax County, and then, both Fairfax and Loudoun. Among the affairs of Loudoun County left unfinished at the time of his death was the purchase of a County Seal, and the law suit prosecuting Loudoun Justice Aeneas Campbell for his failure to complete construction of the first County Courthouse. [Landmarks, pp. 138-140; Fairfax, p. 53; FXCOCO, 1749 Book, pp. 52, 125 and 178; see supra, p. 95; supra, Chapter on the County Court].

In 1766, at the conclusion of Loudoun County's first decade, we find a thirty year old attorney named William Grayson entering his appearance at the Loudoun County Court. William Grayson was a son of former Prince William County Justice Benjamin Grayson and the older brother of eventual Cameron parish Rector Spence Grayson. He rapidly advanced to the position of Deputy King's Attorney for both Loudoun and Fairfax when Hugh West died in 1767, despite the Loudoun County Court's recommendation of attorney William Ellzey. During the Revolution William Grayson organized a regiment of Continental soldiers, he was elected to represent Virginia in the Continental

Congress from 1784 to 1787, and he represented the new State of Virginia in the U.S. Senate in 1789 and 1790. His replacement in the U.S. Senate was none other than James Monroe. In 1792, two years after his death, Grayson County Virginia was named to honor the second colonial King's Attorney of Loudoun County. [Landmarks, p. 156; FXCOCO, 1768 Book, p. 18].

The procedures for examining prospective attorneys and the issuance of licenses to practice law, and regulations governing and the maximum allowable attorney fees in Virginia Courts, were all codified in laws enacted by the Virginia Assembly as early as March of 1642-43, during the reign of King Charles I. The 1745 Assembly viewed "the great number of ignorant and unskilful [sic] attornies practicing in the county courts ... [as] a grievance to the country, in respect of their neglect and mismanagement of their clients causes," and imposed stringent regulations to control the practices in the County Courts. The law instructed the Governor's Council to form a committee of learned attorneys who thereafter were "to examine into the capacity, ability, and fitness of such persons [who] apply for a license to practice as attornies," and every applicant was obliged to produce "a certificate from some county court ... of his probity, honesty, [sic] and good demeanor." The new regulations also mandated the payment of an application fee of 20 shillings (£1). [Hening, I/275 and V/345].

By 1757 the Assembly enacted measures to prohibit felons from becoming attorneys, punish the unlicensed practice of law, and allow the General Court to suspend "attornies misdemeaning themselves." The county courts could exercise discretionary authority and require attorneys to post security for their good behavior, or punish contempt by any "misdemeaning" attorneys through the imposition of a fine. The reader will note the numerous fines that the Loudoun Court imposed on Francis Dade, Esq., which suggests attorney Dade had earned a reputation as the "bad boy barrister" of the Northern Neck. Attorney Dade was disbarred in both the Loudoun and Fairfax County Courts about the same time, shortly before he moved to Maryland around 1766. [Hening, VI/142-143 and VII/398-399; Fairfax, p. 73].

In April of 1757, only months before Loudoun County was created, the Virginia Assembly revised the Acts of 1745, 1748 and 1754 "regulating the practice of attornies" and restored to non-Tidewater attorneys the privilege of arguing the same case in both their county court and then on appeal in the General Court. While this measure also allowed Williamsburg's General Court attorneys to practice in the more remote county courts like Loudoun, they influenced the Assembly to reverse the policy in 1761. In order to obtain an attorney's license, an applicant was required to: obtain a certificate from a county court where he intended to practice wherein the county court verified the applicant's "probity, honesty, and good demeanor"; pass an examination given by a select group of attornies practicing in the General Court (predecessors to the modern Virginia Board of Bar Examiners); and pay a 20 shilling examination fee. Upon selection by the examiners, the applicant was required to subscribe the oaths of abjuration and "the test," as well as "the oath of an attorney, as follows to-wit: *I 'A.B.' do swear, that I will truly and honestly demean myself, in the practice of an attorney, according to the best of my knowledge and ability.- So help me God."* [Hening, VI/140-141, VII/124, VII/397-401 and VIII/198].

Aside from the two King's Attorneys, only seven other lawyers were licensed to practice in the Loudoun County Court before 1766. Benjamin Sebastian was an Alexandria merchant and a fixture at the Loudoun Court who traded in Loudoun real estate and represented other Alexandria merchants; William Ellzey was a Cameron parish vestryman whose family had long been associated with the at Dumfries merchants; James Keith was from Fairfax and briefly represented the trading firms located at Colchester; Lee Massey, from Fairfax, advanced to become a County Justice of, first, Fairfax and then Loudoun, and ultimately accepted the Rectory of Truro parish; Francis Dade, brother of Fairfax County Justice Townsend Dade, fell into disfavor with the various Potomac interests, and apparently became a journeyman attorney before he was disbarred in the Virginia courts; Cuthbert Bullett, from Prince William, briefly represented the Dumfries and Occoquan merchants; and, George Johnston, from Fairfax County, served in the Virginia Assembly and represented Potomac and Colchester merchants in the courts before his death in 1768.

During the two decades before 1776, attorney fees for all attorneys practicing in the Virginia county courts were regulated according to the following schedule:

"for an opinion or advice, where no suit ... shall be

brought ... ten shillings; and in any suit at common law ... or by petition, fifteen shillings; in all chancery suits, or ... actions, where the title or bounds of land ... come in question, thirty shillings; on a petition of a small debt seven shillings and six pence; and any lawyer for attending a survey in the country, for every day ... one pound one shilling and six pence."

Virginia law, enacted in 1745, allowed for the recovery of attorney fees when a litigant won a case, by including 15 shillings or 150 lbs. of tobacco "in the bill of costs ... if the party employed [an attorney] ... except where the [case] shall be brought by petition." In the statute of 1757, county court Clerks were instructed to "tax" attorney fees in the bill of costs that was entered on all final decrees in their court, with payment of the fees to be allowed in either tobacco or money. For this purpose only, 20 shillings (£1) was declared to equal 200 pounds of tobacco in value. [Hening, V/344, VII/124-125, VII/397-401, VIII/184-185 and VIII/385.]

By statute, the 1748 Virginia Assembly instructed every county court "to provide, at the charge of their county," a County Seal. Despite this requirement, the colonial County Court did not take action to obtain a Loudoun County Seal until 1759, two years after incorporation. The Court was still making arrangements with Loudoun's King's Attorney Hugh West for the purchase of the Seal late in 1762, but there is no record that his efforts met with success before his death in 1767. The County Court may have simply forgotten about the Seal until 1771, when Loudoun Justice and Leesburg silversmith Stephen Donaldson took the commission to manufacture the first County Seal. [Hening, V/462; infra, The Record, pp. 104 and 106; LDCOCO, Book E, pp. 166 and 385].

The Loudoun Record

July 12, 1757 - [On the first day of the new County Court] - Charles Binns receives his Commission from "Thomas Nelson, Esqr., Deputy Secretary of this Colony," and takes the Oaths of the "Clerk of this Court." Book A, p. 2.

July 12, 1757 - Hugh West, Benjamin Sebastian, William Ellzey and James Keith each presents his Certification and takes the Oaths of an Attorney at Law. Book A, p. 2.

August 9, 1757 - Lee Massey Gent. [a future Loudoun Justice] takes the Oaths of an Attorney at Law. Book A, p. 4.

August 10, 1757 - In the years before the American Revolution, the Virginia courts awarded judgment interest to successful plaintiffs at the rate of 5% per annum. Book A, p. 5.

August 10, 1757 - Throughout the 1757-1766 decade, witnesses are awarded 25 lbs. of tobacco per day for their appearance to give testimony at Court, and an additional 1½ lbs. of tobacco for each mile when travelling from and back to another County. Book A, p. 6; infra, the Chapter on the Sheriffs.

September 14, 1757 - Hugh West receives his Commission and takes the Oaths required of the Kings Deputy Attorney for the County. Book A, p. 19.

December 13, 1757 - Itemizing the County Levy, a Debit is listed for "Charles Binns Clerk [of Court] for [his salary for Public Service] ... 1,248 [lbs. tobacco, of the value of about £8 in currency]." Book A, p. 54.

December 13, 1757 - In the itemization of the County Levy, a debit is listed for "... Hugh West Deputy [King's] Attorney as a Salary ... 2,000 [lbs. tobacco- about £12½]." Book A, p. 55.

May 9, 1758 - Francis Dade Gent. takes the Oaths of an Attorney at Law. Book A, p. 98.

June 13, 1758 - "Ordered that William West agree with a Workman to build a Book Press and Writing Desk for the use of the Clerks Office." Book A, p. 113.

June 15, 1758 - Jacob Pfhaw (Jacob Faw), a former ordinary keeper in Alexandria who is identified as a "saddler," for £4, subscribes Lot #27 in "George Town," the future Leesburg Courthouse lot. LDCODB, Book A, p. 89.

June 15, 1758 - The Governor and his Council, meeting in Williamsburg, "having this Day taken under Consideration the most proper Place for establishing the Court House of Loudoun County, it appearing to them that the Plantation of Captain Nicholas Minor was the most convenient Place and agreeable to the Generality of the People in that County ... accordingly Order'd That the Court-house for the said County be fixed on the Land of the said Minor." Council, VI/103.

July 11, 1758 - "Ordered that the Sherif [sic- meaning Aeneas Campbell] ... Advertise for Workmen to build a Courthouse to meet here at the next Court to agree for the same." Book A, p. 131.

August 9, 1758 - In response to an Order of the Governor's Council, the Loudoun County Court orders that: "A Courthouse to be built for this County on the Lands of Nicholas Minor Gent. after the following Dimensions, to-wit, To be of Brick 40 by 28, Jury room 16 by 16 with an outside Chimney and fire place 8 feet in the clear, from the foundation to the Surface 2 feet, from the Surface to the Water table 4 feet, from thence to the Joist 10 feet. The Joiners and Carpenters Work to be in the following manner all the framing to be of white Oak, the Windows well framed and Cased to consist of 24 lights each 8 by 10, five Windows in the Courthouse two on one side, two in the end where the Justices sit, & one in the side on which the Jury room is built, two Windows in the Jury room - opposite to each other. the Sashes to be made of well Seasoned Pine of at least 1¼ Inches after they [are] wrought, pannelled [sic] Window shutters with Hooks & Bolts. The Doors to be of pannelled Work of proper stuff well seasoned, the front to be 8 by 4½ folding with proper Bolts and Locks. Two Galleries for Juries with Stairs leading to each from the Floor raised to a proper height sufficient for a person to walk under with Rails and Banisters. the Justices seat to be Circular raised to a proper height, with a Lawyers Barr and both railed and Bannistered. the floor of the Courthouse 5 feet before the Lawyer's Barr to be laid with Inch Plank together with the Jury room, which is to be finished above Stairs with two Dorman Windows, a small Stair Case leading thereto faced in the most convenient place for that purpose. the floor of the Courthouse from 5 feet from the Lawyer's Barr to be laid with Bricks or Tyle [sic] made of the dimentions [sic] of 8 by 8, & to finish in whole in a Workman like manner. likewise two Boxes for the Sherif and his Deputy fixed at the foot of each of the Stairs leading to the Juries Galleries - Ordered that Nicholas Minor, James Hamilton and William West, Gentlemen, Advertise for Workmen to meet them at some convenient place in this County on any day by them to be appointed ... [before] the 25th day of next Month with their Plans to undertake the said Building according to the above dimensions ... to the lowest bidder ... [requiring] Bond with sufficient Security ... [for] performance of the said work within such time as [the named Commissioners] think convenient." Book A, pp. 142-143.

September 12, 1758 - Cuthbert Bullet, Gent., takes Oaths as an Attorney at Law. Book A, p. 158.

September 12, 1758 - "Ordered that the Courthouse for this County be Built on a Lott of Captain Nicholas Minor's No. 27 and 28 and that he Convey the same to William West & James Hamilton, Gent., as Trustees in & for the use of the said County." Book A, p. 162.

September 13, 1758 - "Aneas Campbell Gent. [apparently low bidder] undertook the building of the Courthouse for the sum of £365 Current Money to be paid him at two equal Payments, to-wit, one half on the first of August next [in 1759] ... the other half [on August 1st] in the year 1760." Book A, p. 166.

November 14, 1758 - A County Levy lists a debit to "Aneas Campbell ... in part for building a Courthouse for this County ... 21,900 [lbs. tobacco]," as the first installment for construction of the Courthouse. Book A, p. 177.

June 14, 1759 - Hugh West [the Deputy King's Attorney] is authorized to obtain the County Seal. Book A, p. 256.

September 12, 1759 - "Ordered that Nicholas Minor, William West and Josias Clapham from time to time make Alterations ... to building the Courthouse." Book A, p. 291.

November 14, 1759 - In itemizing the County Levy, a debit is listed for "Nicholas Minor Gent. for the use of his House for holding Courts ... 1200 [lbs. tobacco]." Book A, p. 303.

January 29, 1760 - Francis Peyton attended the Prince William Court for two days as a witness for Francis Mountain, against William Powell, "travelling from Loudoun County ... forty-five miles." PrWmCOA, (1760)/19, p. 292.

June 24, 1760 - James Lane attended court in Prince William County for two days as a witness for John Diskin, against Edward Conner, "travelling from Loudoun County ... twenty-five miles." PrWmCOA, (1760)/20, p. 193.

August 13, 1760 - William West and Francis Peyton are appointed "To Inspect the Office of the Clerk of this Court and to Report ... the Condition in which they find the Papers and Records." Book A, p. 391.

November 12, 1760 - In the itemization of the County Levy, a debit is listed for "Nicholas Minor ... the hire of his Home for holding Courts ... 1,000 [lbs. tobacco]." Book A, p. 404.

March 10, 1761 - "Charles Binns Clerk of this Court took the Oaths to his Majesty's Person and Government ... Subscribed the Abjuration Oath and ... the Test." This renewal of Oaths was probably occasioned by the receipt of a new Commission, which would have been issued after King George III assumed the throne. Book A, p. 427.

March 10, 1761 - Attorneys at Law Hugh West, William Ellzey and Francis Dade renewed their Oaths "to his Majesty's Person [newly enthroned George III] and [his] Government ..." Book A, p. 427.

March 11, 1761 - Benjamin Sebastian, of Alexandria, produces his Commission and takes the Oaths of an Attorney at Law. Book A, p. 433.

June 11, 1761 - In anticipation of the lapse of Jacob Faw's old deed to Lot #27, a deed from Nicholas Minor Gent. for the Courthouse properties, town Lots #27 and #28, to "Francis Lightfoot Lee the first Justice named ... and the rest of the Justices" of the Peace named in the Commission for the County, is proved and ordered recorded. Book A, p. 461; LDCODB, Book B, p. 149.

October 13, 1761 - At the last Loudoun Court session of the first year in the reign of George III, the preface for the Orders reads: "At a Court held for Loudoun County at the Courthouse ... In the first Year of the Reign of our Sovereign Lord George the third by the Grace of God of Great Britain, France and Ireland, King Defender of the Faith &c. ... Before his Majesty's Justices of the Peace for the said County." Book A, p. 525.

November 11, 1761 - In the itemization of the County Levy, a payment is listed to "Charles Binns for 2 Record Books & payg. [paying a] Wagener [sic] for bringing the same 45/ [shillings] in Tobo. is [rated at] ... 360 [lbs. tobacco]." Book A, p. 533.

November 12, 1761 - "Ordered that Nicholas Minor Gent. and John Moss Junr. Agree with Workmen to Clear away the Bricks and Dirt about the Courthouse and likewise for building a Necessary House and Posting and Railing in the Courthouse Lott and ... Account at ... the next Levy." Book A, p. 544.

May 11, 1762 - George Summers produces his Commission in open Court and takes the Oaths of a "Deputy Clerk of this Court." His Commission confirms a previously existing working arrangement. George Summers was assisting Charles Binns and living at the Binns Rokeby plantation home as early as 1760. Summers continued in this capacity through 1765, and eventually was appointed as a Loudoun County Justice, in 1768. Book A, p. 588; LDTX/1, pp. 5, 12 and 38; LDCOCO, Book D, pp. 90 and 92.

June 21, 1762 - Charles Binns pays Alexandria merchants "Carlyle & Dalton" for three large record books for the Loudoun County records, the total sum of £7, 4 shillings being rated in tobacco, at 12/6 per hundred, to a total value of 1152 lbs. of tobacco. This means each large County record book had an original cost of £2.8. Clerk's Fee Book for 1762, last page.

July 15, 1762 - "Ordered that the Sherif pay [Leesburg carpenter] Thomas Pritchard towards Railing in the Court house Lott &c. the ballance ... to be applied to the purchase of a Seal for the use of this County." Book B, p. 25.

August 13, 1762 - "Hugh West [Deputy King's Attorney] and Francis Dade [an attorney practicing in the Loudoun Court] having Misbehaved themselves before this Court and disregarded the Court's repeated Admonitions ... for such their Ill Behavior and Contiemacy [sic- contempt] be fined each of them [£5] ... Hugh West and William Ellzey his Security [gave bonds totalling £75 that] Hugh West shall be of good Behavior for the space of one Year ... Francis Dade failing to give such Security ... be committed to the Custody of the Sherif there to remain until he shall give such Security." Book B, p. 51.

October 25, 1762 - The annual levy of Truro parish, in Fairfax County, includes a payment of 1200 lbs. of tobacco to Hugh West, Deputy Kings Attorney. This is a clear indication that Hugh West continued to serve as King's prosecutor in Fairfax County after Loudoun was formed. Truro, p. 85.

November 10, 1762 - In the County Levy, a debit is listed, "To ... Charles Binns, Clerk, for public Services ... 1248 [lbs. tobacco]." Book B, p. 73.

November 10, 1762 - "Ordered ... William West Gent. late Sherif [having just stepped down from office] pay ... £6 to Hugh West [King's Attorney] ... to apply the same to the purchase of a Seal for this County." Book B, p. 75.

November 25, 1762 - In Williamsburg, "A Petition of Charles Binns, Clerk of Loudoun County, praying some Alteration as to his Fees, was presented to the House [of Burgesses] and read. [The Assembly] Ordered, That the said Petition be referred to the Consideration of the Committee of Propositions and Grievances; that they examine into the Allegations thereof, and report ... with their Opinion thereon." Assembly, (1761) p. 114.

December 10, 1762 - The Virginia Assembly, in session in Williamsburg, after receiving an unfavorable Committee report, resolves "That the Petition of Charles Binns, Clerk of Loudoun County praying that the Deduction from the Tobacco Fees of his Office, for making the same convenient, may be lessened, be rejected." Assembly, (1761) p. 145.

April 14, 1763 - Francis Dade is fined 5 shillings for swearing one Prophane Oath [sic], ie., "By God." Book B, p. 111.

August 10, 1763 - "Pursuant to Law ... [Loudoun Justices] George West and Charles Tyler are appointed to Inspect the Office of the Clerk of this County and Report to Court the Condition in Which they find the Papers and Records." Book B, p. 200.

November 9, 1763 - In the itemization of the County Levy, a debit is listed "To ... Hugh West Deputy King's Attorney his Salary ... 3,000 [lbs tobacco - valued at £18, 15 shillings]." Book B, p. 266.

March 14, 1764 - "Ordered that William West Gent. deliver to Leven Powell Gent. the Body of Laws together with Mercers Abridgement ... belonging to this County." William West Senr. had not returned to sit on the County Court after his term as Sheriff and was in "retirement," having removed to his property above the Beaver Dam Branch of Goose Creek. Book B, p. 283.

April 11, 1764 - George Johnston [Senr.], takes the Oaths of an Attorney in the Loudoun County Court. Book B, p. 335.

June 15, 1764 - It appears that a new assistant Clerk takes over as scribe in the Court Order Books. Book B, p. 383.

September 12, 1764 - "Ordered that [attorney] Francis Dade be fined Five Pounds [£5] for his ill behavour [sic] before the Court in threatening to Fight John Heryford and beat him when ever he met him out of the Verge of the Court." Book B, p. 435; see Glossary.

September 12, 1764 - The Loudoun Court "Ordered that [attorney] Francis Dade be committed to the Stocks there to remain until the Rising of the Court for Grossly misbehaving before the Court and being Drunk some time after his being fined [earlier the same day]." Book B, p. 436.

Friday, September 14, 1764 - "Ordered that Francis Dade be fined Fifty Pounds [£50] for his Opprobrious [shameful] and Abusive Language at the Bar." [This followed a ruling giving Charles Binns, Clerk of Court, judgment against Dade for a "Debt due by Account," for £1, 12 shillings]. Book B, p. 461.

September 14, 1764 - Loudoun attorney "Francis Dade, coming into Court in the evening and making proper Concessions ... the fine imposed on him this morning [£50] be Remitted." Book B, p. 471.

November 13, 1764 - In the County Levy, a debit is listed, "To ... Charles Binns, Clerk for Public Services ... 1248 [lbs. tobacco]." Book B, p. 495.

November 13, 1764 - In the County Levy, a credit is listed for "Hugh West, Deputy Kings Attorney his Salary ... 3,000 [lbs. tobacco]." Book B, p. 495.

November 14, 1764 - In the itemization of the County Levy, a debit is listed for a payment "To ... [Loudoun County Justice] John Moss Junr. for attending [supplying] the Courthouse with Wood and Water for one year ... 1,000 [lbs. tobacco - valued at £6, 5 shillings]." Book B, p. 497.

April 9, 1765 - Charles Binns, the Clerk of Court, charges 200 lbs. of tobacco for "attending an exam Court agt. [against] John Ream for Felony." There was no other entry for John Ream, who apparently was found not guilty at this hearing. Clerk's 1765 Fee Book, last page; infra, Chapter on Criminals.

June 13, 1765 - Clerk of the Court Charles Binns charges 200 lbs. of tobacco for "attending an exam Court agt. [against] Mary McDonald for Felony." Clerk's 1765 Fee Book, last page; and see infra, Chapter on Crimes.

August 12, 1765 - Charles Binns, Clerk of the Court, charges 200 lbs. of tobacco for "attending an exam Court agt. [against] John Castle for Felony." Clerk's 1765 Fee Book, last page.

August 13, 1765 - "Anthony Russell [as a witness] ... against Benjamin Grayson, having attended Court two Daies [sic] ... Ordered that the said Benjamin pay him fifty pounds of Tobacco for the same the Cause being Continued till the next Court at his Cost." Anthony Russell was a former Loudoun County Justice and this Benjamin Grayson was a Justice in Fairfax County. Book C, p. 17.

September 11, 1765 - "Ordered that the Bond given [by Loudoun Justice Aeneas Campbell] ... for building and finishing the Courthouse ... be put in Suit in the General Court [in Williamsburg] for the nonperformance of the Covenants therein mentioned." Book C, p. 49.

October 7, 1765 - Charles Binns, Clerk of the Court, charges 200 lbs. of tobacco, "gross," and 160 lbs. of tobacco net, "To attending an exam Court agt. John Mares [sic- John Maris ?] for Felony." Clerk's 1765 Fee Book, last page.

November of 1765 - On the tithable list returned by James Hamilton, absentee landowner John Mercer is identified as an Attorney. LDTX/1, p. 35.

November 11, 1765 - In the itemization of the County Levy, a debit is listed: "To ... Hugh West Prosecutor for the King as a Salary ... 2,000 [lbs. tobacco - valued at £12, 10 shillings]." Book C, p. 72.

November 11, 1765 - In itemizing the County Levy, debits are listed: "To ... Charles Binns, Clerk, for Public Service ... 1,248 [lbs. tobacco] ... John Moss Junr. Gent. for keeping and cleaning the Courthouse ... 1,000 [lbs.t.] ... [and] John Heryford for finding Candles and Necessaries [for the Courthouse for] three years [probably 1763-65] ... 200 [lbs.t.]." Book C, pp. 72-73.

November and December of 1765 - No General Courts or Loudoun County Courts are held during these two months. This was a measure of civil disobedience that was adopted throughout the Virginia Colony in response to the imposition of the Stamp Act. Book C, p. 73.

May 12, 1766 - With the repeal of the Stamp Act, a resumption of business was contemplated in the Loudoun County Court and "... a Question being put whether the Court would proceed to business in general [was] ... Resolved in the Affirmative." Book C, p. 75.

September 8, 1766 - William Grayson takes the Oaths of an Attorney at Law in the Loudoun Court. Book C, p. 185.

October 14, 1766 - "James Clemmons a Witness for John Griffith ... duly summoned ... and failing to appear ... [is] fined [350 lbs.] of tobacco ... for such his contempt." Book C, p. 209.

November 11, 1766 - In the itemization of the County Levy there is a debit listed for "Law Books [that were purchased] for the use of the County ... [costing] 3035 [lbs. of tobacco, ie., about £19]." Book C, p. 220.

November 12, 1766 - Charles Binns, Gent., the Clerk of the Loudoun County Court, who was presented by a Grand Jury for swearing a Profane Oath, is noted as "known to be a Person abhorring such detestable words or Language ... the Presentment ... is dismissed." Book C, p. 225.

Constables of the County

The term Constable was derived from the Roman title of Constabularius - originally, an officer of the horse. In feudal times, the English Constables were generally charged with keeping the King's peace within their respective hundred or franchise. The English office of Constable came into use in colonial Virginia at the time of the creation of the Virginia county court system of local government in 1634. As in England, a Constable in the Virginia colony was an officer of his county court, appointed directly by the Justices of the court, with the general duty of policing and keeping the peace in his precinct or district within the county. While the traditional role of the county Constable was that of a minor functionary in the colonial system of justice who assisted in giving court and militia notices, from time to time the Virginia Assembly assigned new responsibilities. For example, when the Assemblies of 1642-43 and 1647 required every Virginia field worker to plant two acres of corn, the county Constables were instructed to view the fields and report any deficiencies to their county courts. A hundred years later, in 1748, Constables were given similar duties when the Assembly prohibited second crops of tobacco. County Constables were instructed to view "all the fields and places whereon tobacco shall be planted or tended" in order to discover any violations. The county courts were directed to pay their Constables for viewing the tobacco fields "in proportion to the number of tithables in their respective precincts," assessing one lb. of tobacco on each tithable resident in the annual county levy. [Black, p. 383; Hening, I/246, I/344 and VI/51-53].

The role of Virginia's county Constables was gradually expanded to include responsibilities far removed from the viewing of planted fields. Between 1735 and 1755, county Constables were given supplemental powers and duties: to search on private property for and seize unlawfully hunted deer skins; to arrest participants, and otherwise suppress, unlawful slave meetings; and, to impress men and horses into their command to expedite the safe return of servants, slaves and deserters. Ferry operators were instructed to give priority to Constables who had custody of a runaway slave or servant or a deserting militiaman, but the 1757 militia patrolling laws relieved Constables of their duty to suppress unlawful slave meetings. In 1765, the laws controlling servants and slaves were changed and Constables were also relieved from their duties in the processing and return of runaways. [Hening, V/60-63, VI/109, VI/367, VI/563, VI/22, VII/104 and VIII/136; infra, Chapter on Servants and Chapter on Slaves].

When the Virginia Assembly recodified the laws and regulations of the county courts in the 1740s, Constables were identified among the county officers who could properly serve writs of attachment and execution in colonial "small claims" cases, where less than 25 shillings was at issue. The 1745 Assembly established a comprehensive fee schedule for the several county officers that was in force and operative for the entire 1757-1766 decade. In giving the schedule, the Assembly recited the various duties usually undertaken by colonial county Constables, and the fees that Constables were normally paid for each action:

"*... To the Constable.*	*[lbs. tobacco]*
For serving a warrant,	*10*
... summoning a witness,	*5*
... summoning a coroner's jury, and witnesses,	*50*
... putting [a criminal] into the stocks,	*10*
... whipping a servant; to be paid by the owner, and repaid by the servant,	*10*
... serving an execution, or attachment, returnable before a justice,	*10*
... serving an attachment, returnable to the county court, against the estate of a debtor ... [who is] removing his effects out of the county,	*30*
... whipping a slave; to be paid by the overseer, if the slave is under an overseer, if not, by the master, one shilling, or,	*10*
... removing any person, suspected to become chargeable to the parish; to be paid by such parish, for every mile,	*2 ...*

... [and] the same for returning." This fee schedule was modified by the 20% abatement of Loudoun's officer fees included in the 1757 incorporating statute so that, for example, a Loudoun County Constable serving a warrant was entitled to a fee of 8 lbs. of tobacco. The official exchange rate in Loudoun County, as set by the Virginia Assembly in 1759, established 8 lbs. of tobacco as the legal equivalent of one shilling. [Hening, V/340, V/493-495,

VII/149 and VII/292; see infra, Chapter on Cameron Parish].

Contrary to what one might anticipate, service as one of the Constables in colonial Loudoun did not normally lead to advancement to a higher office or an appointment to the County Court. A rare exception was Benjamin Grayson (one of three prominent men in the Northern Neck with the name), who was a Constable in western Fairfax County when Loudoun was created, served for two months as a Loudoun County Constable, and was then advanced to the Loudoun Court as a County Justice in December of 1757. Another former Fairfax County Constable in the "Loudoun" section, Thomas Sorrell, served briefly as one of the earliest Trustees for Leesburg. Jacob Remey Junr., who was a Loudoun Constable in the far southeast section of the County (now Fairfax) from 1760 to 1761 and again from 1765 to 1766, was elected to the reformed Cameron parish Vestry when Shelburne parish was created in 1771; and John Lewis, the Cameron parish Clerk at Broad Run Church in 1764, had served as a Loudoun County Constable from 1761 to 1762. But these men were exceptional. In fact, the four dozen individuals who were appointed to serve as Constables in Loudoun County during the 1757-1766 decade were, almost to the man, simple yeomen, tenant farmers and tradesmen. They were representative of the growing middle class that constituted the majority of freeholders in colonial Loudoun. Regardless of the practice elsewhere in Virginia and the other colonies, it is apparent that the Loudoun County Court was intent on expanding the circle of leadership in the county to include men of relatively modest means.

Surprisingly, the Constable position was lightly regarded by many of the men who held the office - evidenced by more than one reference to a Constable "who is run away." And remarkably, in 1765 and 1766, five members of the extended Jones family were appointed Constable in western and northern Loudoun.

The map on the following pages, in seriatim, shows the various Constable districts that the Loudoun Court divided the county into in 1765-1766, and we have arbitrarily labelled the districts {A} through {H}. In the course of compiling The Record for this chapter, every effort has been made to ascertain the precinct that was assigned to each individual Constable, noted with certainty after 1765. In all likelihood, the Constable districts before 1765 were fairly similar to those portrayed in the map.

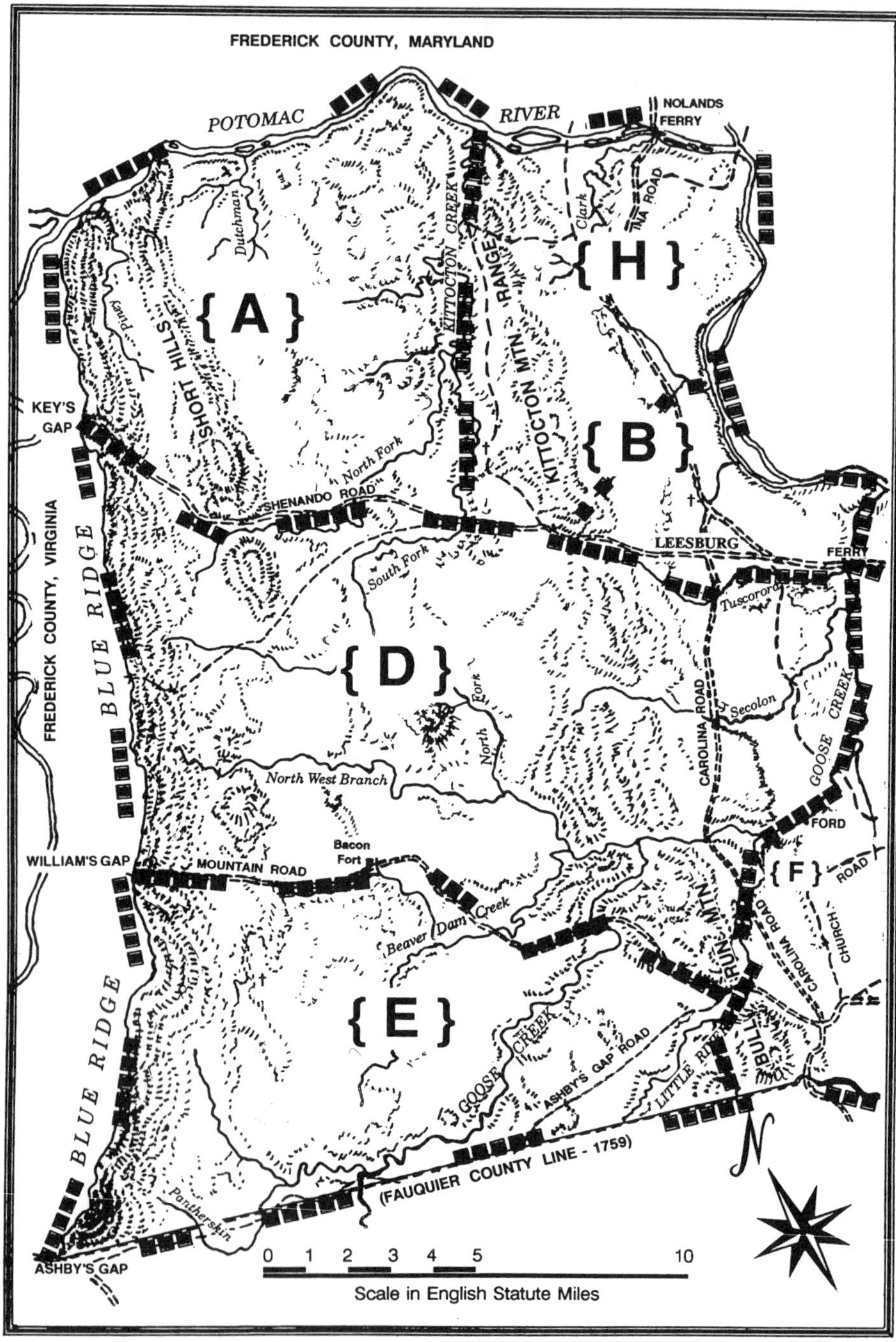
FREDERICK COUNTY, MARYLAND
POTOMAC
RIVER
NOLANDS FERRY
{A}
{B}
{D}
{E}
{F}
{H}
SHORT HILLS
KITTOCTON CREEK
KITTOCTON MTN. RANGE
Dutchman
Clark
KEY'S GAP
FREDERICK COUNTY, VIRGINIA
BLUE RIDGE
North Fork
SHENANDO ROAD
South Fork
LEESBURG
FERRY
Tuscorora
Secolon
CAROLINA ROAD
GOOSE CREEK
North West Branch
North Fork
FORD
Bacon Fort
WILLIAM'S GAP
MOUNTAIN ROAD
Beaver Dam Creek
CHURCH ROAD
BULL RUN MTN.
GOOSE CREEK
ASHBY'S GAP ROAD
LITTLE RIVER
(FAUQUIER COUNTY LINE - 1759)
Panther skin
ASHBY'S GAP
N
0 1 2 3 4 5 10
Scale in English Statute Miles

-LOUDOUN COUNTY - VIRGINIA-

CONSTABLES PRECINCTS
circa 1760 - 1766

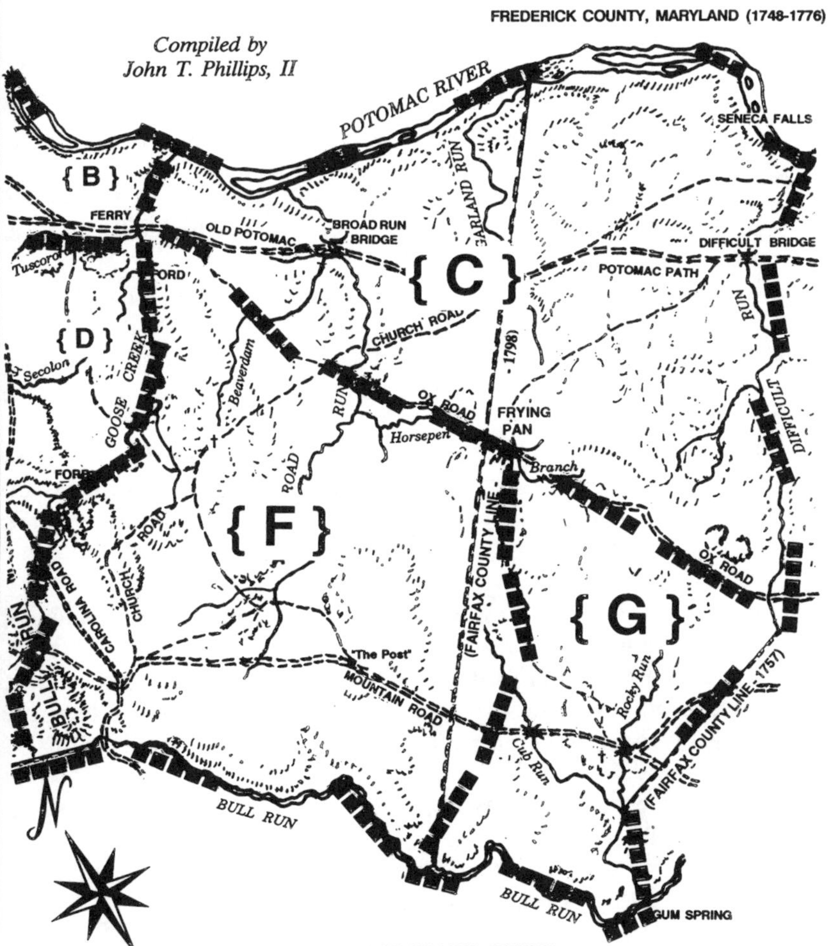

July 12, 1757 - Benjamin Grayson {D?}, William Owsley {F}, David Davis {B}, Samuel Compton {A}, John Ellzey {C}, and Samuel Combs {B}, are each appointed to the Office of County Constable. At the time Loudoun County was created, William Owsley was serving in his district as a Fairfax County constable along the mountain road, having been appointed in March of 1757. Book A, p. 2; FXCOCO, 1756 Book 2, p. 11.

August 10, 1757 - William Lewis is named a new County Constable. Book A, p. 11. {G}

September 13, 1757 - William Landrum is appointed Constable replacing Benjamin Grayson. Book A, p. 16. {D?}

October 12, 1757 - A Complaint of William Dodd against Samuel Compton "for neglect of his Duty [as Constable] is dismissed." Book A, pp. 12 and 34. {A}

August 8, 1758 - The tithables list of Francis Peyton identifies William Owsley as a Constable {F}. LDTX/1, p. 1.

November 14, 1758 - Thomas Connell is appointed Constable replacing William Lewis. Book A, p. 179. {G}

November 15, 1758 - William Norris is named a new County Constable {E}; and, William Stephens is appointed Constable {F} replacing William Owsley. Book A, p. 180.

December 12, 1758 - Thomas Cartwright is appointed Constable replacing David Davis {B}; and, George Fling, who will serve in his office through 1762, is appointed Constable {C} replacing John Ellzey. Book A, p. 183; and infra, p. 115.

February 14, 1759 - Joseph Hutchison is appointed Constable {F} replacing William Stephens. Book A, p. 192.

March 13, 1759 - Benjamin Shacklett is appointed Constable replacing Samuel Compton. Shacklett probably served as Constable in his precinct until 1761, when he is replaced by David Smith. Book A, p. 209; and see, LDTX/1, p. 11. {A}

April 10, 1759 - Nathan Williamson is named a new County Constable. Book A, p. 231.

May 9, 1759 - Christopher Perfect is appointed Constable {B} replacing Samuel Combs. Book A, p. 239.

August 14, 1759 - Francis Malbrough [sic - Francis Marbury] is appointed a Constable {E} replacing William Norris. Book A, p. 265.

September 11, 1759 - William Landrum is discharged from the Office of Constable. Book A, p. 284. {D?}

September of 1759 - William Norris is identified on the tithable list returned by Francis Peyton as a [former] Constable {E} for the precinct along the mountain roads west of Little River; and, George Fling is a Constable {C} on the list returned by Richard Coleman. LDTX/1, p. 2.

March 11, 1760 - James Leith is appointed Constable {F} replacing Joseph Hutchison. Book A, p. 325.

August 12, 1760 - Jacob Remey Junr. is appointed Constable replacing Thomas Connell. Book A, p. 384. {G}

September of 1760 - Christopher Perfect is identified as a Constable {B} on the tithable list returned by James Hamilton; Francis Marbury is a Constable {E} on the return of Francis Peyton; Thomas Connell is a [former] Constable {G} on the list of James Lane; and, William Veal, who had been appointed by the Fairfax County Court, is identified on the "Cameron parish" tithable list as a Constable. LDTX/1, pp. 5, 6, 7 and 8.

February 10, 1761 - James Saunders is appointed Constable replacing Francis Marbury [aka Francis Malbrough] {E}. Later that year, Saunders is identified as a Constable, exempt from the levy, on the tithable list returned by William West. Book A, p. 411; and, LDTX/1, p. 14.

June 11, 1761 - William Hutchison is appointed Constable {F} replacing James Leith. He is identified as a Constable and exempt from the county levy on the 1761 tithable list of Francis Peyton. Book A, p. 464; and, LDTX/1, p. 15.

August 11, 1761 - John Lewis is named a new County Constable {F/G} for the part of Loudoun "below Goose Creek." Book A, p. 481.

August 11, 1761 - Benjamin Cockrill is appointed Constable {G} replacing Jacob Remey Junr.; and, Hugh Black is "appointed a County Constable [{D}]." Book A, p. 482.

September of 1761 - Christopher Perfect is again identified as a Constable {B} on the tithable list returned by James Hamilton. LDTX/1, p. 9.

Tuesday, October 13, 1761, "In the First Year of the Reign of King George the Third," ... David Smith is named a new Constable for the County. Book A, p. 525. {A}

March 12, 1762 - David Smith is again appointed as a County Constable. Book A, p. 579. {A}

Friday, May 14, 1762 - Robert Bland is appointed a Constable {G} replacing Benjamin Cockrill, and is so identified on the 1762 tithables lists. Book A, p. 610; and, LDTX/1, p. 19.

July 13, 1762 - John Davis is appointed a Constable replacing George Fling. Book B, p. 2. {C}

July 15, 1762 - "John Evins" [sic] is appointed Constable {D} to replace Hugh Black "who is run away." Book B, p. 25.

August 10, 1762 - John Gist is appointed a Constable replacing John Lewis. Book B, p. 28. {F/G}

September 15, 1762 - Sylvester Gardner is appointed Constable {F} replacing William Hutchison. Book B, p. 55.

September of 1762 - John Evans is identified as a Constable {D} on the tithable list returned by James Hamilton [Loudoun County "List No. 2"]; George Fling is named a Constable on the "Cameron parish" list; Robert Bland {G} [on Loudoun County "List No. 1] and David Smith {A} are identified Constables on the tithables lists. Sylvester Gardner is noted as a Constable, and John Lewis is also noted as a [former] Constable on the list of Charles Tyler [his Loudoun County "List No. 4"]. LDTX/1, pp. 18, 19, 20 and 22; and, see the Property Tax Lists, 1757-1799, in undated MS series, at pp. 1355-1359.

December 15, 1762 - Ezekiel Jenkins is appointed a Constable replacing John Davis. Book B, p. 78. {C}

April 12, 1763 - Richard Spurr is appointed Constable replacing Ezekiel Jenkins. Book B, p. 86. {C}

April 13, 1763 - John Ethall is appointed Constable replacing James Saunders. Book B, p. 107. {E}

August 9, 1763 - John Dodd is appointed a Constable replacing John Evans. Book B, p. 196. {D}

September 15, 1763 - William Ross is named a new County Constable. Book B, p. 254. {A/B}

March 13, 1764 - Joshua Willson is named a new Constable "in the upper part of the County," [ie., north and west of Goose Creek]. Book B, p. 278.

March 14, 1764 - William Stephens is once again appointed as a Constable, this time "in the upper part of the County," probably replacing John Dodd. Book B, p. 283. {D}

March 14, 1764 - William Saunders is appointed Constable replacing David Smith. Book B, p. 286. {A}

April 12, 1764 - Richard Spurr is still serving as a Constable. Book B, p. 350. {C}

June 10, 1764 - John Dodd is identified as a Constable on the tithable list returned by Nicholas Minor. LDTX/1, p. 25.

August 15, 1764 - William Ross is still serving as a Constable. Book B, p. 410. {A/B}

September of 1764 - Christopher Perfect is still identified as a Constable {B}, but not noted as exempt from the levy [sic- ?], on the tithable list returned by Nicholas Minor; William Ross is given as a Constable {A/B} on the same list. LDTX/1, p. 27.

October 9, 1764 - Richard McPhearson is appointed Constable replacing William Stephens, "who is run away." Book B, p. 472. {D}

October 9, 1764 - Robert Bland is still serving as a Constable. Book B, p. 474. {G}

March 13, 1765 - "Ordered ... the Several Constables heretofore appointed for this County be discharged from their ... Offices." Book B, p. 533.

March 13, 1765 - Joseph Jones, new Constable "from the Blue Ridge down the road that leads to Vestals [Keys'] Gap to the lower Kittocton Creek and down the said Creek to Potowmack River," {A}; Richard Stewart, new Constable "from Kittocton Creek with the main Road to Tuscarora Run down the said Run to Goose Creek and down the said Creek to Potowmack River," {B}; Steerman Chilton, new Constable "from Goose Creek with the Ox road to the County Line thence down Difficult Run to Potowmack River," {C}; John Ethall, the new Constable "from Williams' Gap to Vestal's [sic - Keys'] Gap and down the Main roads, from each Gap to Goose Creek," {D}; Daniel Jones, new Constable "from Williams' Gap to Little River then with Little River to the County Line and with the County Line to the Blue Ridge," {E}; John Hall, new Constable "from the Little River to Cub Run the Ox Road and the County Line," {F}; and, Jacob Remey Junr., new Constable "from Cub Run to the Ox Road Fairfax & Fauquier [sic - meaning the Prince William] Lines," {G}. Book B, p. 534.

April 11, 1765 - A Complaint of Richard Stewart, against John Fanning "for obstructing the said Richard as a Constable ... fully heard ... dismissed." Book B, p. 574. {B}

August 13, 1765 - Richard Stewart is still serving as a Constable {B}. Book C, p. 18.

September of 1765 - Steerman Chilton is identified as a Constable {C} on the tithable list returned by Nicholas Minor; Daniel Jones is given as a Constable {E} on the list of Levin Powell; John Hall is a Constable {F} on the list of Francis Peyton; Joseph Jones is a Constable {A} on the list of James Hamilton; Jacob Ramey Junr. is a Constable {G} on the list of Fielding Turner; and, John Ethell is a Constable {D} on the list of William Carr Lane. LDTX/1, pp. 28, 32, 33, 35, 39 and 40.

May 12, 1766 - Reubin Suttle is appointed Constable replacing John Hall, {F}; and, John Goram Junr. is appointed Constable {G}, replacing Jacob Remey Junr. Book C, p. 76.

May 12, 1766 - Stephen Rozel is appointed Constable replacing John Ethell, "deceased." Book C, p. 77. {D}

June 9, 1766 - Jacob Jones is appointed as the new County Constable "from the line on the Blue ridge thence down the great Road to Catocton Creek ... to the River ... [replacing] Joseph Jones." Book C, p. 80. {A}

September 9, 1766 - James Jones is appointed as the new County Constable "from Potomack River near the mouth of Kittocton and from thence to the Great Limestone thence with Potomack and binding with Kittocton Mountain westward." Book C, p. 190. {H}

October 13, 1766 - William Taylor Jones is appointed as the new Constable "from Williams' Gap to little River ... to the County Line ... thence to the Blue Ridge [replacing] Daniel Jones." Book C, p. 206. {E}

November 13, 1766 - Joseph Hopkins is appointed Constable replacing James Jones. Book C, p. 229. {H}

Maintaining Morality and the Roads
The Grand Jury

The grand jury was another device of the English court system that was adopted in the Virginia colony around the time of the formation of the Virginia counties in 1634. In the 1640s, the Assembly formally established the Midsummer and March sessions of all county courts as the appropriate times for grand juries to be empaneled to "enquire of the breach of all penal laws and other crimes and misdemeanors not touching life or member." Aside from a brief experiment (after the civil war, during Parliament's rule) with the seating of grand juries at every county court session in 1658, grand juries in colonial Virginia were empaneled twice each year in every county "to receive all presentments and informations" concerning violations of the penal laws and "to present the same to the court." The law enacted in March of 1661-62 instituted the requirement that presentments be based on "the certaine [sic] knowledge of any [one] of them," and moved the grand jury courts on the calendar to April and December court sessions. A Virginia law enacted in 1667 instructed the county courts to convene and swear in at least one grand jury of inquest every year before the conclusion of their April court, but many apparently failed to do so. The 1677 General Assembly, noting that "the true intent and meaning [of the grand jury law had by then] become generally neglected and unexecuted," imposed a fine of 2,000 lbs. of "tobacco and cask" on the Justices of the county courts "for every such omission" in failing to call a grand jury. [Hening, I/304, I/463, II/74 and II/407].

The provisions for seating colonial grand juries, and their responsibilities, remained essentially unchanged for seventy years until the 1748 Virginia Assembly completely revised the laws regulating grand juries and petit (trial) juries. After June of 1751, with but a few exceptions, every county court in Virginia convened a grand jury during each May and November county court session. The new law specified that:

> *"every county court shall cause twenty four [24] freeholders of their county, not ordinary keepers, constables, surveyors [or overseers on the] highways, or owners or occupiers [ie., operators] of a mill ... to*

be summoned to appear ... out of which shall be impanelled a grand jury of fifteen at least ... to enquire [sic] into the breach of penal laws, and make presentment of the offenders, but shall present such offences and breaches only ... committed within the space of twelve months before ... any presentments of their own knowledge, upon the information of [any] two of their own body ... [and] when they make presentment upon information of any other person ... to write the names of the informers ... county courts shall have full power and authority to hear and determine all offences made penal by the laws of this colony [regardless of the severity of] ... the fines ... thereby inflicted ..."

As with petit jurors, any grand juryman who did not answer a summons to court was fined 400 lbs. of tobacco, ie., £2½ or 50 shillings, which was 50 lbs. of tobacco more than the fine imposed on a witness who failed to appear when summoned. The grand jury was not required to use any special form in the presentment of an offender to the county court and, in instances where the penalty for an offence under presentment was less than £5, the county court was to "summon any person so presented" and proceed to trial of the matter "without the formality of a jury." Since the "formality" of a jury trial was not necessary, occasional delays between the grand jury presentment and the trial must have been caused by an inability to obtain service on the accused. Between 1748 and 1752 the Fairfax County Court met in quarterly sessions at colonial Springfield. During that period, June and December were designated as the months for grand jury sessions, but the Fairfax quarterly court law expired at the end of 1751. The Fairfax County Court removed to Alexandria and returned to a schedule of monthly sessions in the spring of 1752, and a May and November grand jury schedule was resumed. The same May and November schedule was in effect for the Loudoun County grand juries in and after 1757. [Hening, V/540, V/523-526 and VI/210; supra, Chapter on the County Court; infra, p. 128].

As noted elsewhere, the term "freeholder" had a special meaning in colonial Virginia, and status as such was determinative of one's right to vote in the election of Burgesses, as well as of eligibility to serve on the bi-annual county grand juries, the

Episcopal parish vestries, juries that condemned land for the use of grist mills and juries in the General Court in Williamsburg. Thus we can properly assume, regardless of the absence of extant deeds, leases or any other documents of proof, that all of the grand jurors identified in The Loudoun Record, (excepting only the John Davis who was involved in the controversy in 1759) either owned outright, held a life estate interest in, or a lifetime lease of: at least 100 acres of unimproved Loudoun County lands; 25 acres in Loudoun County that contained a plantation house; or, a town lot and a house in Leesburg. We note with some interest that John Carlyle, a resident of Alexandria, made no objection and presented himself under a summons, prepared to serve as a grand juror, in November of 1761. Ordinary keepers and the surveyors of the roads were specifically excluded from duty on the grand juries, probably because they were the most frequently cited individuals in grand jury presentments. [supra, Chapter on Loudoun's Burgesses; infra, The Record, pp. 128-130].

The 1748 Assembly also revised the penalties for colonial officials who failed to bring in a grand jury, imposing a fine of 1,000 lbs. of tobacco and cask on any Sheriff who failed to return a panel of grand jurymen in either May or November, with an additional fine of 400 lbs. of tobacco on every individual Justice of a county court who failed to order that a grand jury be summoned. These infractions were to be tried in the General Court with the proceeds of all fines to be applied "for the benefit of the county," by lessening the annual levy. The Record reveals the unexplained failure of Sheriff Nicholas Minor (May of 1761), and Sheriff William West (November of 1762), to seat grand juries. What happened next is subject to speculation because, sadly, Tarleton's British raiders destroyed most of the colonial General Court records during the Revolution. Loudoun's colonial residents took participation on their grand juries very seriously; only one of the fifteen county grand juries that was legally empaneled in Loudoun before 1767 was comprised of the minimum number of jurors. [Hening, V/524; infra, @ p. 123; see the Table, infra, p. 133].

The Loudoun Record shows us that service as a Foreman of the bi-annual grand jury was a stepping-stone position for many men in the political ascendence in colonial Loudoun. Of the baker's dozen who served as Foreman in Loudoun's first decade, six of the men were later advanced to the position of Loudoun

County Justice: John Moss Junr., William Carr Lane, Elijah Chinn, Stephen Donaldson, Vincent Lewis and Charles Eskridge. Another three Foremen were sons of County Justices who never advanced to the bench themselves. Of those nine, five were subsequently elected and served as an Episcopal Vestryman for Cameron parish: Moss, Lane, Chinn, Lewis and Jeremiah Hutchison. On the other hand, while several Episcopal Vestrymen served on grand juries over the years, none served as Foreman. And Vincent Lewis resigned his position on the Cameron parish vestry before he served as Foreman three times in 1759 and 1760. John Moss Junr. had been recommended to the Governor and was awaiting appointment as a Justice when he served as Foreman in May of 1762. Elijah Chinn and, to a greater extent, William Carr Lane both established their credentials for service on the parish vestry by bringing in extensive presentments for violations of the morals and church laws. [see supra, Chapter on the County Court; and infra, Chapter on Cameron Parish].

Episcopal parish Churchwardens and ministers were legally obligated to "visit" with the county court and present their charges involving immoral behavior once each year, but this did not relieve the county's grand jurors of their equivalent obligation. In fact, because of the large number of "dissenting" congregations in the county, the importance of the grand jury presentments was undoubtedly magnified in Loudoun County. Drunkenness and swearing were two "morals" offenses that had the attention of the Virginia Assembly from the earliest days of the colony, the former due to a concern for industry and the latter arising from a sense of English propriety. Prior to institution of the county court system in Virginia, the Governor and his Council attempted to fight immorality through the issuance of proclamations. In February of 1631-32, the "laws of England agaynst drunkards" were enacted, imposing a fine of 5 shillings on the wayward. The Assembly, at the same session, determined that "whosoever shall sweare an oath" would be fined 1 shilling for the offense. Eventually, the potential fines for public drunkenness, swearing and the like were increased to fifteen shillings and corporeal punishment. [Hening, I/126 and I/167, Acts XXXI-XXXII; and see infra, the Chapter on Cameron Parish].

As the colony grew, reenactment of other English laws confirmed a wide range of offences in the colonial moral code.

Adultery, whoring, fornication and working on the Sabbath were all considered criminal acts of varying degrees of severity. When Churchwardens brought in a list of persons:

> *"... prophaning God's name, and his holy Sabbaths, abuseing his holy word and commandments ... [and those who] soever abuse themselves with the high & foule offences of adultery, whoredome or fornication or with the loathsome sinne of drunkennes in the abuse of God's creatures ... [sic],"*

the county court usually referred the charges to the next grand jury for further action if the Churchwardens did not initiate suit. Loudoun grand juries also addressed the penal infractions arising from bastard births and breaches of the peace, as well as violations of the ordinary licensing and gambling laws. The Loudoun Record is replete with charges against men who served liquor to their neighbors without the benefit of an ordinary license, an offence that was also referred to as "keeping a tipling house" or "selling liquor by the small measure." The Record of the May 1762 grand jury also notes the charges that were brought against participants in Leesburg's first "riot," but is surprisingly silent regarding the brawl that resulted in John Owsley's death in 1764. [Hening, I/240-241; infra, Chapter on Crimes and Punishment, Chapter on Ordinaries, and Chapter titled Dirty Laundry].

During the French and Indian Wars, as the colony struggled to meet extraordinary military expenditures, the collection of Virginia's new property taxes increased in importance. In 1761, the county grand juries were brought into the tax collection process. Initially the law instructed county courts:

> *"at the time of swearing a grand jury ... in the month of May annually, [to] particularly give it in [the] charge to such [grand] jury [the duty] to enquire [into those] who have failed to ... account [for] their wheel carriages and also of their lands."*

Before 1763, an offender was subject to a steep £10 fine under the tax list law, and a summons based on a grand jury presentment "for such offence" was prosecuted "without the formality of a jury." Whether it was a matter of active civil disobedience, or simply an oversight, it is a striking coincidence that Sheriff Minor failed to bring in a Loudoun grand jury to make presentments on the lists in May of 1761, and was removed from office shortly thereafter.

In November of 1761, with William West as Sheriff, the Loudoun grand jury once again was not sworn in when a substantial number of jurymen failed to appear although duly summoned. The first full presentment of Loudoun tax list "concealers" was finally undertaken by the grand jury in May of 1762, and the next May grand jury followed suit. Confusion over the enforcement provisions of the law might have caused intentionally sloppy handling at the county level, and in 1762 the Virginia Assembly addressed the crisis by revising the penalties to which "concealers" were subject. Beginning in 1763, the fines for avoidance of a land tax list were set at 20 shillings [£1] for every 100 acres, with a fine of 30 shillings for each axle of a wheeled chair or coach that was omitted from the carriage list. The "several clerks of the county-courts" were, thereafter, instructed to deliver:

> *"to the [November] grand-jury ... a list of the lands, tithables, and wheel-carriages taken in his county that year and the presiding justice then present in court [was to] charge the grand-jury to examine the said list, and to present every concealor [sic]."*

Prosecutions based on grand jury tax list presentments were to continue to be heard "without the solemnity of a jury," but the reduction in fines and other specific measures in the law calling for grand jury action had the desired effect. Starting in September of 1763, Loudoun County landowners took great pains to comply with the law and thereafter grand juries were obliged to present only a few tax list "concealers." Subsequently, the Loudoun County Court refused to meet and accordingly did not seat a grand jury in November of 1765, when the entire Virginia colony was actively involved in various measures of civil disobedience in response to Parliament's imposition of the Stamp Act. [Hening, VII/78, VII/264-265 and VII/540-541; infra, The Record, pp. 129-130 and 132; infra, the Chapter on Colonial Taxes].

Before the county courts were created in Virginia, roads were laid out upon the order of the Governor, at the direction of commissioners of the monthly courts, or simply when parishioners were in agreement. In 1657-58, the Virginia Assembly vested the various county courts with full responsibility for the dedication, clearing and maintenance of all roads, bridges and "general ways" from county to county and to and from the churches, "as in England." The county courts were also instructed to annually appoint "surveyors of highwaies," who in turn, with the assistance of the "hands" living along the roads, would be responsible for maintaining all of the public roads and bridges. Only ferry keepers, the masters of two or more tithable male laboring slaves and ironworkers were exempted from lending a helping "hand" in the maintenance and repair of the roadways. It became customary for county courts to appoint an "overseer" for maintenance when replacing a road "surveyor" on a well-established road. Surveyors, overseers and "hands" on the county roads all answered to the county courts. [Hening, I/199, I/436, VI/66 and VI/137-138].

The Virginia Assembly's 1748 "Act concerning Highways" was the law of Virginia at the time Loudoun was created, and with some 1762 amendments, in force throughout the 1757-1766 decade. Anyone blocking or obstructing a road was subject to a ten shilling fine. Surveyors and overseers of the roads were required:

> *"where two or more cross roads of highways meet ... [to] cause to be erected, and keep in repair from time to time, in the most convenient place where such roads join, a stone or post, with plain inscriptions ... in large letters, directing to the most noted place which each of the said joining roads leads."*

The law called for a fifteen shilling fine to be imposed for every month that a post at a fork in the roads was found to be wanting or when a surveyor failed to properly maintain his roadway, but the Loudoun County Court adopted the practice of assessing a standard fine of 15 shillings for inadequate road maintenance regardless of the number of months that the road was alleged to be found in disrepair. The reader will note that either the road surveyors neglected their duties with regularity or the colonial roads in Loudoun were in constant, heavy use and deteriorated rapidly, because the poor condition of the roads was invariably a central concern of the grand juries in their in bi-annual presentments to the county court. The Assembly amended the Virginia road laws in November of 1762 to allow any judge of a county court, acting alone as a Justice of the Peace, to return a judgment against a surveyor of the roads who failed to maintain his road in good repair. Implementation of this procedure does not seem to have lessened the vigor of the Loudoun grand jury in the pursuit of neglectful surveyors and overseers of the county roads. [Hening, VI/64-69 and VII/578; see infra, The Record, pp. 130 and 132; infra, Chapter on Bridges, Fords and Ferries].

The numerous and extensive court orders involving the dedication, oversight and maintenance of the colonial roads generated in the Loudoun County Court give this author cause to defer the full treatment of the subject to a future volume. Accordingly, the information that is presented hereinafter regarding the Loudoun County roads is limited in scope to those references involving presentments of the grand juries and the identification and location of churches, mills, ferries and other infrastructure features. [infra, Chapter on Grist Mills, Chapter on Bridges, Fords and Ferries, and Chapter on Leesburg].

The Loudoun Record

November 8, 1757 - The first Loudoun County grand jury is empaneled with Ezekiel Hickman as Foreman, and George Chelton, Thomas Fields, Samuel Mobley, David Richardson, Dorman Henson, Christopher Perfect, John Sinclair, Joshua Gore, Jacob Lasswell, Thomas Awbrey, Francis Wilks, Thomas Shores, Robert Wood, Pierce Noland, Joseph McGeach, Hugh Caldwell and Samuel Jenkins as the [18] Jurymen. Book A, p. 39.

November 8, 1757 - The first Loudoun grand jury presents charges against "Thomas Kelly ... Peter Noland ... and John Wells ... for being common Drunkards ... Rachel Steare alias Rachel Lynham ... for being drunk on a Sabbath Day ... [and] John Murra for cohabiting with Negro Sue belonging to Mr. Henry Taylor." Book A, p. 41.

December 14, 1757 - On a "Presentment of the grand jury against Rachel Steere, alias Lynham, for being Drunk on a Sabath [sic] Day ... [she is fined] five shillings" for the benefit of Cameron Parish. Book A, p. 57.

April 12, 1758 - Peter Noland, charged "with being a Common Drunkard," is fined 15 shillings for the Churchwardens to use to benefit the poor of Cameron Parish. Book A, p. 95.

May 9, 1758 - The second County grand jury is empaneled with Elijah Chinn as Foreman, and Ezekiel Hickman, John Osborn, Joseph McGeach, Richard Roberts, Francis Elgin, John Sinclair, Benjamin Mason, Thomas Connell, John Davis, John Owsley, Daniel Hutchison, John Hutchison, Jacob Ramey, Thomas Owsley, William Ross, Nicholas Osborn, John Ethall and Edward Harding, the [19] Jurymen. Book A, p. 98.

May 9, 1758 - The second Loudoun grand jury presents charges against: "Barbary Ramey [sic] for having a base born child within six months last past ... James Whaley Junr. for Absenting from his Wife and taking up with another Woman &c. his Wife's Sister and having a base born child by her within six months last past ... John Johnson Junr., James Goulding, and Aneas Campbell [the Loudoun County Sheriff !] each for swearing Oaths ... Charles Chinn for Cohabiting with Sith Davis ... Ann Vines for having a base born child," and several Surveyors of the Roads for not erecting signs and posts at the forks of their roads. In November of 1759, all of these Presentments are Quashed due apparent irregularities in the seating of the grand jury. Book A, pp. 98-99.

November 14, 1758 - A grand jury is empaneled with Edward Conner as Foreman, and Ezekiel Hickman, Adam Mitchell, Jacob Remey, Jacob Remey Junr., Joseph Hutchison, Francis Summers, Vincent Lewis, William Norris, John Owsley, Thomas Owsley, William Trammell, Christopher Perfect, Joshua Gore, Jacob Lasswell and Robert Thomas the [16] grand jurors. Book A, p. 175.

November 14, 1758 - The third Loudoun grand jury presents charges against: "Peter Noland for Cohabiting with Elizabeth Grant ... Mary English for having a base born child ... Thomas Fields ... James Wheelock ... [and] William Owsley for swearing ... Charles Chinn for Cohabiting with Syth Davis ... and the Surveyor of the Road from Frying Pan to the Beaver Dam [sic - Broad Run Church] ... for not keeping the same in repair." Book A, p. 175.

May 8, 1759 - The County grand jury is empaneled, with Vincent Lewis as Foreman, Benjamin Mason, John Lewis, Thomas Pritchard, Elijah Chinn, Thomas Triplet, Charles Chinn, Jacob Remey, Joseph McGeach, Thomas Owsley, George Chelton, Moses Botts, Thomas Squires, Jacob Reed, James Buckley and Thomas Fields as the [16] jurymen. Book A, p. 233.

May 8, 1759 - The Loudoun grand jury presents charges against: "Elizabeth Gipson for Petty Larceny ... Rachel Duncan ... [and] Lydia Dodd [each] for having a base born child ... [and] John Davis ... [and] Jacob Lasswell ... for selling of Liquor by retail small measure ... [without a license]." Book A, p. 233.

November 13, 1759 - A new County grand jury is empaneled with Vincent Lewis as Foreman, Charles Eskridge, Jeremiah Hutchinson, Benjamin Mason, John Herryford, Thomas Owsley, Ezekiel Hickman, Jacob Lasswell, Thomas Stump, William Norris, Joseph Jones, Thomas Pritchard, William Owsley, George Chelton, Edward Harden, James Spencer and John Owsley the [17] Jurymen. Book A, p. 299.

November 13, 1759 - The Loudoun grand jury presents: William Hardy, on the testimony of John Morse Senr. [sic - Loudoun Justice John Moss Senr.], charged with swearing and being drunk ... "James Whaley the Younger" for unlawfully cohabiting with Barbary Remy [sic] his wife's sister, charged by Jacob Remey Senr. ... Elizabeth Tapman, Chloe Poor, Mary Franks and Sarah Roberts for having base born children ... James Wheelock, James Leith and John Calahan [sic] for Fighting on the Sabath Day ... John Davis, farmer, for not keeping the Road between William Shreives and the Gum Spring, and for keeping a Tipling house ... John Barrett for cohabiting with Mary Franks ,... the Surveyor of the [Mountain] Road for not keeping a Post at the fork [below Rocky Run] near Edward Porters where one Road leads to Alexandria and the other to Occoquan ... and, Mary Proctor for living at Thomas Kelly's and cohabiting with one of Kelly's Negroes. Book A, pp. 299 and 300.

November 16, 1759 - "Upon an Information" brought by the Churchwardens but based on a presentment of the May 1758 grand jury, James Whaley Junr. is tried by a jury and found "Guilty of the premises," that is to say, deserting his wife and fathering a child by his sister-in-law. Book A, p. 314; and see infra, Chapter on Base Born Children.

November 16, 1759 - On the "Motion of William Ellzey to Quash the Presentments of the grand jury made in May Court [1758] Suggesting that John Davis one of the said Jurors was no Freeholder ... Hugh West Deputy Attorney for his Majesty for this County objected ... but was Overruled by the Court ... Ellzey and Thomas Pritchard were sworn and proved the said Davis to be no Freeholder ... said Presentments were thereupon Quashed ... West on his Majesty's Behalf prayed an Appeal to the next General Court [in Williamsburg] which is granted." Ellzey was attorney for James Whaley, who had just been fined £10 in a jury trial for fathering a base born child. Book A, p. 315; and see supra, Chapter on the County Court, and infra, Chapter titled Dirty Laundry.

May 13, 1760 - A County grand jury is empaneled with Thomas Sorrell as Foreman, Charles Eskridge, Jacob Ramey, George Taylor, Joseph McGeach, Hugh Caldwell, Henry Taylor, Thomas Lewis, John Trammell, Thomas Owsley, Robert Wood, Cornelius Donohue, George Vandever, Thomas Stump, Joshua Gore and Thomas Pritchard the [16] Jurymen. Book A, p. 343.

May 13, 1760 - The grand jury presents charges against: "John Reily for a Breach of the Sabath ... John Davis for not keeping the Road between Goose Creek and [the Gum Spring on] Broad Run ... [and] William Shreive for not having the Road from his House to Goose Creek in repair." Book A, p. 343.

June 12, 1760 - "The Presentment of the grand jury against Thomas Fields [in 1758 for swearing] for reasons appearing to the Court is dismissed ... The Presentment ... against Charles Chinn [in 1758 for cohabitation] is Continued to the next Court ... The Presentment ... [in 1758 for swearing] against William Owsley is Discontinued [ie., dismissed]." Book A, p. 368.

June 12, 1760 - "The Presentment of the grand jury against Thomas Kelly [in 1757 for being a drunkard] is Discontinued."; and, based on a 1759 Presentment for having a base born child, a warrant for Sarah Roberts is "returned, not found." An alias Summons for her arrest and appearance at the next Court is authorized. Book A, p. 369.

June 12, 1760 - James Wheelock, James Leith and John Kellihan are each "Presented ... for Fighting on the Sabath day ... [and fined] 5 shillings or [50 lbs.] of Tobacco to the use of the Poor of [Cameron] Parish." Book A, p. 369.

June 12, 1760 - Based on the grand jury Presentments in November of 1759 and May of 1760 against: "John Davis, Farmer ... for not keeping the Road ... between William Shreive's and the Gum Spring [via Dawson's ford of Goose Creek] ... [and] William Shreive for not having the Road from his House [near Secolon's branch] to Goose Creek in repair ..."; each is fined the standard 15 shillings "to the use of [Cameron] Parish" when they fail to appear. Davis may have been outside on the Courthouse lawn when the Court first ruled against him, because the Court appears to have promptly reversed itself upon hearing Davis explain his absence. Book A, pp. 369-370.

November 11, 1760 - A grand jury is empaneled, with Vincent Lewis as Foreman, and Joshua Gore, Thomas Connell, William Ross, Benjamin Mason, Daniel Hutchison, Stephen Emry, Joseph McGeach, Thomas Stump, Thomas Gore, Edward Harden, David Smith, George Chelton, Thomas Owsley, James Abbet, Jacob Lasswell and Joshua Duncan the [17] Jurymen. Book A, p. 403.

November 11, 1760 - The Loudoun grand jury presents their charges against "Sarah Owsley for having base Born Children [in the last six months, apparently twins]." Book A, p. 403.

May of 1761 - Sheriff Nicholas Minor fails to call a grand jury.

November 10, 1761 - "The Sheriff [William West] having returned a Panel of the Grand Jury, to-wit, Vincent Lewis, John Carlyle, Thomas Owsley, Benjamin Mason, Joshua Gore Junr., Jacob Remey, Henry Wisheart, Thomas Sorrell, John Moss, Henry Moore, Henry Taylor, Owen Roberts, John Hall, John Smarr, Elijah Chinn, Thomas Connell, Francis Summers, George Headen, and William Trammell, [19] Freeholders of the County of Loudoun to serve as a Grand Jury for the said County at this Court who being solemnly called ...

... the following [12] Persons so Summoned did not appear Vizt. Vincent Lewis, Henry Wisheart, John Moss [Junr.], Henry Moore, Owen Roberts, Samuel Compton, Edward Garrett, John Hutchison, Walter Williams, Elijah Chinn, Francis Summers and George Headen by means whereof fifteen Freeholders did not appear so that no Grand Jury could be Sworn ... Ordered that each of the above Persons ... be Fined [400 lbs.] of Tobacco to the King." Book A, p. 530; and see supra, @ p. 120.

May 11, 1762 - A new County grand jury is empaneled with John Moss [Junr.] as Foreman, Thomas Connell, Vincent Lewis, Benjamin Mason, Thomas Owsley, Jacob Remey Junr., Daniel Hutchison, Francis Summers, John Hall, John Smarr, Gilbert Simpson Junr., William Ross, Thomas Sorrell, Charles Chinn and John Cargill the [legal minimum of 15] Jurymen. Book A, p. 584.

May 12, 1762 - "The Grand Jury sworn Yesterday returned into Court and Presented --- [after an extensive enumeration of Loudoun landowners and two-wheeled chair owners who were omitted from the tax lists] ... William Beevers [sic] of this County for stoping the Road adjacent to his House ... likewise said William Beevers for keeping a Tipling House ... Robert Bland ... John Lewis ... John Hooms ... Daniel Diskins ...[and] Jacob Remy [sic] [each] for swearing four Oaths within two months last past ... William Furr ... [and] John Minor [each] for swearing one Oath ... Silvester Gardner ... John Morriss, Mountain [ie., the one living on a mountain] ... John Hallox ... William Lankford ... Joseph Stephens ... [and] William Debell [each] swearing two prophane Oaths within two Months last past ... Blue Ridge John Davis [distinguishing him from the 'farmer'] ... and John Morris Mountain [sic - again!] [both] for swearing ... Joseph Moring for swearing three Oaths & being Drunk this Day ... [and, based on] An Indictment against Samuel Davis Junr., John Davis, William Furr & William Allen for a Riot, [the grand jury reports] a True Bill against John Davis,

William Furr & William Allen & not a true Bill against Samuel Davis --- And then the said grand jury having nothing further to Present were Discharged. --- Ordered that Process issue against the severeal [sic] Persons this Day Presented & Indicted by the Grand Jury to cause them to come here at the next Court to Answer the Presentations against them respectively." Book A, pp. 595-600; see infra, the Chapter on Colonial Taxes, and the Chapter on Loudoun Tax Lists.

November 10, 1762 - No grand jury is sworn at this Loudoun County Court session, possibly due to some confusion arising from the lapsing of Sheriff William West's Commission. Book B, p. 72.

April 12, 1763 - Following the usual procedure for calling a grand jury, it was "Ordered that the Sheriff Summon Twenty four of the most Capable Freeholders of this County to appear here on the second Tuesday in May next to serve as a Grand Jury of Inquest for the Body of this County." Book B, p. 85.

May 10, 1763 - "William Carr Lane, Foreman, Vincent Lewis, Thomas Owsley, John Cargill, Elijah Chinn, Joseph Hutchison, Francis Elgin, Jacob Remey, Thomas Lewis, Richard Conner, John Thomas, Samuel Conner, Joshua Gore Junr., Benjamin Shrieves, Robert Popkins, William Ross, Joseph Caldwell, Owen Roberts, Richard Keen and John Dodd were Sworn [in as] a Grand Jury of Inquest [of 20 jurors] for the Body of this County and having received their charge went out of Court." Book B, p. 122.

May 11, 1763 - The Loudoun grand jury presents charges against: "Overseer of the Road leading from John Keen's Spring to broadrun Church for not keeping the same in lawful repair ...; Overseer of the Road leading from Lime Stone to the fork of the Roads by where John Markley now lives [on the Potomac Path near Goose Creek] for not keeping the same in lawful repair ...; Overseer of the Road leading from Leesburg to Wm. Dodd's ... also the Overseer of the Road leading from Wm. Dodd's to the Catocton Creek for not keeping the Said Roads in lawful repair ...; Hannah Oxley for bearing ... one Base Born Child ...; Christopher Perfect ... John Minor ... Fleming Patterson of Leesburg ... [and] Ferdinando O'Neal ... [each] for a Prophane Swearer ... Thomas Avery [sic-Thomas Awbrey] for Swearing one Oath and getting Drunk ... Thomas Kelley ... [and] Charles Martin [each] for getting Drunk once within one month last past ... Sampson Turley ... George Vandiver ... Robert Stephens Senr. ... William Lansitt ... James Ecton ... [and] Joseph Pooler ... [all] of this [Cameron] Parish ... for Absenting himself from his Parish Church one Month last past by the knowledge of Two of us ... [and] Andrew Adam for Fornication and Cohabitation with Catharine Stewart within six months last." Book B, pp. 131-137.

November 8, 1763 - A grand jury is empaneled: Joseph Hutchinson, Foreman, Benjamin Mason, Daniel Hutchison, Benjamin Hutchison, Thomas Owsley, William Beavers, Thomas Beavers, William Triplett, Daniel Triplett, John Cargill, John Smarr, Samuel Conner, Daniel Jones, Jacob Reed, Benjamin Shrieve, Jonathan Monkhouse and John Cavins the [17] Jurymen. Book B, p. 262.

November 8, 1763 - The grand jury presents: "John Herryford, Overseer of the Road from Leesburg to Trenary's for not keeping the same in lawful repair ...; Overseer of the Mountain Road from Little River [east] to Piny

Branch for not keeping the same in lawful repair ...; Charles Chinn Overseer of the Road [to Ashby's Gap] from Daniel Adams' [ford on Goose Creek] to the Blueridge for not keeping the same in lawful repair ...; [and] Charles Eskridge, Overseer of the [Mountain] Road from Cub run down by Rockey run Church for not keeping the same in lawful repair." Book B, pp. 262-263.

November 9, 1763 - "The Presentment of the Grand Jury against Elijah Chinn for swearing one Prophane Oath is Dismissed (the Fine [which was usually 15 shillings] being paid) and It is Ordered that he pay the Costs of the Prosecution." Book B, p. 264.

May 8, 1764 - Sixteen jurors are empaneled with Greenberry Dorsey as Foreman, and William Neving, Richard Vallendingham, Thomas Lewis, Samuel Compton, Nicholas Osborn, Daniel Hutchison, Jacob Remey, William Buckley, John Cargyle, Benjamin Shreive, William Beavers, Robert Popkins, Thomas Middleton, Samuel Conner and Thomas Owsley composing "a Grand Jury of Inquest for the Body of the County." Book B, p. 354.

May 8, 1764 - The Loudoun grand jury presents charges against: "James Coleman for not keeping the Road in lawful repair from Sugar Land run to Broad run within one Month last past ...; Overseer from Broad Run to Hough's Mill road [at Goose Creek] within one month last past ...; Overseer of the [Potomac Path] from Leesburg to Sugar Land Run ...; [and] Overseer of the Road between Leesburg and Mr. Dodd's for not keeping the said Road in lawful repair within two Months last past." Book B, p. 354.

November 13, 1764 - A County grand jury is empaneled with John Berkley as Foreman, and Adam Mitchell, John Thomas, Jacob Remey, Benjamin Shreve, John Cargill, Elijah Chinn, Samuel Compton, Nicholas Osborn, Daniel Jones, John Little, Joseph West, Thomas Shore, William Triplett, Thomas Owsley and David Smith the Jury of sixteen members. Book B, p. 492. The Foreman, John Berkley, had married Susanna Linton, the widow of former Fairfax ["Loudoun"] County Justice Moses Linton. FXCOCO, 1749 Book, p. 418.

November 13, 1764 - The Loudoun County grand jury presents charges against: "The Overseer of the Road that leads from Little River to Ashby's Gap as far as Goose Creek for not keeping the same in lawful repair within one Month last past ...; Overseer of the [Potomac Path] from ... Broad Run to Leesburg for not keeping the same in Repair, by the Information [ie., complaint] of Benjamin Sebastian ...; [and] Overseer of the Road from William Dodd's to the Kittocton for not keeping the same in repair to the knowledge of two of us within two Months last past." Book B, pp. 492-493.

May 13, 1765 - A new County grand jury is empaneled with Charles Eskridge as Foreman, and "Francis Wilks, John Wilks, Thomas Awbrey, John Sinclair, Thomas Pritchard, James Abbett, Robert Popkins, Samuel Compton, Nicholas Osborn, John Jones, Thomas Shore, Jacob Remey, Daniel Hutchison, John Hutchison, Francis Summers, Benjamin Mason, Thomas Beavers, Thomas Self & Griffith Evans were Sworn a Grand Jury of Inquest [of 20] for the Body of [Loudoun] County." Book B, p. 570.

May 13, 1765 - The Loudoun grand jury presentments include charges against: "The Overseer of the [Mountain] Road from Little Rockey Run to Hutcheson's Post [sic] for not keeping the same in Repair; Samuel Conner for Stopping the Road by erecting a [fence along his] Lane ... within two Months last past ...; Overseer of the [Potomac Path] from Leesburg to Goose Creek for not keeping the same in Repair within Two Months last past ...; Overseer of the [Potomac Path] from Broad Run to Sugarland Land [sic] Run for not keeping the same in Repair within Two Months last past ...; Overseer of the [Mountain] Road from Williams' Gap [down] to the new [Roszell's] Church for not keeping the same in Repair within Two Months last past ...; Overseer of the [Shenandoah] Road from William Dodd's to Kittocton for not keeping the same in Repair within Two Months last past ...; Overseer of the [Shenandoah] Road from the Gap of the Short hill to the Top of the [Blue] Ridge [at Keys' Gap] for not keeping the same in Repair within Two Months last past ...; Joseph Stephens ... James Butler ... Charles West ... John Tyler ... Robert Stephens ... Dennis Dallis ... Samuel Creswell ... [and] William Barnaby Seares [each] for unlawful Gaming on the Sabbath [all] by the Information of James Whaley ...; [and] John Minor for Swearing Two Prophane Oaths ...; [and] Martin Sehon [sic] for swearing one Prophane Oath ... by the knowledge of two of us -." Book B, pp. 570-571.

November of 1765 - No grand jury is empaneled, an exercise of civil disobedience practiced throughout Virginia in protest against the Stamp Act.

May 12, 1766 - Another Loudoun County grand jury is empaneled, with Jeremiah Hutchison as Foreman, Benjamin Hutchison, Francis Summers, William Whitely, William Rust, Richard Eskridge, Thomas Beavers, John Smarr, William Smith, Robert Popkins, Stephen Donaldson, James Abbott, Samuel Mobley, William Molton, James Saunders, Jacob Reed and John Wilks the [17] Jurymen. Book C, p. 75.

May 12, 1766 - The County grand jury presents the "Surveyor of the Road from Nathan Spencer's to the Tuskorora [sic] ... [and the] Surveyor [on the Mountain Road] from little River to the Piney Branch," both for not keeping their roads in proper repair. Book C, p. 75.

Monday, November 10, 1766 - A new County grand jury is sworn in: Stephen Donaldson is Foreman, with John Wilks, Francis Wilks, John Butcher, Peter Romaine, Thomas Fields, Thomas Shore, Thomas Gore, William Whiteley, John Smarr, Robert Sandford, John Thomas, Samuel Mobley, Stephen Emery, Robert Popkins and Owen Roberts the [16] Jurymen. Book C, p. 219.

November 11, 1766 - The Loudoun grand jury presents charges against: "[Samuel Duncan] Overseer of the [Mountain] Road from Snickers Gap to Bacon Fort ... [and] Overseer of the [Mountain] Road from little River to Piney Branch and from thence to the fork of the [Mountain] Road at John Homes' [below Rocky Run] ... [both] for not keeping the same in proper repair within two months last past ... [and] Charles Binns Gent. [the Clerk of the Loudoun County Court !] for swearing one Profane Oath." Book C, p. 223.

LOUDOUN COUNTY GRAND JURY FOREMEN, 1757-1766

November 8, 1757	EZEKIEL HICKMAN as Foreman, [18]
May 9, 1758	ELIJAH CHINN as Foreman, [19]
November 14, 1758	EDWARD CONNER as Foreman, [16]
May 8, 1759	VINCENT LEWIS as Foreman, [16]
November 13, 1759	VINCENT LEWIS as Foreman, [17]
May 13, 1760	THOMAS SORRELL as Foreman, [16]
November 11, 1760	VINCENT LEWIS as Foreman, [17]
May of 1761	no Grand Jury called
November 10, 1761	no Grand Jury sworn
May 11, 1762	JOHN MOSS [Junr.], Foreman, [15]
November 10, 1762	no Grand Jury sworn
May 10, 1763	WILLIAM CARR LANE, Foreman, [20]
November 8, 1763	JOSEPH HUTCHINSON, Foreman, [17]
May 8, 1764	GREENBERRY DORSEY, Foreman, [16]
November 13, 1764	JOHN BERKLEY as Foreman, [16]
May 13, 1765	CHARLES ESKRIDGE, Foreman, [20]
November of 1765	no Grand Jury empaneled
May 12, 1766	JEREMIAH HUTCHISON, Foreman, [17]
November 10, 1766	STEPHEN DONALDSON, Foreman, [16]

[#] - Designates the number of jurymen who were seated.

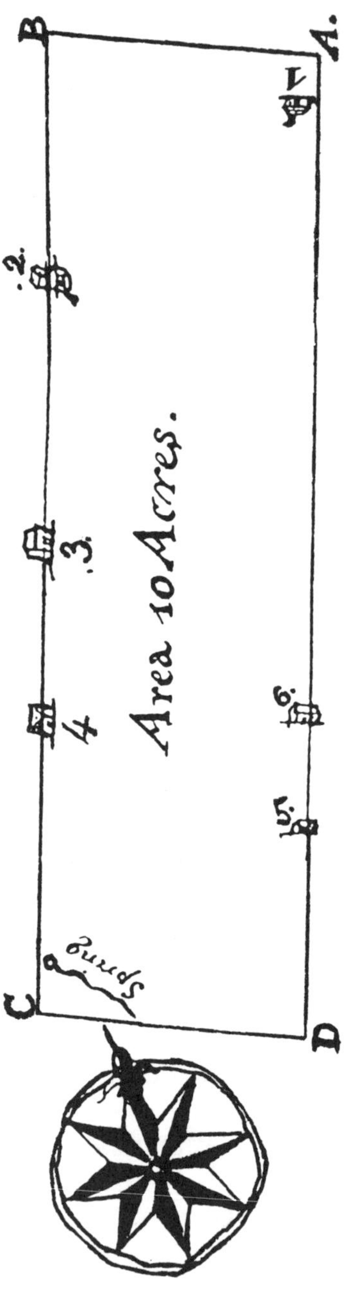

Legend given for Plat of 10 acres:
"Figure ...
1- represents the Prison or Goal [sic] [on Leesburg Lot #28]
2- [John] Miller's Stable and Dwelling House a Tenant to Mr. [Aneas] Campbell ... [on Leesburg Lots #19 and #20]
3- Mr. [John] Hough's Cow house [on Leesburg Lot #13]
4- Mr. [Joseph] Janney's Stable [on Leesburg Lot #4]
5- Daniel Miller's Old Smiths Shop [on Leesburg Lot #6]
6- Mr. [John] Patterson's Stable [on Leesburg Lot #11] ...
A - a stake and a stone by the prison ... [Lot #28]
B - a ... stake in John Hereford's [Leesburg] lot ... [#32]
C - a stake in Mr. [Andrew] Adam's meadow ... [65' south of the south line of Leesburg Lot #66]
[note: the head of the spring detailed on the plat is 118' south of Royal Street, and roughly 10' east of Lot #65, on Lot #66] ...
D - a stake ... [65' south of the south line of Leesburg Lot #68]
[note: AB and CD are 348½ feet; BC and AD are 1,254 feet long]

I have laid off the Prison Bounds ... July 4th, 1765 ... George West ..."

[LDCODB, Book D, p. 574; see LDCODB, Book A, p. 186; and see infra, Chapter on Leesburg, Plat of Leesburg Town Lots]

Historically, the Sheriff of every English shire, or county, was appointed by the Crown - and charged with the responsibility of transacting the public business for his shire. Alternately, the Sheriff was called "bailiff" or "vice-come," his latin title, and his jurisdiction was known, both then and now, as his "bailiwick." By the time the county court system was inaugurated in Virginia in 1634, the office of county Sheriff had already been introduced to replace the marshals on the various plantations. Among their duties, Sheriffs conducted elections of the representatives for the House of Burgesses, read public notices from the Governor and the Assembly on their Courthouse steps, collected taxes and levies for the King and county, maintained the peace at the county court sessions, had primary responsibility for supervising the County Gaol (meaning and pronounced "jail"), and conveyed prisoners to Williamsburg for their trial in cases of capital offence - where the penalty would be the loss of life or a limb. [Black, pp. 809 and 1543; Hening, I/125 and I/132-133; see Glossary].

The colonial Governor of Virginia, in his capacity as the King's representative, appointed Sheriffs annually from among the Justices of the Peace serving in each County. Of the local offices the position of County Sheriff was potentially the most lucrative and was certainly the most powerful. Virginia experienced a growth in party politics as the colony matured, giving cause for the 1658 enactment of a law fixing the order of succession: "the Sherriffes [sic] place shall after this yeare be conferred on the first [County Justice listed] in Commission, and so devolve to every commissioner in course." In time, as deaths and refusals to qualify caused difficulties, Virginia Governors learned to rely on the nominations that sitting county court Justices continued to offer annually to guide the appointments for the office of Sheriff. The customary practice, originally instituted in 1656, was reinstated by the 1705 Assembly. Thereafter, Governors appointed new Sheriffs annually from a slate of three nominees offered by each of the county courts. [Hening, I/392, II/21, II/78, III/246 and V/489].

The slate of nominees for Loudoun's Sheriff during the 1757-1766 decade was invariably headed by a first-term Sheriff or the next most senior Justice, and then included the following two ranking Justices from the Commission of the Peace. Before 1767, Governors followed the Loudoun Court's recommendations on five of the seven slates that were recorded. Out of concern for the renewal of factionalism on some of the county courts, the 1759 Assembly codified an unofficial practice, limiting every Sheriff "in his office [to] two years next succeeding each other ... and no longer." Citing a desire to retain Sheriffs in office until "they have completed the collection of his majesty's ... publick taxes of the year," the 1763 Assembly amended the term limit law, fixing October 25th as the date for "the general appointment of Sheriffs" except in instances of misconduct or death. This Act allowed for the continuance in office of interim Sheriffs for part of a third year so that all terms would end in October. Thereafter Commissions for the Loudoun Sheriff were normally presented in the November county court. [infra, the Table @ p. 155; Hening, VII/643-644].

As suggested elsewhere, the County Coroner in colonial Virginia was something of an alternate Sheriff. Coroners had the legal responsibility for serving process when a Sheriff was party to an action; they charged identical fees and were entitled to serve as the Sheriff's legal replacement in a number of situations. All four Coroners who served in Loudoun from 1757 to 1765, Justices Nicholas Minor, Josias Clapham, Charles Tyler and Philip Noland, advanced to the position of Sheriff shortly after completing their term as Coroner. By 1772, the Assembly had observed that "long continuance of Under-Sheriffs in office [had allowed them to] gain undue influence," and banned the Under-Sheriffs from service "for any longer time than two years successively without the consent and approbation of the[ir county] court." This concern may or may not have been felt in Loudoun, but one can not deny the fact that the Under-Sheriffs who served the longest in the 1757-1766 decade (Leven Powell, John Moss Junr., John Minor and Charles West), and three other Loudoun Under-Sheriffs from that decade (Craven Peyton, Thomas Lewis and Simon Triplett), all advanced rapidly to the office of Loudoun County Justice. And Francis Peyton, a Justice and one of Loudoun County's first Under-Sheriffs in 1757, became the Loudoun Sheriff in 1766 without having served first as the County Coroner. [infra, Chapter on Coroners; see infra, the Table on p. 155; Hening, V/492, V/504 and VIII/524-525].

Aside from the practical utility in having the power inherent in the office shared among the various leaders of the community, everyone serving as Sheriff was disqualified from election to the Assembly for the two years following his term of office, and the official demands on the Sheriff undoubtedly took up a great deal of time. The latter two reasons may have caused Loudoun Justices of the Quorum Anthony Russell and Fielding Turner to refrain from seeking the Sheriff's position in 1757, or Justice George West to avoid appointment in 1765. Russell and Turner, and one of Loudoun's first Burgesses, James Hamilton, were the three most senior Loudoun Justices passed over when the Governor chose Aeneas Campbell, a relatively recent arrival on the Potomac piedmont, as Loudoun's first Sheriff. As with all subsequent Loudoun Sheriffs, Campbell, after taking the several oaths of office as a County Justice, was sworn in as Sheriff and gave additional "oaths ... [took the] test ... and oath appointed by the Tobacco law" for the collection of taxes. Typical of the county Sheriffs' duties, at the May court in 1759 Sheriff Aeneas Campbell was obliged to stand "at the door of the Courthouse" and read the public notice of a new law requiring all colonists to assist in the compilation of tax lists in every county "within the proprietary of ... Lord Fairfax." [Hening, VII/264 and VIII/316; Glossary].

Nicholas Minor followed Campbell as Loudoun County's second Sheriff, and he was commissioned in due course in 1759. No commission was issued in 1760, probably as a result of the government's distraction with the French and Indian incursions on the Virginia frontier. In 1761, as Sheriff Minor's term was drawing to a close, he neglected to summon a Grand Jury in the May court, perhaps in protest over the new enforcement provisions of the land tax laws or possibly as a result of the confusion arising from the tardy renewal of his commission. No county court had been held the previous month to order that the jury be summoned, but we can only speculate on the true cause of Minor's omission. When the new Sheriff's Commission arrived for William West early in the fall of 1761, an unusually large number of Under-Sheriffs were appointed as Deputies, further evidence of the impact that the French War may have had on day-to-day life in Loudoun. [see supra, Chapter on the Grand Jury].

William West's appointment in 1761 to the office of Loudoun County Sheriff established a high water mark in the ascendancy of the West family in the Potomac piedmont. At that point in time, William West's brother John West was representing

Fairfax in the House of Burgesses, one nephew, George West, who had married the niece of Leesburg founder Nicholas Minor, was the County Surveyor for both Loudoun and Fairfax, while another nephew, Hugh West [Junr.], a former Virginia Burgess, was also serving as the Deputy King's Attorney (prosecutor) for Loudoun and Fairfax. The concentration of power in one family, or the failure to seat Grand Juries in 1761, may have been the reason that William West was not returned as Sheriff despite being listed first on the nominating slate in 1762. The third listing that year, of George West, could have served to remind the Governor of the West family's growing influence. We also note that the 1761 and 1762 slates give us the first hint of Justice Richard Coleman's declining health and last illness in 1762, when Coleman was omitted from his expected place on the list of nominees for Loudoun Sheriff. Coleman died a year and a half later, early in 1764. George West was placed first on the slate for Sheriff in 1764 but was not appointed. Nomination of the County Surveyor may have caused confusion in the Governor's office, or West may have expressed an interest in standing for election to the Assembly, and no Sheriff's commission was issued that year, causing Josias Clapham's term to continue into an unusual third year despite other irregularities that were becoming painfully apparent. [Landmarks, pp. 138-140; infra, pp. 141 and 151; infra, Chapter on Ordinaries, and Chapter on Deaths; supra, Chapter on the County Court].

The Sheriff was one of only three salaried County officials, the other two being the Clerk and the Deputy King's Attorney. In the colonial period, standards of pay for Virginia's Sheriffs and the guards at county gaols remained stable. An Act of the Virginia Assembly established the Sheriff's basic annual salary:

> *"For all public services of the Sheriff; attending the courts of claims and grievances, impannelling [sic] grand-juries, publishing of writs for electing of Burgesses, and attendance; serving all public orders of court ... and all other public and county service: To be levied annually, by the Justices, on the County; besides cask, 1200 [lbs. of tobacco]."*

With the cask allowance of 4%, the salary for the Loudoun Sheriff was a total of 1248 lbs. of tobacco, or the equivalent in Loudoun County of just under £8 for each year of service. In addition, the

Assembly's fee schedules for county officers enumerated the various other responsibilities and fees of the Sheriffs:

"... To the Sheriff	*Pounds of tobacco*
For an arrest, bond and return,	*30 ...*
... pillorying any person [ie., convict],	*20 ...*
... putting [a convict] into the stocks,	*10 ...*
... ducking [sic - dunking] any person,	*20 ...*
... putting [a defendant] in prison, and releasement,	*20 ...*
... serving a summons upon a petition ...	*15 ...*
... summoning and impannelling [sic] a jury ...	*50 ...*
... going to Williamsburg, for a commission ... every mile ...	*2 ...*
... removing of every criminal, from the County goal [sic], to the public goal [in Williamsburg] ... for every mile,	*5 ...*
... removing a debtor [to Williamsburg] ... for every mile,	*2 ...*
... summoning a jury upon any inquisition [or] survey ...	*150 ...*
... every days attendance upon a jury in the country ...	*50 ...*
... serving an attachment upon the body [under oath],	*30 ...*
... whipping a servant ... repaid by the servant,	*20 ...*
... whipping a free person ... paid by such person ...	*20 ...*
... whipping a slave ... paid by the county ...	*20 ...*
... serving an execution for any debt due in tobacco, 5% for the first 1,000 [pounds]; 2% for all above ... in money, 5% upon the first £100; and 2% for all above ...	
... selling a servant at public outcry ... and all fees incident,	*20 ...*
... keeping and providing for a debtor, in goal, each day,	*10 ...*
... keeping and providing for a runaway [servant or slave], or criminal, in goal, each day; ... paid by the County ...	*5 ...*
... serving a Justice's warrant,	*10 ...*
... summoning a witness before a Justice,	*5 ."*

The Virginia law providing for Loudoun's organization in 1757 also required an abatement or allowance of 20% of the Sheriff's fees "for tobacco due in the County of Loudoun." Similar fees were abated by 10% in Fairfax County. Thus, fees assessed by the Loudoun Sheriff were abated by 1 lb. for every 5 lbs. on the above schedule. On complaints prosecuted by the Churchwardens or arising from Grand Jury presentments, the Sheriff was to assess his fees only if the individual was convicted, and then to charge the "convict." Sheriffs were instructed to collect the outstanding Clerk's, Surveyor's and Sheriff's fees beginning around the 20th of January each year. If the demanded fees were not paid by the following 10th of April, the Sheriff was fully empowered "to make distress and sale of the slaves, goods, and chattels, of the party so refusing or delaying payment." By the end of May, every Sheriff was required to render a full account with Clerk and Surveyor of his county "for all fees put into his hands ... and pay the same [after deducting] 6% for collecting," and by June 10th, account and pay to the Virginia treasurer all land and poll tax assessments "after deducting [5%] for each Sheriff's salary in collecting." Sheriffs were also entitled to 200 lbs. of tobacco, "or 20 shillings for the taking up" of a recovered runaway along with all of the other scheduled Sheriff's fees. [Hening, I/266, V/337-339, V/342-343, VI/365-367, VII/148-149, VII/292 and VIII/266-267].

The Sheriff's income was supplemented by collection fees for the annual County levy, the Virginia public levy and the Virginia militia taxes. These supplements varied with the size of the County levy, whether extraordinary public expenses were budgeted, the number of tithables in the county and, for taxes assessed against landowners, the tax on Loudoun acreage in a given year. When the first Courthouse and a new jail were under construction in 1758, Sheriff Aeneas Campbell was entitled to a £20 fee for collecting the County levy, while Sheriff Charles Tyler earned only £1½ for collecting the County levy in 1765. Between those extremes, fees for the County levy normally doubled the Sheriff's basic annual salary with a supplement of about £7½. Colony-wide tithable taxes, imposed to defray military expenses and retire Virginia's French War paper money, generated another 5% fee for the Sheriffs. And land taxes, instituted in 1758 as another part of the French and Indian War financing scheme, brought the Loudoun Sheriff additional collection fees of between £5 and £20 a year. Collection fees would have totalled at least £30 in fee income for Sheriff Nicholas Minor in 1761, but Sheriff Tyler was entitled to £31¾ just for collecting the Virginia levy in 1765. Annual collection fee income of the Loudoun Sheriffs grew to average £55 by 1767. [Hening, VII/77-79 and VII/258-259; infra, Chapter on the County Levy, and Chapter on Colonial Taxes].

The Sheriffs handled large amounts of cash and bills of exchange while transacting the public business, and Virginia law required that every Sheriff "give bond and security for the due collection and payment" of Virginia's public levy, and other tithable and property taxes imposed by the Assembly "to be collected by him the year ensuing." Loudoun deed books are full of the performance bonds of colonial Sheriffs and their securities, solemnly recorded in keeping with Virginia law. In the early years of the county, the sureties were almost always senior Justices of the Court, and the exceptions were invariably men who were destined for appointment to the Court. [Hening, VII/79, VII/395, VII/544 and VIII/181; infra, The Record, pp. 150 and 153].

Irregularities in the collection of war taxes on property and/or the Virginia public levy may have led to the abrupt dismissal of Sheriff Nicholas Minor in 1761, Sheriff William West in 1762 and Sheriff Josias Clapham in 1765. In establishing the public levy for November of 1762, in the same month that Sheriff Clapham took office, the Assembly indicated that Loudoun was not among the counties then in arrears. By the end of Clapham's two year term in office, the arrearage in Loudoun's share of the Virginia tax levies was so sizeable that the 1764 Assembly felt compelled to enact a law directing:

> *"the [Loudoun] Sheriff ... [to] sell the tobacco levied in his county ... at Dumfries, on the next court day of Prince William county [which was the 1st Monday] in July [1765] ... which tobacco shall be fairly sold, to the best advantage, between the hours of one and three, and in lots of not more than ten thousand, and ... the [Loudoun] Sheriff ... [shall] account for and pay the same to ... the Treasurer [of Virginia] ... before ... September [10, 1765]."*

Before Sheriff Clapham could do any further damage, Governor Fauquier removed him from office. In an unusual mid-winter appointment (in February of 1765), a Sheriff's Dedimus arrived in Leesburg with County Surveyor George West, next on the slate, passed over and Charles Tyler commissioned, replacing Clapham. Sheriff Tyler apparently acted immediately to correct the situation, collecting the public and county levies in a timely fashion, selling Loudoun's transfer tobacco at Dumfries in July as directed and accounting for and paying the balance to the Virginia Treasurer in Williamsburg by that September. When the Assembly met again in October of 1765, their Act dealing with the collection of Virginia taxes shows that Loudoun County was no longer in arrears. That year, with Sheriffs throughout the colony trying to take advantage of an inflation in tobacco prices, an additional requirement was imposed requiring "every Sheriff [in Virginia to] render an account, upon oath, before the court of his county ... of what tobacco or money" he collected, instructing the sale of the tobacco or payment of money collected "without shifting or exchanging the one for the other." Loudoun's tobacco was again scheduled to be sold at Dumfries, this time at the 1766 August court days for Prince William. The strain of the extraordinary tax collections may have pushed Charles Tyler to an early grave - although the Loudoun Court requested his reappointment in June of 1766, the Dedimus was not recorded in November and Sheriff Tyler was replaced by Francis Peyton, probably at Tyler's request, that December. Charles Tyler died just two months later. [Hening, VII/78, VII/148, VII/509, VII/544, VIII/39-40 and VIII/178-181; see supra, Chapter on the County Court, and Chapter on the Grand Jury; infra, Chapter on Colonial Taxes].

One of the primary functions of the Sheriff's office, and a substantial source of his fee income, was the service of summons on jurymen, defendants and witnesses alike. A county Clerk anywhere in the colony could direct a summons to any Virginia Sheriff "where such witness lives" - in this manner Virginians could be compelled to attend any county court in the colony, regardless of distance. Before 1736, witnesses were allowed either 40 or 60 lbs. of tobacco for each day that they were in attendance at a court while under summons; after 1736 the witness fee was reduced to 25 lbs. of tobacco per day - the standard fee that was still allowed at the time of the Revolution (regardless of any other business the witness might have at the court). "Every person residing in and summoned out of another county" was entitled to an allowance for mileage and ferry charges. While a witness was coming to, attending or returning home from court, he was "privileged and free from arrest or imprisonment." A contempt citation was warranted against any witness who failed to appear after being summoned - the standard fine of 350 lbs. of tobacco was established in 1696 and not altered for nearly a century. [Hening, II/23, III/144, III/299, III/514, IV/523, V/480, V/504-505 and VI/338; see infra, the Chapter on Non-Residents].

In March of 1661-62, in the 14th year of the reign of Charles II, the Assembly instructed "every County ... [to] sett up a pillory, a pair of stocks, and a whipping post, neere the courthouse and a ducking stoole [sic]." The authority for County jails was continued in essentially that form for the next century, until the recodification in 1748 required every county court to provide for "one common goal [sic] and county prison, well secured with iron bars, bolts, and locks, and also one pillory, whipping-post, and stocks." That law made the construction and use of dunking stools a local option, allowing county courts the discretion "to cause a ducking-stool [sic] to be built in such convenient place as they shall direct." Construction of a gaol and pillory was one of the first orders of business for the new county court when Loudoun was created. Sheriff Campbell inaugurated what became an annual ritual for new Loudoun Sheriffs when he "protested against the Sufficiency of the Gaol" at the time he took Office in 1757. While the outright absence of a jail explains Campbell's objection, and the first four Loudoun jail structures (in use until the onset of the American Revolution) were all in a nearly constant state of renovation, the real cause for the annual complaint of the Sheriffs is found in Virginia's colonial law. By noting an official objection, a Sheriff was shifting legal liability for any insufficiency of the Loudoun gaol squarely onto the shoulders of the other Justices, thereby insulating himself from any civil liability for an escape. [Hening, II/75, II/166-167, V/507-508 and VI/345].

The modern reader might rightfully be confused by occasional references in The Record using an archaic English expression - the "prison (or gaol) bounds." The colonial usage developed from the English custom of allowing "prisoners" of good character to go at large within certain boundaries after giving the proper security to remain within the "bounds." Colonial officials were concerned by outbreaks of "gaol fever," a virulent form of typhus, and smallpox. The knowledge that a dose of fresh air and sunshine was often a suitable tonic was reason enough to continue the "gaol bounds" custom in Virginia. County courts were directed "to mark and lay out the bounds and rules of their respective county prisons, not exceeding ten acres of land," around their county jails. The 1748 Assembly further directed that:

> *"every prisoner, not committed for treason, or felony, giving good security to keep within the said rules, shall have liberty to walk therein, out of the prison, for the preservation of his or her health, and keeping continually within the said bounds shall be adjudged in law a true prisoner."*

The survey of Loudoun's first prison bounds, nine acres around the small jail at Raspberry Plain, was recorded in May of 1758. After the second jail was constructed, the survey of ten acres for a new prison bounds "round the Gaol" in Leesburg was recorded in November of 1759. Loudoun's yeoman farmers (like Charles Griffith in 1763), occasionally mortgaged their farms as collateral for their good behavior while at liberty "in" the Leesburg jail. [Black, p. 809; Glossary; Hening, V/508 and VIII/260; infra, The Record, pp. 148, 149 and 151; infra, Chapter on Servants].

In 1765, the Loudoun Court found that the "Prison Bounds formerly laid off for this County [in 1759] are very inconvenient," (probably because the town spring on Lot #66 was outside of the bounds), and ordered that a new ten acre tract be surveyed. The new jail bounds were platted on July 4, 1765, and recorded that August. Two months later, the 1765 Assembly adopted an Act in response to a growing concern for "the escape of debtors out of the prison rules [bounds]" throughout Virginia. The new law directed county courts "to mark and lay out the bounds and rules of their respective county prisons, not exceeding ten, nor less than five acres of land, adjoining to such prison, which marks and bounds shall be recorded." This law clarified the procedures for the issuance of escape warrants against anyone "who shall have obtained the liberty of the prison rules, by giving bond and security ... and go[ing] out of the same," and limited the liability of Sheriffs and Coroners, for the debts of an escapee, to instances where "the security ... named in the bond ... of such prisoner ... shall afterward be found to have been insufficient." Loudoun's new prison bounds conformed to the statutory requirements and another survey was not required. The reader will note that the Leesburg ordinaries along King Street were all included within both the 1759 and 1765 prison bounds, where misdemeanor offenders and debtors "in jail" were free to preserve their health. [see supra, the 1765 Plat @ p. 134; infra, The Record, p. 152; Hening, VIII/118-123].

Loudoun's first jail was a modest log affair, twelve feet square, erected at the Raspberry Plain plantation home of Sheriff Aeneas Campbell. This structure was apparently built by John Trammell Junr. late in 1757. Trammell had previously constructed a bridge across Broad Run for Fairfax County [in "Loudoun"] on the Potomac Path. In 1757 the Loudoun County Court appointed Commissioners to review the status of construction, who found the building efforts at both the jail and the bridge to be "insufficient." The following fall, Trammell's work on the jail was appraised at only £6, presumably including materials. Previously, without any substantiation, it has been mistakenly suggested that a ducking stool was in operation at Sheriff Campbell's Raspberry Plain plantation pond. To the contrary, the Loudoun County Court, in the exercise of its discretion in the matter, authorized neither the construction nor the use of a ducking stool in Loudoun County until shortly before the Revolution, almost fifteen years after the second County jail had been built in Leesburg. On the other hand, as The Loudoun Record reveals, the pillory and whipping post were frequently put in use by the county court and the Loudoun Sheriff during the 1757-1766 decade. [Hening, V/508; supra, Chapter on the County Court; contra, Legends, pp. 102 and 170; and see infra, Chapter on Crimes and Punishment].

When Leesburg was established as the seat of Loudoun County's colonial government and construction on the first County Courthouse began in 1758, the Loudoun County Court arranged for the construction of a more convenient county jail. The court directed that the jail, pillory and stocks that were to be constructed in Leesburg were to be the same dimensions as their counterparts that had been built for Fairfax County in 1752 and were then in active use in Alexandria. In any event, when the contract was let for construction of the second county jail the Loudoun County Court hired a contractor from Fairfax, Daniel French [3rd], a contemporary of George Washington, builder of the (surviving) Pohick church in Truro parish and eventually a Fairfax County Justice, to construct the Leesburg jail. The contract price of the new jail, including stocks, was £83 and it was erected on the "back" of the County's public town Lot #28, as evidenced by surveys of the Leesburg prison "bounds" that were recorded in 1759 and 1765. At the time that the jail contract was let, the construction cost of wooden buildings in Leesburg was only about 2 shillings per square foot. If the heavier wood construction of a jail had been at or near double the cost, the first Leesburg jail would have been about 400 or 500 sq.ft. in size. Completion was scheduled for August of 1759, but Mr. French was obliged to continue finishing work at the jail that winter, even after the new jail had been put in service. Repairs and new locks were ordered in the summer of 1761 and again, after Loudoun's first jail-break, in the summer of

1766. Loudoun's first jail in Leesburg burned down at the end of December in 1766 or early in January of 1767, and was replaced, temporarily, by a 12' square log structure built beside the location of the burned-out building. A fourth county jail, the third in Leesburg, was put in use by June of 1769, when the temporary structure was sold at auction and removed from the County lots. [Fairfax, p. 59; infra, The Record; LDCOCO, Book D, p. 238].

Early in 1759, while the first jail was still in use, Thomas Deane was charged with the felony of counterfeiting and passing a £10 Virginia Note. Deane was to be conveyed to Williamsburg for trial, and the occasion spurred the county court to authorize a payment to Leesburg blacksmith Daniel Davis for the manufacture of two pair of iron handcuffs. A third pair was made for the use of the County in 1766 by Jacob Shilling. [infra, The Record, pp. 149 and 153; infra, the Chapter on Crimes and Punishment].

Guards were hired at the Loudoun jail only on those rare occasions when dangerous individuals - rapists, counterfeiters, murderers and felonious thieves - were being held pending trial. A full-time jailer was not employed until around 1770. The contemporary attitude toward imprisonment, in the 1700s, was that a prisoner could pay for his food and keep or starve, and jailers were thus entitled to compensation from their wards. During the 1757-1766 decade, Loudoun County normally paid guards serving at the jail 20 lbs. of tobacco, the currency equivalent of 2 shillings and 6 pence, for each night of guard duty. On occasion, a salary of 25 lbs. of tobacco would be authorized, presumably for guarding a more dangerous or disreputable character.

The Record gives us news of Loudoun's first jail-break when Sheriff Charles Tyler was instructed to "raise the force of this County and take Patrick McKenzey who broke the Gaol" in 1765. McKenzey, a Potomac ferryman, had been in and out of trouble for several years. The official reason for McKenzey's incarceration at the time of his escape does not appear, but it must have been for a capital offence and his guilt certain (at least in his own mind), because McKenzey did not wait for his arraignment in the county court. Shortly after Loudoun County's first jailbreak, we learn of Patrick McKenzey's death - a good indication that colonial Loudoun's first posse took its business very seriously. [infra, p. 152; see infra, the Chapter on Crimes and Punishment, the Chapter on Ferries, and the Chapter on Coroners and Deaths].

July 12, 1757 - On the first day of the new Loudoun County Court - The Governor's Commission for Aneas Campbell is presented and he takes the Oaths as the first Sheriff of Loudoun County; and, Francis Elgin and Francis Peyton take their Oaths as his Under Sheriffs. Book A, p. 2.

July 12, 1757 - Aneas Campbell, Loudoun's first Sheriff, "protested against the Sufficiency of the Goal [sic] for this County." Book A, p. 2.

July 12, 1757 - It is "Ordered that James Hamilton Gent. agree with Workmen to build a Prison twelve feet square." John Trammell Junr. gets the contract. Book A, p. 4; and see infra, The Record @ p. 148.

August 9, 1757 - Daniel McCarty, a former Sheriff of Fairfax County, is a witness at the Loudoun Court, "coming fifty Miles from Fairfax County and returning." Book A, p. 6.

October 11, 1757 - Leven Powell takes the Oaths of an Under Sheriff. Book A, p. 25.

October 12, 1757 - John Moss and Thomas Sorrell are appointed to view and report on the Prison. Book A, p. 36.

November 9, 1757 - A "Complaint of Aneas Campbell, Sheriff ... [against William Trammell] for refusing to ... Assist when ordered to guard Robert Colclough ... William Trammell is fined 10 shillings for such," William Colvin and Samuel Awbrey are discharged. Book A, pp. 25 and 52.

December 13, 1757 - The itemization of the County Levy lists debits for: "John Doories for going to Williamsburgh for Sherifs Commission ... 600 [lbs. tobacco, ie., payment for a round-trip totalling 300 miles] ... the Sherif [sic] [Aneas Campbell for his salary] for Public Services ... 1,248 [lb.t.] ... To 6 PerCt. [percent] on 26816 lbs. Tobacco for Sheriff's collection ... 1609 [lb.t., ie., about £10, and] ... To a Depositum [ie, a credit forward] in the Sheriff's hands ... 357 [lb.t.]." Book A, pp. 54-55.

December 14, 1757 - Loudoun Justices James Hamilton and Anthony Russell enter themselves as Sureties on bonds for Aneas Campbell's faithful performance of his duties as Sheriff in collecting the county levy and the colonial taxes imposed "for the better protection of the Inhabitants of the Frontiers of this Colony." LDCODB, Book A, pp. 45-46.

December 13, 1757 - In the itemization of the first County levy, without additional explanation, Joseph McGeach, Thomas Lewis, John Shepherd, Benjamin Edwards, William Ross and William Woolard are each paid 25 lbs. of tobacco. This is the sum usually paid for guarding a prisoner in the County jail for one day. Book A, p. 55; and see supra, p. 146.

December 14, 1757 - John Moss and Thomas Sorrell report that the "Prison ... [is] insufficient ... [and] not agreeable to the Bond." Book A, p. 62.

May 9, 1758 - George West, "The Surveyor of this County, returned a Platt of the Prison bounds ... nine Acres of Land adjoining to the Prison built at Mr. Aneas Campbell's." Entered in the Order Book, this Plat shows a square tract with the Gaol to the north of "Mr. Campbell's House" at Raspberry Plain, in the center of the 9-acre tract. Book A, pp. 84 and 103.

July 11, 1758 - William Owsley takes the Oaths of an Under Sheriff. Book A, p. 129.

July 11, 1758 - Aneas Campbell, Nicholas Minor and Fielding Turner are recommended to the Governor as Loudoun's slate of nominees as "proper persons to execute the Office of Sheriff of this County." Book A, p. 130.

August 2, 1758 - James Dozer is serving as an Under Sheriff of Fairfax County. [HDC]

August 2, 1758 - In Fairfax County, based on a warrant issued from the Loudoun Court, James Goulding is arrested "and [held] in Fairfax Goal" [sic] [in Alexandria] for a judgment debt owed to James Ingoe Dozer. [HDC]

August 8, 1758 - Charles Broadwater is the "late [former] Sherif of Fairfax County." Book A, p. 134.

August 9, 1758 - It is "Ordered that Nicholas Minor, James Hamilton and William West, Gentlemen, Advertise for Workmen to meet them at some convenient place in this County on any day ... [before] the 25th day of next Month with their Plans to undertake ... [construction of] a Prison and Stocks of the same Dimensions of those in Fairfax County for this County - to the lowest bidder ... [requiring] Bond with sufficient Security ... [for] performance of the said work within such time as [the Commissioners] think convenient." Book A, p. 143.

August 10, 1758 - "John Moss, Thomas Sorrell, Joseph Yeats ... Report of the Prison built at Aneas Campbells ... the Timber work Cost &c. to be worth 950 lb. Tobacco but for the intended use (as a Prison) we judge it insufficient ... John Trammell be allowed [950 lb.] of Tobacco for the workmanship &c. of the said Prison." Book A, p. 155.

September 13, 1758 - The same day that the contract for construction of the Courthouse in Leesburg is let, it is "agreed with Daniel French Gent. [of Fairfax County] for the building of the Goal and Stocks ... for ... £83 Current Money ... [to be] paid him ... before [August 20, 1759]." Book A, p. 166.

November 14, 1758 - In the County Levy, debits for the guards at the jail for prisoner John Walker are listed: Thomas Cartwright, Robert Boyd, Francis Elgin, Joseph McGeach, William Wollard, William Brooks, Stephen Emery, William Heath, Jonathan Mercer, Daniel Davis and John Shepherd. Debits are also listed for the payment of the men who guarded prisoner Robert Colclough at the jail: Thomas Cartwright, Robert Wood, Jacob Reed, Edward Harding, Hugh Johnston, Samuel Mobley, John Poultney and John Shepherd. Book A, pp. 176 and 177.

November 14, 1758 - In the itemization of the County Levy, a debit is listed for "Daniel French for building a Prison ... 9,960 [lbs. tobacco]." This payment is the equivalent of £62, 5 shillings. Book A, p. 177; supra, @ p. 145.

November 15, 1758 - It is "Ordered that the Sherif ... pay ... [25 lbs.] of Tobacco to Moses Lasswell for ... guarding the Prison over John Walker twenty four hours." Book A, p. 180.

March 13, 1759 - It is "Ordered that the Sherif ... provide sufficient Irons for the better securing of Criminals in his Custody." Book A, p. 207.

August 15, 1759 - "Ordered that the Sherif ... discharge Elizabeth Gibson out of his Custody." Book A, p. 269.

August 16, 1759 - James Dickson is the Sheriff of Frederick County, Maryland. MdGaz., No. 745, p. 3, col. 1.

September 11, 1759 - Nicholas Minor receives his Commission "from the Hon.ble the Lieutenant Governor" and takes the Oaths of the Office of Sheriff. Loudoun Justices Richard Coleman and Josias Clapham enter themselves as Sureties on the usual bonds for the faithful performance of the office. Book A, p. 284; and, LDCODB, Book A, pp. 331-334.

September 11, 1759 - John Moss Junr., John Minor and Leven Powell, upon the Motion of Sheriff Nicholas Minor, each take their Oaths as Under Sheriffs. Book A, p. 285.

September 12, 1759 - "Nicholas Minor, Gent., Sherif ... Protested against the Sufficiency of the Goal." Book A, p. 292.

September 13, 1759 - William Owsley renews his Oaths as an Under Sheriff. Book A, p. 294.

November 13, 1759 - "Ordered that the Surveyor ... lay off the Prison Bounds round the Goal [sic] [in Leesburg] ... not exceeding ten Acres." Two days later the plat is returned to Court. Book A, pp. 301 and 309; and see infra.

November 13, and November 14, 1759 - In the County Levy, debits for the payment of the guards, of prisoners Thomas Dean and William Robinson, at the prison are listed: William Wollard, John Thomas, Francis Elgin, Samuel Cartwright, Richard Allen, Thomas Cartwright, Thomas Hamilton, James Saunders, Ezekiel Hickman, John Shepherd, William Ross, George Scott, John McCarty, Cornelius Donohue, Edward Harden, Daniel Davis, Jacob Fouch and Hugh Black. Book A, pp. 302 and 303.

November 14, 1759 - In the itemization of the County Levy, a debit is listed for "Daniel Davis [a blacksmith] for making 2 pr. [pair of] hand Cuffs for Criminals as per acct ... 80 [lbs. tobacco]," ie., 10 shillings in currency. Book A, p. 304.

November 14, 1759 - Fielding Turner, William West and Benjamin Grayson report that the Prison is not sufficient and requires additional work: "each Hearth to be laid with Brick or Stone 2 foot deep ... the plank butting the Fireplace to be taken off nine inches ... Chimney to be raised three foot higher ... outside Locks to both Doors, a Trough and passage to carry of the Excrements of Prisoners." Book A, pp. 298 and 305.

November 14, 1759 - John West is a former "Sherif of Fairfax" County. Book A, p. 305.

November 15, 1759 - George West, "Surveyor of this County, returned a Platt of the Prison Bounds in Leesburgh [sic]" around the new jail on the back of town lot #28. The plat shows a rectangular area of about 10 acres bounded by "Daniel Davises" blacksmithy at the northern marker on lot #36 and "Janney's Stable," probably on Joseph Janney's town lot #4, at the southwest marker. The two are connected by a line designated as S22'W58. The northern jail boundary is represented by a line extending east from Davis', noted as S68'E27. This author suggests that compass directions, parallel to the streets, are supplemented by distances, in poles, which accounts for a ten-acre area, with the north-south boundaries lines 957' long and the east-west boundaries 445½' long. The western jail boundary must have extended down the western lines of Leesburg town lots #4, #13 and #20 and through the middle of lots #29, #32, #33 and #36. Book A, p. 309; infra, Town Plan illustration in the Chapter on Leesburg. For a comparison, see Plat of the Leesburg Prison Bounds in 1765, supra @ p. 134.

May 27, 1760 - Leven Powell is sworn in as a Sub-Sheriff in Prince William County. PRWMCOA, (1760) vol. 20, p. 142.

August 11, 1760 - John Rhodes is the Fairfax County Sheriff. [HDC]

August 12, 1760 - "Aneas Campbell, late Sherif of this County," is fined 5 shillings for his Neglect of Duty in failing to return Writs of Execution on behalf of John Mercer against John Owsley and William Owsley. Note: William Owsley was one of Campbell's Sub-Sheriffs. Book A, p. 386; infra, p. 155.

August 13, 1760 - Nicholas Minor, William West and Richard Coleman, Gent., are recommended for appointment "to Execute the Office of Sheriff of this County." Book A, p. 391.

November 12, 1760 - In itemizing the County Levy, debits are listed for "a Horse impressed to carry Dickson Hall a Prisoner to the Public Goal [sic] ... 480 [lbs. tobacco] ... [and] Thomas Thompson guarding the Goal over Chas. Cole 24 Hours ... 25 [lb.t.]." Book A, p. 404.

November 12, 1760 - Fielding Turner, Richard Coleman and Josias Clapham enter the usual bond for Nicholas Minor for the performance of his Sheriff's duties. LDCODB, Book B, p. 61.

March 10, 1761 - Nicholas Minor apparently receives the renewal of his Commission and renews his Oaths as the Sheriff of Loudoun. Book A, p. 427.

March 10, 1761 - John Moss Junr. and John Minor renew their Oaths as Under Sheriffs. Book A, p. 427.

June 9, 1761 - It is "Ordered that James Hamilton and Nicholas Minor Gent. [Loudoun Justices] Agree with Workmen to Repair the Prison built for this County." Book A, p. 454.

June 11, 1761 - Based on the deed from Nicholas Minor to the Loudoun County Justices, "the Court House and Prison now stand" on Leesburg Lots # 27 and 28. LDCODB, Book B, p. 149.

July 14, 1761 - William West, Richard Coleman and Josias Clapham are recommended for appointment to "the Office of Sherif of this County." Book A, p. 481.

September 8, 1761 - Justice William West takes the Oaths of Loudoun Sheriff; James Hamilton, Richard Coleman, Nicholas Minor and Hugh West all enter into the usual bond for full performance of the new Sheriff's duties, and a new bond for collection of a new Virginia "publick levy"; and subsequently, William West Junr., John Moss Junr. and John Minor take their Oaths as Under Sheriffs. Book A, p. 491; LDCODB, Book B, p. 258; and see Hening, VII/395.

September 9, 1761 - William West, Sheriff, registers his protest against the Gaol as "not sufficient to confine those who shall therein be committed." Book A, p. 503.

September 10, 1761 - Craven Peyton and Charles West take the Oaths as Under Sheriffs, at the request and on the Motion of William West, Sheriff. Book A, p. 513.

November 11, 1761 - In the County Levy, a debit is listed to "Joseph West for Halling Stone & Underpining the Prison £10 ... in Tobo. at 12/6 per Ct. is ... 1600 [lbs. tobacco, ie., £1 is valued at 160 lbs. of tobacco]." Book A, p. 533.

February 9, 1762 - Hugh West enters himself as Security on Sheriff William West's bond for the proper collection of the annual levy on tithables. LDCODB, Book C, p. 137.

July 14, 1762 - William West Junr. makes an Affidavit of service on the tenant in an eviction action. Book B, p. 9.

July 14, 1762 - William West, Josias Clapham and George West are recommended as "proper persons" to be appointed as Sheriff. Book B, p. 11.

November 9, 1762 - Josias Clapham takes the Oaths as Loudoun Sheriff, with Nicholas Minor and Philip Noland entering as his Securities on the Bonds that are normally given by the new Sheriff. Book B, p. 69.

November 9, 1762 - "Josias Clapham Gent. Sheriff ... Protested against the Sufficiency of the Gaol." Book B, p. 70.

November 10, 1762 - In the County Levy, a debit is listed, "To ... Malcum McMurry" for guarding prisoners at the County Gaol. Book B, p. 73.

November 10, 1762 - John Moss Junr. [who is also a junior Loudoun County Justice] renews his Oaths as an Under Sheriff. Book B, p. 74.

April 12, 1762 - Brothers William West [Junr.] and Charles West take the Oaths of Under Sheriffs. Book B, p. 86.

May 11, 1763 - William Moss takes the Oaths of an Under Sheriff. Book B, p. 126.

August 10, 1763 - Josias Clapham, George West and Charles Tyler are recommended for appointment to the Office of Sheriff "for the ensuing Year." Book B, p. 197.

September 16, 1763 - Charles Griffith deeds 400 acres to Hugh West, as collateral for West "becoming his security for [staying within] the prison bounds of County Loudoun in an action of debt." LDCODB, Book D, pp. 97-100.

November 9, 1763 - Among the itemized debits listed on the County Levy is the salary of "Josias Clapham Gent. Sherif for public Service and cash ... 1248 [lbs. tobacco]." Book B, p. 266.

February 14, 1764 - Josias Clapham, the Loudoun Sheriff, with John Moss Junr. and John Minor as his sureties, enters into the usual bonds for the Sheriff's proper collection of taxes and levies. LDCODB, Book D, pp. 56-57.

February 14, 1764 - John Minor renews his Oaths as an Under Sheriff. Book B, pp. 270-271.

August 14, 1764 - George West, Charles Tyler and Francis Peyton are the nominees slated for appointment as the next Sheriff. Book B, p. 408.

November 13, 1764 - In the itemization of the County Levy a debit is listed "To ... the ensuing Sherif for Public Service ... 1248 [lbs. tobacco]." This is a clear indication that a new Sheriff's Commission was expected and overdue. Book B, p. 495.

November 13, 1764 - In the County Levy, debits are listed: "To ... Jacob Shilling ... William Bowling ... Francis Chelton [and] Richard Stewart," each for guarding prisoners at the County Gaol. Book B, p. 495.

November 14, 1764 - In the itemization of the County Levy, a debit is listed, "To ... Josias Clapham ... [in payment on account] for providing for Prisoners and Criminals ... 1,992 [lbs. tobacco]." Book B, p. 497.

December 12, 1764 - John Palmer Junr. sues "Thomas Speake, Gent. late Sherif of Frederick County." Book B, p. 516.

February 12, 1765 - Charles Tyler is Commissioned and gives his Oaths as Sheriff; and, Thomas Lewis and John Tyler take the Oaths of Under Sheriff. Book B, p. 518.

February 12, 1765 - "Charles Tyler, Gent., Sherif ... protested against the Sufficiency of the Goal [sic] built for this County." Book B, p. 518.

March 14, 1765 - John Minor and William Moss renew their Oaths as Under Sheriffs for the County. Book B, p. 535.

June 13, 1765 - "The Court being of the opinion that the Prison Bounds formerly laid off for this County are very inconvenient ... Ordered that the Surveyor do lay off for the said Bounds ... Vizt. Beginning at a stone near the Prison thence a Streight line crossing the street to a Stake in John Heryford's Lot thence as far down the Town as to Include Ten Acres of Land, and Nicholas Minor Gent. is to accompany the Surveyor to direct him in the same and the former Rules to stand till surveyed & Plat returned." Book B, p. 671; see the Plat of the 1765 Prison Bounds, supra @ p. 134.

June 13, 1765 - Christopher Perfect takes the Oaths of an Under Sheriff. Book B, p. 671.

August 12, 1765 - Charles Tyler, Francis Peyton and John McIlhaney are recommended to the Lt. Governor for appointment "to Execute the Office of Sheriff." Book C, p. 6.

August 13, 1765 - A Plat and a Report of the ten acres surveyed for the Prison Bounds in Leesburg are returned to the Court and recorded. Book C, p. 18; LDCODB, Book D, p. 574.

August 14, 1765 - Simon Triplett takes the Oaths of an Under Sheriff. Book C, p. 27.

September 11, 1765 - It is "Ordered that the Sheriff [Charles Tyler] raise the force of this County [ie., a 'posse'] and take Patrick McKenzey who broke the Gaol." Book C, p. 51.

November 11, 1765 - In the County Levy, a debit is listed: "To ... Charles Tyler Sherif for Public Service ... 1,248 [lbs. tobacco]." Book C, p. 72.

November 11, 1765 - In the County Levy, debits are listed for guards at the Gaol: "Thomas Pritchard [guarding] over Mary Duffy and Mary McDonald ... Jacob Shilling [guarding] over John Mares, Benjamin Warford, Mary Duffy and Mary McDonald ... Richard Stewart [guarding] over Benjamin Warford ... [and] Thomas Cartwright, Alexander Bowling, Richard Stewart and Jacob Shilling [each paid as a guard for] one Night." Warford apparently was imprisoned for a judgment debt, since there was no criminal prosecution recorded. Book C, pp. 72-73.

June 10, 1766 - "Ordered that James Hamilton, Nicholas Minor and Charles Tyler Gent. agree with Workmen to repair the Prison ... and purchase Locks for the same." Book C, p. 86.

June 11, 1766 - Loudoun County Justices Charles Tyler, Francis Peyton and John McIlhaney are again slated as the nominees for appointment "to Execute the Office of Sheriff." Book C, p. 109.

October 15, 1766 - The Court Orders note: "Thomas Pritchard having finished the repairs of the Prison," giving additional evidence that Pritchard had, by this time, firmly established himself as Leesburg's primary builder/developer. Book C, p. 215; infra, Chapter on Leesburg, Chapter on Trades.

November 11, 1766 - In itemizing the County Levy, debits are listed, for guarding the Gaol: "To ... Martin Seahorn over John McCollom ... Gasper Smith over James Thomas ... Jacob Shilling over James Thomas ... [and] Alexander Mcintire over John McCollom." James Thomas appears to have been jailed for a judgment debt, since there was no criminal prosecution of him on record. Also in the County Levy is a debit "To ... Jacob Shilling [apparently a blacksmith] for a pair of Handcuffs ... 40 [lbs. of tobacco]," ie., valued at 5 shillings. Book C, p. 220.

November 13, 1766 - "Ordered ... the Sherif ... pay to [former Sheriff] Josias Clapham ... [1,600 lbs.] tobacco, being for credit of Ten Pounds [in currency] ... for the Sale of Horses to carry Criminals [probably John Lewis and Francis Kennedy] to Williamsburg when [Clapham] was Sherif." Book C, p. 230.

December 9, 1766 - Francis Peyton Esqr. receives his Commission, originally issued by the Governor on October 25, 1766, and takes the Oaths as the new Sheriff of Loudoun County. Leven Powell, Stephen Donaldson, Elijah Chinn and Sampson Turley, all of whom were either a sitting or future County Justice in Loudoun and Fairfax Counties, entered themselves as Security on Peyton's Sheriff's bonds. LDCODB, Book E, p. 280.

December 9, 1766 - Craven Peyton, Thomas Lewis and Christopher Perfect each takes the Oaths of an Under Sheriff and is sworn into office. Book C, pp. 231 and 232.

Late in December of 1766 or the first days of 1767, the Loudoun jail "burnt down." Construction of a new County jail, and a temporary structure for the housing of prisoners, are the first orders of business in the Loudoun County Court sessions conducted in January, 1767. Book C, p. 233.

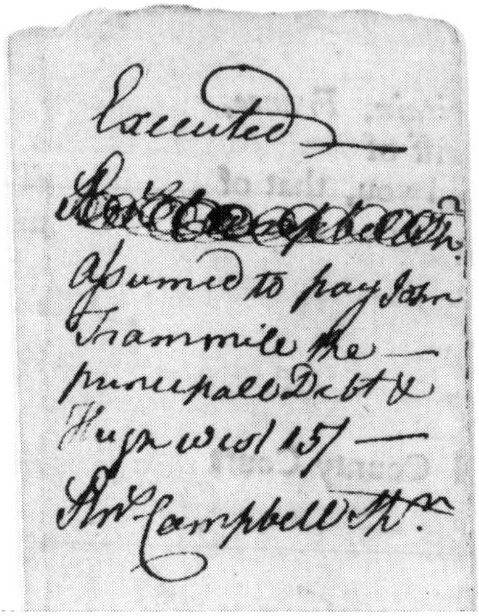

Executed
Assumed to pay John
Trammile the
principall Debt &
Hugh West 15/ —
An^s Campbell Sh^r

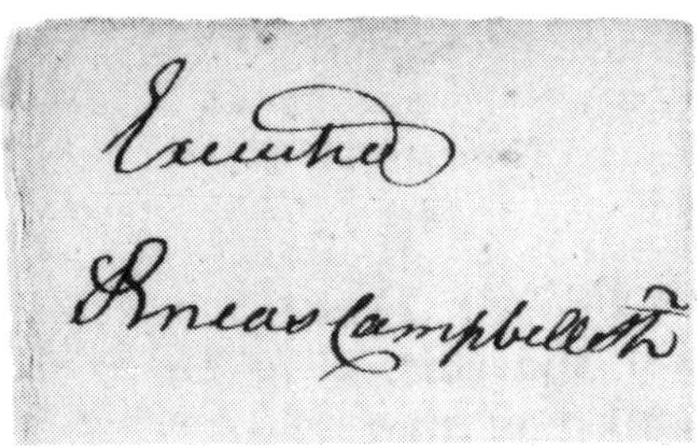

Executed
Aneas Campbell Sh^r

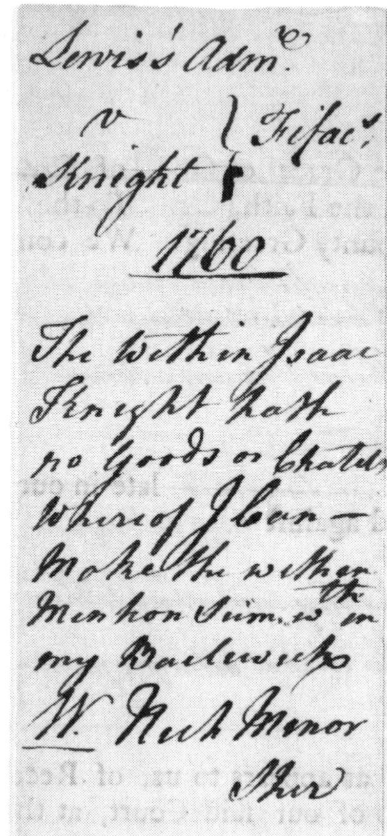

Lewis's Adm^x
v } Fi fac^s
Knight }
1760
The within Isaac
Knight hath
no goods or Chatels
whereof I can
make the within
mention Sum w in
my Bailiwick
W. Nich Minor
Sher

The signatures of the first two Sheriffs of Loudoun County, Aneas Campbell and Nicholas Minor, appear above on the returns of attachments and warrants issued by the Loudoun County Court in three cases in 1758 and 1760. In the case of John Radcliff vs. Thomas Williams Wells, in May of 1758, Sheriff Campbell noted: "Executed - Assumed to pay John Trammill [sic] the principall Debt & Hugh West 15/ [shillings, attorney fees]." In the case of James Layton vs. Ezekiel Hickman in June of 1758, Loudoun Sheriff Campbell noted that the warrant for the arrest of Hickman was "Executed," and signs his full name. In the case of Elizabeth Lewis, suing as the Administratrix of the Estate of Stephen Lewis, vs. Isaac Knight, Sheriff Minor noted in February of 1760 that "The within Isaac Knight hath no goods or Chat[t]els whereof I can make [sell for] the within mention[ed] Sum w[i]thin my Bailiwick. W. [Witness.] Nich[olas] Minor, Sher[iff]." [HDC]

Loudoun County Sheriffs and Under-Sheriffs, 1757-1766

Year	Sheriff	Under-Sheriffs
1757-59	Aneas Campbell	Francis Elgin, Francis Peyton, Leven Powell,
1758-59	"	William Owsley
1759-61	Nicholas Minor	John Minor, John Moss Junr., William Owsley, Leven Powell
1761	"	John Moss Junr., John Minor
1761-62	William West	John Minor, John Moss Junr., Craven Peyton, Charles West, William West Junr.
1762-64	Josias Clapham	John Moss Junr., Charles West
1762-63	"	William West Junr.
1763-64	"	William Moss
1764-65	Josias Clapham	John Minor, John Moss Junr., William Moss, Charles West
1765-66	Charles Tyler	Thomas Lewis, John Minor, William Moss, Christopher Perfect, Simon Triplett, John Tyler,
1766-67	Francis Peyton	Thomas Lewis, Christopher Perfect, Craven Peyton

When no new Commission was recorded, the author assumes that the Sheriff and his Deputies continued in their duties.

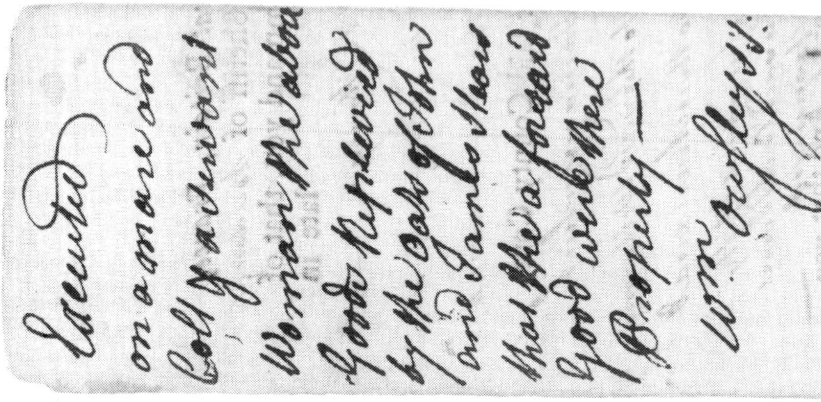

Executed on a mare and Colt of a servant woman the above goods Replevied by the Oath of John and James Stears that the aforesaid goods were there property — Wm. Owsley S.S.

No Effects within my Bailiwic

Leven Powell S.Sh.

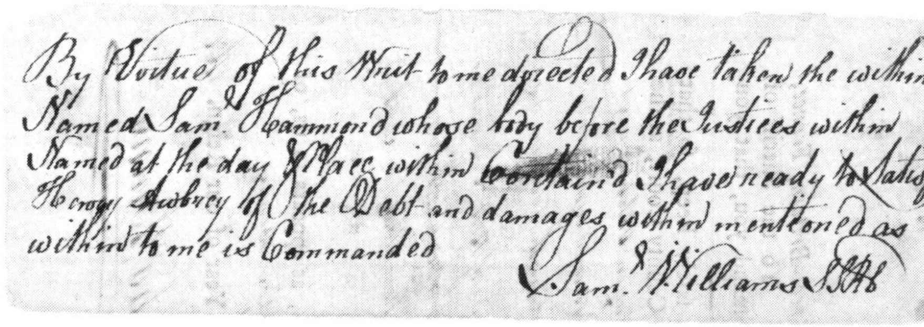

By Virtue of this Writ to me directed I have taken the within Named Sam. Hammond whose body before the Justices within Named at the day & Place within contained I have ready to Satisfy Henry Awbrey of the Debt and damages within mentioned as within to me is Commanded

Sam.l Williams S.Sh.

In July of 1760 in William Heth vs. Philip Lynham, a slander case, Loudoun Under Sheriff William Owsley noted that he "executed [a writ of fifae] on a mare and Colt & a servant woman the above goods Replevied by the oath of John [Stears] and James Stears that the aforesaid good were there [sic] property-." One of Loudoun's original Under Sheriffs, Leven Powell returned a writ noting "No effects within my Bailiwic." Samuel Williams, a Richmond County Sub-Sheriff, indicated that he arrested Samuel Hammond and that he would deliver him bodily to the Loudoun County Court "to Satisfy Henry Awbrey [a judgment creditor] of the Debt and damages" itemized in a Loudoun warrant. *[HDC]*

In the years before Virginia's Great Charter, criminal offences in the colony were tried by the military Governor and his lieutenants. By 1634, the Governor's "court" was known as the Quarter Court, the name deriving from the practice of holding sessions on a quarterly schedule. Despite the creation that year of the county courts, then known as monthly courts, the Quarter Court retained exclusive trial jurisdiction over all major crimes, such as piracy, traitorous behavior or the commission of a felony. In 1643, the Quarter Court was retitled the "General Court," and the title of that court, which conducted its jury trials in the colonial capital (first Jamestown and then Williamsburg), was retained for the supreme judicial body in Virginia until the time of the American Revolution. Aside from handling appeals from the county courts in civil matters and the trials of large estate cases, the General Court conducted the felony trial of every white colonist who was accused of a crime that involved a capital offence, "where the judgment upon conviction shall be for the loss of life or member [body part]." The execution of white criminals by hanging, sometimes followed by a drawing and quartering of the body, was carried out at the colonial capital. A more genteel or at least less painful execution, beheading, was generally reserved for only the King and his peers of the realm. [Hening, I/313, III/504-516 and V/491; supra, Chapter on the County Court].

As settlements expanded into Virginia's frontiers, judicial practices evolved to deal with increasing distances between county courts and the capital. One result, in dealing with all kinds of crime, was the increasing importance of the individual Justices of the Peace and the county courts. By the 1700s, county Justices, acting individually, were authorized to issue a warrant to cause "any traitor, felon, pirate, rioter, breaker of the peace, or other criminal offender to be apprehended" immediately. When a colonist was arrested on a felony warrant, the county court would convene an arraignment hearing on short notice - sometimes holding session on a weekend. Taking the role of the General Court's grand jury, the county court would proceed to take the testimony of witnesses. Where the evidence was deemed sufficient to warrant a felony trial, the defendant would be returned to the

Loudoun jail in the custody of the Sheriff, and then conducted on to Williamsburg at the earliest opportunity. The Loudoun Court would determine which witnesses had given probative evidence, and place them under bond, requiring crucial witnesses to travel to Williamsburg for the trial. Loudoun County witnesses at the General Court were reimbursed £2 for total mileage, and 7½ shillings per day "until discharged." A second potential outcome at a county court arraignment was the determination that the accused was not guilty of a felony, but apparently guilty of a misdemeanor. Since defendants had a right to trial by jury, the accused had the option of either insisting on his right, resulting in his return to the custody of the Sheriff to await trial, or accepting the sentence meted out by the arraignment court. Instances of both alternate results appear in The Loudoun Record. At the time of arraignment in the county court, when evidence was found altogether wanting, an accused could be found not guilty and given his liberty. This was not an uncommon event in Loudoun County in the 1757-1766 decade; ten of about two dozen capital cases had this result, including two colonists accused of murder, two accused of horse theft, and one accused of counterfeiting. The most striking of these was the release of Loudoun troublemaker Charles Cole, when the county court noted that the principal witness giving evidence against Cole in a murder case, Mary Winde, was a convict servant. [Hening, V/480 and V/495].

An emphasis was placed on substance over form in the colonial county courts. County courts had jurisdiction over all penal violations, regardless of the amount of the potential fine. When a maximum penalty did not exceed £5, county courts were authorized to ignore any objections "by reason of any default ... or want of form, in any writ," and to "proceed and give judgment according to the very right of the cause." Since there was no appeal of a ruling under £10, the county court had a great deal of latitude within which to fashion justice. Regardless, there was no evident predisposition in favor of the prosecution in Leesburg's colonial Courthouse. Criminal prosecutions in Loudoun from 1757 to 1766 ended in nearly as many acquittals as convictions. And of the sixty colonists accused of a crime in Loudoun before 1767, twenty defendants were acquitted outright and another twenty had the charges reduced by the county court or were found guilty only on lesser charges. [Hening, V/500 and V/523].

Larceny, and theft in general, was the most common type of criminal charge at the colonial Loudoun Court, amounting to fully half of the criminal prosecutions in Loudoun in the 1757-1766 decade. We note with some surprise that the theft of a horse bell was frequently at issue. The maximum sentence that the county court could, and did, mete out for a misdemeanor conviction was 39 lashes on the bare back "well laid on." The reader might well imagine the spectacle on the Courthouse lawn in June of 1765 occasioned by Sheriff Charles Tyler parading Mary Duffy and Mary McDonald to the whipping post, tying their hands above their heads, stripping them to the waist, and "laying on" the sentence of 39 lashes on the bare back, as the Loudoun County Court had directed.

As noted elsewhere, if a servant was convicted of a criminal offence after 1753, "where free persons are punishable by fine, servants shall be punished by whipping after the rate of twenty lashes for every five hundred pounds of tobacco or fifty shillings." The Assembly went on to prohibit the imposition of more than forty lashes at one time on any servant. The Assembly of 1753 also provided, in The Servants and Slaves Act, that anyone stealing "any negroe, mulattoe, or Indian slave, whatsoever" would be treated as a felon and subject to the death penalty, without the benefit of clergy. Thus, John Maris would have been sent to Williamsburg to be tried for the theft of a slave and hanged there if found guilty, had the Loudoun Court not extradited him to Maryland in 1765. The extradition of John Maris was not Loudoun's first -- his was preceded by the extradition to Maryland of John Fouch and Jacob Fouch on theft charges in 1758. [Hening, VI/359-360 and VI/369; infra, The Record, p. 171].

Loudoun County's first capital crime, Robert Colclough's rape of his daughter Charity in 1757, ended in Colclough's execution in Williamsburg that winter. His death was noted, without further remark, in the Loudoun Order book early the next year, abruptly terminating a divorce case that Sarah Colclough had initiated. Their son, Alexander Colclough, inherited the family lands near Bull Run. Over the course of the 1757-1766 decade, the Loudoun Court arraigned a total of eleven accused felons and sent them to Williamsburg for trial. Ten of them were never heard from again. The most frequent capital offence arraigned in Loudoun County in the first decade was the counterfeiting of

Virginia Treasury notes, with five offenders packed off to their destiny. Three horse thieves were sent to Williamsburg for trial, and two women were also sent, accused of the capital crime of breaking and entry theft (of a pewter dinner service). Only one accused murderer, Francis Kennedy, was tried in Williamsburg in the Loudoun's first decade. His story, and the vivid description of Cameron parish vestryman John Owsley's death during a melee in 1764, are set out in The Record and are strongly recommended to the reader. The jury in the General Court trial returned a verdict of capital murder against Kennedy, and only the King's Royal Pardon could save Kennedy from a death sentence. Governor Fauquier corresponded with London while Francis Kennedy spent a year in the public gaol in Williamsburg, before the King's Pardon was finally issued. [infra, The Record, pp. 164 and 169-171; Grants, E/165 and I/53; infra, Chapter on Familial Relations, and Chapter on Coroners, Deaths and Estates].

With the advent of issuance of large quantities of paper money to finance Virginia's military efforts during the French and Indian Wars (over £165,000 in Virginia Treasury notes in the three years before March of 1759), and a corresponding increase in the opportunity for mischief, the Assembly determined that:

> *"if any person ... shall forge or counterfeit, alter or erase, any such treasury note[s], or shall tender in payment by way of barter or otherwise ... knowing the same to be forged ... [the offender] shall be adjudged a felon, and shall suffer [death] as in cases of felony, without benefit of clergy."*

Loudoun's first experience with the counterfeit notes involved charges against ordinary keeper and Baptist elder Samuel Butcher. Despite his acquittal, the experience of receiving counterfeit notes and his subsequent arraignment may have resulted in the closing of Butcher's ordinary at The Gap. [Hening, VII/19, VII/167-168, VII/177 and VII/260-263; infra, the Chapter on Ordinaries].

By 1748, the Virginia Assembly had noticed that:

> *"... the crime and offence of stealing horses is of late ... more frequent, especially in the frontier counties, to the great detriment ... of many of his majesty's good subjects ... [enacted a law to] encourage ... [Virginia colonists to] vigorously endeavor the apprehending of such malefactors."*

The new law authorized a £10 reward for every person "who shall apprehend, and take any person guilty of the stealing of a horse," and a £50 reward to the estate of the person "endeavoring to apprehend, or making pursuit ... being so killed" by a horse thief. The transport of "led horses" was, thereafter, closely watched, and the Assembly went even further, acknowledging in an Act that:

> *"a great number of persons make a trade ... receive and buy of such felons the horses ... [transported intra-colony,] any persons [shown to] ... receive, or buy, any horse ... knowing the same to be stolen; ... harbour or conceal any horse-stealer knowing[ly] ... by the testimony of one or more credible witnesses ... [shall] suffer the pain of death, as a felon."*

Even if the principal was not apprehended, county courts were allowed to prosecute accessories "buying or receiving any stolen horse," to impose fines, "imprisonment, or other such corporal punishment as the court shall think fit to inflict." The theory of double jeopardy was incorporated in the enforcement provisions. In an attempt to resist "great frauds ... committed in taking up and concealing stray horses," the 1762 Assembly, awkwardly, provided that only freeholders or tenants for years were allowed to take up and claim stray horses. [Hening, VI/128-131 and VII/545-548].

Legislation enacted by the Virginia Assembly after 1692 reflected an increasing concern for internal security, incidents of slave "rebellion" and crimes committed by slaves. In 1748, special procedures were adopted for the trial of slaves who were charged with commission of a felony or capital crime. Once a County Sheriff gave the proper notice of such a case, the Governor was authorized to issue a special Dedimus of Oyer and Terminer to the disinterested Justices of the particular county court where the slave was arraigned and being held in jail. The Special Dedimus would specify the slave by name and authorize the county court to conduct the trial. The only time that a negro, mulatto or Indian was permitted to give evidence in a criminal case in a Virginia court was when a slave was on trial. Accused slaves were not entitled to a trial by jury, but were afforded the protection of the normal rules of procedure for arraignment and trial, and the requirement that evidence be obtained from credible witnesses. The standard procedure whereby only the slaves, and not whites, who were convicted felons were sentenced in a colonial county court and then executed locally, explains what is otherwise a misleading inconsistency in the Loudoun Court records. [Hening, III/102, IV/127 and VI/104-112; Glossary; Justices, p. 53].

In 1765, the Virginia Assembly revised the procedures for the trial of slaves, citing "much unnecessary expense and trouble [occasioned by the requirement of] sending to the Governour [sic] [for a Dedimus] for the trial of each particular slave, which commissions issue [as a matter] of course to the Justices of the County." Thereafter, the Governor was authorized to include a General Dedimus of Oyer and Terminer for each county at the same time that a Dedimus and Commission of the Peace was issued, "empowering [all county courts] to try, condemn, and execute, or otherwise punish or acquit, all slaves committing capital crimes within their county ... at any time that there shall be occasion." The 1765 law contained a delaying clause and did not go into effect until the King gave his consent to the measure late in 1767. In November of 1767, Governor Fauquier began the issuance of a General Dedimus of Oyer and Terminer to each of the counties, but his last illness interrupted the process. The first General Dedimus for Loudoun was finally issued in June of 1768 by Governor Botetourt and was, thereafter, the authority for the criminal trials of slaves in Loudoun. [Hening, VIII/137-139; Justices, p. 87; see infra, Chronology and Glossary Appendices].

A Special Dedimus from Governor Fauquier authorized the first trial of a slave in the Loudoun County Court on June 28, 1760. After finding that a slave named James was guilty of breaking and entering and stealing goods valued at 35 shillings from the house of Mary English, Loudoun's County Court granted James the "benefit of clergy" and ordered the administration of 39 lashes at the whipping post. The Loudoun Justices may have mistakenly applied the law governing commutation in this case. When benefit of clergy was extended to a slave convicted of a capital crime, the slave was supposed to "be burnt in the hand, by the goaler, in open court," and the law denied slaves the benefit of clergy when, among other serious crimes, a house was broken and entered and goods valued in excess of twenty shillings were taken. All of the Loudoun Justices were slave owners and must have been aware of the laws regulating the institution, leaving us to conclude that the Loudoun Court intentionally chose to err in the direction of leniency. There were no other slaves accused of capital crimes in Loudoun before 1766, but this was not the only occasion on which the early Loudoun Court displayed compassion. While the colonial law did not allow special bail "in any suit brought upon a penal law," in June of 1762, the Loudoun County Court released Mary Rogers on bail in the custody of her husband James Rogers prior to her trial in Williamsburg. [Hening, V/496 and VI/106; and supra, Chapter on the County Court].

From the early days of the colony, the Virginia Assembly exhibited a special concern for the otherwise obscure crimes of stealing or killing hogs. Even wild hogs were considered a scarce resource and they were protected and reserved as rewards for colonists who killed wolves. In 1642, it was considered a felony to kill a domesticated hog owned by another. In 1647, the crime was downgraded from a felony to a misdemeanor, shifting the trial of these matters to the county courts, but substantial fines of 2,000 lbs. of tobacco were imposed on the offenders, with half going to the owner and half to an "informer." If unable to pay the fine, the offender was required to render a total of two years of personal service as a servant to the hog's owner. [Hening, I/244 and I/350-351; see infra, Chapter on Agriculture].

The law had evolved considerably in the intervening century when the Assembly enacted "An Act against stealing Hogs" in October of 1748. This comprehensive Act, which went into effect in 1751, was still in force during the first decade of Loudoun's existence, from 1757 to 1766. It created a series of increasingly severe penalties for repeat offenses, and distinguished between free persons, servants and slaves. "[I]f any person not being a slave, shall steal any hog, shoat, or pig ... for the first offence ... twenty-five lashes, well laid on, at the public whipping post of the county." The offender had the option of avoiding the whip by paying £10 "current money to the use of the same county, towards lessening that county levy." For the first offence, slaves were to receive thirty lashes at the whipping post, without avoidance. At a second offence, all offenders were to stand in the pillory for two hours on a court day, with their ears nailed to the pillory, "and at the end of two hours, have the ears cut loose from the nails." The law provided that "if any person whatsoever, shall be the third time convicted of hog stealing, every such offender ... shall suffer death without the benefit of clergy." This meant that trial of a second or third offence was conducted in the General

Court, after a county court "arraignment." On either a first or second offence, every non-slave offender was also held liable to the owner of the hog, and any "informer," for a total penalty payment of 400 lbs. of tobacco. As with other penal fines, servant offenders were to repay their masters "for the same and costs of suit by further service ... at the rate of one hundred fifty pounds of tobacco for one month's service." Joint offenders were each to suffer the full legal penalties, even if only one hog was involved. In 1763 in the Loudoun Court, Samuel Jenkins, Silvanus Lay and Emanuel Lay were, together, convicted of hog stealing, as first offenders, and each paid the £10 fine rather than accepting the whip. [Hening, VI/121-124; infra, The Record, p. 169; Glossary].

The Loudoun Record

September 1, 1757 - Robert Colclough is charged with "Felonious committing [sic] a Rape on the Body of Charity Colclough [his] daughter." Colclough was sent to Williamsburg for his trial in the General Court, where he was "convicted of Felony and Executed for same." Book A, p. 12; Grants, I/53.

March 15, 1758 - Elizabeth Slade, brought into Court on charges of "stealing Coleworts out of Samuel Jenkin's Garden," with Elizabeth Bright and Ann O'Bryant testifying, Elizabeth Slade is found not guilty, discharged and released. Book A, pp. 77-78; and see Glossary.

April 11, 1758 - The Prosecution against John Thomas, for stealing an Auger belonging to David Davis, after testimony, is dismissed. Book A, pp. 77 and 82; and see Glossary.

August 18, 1758 - John Walker, who is brought before the Court "on Suspicion of his Stealing a Three Pound Bill the property of Henry Taylor ... [on the testimony of] William Whitely and Andrew Adams ... [is charged with] a Misdemeanor ... [he is bound over to the custody of the Sheriff until] his trial ... [to be held] at the next Grand Jury." Book A, p. 156.

October 10, 1758 - John Thomas, "charged with stealing about forty shillings ... and one Lance the property of Caleb Davis ... Joseph Janney, Christopher Perfect, Andrew Adams, John Moss Junr. and John Minor [all testifying, he is found] ... Guilty of a Misdemeanor ... Ordered ... John [Thomas is to] give Security for his good Behavior." Book A, p. 167.

October 16, 1758 - In the first case of an extradition ordered by the Loudoun County Court, John Fouch and Jacob Fouch are brought before the Court "on Suspicion of ... stealing of a Plough Share and Colter and an Iron Pott the property of Sarah Orton ... it appearing that the Felony was committed in ... Maryland ... [the Loudoun County Court orders them to] be sent [to Maryland] for their Trial ... [and they are then] ... Ordered [to be taken] into the [custody] of an Officer of the Court," meaning the Sheriff and his Deputies, for transfer to Maryland authorities. Book A, pp. 167 and 173-174.

November 14, 1758 - Elizabeth Slade, is tried by the Grand Jury "on Suspicion of her being Guilty of felonious stealing a Hat the Property of Ann Smith," with Mary Ruttery testifying against her, she is acquitted of the Misdemeanor and discharged. Book A, pp. 112 and 175.

November 28, 1758 - Charles Cole is brought before the Loudoun Court on the "suspicion of ... Murder of Margaret Davis ... [Coroner] Nicholas Minor, David Davis and Cornelius Donnohue [testifying] ... Mary Winde, the principal Evidence [witness] against [Cole] is a Convict ... thereupon [Cole] is Acquitted." Book A, p. 182/2.

February 13, 1759 - Elizabeth Botts, "charged with entering the Loft of William Owsley and taking ... about eight Barrels of Corn of the Value of £3 ... Syth Botts [testifying] ... the Prosecution be dismissed." Book A, p. 189.

March 13, 1759 - Samuel Butcher is charged "on Suspicion of ... Passing of in Paiment [sic] to Joseph McGeach a Counterfeit five Pound Bill of the Currency of this Colony ... Acquitted and discharged." Book A, pp. 206-207.

March 14, 1759 - Thomas Deane, charged on "Suspicion of ... Counterfeiting and passing of in Payment a Ten Pound Bill of the Currency of this Colony ... John Davis and William Owsley [testifying, the case is bound over] ... to the General Court [in Williamsburg] for further Trial ... [Deane is] remanded to Goal." Book A, p. 217; see supra, Chapter on the County Gaol.

May 8, 1759 - Elizabeth Gibson, "charged with stealing a parcel of Wooll [sic] and other things the property of Garritt Fitzgerald ... Elizabeth Fitzgerald and Margaret Wright [testifying] ... a Jury ... say upon their Oath that [Gibson] is Guilty of the Felony [sic] ... [and impose] a fine ... in the sum of twenty five shillings." Book A, pp. 190 and 236.

August 14, and September 1, 1759 - John Moore, charged with "Stealing two Mares and Colts the properties of Peter Bedinger and David Loyd [both of Frederick County], and sundry other things belonging to William Mead, Mary Jannings, William Pearle and Benjamin Shrieves ... said he was Guilty ... Francis Padgett [testifying against him, he is] sent for further Trial to the ... next General Court [in Williamsburg] and thereupon he is remanded to Goal." Book A, pp. 265 and 282-283.

November 12, 1759 - William Robinson and Thomas Simmonds, charged with "Stealing a Pewter Plate the Property of Ambrose Nelson ... Elizabeth Simmonds, Ann Knight, Monikey Simmonds and John Anderson [testifying, defendants are found] ... not Guilty ... Acquitted &c." Book A, p. 297.

January 14, 1760 - Dixon Hall, charged with "stealing a Horse the property of Sarah Smith of King George County ... Angel Jacobus Jordan and George Jordan of Stafford County, Richard Smith of King George County, and

Russell Willson and John Waters [testifying] ... [Hall is held for trial] at the next General Court ... remanded to Goal." Book A, p. 321.

June 17, 1760 - Pierce Butler [aka Peirce Butler] is arraigned before the Loudoun Court and charged with "Stealing a Mare ... and an Iron Kettle and Bell." The felony charges are dismissed, and Butler is apparently allowed to post bond for his good behavior and appearance at trial on the misdemeanor charges. Book A, p. 380; see infra, entry for November 12, 1760.

June 28, 1760 - John Riley, who allegedly "Assaulted Frederick Poyer by striking at him with a stick and by force took from the said Frederick one Riffle Gun and carried the same away contrary to the Peace ... [is found] not Guilty of a Felony ... [the Court setting trial] for Misdemeanor ... here on the second Tuesday in November." Riley, his attorney Francis Dade, and his Securities Griffith Meyrick and David Smith, post bonds totalling £200 to guarantee his appearance at trial. Book A, p. 381.

June 28, 1760 - Hugh West, Deputy Kings Attorney, presents charges against "James a Negro Man Slave belonging to Thomas Gant of Prince Georges County ... Maryland ... [that] on the tenth Day of June [1760] the aforesaid James broke and entered the House of a certain Mary English ... and Feloniously took one large Snuff Box of the price of three shillings, three pair of Silver Sleeve Buttons [worth] five shillings, three Handkerchiefs [worth] ten shillings, one silver Thimble [worth] two shillings, one pair of Silver Studs [worth] two shillings, five Ribbon head knots [worth] Ten shillings, one Pen knife [worth] one shilling, one Lace [worth] three pence, one Pin Cushion [worth] five pence and ten Needles [worth] ten pence ... in the whole amounting unto one Pound [£1] fourteen shillings and six pence ... Hugh Fouch and Mary English [testifying, James is found] ... Guilty ... the Offence aforesaid being within the benefit of Clergy ... [he is sentenced to receive] at the public Whiping Post [39] lashes on his bare Back well laid on." Book A, pp. 382-383; and see Glossary.

August 27, 1760 - Thomas Donohoe is brought before the Court "on suspicion ... of Felony ... Mark Chelton, James Goulding and Daniel Reedy [testifying, Donohoe is bound over for trial of a misdemeanor to be held] ... here [in Leesburg] on the second Tuesday in November next." There is no additional information, or the final disposition, recorded. Book A, p. 400.

November 12, 1760 - "John Riley was bound by recognizance [bond] to appear ... came not [for his trial] ... Ordered by the Court that Hugh West Gent. Deputy [King's] Attorney Prosecute the said Recognizance against Francis Dade, Griffith Meyrick and Davis Smith Securities [on Riley's appearance bond, having a total penalty in the sum of £200] for the said John Riley's Appearance." Book A, p. 402; and see supra, entry for June 28, 1760.

November 12, 1760 - Pierce Butler [aka Peirce Butler], who was initially charged with "Stealing a Mare the property of Adam Payne and an Iron Kettle and Bell the property of Charles Burkom [of Frederick County, with] ... John Daughedy [sic- of Frederick County], John Haven and Mary Haven [all testifying, a jury finds Butler] Guilty of [the misdemeanor of] Stealing a horse Bell," and Butler is fined Fifty shillings and required to post a Bond for his good behavior. Book A, p. 407; and see supra, entry for June 17, 1760.

December 31, 1760 - Joshua Morgan is charged with "stealing a Mare the property of Christopher Bealor of Frederick County ... [with] William Sewell and William James [both of Fairfax County] and Christian Harnes [testifying witnesses], Christopher Bealor and Benjamin Bealor ... [who were also] summoned [as witnesses] but did not appear ... [Morgan is indicted by the Loudoun Court for felony theft and bound over for trial] at the General Court in Williamsburg." Book A, pp. 408-409; see supra, entry of June 28, 1760.

June 10, 1761 - James Kanneday, [aka James Kannaday], charged with "Stealing a Shirt, a Waistcoat and some Stocking thread the property of Henry O'Daniel ... Mary O'Daniel and Sarah Ponel [testifying, Kanneday is found] ... Guilty of a Misdemeanor ... Ordered that he give Security for his good Behavior." The next day he posted a good behavior Bond and was released from custody. Book A, pp. 459 and 463.

July 14, 1761 - Jacob Shilling, charged with "taking a Bell on the Kings highway the property of Robert Worthing ... Jacob is [found] not Guilty of the Fact laid to his charge ... acquitted & discharged." Book A, p. 478.

October 13, 1761 - Charles Cole, charged "with the Felonious Stealing [of] one Earthern Stone or Delph Mugg ... and one Glass Pocket Bottle ... the property of James Vessell ... [Cole is found] not Guilty ... prosecution be dismissed." Book A, p. 527.

November 9, 1761 - Charles Cole is charged with "Stealing a Great Coat the property of William Dodd, one fine shirt the property of William Baker, one handkerchief the property of John Heryford, one handkerchief the property of James Vessell, one Great Coat the property of John Moss, two handkerchiefs the property of John Davis and one shirt the property of John Dodd ... Margaret Heryford, Catherine Dodd, Robert Silwood, Sarah Vessell, John Thomas, John Chiles and Benjamin Hisket [all testifying against him, Cole is found] ... Guilty of Petit Larceny in Stealing a shirt the property of John Dodd and a handkerchief the property of John Heryford ... the value of eleven pence ... [Rather than insisting on his right to a jury trial, Cole submitted] to the Judgment of the [Loudoun County] Justices sitting ... [is to be given] ten lashes on his Bare Back and [then ordered to] stand in the Pillory ten minutes." Book A, pp. 527-528.

November 11, 1761 - John Wells, charged and tried with "Felonious stealing two narrow Axes and two drawing knives the property of John Trammell ... William Trammell, Samuel Patterson, Thomas Phillips and Patrick McKenzey [all four from the 'Lost Corner' area, testifying] against him ... [Wells is found] Guilty of a Misdemeanor ... Ordered that he enter into Recognizance [bond] ... for his good Behavior." Book A, p. 531.

March 10, 1762 - Patrick O'Cain, charged with "Stealing on the last Night a Bridle and Saddle the property of John Cargyle [sic - either John Cargill or John Carlyle], a Bridle the property of John Sasser and a Bridle the property of William Beavis, one Bell and a Petticoat the property of John Davis ... he confessed that he was thereof Guilty ... [sentenced to receive] at the Public Whiping Post thirty Lashes on his Bare Back well laid on." Book A, p. 563.

March 23, 1762 - William McDaniell, charged with "Forging of five Treasurer Notes two of ... Ten shillings each and three of ... Five shillings each ... Henry Moore, Daniel Deskins, Burkett Jett, Charles Eskridge, James Whaley, John Miller, William Sears and John Goddard [all from the Rocky Run area on the Mountain Road, testifying, McDaniell is found not guilty of felony but] ... Guilty of a Misdemeanor ... [sentenced to have] twenty Lashes Well laid on." Charles Binns records his fee for the trial as 200 lbs. of tobacco for "attending and examining." Order Book A, p. 582; Clerk's 1762 Fee Book, last page.

May 11, 1762 - Samuel Jenkins, Silvanus Lay and Immanuel Lay are charged by James Whaley with "Stealing of a Hogg ... Moses Thomas, William Suddith, Richard Spurr, Mary Golly, Mary Smith, James Coleman and Robert Stephens [all testifying]," the defendants are bound over to the Sheriff's custody for their trial at the next County Grand Jury. Book A, p. 586.

June 1, 1762 - Mary Rogers and Margaret Walker are charged with the felony of "breaking open Clater Smith's House and stealing thereout Pewter ... Vizt. [two] Basons, one Dish, [six] Plates and one Butter Pot ... Elizabeth Hedgbrough [testifying]." They are both bound over for a felony trial in Williamsburg, with "Margaret Walker remanded to Goal" and Mary Rogers allowed to post Bond for her appearance with her husband James Rogers as Security. Loudoun Clerk Charles Binns records his fee as 200 lbs. of tobacco for attending the trial. Order Book A, p. 624; Clerk's 1762 Fee Book, last page.

June 3, 1762 - Piers Butler is charged with "High Treason" on the complaint of "John Mucklehaney Gent.," found "Guilty of a Misdemeanor" and required to give Security and post a Bond for his good behavior. The Clerk's fee is 200 lbs. of tobacco. Order Book A, p. 624; Clerk's 1762 Fee Book, last page.

June 8, 1762 - On an appeal to the full Loudoun County Court, "Patrick McKenzie [claiming he was] Convicted of Gaming contrary to Law [by] ... Nicholas Minor and James Lane Gent. Justices ... Patrick Appealed to the Court ... Patrick not appearing ... the Judgment ... [was] affirmed ... the Churchwardens of Cameron Parish recover ... for the use of the Poor ... the sum of Five Pounds Current Money with Costs &c." Book A, p. 628.

June 10, 1762 - "Ordered that [attorney] William Ellzey receive from the Counties of Surry, Sussex, Southampton, Lancaster & King William the Tobacco due from the said Counties respectively to this County for their several Proportions of Criminals." Book A, p. 635.

August 30, 1762 - John Wollamsley [sic- alias John Walton ?] is charged "of Robbing Christopher Perfect a Constable in his Office, of a Mare ... Robert Popkins and Sarah Vessells [testifying] ... he is acquitted and discharged." Charles Binns' fee for "attending and examining" at the trial is 200 lbs. of tobacco. Book B, p. 53; Clerk's 1762 Fee Book, last page.

December 14, 1762 - John McGinnis is charged with "Stealing a Cock [a fighting chicken, or gamecock] the property of Robert Hamilton ... Sarah Berkley [testifying, McGinnis is found] ... Guilty for suffering disorderly Behavior in his House ... ordered to give Security for his good Behavior." What a gamecock was doing at McGinnis' ordinary, we can only guess. Book B, p. 77.

April 12, 1763 - James Vessells, charged with "felony ... Craven Peyton, Aneas Campbell, Gent., John Moss Junr. [three of the Loudoun Justices], Micajah Powell and Daniel Lawrence [all five testifying, the Court finds that Vessells is] ... not Guilty ... Acquitted and discharged." Book B, p. 84.

April 12, 1763 - Frederick Grider Junr., Zachariah Thomas and Philip Arrants are charged with "making & passing base or Counterfeit Money ... Israel Thompson and Ann Thompson his wife (Quakers) ... John Newlan, Thomas Pursley and James Buffenton [all residents at the Gap of Short Hill, testifying]," the defendants are bound over for trial in Williamsburg. Book B, p. 84.

April 15, 1763 - Patrick McKenzey, charged "with the felonious taking [of] a Bell, a Bell Collar, and Buckle the property of William Schooley ... Sylvester Tipton and John Wells [testifying against him, McKenzey is found] ... not Guilty ... he is Acquitted and discharged" from custody. Book B, p. 112.

May 12, 1763 - A jury finds John Walmsley [aka John Walmsly] guilty of "committing a Perjury in [falsely] Swearing to a Plea," Walmsley "prays that the Judgment may be Arrested and staid [sic] &c.." Book B, pp. 72 and 150.

May 12, 1763 - After no Grand Jury is convened in November of 1762, Silvanus Lay, Abraham Lay, Emanuel Lay and Samuel Jenkins are finally tried for hog stealing. James Hook, Thomas Pritchard, Hugh French, Benjamin Mason, James Spencer, Benjamin Hough, Joseph West, Thomas Connell, Daniel Miller, Joseph Jones, John Lewis and John Sinclair all testify against them. A jury finds Abraham Lay not Guilty and the other three Guilty. Silvanus, Emanuel and Samuel are sentenced to receive twenty-five lashes "on their bare back well laid on." Their Motions for Appeal are rejected by the Court, and each of them, in order "to avoid the Whipping paid down ... the sum of Ten Pounds [in Virginia currency]." Book B, pp. 154-155; and see supra, entry for May 11, 1762.

May 24, 1763 - Elizabeth Griffin, charged with "Stealing one Dollar of the value of five Shillings and nine pence Current Money [ie., £1 = $3.48] the property of John McGinnis ... John McGinnis and his wife Sarah McGinnis, Barbara Zeahon and Mary Zeahon [all testifying, Griffin is found] ... not Guilty ... She is Acquitted and Discharged" from custody. Book B, p. 158.

March 14, 1764 - Alexander Bowling and John Fouch are charged with "Stealing an Ax the property of Hugh Fouch ... Jacob Shilling, James Abbett and James Ross [testifying, both of the defendants are] acquitted and discharged." Book B, p. 281.

August 16, 1764 - John Lewis is charged with "Passing Counterfeit Treasury Notes of this Colony ... Kitchen Prim, George Russell and Ann Russell [testifying, the Loudoun Court rules that Lewis] ... ought to be tried on the Sixth Day of the next General Court [in Williamsburg] and thereupon he is remanded to [the Sheriff and the Loudoun] Goal." Book B, p. 430.

August 22, 1764 - [Leesburg Doctor] John Urquhart is charged with "Stealing one pound of Tea the property of Joseph Craig ... Craig failing to appear ... [Dr. Urquhart is] acquitted and Discharged." Book B, p. 431.

October 8, 1764 - In the arraignment of Francis Kennady [Francis Kennedy], charged in "the murder of John Owsley of this County ... [with witnesses] Newdigate Owsley, Sarah Owsley and William Patterson [testifying, Kennady was bound over] ... to be tried for the [murder] at the next Court of Oyer and Terminer to be held at the Capitol in Williamsburg on the second Tuesday in December [1764]." Book B, p. 472; see infra, entries for 1765-1766.

December 20, 1764 - After hearing of a verdict in a jury trial before the General Court in Williamsburg, Governor Fauquier writes to Virginia's agent in London, James Abercromby, initiating a correspondence aimed at obtaining a Royal Pardon for Loudoun's Francis Kennedy. Fauquier Papers, Vol. 3, p. 1198.

February 26, 1765 - Regarding the Francis Kennedy case, James Abercromby, Virginia's agent in London, advises Virginia Governor Fauquier "to write the Lords of Trade [since] the King requires [information of] all circumstances in cases of Murder." Letterbook, pp. 426-427.

June 13, 1765 - Mary Duffy and Mary McDonald, who are convict servants, are charged with "Stealing several Pennsylvania Bills & several Dollars to the amount of Twenty odd pounds [currency] the Property of [two Loudoun County merchants] Joseph Janney & Joseph Hough ... [with] John Moss, Patrick McCarty, Bridgett Sheeley, Matthew Campbell and Jemima McCarty [all giving testimony] ... it appearing to the Court that Charles Secrest was concerned in the same being a Partner [in the commission of the crimes] ... Ordered that the said Mary Duffy and Charles Secrest each of them receive on their bare Backs [39] Lashes Well laid on ... Mary McDonald be pillored [sic] [on the Courthouse lawn] fifteen Minutes and receive on her bareback [39] Lashes well laid on at the Common Whipping Post." Book B, pp. 672-673.

August 1, 1765 - In a long-delayed letter, finally read by the Board of Trade in London on September 24th, Governor Fauquier writes that "Francis Kennedy was tried [before the Virginia Council in December of 1764] at a Court of Oyer and Terminer in which I did not sit, but he was recommended ... for Mercy by the unanimous Voice of the Court." In his letter, the good Governor provides us with a detailed account of the occasion of John Owsley's death, which, being a singular event in the early life of Loudoun County, bears repeating:

> *"On the Trial of Francis Kennedy for the Murder of John Owsley - The Case by the Evidence of Sarah Owsley Wife of the deceased and one other Witness ... Owsley, his Wife and the said Kennedy with several others happening in Company, a Quarrel ensued, upon which they all got to fighting. Kennedy receiving a blow from some[one] of the Company with a Club; he in order to defend himself drew his knife, with which he cut the forehead of the said Owsley, and then stabed [sic] him in the Thigh which unfortunately cut some principal Artery, the bleeding of which ... Owsley in a few hours died ..."*

In the official justification of his request for the King's Royal pardon for Francis Kennedy, Governor Fauquier went on to remark that, as:

> *"the Affair was transacted in passion ... Kennedy not having time for cool reflection, and [there being] no premeditated Malice between [Kennedy and Owsley ... the Council, sitting as*

a Court, was unanimous in its] Opinion ... that the Jury should have found him guilty of Manslaughter and not of Murder." Fauquier Papers, Vol. 3, pp. 1226 and 1270.

October 7, 1765 - John Maris, charged with "Stealing a Negro Man Slave named Abram belonging to the Estate of George Eskridge, deceased ... Peter Mullins, Richard Eskridge, Burdit Eskridge, John Goram Junr. and Thomas Marbury [all testifying, for trial Maris is] ... sent to ... Maryland where the Fact was committed ... in Dorset County." Book C, p. 58.

November 8, 1765 - The Board of Trade advises Virginia Governor Fauquier that "His Majesty having been graciously pleased ... to extend His Royal Mercy and Pardon to Francis Kennedy" of Loudoun County. The Royal Pardon for Kennedy was to be enrolled among a listing of the pardons for prisoners at England's infamous Newgate prison. Fauquier Papers, Vol. 3, p. 1302.

April 14, 1766 - William McCaffrey, who is charged with "taking some Quantity of Wheat & sundry other things ... of Charles Chinn ... [the Court finds] the Proceedings [are] Illegal ... [the case is] Dismissed." Book C, p. 74.

May 12, 1766 - Jeremiah Foster is appointed Surveyor of the Mountain Road "from Rogue's Road [sic- the Carolina Road at West's Ordinary] to Piney Branch [near the Cameron parish glebe]," with Justice William Carr Lane appointed to assign the hands for road work. This appears to be the first official reference to the "Rogue's Road," the moniker that was given to the colonial Carolina Road after a certain banditti element has begun to make their presence felt between Leesburg and Haymarket. Book C, p. 77.

June 28, 1766 - Richard Pearl is found guilty of the misdemeanor theft of "a narrow Ax the property of Thomas Dodd," based on the testimony of John Dodd, Patrick Bruff and George Squires. The Court orders Pearl to post a personal recognizance bond. Book C, p. 138.

July 12, 1766 - John McCollum is found Guilty of Petit Larceny in "stealing one Saddle of the Price of thirty five Shillings the property of John Fanning," based on the testimony of John Fanning, Martin Lehon [sic] and Richard Coombs. McCollum is sentenced to have "thirty-nine Lashes on his bare Back well laid on ..." at the "public Whiping Post." Book C, p. 139.

October 13, 1766 - Zachariah Hurley, brought before the Court "on Suspicion of .... the Murder of William Snider ... Thomas Price, Henry Snider, Adam Counts and Robert Jackson [all testifying] ... the said Zachariah is [found to be] not Guilty of the Murder." Book C, p. 205.

October 13, 1766 - In "Proceedings ... against James Herryford for [beating and the] Abuse [of] Jane Macintire the wife of Alexander Macintire ... [after the testimony of the parties is taken and] fully heard ... [the case is] dismissed." Book C, p. 207.

November 13, 1766 - John Butler, brought before the Court "For Hogstealing ... [the Court finds] the Proceedings are illegal ... [and the case is] dismissed." Book C, p. 230.

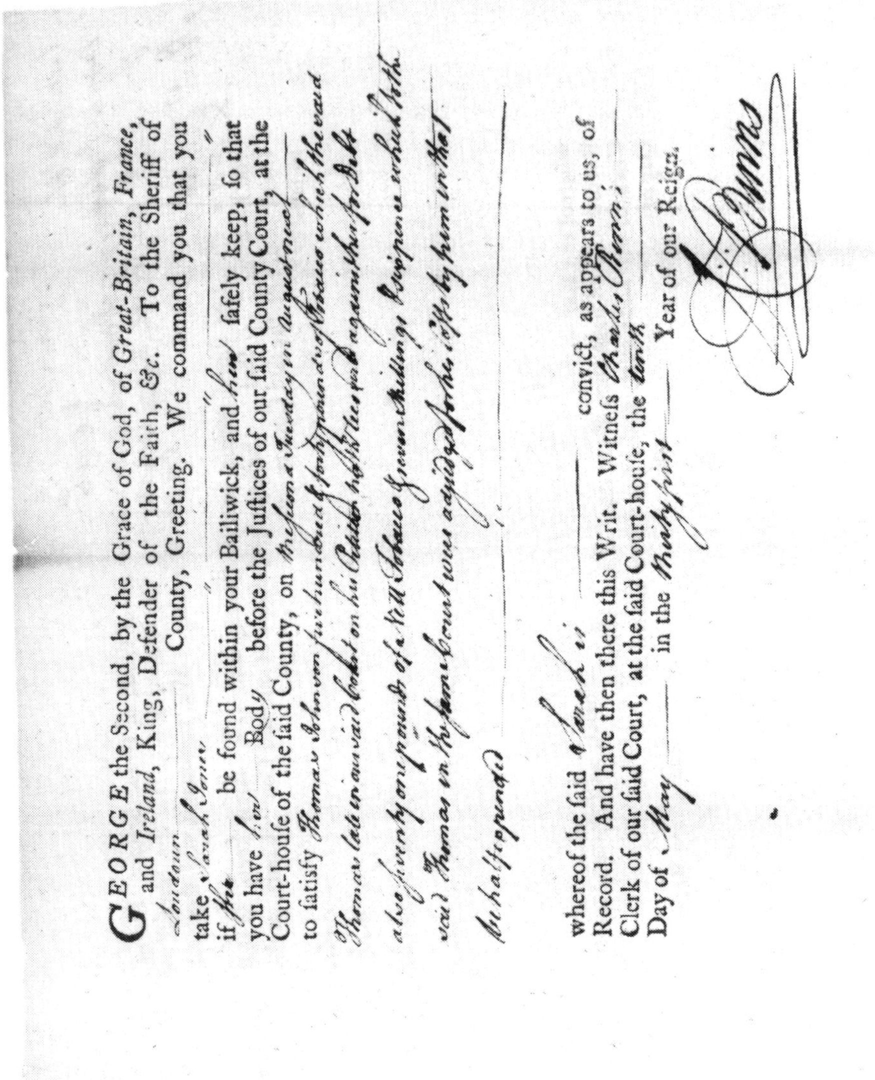

GEORGE the Second, by the Grace of God, of *Great-Britain, France,* and *Ireland,* King, Defender of the Faith, *&c.* To the Sheriff of Loudoun County, Greeting. We command you that you take Sarah Jones if she be found within your Bailiwick, and her safely keep, so that you have her Body before the Justices of our said County Court, at the Court-house of the said County, on the second Tuesday in August next to satisfy Thomas Johnson five hundred & forty pounds of Tobacco which the said Thomas lately in our said Court [illegible] against her for debt also [illegible] shillings & [illegible] pence which to the said Thomas in the same Court were adjudged for his costs by him in that behalf expended whereof the said Sarah is convict, as appears to us, of Record. And have then there this Writ. Witness Charles Binns, Clerk of our said Court, at the said Court-house, the tenth Day of May in the thirty first Year of our Reign.

C. Binns

This Arrest Warrant was issued on May 10, 1758 for Sarah Jones, a judgment debtor, and returned by Loudoun's first Sheriff Aeneas Campbell, who noted that the warrant was "Executed, the Body in Custody." Sarah Jones became Loudoun County's first bankrupt individual (then called an "insolvent debtor"). Three weeks after she had been jailed on this warrant for debts totalling a little under £4½, Sarah Jones petitioned the Loudoun County Court from gaol, declared herself "insolvent," gave the Court a list of her property for the benefit of her creditors, and was released from the Loudoun jail. See infra, pp. 175-178 and 181. [HDC]

Debtors, Insolvents and Peace Bonds

The expeditious resolution of commercial disputes and the determination and collection of just debts were primary causes for the organization of the colonial justice system in general, and Virginia's county court system in particular. English merchants and their colonial factors (agents) had a deep and abiding interest in the subject, and they exerted a constant influence, through the King's Board of Trade, to insure that colonial book debts were translated into acceptable trading profits. The everyday business of the colony was reflected in the law suits that were brought in the county courts. There were so many law suits regarding debts during Loudoun's first decade that time constraints compel the identification and discussion of but a small representative sample.

"For the more speedy recovery of small debts," all cases under £5 that were brought to a county court on a sworn petition were decided "without the solemnity of a jury." A controversy involving less than 25 shillings was the colonial equivalent of a small claim and was resolved by any individual county Justice. No records of "small" cases survive except in rare instances where one litigant demanded a re-hearing before the full county court, claiming that a larger sum was at issue. Colonial law encouraged the resolution of disputes while they were small. Inn keepers generally could not collect book debts over 20 shillings for liquor sold in an ordinary, surveyors of land could not accept promissory notes in payment for their services, and almost all civil fines were under the jurisdiction of a single Justice. Even so, actions to recover debt constitute roughly 90% of entries in the Loudoun County Court Order books. In the 1760s, it was not unusual to find Loudoun's colonial residents litigating on one account in Court and, at the same time, trading with their adversary on a new account. Short of literally transcribing those volumes of records (a task foregone at this juncture), there is no way that anyone can undertake a complete study of the many legal actions for the recovery of debts in colonial Loudoun. [Hening, V/498 and VI/66; infra, Chapter on Ordinaries; but contra, Democracy].

Colonials in Loudoun did not have to travel very far to borrow money or trade on credit. Proprietors of the Loudoun ordinaries, when they could find the space, would stock the farming and hunting implements, hardware and grocery items that were in demand in their neighborhood. Merchants and importers based in Colchester, Alexandria, Dumfries, and Frederick, Maryland, and from as far away as Philadelphia, sent or appointed agents or formed partnerships with Leesburg residents to facilitate trading at the monthly sessions of the Loudoun County Court. The large majority of debt cases in colonial Loudoun were for small sums, but court-goers occasionally would be treated to a controversy of seemingly vast proportions. Two Leesburg merchants and land speculators were Loudoun County's largest debtors in the 1760s. Englishman Fleming Patterson (brother and business partner of the Earl of Tankerville's land agent), and Craven Peyton (scion of a tidewater family of tobacco magnates and owner of Leesburg's largest colonial ordinary), each used their extensive land holdings as collateral, and the good offices of friends in Alexandria trading houses, to obtain large sums from London financiers. [see Democracy, pp. 102-108 and 121].

The 1748 Assembly adopted the law that governed creditor-debtor rights during Loudoun County's first decade. One extraordinary recourse that was available to colonial creditors was the preliminary attachment of an alleged debtor's assets. If the initial court summons of a debtor was returned "not found," a creditor had the option of reissuing the summons or proceeding directly with an attachment of the debtor's goods and property, before judgment in his case! Individual Justices were empowered to grant pre-judgment attachments against property and the estate of any debtor when, "upon complaint to him made by any person, [he was told that a] debtor [was secretly] removing out of the county and conceals himself." If a debt was over 25 shillings, the Sheriff would be directed to "levy ... upon the slaves, goods and chattels of the party absconding, wherever the same shall be found" and, to summon any garnishee to appear at the next county court "to answer upon oath what he or she is indebted unto such party, and what effects" of the debtor were in the garnishee's possession. The Sheriff, a deputy (called a Sub-Sheriff) or any county constable could then pursue and seize the effects of the debtor anywhere in Virginia, without a formal petition of the creditor. The Sheriff reported directly to the Justice that was named in the writ in a "small" case, or to the next full county court when the amount in controversy was over 25 shillings. An indemnity bond from the creditor, for double the debt claimed, was the only other prerequisite to issuance of the colonial prejudgment writ of attachment. [Hening, V/489-508, @ V/492-494].

Debtors and garnishees could redeem attached property before a law suit went to court by appearing, with another creditworthy individual acting as surety, and posting a bond with the Sheriff that required the debtor's or garnishee's appearance at court for the hearing of the case. The debtor and his security would be bound "to abide by and perform the order and judgment of such court." In instances of redemption, the Sheriff was personally liable for an insufficient bond or security, so property redemptions were surely undertaken at full arm's length. When an execution was made against a debtor's "estate," within five days or as late as "at the time of sale ... [the debtor could] tender sufficient sureties approved of by the creditor ... to pay the [judgment] debt and costs, with lawful interest," and have his property restored to his possession. [Hening, V/493 and VII/641-642].

"Under the common law of England, and divers acts of Parliament," a creditor with a judgment from a court of record (a county court in colonial Virginia) could, "at [his] election prosecute writs ... within the year ... taking the goods, lands, or body of the person or persons against whom such judgment [was] obtained." A judgment that was more than one year old was considered stale, and an unsatisfied creditor presumably had to return to court to obtain a new judgment. "Taking the body" meant, literally, just that. As in England, a judgment debtor could be jailed until either his debts were paid or a secured bond was posted for the benefit of his creditors. When a colonial debtor was jailed, if he could not find a security for his obligations and refused to declare himself "insolvent," the debtor could, at the option of his creditor, be held in jail indefinitely. Prisoners in jail customarily paid for their own keep, which included processing and release fees and all daily jailer charges. There were so many debtors in Virginia jails when the colonial capital was moved to Williamsburg in 1700 that authorities were compelled to build a public prison expressly to house the debtors. The 1705 Assembly revised the debtor laws to allow for the release of insolvents after "only" three months in jail. [Hening, III/385-389 and V/527; Democracy, pp. 102-112].

The procedure whereby a colonist became surety on a bond to guarantee the payment of the judgment debts of another was known as giving a "special bail" or "mainprize." Any plaintiff could request that a "defendant ... be held to special bail." County courts had the discretion, upon a motion and showing of cause, to commit defendants "in[to] the custody of the Sheriff 'till such bail be given." When judgment was given in a case where a "specialty" bond had been given, a common occurrence in the Loudoun Court up to 1766, the penalty amount of the bond (double the debt) was given for the judgment, with a proviso entered that the judgment could be discharged by the voluntary payment of the debt with interest. If the debtor then failed to pay or surrender himself for arrest after an adverse judgment, the surety on the "special bail" was subject to arrest and imprisonment in the debtor's stead. When the principal debtor surrendered himself to the court, the bailment was discharged. Special bail was only allowed in civil cases, and not in criminal cases. [Hening, IV/406 and V/495; for example, see re Linton and Simms, infra, @ pp. 184-185].

Virginia's 1705 insolvency law also formalized a practice that had been followed throughout the 1600s. An insolvent could retain a suit of clothing, valued at less than 50 shillings, and his set of militia arms as exempt from his creditors' claims. The 1726 Assembly, accounting for a widespread need for skilled artisans, allowed an insolvent a set of tradesmen's tools and additional wearing apparel as exempt property. During the French War, the "estate" of every Virginia soldier was exempted from attachment for debts of under £10 or 2,000 lbs. of tobacco. Before 1714, essentially all of a debtors assets, except for lands, were subject to sale at public outcry. This meant that when a Sheriff seized goods or slaves under an attachment based on a judgment debt, he could proceed to sell the property on fairly short notice if there was a ready buyer. In 1734, Parliament determined that all lands in the colonies would be subject to public auction for the satisfaction of debts, prompting an increased use of "entail" covenants in Virginia real estate conveyances. [Hening, III/385-389, IV/151, IV/452 and VI/521-530; see Chapter on Militia, supra, @ p. 70].

Virginia's colonial usury law of 1730 set the allowable interest rate at 6%. Legal interest was reduced to 5% by the 1748 Assembly, the maximum allowable interest rate that was in force at the time of the American Revolution. A 5% interest rate was imposed on every judgment of the colonial Loudoun County Court. [Hening, IV/294 and V/101; see, Democracy, p. 111].

The Assembly composed and codified standard forms for the writs of execution that were used against debtors in Virginia. The cotton rag paper that was used for the forms had the King's Coat of Arms and Seal in the watermark and was supplied from London under Royal contract. After printing presses were brought to Virginia in the 1720s, these forms were printed in Williamsburg and then made available to Virginia's county clerks. Loudoun County's first Clerk, Charles Binns, must have obtained a stack of these printed forms when he took office. The earliest Loudoun Court documents that have survived for our examination were, for the most part, composed on these standard forms. [Hening, V/522 and V/527; supra, Arrest Warrant on p. 172; generally, see HDC; but see Order Upon an Attachment, infra, p. 187].

By 1726, the incarceration of judgment debtors had become such a burden on the Virginia colony that the Assembly enacted a new colonial "insolvency" law, providing that debtors could be released after spending three weeks in jail if they surrendered all of their assets to the county Sheriff. A public allowance of 6 pence per day (the price of a night in an ordinary) was granted to jailers "where any such prisoner shall be so poor as not to be able to maintain and subsist [ie., pay for] himself ... in prison." Unless the judgment creditor posted a bond for the costs of the prison fees that were anticipated past the third week, the Sheriff was supposed to release the debtor from his custody. Most Loudoun County debtors were housed in the Leesburg jail, but the east wing of the Williamsburg jail was still "appropriated and kept for the receiving and safe keeping of debtors" during the 1750s. [Hening, IV/151-167, V/522 and VI/135].

"For the relief of insolvent debtors," the 1753 Assembly provided that an insolvent who had been in jail for 20 days could be released from custody if he delivered a schedule of his entire estate, which would be sold for the benefit of his creditors. The debtor was required to swear or affirm that the schedule was a "just true and perfect, account and discovery of all the estate, goods and effects ... anywise belonging, and [all] such debts" that were owed to him. As a practical matter, insolvents often had to wait in jail for five or six weeks for the next county court session, like Loudoun County's John Anderson did in 1765. To assist merchants in identifying debt-troubled colonists, every county clerk transmitted "a true copy of all proceedings in [their county] court" to the clerk of the General Court within a month of the discharge of an insolvent. Unlike today, a discharge for insolvency did not wipe out the insolvent's debts unless the property that the debtor surrendered was of sufficient value. Judgment creditors could and did "have execution against any lands or tenements, goods or chattels which such insolvent person" acquired or was found to possess after the declaration of insolvency. [Hening, VI/136, VI/342-344 and VII/549; see infra, p. 185].

The 1762 Assembly, following the lead of Richard Henry Lee, attempted to liberalize the insolvency laws to enable debtors to retain more of their assets, provide for proportional distribution to creditors, and allow for the full discharge of all debts in the process. But the next session, five months later, thought the new law would be "injurious to the credit of this colony, and ... of evil consequence to the trade thereof," and voided the Act before its effective date. The King's colonial Board of Trade issued a contemporaneous rejection of the new law, which would have given the same result. [Hening, VII/549-562 and VII/643].

Sheriffs would assist any creditor with a fresh court order and a writ of attachment in the collection of their judgment debt. Where there was an arrears of quit-rents, public levies or officers' fees, Sheriffs were also instructed to "make distress for the same, upon the slaves, goods or chattels of the person or persons so chargeable, and make a sale thereof ... to be accounted for and paid by such Sheriff," after taking an allowance of 6% "for collecting and paying the same." Virginia's colonial Sheriffs and county jailors were not particularly happy to see anyone declare themselves insolvent. The 1765 Assembly specified that a Sheriff's commission in an insolvency was limited to a percentage of the total value of the scheduled assets surrendered, regardless of the net worth of any special bail or surety, or the penalty value of any bond that had been given. Thus, a declaration of insolvency often meant that the Sheriff or county jailor could take only a nominal fee for his troubles. [Hening, III/385-389 and VIII/122-123].

Sheriffs could be held accountable for the obligations of debtors they had arrested who subsequently escaped and, of course, where a debtor's assets were attached and auctioned but the proceeds were not paid to the creditor. By 1765,

> *"many controversies and disputes [had] arisen concerning the duty of Sheriffs upon prisoners in*

execution for debt escaping and going at large out of the prison rules [bounds], where they obtained the liberty of the same by giving bond and security."

New procedures were adopted. In the event that a debtor escaped from jail, the Sheriff was required to go to one of the county Justices immediately, apply "for an escape warrant to retake such prisoner," and then give notice to the creditor "at whose suit [the debtor had been] in custody." The creditor had the option of proceeding in court against the security for the bond of the debtor, and the creditor could claim against the Sheriff if the security who was "taken [for] such prisoner for the liberty of the prison rules shall afterwards be found to have been insufficient." [Hening, V/496, VI/344 and VIII/118; re prison rules and bounds, see Chapter on Sheriffs and the Gaol, supra pp. 143-144].

As early as 1736, jail-breaks of colonial debtors caused concern in the Virginia Assembly. Incidents of debtor escapes from various county jails eventually led the 1766 Assembly to enact specific provisions "for the punishment of persons who ... assist prisoners for debt to escape." Thereafter, anyone aiding an escape attempt, or causing "to be conveyed into any gaol or prison any instrument or arms whatever, proper to facilitate the escape of any prisoner," would be subject to a fine and imprisonment. If the offender could not pay the fine that was imposed, he was to "receive on his bare back twenty-one lashes well laid on." A standard one year statute of limitations was imposed for the prosecution of an offence. [Hening, IV/487 and VIII/240-241].

The 1748 Assembly provided for the restraint of "divers idle and disorderly persons ... [who] frequently strole from one county to another, neglecting to labour ... by their idle and disorderly life, rendering themselves incapable of paying their levies." Thereafter, "strolling persons" and able bodied persons,

"loitering, and neglecting to labour for reasonable wages; all persons who run from their habitations, and leave wives and children; ... and all other idle, vagrant, or dissolute persons, wandering abroad ... shall be ... adjudged rogues and vagabonds."

A rogue was treated and punished like a runaway servant and, at the direction of any individual Justice of the Peace, was to be whipped and then conveyed by the constables to the parish "where he ... did last reside." At his home county, a vagrant was held in jail until he gave "sufficient security [ie., a bond] for his ... good behavior, and for betaking himself ... to some lawful calling or honest labour." Vagrants who had failed to establish a residence by living in any parish for one full year were jailed and tried in the county where they were arrested. County courts could sell a vagrant "[in]to service, on wages, for the term of one year" if he failed to give proper security. A vagabond of "such evil repute, that no person will receive him ... into service," was summarily given 39 lashes at the public whipping-post. Absolom Mullenax, the first prosecution in Loudoun under the vagrancy statutes, was released from the Raspberry Plain jail on a recognizance bond in October of 1757, but then disappeared from Loudoun County. [Hening, VI/29-33 and VII/549; re runaways, see infra, Chapter on Servants, and Chapter on Slaves].

Virginia's county court Justices could require the posting of a bond with surety in a number of other circumstances: for the performance of a public construction contract; as a condition for the release of attached assets; to guarantee an appearance at trial; and to guarantee good behavior. The latter was commonly called a "Peace Bond." Based on the prohibition against "disorderly persons" in the "Rogues Statute," Peace Bonds came into fashion in Loudoun County in 1764.

The Record contains an interesting narration of Leesburg's first "riot," which took place in February of 1762, during the Loudoun County Court Days. One "rioter," John Davis, would be ruled "a common Disturber of the Peace," be required to post several good behavior bonds, became an object of contempt in the Loudoun community when a posse was organized for his arrest in 1764, and ultimately be prosecuted on his bond for additional public disturbances. Sometimes, family feuds got out of hand. John Galloway's children were cited in 1761 on the complaint of William Trammell, and two years later Galloway took revenge with a complaint against William's brother. The first Loudoun County prosecution on an appearance bond apparently occurred in 1763, when John Trammell failed to answer Galloway's complaint. When the terms of a peace or appearance bond were violated, the County Court would order the Deputy King's Attorney, Hugh West, to prosecute the bond. As in modern times, this amounted to suing the sureties if they did not pay the penal amount of the bond voluntarily. [infra, The Record, pp. 182-184].

Peace Bonds were required of the high and low alike. The Loudoun County Court frequently required a recognizance bond of any "disorderly person" who was disturbing the peace. After Cameron parish Churchwarden John Owsley was accidentally killed in a tavern brawl in 1764, personal disputes ended up in front of the County Court with increasing frequency. Colonial Loudoun's "bad boy barrister," Francis Dade, was brought in to answer the charges of Leesburg innkeeper John Herryford; even William West, an ordinary keeper and a retired Loudoun Justice, was required to post a bond for <u>his</u> good behavior. The trend continued throughout 1765, but there were fewer incidents involving tavern keepers. [infra, The Record, pp. 184-184; re Dade, Chapter on Attorneys, supra, @ pp. 100 and 107; re Owsley, Chapter on Crimes, supra, @ p. 169-170].

The Loudoun Record

August 10, 1757 - Throughout the latter part of the Colonial period, Judgment interest is awarded to successful plaintiffs in Virginia's county courts at the rate of 5% per annum. Book A, p. 5.

October 11, 1757 - Absolam Mullenax is charged by Ezekial Hickman and William Williams "with being a Stroling Person and not taking any care for a Livelyhood ... [he is] discharged" on his Recognizance. Book A, pp. 27-28.

November 8, 1757 - Anthony Parker and his wife Margaret Parker give a Peace Bond to satisfy the Complaint of Elizabeth Gibson. Book A, p. 42.

April 12, 1758 - "Petition of Thomas Johnson against Sarah Jones for a Debt due by Account. Hugh West Gent. [as the attorney for Johnson] became Security to pay the Clerk's and Sheriffs fees ... fully heard ... the Plt. recover against the said Deft. [540 lbs.] of Tobacco [worth about £3] and his costs ... including seven shillings and six pence for a Lawyer's fee." Book A, p. 96; and see Chapter on the Courthouse, Clerk of Court and Attornies, supra, p. 102.

June 14, 1758 - "Sarah Jones a Prisoner ... [in debt for about £4] at the suit of Thomas Johnson ... having remained in Goal [over 20] days, delivered a Schedule of her Estate and took the Oath ... for Insolvent Debtors ... [and was released from jail]." Book A, p. 119; see her Arrest Warrant, supra, p. 172.

July 11, 1758 - George Chelton and William Murphey are required to enter Peace Bonds to satisfy the Complaint of Thomas Kelley. Book A, p. 132.

July 12, 1758 - On a Writ of "Fifae" [sic- Fieri Facias, an attachment] issued against the goods and possessions of Philip Lynham, for a judgment debt;

William Owsley, a Loudoun County Sub-Sheriff, remarks on his return to the Court that "a mare and colt & a servant woman the above goods [were] replevied by the oath of John Stears and James Stears that the aforsaid [sic] good[s] were there [sic] property [ie., and not the property of Lynham]." [HDC]

September 26, 1758 - A Writ of Fifae [an attachment] is issued on the goods of William Berry for the judgment debt of 750 lbs. of tobacco and costs, owed to [Judge] Anthony Russell. Sub-Sheriff William Owsley noted that the writ was "Executed and the goods on hand [not sold] for want of Buyers." [HDC]

May 8, 1759 - "Thomas Botts ... in Prison ... twenty Daies [sic] ... delivered in a Schedule of his Estate and took the Oath ... for Insolvent Debtors." It was then ordered that Botts be released from jail. Book A, p. 235.

June 12, 1759 - Henry Rhoads is required to enter a Peace Bond to satisfy the Complaint brought against him by Andrew Adams. Book A, p. 246.

September 12, 1759 - "Aneas Campbell [immediate past Sheriff] ... delivered over to Nicholas Minor, Gent. ... present Sherif the following Prisoners ... on certain Writs of Executions Vizt. - Thomas Phillips at the suit of Ann Talbot for £22.4.6, 580 lb. tobo., [for] Debt, 15 shill. and 143 lb. tobo. costs ...; [and] James Compton at the suit of Robert Maxwell & Edward Maxwell for £1.3.6 [Pound.Shilling.Pence] & 905 lb. tobo." Book A, p. 292.

March Court of 1760 - In the case of Joseph Jones vs. Morris Turner, John Moss Junr., Sub-Sheriff, serves an attachment on "one Blanket and sheet, [belonging to Turner] and on his return to the Court notes that he "sold the goods within Ordered for two shillings & six pence in Money ..." [HDC]

June 10, 1760 - Pearce Butler is required to give a Peace Bond to satisfy the Complaint brought against him by John Haven. Book A, p. 362.

June 17, 1760 - In Ellzey vs. Whaley, on a warrant issued for the arrest of James Whaley for a judgment debt, Loudoun Sub-Sheriff John Minor Junr. notes on his return to Court that Whaley was "Not found [in my Bailiwick] ... Whaley lives near Frying Pan [then in eastern Loudoun County]." [HDC]

August 13, 1760 - "George Tavener ... in Prison for [over 20 days] ... delivered in a Schedule of his Estate and took the Oath ... for Insolvent Debtors ... that the Sherif forthwith set the said George at Liberty." Book A, p. 387.

February 10, 1761 - John Galloway Senr., on behalf of his infant children John Galloway Junr. and Mary Galloway, is required to enter a Peace Bond in satisfaction of the Complaint of William Trammell. Book A, p. 410.

October 13, 1761 - The Court discharges James Vessell from the "Complaint of Charles Cole, Labourer, against him for Breach of the Peace ... Cole failing to appear ..." Book A, p. 526.

February 9, 1762 - James Vessell is required to post a Peace Bond for his good behavior, on the complaint of Robert Hamilton. Book A, p. 553.

February 10, 1762 - "Samuel Davis Junr., John Davis, William Furr and William Allan ... behaving in a Riotous manner in breaking his Majesty's

Peace ... on the ninth day of this Instant in the Night time ... William Baker, William Winn, Archibald Crawford, Martin Armstrong, William West, Craven Peyton, Catharine Dodd, William Dodd and John Winn [all testifying]," all of the defendants are required to post a Peace Bond and give Security for their good behavior while awaiting trial at the next Loudoun Grand Jury. Book A, p. 556.

May 12, 1762 - "Samuel Davis [Junr.] of this County, Labourer, ... the Indictment against him Not a true Bill," he is discharged. John Davis, on the Indictment of the Grand Jury, is ordered to give "Security for his good behavior," posts a bond and is released from the Sheriff's custody. Book A, p. 600.

June 8, 1762 - John Thomas posts Security and gives a Peace Bond for his good behavior "on a Conviction for unlawful Gaming." Book A, p. 630.

July 13, 1762 - John Simms obtains a judgment against Thomas Eaton for £1, 19 shillings and 11 pence. Eaton's goods, including "one Cobler's Box, three shoe tacks and three Weavers stays," are attached. Book B, p. 2.

August 12, 1762 - Aneas Campbell obtains a judgment against Joseph West for £19, and an a attachment is "executed on one shoe awl" that is the property of West. Book B, p. 37.

August 12, 1762 - William Atterberry and John Morris are entered as Securities for the appearance of James Rogers in a case in debt. Book B, p. 39.

August 12, 1762 - Merchant Thomas Sligh obtains a judgment against Ralph Broadax, with a jury awarding 10,909 lbs. of tobacco [ie., roughly £68 Sterling!] as his damages. Book B, p. 46.

August 13, 1762 - When William Murphey obtains a jury verdict awarding him £20 for damages against Thomas Stump as the Executor of Robert Booth, deceased, the Loudoun Court finds that "the Damages are excessive a New Trial is granted ... at the next Court." Book B, p. 48.

December 15, 1762 - Constable Christopher Perfect, was required to post a Peace Bond on the complaint of Christopher Canouse. Book B, p. 81.

June 14, 1763 - Philamon Chesser, on the Complaint of Mary Miller, the wife of John Miller, is required to give "Security of the Peace for his good Behavior ..." Book B, p. 161.

June 15, 1763 - William Goolsberry, on the Complaint of Samuel Watts for a Breach of the Peace, is required to give Security and post a Peace Bond. Book B, p. 169.

July 12, 1763 - John Trammell, who was "bound by [his Bond] ... to answer the Complaint of John Galloway and Isabella Galloway his Wife against him for Breach of the Peace ... but came not ... Ordered that Hugh West [Kings Attorney] ... Prosecute the Recognizance." Book B, p. 192.

August 11, 1763 - Ralph Braddock, an insolvent in Prison for over 20 days due to a judgment in favor of merchant Thomas Sligh for debts, delivered a Schedule of his Estate for the benefit of his Creditors, gave the Oaths required of insolvent debtors, and was discharged and released from jail. Book B, p. 214.

October 11, 1763 - "Peter Smith ... [an insolvent] in Prison upwards of twenty Daies ... delivered in a Schedule of his Estate and made Oath ... Ordered that the Sherif forthwith set the said Peter at Liberty." Book B, p. 258.

November 8, 1763 - "Francis Shelton ... [an insolvent] in Goal upwards of twenty Daies ... delivered in a Schedule of his Estate and made Oath ... [he is set] at Liberty." Book B, p. 262.

November 9, 1763 - John Owsley and William Chelton, both "brought before the Court for a breach of the peace ... [with] William Luckett, John Herryford, Thomas Owsley and George Vallandingham [testifying, Owsley and Chelton are required to] ... give Security [Bond] for [their] good Behavior," for a period of one year. Churchwarden Owsley's apparent propensity for riotous behavior results in his untimely death the following fall. Book B, pp. 264-265; and see, Chapter on Crimes and Punishment, supra, @ pp. 169-170.

February 15, 1764 - "Ordered that the Sherif ... raise the Posse of the County and take John Davis (son of Samuel Davis) into his Custody ... who is a common Disturber of the Peace and him safely keep until he give Security for his good Behavior." Book B, p. 277.

March 13, 1764 - John Davis, after his arrest by the Sheriff and the County posse, for disturbing the Peace, is required to give Security for his good Behavior. Book B, p. 279.

June 15, 1764 - "Ordered ... Hugh West, the Deputy Kings Attorney ... prosecute a Recognizance against John Davis and his Securities for the Breach [of the conditions of the Bond, ie., a Breach of the Peace]." Book B, p. 396.

August 14, 1764 - John Mattox, on the Complaint of Thomas Simmonds, posts a Peace Bond for his good behavior. Book B, p. 408.

October 10, 1764 - The personal effects of Daniel Lawrence are attached, listed, and ordered sold to satisfy his judgment debts. Book B, p. 485.

October 10, 1764 - Francis Dade, on the Complaint of John Heryford, is required to post a Peace Bond for his good behavior. Book B, p. 489.

November 14, 1764 - William West [Senr., the former Loudoun County Justice!] is required to give Security for his good Behavior and post a Peace Bond on the complaint of Ferdinando O'Neale. Book B, p. 500.

April 8, 1765 - Amos Jenkins, on the complaint of Joshua Jones, is required to post a Peace Bond, with Hezekiah Boone and Henry Oxley Junr. as the Securities for his good behavior. Book B, pp. 539 and 548.

April 8, 1765 - George Chilton [sic - George Chelton] is required to give Security for his Good Behavior and post a Peace Bond on the complaint of Edward Taylor. Book B, p. 542.

May 6, 1765 - John Linton, the special bail for Benjamin Grayson on a judgment debt to John Dalton and John West Junr. of Alexandria, was arrested when Grayson failed to pay. "[A]t the request of John Linton and [to] prevent [him] from being committed to Gaol," Linton mortgages 509 acres on Broad Run, "whereof Benjamin Sebastian hath a plantation [slave quarter]," as collateral to guarantee Grayson's payment of the judgment. LDCODB, Book E, p. 15.

June 10, 1765 - Thomas Wood, "brought before the Court [by the Sheriff, one would assume] for Breach of the Peace," is required to give Security for his good behavior and post a Bond. Book B, p. 624.

June 10, 1765 - The personal property of William Winn is attached and ordered sold to satisfy a judgment debt to Daniel Baley. Book B, p. 627.

August 12, 1765 - George Turner is required to enter a Peace Bond for his good behavior, on the Complaint of John Anderson. Book C, p. 2.

August 12, 1765 - Jonathan Buckalew is required to enter a Peace Bond for his good behavior, on the Complaint of Mary Butcher. Book C, p. 3.

September 10, 1765 - John Anderson "is Committed ... to the Custody of the Sheriff ... to remain in the common Gaol for Debtors until [he pays a judgment or posts an appropriate bond]." Book C, p. 44.

October 14, 1765 - "John Anderson ... in Prison [for about 5 weeks] ... delivered in [to Court] a Schedule of his Estate [to be] ... Vested in [his] Creditors ... the Sheriff ... set John Anderson at Liberty." Book C, pp. 61-62.

May 12, 1766 - The Grand Jury returns a Presentment of charges against: "Robert Bland for a breach of the Peace committed on the body of James Leith." Perhaps a bloody nose, or worse. Book C, p. 75.

June 3, 1766 - John Simms gives Ferdinando O'Neal a bill of sale for a bull, cows, hogs, horses and furniture. "The substance ... is that Ferdinando O'Neale is the special bond for John Simms [a defendant] at the suit of Gerrard Alexander ... if Ferdinando O'Neale be saved harmless in the aforesaid bailship then the above ... sale is ... void." LDCODB, Book E, p. 82.

June 9, 1766 - Easter Connell complains against William Furr for a breach of the peace. Book C, p. 80.

June 10, 1766 - After Patrick McCarty defaults on a promise to pay £12, William Ross records a bill of sale for the collateral that had been given, which includes "one loom ... and one trunk." LDCODB, Book E, p. 83.

June 14, 1766 - "Michael Vanbuscart [sic] ... in Prison [over 20 days] ... delivered in a Schedule of his Estate ... for the benefit of the Creditor ... Vanbuscart [is set] at liberty." Book C, p. 140.

August 12, 1766 - Rose Hall brings a Complaint against James Hall for a breach of the Peace. Book C, p. 148.

August 12, 1766 - George McDonald, for a "Just [judgment] Debt" of £10, 13 shillings and 5½ pence "owing to Mssrs. Hunter, Campbell and Company," warrants that his horse, cattle, 50 hogs, "a rifle gun and a smooth boor [sic]," are worth more than the balance that he owes. LDCODB, Book E, p. 150.

September 9, 1766 - James Allan, on the Complaint of Mary Pitts, is required to enter a Peace Bond for his good behavior. Book C, p. 189.

September 9, 1766 - "Leonard Marbury ... in Prison ... delivered in a Schedule of his Estate [he is] ... set ... at Liberty." Book C, p. 191.

October 17, 1766 - Richard Eskridge pledges 455 acres at Cub Run to secure some £144 in account debts to John Glasford & Archibald Henderson, merchants of Glasgow, "in the Kingdom of Great Britain." Alexander Henderson, their factor at Colchester, took the mortgage. LDCODB, Book E, pp. 344-352.

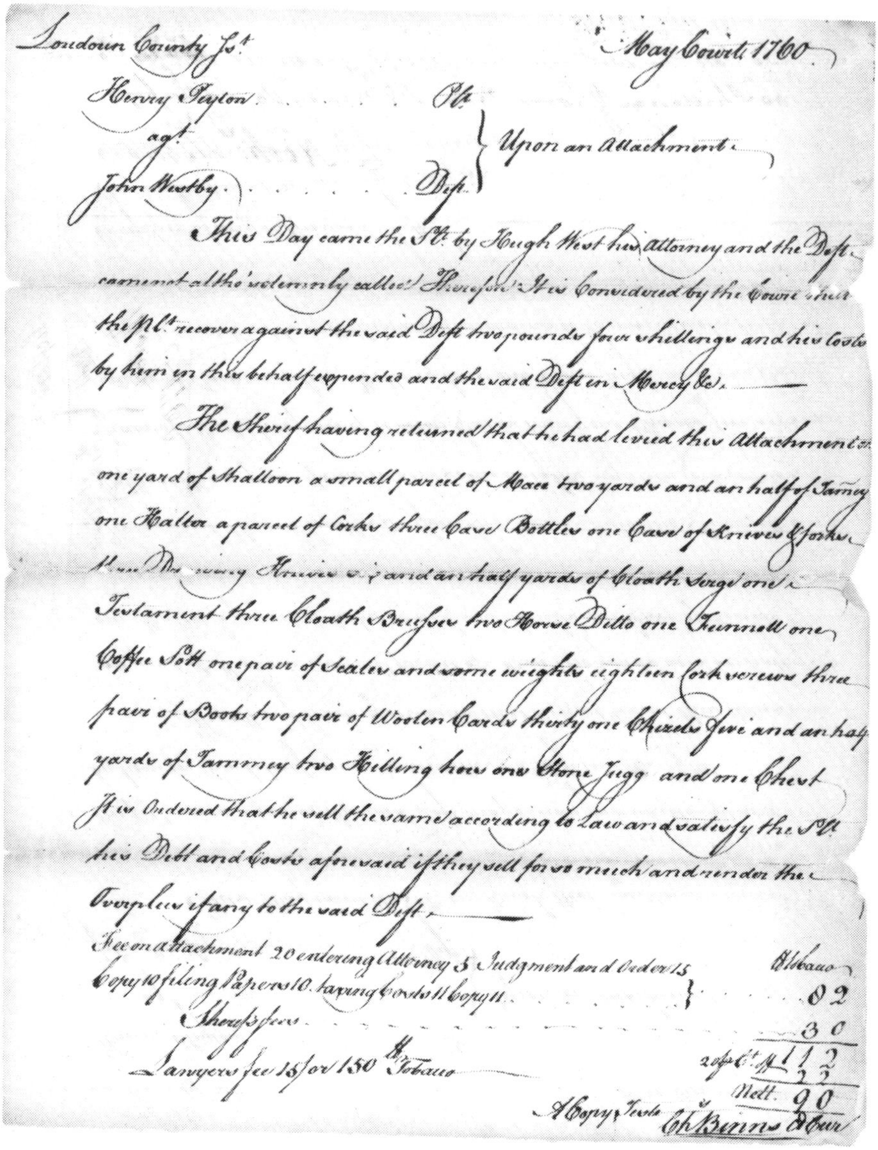
Loudoun County Sct. May Court 1760

Henry Peyton ... Plt.
agt. } Upon an Attachment.
John Westby ... Deft.

This Day came the Plt. by Hugh West his Attorney and the Deft. came not altho' solemnly called Therefore It is Considered by the Court that the Plt. recover against the said Deft. two pounds four shillings and his Costs by him in this behalf expended and the said Deft. in Mercy &c.

The Sheriff having returned that he had levied this Attachment on one yard of Shalloon a small parcel of Mace two yards and an half of Tammy one Halter a parcel of Corks three Case Bottles one Case of Knives & forks three Pruning Knives 2 and an half yards of Cloath Serge one Testament three Cloath Brushes two Horse Ditto one Funnell one Coffee Pott one pair of Scales and some weights eighteen Cork screws three pair of Boots two pair of Woolen Cards thirty one Chizels five and an half yards of Tammey two Hilling hoes one Stone Jugg and one Chest It is Ordered that he sell the same according to Law and satisfy the Plt. his Debt and Costs aforesaid if they sell for so much and render the Overplus if any to the said Deft.

Fee on attachment 20 entering Attorney 3 Judgment and Order 15 Copy 10 filing Papers 10. taxing Costs 11 Copy 11 } ... lb Tobacco 82
Sheriffs fees ... 30
Lawyers fee 15/ or 150 lb Tobacco — 20 pr Ct. lb 112 / 22
Nett. 90

A Copy Teste Chs. Binns Clk.

The Order granting execution "Upon an Attachment" shown above was issued in the case of Henry Peyton vs. John Westby in the May Court of 1760. On the reverse side of the Order, in his return to the Loudoun Court, Sheriff Nicholas Minor noted: "I have sold the within Mentioned goods for Six Pounds [£6] Three Shillings & four Pence & [I am] Ready to Satisfy." The Order provides detailed lists of the goods that were attached and auctioned, and the fees and costs assessed in the case. *[HDC]*

Agriculture and Colonial Economics

The exploration and settlement of Virginia was a direct consequence of British attempts to locate and obtain mineral wealth, but agriculture was the backbone of colonial Virginia's commerce. The extraction of raw materials, initially furs, and subsequently iron, was elemental to the growth and development of the Virginia colony. But furs were rapidly replaced by tobacco as Virginia's primary export, and production of "the stinking weed" eventually became so fundamental to the Virginia economy that, by 1715, the colony's entire financial structure was backed by warehoused tobacco. Wheat flour, iron, barrel staves and beef played increasingly important commercial roles as exports from the Potomac as the region matured throughout the 1700s.

Furs and hides were the first commodities exported from the Potomac region. The absence of European settlements prevented tobacco from gaining a solid position in Potomac trade before 1650. Beaver and otter pelts, which were bringing large revenues and were the staples of the Potomac trade, were not affected by bans on the exportation of various kinds of hides. During the English Civil War, the Assembly briefly stopped the exportation of all hides and leather products. Loudoun's bison herd was hunted to extinction by the mid-1600s, and stocks of other game on the piedmont were severely impacted by expanding English settlements around the turn of the century. All the same, the remarkable number of "beaver dam" branches, on practically every creek in Loudoun County, serve as reminders of the likely abundance of that species when European settlers seated the Loudoun piedmont in the 1720s and 1730s. The leather industry was alive and well in colonial Loudoun. During the 1760s, a number of tanneries would have been clearly seen and smelled, all over Loudoun as well as in the town of Leesburg proper. [Hening, I/174, I/199 and I/307; re cordwainers, see infra, Chapter on Trades, and Glossary].

Tobacco had become Virginia's dominant export crop very shortly after John Rolfe initiated its exportation in 1614. In the 1720s, Virginia export production averaged 40,000 hogsheads, about 20,000 tons, of tobacco per year. Virginia's planters maintained roughly the same level of production up to the time of the Revolution. Tobacco production in modern-day Virginia has receded to the area south of Louisa and Caroline Counties, but in the mid-1700s, "new fields" of crop tobacco were being planted all over Virginia's Northern Neck, including the Loudoun piedmont below the Kitoctin-Bull Run range of mountains. The value of tobacco, as with other crops, was influenced by the quality of the product, the seasonal moods of mother nature, fluctuations in demand in European markets, and the industry, or greed, of the colonial planters. Over-planting, good and bad growing conditions, and economic depression in England often combined to wreak financial ruin on Virginia cultivators. [Jamestown, pp. 37-42].

In 1639, the inspection of export tobacco was instituted with a law instructing overseers of the plantations to inspect and swear to the quality and quantity of their crop before allowing a shipment to leave their pier. Virginia's 1640 Assembly regulated tobacco prices, directing that the 1640 crop was "not to be sold under 12 pence per [lb.], and 2 shillings per lb. [for the] next year's crop." A little over 120 years later, Loudoun planters would be delighted when 1 lb. of their tobacco could command 2 devalued pennies. After 1650, colonial Assemblies frequently intervened to ban the planting of second crops when prices were depressed. The Virginia colony banned second crops of tobacco a number of times during the following century. In some cases, the population of a precinct could be determined indirectly because constables, who were viewing the fields for double plantings, were paid on the basis of the number of residents in their district. In Loudoun, for example, in 1766, Steerman Chilton was paid 284 lbs. of tobacco for viewing fields because 284 tithable individuals were living in his precinct. [Hening, I/226 and I/399; infra, @ p. 212; for a Map of Tithable Precincts, infra, Chapter on Tax Lists].

The most significant initiative in Virginia's regulation of tobacco was the institution of a public tobacco warehouse system. These warehouses, privately owned and operated under exclusive licenses issued by the Assembly, effected the uniform inspection of the export crop and tended to offset the monopoly purchasing power of the shipping masters. This had the twin results of raising and stabilizing the price of export tobacco. Warehouse owners issued "transfer receipts" that were essentially demand notes on the inventory of the tobacco deposited in their warehouse. The Assembly acted as guarantor of warehouse operations. In 1752, after "high wind and rain and the overflowing of the tide" had destroyed large quantities of warehoused tobacco, the Assembly provided for the public reimbursement of losses. After the public warehouse system was formalized in 1713, tobacco prices were less erratic although droughts, hurricanes and economic depressions continued to have their effect on the colonial market price. In 1758, in the middle of the French and Indian War, at a time when extended droughts were also taking their toll, tobacco prices went as high as 30 shillings per hundred weight - over 250% of the official exchange value! [Hening, IV/247-271, IV/487, V/537, VI/154, VI/168, VI/236-237, VI/467, VI/478 and VIII/100; Democracy, pp. 114-118; GW Papers, V/315; infra, p. 192].

Stocks of coin of the realm and other "hard" currencies were nearly nonexistent in the Virginia colony, so much so that the premium value of "Sterling" coinage had to be legislated - at 125% of nominal value. Various tax incentives that were instituted as "an encouragement to import ... gold and silver coin ... into this colony and dominion" met with limited success. English copper coinage was not introduced into Virginia until the mid-1770s. Transfer receipts were simply the most convenient medium of exchange that colonials had; as a result warehouse receipts became Virginia's primary currency almost overnight once the public warehouse system was introduced. Warehouse notes were accepted throughout Virginia in the payment of any debt or obligation, including the King's quitrents, and substituted for coinage until after the Revolution. The 1748 Assembly formally adopted tobacco transfer receipts as currency, providing that, wherever payable with tobacco, levies, quitrents and officer fees:

> *"shall be paid and discharged by transfer notes ... paid in some warehouse in the county ... In any county where no public warehouse is established, [levies, quitrents and fees] shall be paid at some warehouse in the next adjacent county."*

Tobacco warehouse receipts were accorded the same protection given to other forms of specie, and forgery of a receipt was punishable as a felony, by death. [Hening, IV/79, VI/168-171, VII/262, VII/271 and VIII/107; contra, Democracy, p. 115].

In the 1730s and 1740s, "Loudoun" planters hauled or rolled their tobacco to one of three public warehouses: Valentine Peyton's warehouse at the falls on the Occoquan; the West family's warehouse at Hunting Creek (also known as Belhaven, and later as Alexandria); or, Thomas Lee's warehouse at the Little Falls of the Potomac. Receipts from those warehouses, and another warehouse at Pohick, circulated freely in Loudoun.

Thomas Lee built both his career and a personal fortune upon the extension of tidewater commerce into the upper Potomac and Ohio river basins. In the furtherance of his ambition, Lee fostered settlements at the Sugarlands, in the branches of Broad Run, and above Goose Creek. Thanks, in part, to Thomas Lee's efforts, rolling roads between the Sugarlands and Little Falls (modern Rte. 7 and Rte. 193) were already in active use by the mid-1730s when the Fairfax family manors were created. One element of Lee's vision was a seat of commerce at the head of navigation on the Potomac. Lee's efforts were rewarded in 1742 when the Assembly, responding to the rapid growth of settlements in Loudoun all along the Potomac, licensed the Lee tobacco warehouses at the Little Falls. After inheriting the Little Falls warehouses in 1750, Philip Ludwell Lee rehabilitated the facility. But the location did not permit larger ocean-going vessels access, and tobacco often had to be floated further downriver for reloading onto Atlantic shipping. [Lee, p. 121; Grants, Book C, folio 60; infra, Chapter on Leesburg and Chapter on Population].

By the mid-1750s, tobacco warehouses at Occoquan had been in use, off and on, for two full decades. They had been situated at the terminus of the Mountain Road primarily to serve the "Loudoun" planters above Rocky Run. The 1759 Assembly determined that "the quantity of tobacco brought to Peyton's warehouse ... [was] so small that the keeping up an inspection ... [would] be of no benefit or advantage to the public," and Peyton's license was revoked. In the late 1750s and early 1760s, merchants from Occoquan and Dumfries competed with Alexandria traders by establishing satellite warehouses at Leesburg, where Loudoun tobacco, wheat flour and corn were prepared for shipment down either the Mountain Road or the Ridge Road. By 1761, tobacco planters in southeast Loudoun petitioned to the Assembly for the authorization of new warehouses at Murray's landing at Quantico. John Ballendine had developed an industrial complex at Occoquan where forges, mills and bread ovens prepared supplies for ocean-going vessels, but the Occoquan had silted up, and the tobacco warehouses there were "in a ruinous condition and ... [deemed]

inconveniently situated." The 1762 Assembly directed that "new warehouses [be] erected at ... Colchester." Thereafter, Loudoun residents near the Mountain Road used the "Colchester Road," or a relatively new back route to Alexandria known as the "Braddock Road," for the transport of their crops and goods to Potomac shipping. Mercantile operations around Leesburg were re-focused along the Ridge Road above the Potomac and, increasingly, were dominated by the merchants of Alexandria and Georgetown. After the Colchester warehouse began operations, tobacco receipts from all four Fairfax warehouses, and Prince William's Quantico warehouse, passed as "Virginia money" in Loudoun County. [Hening, IV/381, VI/173, VII/310, VII/530-531 and VIII/508; Landmarks, pp. 402 and 408; infra, The Record, @ p. 207].

In 1738, Virginia's frontier counties in the Shenandoah valley, Frederick and Augusta, were removed from the tobacco receipts standard. Residents were allowed to pay all public fees and levies with either coin or currency. In the 1750s, the cash payment provision was extended to Bedford and Halifax counties, and to Norfolk and Princess Anne Counties during severe tobacco crop failures in 1755. Witness fees at the county courts could also be discharged with cash "in any county where the levies and officers fees [were payable in cash] ... at the same [exchange rate] as the levies." During the French and Indian War, Stafford County, noting that trade and credit were stagnant, unsuccessfully petitioned for authority to allow the payment of debts with land, slaves or other goods, subject to a reasonable valuation. Loudoun County was put on a cash basis shortly after it was created. The Virginia Assembly directed that, effective December 2, 1759:

> *"Whereas the inhabitants of Loudoun ... make but little tobacco, and many of them none ... whereof they are subject to great impositions in discharging their public dues and officers fees ... [it is] lawful ... for all and every person ... chargeable with any tobacco for public dues or officers fees ... to discharge the same in money at twelve shillings and six pence per hundred [weight of tobacco]."*

This set Loudoun County's official valuation of 1 lb. of tobacco [hereinafter, "lbt."] at 1½ pence, or 3 farthings. The entire Virginia colony was placed on a "cash" basis in 1762, largely as a consequence of the availability of huge sums of Virginia Treasury notes that had been issued to finance the colony's military efforts in the French War. Thereafter, Virginians could pay "secretaries, clerks, sheriffs, surveyors or other officers ... either in tobacco ... or in money," at the exchange rate of 16 shillings and 8 pence, or 200 pence, for every 100 lbt.s. The old valuation rate, 150 pence per 100 lbt.s, was maintained in several piedmont counties including Loudoun, Halifax and Bedford, while the valley frontier counties, Augusta, Frederick and Hampshire, had a new exchange rate of 100 pence per 100 lbt.s. [Hening, VI/369, VI/502, VII/292, VII/384-386 and VIII/178; Assembly, (1752) p. 428].

The Assembly's establishment of official exchange rates did not eliminate the ability of county courts and individuals to take notice of the relative value of tobacco on the fair market. Despite the overall success of the warehouse system, the value of transfer tobacco (and transfer notes) varied with the political climate and growing conditions. While the official exchange rate was 12 shilling, 6 pence per 100 lbt.s, the 1753 Fairfax County Court calculated payments for public works at 8 shillings per 100 lbt.s - a 36% devaluation of tobacco. In 1754, demand for tobacco dropped so precipitately with the onset of the French War that the price of exchange tobacco fell by 55%. Planters in Norfolk and Portsmouth had such poor harvests in 1755 and, as a consequence, tobacco notes were so scarce that the Virginia Assembly put the colony's largest port complex on a cash basis that year. In 1757, George Washington noted that 8 hogsheads (about 4 tons) of his tobacco brought £57 Sterling upon delivery in London, roughly 18 Virginia shillings per 100 lbt. - 150% of the official value. And in the course of setting the county levy in 1758, the Loudoun County Court acknowledged that the value of transfer tobacco was higher than the official rate of exchange, requiring 16 shillings, 8 pence to offset 100 lbs. of transfer receipts. But in 1760, and again in 1765, the Loudoun Court returned to the official formula in setting the value of tobacco notes. [Fairfax, p. 57; GW Papers, IV/402; infra, The Record, pp. 205, 206, 207 and 210].

Transfer receipts were unique among currencies in that they depreciated by 1% per month for the first six months after their issuance - a storage fee that was credited to the proprietor of the warehouse when the receipt was presented for redemption. While the market rate of tobacco fluctuated, the rate of exchange for tobacco notes remained constant in Loudoun County inns and taverns; a transfer receipt for eight lbs. of tobacco had a value of one shilling. Values of different colonial currencies, relative to "Virginia money," varied in time and with the distance from the point of redemption. The Loudoun County Court, in one of its first official acts in 1757, indicated that £5 of Pennsylvania money was equal in value to £4 of Virginia currency. The notes of colonial Maryland also circulated in Loudoun County, apparently trading at about a 10% discount during the 1760s. [Landmarks, pp. 421-422; see generally, infra, Chapter on Ordinaries].

Colonial financing of the French War in the 1750s and 1760s brought about the issuance of Virginia Treasury notes, which "pass[ed] as a lawful tender, in payment of any debt, duty or demand ... except for the payment of his majesty's quit-rents." Virginia Treasury notes were backed by the expectation of future tax revenues and were designed for retirement during the 1760s. The Virginia Assembly specified that proceeds of increased annual poll and property taxes were to be applied to retire the notes. [Hening, VII/167; infra, Chapter on Colonial Taxes].

Parliament, concerned with the spread of paper money issues in the American colonies and fearing the depreciation of colonial notes with an attendant loss on colonial book debts, restricted the "legal tender" of the colonial paper money in 1764. When the Virginia Assembly enacted the Treasury note plan, fines were imposed on anyone who attempted to depreciate Treasury notes by demanding a "higher difference of exchange ... [or using] any other device, means or method ... whereby the credit of the said notes may be impaired." The widespread use of Treasury notes inspired the criminal element. Despite elaborate procedures that had been instituted, counterfeiting and forgery of Virginia Treasury notes were the most frequently committed felony offenses in Loudoun County from 1757 to 1766. Only a few colonists would have cause to suspect that John Robinson, Virginia's Treasurer, would misappropriate £100,000 in "retired" Treasury notes and leave Virginia on the verge of a financial disaster upon his death in 1766. This situation forced the Assembly to impose additional poll and property taxes and extend retirement dates of Treasury notes, some issues by six years. With austerity measures in effect, Virginia paper money issues were reduced from a high of £540,000 during the French War down to £55,000 by 1773. The substantial tax increases and attendant contractions of the Virginia economy set off an emigration toward the southern and western frontiers in the decade before the Revolution. Fresh land was more "affordable" and the King's tax collectors were not so near at hand in the Carolina, Kentucky and Ohio frontier settlements. [Democracy, pp. 114-115; Hening, VII/259-261; re counterfeiting, see Chapter on Crimes, supra @ p. 159; re scandal, The Record infra, @ pp. 210-212; infra, Chapter on Colonial Taxes].

Colonial paper money was not the only type of currency to suffer from exchange variations. Gold coins of the German empire were so debased that the 1762 Assembly devalued all such coinage by 15%, from 60 pence to 51 pence for a pennyweight "and no more." Remarkably, the "dollar" (a Spanish coin often minted in Scotland) maintained a steady value. In 1763, the Loudoun County Court valued a dollar at 5 shillings, 9 pence. When the Continental Congress authorized issuance of paper money to finance the Revolutionary army, colonial currencies were to be redeemed in Spanish Milled Dollars. During the Revolution the official exchange rate used by Continental army paymasters was 6 shillings to the dollar - only a 4% change in 15 years. Do we dare to suppose that the American dollar was adopted as our national currency thanks, in part, to the historic stability of it's namesake? [Hening, VII/575-576; and see infra, p. 209].

The Virginia Company had never planned on a one-crop economy. The early leaders of the colony were duly alarmed when colonists abandoned the planting of grain crops in favor of tobacco. In an attempt to encourage the cultivation of corn the year after the first Indian massacre, the 1624 Assembly removed price controls. Due to the preöccupation with tobacco, occasional crop failures, or Indian warfare, the Assembly repeatedly noted a "great scarcity of corn" during the next fifty years. Price controls were, alternately, reimposed and removed. Finally, the Assembly required every colonist to plant two acres of corn annually. [Hening, I/125, I/347, I/152, I/173, I/197 and I/419].

In colonial Virginia, alternate crops generally meant anything but tobacco, hides or corn. The staple commodities - wine, wheat, hemp and flax - and various kinds of "arts and manufactures" - glass, silk, tar, iron and saltpeter - were all the objects of encouragement at one time or another. The Assembly instituted financial promotions for the domestic production of wine, flax and hemp in the 1630s. Export crops were also encouraged, through the payment of "premiums" in either cash or tobacco. Silk and "English wheate" were added to the list of promoted export items in 1658. Unfortunately, most colonial promotion schemes seem to have been written with the large plantation owners in mind. The requirement of large quantities of production, for modest rewards, invariably gave little or no incentive to small farmers. [Hening, I/192, I/218 and I/471].

Virginia's grain production steadied around 1690 and, with wars disrupting crop production on the European continent, corn and wheat prices rose dramatically during the 1700s. Colonial slavery was expanding during the same period. The increased investment caused tidewater planters to exert greater effort to insure steady production of food crops. An Act of the 1755 Assembly is typical of the regulations that were imposed when "great scarcity of Indian corn" was anticipated in the 1700s. A price ceiling on "corn or meal of the same" was set at 12 shillings, 6 pence for a 220 lbs. barrel (1½ lbs. of corn for one English penny), along with a steep £5 penalty for price gouging. The ceiling remained in effect until October of 1756, when the next fall harvest was to arrive at market. The price limit was imposed immediately after General Braddock's disaster at Pittsburgh, at a time when the Assembly was consumed with the planning of military procurement for the ongoing frontier war with the French. Twice during the French and Indian War, the exportation of corn was banned "by reason of the shortness of the crop of corn and other grain occasioned by the extraordinary drought ... the greatest distress" being observed in Virginia's southern and western frontier settlements. [Hening, VI/553-554 and VII/312; infra, @ p. 208].

Farming was considered to be a noble, profitable pursuit, particularly during the several decades preceding the American Revolution. Loudoun colonials who were successful merchants, millers, carpenters and ordinary keepers all appear to have preferred the title of "planter" or "farmer." Notable among them, Leesburg ordinary keeper John Heryford aspired to the title of "planter" despite the success he enjoyed with his tavern across King Street from the Loudoun Courthouse, while Mahlon Janney, the owner of Janney's mill, preferred to call himself a "farmer." [Virginia, p. 63; infra, The Record, pp. 206 and 208].

Beginning in 1671, the Virginia Assembly encouraged the production of wheat by providing for reduced tolls (charges) on wheat flour ground in Virginia's grist mills. The colonial government's encouragement of wheat production was apparently needed no longer by 1751, when the Assembly finally equalized the grinding tolls for corn and wheat. Early settlers who moved to Loudoun from the north and west had never been wed to the tobacco culture of the Virginia tidewater. Many of them were either emigrants or first generation colonists, and they brought the agronomics and husbandry of Germany, Scotland, Ireland and Wales with them to the Loudoun piedmont. Corn was the staple grain across most of Virginia in the mid-1700s, but wheat was the primary grain crop in the Shenandoah valley and on Loudoun County farms. By the time Loudoun County was formed, wheat was such an important cash crop that Virginia Governor Dinwiddie lifted an embargo that had been imposed by Lord Loudoun. Over 50,000 bushels of Virginia wheat were shipped to Britain in 1757 despite a severe drought. With the market price of wheat ranging around 4 shillings per bushel in the 1760s, high average yields of 20 bushels to the acre (£4 gross per acre), and the average rent on the Loudoun manor lands at only £4 a year for 200 acres, it is easy to imagine how an industrious colonial could turn a tidy profit farming in Loudoun County. Export trade out of Alexandria's seaport was already shifting toward the primacy of wheat flour by the mid-1760s. [see infra, Chapter on Grist Mills; ColVa, p. 708; Landmarks, pp. 397-481; Frontier, pp. 27-29; Democracy, p. 20].

Virginia colonists were encouraged to plant orchards and vineyards as early as 1636. Fruit was a primary ingredient in the production of brandy - a favorite colonial beverage. Standard covenants in most of the farm leases on manor lands in Loudoun County required the planting of acres of apple and peach trees. As a consequence, large areas of Loudoun, from Difficult Run to the Sugarlands along the Potomac Ridge Road and between Kitoctin Mountain and the Blue Ridge, must have seemed as one vast orchard. During the French and Indian War, after years of warfare with the French, Virginia faced shortages of all kinds of European goods including wines. The 1762 Assembly upgraded premiums that were being paid, and formally inaugurated a Virginia Wine Competition in order to encourage the domestic manufacture of wines. Loudoun's colonial orchardists did not incorporate vineyards within their plans. The vintner nearest to Loudoun County grew his grapes on the hill overlooking the port of Colchester. [Hening, I/226; re leases, see infra, Chapter on Lands; re colonial winemaking, see infra, Chapter on Trades].

The growth of domestic industries in the Virginia colony throughout the 1600s, and increasing colonial access to European markets through the construction and use of their own trading vessels, caused a great deal of concern in mercantile circles in London and Glasgow. In 1651, Parliament attempted to limit direct European trade with the colonies by requiring the shipment of all Virginia exports in English ships. The imposition of the "Navigation Acts," and their resurrection by another Parliament a century later, would have a profound effect in shaping the attitudes of colonial planters during the years leading up to the American Revolution. In 1699, with the imposition of the Wool Act, Parliament initiated a series of ultimately self-destructive efforts to restrain colonial industries from the manufacture of goods and other "things produced in England." In 1706, when colonial production was allegedly harming English industries, the King's Board of Trade actually instructed Virginia's Governor Nott to discourage the planting of cotton and flax. [ColVa, p. 369].

The production of flax was first banned in Virginia in 1632, not because English industry was being effected, but as a measure to encourage the production of food stocks. This was at variance with the prevailing attitude in colonial Assemblies, where the production of both flax and hemp was regularly encouraged. Bounties were offered for the production of fibers throughout the 1700s, but it seems that only the more affluent Virginians were in a position to take advantage of the promotions. For example, in 1730, William Byrd obtained a Certificate for his production of 26 "gross hundreds" of hemp, which entitled him to a bounty of a mere £5, 4 shillings. In response to another promotion, Loudoun Justice Josias Clapham certified that he had produced 163 lbs. of flax at his Lost Corner plantation in 1762. Meanwhile, small farmers, like Loudoun's Daniel Mittenger, regularly cultivated flax but did not bother with the Assembly bounties. [Hening, I/218 and IV/302; infra, The Record, @ pp. 208 and 210].

During the 1700s, Virginia Assembly promotions, (often under instructions from the Admiralty or the King's Board of Trade), focused on export products that were of the greatest military utility to the British Empire - tar, turpentine and hemp (for rope). These items were not produced in Loudoun County in any commercial quantities, but increased regulation came along with the increasing diversity of Virginia's exports. The length and width of barrel staves were codified. Inspection programs were instituted for all kinds of products - pork, beef, flour, tar, pitch, turpentine, and barrel staves - that were exported from the colony. Certificates of inspection and purity were required for all cargos on vessels leaving the colony, and ship's captains were required to produce the certificates for the King's Customs Officers before their ship would be cleared for exit. [Hening, IV/302, VI/144-146, VI/233-235 and VIII/143-154; and ColVa, p. 72].

The Virginia Inspection Acts that were in force during the 1757-1766 decade imposed regulations on "every person making, or causing to be made, wheat flour intended for exportation." Flour barrels were to be branded with, among other things, an 'L,V' for Loudoun County, Virginia, the first letter of the christian name and the entire surname of the inspector, the weight of the barrel and a distinction of the fineness of the flour. Inspector's fees were also regulated: "for every barrel of flour, containing two hundred and twenty pounds nett, or less, three pence; and for every cask of greater weight, six pence." The 1766 Assembly encouraged the exportation of wheat flour, reducing inspector's fees on export flour to "one penny half-penny for every cask or barrel of flour by him inspected and marked," regardless of barrel size. [Hening, VI/148-149, VII/40, VII/570-574, VIII/143 and VIII/198; see infra, Chapter on Mills].

Loudoun County's first inspectors, appointed early in 1758, were Quaker leaders John Hough and Francis Hague. They both served in that office until the fall of 1761, when John Hough sponsored their replacements, John Newland and William Baker. John Newland was a tenant on the Piedmont Manor, and was convenient to all of the mill owners in the Kitoctin valley. Newland, however, apparently found better prospects and moved north to Frederick County, Maryland without waiting for the appointment of his replacement. William Baker, a Quaker, bought the vacant lot on Loudoun Street next door to John Hough in Leesburg, where Baker was still residing long after he resigned as inspector. Baker's replacement, Loudoun Justice Francis Peyton, was appointed Inspector of Flour in 1766. Curiously, both initially and when Peyton renewed his oaths in June of 1767, there was no mention of the inspection of other commodities that had been listed in the Export Inspection Acts. It would seem that wheat flour had already obtained its position as the dominant export product of colonial Loudoun by the mid-1760s! Peyton's appointment is remarkable in another respect, reflecting the growth of grist mill operations outside of the Kitoctin valley and, more particularly, in the Goose Creek basin. [LDCOCO, Book C, p. 278; see infra, The Record, pp. 206, 207 and 212; and generally, see infra, Chapter on Grist Mills].

From the colony's inception, the standard weights and measures, officially, were supposed to conform to those adopted by the British Parliament. In 1654, the Virginia Assembly noticed a "great abuse and deceit by false styllyards [sic - steelyards are hanging, single-arm balance scales]." Each county was thereupon instructed to "procure and keep att the court house sufficient weights to try ... all styllyards [sic]." [Hening, I/331 and I/391].

Commercial difficulties arose when multinational trading increased in Virginia ports in the early 1700s. The non-uniformity of European measures led to misunderstandings and allegations of fraud. The 1734 Assembly felt compelled to adopt an "Act for more effectual[ly] obliging Persons to buy and sell by Weights and Measures according to the English Standard," and reaffirmed "one weight, one measure, one yard, and one ell, according to the standard of the Exchequer, in England" as the official weights and measures for Virginia. The 1734 Assembly also provided that:

> *"[By 1737] the justices of peace of every county ... provide, at the charge of their ... counties, brass weights, of half hundreds, quarterns [¼ of a 'stone', or 3½ pounds], half quarterns, seven pounds, four pounds, two pounds, and one pound weight ... And measures, of bushel, half bushel, peck, and half peck, dry measure ... And gallon, pottle [sic - a 'pot' measure, or half-gallon], quart, and pint of wine measure ... with proper scales for the weights."*

A keeper of standards was appointed in each county, "to which all persons [in the county] may resort, for trying their weights and measures." When a weight or measure was "found to agree with the standard," it was marked and sealed. A fee of one shilling was allowed to the county's keeper of standards for certifying a steelyard, and four pence for trying and sealing any weight or measure. [Hening, IV/406-407; re "ell" see infra, Glossary].

In the normal course of doing business, the mill operators, ordinary keepers and merchants of Loudoun County obtained and used either a partial or full set of the official weights and standards. As early as 1705, Virginia's ordinary keepers had been required to obtain a sealed set of the liquid measures, and mill owners had to have "sealed measures" of a half bushel, a peck, and a toll dish. The 1742, 1748 and 1764 Assemblies also instructed the owners of the public tobacco warehouses to provide "a sett of small weights ... the same ... [as] provided for the standard weights of each county," and a "good and sufficient pair of scales" that could weigh up to 1,200 lbs., before 1764, and 1,500 lbs. after 1764. This was in keeping with the requirement that all hogsheads of export tobacco were "to contain [950 lbs.] of tobacco [net] ... at the least." [Hening, III/336, III/395, V/150, VI/182 and VIII/85-91].

For Loudoun's first dozen years, Justice Nicholas Minor maintained the County's official "Weights and Measures." In 1758, Minor and fellow Loudoun Justice Josias Clapham arranged the purchase, through Alexandria merchants Carlyle and Dalton, of Loudoun's first set of standard measures. The set was apparently delivered to Minor's custody in 1759. In 1768, about the same time that Nicholas Minor moved east of Goose Creek, Leesburg silversmith Stephen Donaldson was appointed as the new "Keeper" of the County Weights and Measures. The original set of Standards was incomplete, or something happened to them around 1772, when County Justice Leven Powell was appointed to obtain "a half Bushell, a Peck, and half Peck" measures which were to be used as the new Standards for the county. [see infra, The Record, p. 206; LDCOCO, Book D, p. 134, and Book E, p. 385].

Weighing produce was one thing. Transporting produce, and ones self, to market or to the county court was something different. Visitors in the colony found it remarkable that "even the most indigent [Virginian] has his saddlehorse, which he rides to every place." The primary mode of 18th century transportation usually had a mind all it's own, and the loss and recovery of stray horses was a constant exercise, all over colonial Virginia. Before 1762, "freeholders, house keepers and overseers" were authorized by law to "take up" stray horses. Once found, a stray was appraised by three "honest housekeepers" and, when valued over £1 as nearly every horse should have been, the description and circumstances of the stray were advertised in the *Virginia Gazette*. Advertising charges were regulated, limited, in this instance, to a total of 3½ shillings for three listings. If no one claimed a stray within six months of the date of appraisal, title to the horse vested in the "taker up." The 1748 Assembly expressed concern for "divers vagrant people travel[ling] through this colony, from the northern provinces, to the southern, pedling [sic] and selling horses ... [who] often take away with them, the cattle of the inhabitants." The Assembly attacked the problem headlong, imposing a £10 duty on every horse "imported, or brought into this colony, for sale." "Persons ... moving their families and effects ... to reside" in the south were exempted from the duty. Virginia Governors regularly appointed collectors who were "resid[ing] near the frontiers," but records of the Loudoun collectors have yet to be identified. [Hening, VI/124-128 and VI/133; Democracy, p. 21].

The 1762 Assembly addressed "great frauds ... by ill-disposed people ... in taking up and concealing stray horses ... afterwards advertising them by false and imperfect descriptions." Thereafter, stray horses that were found anywhere in Virginia were to be taken immediately "before some Justice of the Peace of the county." The Justice, after confirming that an animal's markings had not been changed, would write out a full description of the stray in an order intended for local publication. Descriptions would then be "publickly affixed at the court-house ... on two several [monthly] court days next after" the viewing by the Justice. Three, or perhaps even as late as six, months after the "taking up," if the owner had not claimed his property, the finder would go through the old appraisal and *Virginia Gazette* publication process in order to clear his title to the animal. Similar procedures were instituted for stray cattle, sheep, goats and hogs. Rewards were fixed at 5 shillings for a horse or head of cattle, one shilling for a sheep, goat or hog, and publication fees were changed - to 5 shillings for 4 listings. A new £10 fine was imposed on every "taker up" who avoided the viewing and publication process, or "used" a stray before obtaining an appraisal. The penalty for an unauthorized person taking up a stray was increased from £1 to £5, but a tenant who had a lease for three or more years, like a freeholder, was authorized by the 1762 law to take up strays "on his own plantation, or at his place of residence." [Hening,

VII/545-548; re "freeholder" see, infra, Glossary; re horse stealing, see supra, Chapter on Crimes, @ pp. 160-161].

For over two centuries, beef and dairy cattle have been important agricultural stock in Loudoun County. Colonial husbandmen marked or branded their livestock. Following the custom of the time, the usual method of branding cattle was the notching of particular ear markings. Justice Aeneas Campbell had a rather exotic mark - branding a "Poplar leaf in each ear." Livestock ear marks were announced for the record at county court sessions and recorded in the order books, testimony to both the importance of their livestock and the breadth of the beef and dairy industry in colonial Loudoun. In light of the large number of colonial farmers who recorded livestock markings in the Loudoun County Court, only a representative sampling of the record is presented herein. [infra, The Record, p. 207].

During the French and Indian War, Virginia's Export Inspection laws for beef and pork were unnecessary and had been allowed to lapse. "Found useful and beneficial to the trade and export of this colony," the law was re-instituted in August of 1763, and was in effect through 1773. County courts were instructed to appoint one or more "fit and able" residents as inspectors, annually at either the August or September county court days. The new law was applied to "every barrel of pork or beef packed within [Virginia] for sale or exportation," which was to "contain at least [220] pounds of good clean, fat [sic!], sound, merchantable meat, well salted between each layer, well pickled, nailed and pegged ... allowing only [2½%] for shrinkage or loss of weight." For some reason, the Loudoun County Court apparently failed to appoint inspectors of beef as required by law. [Hening, VII/570-573].

In the reign of Charles I, the 1632 Assembly encouraged the elimination of predatory wolves by legislating that "whosoever shall kill a wolfe ... for every wolfe so kild, to kill also [as a reward] one wild hogg and take the same for his owne use [sic]." The 1646 Assembly, probably in response to an increasing scarcity of wild hogs, amended the law to grant a public reward of 100 lbt. for each wolf killed, "to bee raised out of the county where the wolfe is killed." At the time, this sum would have represented the greater part of the costs associated with importing a wife into the colony. The 1658 Assembly granted all of the county courts discretionary power to "augment the reward appointed for killing wolves," but this local power was seldom exercised. The reward for killing an adult wolf in Virginia, with few exceptions, was 100 lbt.s until the American Revolution. [Hening, I/199 Act XLIX, I/328, I/395, I/456 and IV/302; and see, ColVa, p. 71].

The 1748 Assembly recodified applicable Virginia law in "An Act for giving a reward for killing Wolves," which was in effect from 1757 to 1766, during Loudoun County's first decade. The reward for an adult wolf was reiterated as "one hundred pounds of nett tobacco," with the reward for a wolf under six months old set at half that amount. Individual Justices of the Loudoun County Court were authorized to grant a certificate to any hunter who produced the whole head of a wolf and gave the following oath:

> *"I '---' do swear that this head by me now produced is the head of a wolf ... first taken and killed within the county of 'Loudoun' in Virginia; and that I have not, wittingly or willingly spared the life of any bitch wolf in my power to kill. So help me God."*

The penalty for giving a false oath in obtaining a wolf certificate was substantial - 1,000 lbt.. The Assembly established a system for the rewards whereby a county initially paid the marksmen and was then reimbursed through a proportioning of the next colony-wide "public levy." One can imagine the spectacle at the County Court when Israel Thompson, a Quaker from The Gap, having neglected to obtain a Certificate from one of the Justices prior to the laying of the County levy in December of 1757, displayed a wolf's head in open court in order to qualify for his reward. Thereafter, at least through 1766, after killing a wolf, Loudoun residents would locate the nearest Justice and obtain a Certificate for their trophy. In 1765, rewards for killing wolves in Loudoun County, and neighboring Fauquier, Frederick, Hampshire and Prince William, were doubled. These additional rewards were almost immediately determined to be unnecessary in the northern piedmont, and the 1766 Assembly revoked the bonus for Loudoun County, and for neighboring Fauquier County as well. Despite the brevity of its availability, two Loudoun colonials, John Whitacre and George Buckalue, each collected the additional reward for killing a mature Wolf. The court records also give testimony to the expertise of another man, Samuel Jenkins (a resident of the Great Falls area), as colonial Loudoun's wolf hunter par excellence. [Hening, VI/152, VIII/147-148 and VIII/200; see infra, pp. 205-210].

Boars and wolves were not the only wild animals to be regulated in colonial times. To further the "better preservation of the Breed of Deer and [for] preventing unlawful Hunting" on private lands, the 1738 Assembly established deer hunting seasons. Buck season was limited to August through November, and does were to be taken only from October to December. The Assembly also outlawed fire hunting of deer. [Hening, V/62 and V/430].

Leesburg, as the site of the monthly County Court sessions, was the hub of commercial activity in colonial Loudoun. During monthly Court days, the entire community would meet friends, conduct business, exchange news, market produce, place orders for imported goods and, perhaps, find a bargain in the Sheriff's "outcry" sales of debtors' possessions. By reviewing commercial transactions that took place in Loudoun in the 1760s, we can obtain a sense of the relative value of various items. For example, the value of one month of labor from an indentured servant under contract was at least £1, or 160 lbt.s. Commodities were packed into barrels, or hogsheads, for shipment or storage. The standard allowance for the cost of making "cask" was 4% of the value of the goods although a hogshead, the large barrel itself, was widely understood to cost no more than 4 shillings to make. For £2, you could purchase one head of cattle, or 2 sheep, or 6 hogs, or 6 bushels of wheat, in the markets at Court days. A vacant ½-acre lot on Cornwall Street in Leesburg could cost as little as £4, even as late as 1780, while military suppliers were getting an inflated £3 or £4 per head of cattle at the height of the French War. A steady working mount, with saddle and reins included, could be had for under £10. A four-year contract for an unskilled indentured servant might be purchased for about £20. An improved ½-acre in Leesburg, with a small frame house on the lot, could cost £40; while an unimproved 300-acre tract or an unskilled, field-hand, slave would have been about the same price. [Hening, VII/25, VIII/91 and VIII/178; infra, p. 206; Democracy, p. 21; infra, Chapter on Slaves, and Chapter on Leesburg].

Commodities that were in the flow of colonial commerce reflect the industries and lifestyles of the Potomac river region as a whole. For this reason, ships' manifests from the second half of 1766, representing between ¼th and ½ of all imports and exports in the Potomac river that year, are included in The Record. These manifests document a period of colonial economic growth. Taken as a whole, they suggest the quantities and types of goods that were traded in the Potomac during the decade before the Revolution.

Exports in 1742 for the entire Virginia colony, ranked in order of value, were: 1- 34,000 hogsheads (about 1,000 lbs. each, or 17,000 tons) of tobacco; 2- 20,000 barrels (over 2,000 tons) of pork and beef; and, 3- 100,000 bushels of corn. Other major exports were: 100,000 barrels of pitch, tar and turpentine; 900 tons of pig iron (mostly processed Maryland ore); and 20,000 deer and beaver skins. Wheat and barrel staves were still minor exports for the Virginia colony as a whole, but they were quickly gaining importance and within three decades would become the primary exports of the Potomac piedmont region. [ColVa, p. 529].

Using the ships' manifests from 1766 as a guide, annual exports of Potomac production in the mid-1760s probably totalled: 1,300 tons of tobacco, with a total value of about £20,000; 500 tons of pig and bar iron; 100,000 barrel staves, valued at perhaps £2,000; and 100 tons of wheat flour. Aside from 3,000-5,000 parcels of "sundry European goods" and large quantities of plow shares, nails and frying pans, annual imports into the Potomac region would have included: 30,000-60,000 gallons of rum; 20 tons of sugar; 10 kiloliters of salt; 10,000-20,000 gallons of Madeira wines; and between 400 and 600 indentured and/or convict servants. [see infra, in seriatim, pp. 210-212].

The Loudoun Record

July 2, 1757 - Robert Stukesbury, Senr. is identified as a yeoman. LDCODB, Book A, p. 28; and see infra, Glossary.

August 10, 1757 - The Loudoun Court rates £5 of Pennsylvania currency to be equal in value to £4 of Virginia currency. Book A, p. 5.

August 31, 1757 - William Hatcher is referred to as a planter on the Northeast branch [Crooked Run] of Goose Creek. LDCODB, Book A, p. 24.

October 28, 1757 - Thomas Gore is identified as a husbandman [ie., a marshal of livestock]. LDCODB, Book A, p. 31.

December 13, 1757 - In the County levy, debits are listed for: "William Mead Junr. [and] John Piles [both] as per Certificate ... 100" lbs. of tobacco. These appear to be payments for killing wolves. Book A, p. 55.

December 14, 1757 - "Ordered ... the Sherif ... pay to Israel Thompson 100 lb. tobacco [the reward] in discharge of a Wolf's head." Book A, p. 63.

February 17, 1758 - James Abbett is a yeoman; John Hough is a farmer; Daniel Davis is a yeoman; Andrew Link is a yeoman; and, John Poultney is a farmer. LDCODB, Book A, pp. 70, 78, 81, 83 and 96.

March 15, 1758 - Joseph Yates and Mahlon Janney are farmers. Book A, p. 73; and, LDCODB, Book A, p. 59.

March 15, 1758 - "Ordered ... Nicholas Minor or Josias Clapham Gentn. agree with John Dalton, Gent., [an Alexandria merchant] for necessary Weights and Measures for a Standard for this County .." Book A, p. 74.

March 15, 1758 - John Hough and Francis Hague are appointed "to Inspect the Package and Weigh all Pork, Beef ... the filling of all Tar Pitch and Turpentine packed ... [within] and intended for Exportation [from] this County." Book A, p. 78; and see infra, Glossary.

April 11, 1758 - In a recorded deed of transferred property, 7 cattle are valued at £7, and 17 hogs are valued at £3. DALD, (1758) p. 13.

June 12, 1758 - Thomas John is a farmer. LDCODB, Book A, p. 148.

August 10, 1758 - John Hough and Francis Hague, ie., "the Present Inspectors of Pork, Beef &c. in this County are Continued [in that position] for the ensuing Year." Book A, p. 154.

November 14, 1758 - In the County Levy, debits are listed for Wolves heads: "To ... Samuel Jenkins ... for 7 young Wolfs heads ... Thomas Owsley ... Leven Powell ... [and] Peter Huggins ... [each] for a Wolfs head ... [and] Ann Stephens ... for 3 young Wolfs heads," with payments listed at 50 lbt.s for each young wolf and 100 lbt.s for each mature wolf. Book A, pp. 176 and 177.

November 14, 1758 - In the County Levy, the Loudoun County Court rates £1 of Virginia currency to be equal in value to 120 lbs. of tobacco [ie., with 240 pence in £1, 100 lbt.s equal 200 pence]. Book A, p. 177.

March 11, 1759 - Thomas Pritchard is referred to as a farmer. LDCODB, Book A, p. 363.

March 14, 1759 - In Assembly, "A Bill to enable the Inhabitants of the County of Loudoun to pay their public Dues and Officer Fees in Money, was read a second Time, and committed to [a committee of] Mr. Francis Lightfoot Lee, Mr. Hambleton [sic - James Hamilton] and Mr. Walker." This "Mr. Walker" was Thomas Walker, the son-in-law of Lord Fairfax. Assembly (1758), pp. 88 and 93.

March 17, 1759 - Francis Lee reported: the committee "made several Amendments [to the Loudoun "money" bill]." He then delivered the Bill "with the Amendments," which was engrossed for a third reading. Assembly (1758), p. 98.

April 5, 1759 - Lt. Governor Fauquier gives the Crown's assent to the Loudoun "money bill." Assembly (1758), pp. 106 and 118.

August 15, 1759 - "Ordered that the Sherif ... pay unto John Carlyle Gent. [a senior Fairfax County Justice, Colonel of Fairfax militia, Alexandria merchant and John Dalton's business partner] ... £25 ... for Standards, Weights and Measures for this County." Book A, p. 267; supra, March 15, 1758 entry.

August 15, 1759 - An accounting of the estate of John Poultney values his "riding horse, saddle and bridle at £9.10.0, [and a] Silver Watch & two pair of Silver Buckles at £13." LDCOWIL, Book A, p. 18.

November 13, 1759 - The Grand Jury brings a presentment against "the Surveyor of the Road for not keeping a Post at the fork of [Mountain] Roads near Edward Porters [below Rocky Run] where one Road leads to Alexandria and the other to Occoquan Warehouse." Book A, p. 300.

November 14, 1759 - In itemizing the County Levy, debits are listed for Wolves heads: "To ... Thomas Pritchard ... Joseph Janney ... Thomas Owsley ... [and] Leven Powell ... [each] for a Wolf's head ... 100 [lbs. tobacco]." Book A, pp. 302, 303 and 304.

November 16, 1759 - Henry Taylor, "of Loudoun ..." is identified as a "Planter." Book A, p. 310.

March 11, 1760 - The Loudoun County Court restates the value of tobacco: 100 lbs. of tobacco is valued at 12 shillings, 6 pence. Book A, p. 323.

May 12, 1760 - In a deed selling 568 acres of land on the south fork of the Beaver Dam branch of Goose Creek to George Burson "farmer," Thomas John is now identified as a yeoman. LDCODB, Book A, p. 392.

May 14, 1760 - On the "Motion of Charles Binns [the Clerk of Court] ... his Ear Mark is ... Recorded Vizt. A crop and a slit in the left ear and a swallow Fork and Underkeel in the right Ear." Book A, p. 349.

June 12, 1760 - Henry Ansley is a farmer. LDCODB, Book B, p. 8.

August 14, 1760 - Hugh Black "of Loudoun County near George Town [sic - ie., near Leesburg], Yeoman." Book A, p. 397 and Book B, p. 173.

November of 1760 - In the 1760 tithables list returned by William West, one John Davis is identified as a farmer, probably to distinguish him from another who is not. LDTX/1, p.4; and see, Order Book A, p. 468.

November 12, 1760 - In itemizing the County Levy, a debit is listed for "Ezekiel Jenkins for two young Wolves heads as per Certificate ... 100 [lbs. tobacco]." Book A, p. 404.

November 12, 1760 - "Francis Wilks, his Ear Mark [for livestock] ... a Swallow Fork in the right Ear and a Crop in the left Ear." Book A, p. 406.

March 12, 1761 - "On the Motion of Aneas Campbell his Ear Mark is Ordered to be Recorded, vizt., a Poplar Leaf in each Ear." Book A, p. 449.

March 19, 1761 - Various Petitions, from Loudoun, Fairfax and Prince William County farmers and merchants, request that new tobacco warehouses be authorized "to [at] Murray's Landing on Quantico." Assembly (1758), p. 219.

June 10, 1761 - The livestock of Ann Murphey are all marked "with a crop in the right Ear and a slit in the left." LDCODB, Book B, p. 140.

September 8, 1761 - Jacob Phaw, or Jacob Faw, is identified as a farmer. LDCODB, Book C, p. 15.

September 9, 1761 - "John Newland and William Baker ... able Persons residing in this County [are appointed] to Inspect the Package and Weigh all Pork, Beef ... also the filling of Tar Pitch and Turpentine ... for Sale or

Exportation & also to Inspect and Weigh all Wheat Flower made & intended for Exportation within this County." Book A, p. 503; and see infra, Glossary.

October 13, 1761 - Jonas Potts, farmer, buys 122 acres on the north fork of the Kitoctin from Jonas Potts, blacksmith. LDCODB, Book C, p. 27.

November 12, 1761 - "John Owsley of Loudoun County" is identified as a "Planter." Book A, p. 541.

May 14, 1762 - Jonathan Price, William Jones, Edward Harden and John Popkins are to view the route for a new "Road from Jenny's [Janney's] Mill [at Waterford, east over Kitoctin Mtn.] into the main [Carolina] Road leading from Leesburgh [sic] to Clapham's & Noland's Ferries." Book A, p. 622.

June 10, 1762 - George Chelton and Samuel Winn are "Planters." Book A, p. 636 and Book B, p. 398.

July 8, 1762 - The Governor and his Council, in a meeting at Williamsburg, "having taken under consideration the Scarcity of Indian Corn, it was Order'd, that a Proclamation issue to Prohibit the Exportation thereof until further order made." Council, VI/228.

July 13, 1762 - The Loudoun County Court Orders that "On the Motion of John Dodd his Ear Mark is Recorded as follows, vizt., a Crop in the right Ear and an underbit in the left." Book B, p. 1.

July 13, 1762 - "On the Motion of John Carr his Ear Mark is Ordered to be Recorded vizt., a Swallow fork in each Ear." Book B, p. 2.

August 12, 1762 - On the "Motion of David Smith his Ear Mark [for his livestock] ... Recorded vizt. A crop and Slit in the left Ear and an Overkeel in the Right." Book B, p. 47.

November 10, 1762 - The County Levy lists a debit "To ... Thomas Williams ... for one old Wolf's head ... 100 [lbs. tobacco]." Book B, p. 73.

November 18, 1762 - Petitions to the Assembly of "sundry inhabitants" of Fairfax and Loudoun County requesting that "the public warehouses for the Inspection of Tobacco at Occoquan be discontinued, and that new Warehouses ... [be] established at the Town of Colchester ... [are found] reasonable. [The Assembly Orders that a] Committee amend the Act ..." Assembly (1761), p. 99.

March 24, 1763 - William Allan, formerly of Hunterdon County in West Jersey, and John Violett, are identified as "Loudoun Planters." LDCODB, Book C, pp. 584 and 592.

April 12, 1763 - Josias Clapham displayed "a Sample of flax of one pound weight," and certified that in 1762 he produced 163 lbs. of flax from one acre on his Plantation. Book B, p. 88.

April 13, 1763 - Nicholas Osborn is identified as a Yeoman of Loudoun. Book B, p. 94.

April 13, 1763 - "John Heryford of Loudoun County, Planter." Book B, p. 103.

May 1, 1763 - William Trammell is identified as a Loudoun County "Farmer." LDCODB, Book C, 660.

May 10, 1763 - Daniel Conner is identified as a farmer living near the head of Elk Lick Run. LDCODB, Book D, p. 185.

May 10, 1763 - "Isaac Nichols of Loudoun County ... Yeoman." Book B, p. 123.

May 12, 1763 - "George Russell of Loudoun County, Planter." Book B, p. 141.

May 24, 1763 - The Loudoun County Court determines that: "[O]ne Dollar [is] of the value of five Shillings and nine pence Current Money [of Virginia]." In other words, at the time £1 = $3.48 in Loudoun. Book B, p. 158.

June 14, 1763 - The Ear mark "of Daniel Jones [for his livestock is recorded] ... a half crop and a nick under the Left Ear." Book B, p. 159.

June 14, 1763 - The Ear mark "of Thomas Lewellen [for his livestock] ... Recorded vizt. a smooth Crop in the right Ear." Book B, p. 159.

October 29, 1763 - William McKnight of Loudoun is identified as a yeoman. LDCODB, Book D, p. 479.

November 8, 1763 - "On the Motion of James Garey his Ear Mark is Recorded as follows, a Crop and a slit in the right Ear and a slit and an underkeel in the left." Book B, p. 263.

November 9, 1763 - In the County Levy a debit is listed "To ... Thomas Williams for one Old Wolf's head ... 100 [lbs. tobacco]." Book B, p. 266.

April 12, 1764 - John Bishop, a defendant, is a "Planter of Loudoun County." Book B, p. 343.

May 7, 1764 - Samuel Harris of Loudoun is identified as a "Farmer." LDCODB, Book D, p. 178; and, DALD, (1764) p. 48.

June 15, 1764 - "Thomas Williams Wells, of Loudoun County, Planter." Book B, p. 397.

August 14, 1764 - "Francis Heronimus of Loudoun County, Farmer." Book B, p. 408; see infra, Chapter on Various and Sundry and the Unusual.

September 12, 1764 - "John Compton of Loudoun County, Planter." Book B, p. 435.

November 13, 1764 - In the County Levy a debit is listed "for one Wolfs head ... by [to] George Buckalew ... 100 [lbs. tobacco]." Book B, p. 495.

February 12, 1765 - The livestock Ear mark "of William Musgrove [is] Recorded Vizt. a Crop and one Slit in the Right Ear and an underkeel in the Left [Ear]." Book B, p. 517.

June 12, 1765 - "Joseph Stephens, Farmer" is a defendant at Court. Book B, p. 642.

August 13, 1765 - John Evans is now identified as a "Farmer of Loudoun." Book C, p. 18.

September 12, 1765 - In a lease for a 200 acre farm at Broad Run, George William Fairfax agrees with John Hutton to accept wheat in exchange for rent at the rate of 2½ shillings per bushel. LDCODB, Book E, p. 25.

October 28, 1765 - In a chattel mortgage (a loan secured by personal property), Joseph Longley and Kitchen Prim agree that 40 bushels of wheat are worth £6 in currency [ie., 3 shillings to the bushel]. LDCODB, Book E, p. 22.

September 12, 1765 - Loudoun County Justice John McIlhaney is identified as a farmer. LDCODB, Book D, p. 707.

November 11, 1765 - In the County Levy, a debit is listed "To ... Samuel Jenkins ... for one Wolf's head ... 160 [lbs. tobacco]." Book C, p. 73.

November 11, 1765 - The Loudoun County Court rates £1 of Virginia currency equal to the value of 160 lbs. of tobacco. This restates and confirms the official exchange rate that was established for Loudoun by the 1759 Assembly, ie., 100 lbs. of tobacco was valued at 12 shillings, 6 pence. Book C, p. 73; see supra, this Chapter, @ p. 191; but see November 14, 1758 entry, supra, @ p. 205, 206.

Sunday, May 11, 1766 - Virginia's Treasurer, John Robinson, dies in Williamsburg. This sets the stage for a precipitous economic crisis in Virginia, following revelations of an enormous financial scandal. Assembly, (1766) xxi.

June 10, 1766 - Isaac Dillon is a farmer. Book C, p. 97.

June 10, 1766 - Isaac Wright is a farmer. Book C, p. 98.

June 10, 1766 - Henry Aylon [sic] is a planter. Book C, p. 98.

June 12, 1766 - Joseph Yates and Mahlon Janney [the miller!] are both identified as farmers. Book C, p. 119.

June 13, 1766 - Joseph Stephens is a farmer. Book C, p. 136.

June 14, 1766 - The schooner *Patowmack,* captain Henry M'Cabe [the future owner of a large tract around Leesburg], arrived in the South Potowmack, from Philadelphia, with a cargo of 7 casks of tin ware, 4 casks and 3 kegs of nails, 12 dozen sickles, 2½ dozen scythes, one dozen hoes, one bundle of waggon boxes, one barrel of resin, one barrel of tar, 3 hogsheads, 6 tierces, 5 bales, 11 boxes, 2 cases and 3 trunks of European goods, one bundle of frying pans, 23 bundles of steel, one hogshead of molasses, one quarter-cask of wine, 6 barrels of loaf sugar, 23 hogsheads of rum, 23 barrels of muscovado sugar, 3 boxes of soap, one bundle of plat hats, and one passenger. VaGaz/R, No. 10, July 18, 1766, p. 3, col. 2.

June 14, 1766 - The ship *Northumberland,* with captain Henry Parry [sic - Henry Perry?], is reported to be "a New Ship [launched] from the Stocks." VaGaz/R, No. 10, July 18, 1766, p. 3, col. 2.

June 23, 1766 - The brigantine *Adventure,* with captain Thomas Adam, arrived in the South Potowmack, from Hampton, with a cargo of 20 tons [sic - this was almost certainly intended as "tuns"] and 54 gallons of Portugal wine. VaGaz/R, No. 10, July 18, 1766, p. 3, col. 2; see infra, Glossary.

July 4, 1766 - The ship *Ranger,* captain Hugh Wylie, arrived in the South Potowmack, from London, via Hampton, with a cargo of "sundry European goods and 2 passengers." VaGaz/R, No. 10, July 18, 1766, p. 3, col. 2.

July 13, 1766 - Daniel Mitinger [sic- Daniel Mittenger], in preparation for his removal from Loudoun County, sold his hogs and crops of wheat, corn and flax. LDCODB, Book E, p. 286.

August 12, 1766 - To secure a debt of £10, 13 shillings, Loudoun farmer George McDonald provides a deed of mortgage to Hunter, Campbell & Company, merchants, for his assets: one mare, 5 cattle, 50 hogs, 2 feather beds, a rifled gun and a smooth bore gun. LDCODB, Book E, p. 150.

October 10, 1766 - The ship *Ranger*, this time with John Harbison as the captain, cleared Virginia's district of the South Potowmack bound for London, after registering a cargo of 481 hogsheads of tobacco, 8 tuns [sic - this probably meant tuns, but could have been "tons"] of pig iron, 3 quarter-casks of Madeira wine, 1023 "pipe" staves, 3476 hogshead staves and 7979 barrel staves. See supra, July 4, 1766 entry; VaGaz/PD, November 27, 1766, p. 2, col. 2; see Glossary.

October 15, 1766 - The ship *Jenny,* captain John Hall, entered the South Potowmack, from Hull, with a cargo of 531 parcels of European goods and 3 passengers. Apparently after having miscalculated the season or demand, the *Jenny* cleared the Potowmack district on October 25th, bound for Hampton with 499 parcels of European goods. VaGaz/PD, November 27, 1766, p. 2, col. 2.

October 21, 1766 - The ship *Alexandria,* captain John Montgomery, cleared the district of the South Potowmack, bound for Glasgow, with a cargo of 351 hogsheads of tobacco, 154 tuns [sic] of pig iron, 7 tuns and 13 wt. [weight] of bar iron, 400 hogshead and 10,000 barrel staves, and 1 hogshead and a quarter-cask of Madeira wine. VaGaz/PD, November 27, 1766, p. 2, col. 2; Glossary.

October 23, 1766 - The snow *Keith,* captain William Miller, cleared the Potomack district, bound for Glasgow, with 31 hogsheads of tobacco, and 1 ton [sic] and 17 "wt." of iron bar. VaGaz/PD, November 27, 1766, p. 2, col. 2.

October 25, 1766 - The ship *Nelly,* captain Daniel McKirdy, cleared the district of the South Potowmack, bound for Glasgow, with 100 hogsheads of tobacco. VaGaz/PD, November 27, 1766, p. 2, col. 2.

November 1, 1766 - The brigantine *Adventure,* captain Thomas Adam, entered the district of the South Potowmack, from Barbados, with a cargo of 75 hogsheads and 2 barrels of rum, 26 barrels of muscovado [turbanado] sugar, and 2 bags of cotton. VaGaz/PD, November 27, 1766, p. 2, col. 2.

November 3, 1766 - The *Industry,* captain James Lowes, entered the district of the South Potowmack, from Limerick, with a cargo of 97 passengers and servants. VaGaz/PD, November 27, 1766, p. 2, col. 2.

November 4, 1766 - The ship *Hicks,* captain John Smith, entered the district of the South Potowmack, from Whitehaven and Dublin, with 55 parcels of European goods, and 128 passengers, indented servants and convicts. VaGaz/PD, Jan. 8, 1767, p. 3, col. 1.

November 4, 1766 - Another *Nelly,* with captain James Cuthbert, entered the South Potowmack, from "Greenock," with a cargo of 58 parcels of European goods and one passenger. VaGaz/PD, January 8, 1767, p. 3, col. 1.

November 5, 1766 - John Criswell, of Loudoun County, is identified as a "Farmer" living on the west side of the Folly Lick branch of Sugarland Run. LDCODB, Book E, p. 335-336.

November 5, 1766 - The *Patuxent,* captain David Lewis, cleared the South Potowmack, bound for London, with a cargo of 40 hogsheads of tobacco. VaGaz/PD, Jan. 22, 1767, p. 3, col. 1.

November 7, 1766 - The front edge of a financial scandal begins to unravel as the Virginia Assembly appoints a select committee, which includes Francis Lightfoot Lee, to examine the books in the Office of the late Treasurer, John Robinson, and look into allegations that have begun to circulate regarding irregularities in the colony's books of account. Assembly, (1766) p. xxi.

November 11, 1766 - In the itemization of the County Levy, debits are listed: "To ... John Whitacre ... [and] George Buckalue [each] ... for one old Wolf's head ... 200 [lbs. tobacco]." Book C, p. 220.

November 11, 1766 - In the Levy a debit is listed "To ... Steerman Chilton, Constable ... for viewing Tobacco fields ... 284 [lbt.s]." Book C, p. 220.

November 15, 1766 - Another *Jenny*, from Port Glasgow, captained by Archibald Omey, entered the South Potowmack and registered 198 parcels of European goods and one passenger. VaGaz/PD, January 8, 1767, p. 3, col. 1.

November 17, 1766 - The ship *Swift,* with captain Joseph Thompson, cleared the district of the South Potowmack, bound for St. Christopher's, with a cargo of 356 barrels of "flower", 47 barrels of bread, 1134 bushels of Indian corn, 72 bushels of "pease," one riding chair, 13,000 dressed hogshead staves, 1800 dressed hogshead "headings," 600 white oak hoops and 200 head of live stock. VaGaz/PD, January 22, 1767, p. 3, col. 1.

November 20, 1766 - The ship *Grand Caicos,* captain William Bryan Junr., entered the Potowmack from Bermuda and Turk Island, with 3 hogsheads of rum, one hogshead and 2 barrels of muscovado sugar, 800 bushels of Turk Island salt, and 4,000 lemons and oranges. VaGaz/PD, Jan. 8, 1767, p. 3, col. 1.

December 8, 1766 - Loudoun County Justice Charles Tyler, clearly in anticipation of his own death, liquidates his estate by selling all of his slaves and household possessions to fellow Loudoun Justice Aeneas Campbell and James Nisbett of Prince William County. The 14 head of cattle, along with the other farm animals and household furnishings, brought the considerable sum of £217. LDCODB, Book E, p. 332-334; DALD, (1767) p. 37; and see, Chapter on the Loudoun County Court, supra, @ p. 63.

December 9, 1766 - Justice Francis Peyton is appointed as the new Inspector of Flour for Loudoun County, replacing "William Baker who hath resigned." Book C, p. 232.

December 12, 1766 - In Williamsburg, the consequences of a financial scandal involving practices of the former Treasurer of Virginia are reported to the Virginia Assembly by its select committee: "many Errors and Omissions having been discovered ... at the Death of John Robinson ... there remains due from the [estate of the] late Treasurer ... on the public account, £3,388 ... [in various taxes, licensing fees, import and export duties, a total of] £95,827 ... in the whole ... a Balance due to the Publick of £100,761.7.5." This incredible, shocking shortage in the colony's Treasury resulted from Robinson's illegal practice of re-issuing Virginia treasury notes, that were supposed to have been destroyed when they were redeemed by the Treasurer, as loans to friends in financial distress. Many of the beneficiaries of Robinson's assistance were insolvent and the loans were uncollectible. Surprisingly, this unauthorized "creation" of paper money did not result in an out-of-control inflationary spiral - further evidence that Virginia was constantly being drained of liquid funds in the course of its trading relationship with mother England. Assembly, (1766) pp. xxi-xxii; Democracy, pp. 117-118.

In November of 1645, in the 20th year of the reign of King Charles I, the Virginia Assembly enacted legislation "to rectifie the great abuse of millers," who apparently were charging excessive fees for grinding corn and wheat. In milling parlance grinding fees were referred to as a "toll." The 1645 law instructed millers to accept tolls of no more than "the sixth part thereof ... for grinding any grayne [sic]." Virginia Assembly enactments in November of 1647 and March of 1657-58 continued the 1/6th limit on miller tolls, and added requirements for the installation of new "statute weights and scales" at all mills. In September of 1671 the Virginia Assembly reduced miller tolls for the grinding of "English graine," meaning wheat, to a 1/8th share, retaining the 1/6th toll for corn. Miller tolls were unchanged until 1748 when the Virginia Assembly set the allowable tolls for all grains at a 1/8th portion. This was the legal toll limit in force everywhere in Virginia during Loudoun County's first decade, from 1757 to 1766. [Hening, I/301, Act IV, I/347-348, I/485, II/286, III/401 and VI/58].

Mills and the production of flour grew in importance as the Virginia economy expanded and European sources of flour were interrupted during continental wars. In 1667 the Assembly established procedures for prospective millers to obtain an acre of land on the opposite bank of a waterway where they intended to construct a mill, based on the appraisal of two commissioners. The Virginia Assembly's Act of 1748, "concerning Water Mills," revised the procedures incumbent on anyone intending to erect a water mill in Virginia, with the law becoming effective in 1751. Mill applicants were required to petition their county court for a license. "Where the petitioner's land extends so far, on both sides [of the waterway], as not to affect or overflow the land of any other person," the county court had authority to issue a license for a new mill without further delay. During Loudoun County's first decade the County Court used its authority under this law to issue expedited approval orders to Aneas Campbell on Limestone Run, Joseph Janney on Tuscarora Run, James Lane on Cub Run, John Trammell on Clarks Run, Thomas Dodd on Great Dutchman Run and John Hough on Goose Creek, for the construction of new grist mills. The more usual scenario for the construction of a new mill involved a petitioner who owned land on only one side of the water at the intended mill site. In these situations, Virginia law provided for the condemnation of one acre of land on the opposite bank, based on a mill petition to the county court. The county court was required to instruct the Sheriff to summon a local jury of twelve "freeholders of the vicinage" (meaning twelve "voters," anyone in the locale owning at least a life interest in property in the county), who were to view the site, value the lands, timber and any other property that would be damaged where the lands would "be affected or laid under water," and report back to the court. Provided there were no houses or orchards on the acre affected, the county court was then authorized to approve the construction of the mill, resulting in a conditional transfer of ownership of the identified acre of land. [Hening, II/260-261 and III/401-404; and see infra, pp. 221, 222, 223, 224 and 225].

As a practical matter the Loudoun County Court regularly sent George West, the county Surveyor, to accompany the jury on their viewing, to lay off and set the bounds of the transferred acre. There were only five valuation juries conducted during Loudoun's first decade, and we have given the jury members in The Record herein. The Surveyor's fee for laying off one acre of land for a mill was 100 lbs. of tobacco, or 12½ shillings, paid by the petitioner. The twelve members of the valuation jury were also paid for their attendance, for a total cost of 300 lbs. of tobacco. The Sheriff was entitled to charge another 200 lbs. of tobacco "for summoning a jury upon any survey" and for one day in attendance with the Surveyor and valuation jury. Along with the various Clerk's filing, docketing and recording fees, the process of obtaining an acre of condemned land through the jury valuation method would have cost over £4, the going price for a half-acre lot in Leesburg in 1759. Additionally, the petitioner would be obligated for the assessed value of the condemned acre and any timber or existing improvements that might be lost by flooding. [Hening, V/331-333, V/338 and V/341].

After 1705, mill petitioners were required to begin construction within one year and begin operation within three years of the grant of the license to proceed. If a mill burned down or was carried away in a torrent, the mill proprietor was given similar time limits within which to rebuild without having to renew his original petition for the mill site. Otherwise, by law, the appropriated acre of land would revert to the original owner. Some authorized mills were in fact never built, confusing modern researchers. [Hening, III/403 and VI/55-60; infra, @ p. 224].

The 1714 Assembly required mill dams and retaining walls that also served as causeways or roads were to be constructed to a minimum width of ten feet at their top. This provision was amended in 1748 to require a twelve foot width on the top surface of a bridge or mill dam, with "strong rails to be set up, and kept in repair, on each side of such bridge, passage [or] floodgates." The law contained a grandfather clause for those "already built, ten feet wide, with strong rails to the same, such bridge shall be sufficient so long as it shall be in good repair." In 1762, the Assembly added the requirement that any mill owner constructing a mill dam that was to be traversed by a public road would have to enter a double-indemnity bond with security. The absence of a record or hint of any such bond during Loudoun's first decade leads us to believe that there was no such structure built in Loudoun before 1767. [Hening, VI/67-68, IV/54 and VII/577].

Beginning in 1705 and thereafter through at least 1766, all Virginia millers "having the charge and keeping of any mill" were exempted from service in their county militia. In 1705 the Assembly set up regulations that were in effect and applicable to all mills in operation in Loudoun County during the 1757-1766 decade. Millers who failed to "well and sufficiently grind ... the grain brought to their mills" were to pay a penalty of fifteen shillings to the injured party, along with any court costs involved in the enforcement. Offending millers who were servants or slaves were to be whipped with thirty lashes for a first offence, and forty lashes for a second. All mill owners were required to keep on hand "sealed measures" of a half bushel, a peck, and a toll dish, under penalty of another fifteen shilling fine, paid to "the informer" of the infraction. The Virginia Mill Act of 1748 imposed one additional 'health code' regulation in the milling law, authorizing the neighbors of a mill to kill any hogs that were allowed to run at large on the mill property. The trial of any milling infraction could be had before any individual justice of the peace in the county, which may explain the complete absence of any record of these infractions in the Loudoun Court records for the period despite the existence of a large number of operating mills in Loudoun county. If there were infractions by the millers, either they were not prosecuted or the offending millers did not appeal their sentences to a hearing of the full County Court. [Hening, III/336, IV/119, VII/93, VII/534, III/401-404, and VI/58-59; and see infra, The Record].

A Flour Inspection Act, adopted in 1748 and amended in 1762, was in force during the 1757-1766 decade. "Every person making ... wheat flour intended for exportation" was regulated. Millers and farmers were compelled to certify on oath that their flour was "fine, clean and pure, not mixed with meal or Indian corn, pease [sic] or any other grain or pulse," and have inspectors brand barrels of flour with identifying marks, "the gross, tare and nett weight thereof, and a distinction of the fineness by the words First or Second." Exporters were obliged to pay inspector's fees: "for every barrel of flour, containing two hundred and twenty pounds nett, or less, three pence; and for every cask of greater weight, six pence." [Hening, VI/148-149, VII/40, VII/570-572 and VIII/143; see supra, Chapter on Agriculture @ p. 195].

John Hough, colonial Loudoun's milling "magnate," (he built and operated at least four grist mills before the Revolution), served as one of the Inspectors of flour for the new county from 1757 to perhaps as late as 1761. But in 1765 the Virginia Assembly prohibited any miller from serving as an inspector of flour. At the end of Loudoun's first decade, in November of 1766, the Virginia Assembly also adopted an Act designed to induce the increased exportation of wheat flour, reducing inspector's fees on export flour to "one penny half-penny for every cask or barrel of flour by him inspected and marked." [Mills, pp. 9-10; Hening, VIII/144 and VIII/198; see infra, @ pp. 221 and 224].

When Loudoun County was formed in mid-1757, there were already about a dozen water grist mills operating within its boundaries. Amos Janney (near modern-day Waterford) and Richard Brown (near modern-day Taylorstown) on Kittoctin Creek, and Stephen Lewis on Difficult Run (now in Fairfax County), in the 1730s, were the first three known to have erected a mill on lands that later became part of Loudoun County. They were followed by Willoughby Newton on Great Rocky Cedar Run (now in Fairfax County) around 1746; Richard Coleman on Sugarland Run, John Harle on the Secolon, and John Mercer on Hunger Run of Little River around 1748; Edward Garrett on the Beaver Dam Branch of Goose Creek around 1750; William

Fairfax and Edward Masterson, both on Difficult Run (now in Fairfax County) around 1751; Joseph West on the North Branch of Goose Creek in 1752; and John Hough at the Gap of Short Hill on Kittoctin Creek in 1755. [Marsh, pp. 1, 4, 8 and 49; Lewis, p. 1; FXCOSUR, October 10, 1743; FXCODB, Book B-1, pp. 31, 366, and 373; FXCOCO, 1749 Book, pp. 57, 111, 165, 166, 215, 285, 305; FXCOCO, 1754 Book, p. 318].

The latter is probably the mill identified on the 1756 plat of the Short Hill Gap area showing "Tayloe's Kittoctin Lands," recorded among the Deeds in both Fairfax and Loudoun Counties. While a reference in a 1759 deed to an "old mill" at the Gap has given rise to speculation that the first mill at the Gap was actually operated by Samuel Butcher, there is no record that Butcher ever obtained a mill license, there are no other references to a mill owned or operated at the Gap before Hough's 1755 petition, and Hough's mill at the Gap is reportedly in operation only six months after the 1759 deed. Thus, it would seem more likely that Butcher and Hough were partners in the first mill at the Gap of the Short Hill, built on Hough's 1755 license, and probably operated at first by Samuel Butcher. Only two months before Loudoun County was created, on May 18, 1757, another Loudoun County notable, Josias Clapham, obtained a license from the Fairfax County Court to erect a mill "on his land," probably near the mouth of Kittoctin Creek. [Ibid.; FXCOCO, 1756 Book, p. 101; also see LDCODB, Book A, p. 232; DALD, (1761) p. 57; infra, Chapter on Surveys, Land and Leases; and see infra, The Record, @ p. 222].

The Table at page 229, at the end of this chapter, lists the first official notice of various early Loudoun County mills identified in The Record. The reader will observe that The Record contains several references found in county road orders which prove the existence and/or location of a number of mills. The Hough mill at the Gap of the Short Hill is a good example, since the first official record in Loudoun County of the ownership of the mill is found in a 1759 road order for a new road from the Gap of the Short Hill to Williams Gap. [see infra, p. 222].

The Record provides other information that will be useful to researchers, such as the area of residence of individuals who either served on a valuation jury, had their lands appropriated for a mill, or served on panels that reported the routes of new roads near existing mill sites. [see infra, pp. 227-228].

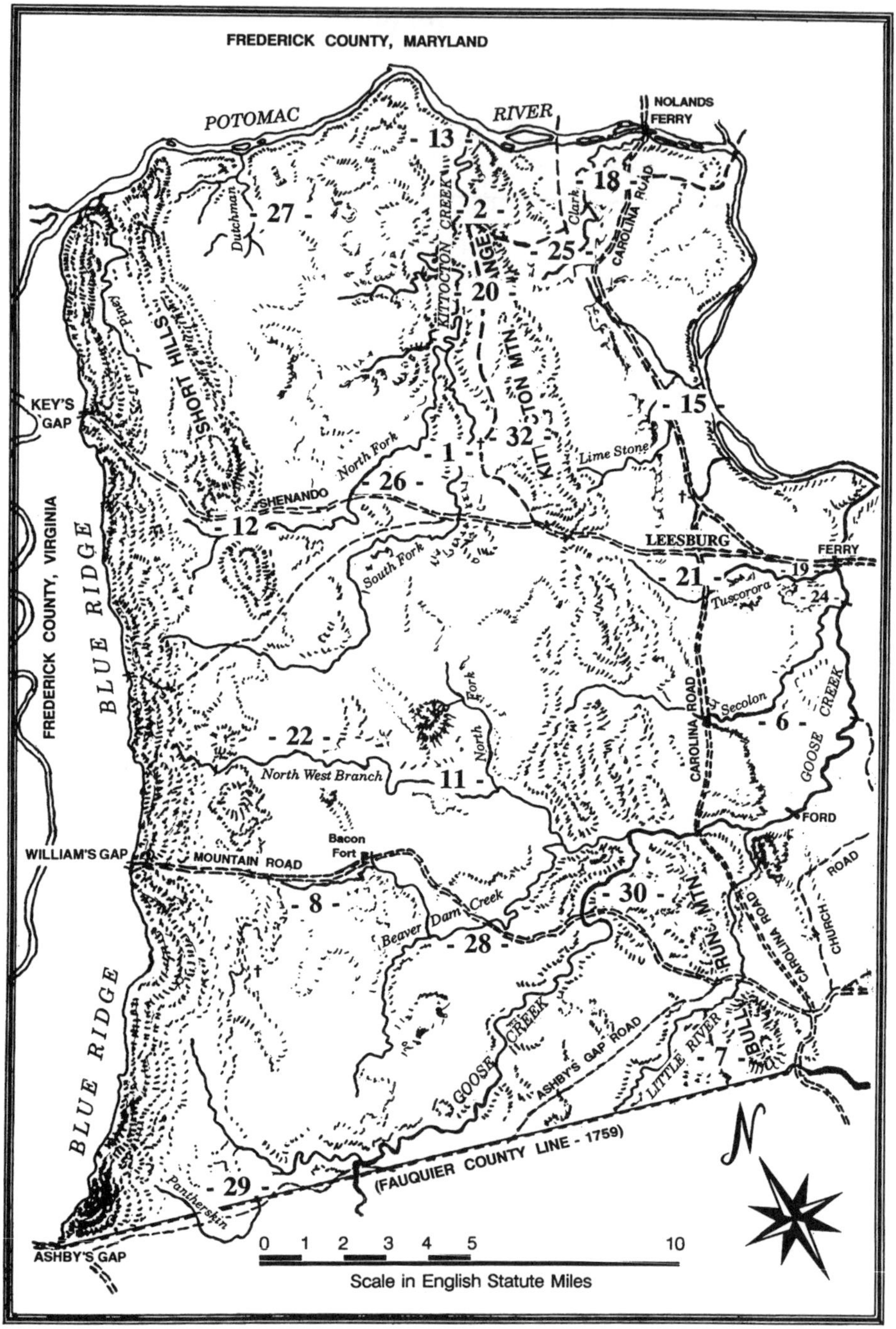
FREDERICK COUNTY, MARYLAND
POTOMAC
RIVER
NOLANDS FERRY
- 13 -
- 18 -
- 27 -
Dutchman
KITTOCTON CREEK
- 2 -
Clark
CAROLINA ROAD
- 25 -
- 20 -
KITTOCTON MTN
SHORT HILLS
Piney
KEY'S GAP
- 15 -
- 32 -
- 1 -
North Fork
Lime Stone
- 26 -
SHENANDO
- 12 -
LEESBURG
FERRY
South Fork
- 21 -
19
Tuscorora
- 24 -
FREDERICK COUNTY, VIRGINIA
BLUE RIDGE
CAROLINA ROAD
Secolon
- 6 -
GOOSE CREEK
North Fork
- 22 -
North West Branch
- 11 -
FORD
WILLIAM'S GAP
MOUNTAIN ROAD
Bacon Fort
- 8 -
- 30 -
Beaver Dam Creek
- 28 -
RUN MTN
CAROLINA ROAD
CHURCH ROAD
GOOSE CREEK
ASHBY'S GAP ROAD
LITTLE RIVER
BULL
- 7 -
BLUE RIDGE
N
(FAUQUIER COUNTY LINE - 1759)
- 29 -
Panthershin
ASHBY'S GAP
0 1 2 3 4 5 10
Scale in English Statute Miles

LOUDOUN COUNTY, VIRGINIA

COLONIAL
GRIST MILL SITES
CIRCA 1730 - 1766

Compiled by John T. Phillips, II

Map Legend for mills west of Leesburg and Little River.

The mills are numbered in the order that they were founded.

Mill Founder	Location in Colonial Loudoun
1- AMOS JANNEY	Kittoctin Creek (now at Waterford)
2- RICHARD BROWN	Kittoctin Creek (now at Taylorstown)
8- EDWARD GARRETT	Goose Creek, Beaver Dam Branch
11- JOSEPH WEST	Goose Creek, North Branch
12- JOHN HOUGH	Kittoctin Creek, at The Gap
13- JOSIAS CLAPHAM	Kittoctin Creek, near the mouth
15- AENEAS CAMPBELL	Limestone Run
18- JOHN POULTNEY	Clarks Run
20- RICHARD ROACH	Kittoctin Creek, "Anderson's" branch
21- AENEAS CAMPBELL	Tuscarora Run
22- ISAAC NICHOLS	Goose Creek, North Branch
25- JOHN TRAMMELL	Clarks Run
26- ISRAEL THOMPSON	Kittoctin Creek, north fork
27- THOMAS DODD	Great Dutchman Run
28- JOSHUA DUNCAN JUNR.	Goose Creek, Beaver Dam Run
29- EDWARD GARRETT	Pantherskin Run of Goose Creek
30- HENRY PEYTON	Goose Creek, west of Little River
32- GEORGE GREGG	sawmill, Kittoctin, Sears (Balls) branch

LOUDOUN COUNTY, VIRGINIA

COLONIAL
GRIST MILL SITES
CIRCA 1730 - 1766

Compiled by John T. Phillips, II

Map Legend for mills east of Leesburg and Little River.

The mills are numbered in the order that they were founded.

Mill Founder	Location in Colonial Loudoun
3- STEPHEN LEWIS	Difficult Run (now Fairfax)
4- WILLOUGHBY NEWTON	Great Rocky Cedar Run (Fairfax)
5- RICHARD COLEMAN	Sugarland Run (on Potomac Path)
6- JOHN HARLE	Secolon Run
7- JOHN MERCER	Hunger Run of Little River
9- WILLIAM FAIRFAX	Difficult Run (now Fairfax)
10- EDWARD MASTERSON	Difficult Run (now Fairfax)
14- [Lee family ?]	horse mill at Horsepen (now Fairfax)
16- JOHN TRAMMELL	Difficult Run (now Fairfax)
17- CHARLES BROADWATER	Difficult Run (now Fairfax)
19- JOSEPH JANNEY	Tuscarora Run
23- JAMES LANE	Cub Run
24- JOHN HOUGH	Goose Creek, lower ford
31- JOHN CARTER	Bull Run, first mill above Sudley ford

See previous page for mills west of Leesburg and Little River.

-LOUDOUN COUNTY - VIRGINIA-

GRIST MILL SITES
circa 1730 - 1766

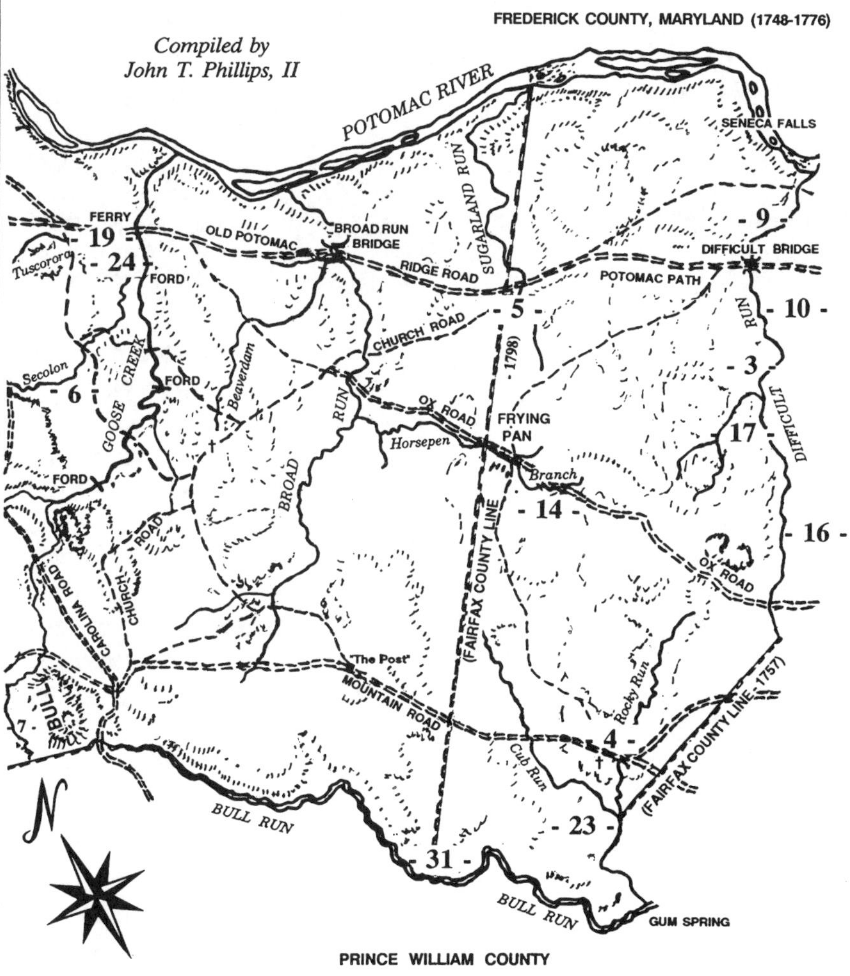

ON the 26th of *Auguſt* laſt, at night, was ſtolen from the plantation of *John Kirk*, of *Lancaſter* county, *Lampeter* townſhip, *Pennſylvania*, a black horſe, upwards of 14 hands high, about 7 years old, paces and trots, has a large ſtar, ſome collar marks, his mane and tail trimmed, but grown long, and branded on the near ſhoulder IC. Another of the ſame ſize and colour, mark unknown. Whoever takes up the ſaid horſes, and thief, and ſecures them, ſo as the thief may be brought to juſtice, and the owner have his horſes again, ſhall have 5l. reward, paid by the ſubſcriber, living on *Kittouton* creek, in *Loudoun* county, *Virginia*.

WILLIAM KIRK.

Probably the oldest surviving structure in Loudoun County, "Hunting Hill," circa. 1734, was originally the home of Loudoun miller Richard Brown. William Kirk married Brown's widow in 1749 and was living there in November of 1763 when he advertised in the *Virginia Gazette* for the return of horses belonging to John Kirk of Pennsylvania. *Courtesy of the Loudoun Museum, Leesburg.*

December 14, 1757 - Two Justices, Nicholas Minor and Josias Clapham, were appointed as special appraisers and ordered to view and value an acre of George West's land on Clarks Run adjacent to the mill belonging to John Poultney. This special commission is very unusual since it was contrary to the law providing for adverse valuation of an acre for a mill, but was probably occasioned by the situation where the owner of the adjacent acre, George West, was also the County Surveyor and a Justice. One could speculate that either John Poultney had agreed to the special proceeding or the new County Court was not fully versed in the application of the milling laws. Book A, p. 61.

March 15, 1758 - A Motion of Aneas Campbell, for "a Water Grist Mill to be built on a stream running through the said Campbell's [Limestone Run] land ... granted." Book A, p. 69.

March 15, 1758 - "One acre of land belonging to [Loudoun Justice and Surveyor] George West Gent. adjacent to [apparently existing] John Poultney's Mill [is] Petitioned for by the said Poultney." Josias Clapham and Nicholas Minor report they "viewed an Acre of Land adjacent to the petitioner John Poultney's Land about [200] yards from [the] Mill as showed to us by John Poultney and Richard Roberts ... [one] acre of Land we adjudge to be of the value of two Pounds [£2]." Poultney probably felt that the appraised price for the acre was too steep, and the Court, less Justices William West and George West, dismissed the petition. Poultney brought another Motion, to have an acre of West's land laid off to include a Ditch to Poultney's Mill, "the same being fully heard by the Court is not granted." Book A, pp. 69 and 70.

March 15, 1758 - "Ordered ... Nicholas Minor or Josias Clapham Gent[lema]n. agree with John Dalton, Gent., [an Alexandria merchant] for necessary Weights and Measures for a Standard for this County." Book A, p. 74.

March 15, 1758 - John Hough and Francis Hague are appointed "as fit and able Persons residing in this County to Inspect the Package and Weigh ... all Wheat Flower made [within] and intended for Exportation [from] this County for the ensuing Year." Book A, p. 78.

June 15, 1758 - Francis Summers, James Lane and James Lane Junr. report their view of a new Road to "continue the Road from Rockey run Church to the Horse Mill, and leading to Frying Pan ... [and from there on] to the Ox Road." Book A, p. 123.

August 10, 1758 - John Hough and Francis Hague, "the Present Inspectors [of Flour] ... in this County are Continued for the ensuing Year." Book A, p. 154.

October 10, 1758 - Francis Hague, John Hough and Mahlon Janney report the route for a new Road "from William Kirk's Mill with the old Road ... to the [Waterford] meeting house ... and to the main [Shenandoah] Road [to

Leesburg] by William Dodds" ordinary. Book A, pp. 159 and 169.

November 15, 1758 - John Poultney and Edward Harding report their view [establishing] a new Road "leading from William Kirk's Mill ... as the old Road goes to a Maple Swamp ... [by marked trees to] Steers old field [by marked trees to] the main [Carolina] Road" near Lucketts. Book A, p. 182/1.

April 10, 1759 - John Hough purchases a 150 acre tract from George William Fairfax, just west of Colonel John Tayloe's section at the Gap of the Short Hill, "by an old mill of Samuel Butcher's." At the time, the £45 purchase price was a much higher price than what one would expect to pay for 150 acres of unimproved land. LDCODB, Book A, p. 263.

June 12, 1759 - Joseph Janney is granted permission to build a mill on behalf of the Honorable Philip Ludwell Lee, Esqr., "on his Lands on Tuscarora Run." Book A, p. 246.

June 12, 1759 - Josias Clapham, Philip Noland, Thomas Awbrey and John Trammell are appointed to view the route for a new "Road from Kirk's Mill by Edward Hardings to Leesburgh." Book A, p. 249.

August 14, 1759 - The route for a new Road is reported "from Williams Gap to Leesburgh ... out of the Road ... at the foot of the Mountain near Compton's Path ... by the south end of the Round Hill ... to Nathan Spencers ... to Jacob Janneys Mill ... into the Great [Shenandoah] Road near Richard Canarys." Book A, p. 264.

August 14, 1759 - Representatives of the Estate of John Poultney sell 305 acres on Clarks Run, "at the head drain near the Great [Carolina] Road ... near a drain of Limestone Run," to [future Loudoun County Justice] Lee Massey. LDCODB, Book A, pp. 20-23 and 320-327.

August 15, 1759 - It is "Ordered that the Sherif ... pay unto John Carlyle Gent. ... £25 for Standards, Weights and Measures for this County." Book A, p. 267.

November 14, 1759 - John Osborn, Nicholas Osborn and Joshua Gore are appointed to view the route for a "Road from John Hough's Mill [at the Gap of the Short Hill] to the foot of the Ridge at Williams' Gap." Book A, p. 304.

August 14, and November 15, 1759 - Richard Roach, a man who was originally known to be a blacksmith by trade, was granted "leave to Build a Mill ... whereon he now lives on Kittocton [Creek]" with an acre apportioned from lands of the Estate of John Colvill, Gent., dec'd. The valuation jury was composed of John Trammell, Edward Hardin, Ezekiel Hickman, Andrew Adam, Richard Roberts, Daniel Davis, Joseph Claypoole, Cornelius Donohue, Hugh Fouch, Michael Stoker, Thomas Squires and Joseph McGeach. They valued an acre of Colvill's land at £1, 5 shillings, and found that "Building the said Mill by Daming [sic] the Water will be of no Damage to any other Lands only the Acre." Attorneys Hugh West and John Patterson, acting for the Earl of Tankerville (the Loudoun Deputy King's Attorney and the agent of the heir of John Colvill), objected to the licensing of the mill and noted an appeal to the General Court. Order Book A, pp. 266 and 308; see, FXCODB, Book B, p. 67.

March 11, 1760 - Aneas Campbell petitions for a Mill on his lands on the Tuscarora, with one acre from Mary Foster ["at this time intermarried with Henry Ansley"]. Book A, p. 324.

March 12, 1760 - John Mcilhaney, Joseph Jones and William Smith report their view of a new Road "from John Hough's Mill [at the Gap] to the mouth of Dutchman's Run ... find that it will not answer for a Road ... but running ... under the short Hill to the River ... one Mile above the mouth of the Dutchman ... the Road is [not ordered]." Book A, pp. 301 and 329.

May 31, 1760 - William Holmes is referred to in a deed of purchase as a millwright, buying land on the north side of Secolon. It seems likely that Holmes was the miller at Aeneas Campbell's new mill on the Tuscarora, since Campbell is the land agent on the deed from Catesby Cocke. The only other mill in that area at the time is the John Harle mill on Secolon, which Andrew Adam had probably bought. LDCODB, Book B, p. 56.

September of 1760 - William West's tithable list identifies Stephen Sebastian as the miller operating Mercer's mill on Little River. LDTX/1, p. 4.

November 12, 1760 - Isaac Nichols petitions to "Build a Mill on the North Branch of Goose Creek and also to have one Acre of Land laid off Adjoining thereto belonging to John Dixon." A survey of the intended site is ordered. Book A, p. 406.

November 12, 1760 - James Lane Gent. obtains leave of Court "to Build a Mill on his Land on Cub Run, It appearing to the Court that the said James is in possession of Lands on both sides of the said Run." Book A, p. 407.

February 12, 1761 - Isaac Nichols obtains a license to build his Mill on the North Branch [probably meaning the northwest branch] of Goose Creek. The Sheriff, valuation jury and Surveyor met on the land on December 4, 1760, and then "laid off" and appraised one acre of John Dixon's land at 10 shillings. The jury consisted of Benjamin Edwards, John Herryford, Thomas Pritchard, Christopher Perfect, Jacob Lasswell, Daniel Davis, Francis Wilks, Hugh Fouch, Joseph West, Daniel Miller, Edward Thompson and Nathan Spencer. We note that many of the men on the valuation jury were living in Leesburg and thereabout, probably riding out for the viewing in the company of Sheriff Nicholas Minor. It is "ordered that the said Isaac Nichols hold the said Acre of Land according to Law." Book A, pp. 406 and 421.

March 10, 1761 - John Osborn is appointed Surveyor of the Road "from [Osborn's] Farm to John Hough's Mill [at the Gap of Short Hill] the most convenient way." Book A, p. 427.

June 9, 1761 - Josias Clapham and John Trammell report a new Road "from William Kirk's Mill to Leesburgh ... brought along by Ralph Braddock's ... to Richard Roberts ... to a Bridge in the main Road nigh Robert Popkin's Fence (above Popkins Plantation)." Book A, pp. 451-452.

August 11, 1761 - Robert Yeldall, Nicholas Osborn and James Connard report a new Road "leading from Potowmack River between the Blue Ridge and Short Hills into the Road that leads to John Hough's Mill" at the Gap of the Short Hill. Book A, pp. 453 and 483.

July 14, and, August 11, 1761 - John Hough is licensed to erect a water grist mill "over Goose Creek ... near where the main Road crosses said Creek at the lower Ford." Sub-Sheriff John Moss Junr. conducted the Surveyor and jury for a viewing of the site on July 31, 1761. The valuation jury, comprised of Benjamin Edwards, John Heryford, James Morray, James Abbet, Philip Connel, Thomas Sorrell, Joseph West, William Dodd, William Berry, Cornelius Donohoe, William Ross and Daniel Miller, valued an acre of the lands of [the children of Samuel] Selden at 20 shillings, and then valued "the Conveniences and timber with the Lands adjacent thereto that may be laid under Water by Daming for said Mill to be of the value of Eleven Pounds [£11] Current Money." As with the valuation jury of the previous December, many of the men on the valuation jury were living in Leesburg and thereabout, and probably rode out for the viewing in the company of Sub-Sheriff John Moss Junr., who also lived in Leesburg. John Hough was not pleased with the prospect of paying the enormous sum of £12 for an apportioned acre, and has the valuation voided in Court the following February. Book A, pp. 478 and 485; and see infra.

September 8, 1761 - John Trammell, Gent., is given leave "to erect, build and finish on [Clarks Run] a Water Grist Mill, where he is Possessed of Land ... on both sides" of the stream. Book A, p. 493.

September 9, 1761 - It is ordered that "the Court doth nominate and appoint John Newland and William Baker as fit & able Persons residing in this County to Inspect the Package and Weigh ... all Wheat Flower made & intended for Exportation within this County." Book A, p. 503.

November 12, 1761 - Samuel Mead, Solomon Hoge, William Wildman, William Hatcher, John Little, William Dodd, Thomas Field, Francis Wilks, Samuel Wilks, John Sims, Robert Stukesbury, Isaac Nichols and Benjamin Poole Petition for a Road to be opened "from Jacob Janney's to Andrew Adam's Mill on Sekolon [sic]." Book A, p. 538.

February 9, 1762 - John Hough petitions for a "Griss Mill" on Goose Creek. A new jury is to value the lands of the "children of Samuel Seldon, Gent. ... on or near the Ford of said [Goose] Creek [at the Potomac Path] leading from Leesburg to Alexandria." Book A, pp. 553-554.

April 10, 1762 - Robert Adam, a Justice in Fairfax County, purchases a 153 acre tract "beginning at a stake by [his] Mill Dam ... on the South side of Siconells Branch." This would appear to be site of Harle's mill, the mill that Andrew Adam had owned. DALD, (1762) p. 2; LDCODB, Book C, p. 390.

May 11, 1762 - Israel Thompson petitioned "to build a Griss Mill on Kittocton Creek [sic] on his Lands," with one acre to be laid off and apportioned from George William Fairfax, Esqr. Sheriff Josias Clapham was directed to summon a valuation jury and the Surveyor to view and determine "the true value of the Acre ... and of the Damages" that any mill flooding would occasion. There is, however, no record of further condemnation proceedings during the next decade. Book A, p. 584

May 11, 1762 - Thomas Dodd obtains a permit from the Loudoun County Court "to build a Mill on his Land on the great Dutchman Run" where he is said to own land on both sides of the Run. Book A, p. 585.

May 11, 1762 - John Steere, John Trammell and William Jones are appointed to "view the most convenient way for a Road leading from Richard Roach's Mill to the Road that leads from William Kirk's Mill to Leesburgh." Book A, p. 585.

May 14, 1762 - Jonathan Price, William Jones, Edward Harden and John Popkins are appointed to site a new "Road from Jenny's [Mahlon Janney's] Mill into the main Road leading from Leesburgh to Clapham's & Noland's Ferries." Book A, p. 622.

June 15, 1762 - Francis Hague sells Mahlon Janney land on the south fork of the Kittockton "just above the mouth of the Tale [sic- tail] race of Mahlon Janney's mill" at Waterford. DALD, (1762) p. 112; LdCODB, Book C, p. 367.

Friday, August 13, 1762 - "Upon the Petition of Benjamin Sebastian against Thomas Phillips (Miller) for a Debt due by Acct. This Day came the Parties in their proper Persons who being fully heard ... the Plt. recover against the Deft. two Pounds and his Costs." Book B, p. 49.

September 15, 1762 - John Steere was "appointed Surveyor of the Road leading from Kirk's Mill to John Popkins's [sic]" and it was also "Ordered that Farlan Ball be appointed Surveyor of the Road leading from Kirk's Mill to [on] the new Road from Noland's Ferry." Book B, p. 58.

September 15, 1762 - "Ordered that George Gregg be appointed Surveyor of the Road ... from Janney's [Waterford] Mill to the Road from Leesburg to Noland's Ferry." Book B, p. 59.

April 12, 1763 - Joshua Duncan Junr. petitions for license to "Erect a Water Griss Mill on the Beaver Dam Run of Goose Creek" with one acre from the lands of Catesby Cocke Esqr. to be valued by a Jury and apportioned. Book B, p. 88.

April 13, 1763 - John Hough is granted, "leave to build a Mill on Goose Creek it appearing to the Court that he has Lands on both sides [of] the said Creek." Book B, p. 105.

May 10, 1763 - Thomas Lamb, Michael VanBuskirk, Adam Winsel and Simon Shoemaker are appointed to determine "the most convenient way for a Road leading from [Thomas] Dodd's Mill [on Dutchman's] to Mahlon Janney's Mill" on the south fork of Kittoctin Creek at Waterford. Book B, p. 124.

May 10, 1763 - Edward Garrett petitions "for leave to Erect a Griss Mill on his Land "on Painter [sic- Panther] Skin run," with an acre to be apportioned from the lands of John Violett and William Allan and valued by a Jury. Book B, p. 124.

June 15, 1763 - "Upon the Petition of John Hough for a Road, from his Grist Mill on the North Fork of Kittockton Creek at the Gap of the Short Hills, to Potomack River opposite or near 'Frail Pain's' [sic]," Samuel Compton, John Osborn, David Potts and Joshua Gore Junr. are appointed to "view the most convenient way." Book B, p. 169.

July 12, 1763 - John Steere and William Jones report that they have "marked out a [new] Road from Roach's Mill to the Road that leads from

William Kirk's Mill road to Leesburg the most convenient way." Book B, p. 192.

August 7, 1763 - George Cunningham, who had moved west to Frederick County Virginia, in the course of selling land he had owned in Loudoun County refers to himself as a millwright. George Cunningham probably helped construct and then worked as the first miller at Jacob Janney's mill south of the Round hill area, which was near his own land. LDCODB, Book C, p. 681.

January 15, 1764 - A deed from Mahlon Janney to Francis Hague recites that Mahlon Janney's mill had been built on land owned by Francis Hague, at Waterford on the east bank of the south fork of Kittoctin Creek. DALD, (1764) p. 39.

February 15, 1764 - Nicholas Minor, Gent., and Benjamin Edwards [without appointee Aneas Campbell] report their view of "the most convenient ways for roads to be opened to John Hough's Mill on Goose Creek ... [reporting] on the way marked by John Mill ... through sundry persons lands ... to John Hough's Mill on Goose Creek ... [and that they] also viewed from Hough's Mill to Morris' Ford and think it convenient a Road should be made there ... [the Court orders that] James Abbett Surveyor of the road from this place [Leesburg] to Goose Creek, [is to] Open the Road from where is turns off the [Potomac Path] leading to Alexandria to the Mill." Book B, pp. 265 and 273.

March 13, 1764 - Henry Peyton petitions "for leave to erect a Water Griss Mill on his Land on the North side of Goose Creek," with an acre of land to be laid off and apportioned from Bryan Fairfax, Esqr.. Sheriff Josias Clapham was directed to summon a valuation jury and the Surveyor to view "the Lands adjacent thereto on both sides the Run which may be effected or laid under Water by building such Mill together with the Timber and other conveniences thereon," but we have no record of further condemnation proceedings during the next decade. This mill, if it was ever built by Henry Peyton, was probably situated on Goose Creek west of Little River and below "a stony ridge open to the Great Mountain." Book B, p. 280; Clerk's 1764 Fee Book, p. 19; and see LDCODB, Book D, p. 285.

March 14, 1764 - Thomas Owsley, William Stevens, Walter Middleton and Elisha Robinson are appointed to view the Road "turned and now opened" by Leven Powell "leading from Mercer's Mill to Ashby's Gap." Book B, p. 286.

April 12, 1764 - William Berry is appointed Surveyor of the Road from Morris' Ford to John Hough's Mill on Goose Creek, with George West to allot the hands. Book B, p. 340.

May 8, 1764 - A Grand Jury presents charges against: "Overseer from Broad Run to Hough's [Goose Creek] Mill road [for not maintaining his road] within one month last past." Book B, p. 354.

May 22, 1764 - Sheriff Josias Clapham conducts a jury and the County Surveyor to their viewing on the Beaver Dam Run of Goose Creek, on the land of Joshua Duncan, and they proceed to lay off and appraise an acre of Catesby Cocke's land for Duncan's Grist Mill. Book C, p. 17.

May 23, 1764 - Sheriff Josias Clapham conducts another jury and the County Surveyor to their viewing (southwest of the site viewed the day before) on

Panther Skin Run, on the land of Edward Garret [Junr.], and they proceed to lay off and appraise an acre of land belonging to John Violett and William Allan, for Garret's Grist Mill. Book C, p. 17.

June 12, 1764 - Josias Clapham, Philip Noland, William Wollard and William Jones are appointed to view a route for a new Road "from John Trammell's [Clarks Run] Mill to the Road that leads from William Douglass' Plantation to David Smiths [and] a Road from the said Trammell's Mill to the Road below Mr. Lee Massey's leading to Leesburgh." Book B, p. 359.

December 12, 1764 - Thomas Connell is appointed Surveyor "from the Mountain Road by Capt. James Lane's [Cub Run] Mill [along the Mountain Road] to the Road leading to Bull Run and that William Carr Lane Gent. allot the hands to work the road." Book B, p. 516.

December of 1764 - One man named Thomas Shepherd, probably the miller at Isaac Nichols' mill on the North branch of Goose Creek, is identified as a millwright. Clerk's 1764 Fee Book, p. 75; see, LDTX/1, (1765) p. 34.

March 11, 1765 - On the "Petition of George West setting forth that John Trammell hath obtained an Order to have a Road ... Opened through [West's Clarks Run] land in a manner very Prejudicial to him leading, from a Machine or Mill which the said Trammell has Erected, into the main Road from Noland's Ferry to Leesburg ... John Moss, John Moss Junr., John Minor and Richard Coombs are appointed to view whether [the road is] Necessary to be opened ... in the mean time that the Surveyor thereof cease opening the same any further." Book B, p. 521.

May 13, 1765 - William Muirhead is appointed the "Surveyor of the Road from where the Ox Road Crosses the ford of Broad Run to John Hough's [Goose Creek] Mill," replacing James Whaley. Book B, p. 574.

July 8, 1765 - Vincent Lewis, Anthony Russell and John Lewis are appointed to view a new "Road from the Gum Spring near Vincent Lewis' to John Carter's Mill." Book B, p. 674.

August 13, 1765 - The Petition of Joshua Duncan, for a license to erect a Grist Mill on the Beaver Dam Run of Goose Creek, is finally granted when the jury viewing, conducted the previous spring and ordered in April of 1763, is returned to the Court. The 1764 jury, composed of William Whiteley, Thomas Owsley, Thomas Squires, Gilbert Simpson, George Taylor, William Cotton, Samuel Conners, John Ethell, Daniel Hunt, James Buckley, James Saunders and Samuel Duncan "value and Appraise one Acre of Land belonging to Catesby Cocke Esq." at "five shillings Current Money ... Whereupon it is Ordered that the said Joshua Duncan hold the said Acre of Land according to Law." Book C, p. 17; see infra, Comment after the next entry.

August 13, 1765 - Another mill Petition, this from Edward Garrett [Junr.], for license to erect a Grist Mill on "Painter Skin Run," is granted when the jury viewing, ordered in May of 1763 and conducted in May of 1764, is returned. The 1764 jury, composed of William Whiteley, Thomas Owsley, Thomas Triplett, James Buckley, John Ethell, James Saunders, Joshua Duncan [Junr.], Thomas Middleton, Josiah Settle, Daniel Triplett, William Cotton and

Thomas Squires "value and appraise one Acre of Land belonging to John Violett and William Allan ... to Fifteen Shillings Current Money ... ordered that the said Edward Garret hold the said Acre of Land according to Law." Book C, p. 17.

[Author's Comment: From the two previous mill-order entries, one could comfortably speculate that Gilbert Simpson, George Taylor, Samuel Conners, Daniel Hunt, and Samuel Duncan, who all served only on the first jury, lived near the Mountain Road above the Beaver Dam branch of Goose Creek in 1764. This "Mountain Road" is now traced, roughly, by the Snickersville Pike. One could just as easily speculate that Thomas Triplett, Thomas Middleton, Josiah Settle and Daniel Triplett were residents further to the southwest, along the road to Ashby's Gap - the roadway now defined, roughly, by modern Rte. 50 - in the area west of what is today known as Middleburg.]

September of 1765 - A tithable list returned by William Carr Lane identifies William Broadhurst as the "Miller for Capt. James Lane" [Junr.] at his mill on Cub Run; and, on the same list, Richard Williams is listed as the miller operating John Carter's new mill at the earliest site of Sudley, on the north bank of Bull Run. LDTX/1, pp. 39 and 40.

June 10, 1766 - Joseph Hough sells John Hough a tract of 150 acres situated on "the north side of a branch that issues from George Gregg's saw mill." Gregg owned lands south of the Sears branch of Kittockton Creek. LDCODB, Book E, p. 77.

December 9, 1766 - Francis Peyton is appointed as the new Inspector of Flour for the County replacing "William Baker who hath resigned." Presumably, John Newland was still serving as the other inspector. Book C, p. 232; see supra, The Record @ p. 224.

Ye Olde Grist Mills of Loudoun County - First mention in Loudoun Records

Date	Owner/operator	Status	Location/adjacent properties/background
12/14/1757	John Poultney	existing	on Clark's Run across from George West
3/15/1758	Aneas Campbell	new Mill	a stream running through Campbell's land
6/15/1758	Lee family [horse mill]	existing	along the road north of Rockey Run Church
10/10/1758	William Kirk	existing	Brown's Mill, north of Waterford Meeting
6/12/1759	Joseph Janney	new Mill	on the lands of Hon. Philip Ludwell Lee, Esqr., on his Lands on Tuscarora Run
8/14/1759	Richard Roach	new Mill	"where he lives on Kittockton [sic]," adjacent to Estate of John Colvill, Gent., dec'd.
8/14/1759	Jacob Janney	existing	east of the south end of the Round Hill
11/14/1759	John Hough	existing	at the Gap of the Short Hill; [petitioned for in Fairfax County in June of 1755]
3/11/1760	Aneas Campbell	new Mill	on Campbell's lands on the Tuscarora, adjacent Mary Foster [Henry Ansley's wife]
11/12/1760	Isaac Nichols	new Mill	on the North Branch of Goose Creek, across from the lands of John Dixon

11/12/1760	JAMES LANE	new Mill	on his land on Cub Run
8/11/1761	JOHN HOUGH	new Mill	on Goose Creek, near the lower ford for the main road, adjacent Samuel Selden's heirs
9/ 8/1761	JOHN TRAMMELL	new Mill	on his lands on both sides of Clarks Run
11/12/1761	ANDREW ADAM	existing	his [Harle's ?] Mill on the "Sekolon"
5/11/1762	ISRAEL THOMPSON	new Mill	Kittoctin Creek, across from G.W. Fairfax
5/11/1762	THOMAS DODD	new Mill	on his lands on the great Dutchman Run
5/14/1762	MAHLON JANNEY	existing	"Jenney's [sic - Janney's]" Mill at Waterford
4/12/1763	JOSHUA DUNCAN JUNR.	new Mill	on the Beaver Dam Run of Goose Creek," adjacent lands of Catesby Cocke, Esqr.
4/13/1763	JOHN HOUGH	new Mill	Goose Creek, Hough owns both banks
5/10/1763	EDWARD GARRETT [Junr.]	new	Panther Skin Run, adjacent Violet and Allan
3/13/1764	HENRY PEYTON	petition	on the north side of Goose Creek, across from the lands of Bryan Fairfax, Esqr.
7/ 8/1765	JOHN CARTER	new Mill	at Sudley ford, on the north bank of Bull Run
6/10/1766	GEORGE GREGG [saw mill]	existing	Kittoctin Creek, south side Sears (Balls) Run

Loudoun County now contains about 517 square miles of land, or roughly 331,000 acres. Between 1757 and 1798, Loudoun included another 115 square miles, for a total of about 405,000 acres. The "extra" area composed an eastern section that included the neighborhoods of Bull Run, Centreville, Chantilly, Dulles, Great Falls, Herndon, Reston and Riverbend in modern Fairfax. [for the early history of Loudoun lands see text in "Opening the Way," supra pp. 5-18, and "Chronology," infra pp. 531-538].

The land tax lists and rent rolls for colonial Loudoun County identify the owners of at least 300,000 acres; the other 100,000 acres was either lost, or hidden, through poor colonial surveying techniques. [Hening, V/422-423; see infra, the Table, "Loudoun's 101 Largest Landowners ...," pp. 259-261].

Reliable surveys were vital for orderly growth and the development of colonial Virginia's expanding frontiers. A series of colonial laws enacted in Virginia between 1624 and 1643 established requirements that every new tract of land be surveyed by an "allowed surveyor," with all surveys duly recorded. As early as 1662, surveyors were instructed to clearly mark the boundaries that they surveyed, so "that none may by ignorance of the bounds intrench [sic] upon anothers right." Every parcel was to be rectangular in shape with a smaller dimension at least one-third the length of the larger dimension, "except where the courses shall be interrupted by rivers, creeks, or unpassable mountains and swamps, or by the bounds of other lands before taken up or patented." [Hening, I/125, I/262-263, II/235 and V/424].

Virginia County Courts were given exclusive responsibility for appointing County Surveyors in 1655. The College of William & Mary was installed as the institutional Surveyor General of Virginia shortly after its founding in 1693. Thereafter, through the Revolution, The College had the exclusive authority to appoint and license all of Virginia's County Surveyors; but the Governor, his Councilors and the Assembly regularly flexed their muscles in the appointments process. Between 1729 and 1787, one-sixth of all surveying fees generated in Virginia were paid to The College, presumably for the maintenance of the surveyor-licensing program. [Hening, I/404; ColVa, p. 777; White Oak, p. 293].

Surveying fees were first regulated in 1624, when a fee of just 10 lbs. of tobacco (hereafter "lbt.") was allowed for every 100 acres surveyed in "every private planter's dividend." Fees were doubled in 1646, revised in 1662, and doubled again in 1666. Any surveyor who charged higher prices, or who refused to survey for the scheduled fees, could be fined up to 4,000 lbt., then about £35. The Assembly imposed additional regulations in 1705; thereafter, chain carriers were to be employed on all surveys in order to ensure that measurements were just and exact, and surveyors were required to maintain note books where they were to record their work. [Hening, I/125, I/335, II/99-100, II/235 and III/330].

Virginia's 1745 law, "for better regulating and collecting certain Officer fees," spelled out the surveyor's fees that were allowed throughout Loudoun's first decade, from 1757 to 1766:

"To the [County] Surveyor.	*Pounds of Tobacco [Lbt.]*
For every survey by him made, plainly bounded ...	
and for a plat [of less than 1,000] acres	*500*
... every [100] acres ... above the first [1,000]	*30*
... surveying a lot in town	*20*
... where the surveyor shall be stopped or hindered	
from finishing a survey, by him begun ...	*250*
... running a [private] dividing line,	*250*
... surveying an acre of land for a mill,	*100*
... running a dividing line between any county or parish; ...	
paid by [the] counties, or parishes, in proportion	
to the number of tithables [under 10] miles ...	*1000*
... And for every mile [of a dividing line] above ten,	*50*

..." An attested copy of a previous entry in the surveyor's book would cost 2/6 (2 shillings, 6 pence). Neither promissory notes nor "money security" were to be accepted in payment for surveying fees. [Hening, V/340, VI/34-36 and VI/171; White Oak, p. 295].

Loudoun was put on a "cash" basis in 1759. Surveying fees were, thereafter, payable alternately in tobacco or specie "at twelve shillings and six pence per hundred" lbt. due, or 15 pence for every 10 lbt. of fees. The Assembly had previously established a 20% abatement of officer fees paid in Fairfax and Prince William; the 1765 Assembly continued the 20% abatement in Loudoun County, but reduced the abatement of fees to 14% in Prince William, and to 10% in Fairfax. [Hening, VII/292, VII/385 and VIII/101].

The 1748 Assembly recodified the regulations governing all County Surveyors. Every Surveyor was required to give a £500 bond, with "two sufficient sureties," for the faithful performance of his duties. All surveyors were directed to "deliver ... a plot and certificate" within five months of each survey, and were prohibited from giving a copy of any survey to anyone but the landowner. Every County Surveyor was also to maintain "a book well bound" to record each survey; when he surveyed land in his own name, he was required to have his book entry witnessed by a County Court Justice. Each June, each County Surveyor was to "return a true and perfect list of all surveys by him made, to his county court clerk's office." However, we have yet to determine whether any of these Loudoun County lists have survived. Upon the death or removal of a Surveyor, the county court was instructed to "retake his book of surveys, and cause the same to be preserved among the county records, or delivered to the next Surveyor." These regulations were re-enacted in 1763 and were still in force while George West served as Loudoun's first County Surveyor. [Hening, VI/33-38 and VII/645; bond, infra p. 249].

Before proceeding to survey a new entry, the surveyor would post a notice at the county courthouse on two successive court days. Citing the large quantities of unpatented land available on the Virginia frontier, and with the stated intent of "preventing disputes," the 1744 Assembly initiated a residency requirement for the County Surveyors of Albemarle, Augusta, Frederick and Louisa. The residency requirement was expanded to include Amelia, Brunswick, Lunenburg and Orange Counties in 1748. In 1763, the Assembly extended the residency requirement to the Loudoun County Surveyor position when it legislated that "every surveyor of lands [in Virginia] shall be [a] resident of the[ir] county." [Hening, V/253, V/382, VI/35-36 and VII/645].

The use of magnetic compasses in colonial surveying subjected the process to considerable error. Surveys were not expected to be entirely accurate - the Virginia Assembly even directed that there should be no penalty for a survey found to be in error by less than 5%. Due to constant shifts of the tectonic plates, the earth's magnetic field varies over time. One result is that, from a surveyor's perspective, magnetic north is constantly "moving." The degree and direction of the movement is known as magnetic variance, or declination. The variance varies with the date of the survey and specific location on the globe. Magnetic bearings on surveys conducted in Fairfax and Loudoun before 1773 evidenced a westward variance from true north. In other words, true north was one or more degrees clockwise from the magnetic bearings given on the early surveys of colonial northern Virginia. Westward magnetic variance was lower as one travelled westward, but higher as one went north, making the calculation of magnetic variances all the more problematical. The 1772 Assembly voiced a concern that "inconveniences have arisen from the inattention of surveyors to the variation of the magnetic needle, in resurveying lands," and specified that, beginning June 1, 1773, surveyors were to "protract and lay down their plats by the true and not by the artificial or magnetic meridian and ... declare ... the true quantity or degree of the variation." [United States Geological Survey ("USGS") Tables of Declination; Hening, VIII/526-527].

Magnetic variances in 1750 have been interpolated for various points of reference all around Loudoun County:

Location	Magnetic declination in 1750
Leesburg, site of the Loudoun Courthouse	West, 2° 12' 44"
Potomac River, at Mount Vernon in Fairfax	2° 12' 56"
Potomac River, mouth of Sugarland Run	2° 18' 54"
Potomac River, site of Poultney's [Noland's] ferry	2° 20' 38"
Potomac River, mouth of Dutchmans Creek	2° 17' 49"
The Gap of Short Hill, at Hillsboro	2° 11' 00"
Mountain Road, site of Bacon Fort	2° 04' 30"
Pantherskin Creek, above Upperville	1° 57' 51"
Carolina Road, site of West's ordinary	2° 05' 26"
Mountain Road, at Rocky Run	2° 06' 23"
Ox Road, east of Horsepen Run	2° 12' 22"
Potomac Ridge Road, at Colvin Run mill	2° 16' 20"
Goose Creek, site of Hough's mill	2° 13' 02"

Before the Revolution, the finest distinction in most surveys was ½°. The most sophisticated field equipment used by colonial surveyors could not discern minute localized variances. Colonial surveyors did notice, and mentioned, that bearings on clearly marked lines appeared to change over time. Changes in magnetic variance over time are referred to as "secular change." Secular change varies from decade to decade and from site to site. USGS tables only go back to 1750, so complicated extrapolations of secular change are required in order to obtain declinations between 1725 and 1745, when most of the early Loudoun surveys were made. After extrapolating secular changes for 1730 and 1740, magnetic variances for the site of the Leesburg Courthouse have been interpolated, through 1780. These values of magnetic declination, rounded to the nearest ½°, can be used to generate "true" values for bearings in old Loudoun surveys, with the caveat that local differences, as discussed, may alter the results slightly:

1730	West, 4°	(West, 3° 48'00")
1740	West, 3°	(2° 57'30")
1750	West, 2°	(2° 12'44")
1760	West, 1½°	(1° 32'37")
1770	West, 1°	(56'57")
1780	West, ½°	(27'39")

Exercise the appropriate caution when comparing the metes and bounds recorded in a colonial property description with modern survey data recorded in "true" bearings. [U.S. Coast and Geodetic Survey Publication 40-2, pp. 20-22; refuting White Oak, p. 5].

Old surveys often enable us to determine the original location of major roadways. For example, when Richard Coleman purchased property on Sugarland Run in 1745, his survey located the Potomac Ridge "Road as it goes upward to Goose Creek" and the fording place on Sugarland Run. Capt. Willoughby Newton's 1747 plat showed the Mountain Road, now Braddock Road, "from the Bull Run Mountains down to Occoquan Warehouse," and the various crossings on Rocky Run, Rocky Cedar Run, Round Lick, Flat Lick and Cub Run. [FXCOSUR, p. 17; Cameron, p. 20].

The following men surveyed Loudoun lands before 1767. Each surveyor's [home county] and period of activity is designated:

Nicholas Brent	[Stafford]	1709
Thomas Hopper	[Richmond]	1714-1723
Thomas Thompson	[Westmoreland]	1715
Henry Netherton	[Stafford]	1716
John Savage	[Stafford-Pr.Wm.]	1723-1731
James Thomas	[Westmoreland]	1727-1739
John Warner	[King George]	1727-1745
John Awbrey	[Pr.Wm.-Loudoun]	1731-1742
Amos Janney	[Pr.Wm.-Loudoun]	1730s-1750
John Grant	[Stafford]	1739-1741
Thomas Davies	[Prince William]	1740-1742
William West	[Fairfax-Loudoun]	1741-1765

George Byrne	[Prince William]	1742-1761
Daniel Jenings	[Fairfax]	1742-1764
Jacob Lasswell	[Fairfax-Loudoun]	1743-1749
James Genn	[Prince William]	1745-1749
Guy Broadwater	[Fairfax]	1748-1750
John Baylis	[Prince William]	1748-c.1769
John Hough	[Loudoun]	1751-c.1780
George West	[Fairfax-Loudoun]	1754-c.1780
William West Junr.	[Loudoun]	1759-1763
John Moffitt	[Fauquier]	1759-1772
William Carr Lane	[Loudoun]	1763-c.1770
John Mushett	[Prince William]	1765-c.1770
William Hough	[Loudoun]	1766-1779

Many prominent colonial Virginians, including George Washington, began their business lives surveying for wealthy patrons. John Warner, John Awbrey and John Hough all surveyed for the Fairfax family. In the mid-1730s, Warner and Awbrey surveyed the manors of Leeds, Shannondale, Piedmont and Great Falls. Shortly thereafter, Amos Janney was engaged to correct some of Awbrey's surveys - which were "found [to be] erroneous." Janney's son-in-law, John Hough, was introduced to surveying on the Janney survey teams of the 1730s and 1740s. [LDCODB, D/286-292; NorNeck, p. 9; Grants, Book F, folio 183].

William West [Senr.], of Fruit Hill, was another Loudoun surveyor who worked on both sides of Goose Creek in the 1740s. The proprietor of West's ordinary on the Carolina Road and a Justice on the first Loudoun County Court, West probably learned surveying as an assistant to Amos Janney. He was installed as an Assistant Surveyor for Fairfax County before 1749. William West conducted surveys everywhere from Pohick in eastern Fairfax up to the Blue Ridge. He surveyed the Cameron parish glebe, and tracts above Goose Creek and at Clarks Run on the Potomac that were eventually acquired by his older brother, Fairfax Burgess Hugh West. Around 1758, William West Junr. followed in his father's footsteps and began working as an Assistant Surveyor for Loudoun County. William Junr.'s career was cut short by his death in the final year of the French & Indian Wars. In 1749, another West, John West Junr., was also enrolled as an Assistant to Daniel Jenings, the Fairfax County Surveyor. John Junr.'s commission contained the proviso that he "neither take Entries nor sign Certificates in his own or the said Daniel Jenings name." His surveying was limited in the 1760s, and by 1765 he was in general disfavor for having "neglected" surveys for several warrants and grants. [Fairfax, p. 26; Hening, VI/35; FXCOCO, (1749) p. 186; Landmarks, p. 277; NorNeck, p. 96; NorNeck WS, IV/118].

When Loudoun County was formed in 1757, yet another West, George West, was named County Surveyor. He was a son of Fairfax Burgess Hugh West. George West platted the town plan for Colchester in 1754; his Commission as the Surveyor of Fairfax County was issued the same year. When Loudoun County was founded, George West was named a Justice on the first Loudoun County Court. He also gave the prescribed oath and posted a bond to the benefit of the College of William and Mary for the faithful performance of his surveying duties, whereupon his Commission as the County Surveyor was confirmed in open court. The imposition of a residency requirement in 1763 did not seem to affect George West. After the mid-1750s, West alternated his residency between his Pea Hill plantation on Goose Creek and his townhouse in Alexandria. As a matter of convenience, Loudoun and Fairfax Counties both appear to have considered George West to be a resident; he continued on as the County Surveyor for both counties for the next dozen years. [The Record, infra pp. 249 and 253; Hening, VII/645; FXCOCO, (1754) p. 62 and (1770) p. 137; White Oak, p. 294; FXCOWIL, Book E, p. 134].

John Hough was an elder contemporary of Washington. He began recording surveys shortly after Amos Janney died. By the 1750s, Hough was active in the Kitoctin valley, platting farm leases in the Fairfax family's 17,000-acre Piedmont manor. As a surveyor, John Hough is probably best known for laying out the town plan for Leesburg in 1758. Solid work for the Fairfax family attracted other distinguished clients. In 1763 Hough was retained as the Loudoun County land agent for the Mercer family. Typical of many surveyors of his time, by 1765, John Hough had acquired more land than any other Loudoun resident, surpassing even Loudoun's First Justice, Francis Lightfoot Lee. He included three of his sons, Amos Hough, John Hough Junr. and William Hough, on his survey teams. As a trusted land agent for Lord Fairfax, a Quaker and a respected leader in the Loudoun community, John Hough obtained a virtual monopoly on the surveying business in northern Virginia during the tumult of the American Revolution.

Generally, colonials acquired fresh land in one of two ways, through the exercise of "headrights" or with "Treasury rights." Headrights confirmed 50 acres for every new arrival in the colony. Treasury rights were purchased outright from the Crown. A third method of acquisition, "Proprietary grants," became the standard in northern Virginia. Buyers obtained "warrants," had acreage surveyed and paid Proprietary "composition fees," to obtain their grants. Grants were recorded in record books at the Proprietary land offices. The headrights system encouraged the titling of small properties, but Royal Treasury patents and the Proprietary grants allowed the formation of vast estates. The central distinction was a non-uniform requirement for title known as "seating." [Hening, IV/37 and V/415-424; Democracy, p. 11; Landmarks, p. 120].

"Seating," imposed as an incentive to put new lands into production, was essential for the perfection of headrights. By the 1700s, headright patentees were required to "clear, tend and work" three acres out of every 50 acres within three years of acquisition. Construction of houses or mills or planting of orchards, involving an expense of not less than £5 for every 50 acres, would also "save lands from lapsing." Patentees who employed a slave or servant for three years in "digging any stone quarry, coal, or other mine" would seat and "save" 100 acres. Once land was seated, it could be left fallow while the owner moved on to take up another new tract. This explains, at least in part, the tendency toward "old field" farming methods that was evidenced throughout the tidewater in colonial Virginia. [Hening, IV/81 and V/417-426].

The second Royal Patent for the Northern Neck, issued by Charles II in 1669, contained a seating requirement. There was, however, no mention of seating when James II issued the third Royal Patent for the Northern Neck in 1688, and Proprietary land agents did not impose seating requirements on any land grant in northern Virginia after issuance of the Brent Town grant in 1687. Thereafter, the Northern Neck grants allowed investors in real estate to acquire and retain vast, undeveloped tracts of frontier land. [Hening, IV/81 and IV/514-523; Proprietary, p. 6].

"Quitrents" were essentially feudal land taxes paid to the King. Collection of quitrents was sporadic, at best, in the early years of the Virginia colony. The Assembly legislated the "first year's payment [of Royal quitrents] at the feast of St. Michael the archangel [September 29,] 1639." A moratorium on the quitrents on newly opened lands was instituted in 1640, with the first quitrents to be paid "seven years after [the] date of patents, [at] 2 s[hillings] per hundred acres ... yearly." With hard currency increasingly scarce, tobacco was accepted in payment of quitrents beginning in 1646, at four lbt. per shilling of quitrents. The Proprietors were released from paying Royal quitrents in 1688. This provision ultimately gave Lord Fairfax the right to an annual quitrent income from nearly five million acres. The 1720s would be distinguished by land agent Robert Carter's "farming" of the Proprietary quitrents. [Hening, I/228, I/280 and I/316].

"Fee rents" and the terms of payment imposed in northern Virginia imitated the Royal quitrents. Lord Fairfax collected "on the Feast Day of St. Michael the Archangel ... the Fee Rent of One Shilling Sterling money for every Fifty acres of land ... and proportionably for a greater or lesser quantity." Quitrents were paid at the Proprietary land offices, or to collection agents appointed by Lord Fairfax. John Minor of Alexandria served as a Proprietary collector on the upper Potomac in the 1740s and 1750s. After Minor's death, John Hough served as the Proprietary collection agent from 1765 until around 1782. Proprietors of the Maryland colony charged quitrents of 2 shillings for 50 acres, double Virginia quitrents, thus stimulating a southward migration across the Potomac River. [Proprietary, p. 10; GW Writings, 2/436 verso; Chapter on Ferries, infra pp. 263-277].

After 1720, the personal property of anyone failing to pay quitrents could be summarily seized and sold. Goods were held for eight days, giving a defaulting landowner one last chance to pay, and then the goods were sold at an "outcry" auction with notices posted only on the day of the sale. By the mid-1700s, tobacco had depreciated by 67% and quitrents could be paid "in current money, or tobacco, at one penny" per lbt.. In 1762, the Assembly found German gold coins to be debased "worse than the Spanish doubloons ... at least [15%]," and disallowed their use in payment of Royal quitrents; but this protection was not given to Lord Fairfax. Early in the Revolution, the 1777 Assembly had a completely different attitude and abolished quitrents in Virginia everywhere except the Fairfax Proprietary. The death of Thomas, 6th Lord Fairfax, in 1781, brought about the extinction of quitrents throughout the Commonwealth of Virginia. [Hening, IV/79-80, IV/521 and VII/576; Proprietary, p. 16; supra, p. 13].

Land held under a Royal patent was subject to "escheat" and could be "lost and forfeited" if quitrents were three years in arrears. Similar provisions were imposed in the Proprietary, but Lord Fairfax often let quitrents fall a decade behind before he declared escheat and issued a new grant. Nonetheless, forfeitures based on the failure to pay the Proprietary quitrents occurred in Loudoun County as late as 1779. The terms of pre-Revolutionary leases clearly indicate that landlords and tenants could and did negotiate who would be obligated to pay the Proprietary quitrents to Lord Fairfax. [NorNeck WS, IV/98; generally, Grants].

The Royal Letters Patent for the Northern Neck contained other reservations that were parroted in Proprietary grants. The King retained title to 20% of all gold and 10% of all silver mined. Proprietors would reserve an additional ⅓rd of "all lead, copper, tin, coal, iron mines and iron ore" in the northern Virginia grants. Royal Patents also conveyed rights to the "fish-roial," (whales and sturgeon), and the "roialties [sic] of hawking and hunting," along with the authority to conduct feudal courts, to the Proprietors. When combined with the transfer of the right to collect quitrents, these provisions substituted Lord Fairfax for the King regarding real property rights in northern Virginia. [Hening, IV/515-520].

Composition fees were a significant part of the Proprietary income from each grant. The fee was five shillings for each of the first six 100 acres, and ten shillings for every 100 acres thereafter. This fee structure explains why so many of the initial Proprietary grants were for about 500-600 acres. Governor Dinwiddie created a political crisis in Virginia, shortly after taking office, by attempting to extract a similar fee - one pistole (a Spanish gold coin valued about 21 shillings) - for placing his seal on every Royal patent in Virginia. [Proprietary, p. 24; Table, infra p. 261].

The traditional English forms of property transfer were continued in America. After obtaining land through either patent or grant, a colonist could convey Virginia real estate very much as we do today by having his deed recorded with the County Clerk. Leases were also supposed to be recorded if they were for the life of a tenant, but this provision was not uniformly adhered to in Loudoun. After 1751, deeds were to be proven in open court by the seller or any three witnesses. Proof was required within eight months if the seller was a resident of the county, otherwise within two years. Proof of a wife's assent could be had via an interview with two Justices of the wife's home county. Late in the colonial period, a "Statute for Transferring Uses" was enacted that required a transfer of "possession" to precede the conveyance of title. This particular law resulted in the recordation of paired "lease and release" deeds. Chain of title had to be contested within thirty years of the initial date of possession, which may explain the large number of contested land cases filed in the March 1764 term of the Loudoun Court. Dower and curtsey, the rights of a surviving spouse in the lands of a deceased, are discussed elsewhere. [Hening, V/408-410 and V/416; text, supra p. 234; The Record, infra pp. 255-256; Chapter on Estates, infra p. 498].

While land was normally purchased outright in private transactions, in rare instances, particularly at public sales and auctions, a purchase might be financed over time. Another usual situation involving a mortgage was when a colonial used property as security to guarantee payment on an outstanding debt. Twice each year, in April and October, county clerks were supposed to deliver lists of new mortgages to the Secretary of Virginia. In Loudoun County, Dr. John Urquhart, Craven Peyton, John Cargill, Richard Eskridge, Jacob Faw and Fleming Patterson each placed a large mortgage on his property before 1770. All but Eskridge were businessmen in colonial Loudoun County's financial center of Leesburg. [Hening, V/411; see generally, LDCODB].

Entail, created under English law in 1285, was a means of conveying land in perpetuity to one's lineal descendants. Entail often resulted in numerous small, unproductive farm units; in 1705, procedures were instituted so that colonists could petition the Virginia Assembly and have land relieved of entail restrictions. The 1734 Assembly modified the practice so that life-owners of entailed lands valued under £200 could have their land surveyed and assessed, file a writ of *ad quod damnum* with the Secretary of the Colony, pay a fee, and obtain clear title. Entail was prevalent among prominent colonial families. In 1751, Thomas Lee's sons inherited thousands of acres of entailed land along the Potomac River between Goose Creek and Little Falls. But entail was involved in only 10% of all land transfers during the 1757-1766 decade. The 1765 Assembly, finding that "large tracts of entailed lands remain uncultivated ... [prescribed the durability of] all leases ... [that were] for the term of [21] years ... for three lives, or for any lesser term." This provision allowed tenants to improve farm properties without fear of eviction in the event of the death of an entailed life-owner landlord. [Hening, III/320, IV/400, V/414 and VIII/183; Democracy, pp. 83-88; Lee, pp. 121-122].

The three-life lease, also known as a "farm lease," was another quasi-feudal practice that was introduced on the manors of northern Virginia. Farm leases had two distinct features: the duration was for the lives of three named persons; and, seating provisions required substantial improvement to the property with structures and orchards. Life-tenants also obtained the right to vote. Each manor had distinctive covenants, depending on the whim, style or design of the owner. Lease covenants might restrict hunting, or require the planting of timothy or pear trees, or the retention of stands of woodland. Loudoun's manors must have improved visibly under the life-tenant system. George Gregg and other modest Loudoun land owners began issuing three-life leases of their own in 1760, with annual rents of £1 for 50 acres. [see Chapter on Burgesses, supra p. 24; for example, LDCODB, B/33].

Virginia Governors issued patents on the Potomac River for 22,800 acres, up to Hunting Creek, by 1657. When the second Proprietary Letters were issued in 1669, Royal patents extended up the Potomac to Four Mile Run, and by 1679 to Little Falls. Royal patents required seating, so settlement of the upper Potomac was delayed by intermittent Indian hostility. The mere issuance of these patents created another conflict that would inhibit settlement in northern Virginia during the 1700s. The issue was title to the Proprietary lands. As early as 1684, "inhabitants of the Northerne neck" who held land under a Royal patent petitioned the Assembly for confirmation of their titles. Their concerns were forwarded to London for James II's "royall consideration," but the King ignored the issue in his 1688 Proprietary Patent. The political conflict over the boundaries of Proprietary lands would fester for another sixty years without resolution. [Landmarks, p. 60; Fairfax, p. 12].

The first great land boom on northern Virginia's piedmont took place during Robert Carter's term as Proprietary land agent. In the last dozen years of Carter's agency, 330+ land grants were issued; over half were issued in 1731 and 1732. Notable colonials invested in land in and around the Loudoun piedmont during this period. Carter obtained 150,000 acres - on Bull Run, along Goose Creek, on Frying Pan branch and at Williams Gap. John Mercer,

Francis Awbrey, Benjamin Grayson and Catesby Cocke took up large grants in the Bull Run and Kitoctin Mountain ranges, and along Kitoctin Creek where Welsh and German homesteaders had staked out claims. [Landmarks, pp. 150, 244 and 273].

Proprietary land offices were moved from Westmoreland to Falmouth, to Belvoir and ultimately to Lord Fairfax's Greenway Court manor, as the frontier expanded westward across northern Virginia. Likewise, placement of the Prince William Courthouse at Occoquan in 1730 and the Fairfax Courthouse at the colonial "Springfield" in 1742 were indicators of the emphasis placed upon piedmont land transactions between 1730 and 1752. [Proprietary, p. 7; Fairfax, p. 17; "Opening the Way," supra pp. 9-12].

From 1727 to 1735 Governor Gooch issued patents for 300,000 acres of Proprietary land, mostly in the Shenandoah valley, despite the strident objections of the Proprietary agents. In the last entry of its kind in Loudoun, Jacob Binks obtained 145 acres "on Tuscarora branch of Goose Creek alias Secoline" with a patent issued "under the Great Seal of the Colony of Virginia bearing the date 1728." In the final settlement of his Proprietary boundaries, "Thomas Lord Fairfax ... consented, before the King in [Privy] Council, that the several ... patents made [in northern Virginia] by the crown ... be confirmed." The 1748 Assembly then reaffirmed the title to northern Virginia lands held under Royal patents, reserving "the [quit]rents and services ... to be paid and performed to the said Thomas Lord Fairfax." [Hening, III/26, VI/519-522 and VI/198-199; LDCODB, D/7, and G/125; text, supra p. 11].

The manors of Piedmont, Great Falls, Shannondale and Leeds were all surveyed for the Fairfax family between 1736 and 1740. Meanwhile, John Colvill acquired the acreage that would become Catoctian manor, and Catesby Cocke, the County Clerk, assessed the land records in his office, found unclaimed warrants and unseated patents, and obtained new grants for 20,000 acres, most of it in Loudoun County. [Fairfax, p. 17; generally, Grants].

Manor lands required active management, which often proved illusive. John Mercer, author of the colonial legal treatise titled *Mercer's Abridgment,* unsuccessfully advertised his 30,000 acres above Bull Run as available for rent in 1752. Catesby Cocke appointed Aeneas Campbell his "Attorney in Fact" for land on Kitoctin Mountain in 1760. News of sweetheart land deals that

Campbell was giving to his neighbors traveled rapidly. The following February, Cocke recorded a revocation of Campbell's agency, citing "divers good causes." [Landmarks, pp. 268 and 369; for example, LDCODB, A/490; The Record, infra p. 251].

John Patterson arrived in Leesburg in 1760, and began his tenure as the land agent, collecting rents and settling accounts, for the Earl of Tankerville. Along with his silent partner, brother Fleming Patterson, he actively engaged in the acquisition of land on his own account. The Loudoun Grand Juries had to remind Patterson to render his tax lists for Tankerville's lands in 1762 and again in 1763. Shortly thereafter, Patterson obtained a warrant in his own name for "waste" land on Great Hunting Creek adjacent to Tankerville's Cleesh manor. When Thomas Colvill learned of Patterson's self-dealing, he recorded objections at the Proprietary land office. Consequently, the Earl of Tankerville appointed Thomas Colvill as his new land agent in 1766. Shortly before he died later that year, Colvill assigned his agency to Loudoun's Surveyor, George West. [The Record, infra pp. 257 and 472-476; Landmarks, p. 277; NorNeck, p. 96; NorNeck WS, IV/118].

Annual rents on three-life leases increased steadily from the £1 for 200 acres charged in 1690 in the Ravensworth tract. In 1730, good bottom land near modern Alexandria was renting at £3 for 100 acres. Around 1757, rent on farm land in the Piedmont, Catoctian and Great Falls manors averaged £2 to £4 for 100-150 acres. Rents had inflated by 1765, and for £1 annual rent, farmers could lease 20 acres in Great Falls manor, 30 acres at Broad Run, on the Wankopin or in Catoctian manor, or 50 acres in Piedmont manor. This was all in sharp contrast to the rent on a house in Williamsburg, then £45 to £60 a year. [Democracy, p. 23; GW Writings, pp. 185-187; White Oak, p. 61; generally, LDCODB].

Only one of every five land owners had more than 500 acres in 1765; two-thirds of all land holdings in Loudoun County were smaller than 200 acres. By 1766, Loudoun farm land was selling for an average of about ten shillings (£½) per acre. Prices on large tracts ranged from £15 to £50 for every 100 acres, while a few improved properties along the Ridge Road (now Rte. 7) at Sugarland Run sold for £1 per acre. Re-sale prices for improved 150-acre three-life leases in the manors kept pace, ranging between £50-100 in the Piedmont manor and £15-20 in the vicinity of Leesburg. [Democracy, p. 14; generally, LDCODB, Book E].

1757 SURVEY OF LOUDOUN - FAIRFAX LINE

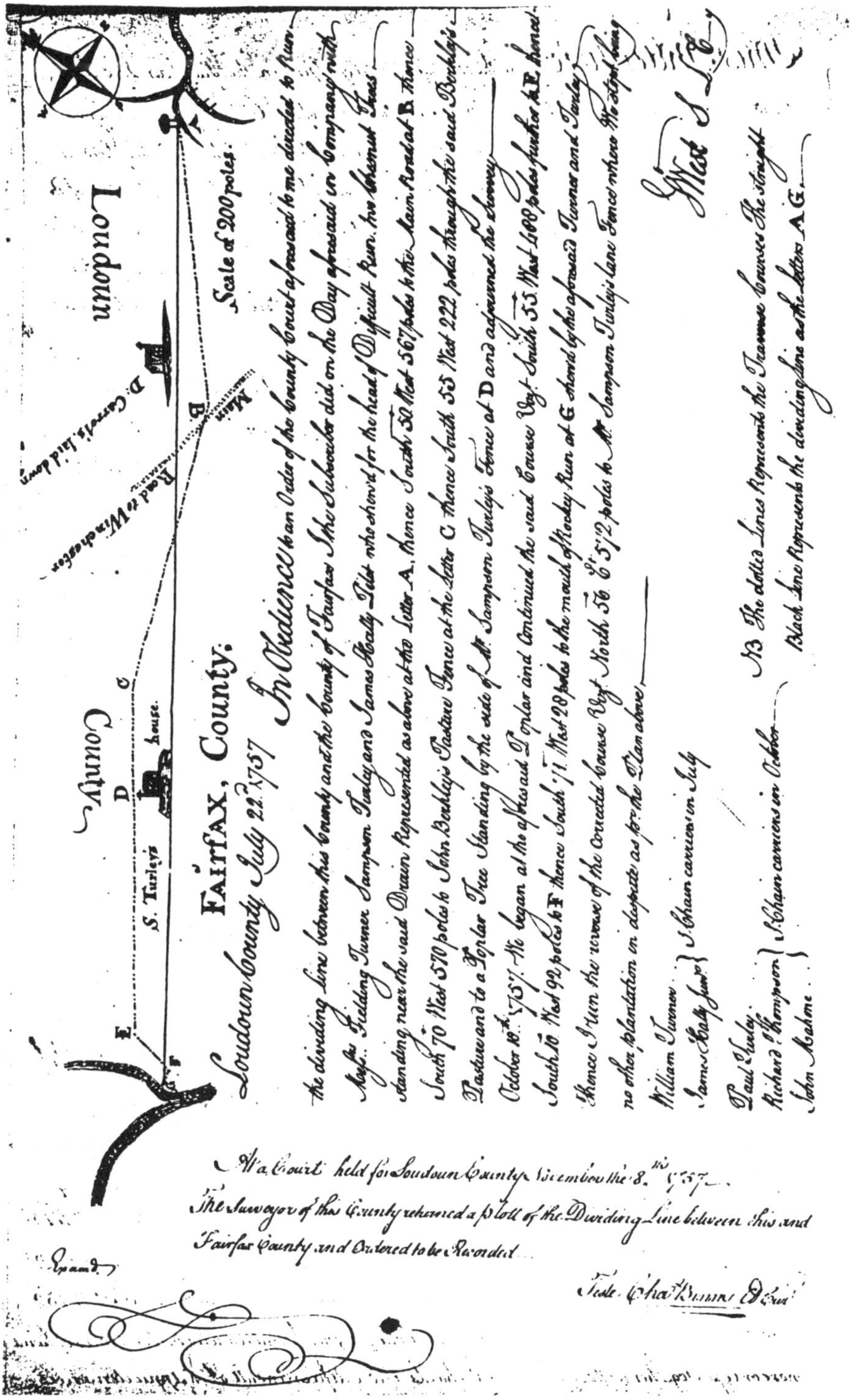

Loudoun

County

S. Turley's house.

D. Carroll's laid down

Road to Winchester

Main

Scale of 200 poles.

A B C D E F

FAIRFAX, County.

Loudoun County July 22d 1757 In Obedience to an Order of the County Court aforesaid to me directed to Run the dividing line between this County and the County of Fairfax I the Subscriber did on the Day aforesaid in Company with Messrs. Fielding Turner Sampson Turley and James Halley Pilot who shew'd for the head of Difficult Run two Chesnut Trees standing near the said Drain Represented as above at the Letter A. thence South 50 West 567 poles to the Main Road at B thence South 70 West 570 poles to John Berkley's Pasture Fence at the Letter C thence South 55 West 222 poles through the said Berkley's Pasture and to a Poplar Tree Standing by the side of Mr. Sampson Turley's Fence at D and adjourned the Survey October 10th 1757. We began at the aforesaid Poplar and Continued the said Course Vizt. South 55 West 408 poles further to E thence South 10 West 92 poles to F thence South 71 West 28 poles to the mouth of Rockey Run at G shew'd by the aforesaid Turner and Turley thence I run the reverse of the corrected Course Vizt. North 56 Et. 572 poles to Mr. Sampson Turley's lane Fence where We stopt being no other plantation in dispute as pr. the Plan above.

William Turner, James Halley Junr. } S. Chain carriers in July

Paul Turley, Richard Thompson, John Mahone } S. Chain carriers in October

J. West S. L. C.

NB The dotted Lines Represents the Traverse Courses The straight Black Line Represents the dividing line as the Letters A G.

At a Court held for Loudoun County December the 8th 1757. The Surveyor of this County returned a plott of the Dividing Line between this and Fairfax County and Ordered to be Recorded.

Examd.

Teste Chas. Binns Clerk

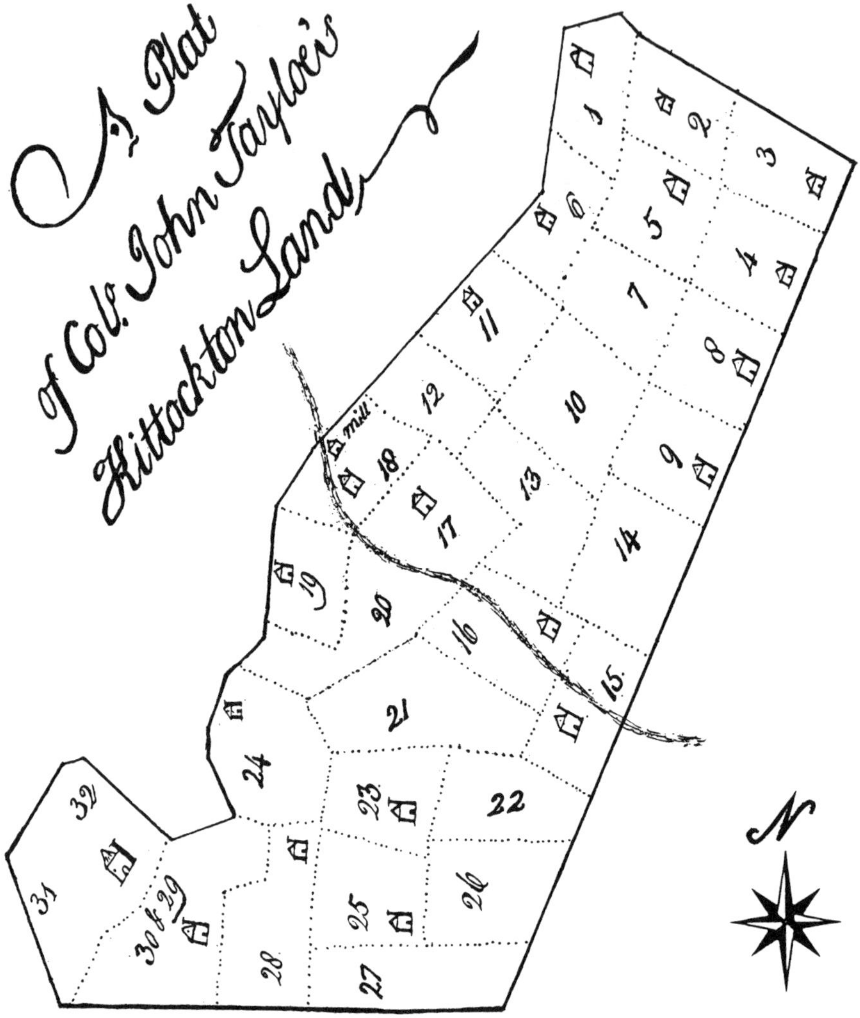

Councilor John Tayloe's Plat of his land at the Gap of Short Hill was recorded in the Loudoun Court Orders in the spring of 1759. The tract was rented out by Col. Tayloe under three-life leases, in lots of about 150 acres each. This Plat shows the location of the mill of John Hough on lot 18, the home of Loudoun Justice John McIlhaney on lots 10 and 11, and the home of Jenkin Phillips Senr. on lots 31 and 32. Several of the leases, including those for the Phillips families on lots 31 and 32, were recorded in Fairfax County in 1756 and early 1757. The McIlhaney family eventually purchased the entire Tayloe tract at The Gap. Book A, p. 232.

July 12, 1757 - "Ordered that George West Gent. run the dividing Line between the Counties of Fairfax and Loudoun on Friday the [22nd] of this [July] and that the Sheriff of this County give Notice to the Magistrates of the said County of Fairfax that they may Attend the same if they please." Book A, p. 4.

August 10, 1757 - "George West produced a Commission to be Surveyor of this [Loudoun] County ... took the Oath ... and acknowledged his Bond to the President and Masters of the Colledge [sic] of William & Mary in Virginia in the sum of One hundred pounds sterling," agreeing to account for his official actions annually at each April County Court and to pay a license commission to The College totalling a "one sixth part of all the fees and profits for Surveying at the rate of Eight shillings current money per Gross hundred [of tobacco]." Charles Binns, the Loudoun County Clerk, and Fairfax attorney Lee Massey serve as Sureties on the bond. The rate of exchange in this bond, at wide variance from the official Loudoun rates, reduced George West's fee obligations to The College by nine pence for every one hundred pounds of tobacco of his surveying fee income. Book A, p. 7; and, LDCODB, A/16.

October 11, 1757 - George West with his brother, Loudoun Deputy King's Attorney, Hugh West, and Lee Massey as his Sureties, gives a £500 bond to "our Sovereign Lord King George the second ..." for the faithful performance of his duties as Surveyor of Loudoun County. LDCODB, A/16-17.

November 8, 1757 - "The Surveyor of this County [George West] returned a Plott of the dividing Line - between this and Fairfax County and [it was] Ordered to be Recorded." Order Book A, p. 41; supra, Survey on p. 247.

November 9, 1757 - "Adam Tuckworth" brings an action in ejectment against "Edmund Duckworth," for one messuage and 50 acres. James Rogers is the tenant in possession. According to witness Francis Elgin, Rogers was served with notice, but did not appear at Court a second time and was evicted under a "Kings Writ of habere facias Possessionem [sic]." Book A, pp. 24 and 53.

December 13, 1757 - In the County Levy, a debit for: "George West, Gent. for running the dividing Line between this & Fairfax County ... 1,000 [lbs. tobacco] ... [and] ... Ditto for paying Chain Carriers ... 60 [lb.t.]." Book A, p. 54; see schedule of rates in text, supra p. 234.

December 13, 1757 - The County levy also includes debits listed for "William Turner [and] ... James Holly Junr. [each of them] a Chain carrier as per account [and] ... James Holly as Pilot [all three, on the survey of the county line, are paid] ... 40" lbs. of tobacco. Book A, p. 55.

March 14, 1758 - A Deed from Richard Roberts to Thomas Green is acknowledged and recorded. Book A, p. 66.

June 12, 1758 - Samuel Butcher purchased over 1200 acres for £100. LDCODB, A/148.

November 15, 1758 - "Ordered ... the Sherif of this County retain in his Hands [671 lbt.] out of the ballance due to Fairfax County for that County's proportionable charge [sic] for running the Division Line between this & the said County of Fairfax." Fairfax County paid 60% of the total cost; thus, George West earned £8, 14 shillings, 9 pence for his 18-mile survey. Book A, p. 180.

March 11, 1759 - George Vandiveere purchases 216 acres south of Goose Creek, for £32. LDCODB, A/363.

March 20, 1759 - In Williamsburg, the Virginia Assembly received "Several Petitions from sundry Inhabitants of the County of Fairfax ... for altering the present Boundaries of the ... Counties of Prince William, Fairfax and Loudoun ... Also a Petition from sundry Inhabitants of the County of Loudoun, to the same purpose ... Also sundry Petitions from divers Inhabitants of the Town of Alexandria ... to the same Purpose ... [the Assembly] Ordered that the said Petitions do lye on the Table [ie., held without action]." Assembly (1758), p. 102.

March 26, 1759 - In the Assembly, Petitions from Prince William, Fairfax and Loudoun, asking for revisions of county boundary lines, are "referred to the Committee of Propositions and Grievances." Fauquier County is created as a result of Committee action on these Petitions. The Petition from Loudoun probably asked that the boundary line with Fairfax County be moved eastward, from Rocky Run to Popes Head, to have all of Cameron parish included within Loudoun County. Assembly (1758), p. 108; infra, Chapter on Cameron Parish.

March 28, 1759 - Before the Lord Mayor of London, England, Charles Bennett, the Earl of Tankerville, designates and appoints "John Patterson of the Parish of Saint James, Westminster, in the county Middlesex, Gent., to depart from England within six weeks and go over to Virginia and there take the possession and management of [Tankerville's] several estates and as Steward, Agent or Manager." The Earl's properties include a 1,600 acre tract on Kitoctin Creek in Loudoun called "Catoctian Manour," and a 6,300 acre estate in Frederick County, Maryland known as "Merryland." LDCODB, C/98-109.

April 10, 1759 - Attending the Loudoun Court, G.W. Fairfax leases 140 acres in the Piedmont manor to Stephen Harlan, on a three-life lease, for annual rent of 16 shillings per 50 acres, due in May. LDCODB, A/268.

December 11, 1759 - "Ordered that the Sherif [Nicholas Minor] ... pay to Charles Broadwater Gent., [a Justice in Fairfax County who was seated on the Fairfax side of Difficult Run] Ten pounds [£10], four shillings and eight pence it being the proportion due from this County to the said Charles for building of Difficult Bridge [on the Potomac Ridge road]." Book A, p. 318.

December 11, 1759 - A three-life lease from G.W. Fairfax to Thomas Wyat recites the usual covenants in the Piedmont manor. Wyat is required to "build a dwelling house ... [20'] long and [16'] wide and other outhouses," and Wyat had the right to "nominate two other persons [on the lease] paying [30] shillings Sterling ... each." Book A, p. 319; LDCODB, A/355.

February 23, 1760 - Jacob Faw, purchased 355 acres on Tuscarora Run, for £10 sterling "and other consideration." LDCODB, A/448.

May 1, 1760 - Aeneas Campbell begins acting in Loudoun County as the Agent, or "Attorney in Fact," for Catesby Cocke, Esqr. [the former Clerk of the Prince William and Fairfax County Courts, and an investor in Loudoun property who was then living near Belvoir]. Book A, pp. 360 and 479-502.

May 15, 1760 - John Mercer appoints Francis Peyton "to receive of my Tenants in the upper part of Loudoun their rents." LDCODB, A/472.

June 12, 1760 - Benjamin Edwards buys 3 acres near Leesburg for £30, southwest of and adjacent to Leven Powell's "lot." LDCODB, B/8.

August 12, 1760 - Samuel Stroud purchased 100 acres west of the Short Hills for £85. LDCODB, B/36.

September 26, 1760 - A deed from Catesby Cocke Esqr. transfers 504 acres above Goose Creek that had been surveyed in 1748 by William West. This was William West Senr., a Loudoun Justice. LDCODB, B/100.

November 20, 1760 - Covenants for a lease in "Catoctian Manour" require construction of a 26'x20' dwelling, "a sufficient [36'x22'] barn or granary," and planting a peach and an apple tree for every acre. LDCODB, C/1.

February 26, 1761 - Catesby Cocke, "for divers good causes," revoked and annulled the 1759 power of attorney he had given to Aeneas Campbell for the management of his lands in Loudoun County. LDCODB, B/205.

May 1, 1761 - John Carlyle, as agent for George William Fairfax, leases 150 acres to Francis Baldwin for three lives - Baldwin's daughter Bathsheba Baldwin, "George William Fairfax Esqr. and his Royal Highness George Prince of Wales [the young son of King George III]" !!! LDCODB, B/200.

August 11, 1761 - A Deed to John Trammell, from widow Margaret Sinclear, for a tract in the Lost Corner, is proven in Court by Aaron Richardson, John Sinclear and John Hanbey [sic], and recorded. Book A, p. 482.

August 11, 1761 - George West, the Surveyor of Loudoun County, reports on his recent survey of the site that had been selected by John Hough as the best location on Goose Creek for Hough's new grist mill. Book A, p. 485.

September 8, 1761 - Leases "for lives" for properties in the Piedmont manor, from John Carlyle Attorney on behalf of George William Fairfax, to tenants Simon Shomaker, Peter Schomaker, George Shomaker, Adam Winsall [sic], Francis Baldwin and James Ross, are recorded. Book A, pp. 494 and 495.

September 8, 1761 - Jacob Phaw purchases 35 more acres on the Tuscarora near the Pyles family, for £6. LDCODB, C/15.

October 12, 1761 - John Hopkins, from Pennsylvania, purchases 670 acres for £345 of Pennsylvania currency. LDCODB, C/23.

November 2, 1761 - A special committee of the Virginia Assembly, including the Burgesses representing Loudoun, Fairfax, Prince William and Westmoreland Counties, is constituted to consider the Petition of Robert Carter for docking entails on some of his lands. Assembly, (1761) p. 20.

January 19, 1762 - James Steer purchases 55 acres near one of the upper forks of Clarks Run, adjacent to Thomas Green, for £40 in Pennsylvania currency. LDCODB, C/138.

February 8, 1762 - William West Junr. (the eldest son of Loudoun Justice William West) surveys a tract of 625 acres that William Ellzey would sell to Loudoun County Justice Anthony Russell, adjacent to and just north of the Cameron parish glebe lands. LDCODB, C/166.

March 10, 1762 - Surveys along Kitoctin Creek are ordered in the land dispute between "The Right Hon.ble Charles [Bennett] Earl of Tankerville," and John Hough. Book A, p. 569.

May 12, 1762 - "Aminidab Goodtitle [pronounced 'I'm in a damn good title ...'], Lessee of John Watson" brings an action against Lewis Ellzey in ejectment for one messuage and 150 acres of Land. A jury finds "Deft. [Lewis Ellzey] is not Guilty of Trespass and Ejectment ... Plt. take nothing ... but for his false Clamour be in Mercy &c." Watson and Ellzey apparently had a boundary dispute at Difficult Run. Book A, p. 595.

May 12, 1762 - A Grand Jury, sitting for the first time in over a year, presents charges against a seemingly exhaustive list of Loudoun landowners living in other Counties, each having failed to render "a List of his Lands to the Clerk's Office of this County: ... William Ellzey of Prince William County Gent. ... Thompson Mason of St. Mary's County Maryland Gent. ... The Revd. Charles Green of Fairfax County ... Colo. George Mercer of Frederick County ... James Mercer, Gent. Attorney at Law at present living in Fredricksburgh ... Landall Carter, [sic - Landon Carter] Gent. of Richmond County ... John Carter, Gent. of Prince William County ... Daniel French, Gent. of Fairfax County ... The Honble. Philip Lud. Lee Esqr. of Westmorland [sic] County ... Colo. Thomas Lee of Stafford County ... Colo. Henry Lee of Prince William County ... Colo. Robert Burwell of York County ... The Honble. John Tayloe, Esqr. of Richmond County ... The Honble. Robert Carter, Esqr. of the City of Williamsburg ... Benjamin Grayson of Fairfax County, Gent. ... Spence Grayson of Prince William County, Gent. ... Lewis Ellzey, Gent. of Fairfax County ... Colo. Catesby Cocke of Fairfax County ... Willoughby Newton [Junr.] of Westmoreland County, Gent. ... John Ariss of Richmond County, Gent. ... Thomas Stone of Prince William County ... Colo. John Carlyle of Fairfax County ... John Berkley of Fairfax County ... Colo. Henry Peyton of Prince William ... Samuel Tillett of Fairfax County ... Capt. Samuel Oldham of Westmoreland County ... The Honble. George William Fairfax now in Great Britain ... Bailey Washington of Stafford County ... Colo. John Baliss [sic] of Prince William County, Guardian of Thomas Blackburn ... Samuel Conner of Fairfax County ... [and] John Turbervile [sic] of Westmoreland County for his Brother (to whom he is Guardian)." Book A, pp. 595-599.

May 12, 1762 - The Grand Jury also presents charges against resident Loudoun landowners "of this County for not rendering a List of his Lands to the Clerk's Office of this County: ... Craven Peyton, Gent. ... Jonathan Monkhouse ... Henry Moore, Gent. [!? - sic] ... Elijah Chinn ... Philip Noland, Gent. ... Enoch Grigsby ... James Spencer ... John Saweer [sic] ... Jacob Remey ... Benjamin Hutchison ... Joseph Hutchison ... Francis Padget ... Robert Sandford ... Silvester Gardner ... Jacob Morris ... Thomas Self ... Wamon Sinkler ... John Hough ... Thomas Clews ... William Buckley ... George Hancock ... Sampson Turley ... Henry Wisheart ... William Triplet ... Daniel Triplet ... Robert Stewksbury ...

Samuel Mead ... John Tramell ... Mahlon Janney ... William Janney ... Robert Bland ... Joshua Gore ... Nicholas Osborn ... William Kirk ... John Patterson, Gent., Agent for the Earl of Tankerville ... Thomas Brown ... Andrew Adams ... Samuel Duncan ... Francis Wilks ... [and] Thomas John." Book A, pp. 595-599.

June 14, 1762 - John Griffy purchases 150 acres from James Hamilton for £30. LDCODB, C/635.

July 14, 1762 - In an ejectment case, James Kennady is a tenant in possession of 241 acres. Book B, p. 9.

August 10, 1762 - For £105 of Virginia colony currency, Mary Janney, a widow, sells 469 acres on the west side of Kitoctin Mountain, "on a barren hill by the [Shenandoah] road," adjacent to the lands of George Atwood, Francis Wilks and William Henry Fairfax, to Jacob Janney. LDCODB, C/362.

August 13, 1762 - "Aminidab Goodtitle, lessee of James Hamilton, Gent." brings a suit against "Ferdinando Badtitle" to try title to 241 acres in Cameron Parish. James Kennedy, tenant in possession, enters himself as defendant. Book B, p. 50.

September 16, 1762 - Charles Bennett, the Earl of Tankerville, brings an action against "John MickleSwamp" for trespass. This appears to be an intentional misstatement and pun on the name of John McIlhaney, the likely defendant. The case is continued to the next Court session. Book B, p. 65.

March 8, 1763 - Lord Fairfax leases 163 acres on the Jeffries Branch to Henry Rector Junr.. The covenants were typical for leases in Leeds Manor. Proprietary "Quitrents and one good fat Turkey or capon ... [were to be] delivered to [Greenway Court] Mansion house," construction of a 20'x16' dwelling House and the planting of "at least 100 apple trees" 30' apart were required during the first three years. Rent was only £2 per 100 acres. LDCODB, C/563.

March 21, 1763 - For £45, George Vandiveer purchases 3 acres at Rocky Run, on the Mountain Road (to Williams Gap). His lot includes a storehouse that had been built by William Jett. LDCODB, C/531.

March 24, 1763 - Shortly before his death, assistant Loudoun Surveyor William West Junr., a first cousin of Surveyor George West and the eldest son of Loudoun Justice William West of Fruit Hill, subdivided a hilly, 1400 acre tract just northeast of the area now known as Mountville, between the Beaver Dam branch and Goose Creek. The entire tract was sold off at the rate of only £10 for each 100 acres. LDCODB, C/584, and D/148-172.

April 11, 1763 - Lewis Massey purchases 200 acres from Jacob Janney for £100. LDCODB, C/495.

May 11, 1763 - The Loudoun Grand Jury, warming to the task, presents a long list of landowners living in other Counties, each "for not entering with the Clerk of Loudoun County the Quantity of Land held by him in the said County according to the Acts of Assembly: ... Willoughby Newton, Gent., of Westmoreland County ... Honble. Robert Carter, Esqr. [Junr., of Williamsburg] ... James Nesbet of Prince William County ... Honble. John Tayloe, Esqr. [of Richmond County] ... John Turberfield, Gent., of Westmoreland ... Baley [sic] Washington of Stafford County ... John Newton of Westmorland [sic] County ...

Mrs. Blackburn, Widow and Relict of Richard Blackburn, dec'd. of Prince William ... John Berkley of Fairfax ... John Carter, Esqr. of Prince William ... Thompson Mason, Gent., of ... Maryland ... Thompson Mason, Gent. ... for Lands belonging to Seldon's Orphans ... John Mercer, Esqr. of Stafford County ... Robert Adams of Fairfax County ... Henry Hampton of Prince William ... William Elzey of Prince William ... Lewis Elzey, Gent. of Fairfax County ... William Grayson of Prince William ... Daniel French of Fairfax County ... Henry Ashton of Westmoreland County ... John Sandford of Westmoreland County ... Thomas Hampton of Fairfax County ... John Rawls of Stafford County ... Henry Peyton of Prince William ... Catesby Cocke of Prince William ... Revrd. Charles Green of Fairfax County ... John Aris of Richmond County ... John Carlyle Gent. of the Town of Alexandria ... Messrs. Carlyle and Dalton of the Town of Alexandria ... Bryan Fairfax, Gent. of Fairfax ... George Wm. Fairfax, Esqr. of Great Britain ... William Douglass of Fairfax County ... Daniel McCarty, Gent., of Fairfax ... William Davis, Fauquier County ... Spence Grayson of Prince William ... Benja. Grayson of Fairfax County ... Isaac Farrow of Prince William ... George Johnston, Esqr., of the Town of Alexandria ... Landon Carter, Gent. of Richmond County ... [and] Thadeus McCarty of Fairfax County." Book B, pp. 131-138.

May 11, 1763 - The Loudoun Grand Jury also presents charges against a long list of resident landowners, "for not entering with the Clerk of Loudoun County the Quantity of Land held by him in the said County according to the Acts of Assembly: ... Robert Sandford ... Jeffrey Johnson ... Persons in the care of Joseph Reed's Estate ... Persons in the care of William Jett's Estate ... William Buckley ... Esther Sinclear [sic - Esther Sinclair] ... Cathrine Shreves ... The Honble. Robert Burwell, Esqr. ... Francis Paget ... William Morland ... Francis Hague ... John Hague ... John Ball ... Evan Price ... Andrew Combs ... Samuel Combs ... John Trammell ... John Stears ... James Stears ... Edward Garret ... John Patason [sic - John Patterson], Agent for the Right Honble. Charles Earl of Tankerville ... Robert Peyton ... Daniel Jones ... Samuel Butcher ... George Busson ... James Stephens ... William Brown ... Mercer Brown ... Joseph Claypool ... John Elbin ... Thomas John ... Henry Wisheart ... James Murray below Goose Creek ... [and] Patrick Mchollom [sic]." Book B, pp. 131-138.

June 13, 1763 - John Hough of Waterford acts as the land agent for three brothers, George Mercer, James Mercer and John Mercer, in the partition and sale of portions of their Loudoun properties. LDCODB, C/624.

June 17, 1763 - "Ferdinando Dreadnaught" lessee of George William Fairfax, Esqr., sues "Timothy Holdfast" in ejectment for one Messuage and tenement and 200 acres of Land. Charles Bennett Earl of Tankerville is entered as the defendant and surveys are ordered. John Patterson apparently brought this action on behalf of George William Fairfax. Book B, pp. 184 and 579.

August 11, 1763 - In a jury trial, James Hamilton wins his dispute with James Kennedy over the title to 241 acres in Cameron Parish, but Kennedy probably continued in possession. Book B, pp. 211-212; see infra p. 256.

September 13, 1763 - "Ordered that ... John Berkley's ... [218] Acres of Land held by him in this County ... [150] Acres of Land belonging to John Hatcher ... [116] Acres of Land belonging to Amos Goodwin ... [and 1,100] Acres of Land held by [Josias Clapham Gent.] in this County ... [all] be added to the Lists taken for this Year." Book B, p. 233; infra, Chapter on Colonial Taxes.

September 14, 1763 - "Ordered that ... [150] Acres of Land belonging to William Trammell ... [877] Acres of Land belonging to John Watts ... Benjamin Shrieve's ... [200 and 245] Acres of Land held by him ... [400] Acres of Land belonging to Nicholas Meese ... Isaac Fouch's ... [230] Acres of Land held by him in this County ... William Ellzey's ... [3,000] Acres of Land held by him in this County ... [all are to] be added to the List taken for this Year." Book B, p. 237.

September 14, 1763 - Upon the motion of John Hough in open Court, it is "Ordered that ... [3,350] Acres of Land belonging to Messrs. George and James Mercers ... be added to the List taken for this Year." Book B, p. 238.

September 14, 1763 - "Ordered that ... [668] Acres of Land belonging to John Hearl be added to the List taken for this Year." Book B, p. 241.

September 15, 1763 - "Ordered that ... [2,755] Acres of Land belonging to Mr. John Carlyle ... [725] Acres of Land belonging to Messrs. Carlyle & Dalton ... [12,648] Acres of Land belonging to George William Fairfax, Esqr. ... in this County ... added to the List ... for [1763]." Book B, pp. 247-248.

September 15, 1763 - "Ordered that ... Charles Bennett Earle [sic] of Tankerville, his ... [12,369] Acres of Land held by him in this County ... [be] added to the List ... for [the tax year 1763]." Book B, p. 251.

October 11, 1763 - "Ordered ... [900] Acres of Land held by William Allen in this County be added to the List taken for this Year." Book B, p. 258.

November 8, 1763 - "Ordered that ... [200] Acres of Land belonging to Isaac Austin ... Jonathan Monkhouse and his ... [760] Acres of Land ... in this County ... [all] be added to the List taken for this Year." Book B, p. 261.

November 8, 1763 - The Grand Jury presents "Jonas Potts ... [and] William Russ ... [each] for not entering with the Magistrates appointed to take List of Tithables the quantity of Land held by him in this County according to the Act of Assembly in that case made and provided." Book B, p. 263.

January 12, 1764 - John Ballendine purchases 194 acres in Loudoun County at the Great Falls, using Maryland currency. LDCODB, D/268.

March 16, 1764 - "Ferdinando Dreadnaught" sues "Timothy Holdfast" in ejectment for one Messuage or Tenement and 200 acres. James Brown enters as the defendant, "Pleads the General Issue, Confesses the Lease Entry and Ouster in the Declaration Supposed, and enters into common Rule to insist on the Title only at [a jury] Trial." No survey is requested. Book B, p. 306.

March 16, 1764 - "Ferdinando Dreadnaught" sues "Timothy Holdfast" in ejectment for one Messuage or Tenement, a Barn, Stables, kitchen and 150 acres. William Trammell, the defendant, "confesses lease entry and ouster ... agrees to insist on the Title only," and asks for a jury trial. Book B, p. 306.

March 16, 1764 - "Ferdinando Dreadnaught" sues "Timothy Holdfast" in ejectment for 150 acres. Ezekiel Jenkins enters as defendant, "confesses lease entry and ouster ...," and asks for a jury trial. Book B, p. 306.

March 16, 1764 - "Solomon Saveall" sues "Simpleton Spendall" in ejectment for three Messuages, 600 acres of Land, 100 acres of Meadow and 50 acres of Pasture. Robert Adam, Gent., enters as the defendant, "confesses lease entry and ouster ...," and asks for a jury trial. Book B, p. 306.

March 16, 1764 - A Certificate of the Examination of Elizabeth Fairfax, wife of Bryan Fairfax, for a Deed to George Washington, Esqr., for 275 acres beside "the main road (now the old road) just at the ford in the lower side of Difficult Run," is recorded. Book B, p. 311; LDCODB, C/458.

March 16, 1764 - "Aminidab Goodtitle" sues "Ferdinando Badtitle" in ejectment for one messuage and 100 acres. Lewis Ellzey, the defendant, is represented by William Ellzey as his attorney. It was "suggested by the Plt's [plaintiff's] attorney that the bounds of the Land are in Question ... Ordered that the Surveyor ... go upon the Land ... on the 12th Day of April next if fair ... Survey and lay out the lands." Book B, p. 313.

May 12, 1764 - Richard Eskridge purchases 315 acres on Licking branch flat lick of Cub Run near Salisbury Plain for £160 in Virginia colony currency. LDCODB, D/448.

June 11, 1764 - For £85, Thomas Umphreys [sic- Thomas Humphreys] purchased 371 acres at Round Hill adjacent to the road leading from Williams Gap to Leesburg. Jenkin Phillips witnessed. LDCODB, D/215.

September 12, 1764 - Lee Massey purchased 13 acres of land, with one boundary said to contain 70 "perches," from his neighbor Robert Popkins. LDCODB, D/292; see Glossary.

September 14, 1764 - "Ordered [6,500] Acres of Land held by Mann Page Esqr. ... be added to the list taken ... this Present Year." Book B, p. 465.

November 13, 1764 - The Grand Jury brings in Presentments against: "Jacob Wildman ... [and] John Hague [of Loudoun] ... for not giving in [their] ... Land in this County [for 1764] ... [and] Thomas Blackburn of Prince William County for not giving in his land in this County [for 1764]." Book B, p. 493.

May 13, 1765 - For £518, Simeon Haines of the New Jersey colony purchases 380 acres on the south side of the south fork of the Kitoctin, adjacent to William Williams. LDCODB, D/433.

May 14, 1765 - "Three Messuages," 4,000 acres of land, 50 acres of meadow, and 50 acres of pasture, is the land subject to a title dispute between "Jonathan Saveall" [apparently a pseudonym for Charles Bennett the Earl of Tankerville] and George William Fairfax. The County Surveyor [George West] is to "Survey and lay off the Land in dispute" on May 28, 1765 "if fair if not the next fair day ... And the Sherif is to Attend the Survey & remove [by] force if any [opposition] shall be offered." Tankerville must have been satisfied with George West's 1765 survey. In August of 1766 George West is appointed as Tankerville's land agent! Book B, p. 579; see infra p. 257; infra, Glossary.

May 14, 1765 - In a counter-suit, "Ferdinando Dreadnaught" [the pseudonym for G.W. Fairfax] brings an action "In Ejectment &c. against Charles Bennett Earl of Tankerville." More surveys are ordered. Book B, p. 579.

May 14, 1765 - The case of "Aminidab Goodtitle" [probably James Hamilton] against James Kennady [sic], on an injunction to evict Kennady, is continued to the next Court. Book B, p. 580.

May 14, 1765 - "Ferdinando Dreadnaught" vs. Ezekiel Jenkins, an ejectment and eviction action, is continued to the next Court. Book B, p. 582.

May 14, 1765 - A lease, from George William Fairfax, Esqr. to George Nixon, is recorded. Book B, p. 582.

August 8, 1765 - William Holmes bought 180 acres east of Kitoctin Mountain, on the upper drains of Secolon, for £260. LDCODB, D/548.

August 13, 1765 - "Ordered that Richard Williams and his ... 570 Acres of Land be added to the List ... this present Year." Book C, p. 18.

August 13, 1765 - "Ordered ... [3,183] Acres of Land Held by William Cocke ... [and 150] Acres of Land held by Frederick Weisell ... in this County be added to the List ... this present Year." Book C, p. 21.

August 13, 1765 - "Ordered that ... [92] Acres of Land held by [Garret Cornelius] in this County be added to the List ... this ... Year." Book C, p. 22.

September 9, 1765 - "[6,500] Acres of Land held by Mann Page Esqr. ... [550] Acres of Land held by Robert Alexander ... [and 530] Acres of Land held by William Payne be added to the List ... this Present Year." Book C, p. 31.

September 10, 1765 - "[Two hundred] Acres of Land held by John Cargell in this County be added to the List ... this Year." Book C, pp. 38-39.

September 11, 1765 - The Loudoun County Surveyor is again ordered to survey the lands in dispute between "Jonathan Saveall" [undoubtedly the Earl of Tankerville, represented by the John Patterson] and George William Fairfax, having failed to perform his duty as ordered the previous May. Book C, p. 50.

September 12, 1765 - In a special covenant of a three-life lease for a 200 acre farm at Broad Run, George William Fairfax agrees "not to raise the Quit rents ... above the sum of Two shillings Sterling." LDCODB, E/25.

September 30, 1765 - Mahlon Kirkbride of Pennsylvania "deputed [his Quaker] Friend William Mead ... to let [rent out] any part of my land ... for any number of years not exceeding fifteen years." LDCODB, E/272.

October 14, 1765 - "Ordered that [127] Acres ... held by John Hendran in this County ... [and 200] Acres of Land held by [Thomas Triplett] ... [all] be added to the List ... taken for this present Year [1765]." Book C, p. 59.

October 14, 1765 - A lease for lives, from George William Fairfax, Esqr. to Henry Toup, is recorded. Book C, p. 60.

October 16, 1765 - "Ordered that George William Fairfax, Esqr., ['that is to say'] his ... [12,648] Acres of Land ... [be] added to the List taken & returned for this present Year." Book C, p. 68.

June 9, 1766 - Charles Bennett, the Earl of Tankerville appoints Thomas Colvill, Gent. as his agent with Power of Attorney. Book C, p. 79.

June 11, 1766 - Surveys are ordered in the land dispute between "Solomon Saveall" and Robert Adam. Book C, p. 103.

July 30, 1766 - Joseph Cadwaleder [sic] purchased 260 acres from Bryan Fairfax for £50. LDCODB, E/116.

August 4, 1766 - Upon receipt of a Power of Attorney from the Earl of Tankerville, Thomas Colvill designates Loudoun's Surveyor, George West, as the agent "to demand and receive from all the tenants of the said Earl [in

Loudoun] ... their several rents and arrearages." LDCODB, E/115.

August 11, 1766 - A deed recorded in Loudoun County confirms that William Hough, one of John Hough's sons, had recently made a survey and plat of subdivision for William West's 644 acre tract on the northeast side of Bull Run Mountain. LDCODB, E/110-115.

August 13, 1766 - John Connell brings a Trespass action against John Dyer. Book C, p. 161.

August 13, 1766 - Michael Hummer is the tenant in possession in an eviction action. Book C, p. 165.

August 17, 1766 - John Edmondson Junr. of Essex County Virginia, "for ... weighty considerations" named Edward Sniggers his agent to collect "of all my tenants [on upper Jeffries Branch, at the Blue Ridge] in Loudoun ... rents due on arrears." LDCODB, E/266; see Table, infra p. 259.

September 8, 1766 - "Ordered ... [150] Acres of Land held by [John Davis] ... be added to List returned for this present Year." Book C, p. 185.

September 9, 1766 - John Cargill mortgaged 193 acres of Loudoun lands for £160. LDCODB, E/197.

September 10, 1766 - Jacob Phaw, or Jacob Faw, mortgaged 153 acres of Loudoun lands for £550. LDCODB, E/238.

October 13, 1766 - "On the Motion of James Caruthers ... Ordered that [247] Acres of Land be inserted in the List returned." Book C, p. 207.

October 14, 1766 - "On the Motion of John Ballendine the following ... Land be Entered on the Lists returned for this present Year vizt. ... McCarty's Quarter ... [ie., 4,175] Acres of Land; ... [and] At Seneca Falls ... [4,000] Acres of Land [sic - belonging to or rented by Ballendine?]." Book C, p. 208.

November 5, 1766 - John Criswell leases a 185 acre farm at Leek Creek on Sugarland Run for 18 years, for an annual rent of £6 "current and lawful money of Virginia." LDCODB, E/335-338.

November 11, 1766 - Jonathan Moore, a resident of New Jersey, appoints Anthony Russell as his agent "to lett a certain tract [in Loudoun County] ... to any persons that he shall think proper." LDCODB, E/271.

November 11, 1766 - The Grand Jury brings in Presentments against: "Robert Burwell, Esqr. ... Thomas Blackburn Gent. ... Mr. John Carter ... John Evans on little River ... Benjamin Grayson ... Capt. William Ellzey ... Edward Harding ... Colo. Thomas Ludwell Lee ... Jonathan Monkhouse ... John Markley ... James Mercer Attorney at Law ... John Oxley ... Craven Peyton Gent. ... [all] for not listing [their] lands for ... 1766." Book C, pp. 223-224.

November 19, 1766 - "A Petition of Robert Bristow of Loudoun County, praying that an Act may pass to dock the Entail of sundry Tracts of Land whereof he is seized in Fee Taille, was presented to the House [of Burgesses] and read; and the Question being put that leave be given to bring in a Bill ... It passed in the Negative [ie., was defeated]." Assembly, (1766) p. 32.

Loudoun's 101 Largest Landowners - 1765

Landowner	(Neighborhood of Primary Holding)	Acres
Robert Carter, [3rd]	(Goose Creek; Frying Pan)	*: 40,000
Thomas, 6th Lord Fairfax	(Leeds; ungranted)	*: 35,000
Geo. Wm. Fairfax, Hon.	(Piedmont-Shannondale)	*: 25,500
Bryan Fairfax, Esq.	(Great Falls; Hogback Mtn.)	*: 16,500
Charles, Earl of Tankerville	(Kitoctin; Difficult Run)	12,369
George Mercer, James Mercer and John Mercer,	(Little River; Kitoctin Creek/Mtn.; Clarks Run)	*: 9,500
Thompson Mason	(Limestone-Leesburg-Potomac)	*: 8,983
John Tayloe, Hon.	(The Gap; Dulles; Mountain Rd.)	8,942
Mann Page, Esq.	(upper Goose Creek; Frying Pan)	6,500
John Semple	(Kitoctin-Potomac; Towlston)	*: 6,100
Landon Carter	(Secolon; Blue Ridge; Bull Run)	*: 5,400
John Hough	(Cub Run-Kitoctin-Leesburg) #	*: 5,050
Thomas Ludwell Lee	(Goose Creek; Difficult)	*: 5,000
Mary [Mason] Selden's orphans	(Exeter-Leesburg)	*: 4,223
Daniel McCarty	(Sugarland on the Potomac)	4,175
Philip Ludwell Lee, Hon.	(Broad Run-Potomac)	*: 3,600
William Lee	(Elk Licking Run-Broad Run)	*: 3,543
John Turberville	(Cub Run-Bull Run)	*: 3,465
Henry Lee, Col.	(Sully at Chantilly-Flat Lick Run)	*: 3,464
Francis Lightfoot Lee	(Horsepen; Difficult Run) #	3,200
William Cocke	(Short Hill-Kitoctin)	3,183
William Ellzey	(Beaver Dam Creek; Broad Run)	3,000
John Augustine Washington	(Blue Ridge)	*: 2,941
John Carlyle	(Sugarland Run basin; Difficult Run)	2,755
Anthony Russell	(upper Broad Run basin) #	2,420
Thomas Edmondson	(Jeffries branch-Blue Ridge)	*: 2,367
William Luckett	(Lucketts-Lost Corner) #	2,336
Griffith Evans	(Sugarland Run-Folly Lick) #	*: 2,211
Andrew Hutchison's sons	(Salisbury Plain) # (tot)	**: 2,175
Willoughby Newton, Capt.	(Rocky Run-Bull Run)	*: 2,160
Isaac Nichols	(N, NW forks of Goose Creek) #	2,080
John Elliott, his heirs	(Cub Run-Salisbury Plain)	*: 1,936
Elizabeth King	(Broad Run-Little Mountain)	*: 1,702
Henry Moore	(Cub Run-Bull Run)	1,588

LOUDOUN'S 101 LARGEST LANDOWNERS - 1765

LANDOWNER	(Neighborhood of Primary Holding)	ACRES
NEWTON KEENE	(Difficult Run basin)	1,500
THOMAS JOHN	(Jeffries branch; upper Limestone) # *:	1,468
JOHN GRYMES	(Cub Run-Elk Lick Run) *:	1,450
DANIEL FRENCH	(Difficult Run)	1,400
MAHLON JANNEY	(Waterford; N fork Goose Creek) #	1,350
JOHN TRAMMELL	(Clarks Run-Lost Corner) #	1,336
LEWIS ELLZEY	(Beaver Dam Creek; Difficult Run)	1,330
PHILIP NOLAND [Junr.]	(Clarks Run-Potomac) #	1,186
JOSIAS CLAPHAM	(Lost Corner on the Potomac) #	1,100
GEORGE GREGG	(Lucketts-Bald Hill; Beaver Dam) #	1,100
WILLIAM WEST	(West's Ordinary-Bull Run Mtn.) # *:	1,080
WILLIAM JONES	(Kitoctin basin) #	1,076
JAMES DILLON	(Kitoctin basin-north of Rock Hill)	1,050
THOMAS BROOKE	(upper Goose Creek-Leeds) *:	1,046
WILLIAM CAVENS	(Kitoctin Mtn.-Woodburn)	1,020
AMOS FOX	(Difficult Run at Ridge Road bridge) #	1,000
MARGARET GREEN, widow	(west side of Goose Creek)	1,000
BENJAMIN HAIT	(Kitoctin Mtn.-Clarks Gap)	973
SIMEON HAINES	(Kitoctin-Rock Hill)	960
GEORGE HANCOCK	(Sugarland Run)	960
SAMUEL BUTCHER	(upper Beaver Dam Creek) #	950
FRANCIS HAGUE	(Waterford-Kitoctin Mtn.-Leesburg) #	950
JOHN PILES	(Belmont-Waxpool; Beaver Dam) # *:	940
CHARLES BINNS	(Rokeby-Secolon) #	902
WILLIAM ALLEN	(Broad Run-North fork) # *:	900
ABRAHAM WARFORD	(Broad Run-Arcola) # *:	900
JOHN WATTS	(unidentified location)	877
JOHN FITZHUGH, Maj.	(Frying Pan-Horsepen) *:	860
JOHN SINCLAIR	(Lost Corner on the Potomac) *:	850
JOSEPH COMBS	(NW fork of Goose Creek) #	845
JACOB JANNEY	(NE, NW forks of Goose Creek) #	800
EDWARD THOMPSON	(NE fork Goose Creek; The Gap)	787
JAMES COLEMAN	(Sugarland Run on Ridge Road)	773
JONATHAN MONKHOUSE	(south of Leesburg-Secolon)	760
HECTOR ROSS	(south side of Hogback Mtn.)	760
DANIEL JONES	(forks of Beaver Dam Creek) *:	751

Loudoun's 101 Largest Landowners - 1765

Landowner	(Neighborhood of Primary Holding)	Acres
Benjamin Berkley	(Rocky Cedar Run-Cub Run)	750
Abel Janney	(Broad Run of Kitoctin-Short Hill)	750
Henry Brown	(Kitoctin Creek-Taylorstown)	728
Carlyle & Dalton, merchants	(Tuscarora Run)	725
Nicholas Osborn	(N fork of Goose Creek)	715
Daniel Conner	(Cub Run-Elk Licking Run)	711
Thomas Waring, Maj.	(Tuscarora Run)	*: 703
William Hatcher	(NE fork of Goose Creek)	700
James Lane, Capt.	(Cub Run basin)	700
William Carr Lane	(Rocky Run-Newgate)	660
Francis Peyton	(Little River; Goose Creek)	650
William Yeardley	(Goose Creek-Jeffries branch)	*: 650
Peter Romine	(Round Hill)	650
James Hamilton	(Kitoctin Mtn.-Hamilton)	645
John Carter	(River Bend-Potomac)	*: 640
William Brown	(North fork of Goose Creek)	634
Chambers Hall	(Beaver Dam Creek)	620
Robert Booth	(Dutchman's Run-Potomac)	*: 600
Joseph Hutchison	(Piney branch of Broad Run)	** 600
John Newton	(Rocky Cedar Run)	600
Kitchen Prim	(Belmont Ridge-Waxpool)	600
William Trammell	(Kitoctin Mtn.-Clarks Run)	586
Spence Grayson	(upper Beaver Dam Creek)	576
Richard Williams	(NE fork Goose Creek; Kitoctin)	570
Vincent Lewis	(Difficult Run)	560
John Dent	(Little River-Wolf Glade)	*: 557
Robert Alexander	(Kitoctin Mtn.-Bald Hill)	550
Edward Dullen	(Lost Corner)	550
John Lewis, estate	(Difficult Run)	550
William Bronaugh	(Cub Run-Rocky Run)	*: 537
William Fitzhugh, Col.	(Sugarland Run-Ridge Road)	*: 535

* - Estimated landholdings were obtained by researching title in property transactions, then adjusting the land tax list entries.

\# - The top two dozen resident landowners are noted thusly.

** - Andrew Hutchison had divided his land between five sons.

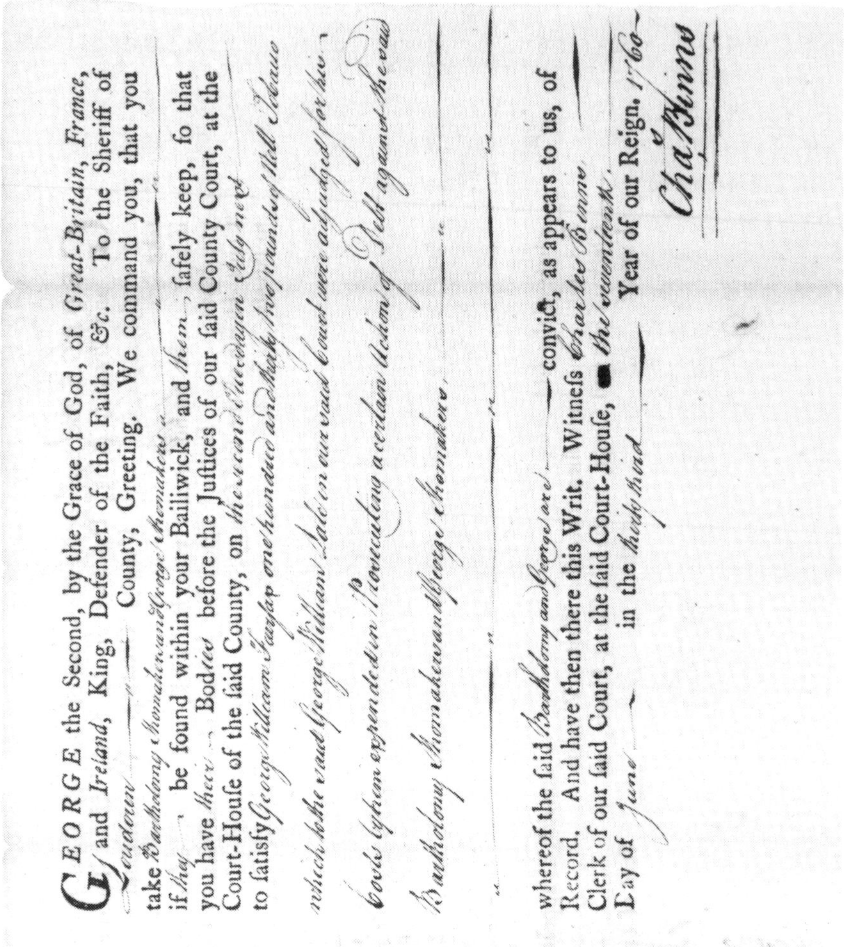

GEORGE the Second, by the Grace of God, of Great-Britain, France, and Ireland, King, Defender of the Faith, &c. To the Sheriff of Loudoun County, Greeting. We command you, that you take Bartholomy Shoemaker and George Shoemaker if they be found within your Bailiwick, and them safely keep, so that you have their Bodies before the Justices of our said County Court, at the Court-House of the said County, on the second Thursday in July next to satisfy George William Fairfax one hundred and thirty two pounds of Nett Tobacco which to the said George William Fairfax in our said Court were adjudged for his costs by him expended in Prosecuting a certain Action of Debt against the said Bartholomy Shoemaker and George Shoemaker, whereof the said Bartholomy and George are convict, as appears to us, of Record. And have then there this Writ. Witness Charles Binns Clerk of our said Court, at the said Court-House, the seventeenth Day of June in the thirty third Year of our Reign. 1760

Cha. Binns

This arrest warrant was issued on June 17, 1760, in the case of George William Fairfax against Bartholomy Shoemaker and George Shoemaker, for the recovery of court costs totaling 132 lbs. of "Nett Tobacco." These costs probably arose from an action for rents due under the Shoemaker family's three-life lease. Several Shoemaker families rented farms from G.W. Fairfax in the area between Lovettsville and Rehoboth Church, in the manor William Fairfax named "Piedmont." The warrant, returned by Loudoun sub-Sheriff John Moss (Junr.), bore the notation "Not found." George William Fairfax's offspring advanced to the title of Lord Fairfax when their cousin, Lord Thomas Fairfax, died childless. [HDC; see The Record in Chapter on Sundry, infra @ p. 525].

In the earliest days of the Virginia colony, Jamestown's military commanders oversaw the construction and maintenance of all new roads and bridges. In 1619 the unicameral Virginia General Assembly, which then included the Governor and his Councilmen, assumed authority for the "King's highway"s, as the dedicated roadways were called. The Assembly, naturally, began to regulate the ferries on the James River shortly thereafter. As the English settlements spread into the back country, the Virginia Assembly's enthusiasm for road making waned. Local control was instituted in 1632 when monthly courts, the predecessors of colonial county courts, were instructed to consult with the resident parishioners when establishing a road. Two years later, when the county system of government was inaugurated, the colony's county courts were given responsibility for the King's highways.

In March of 1655, with the King's permission, the Virginia Assembly first authorized individual county courts to administer the licensing of ferries on the rivers and runs within their county, just as they were charged with the maintenance of their county roads. In the 1700s, the Virginia Assembly directed that "the courts of the several counties, wherein such ferries shall be kept, shall have power to appoint proper boats to be kept at the said ferries, for the convenient transportation of coaches, waggons [sic], and other wheeled carriages." County Courts were also authorized to direct "what boat or boats and the number of hands which shall be kept at each ferry respectively." Anyone operating a ferry for profit without obtaining a license from either the Assembly or a county court would be liable for a civil penalty of £5, with half of the fine going "to the ferry keeper nearest the place," and half going "to the informer." As early as 1673, and continuing until at least 1786, the Virginia Assembly exercised direct authority over the ferries on the Potomac River despite the fact that the entire river was within the Maryland colony's boundaries. Maryland claimed jurisdiction over the Potomac River but apparently did not act to establish or regulate any of the Potomac ferries until 1781. [Hening, I/411, V/66, V/190 and VI/20-23].

The Virginia Assembly encouraged the operation of ferries for the public by extending a number of privileges to ferrymen. By law, the river ferrymen in colonial Virginia were:

> *"free of public and county levies ... all other public services of [militia] musters, constables, clearing highways, impressment and ... things of like nature ... if the [county] court shall find it requisite or useful that an ordinary be kept at any ferry, they may license such ferry keeper to keep ordinary ... [charging] half the fee ... allowed [elsewhere]."*

Ferry operators and their sureties were to give performance bonds of only £20, and were to be paid directly by their county court for ferrying "over the militia of the county on muster days." In return, ferries were to be operated from sunrise to sundown, and ferrymen were obligated to charge only the fees as established by either the Virginia Assembly or the county court. Commanders of the Virginia regiments and their adjutants, express riders with messages for the Governor, and constables returning runaways and deserters, were all to be conveyed at no charge and were given priority in passage. [Hening, VI/20-23 and VII/103].

When Loudoun County was formed in 1757, the colonial County Court assumed regulatory authority over all of the existing roads, bridges and ferries in the new county. The ferries on the Potomac and the ferries and bridges at the more popular fording places on the larger streams and runs, just as in the tidewater, were essential elements of colonial Loudoun's transportation network. The latter enabled the rapid movement of goods to and from markets and shipping centers on the seaboard, while the former were important primarily in easing the transit of people in their migrations into and through Loudoun from the east, north and west. In the half-century before Loudoun County was created, prominent families below the falls on the Potomac engaged in the profitable operation of river ferries to and from Maryland. Among them, the Potomac ferry-founding families and their dates of origin included: Fitzhugh, 1705; Hooe, 1720; Mason, 1732; West, 1740; Herryford, 1740; and Triplett, 1748.

The first ferry on the Potomac River to be based in "Loudoun" was founded by Francis Awbrey Senr. around 1735, shortly before the Virginia Assembly granted his license. Francis Awbrey died in 1742 and Ebenezer Floyd immediately petitioned for a ferry license for a site about two miles east of Awbrey's ferry. Floyd died the same year, but his ferry operation was continued in his absence by son Enock Floyd and partner Richard Poultney. The license for Floyd's ferry was renewed by the 1748 Assembly. Philip Noland Junr., Francis Awbrey's son-in-law, purchased the Conoy Island landing site of Awbrey's ferry and probably resumed operations there before 1745, relying on Awbrey's 1738 ferry license. After building a Quaker meeting house near Winchester in 1747, Robert Harper returned to "The Hole" on the Potomac and established his ferry, but Harper avoided licensing his ferry with the Assembly until 1761. Philip Noland took over the ferry operations at Floyd's and Poultney's landings around 1754, relying on the 1742 and 1748 licenses. Noland was not successful in defending his monopoly position on the Carolina Road in the Assembly sessions of 1756 and 1757, and Josias Clapham, with John Trammell as a partner, obtained an Assembly license in 1757. They began Potomac ferry operations about two miles east of Noland, across from the mouth of the Monocacy. The Awbrey, Floyd, Noland, Poultney and Clapham ferries were all situated between Conoy Island and the Lost Corner in order to capitalize upon north-south trade and migrations along the colonial Carolina Road. [Legends, p. 153; contra, Landmarks, p. 155 n. 31].

Thomas Stump, a Virginia resident on the upper Potomac River who represented a Maryland partnership, began operating Loudoun County's fourth active Potomac ferry around 1760. Stump's landing was situated about a mile west of Dutchman's Creek on the Virginia shore, providing a Potomac crossing to just below what is now Knoxville Maryland, about four miles downriver from Harper's ferry. One of the Maryland partners, Flail Payne Junr., bought out his brother John Payne and asserted a primary interest by 1763. Thereafter the crossing above Dutchman's Creek was known as "Frail Pain's [sic]" ferry. Thomas Stump continued in residence near the Virginia landing, and Payne's ferry served as a primary river crossing for residents of the Gap, Waterford, the German settlements, and the residents of Piedmont and Catoctin manors, in the decade leading up to the American Revolution. Stump and Payne, like Harper, avoided the process of licensing their ferry in Virginia but were never prosecuted in the Loudoun County Court for it. [infra, p. 283; LDCOCO, Book E, p. 245].

Thus, there were at least five locations where ferries operated into Loudoun County on the upper reaches of the Potomac River before 1765. The Loudoun Record provides an ambiguous reference to another ferry that was operated by Patrick McKenzey in 1763, but it seems likely that McKenzey, apparently an itinerant, had been hired to oversee Josias Clapham's ferry at the Lost Corner during the year that Clapham served as the Sheriff of Loudoun County. Patrick McKenzey would meet an ignominious end several years later after leading Loudoun County's first documented jail-break. [infra, p. 282; supra, Chapter on Sheriffs and the Gaol].

Francis Awbrey, the founder of the first Potomac River ferry to be based on land that is today a part of Loudoun County, was Loudoun's first "First Citizen" if ever there was one. He was a senior Justice of the Prince William [Loudoun] County Court beginning in 1731, the first resident "upcountry" Truro parish Vestryman and builder of the Goose Creek Chapel of Ease at Big Spring in 1733, and the Sheriff of Prince William (which included Loudoun) County in 1739. Awbrey was also successful as a real estate speculator - at one time he owned the land where Leesburg, Hillsboro and Arlington National Cemetery were eventually located, as well as the Potomac Path crossing of Goose Creek and most of the best sites in "Loudoun" for Potomac River ferries. On November 6, 1738, acting on "a Petition of divers Inhabitants of Prince William [Loudoun] County, for a Ferry across Potowmack River to Maryland," and the recommendation of their own Committee of Propositions and Grievances, the Virginia Assembly authorized a license for "a new public Ferry ... appointed across Potowmack River, from the Plantation of Francis Awbrey ... over to Maryland; the price for a man seven pence half penny, and for an horse [sic - the same]." The Assembly set rates for wheeled vehicles, using the charge for one horse as the standard: "For every coach, chariot or waggon [sic], and for the driver ... ferriage of [6] horses; ... cart, or four wheel chaise, and the driver ... [4] horses; ... two wheel chaise or chair ... ferriage of [2] horses." The Virginia Assembly was also concerned with the potential for avoidance of Virginia's duties on exported tobacco, and indirectly prohibited the transport of tobacco into Maryland on Awbrey's ferry by specifically disallowing a charge for the ferriage of tobacco. [Assembly, (1738) pp. 326-327; Hening, V/66-67].

Francis Awbrey situated this first "Awbrey's ferry" about two miles downriver from the feature known as Point of Rocks, at the eastern, or lower, end of Conoy Island. Knowledge of Burr

Harrison's report of a 1699 expedition to the Piscataway Indians on Conoy, which noted the "Lower Land, and Little or noe [sic] Bank" on the river, might have led Awbrey to the site. The locale had served Indians for centuries as a convenient place to cross their "Goose River" (the Iroquois name for the Potomac above the falls). Awbrey, no doubt, noted the ancient native landing places on both shores, the pathways up the banks and the remains of an Indian settlement on the ridge above the river when he took out a Northern Neck patent on the land on the Virginia riverfront. At the top of the ridge above his Potomac River ferry operation Francis Awbrey also constructed and operated an ordinary for weary Carolina Road travellers - probably the first tavern in what is today Loudoun County. Both the ferry and the ordinary were active businesses when Francis Awbrey wrote his last will in 1741. [Legends, p. 22; Assembly, (1736) pp. 326-327; Hening, V/66; infra, Chapter on Ordinaries; PrWmCOWIL, Book C, p. 341].

Previous writers have been confused by the references in: Francis Awbrey Senr.'s Will to his ferry and ordinary "at the falls;" the Will of John Awbrey (Francis' son) devising land that he did not own at his father's ferry; Truro parish vestry records from the 1750s referring to "Awbrey's ferry" (John Awbrey's, not Francis') at Wankipin Branch near modern Roosevelt Bridge in Arlington County; Fairfax County records documenting the operation of a ferry on Goose Creek by Henry Awbrey (another son of Francis) from 1754 to 1756; and, Loudoun records proving the founding of a fourth colonial Awbrey's ferry by Thomas Awbrey (yet another of Francis' sons) <u>above</u> Point of Rocks on the Potomac in 1769.

Fortunately, Francis Awbrey's Will identifies the neighbors and tenants on and around his <u>first</u> Awbrey's ferry and ordinary. In 1741 Samuel Hull, the second clerk at the Goose Creek Chapel of Ease from 1736 to 1740, was living on the Potomac River just to the west of the Carolina Road access to the ferry. Francis Awbrey devised 50 acres including the ferry landing and the ordinary, and the adjacent "Hull" tract, to his son Richard Awbrey. Richard Awbrey's 50 acre ferry/ordinary tract was reserved out of a larger, 400+ acre tract left to his brother, John Awbrey (who was living at the eventual site of Leesburg from about 1737 to 1741). "Richard Poutney" was living on the 400+ acre tract in 1741, which had the "ferry [Carolina] road" along its western boundary. Richard and John Poultney, two sons of Rev. William

Poultney of Stafford County, acquired numerous tracts of land above the Lost Corner on both sides of the Potomac in the 1730s and were residents of the Clarks Run area until their deaths in the 1750s. According to contemporary colonial sources, John Awbrey had married badly. Shortly after his father's death he withdrew from the congregation at the Goose Creek chapel and moved forty miles down the Potomac to the area on the Potomac now known as Rosslyn. Sometime during the next two years, John Awbrey took advantage of the liberal language of his father's ferry license and a longstanding family claim to land on Wankipin Branch, and established a second ferry where Roosevelt Bridge now affords a crossing over to Washington D.C. When he died around 1744, John Awbrey contributed to two centuries of confusion by attempting to devise Richard Awbrey's ferry and lands (which he did not own) to his two step-daughters. The step-daughters, having lived on the lower Potomac their entire lives, were strangers to Loudoun County and interpreted their father's bequest to mean the lower Wankipin tract, never bothering with the Loudoun ferry site. But Philip Noland purchased the 400+ acre property surrounding the Loudoun ferry landing in August of 1745 from John Awbrey's widow and probably resumed ferry operations, based on Francis Awbrey's original ferry license, about that time. This deed sets out the metes and bounds of the so-called "larger tract" at the original Awbrey's ferry site, tracing along the winding courses of Clarks Run and giving a definite western boundary, thereby firmly establishing the original route of the Carolina Road near the Potomac as well as the location of Francis Awbrey's 1735 ferry on the river, immediately below and "opposite to Couse [sic- Conoy] Island." [PrWmCOWIL, Book C, p. 341; Truro, p. 72; FXCOWIL, Book A, pp. 60 and 79; Ferry, pp. 42-45; Assembly, (1748) pp. 262 and 325; Stafford County Deeds, Book J, pp. 231 and 241; PrWmCODB, Book B, pp. 242-245; Maryland Wills, Hall of Records, Annapolis, Vol. 6, pp. 222-226; FXCOSUR, pp. 42-44; FXCODB, Book A, pp. 504-507; contra, Landmarks, p. 155].

In May of 1742, shortly after Francis Awbrey's death, the Virginia Assembly licensed several new ferries including one to "be constantly kept ... on [the] Potomack river, from the land of Ebenezer Floyd, in the county of Fairfax [now Loudoun], across the river, to Powel's [sic- John Powell's] landing in Maryland; the price for a man, six pence, and for a horse six pence." Before 1745

Richard Poultney, the former Awbrey tenant and probably one of the ferrymen at Awbrey's first ferry, acquired the lease for a tract of land on the Maryland shore above the mouth of the Monocacy, a tract that John Powell had originally leased in March of 1734.

Ebenezer Floyd apparently married Patience Thacker who, as either the widow or only child, was the heir of Samuel Thacker. Thacker and two partners had acquired a large tract in Virginia near Clarks Run on the Potomac. Floyd and Poultney probably formed a partnership to acquire the ferry boats from Awbrey's executors; after his death in the winter of 1742-43, records of his estate confirmed Floyd's dealings with both Poultney and "Capt. [Francis] Awbrey's Executor." Floyd's widow Patience and his son Enock Floyd must have continued operations at the ferry in partnership with Richard Poultney. In 1750 the Fairfax [Loudoun] County Court referred to "Poultney's Ferry" as the main Potomac River crossing on the Carolina Road. Josias Clapham and Philip Noland purchased the Thacker tract, piecemeal, during the 1740s; and, after Richard Poultney died in 1751, Philip Noland purchased Enock Floyd's interest in the Potomac riverfront section of the Thacker tract. [FXCOCO, 1749 Book, p. 117].

Peter Stephens established a trading post and simple canoe ferry at the confluence of the Potomac and Shenandoah Rivers as early as 1733. After experiencing continuous competition from the Awbrey, Floyd and Noland ferries just downriver, in 1747 Stephens sold his ferry business and the Virginia shorefront (that he did not own) to an itinerant carpenter named Robert Harper. Harper's first surprise was the realization that he had to pay Lord Fairfax a second time for his riverside ferry site. His second greeting at the Potomac-Shenandoah location was a painful visit from the flood stage waters of both rivers in 1748. Harper's ferry, from which the town eventually took its name, was still in operation when Loudoun County was formed in 1757. Harper posted notices offering services to "farmers ... over the Blue Ridge in Loudoun County ... bringing grist to my mill ... [who] will be ferried over the ... Shenandoah river ... free of expense." [C & O, pp. 215-217].

Flooding on the Potomac in 1748, in the aftermath of a major hurricane that scored its mark all over Virginia, carried away the Potomac River ferries. The 1748 Assembly then reissued licenses for ferries everywhere in the colony. Floyd's ferry was relicensed that year although Ebenezer Floyd had been dead for nearly six years. Philip Noland was unsuccessful in Petitioning for his own ferry license that year, forcing him to continue operations from the original site of Awbrey's ferry. Three pence was the usual charge for transporting a man or a horse across a river in Virginia, but one shilling (twelve pence) was a standard charge on the Potomac around Alexandria. Over a dozen ferries were licensed to operate on the Shenandoah and Potomac Rivers in 1748, as listed in the Assembly's rate chart. Most of them were still active when Loudoun County was created a decade later:

"... Potomack.	For Man. [or] Horse.
From Tripplit's land below the mouth of Quantico creek [in Stafford on the Potomac]	*[shillings . pence]* *1 . 6 ...*
From Kersey's landing on Col. Carter Burwell's land, to the land of Col. Landon Carter [on the Shenandoah below Ashby's Gap]	*0 . 3 & ¾*
From Gersham Key's land [on the Shenandoah, west of Keys/Vestals gap], to the land of the Honorable William Fairfax, esq.	*0 . 3 & ¾*
At Williams' Gap, from the land of the Right Honorable the Lord Fairfax, where John Melton now lives [on the Shenandoah] ...	*0 . 3 & ¾*
From the [Potomac] plantation of George Mason opposite to Rock creek, over to Maryland	*0 . 4*
From the plantation of John Hereford, in Daigs neck [above Gunston Hall], over the river ...	*1 . 0*
From Hunting creek warehouse [ie., Bellehaven], to Frazier's point, or Addison's	*1 . 0*
From the land of Ebenezer Floyd [in "Loudoun," at the new Carolina Road crossing] to Powell's	*0 . 6*
From Evan Watkin's landing opposite to Canagochego creek [now I-81 at Williamsport] ...	*0 . 3*
From the land of Hugh West, [at Alexandria] to Frazier's, or Addison's,	*1 . 0 ..."*

The 1748 Assembly established rates for everything that they could imagine that would be transported on a licensed ferry, based on the charge for ferriage of a man or horse:

> *"for the transportation of wheel carriages, tobacco, cattle, and other beasts ... the ferry keeper may demand: ... For every coach, chariot, or waggon, and the driver thereof, ... [as] for six horses ... [for]*

> *every cart, or four wheel chaise, and the driver ... as for four horses ... every two wheel chaise, or chair, as for two horses ... every hogshead ... [or] head of neat cattle, as for one horse ... every sheep, goat, or lamb, one fifth part of the ferriage of one horse ... every hog, one fourth of the ferriage of one horse. According to the prices ... at such ferry respectively."*

Subsequently, the ratable charges for all small livestock were changed so that sheep, goats and hogs all incurred a charge of ¼th the charge for a horse. [Hening, V/189, VI/18-23, VII/126 and VIII/147; Assembly, (1748) p. 288; contra, Landmarks, p. 503].

In July of 1751, Philip Noland consolidated the various Carolina Road ferry operations by purchasing Enock Floyd's claim to the Potomac River section of the Thacker patent. On the deed, Floyd claimed his title as "Enock Thacker alias Floyd" and signed his name "Enock Floyd," presumably as Thacker's grandson and an heir at law of Floyd. Shortly thereafter, Philip Noland relocated his Potomac River ferry operations two miles downriver to the site of the Floyd-Poultney ferry, a location widely known during the Revolution and into modern times as the site of "Noland's ferry." In 1754 Fairfax County ordered the continued maintenance of the Carolina road "from Nolands Ferry to the [Shenandoah] Road at Nicholas Minor's [now Leesburg]." This is proof that, by 1754, Philip Noland had taken over Poultney's well-known river crossing on the Carolina Road across from "Powell's Landing" in Maryland. At harvest time in 1754 another major flood, still known as the "Potomac Pumpkin Flood," washed away a number of the river ferries as well as Indian pumpkin gardens upriver, but both Harper and Noland quickly resumed their ferry operations. [FXCOCO, 1754 Book, p. 63; Landmarks, pp. 503-504; Frontier, p. 32].

Early in April of 1756 and again during the 1757 session of the Virginia Assembly, Philip Noland petitioned Williamsburg:

> *"in Opposition to two Petitions of ... [Josias Clapham] and ... [John] Trammell, which the Petitioner was [mis-!] informed would be presented to the [Burgesses], for putting down [discontinuing] a Ferry established from the Petitioner's [Noland's] Land in ... Fairfax [Loudoun], to Powell's Landing, in ... Maryland ... [which the Burgesses] referred to the Consideration of the next Session of Assembly."*

Two days after they disposed of Noland's Petition, the Assembly seemingly reversed itself and approved a Petition from Clapham, authorizing a ferry "from the land of Josias Clapham [at the Lost Corner] in the county of Fairfax [Loudoun], over the Potowmack [sic] river, to the land on either side [at the mouth] of Monochisey [sic - Monocacy] creek, in the province of Maryland." The Virginia Assembly then "Resolved, That the Petition of Philip Noland, in Opposition to the said Petition be rejected." Clapham clearly gained favor in the Assembly through maneuver; by not asking for the elimination of Noland's, Clapham probably assured his own ferry license. The Assembly set the charges at Clapham's ferry for a man at "four pence, & for an horse the same," undercutting Noland's ferry rates by one-third. Other rates at Clapham's ferry were to be in proportion. Clapham probably asked for a lower rate schedule to compensate for the poor roads leading to his ferry, and as an inducement for Carolina Road traffic to divert to his facility. The language of Philip Noland's Petition confirms that he was already operating his ferry under the Floyd ferry license when Loudoun County was created that year. By the onset of the Revolution, despite spirited competition from Clapham, Noland's ferry site had once again prevailed as the superior Potomac River crossing on the colonial Carolina Road. [Assembly (1756) pp. 352, 425 and 431; Hening, VII/125-127; Landmarks, p. 502].

Colonials used a number of fording places on Goose Creek and the other runs in "Loudoun," but by 1748 the Fairfax County Court had established a public ferry at the Potomac Path (Rte. 7) crossing, just north of the mouth of Tuscarora Creek. The colonial Potomac Path was an old Indian trail that roughly followed the first ridge line about a mile from the Potomac River. Early European explorers and settlers in the area noted the existence of the path in the late 1600s. [Landmarks, p. 98].

When Loudoun County was created in 1757, John Jenkins was the operator of the public ferry that crossed Goose Creek at the Potomac Path. Fairfax County had built, and then maintained, two bridges on the Potomac Path below Goose Creek, at Difficult Run and Broad Run, and a third bridge on the Mountain Road across Cub Run. The first bridge over Difficult Run was built before 1739, and the "bridge [later Colvill's mill] branch" was named for it, but court records from the 1730s have not survived to assist us in confirming its origin. Charles Broadwater probably rebuilt the Difficult Run bridge late in the 1740s, and Colonel Halkett's regiment of Braddock's army certainly used the Difficult Run bridge in 1755. Shortly after Braddock's campaign, the bridge was found to be in need of repairs that cost Fairfax County at least £80. The Difficult bridge was again in need of substantial repair in 1759 and Charles Broadwater, by then a Fairfax County Justice, obliged. Loudoun and Fairfax Counties both contributed to meet the cost, and Loudoun's Justices were active in monitoring the status of the bridge and authorizing the necessary repairs. The Broad Run bridge, sited by Charles Broadwater and built by John Trammel Junr. under the supervision of Francis Hague, had been completed in June of 1753. Fairfax County paid at least £100 for the construction of this bridge. The third public bridge in "Loudoun," at the Mountain Road crossing on Cub Run, was constructed by Jacob Remey in the summer of 1754 under the direction of Justices Anthony Russell and Fielding Turner. Fairfax County paid only 2,650 lbs. of tobacco, the equivalent of about £17, for the little Cub Run bridge. A fourth bridge had been built, perhaps privately, where the Carolina Road (Rte. 15) and the western fork of the Potomac Path, known there as the Shenandoah Road, both crossed the Tuscarora, below a sleepy little crossroads that grew to become Leesburg. A fifth bridge, at the Mountain Road crossing of Little Rocky Run, also appears to have been built before 1758. [Grants, Book E, folios 40-41; FXCOCO, 1749 Book, pp. 196 and 402, 1754 Book, pp. 101 and 423; Fairfax, pp. 57-58; and see infra, The Record, pp. 280 and 285].

Maintenance of the small bridges over the Tuscarora, Cub Run and Little Rocky Run were the responsibility of various of the appointed overseers of the roads. The two large public bridges on the Potomac Path (Rte. 7), over Difficult Run and Broad Run, were maintained in an altogether different manner. The builders of these bridges entered seven-year performance bonds and were responsible for the continual repair of their structures. John Trammell's first bond, initially entered with Fairfax County, expired in June of 1760, indicating with some precision when the bridge at Broad Run was first put in use. Trammell had to make repairs on his bridge in 1756, 1757 and 1759. In June of 1759, after finishing substantial repairs to the structure, Trammell entered a new seven-year bond, and he was called back for repair work under this bond again in 1760 and 1761. By 1764, however, the bridge at Broad Run had fallen into such a state of disrepair that the Loudoun County Court ordered the King's Attorney to prosecute Trammell for nonperformance of his bond at the same time that Loudoun County Justice James Hamilton was contracted with to, essentially, rebuild the structure.

The difficulties that Loudoun County experienced with the Broad Run bridge were not unique in colonial Virginia. In 1762 the Virginia Assembly saw fit to revise the laws for "keeping the publick [sic] roads and bridges in repair," and the reconstruction of the Broad Run bridge in 1764 was conducted under the new law's contractor bonding requirements. After 1762, for all bridges and causeways in Virginia, a double-indemnity bond was required of the contractor and at least one good surety certifying that the construction was to be completed "in a strong substantial manner." Contractors were liable "if any persons ... sustain loss or injury by means of the unskilful [sic] building and not keeping in repair," were responsible for maintaining the bridge "in good repair," and were obligated to rebuild a structure within three months when "such bridge or causey [sic] shall happen to be destroyed, or carried away by tempest or other accident." These stringent bonding requirements undoubtedly drove up the price of public works bridges all over Virginia. [Hening, VII/577-579].

During the 1757-1766 decade, there were four fording places on Goose Creek that were so well-used that they were named. To the west of modern Middleburg, the road to Ashby's Gap crossed Goose Creek at Daniel Adam's ford. Downstream on Goose Creek from Little River, on what was then an alternate, eastern, route of the Carolina Road, Jacob Lasswell's ford and ordinary were situated just downstream from the mouth of Piney Hill Branch. Jacob Morris' ford was situated further north, and very convenient to Loudoun Surveyor George West's Pea Hill plantation, about one mile upstream (south) from the mouth of Sycolin Creek on Goose Creek. John Dawson's ford was situated about equidistant between Morris' and Lasswell's fords, just below a small stream known as the Mill Branch, where modern Rte. 648 would extend southward to intersect Goose Creek.

In the decade before Loudoun County was formed Thomas Evans (1748-51), Edmund Sands (1751-53), Samuel Mead (1753-54), Henry Awbrey (1754-56) and John Moss (1756-57) tended the

Goose Creek ferry. The salary of the Goose Creek ferryman was paid by the Fairfax County Sheriff out of his collections for the annual County levy. The annual salary varied from 1,000 to 2,000 lbs. of tobacco, the equivalent of £8 or £16. The latter amount was then a considerable sum. Edmund Sands was also a good example of the many men of the time who readily changed occupation when the opportunity arose. In 1750, Sands was identified as a cordwainer; the following year he was the keeper at the Goose Creek ferry. And like Samuel Mead, Henry Awbrey and John Jenkins who followed him as ferryman at Goose Creek, Edmund Sands supplemented his other income by operating an ordinary at the public ferry crossing. [FXCOCO, 1749 Book pp. 48, 112, 196, 208, 252 and 473, 1754 Book pp. 287 and 428, 1756 Book pp. 37 and 170; infra, Chapter on Ordinaries; FXCODB, Book B, p. 67; Glossary].

John Jenkins, the ferry keeper at Goose Creek from 1757 to 1759, licensed an ordinary at the ferry in 1758, but Jenkins did not renew his ordinary license and the ferry was discontinued shortly thereafter. Loudoun County businessman John Hough formed a partnership with Alexandria merchant John Carlyle in 1762; they obtained licenses to operate both a Goose Creek ferry and an ordinary at their crossing. However, construction of a proposed Hough mill near the Goose Creek crossing was delayed by a dispute over valuation of the land, and the Hough-Carlyle ferry and ordinary ventures foundered. Finally, in the winter of 1766, Loudoun merchant and planter Joseph Hough obtained a license "to keep a Ferry over Goose Creek at the lower Ford from his Plantation on the lower [east] side of said Creek," with the Loudoun County Court setting his ferry prices at:

> *"seven pence half penny for a Man and Horse ... two shillings and six pence for a Waggon Team and Driver ... one shilling and three pence for a hogshead of Tobacco with Horses and Driver."*

These charges at the Goose Creek ferry were fully double the average ferry charges at most of the river crossings in Virginia at the time. Hough's ferry business probably failed in 1767 when his indentured servant, William Carroll, ran away. Our view of the colonial ferry at Goose Creek fades with Joseph Hough's death in the winter of 1768. [see infra, p. 285].

West of the Blue Ridge there were four ferries across the Shenandoah. Of course, at the northern extreme, Robert Harper did his best to lure Loudoun farmers to his grist mill with free passage. Below the next gap to the south, John Vestal often maintained the Shenandoah ferry crossing on Gersham Keys' land, near the site where his family had been operating a saw mill since 1736. George Washington's company of Virginia militia crossed the Shenandoah at Vestal's ferry on April 8, 1754, paying £ 1.9.0 [ie., 348 pence, the cost of ferriage for 30 men on horseback and another 30 men on foot]. Keys died in 1766. Edward Snickers replaced John Melton as the operator of the ferry below Williams Gap sometime before 1760, investing heavily in the lands between the Shenandoah and the gap that still bears his name. And the ferry on the Shenandoah River below Ashby's Gap, operated as early as 1736 by a man named Kersey, provided access to the valley from southwest Loudoun. [GW Papers, IV; Landmarks, p. 482; Hening, VII/298; Grants, Book E, folios 36 and 42-43].

In October of 1765, the Assembly licensed "a ferry from the land of Thomas Shepherd, at Mecklenburg, in Frederick county [Virginia, now West Virginia] ... over the Potowmack river to his land opposite in the province of Maryland." Rates were set at three pence for ferriage of a man, a horse, a hogshead of tobacco or one head of "neat cattle." This crossing was used by travellers on the Philadelphia Wagon Road and as such was a business threat to the Carolina Road ferry crossings at Philip Noland's and Josias Clapham's. [Hening, VIII/146-147].

Old deeds and surveys indicate the original locations of some of the major roadways and the fording places on various watercourses. In 1737, George Atwood's deed to land between the Short Hill and the Blue Ridge identified the Potomac River site now known as Dixie Bottom as a place "where People crosses over the River." Accordingly, this site is perhaps the earliest identifiable fording place on the Potomac west of Point of Rocks. Lord Fairfax's 1739 plat of his Great Falls Manor shows several locations where the "Sugar Land Rowling Road" (now Rte. 7) crossed the various courses of Difficult Run, including the "bridge branch." A 1740 deed and survey identifies the "Main [Carolina] Road" ford over Clark's Run, due south of Francis Awbrey's Potomac ferry. When Richard Coleman commissioned a survey of his Sugarland Run property in 1745, the plat identified the ford for the Potomac Ridge Road on Sugarland Run. Captain Willoughby Newton's 1747 plat of his lands shows the "rolling road" we now know as, alternately, the Mountain Road or Braddock Road, and it's fords across Rocky Run, Rocky Cedar Run, Round Lick, Flat Lick and Cub Run. And in a turn of the tables, the colonial County Court records for Fairfax and Loudoun Counties assist us in tracing and correcting a recurring mistake on old maps of Virginia's Northern Neck. We can now definitely identify the Fry and Jefferson map of 1755, as revised by British Captain of Engineers John Dalrymple in 1754, as the origin for every subsequent map reference that mistakenly shows an "Avery's Ford" on Goose Creek. Capt. Dalrymple, while en route from the Shenandoah valley to London, mis-labeled the site when he crossed Goose Creek at the Fairfax County public ferry in the summer of 1754. At the time, one of Francis Awbrey Senr.'s younger sons, Henry Awbrey was keeping both the public ferry and an ordinary at the site of the Potomac Path crossing of Goose Creek. Unfortunately, Thomas Jefferson continued and broadened the use of the inaccurate name of "Avery's Ford" on Goose Creek by repeating the reference in his more widely circulated 1787 map of Virginia, even though the residents of Fairfax and Loudoun Counties had never, ever, used the name "Avery" to identify the crossing, and Henry Awbrey had moved to South Carolina around 1757! [Grants, Book D, folio 27 and Book E, folios 40-41, 186 and 188; FXCOSUR, p. 17; Cameron, p. 20; Landmarks, pp. 480 (contra), 519 and 617].

The Record also gives the reader a few hints about the weather conditions experienced by our Loudoun colonials. The bridges, fords and ferries were seriously effected by freshnets several times during Loudoun's first decade - in the spring of 1760, in September of 1764, and again in March of 1766.

The map on the following page gives the locations and periods of operation for the earliest Potomac river ferries that operated between Loudoun County and Maryland.

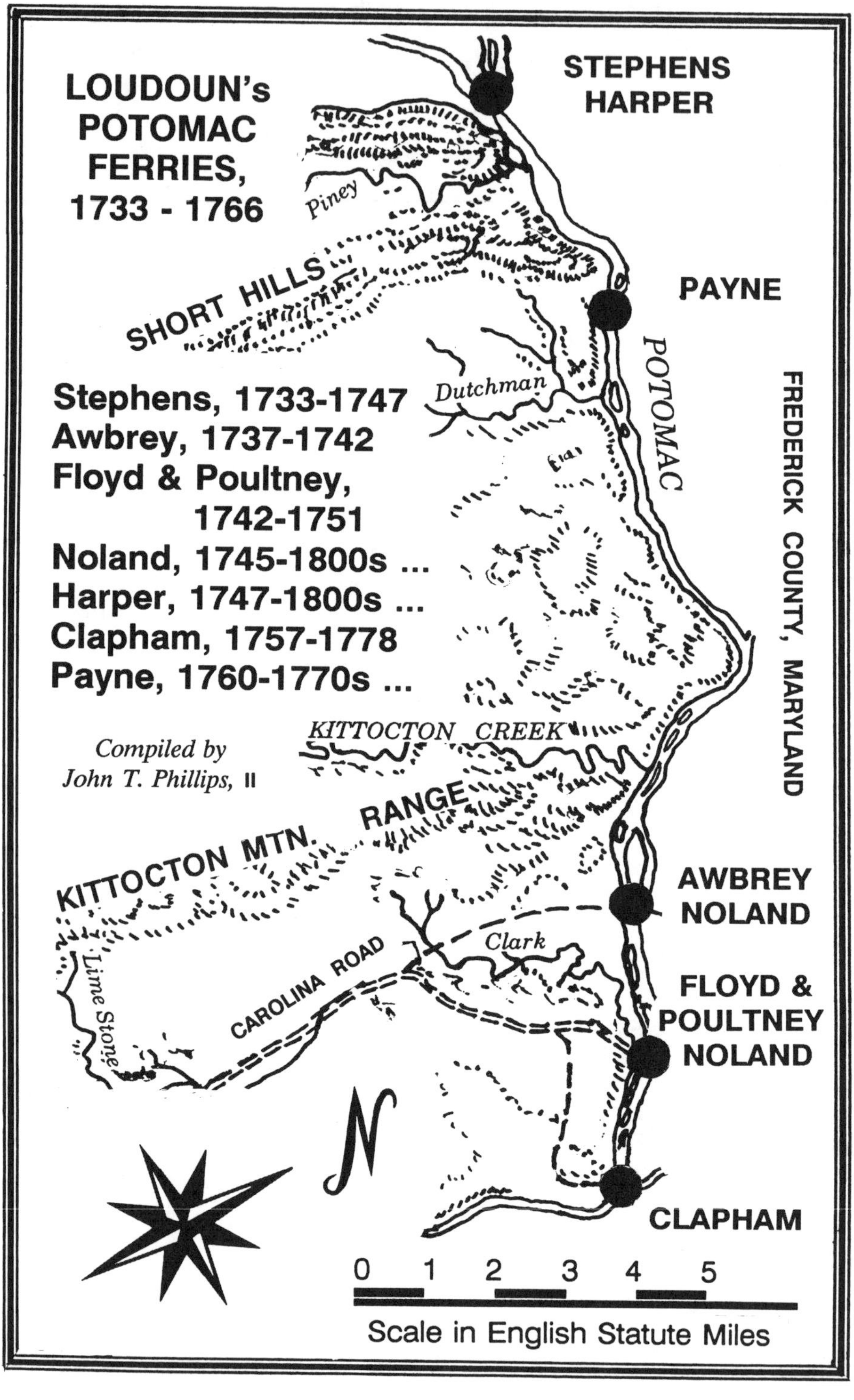

LOUDOUN's POTOMAC FERRIES, 1733 - 1766
STEPHENS
HARPER
Piney
SHORT HILLS
PAYNE
POTOMAC
Dutchman
FREDERICK COUNTY, MARYLAND
Stephens, 1733-1747
Awbrey, 1737-1742
Floyd & Poultney, 1742-1751
Noland, 1745-1800s ...
Harper, 1747-1800s ...
Clapham, 1757-1778
Payne, 1760-1770s ...
KITTOCTON CREEK
Compiled by John T. Phillips, II
KITTOCTON MTN. RANGE
AWBREY
NOLAND
Clark
CAROLINA ROAD
Lime Stone
FLOYD & POULTNEY
NOLAND
CLAPHAM
0 1 2 3 4 5
Scale in English Statute Miles

July 12, 1757 - The Loudoun Court appoints many of the various Surveyors of the Highways: Thomas Sorrell, "[west] from Goose Creek ferry to the [town] run near Capt. Nicholas Minor's;" William Dodd, "[east] from his House to the run near Capt. Nicholas Minor's and that he [Dodd] repair the Bridge over the [Town Run];" and Philip Noland, "from the Great Lime Stone to the said Nolands Ferry across Potomack." Book A, p. 3.

September 13, 1757 - Philip Noland apparently leases his ferry landing on the Potomac to Joshua Pyburn. Noland gives "his leave for said Pyburn [in] selling, shewing [sic] or assisting any person over the Potomac River." The annual rent of 850 lbs. of tobacco, the equivalent of £5, 6 shillings and 3 pence, is exceptionally high for the lease of a 100 acre farm at the time and is a clear indication that Noland's ferry is the true object of the lease. This lease indicates that John Wells had been the tenant ferry operator prior to Pyburn, and Noland appears to have leased Wells another farm nearby rent-free in exchange for Wells' release of his rights to Noland's ferry landing. Pyburn was probably based on the Maryland shore of the Potomac, since he does not appear on Loudoun County tithable lists. LDCODB, Book A, pp. 10 and 17.

October 12, 1757 - John Poultney and David Richardson report a new "Road leading from the Road of Nolands Ferry to the ferry of ... Josias Clapham [at the Lost Corner] ... from the Ford by John Gibsons ... by a Run ... to the main [Carolina] Road about a mile from the River." Book A, pp. 33-34.

November 8, 1757 - The first Loudoun County Grand Jury presents charges against: "John Trammell [Junr.] for not keeping Broad Run Bridge ... in repair," and, "Thomas Lewis Surveyor, for not keeping the [Potomac Path] Road from Goose Creek to Broad run Bridge ... in repair." Book A, p. 41. See also, Chapter on the Grand Jury, beginning @ p. 119, supra, et seq..

April 12, 1758 - Based on a "Petition of the Inhabitants of George Town [ie., Leesburg] praying that the Roads leading from Alexandria to Winchester [the Potomac Path/Shenandoah Road] and [the Carolina Road] from Noland's Ferry [on the Potomac] towards Carolina may be opened to go through said Town in the most convenient manner," the Roads are turned and "established as public Roads." Book A, pp. 52 and 91-92.

April 12, 1758 - The County Court appoints Surveyors for some of the County Roads, including Dempse Carroll [sic] "from little Rockey run down the Mountain Road to the end of the County including the bridge over little Rockey run in the room of James Lane." Book A, pp. 91-92; and see Glossary.

May 9, 1758 - The Second Grand Jury presents "the Surveyor of the [alternate route of the Carolina] Road from Mr. Clapham's ferry to the fork of Nolands [ferry] Road for not having [the road] in Repair." Book A, p. 99. And see Chapter on the Grand Jury, beginning @ p. 119, supra, et seq..

June 14, 1758 - John Radcliff [sic] is appointed as overseer of the Carolina Road "from the Ford of Sicolons Branch near his [Fence] to little River ... [Justice] William West Gent. [is to] allot the hands." Book A, pp. 118-119.

June 14, 1758 - It is "Ordered that ... Thomas Sorrell clear the [Shenandoah] Road from George Town [ie., Leesburg] to Goose Creek at the Ferry and that [Loudoun Justice] William West Gent. [is to] allot the hands to work on the said Road." Book A, p. 122.

June 14, 1758 - Jacob Morris is appointed overseer of the road "from Morris' ford [on Goose Creek] to broad run Chappel ... George West [to] allot the hands." Book A, p. 122.

November 14, 1758 - A Loudoun Grand Jury Presents charges against the "Overseer of the Road from Limestone Run to Goose Creek Ferry," and, the "Surveyor of the Road from Frying Pan to Difficult Bridge." Book A, p. 175. And see Chapter on the Grand Jury, beginning @ p. 119, supra, et seq..

November 15, 1758 - Benjamin Grayson, Thomas Sorrell and William Ross report a new Road "leading from ... George Town [sic] along the new Road to a glade between John Moss' and Thomas Sorrells then leaving said Road ... to the East end of Benjamin Shreives ... to the same end of William Shreives Plantation thence to the West end of John Dawsons Plantation to Dawsons Ford [on Goose Creek] thence along an old road by Mr. Ellzeys Plantation and so by Vincent Lewis' ... John Davis [is appointed the] Overseer [of the road] from Siccolon [across Dawson's ford] to Vincent Lewis' Road." Book A, p. 180.

May 8, 1759 - It was "Ordered that Richard Coleman, Benjamin Grayson and Josias Clapham ... agree with Workmen to repair the Bridge over Broad run."; and that "Nicholas Minor join with a Commissioner of Fairfax County to agree with Workmen to repair the Bridge over Difficult Bridge [sic]." Book A, p. 234.

May 8, 1759 - William Stephens and James Bartley report a new Road "from [Daniel] Adam's Ford on Goose Creek [west of modern Middleburg] to [meet the Mountain Road] where the Road crosses little River [at modern Aldie] ... from the Ford of Adam's down [east] to the Mountain Road by [way of] John Champs ... [sic - John Champe Junr.] appointed Overseer ... Francis Peyton [is to] allot the hands to work thereon." Book A, p. 235.

June 12, 1759 - "John Trammell [Junr.] ... undertook to keep in repair for Travellers the Bridge over Broad run ... [until] June 1760." Book A, p. 245.

November 13, 1759 - The Grand Jury presents charges against: "Philip Noland for not keeping the Road according to Law between Nolands Ferry and the great Limestone, [and] ... Josias Clapham Gentl[eman]. for not keeping a [sign] Post at the fork of the Roads between the said Claphams and Philip Nolands ... [and] John Davis, farmer, for not keeping the Road ... between William Shrieves [at Sicolons branch] and the Gum Spring." Book A, pp. 299. And see Chapter on the Grand Jury, beginning @ p. 119, supra, et seq..

November 14, 1759 - John Davis, a farmer cited the previous day for not keeping his road, was continued as Overseer of a portion of the road "from Dawson's Ford to Vincent Lewis' ... [with Loudoun Justice] Fielding Turner [to] allot the hands [for the road]," and William Shreive was appointed Overseer of the section of the road "from Siccolons Run to Dawson's Ford." Book A, p. 304.

December 11, 1759 - "Ordered that the Sherif [sic - Nicholas Minor] ... pay to Charles Broadwater Gent., [a Fairfax County Justice who was seated on the east side of Difficult Run] [£10], four shillings and eight pence it being the proportion due from this County to the said Charles for [re-]building of Difficult Bridge" [on the King's highway known as the Potomac Path]. [With the Fairfax County Court contributing £15, 5 shillings, 4 pence, the total cost of repairs to the Difficult Run bridge was £25½ in 1759.- JP2.] Book A, p. 318.

March 12, 1760 - John Mcilhaney, Joseph Jones and William Smith report their view of a new Road "from John Hough's Mill to the mouth of Dutchman's Run ... it will not answer for a Road, neither can any Ferry be kept there, but running through John Muckelhany's Plantation ... to the River opposite to John Payne's [in Maryland] about one Mile above the mouth of the Dutchman ... Road is Quashed [not ordered]." Book A, pp. 301 and 329.

June 11, 1760 - Benjamin Edwards is appointed Overseer of the Road "from Leesburg to Goose Creek" replacing Ezekiel Hickman, and the road hands under the direction of Benjamin Edwards and Thomas Lewis are Ordered to "assist in clearing the Ford where John Jenkins formerly kept Ferry [Goose Creek on the Potomac Path, at the mouth of the Tuscarora]." Book A, p. 366.

June 12, 1760 - Acting on a 1759 presentment against "Philip Noland ... for not keeping the [Carolina] Road Between Noland's Ferry and the great Limestone ... [fined the standard] 15 shillings ... to the use of [Cameron] Parish." Book A, p. 368.

June 12, 1760 - "The Presentment[s] of the Grand Jury against the Overseer of the Road [ie., the Potomac Path] from Frying Pan [sic] to Difficult [Run] Bridge ... [and the] Overseer of the Road from Limestone to Goose Creek Ferry ... [the presentments are both] Discontinued." Book A, p. 368. Also see Chapter on the Loudoun County Grand Jury, beginning @ p. 119, supra, et seq..

August 13, 1760 - William Starks, Gabriel Adams and John Jenkins are appointed to determine "the most convenient way to cross Broad Run at the old Ford." Book A, p. 390.

September of 1760 - On the tithable list returned by George West, the hands at Philip Noland's ferry appear to include William Parsons, Charles Stafford and two slaves named George and Jack, identified as "Ferrymen"; and, on the list of James Hamilton, Patrick McKenzie is listed working with Thomas Stump at his landing above Dutchman's Creek. LDTX/1, pp. 3 and 4.

November 11, 1760 - A Grand Jury presents charges against: "Josias Clapham for stoping [sic] and not having the Road to his Ferry or Ford open and in good Repair within the six months last past." Book A, p. 403. And see Chapter on the Grand Jury, beginning @ p. 119, supra, et seq..

November 12, 1760 - It is "Ordered that [Loudoun County Justices] Nicholas Minor, Richard Coleman and Josias Clapham Agree with Workmen to repair Broad run Bridge and take Bond with Security for keeping the same in Repair for seven Years." Book A, p. 407.

June 9, 1761 - John Peake, Andrew Adam and George West are appointed to view the route for a Road "from Morris' Ford to the Road that leads to Dawson's Ford." Both fords are crossings on Goose Creek. Book A, p. 450.

June 11, 1761 - William Triplett, Daniel Adams, William Smith and Thomas Lewis are appointed to view the route for a new "Road from the Ford of Little River [ie., at modern-day Aldie] to Ashby's Gap." Book A, p. 465.

June 11, 1761 - Henry Taylor, William Smith, Thomas Lewis and Robert Wood are appointed to view the route for a "Road from Lasswell's Ford [on Goose Creek] to the Mountain Road by Robert Wood's." Book A, p. 465.

August 11, 1761 - Samuel Smith, William Smith and Thomas Stump are appointed to view the way for a new "Road from Thomas Stump's [Potomac River] Landing to Leesburg." Book A, p. 483.

September 10, 1761 - "Ordered that the Surveyor of the Road between the Sugar Land Run and Broad run and the Surveyor between Broad run and Goose Creek Clear a Road [meaning a ford] over Broad Run just below the Bridge." Book A, p. 521.

September 10, 1761 - "Ordered that Hugh West put in suit a Bond from John Trammell ... for [not] keeping in repair the Bridge over Broad Run." Book A, p. 522.

September of 1761 - The tithable list returned by Loudoun Justice and ferry owner Josias Clapham, identifying the residents of the "Halling's Corner" section of the County, shows Patrick McKenzey listed next to "George Campbell and John Campbell, [two] ferrymen"; and on the same list, William Parsons is identified as still working for Philip Noland, but no ferrymen or slaves are listed. We suppose that Clapham listed the Campbells, even though they were exempt, because they were operating his ferry, but did not bother to list the exempt ferrymen who were operating Noland's ferry. LDTX/1, pp. 14 and 15.

November 11, 1761 - In the County Levy, a debit is listed "To ... John Tramell [sic - Junr.] ... for keeping Broad Run Bridge in repair seven years ... 7120 [lbs. tobacco]." Book A, p. 533.

February 9, 1762 - "John Carlyle, Gent. & John Hough ... have leave to keep a Ferry from the lower side of Goose Creek in this County to the usual Place of Landing on the upper side of the said Creek on the road leading from Leesburg to Alexandria ... the Land formerly belonging to Ann Mason, Widow and now ... the Land of the children of Samuel Selden." Book A, pp. 553-554.

February 9, 1762 - "Ordered that the Surveyor of the Road from Leesburg to Goose Creek clear the Road to the usual Ferry Landing [on the Potomac Path] at the Mouth of Tuscarora." Book A, p. 554.

February 9, 1762 - Samuel Smith, William Smith and Thomas Stump report a new Road "from Thomas Stump's Landing to Leesburg ... markt it agreably [sic] ... through Colo. Fairfax's [Piedmont Manor] Land ... William Smith appointed Surveyor ... John Mucklehany [to] Allot the hands." Book A, p. 554.

September of 1762 - The county tithable lists for 1762 include an entry for a slave owned by William Starks named "Boatswain." [Could he have been a ferryman ?] LDTX/1, p. 20.

May 11, 1763 - The Grand Jury presents charges against the "Overseer of the [Potomac Path] leading from the lower ford of Goose Creek to Leesburg for not keeping the same in lawful repair in one month last ..." Book B, p. 131. And see Chapter on the Grand Jury, beginning @ p. 119, supra, et seq..

May 11, 1763 - The Loudoun Grand Jury charges the "Overseer of the Road leading from the Fork of the Road to Mr. McKenzey's Ferry for not keeping the same in lawful repair in one month last past by the Information of Josias Clapham [who was not on the Grand Jury]." Book B, p. 134. And see Chapter on the Grand Jury, beginning @ p. 119, supra, et seq..

June 15, 1763 - John Hough petitions for a Road from his Grist Mill at the Gap of the Short Hills to the Potomac river, "opposite or near 'Frail Pain's' [sic]." This is the first recorded reference to Payne's ferry, which was using Thomas Stump's landing above Dutchman's Creek. Book B, p. 169.

November 8, 1763 - A Grand Jury brings presentments against the "Overseer of the Road from Dawson's Ford on Goose Creek to [the] Broadrun [sic- church] road for not keeping the same in lawful repair." Book B, p. 262. And see Chapter on the Grand Jury, beginning @ p. 119, supra, et seq..

November 9, 1763 - In the County Levy, a debit is listed for a payment "To ... Jonathan Monkhouse for Timber for the use of the County ... 9/[shillings] in Tobo. @ 12/6 per Ct. ... 72 [lbs. tobacco]." This timber was probably used for a bridge on either the King Street crossing of the town branch of the Tuscarora or the Carolina Road crossing further south over Secolons, both near Monkhouse property. Book B, p. 266.

December 13, 1763 - A deed from John Hough to Daniel Hunt describes a tract beginning "in a gulley on the north side of the main [Carolina ?] road to Lasswell's ford on Goose Creek." LDCODB, Book D, pp. 61-66.

February 14, 1764 - The Loudoun Court "Ordered that Hugh West ... prosecute a Bond ... against John Trammell for not keeping Broad run Bridge [along the Potomac Path] in repair." Book B, p. 270.

February 14, 1764 - "Ordered that Benjamin Sebastian, Hugh West, William Douglass and John Moss Junr. ... agree with Persons to repair Broad run Bridge." Book B, p. 270.

February 14, 1764 - Nicholas Minor and Benjamin Edwards [sans co-appointee Aeneas Campbell] report the route for a new Road from Hough's Mill [on Goose Creek!] to Morris' Ford [also on Goose Creek] and indicate that they "... think it convenient a Road should be made there." Book B, p. 265.

April 12, 1764 - William Berry is appointed Surveyor of the Road from Morris' Ford to John Hough's Mill, both on Goose Creek. George West is appointed to allot the road hands. Book B, p. 340.

May 8, 1764 - A Grand Jury presents charges against "Henry Brewer of ... Loudoun [County] for not keeping the [Potomac Path] in lawful repair from Sugar Land Run to Difficult Bridge, within one month last past." Book B, p. 354. Also, see the Chapter on the Loudoun County Grand Jury, beginning @ p. 119, supra, et seq..

June 10, 1764 - In the tithable list returned by Nicholas Minor, one of the slaves owned by Josias Clapham is identified as "Jack a Ferryman." In 1760, Jack had been listed as one of the slaves working at Noland's ferry. LDTX/1, p. 26; supra, p. 281.

June 13, 1764 - John Miller is appointed Surveyor of the Road "from the Great Limestone to Philip Noland, Gent., his Ferry," replacing Philip Noland. Book B, p. 367.

August 14, 1764 - Loudoun County Justices Nicholas Minor, George West and Philip Noland are appointed as a committee to view and determine "in what manner broad run bridge is done [repaired]." Book B, p. 405.

October 10, 1764 - "Ordered that the Surveyors of the [Potomac Path] from Sugar Land Run and from Goose Creek to Broad Run with their Hands [residents assigned to help on the road] make Proper Causeways at each end of Broad Run Bridge"; and "the Surveyor of the [Potomac Path] from Leesburg to Goose Creek Clear and open the ford and open a Passage for the Water to flow down the said Creek." Book B, p. 491.

November 13, 1764 - Grand Jury presentments include charges against the "Overseer of the [Potomac Path] from Difficult Bridge to the Sugarland run ... for not keeping the same in Repair, by the Information of Benjamin Sebastian." Book B, pp. 492-493. And see Chapter on the Grand Jury, beginning @ p. 119, supra, et seq..

November 13, 1764 - In the County Levy a debit is listed "To ... James Hamilton for repairing Broad Run Bridge as Per Agreement, £95 @ 12/6 Per Ct. [ie., 12 shillings and 6 pence are valued at 100 lbs. of tobacco] ... 15,200 [lbs.t.]." Book B, p. 495.

November 14, 1764 - James McGrew is appointed Surveyor of the road "from Mr. Clapham's Ferry Landing [west] to the fork of the Roads," replacing John Trammell. Book B, p. 499.

April 8, 1765 - David Smith is appointed "Surveyor of the [Carolina] Road from the Great Limestone [north] to Noland's Ferry," replacing John Miller. Book B, p. 536.

May 13, 1765 - William Beavers is appointed "Surveyor of the Road from Dawson's ford to the Road by the Gum Spring," replacing George Ashford. Book B, p. 572.

May 13, 1765 - Loudoun Grand Jury presentments include charges against the "Overseer of the [Potomac Path] from Goose Creek to Broad Run Bridge for not keeping the same in Repair within Two Months last past ... [and the] Overseer of the [Potomac Path] from Sugarland Run to Difficult Bridge for not keeping the same in Repair within Two Months last past." Book B, p. 570.

May 13, 1765 - William Muirhead is named "Surveyor of the Road from where the Ox Road Crosses the ford of Broad Run to John Hough's [Goose Creek] Mill." Book B, p. 574.

April 10, 1765 - John Markley is appointed "Surveyor of the Road from Leesburg to the ford of Goose Creek towards Alexandria," replacing Craven Peyton, Gent.. Book B, p. 559.

June 12, 1765 - Anthony Russell and William West are appointed to establish the route for a "Road leading [to the southeast] from Dawson's ford so as to Intersect the Church Road about [near] Thomas Beaver's." Book B, p. 647.

September of 1765 - In the tithables lists returned by Philip Noland, adjacent to Sinclair and Awbrey on the Potomac river, Lewis Massey and "Negro George" are both identified as ferrymen, probably at Noland's ferry, while the next tithable listing, for Patrick McKenzy [sic] [a former ferryman at Thomas Stumps' landing and subsequently the operator at Clapham's ferry], lists no occupation. LDTX/1, pp. 36-37.

November 11, 1765 - In itemizing the County Levy, a debit is listed for a payment "To ... Isaac Fouch for Timber for a Bridge ... 30 [lbs. tobacco]." This bridge is almost certainly on the Carolina Road, either on Sycolin Creek near Fouch's home or at the crossing of the town branch of the Tuscarora. Book C, p. 73.

April 14, 1766 - "Ordered ... the Surveyors of the Roads [along the Potomac Path] above and below Broadrun Bridge join to disengage the Trees and Lumber Lodged against the said Bridge." Book C, p. 74.

April 14, 1766 - "Ordered that John Moss Junr. ... with George William Fairfax, Esqr. [a senior Justice on the Fairfax County Court] ... agree with Workmen to repair Difficult Bridge." Book C, p. 74.

May 12, 1766 - The Loudoun County Grand Jury presents charges against the "Surveyor of the [Mountain] Road for not keeping the Bridge over Little Rocky run" in proper repair. Book C, p. 75. And see Chapter on the Grand Jury, beginning @ p. 119, supra, et seq..

September of 1766 - The tithable list returned by Philip Noland names the ferrymen at Noland's ferry as Samuel Arwin [sic- Samuel Irwin ?] and "Negro George," who seems to have become a fixture at the ferry. LDTX/1, p. 41.

October 14, 1766 - "Ordered that Nicholas Minor and John Moss Junr. ... in Company with two of the Justices of Fairfax [County] ... examine the work done to difficult Bridge [on the Potomac Path]." Book C, p. 208.

November 13, 1766 - "Joseph Hough on his Motion ... [is] allowed to keep a Ferry over Goose Creek at the lower Ford from his Plantation on the lower side of said Creek ... [and is permitted to set his prices as follows:] ... seven pence half penny for a Man and Horse ... two shillings and six pence for a Waggon [sic] Team and Driver ... one shilling and three pence for a hogshead of Tobacco with Horses and Driver." Book C, p. 230.

Advertiſements.

WHEREAS I have received certain and frequent information that I am injured to the amount of a large ſum of money annually, by the indulgence ſhown to the keepers of ordinaries, in not compelling them to renew their licenſes, according to law: This is to deſire that the Judges on the reſpective Benches would take care that juſtice is done to the country as well as myſelf in this point, by directing that the Clerk of the Court keep a correct regiſter of the dates of the licenſes granted, and report to the Court the time of the expiration of each licenſe. And the King's Attornies are hereby required to preſent, and proſecute, all ſuch offenders againſt law as ſhall preſume to keep open ordinary, and ſell liquors, after the expiration of the term for which the laſt licenſe was granted.

FRANCIS FAUQUIER.

This notice from Governor Fauquier, originally placed in the *Virginia Gazette*, was published by Purdie and Dixon on November 17, 1766. The Governor's concern for the collection of ordinary licensing fees throughout the Virginia colony should not have extended so far as Loudoun County. The Record in this chapter, infra, shows that the Loudoun County Court and County Clerk Charles Binns were diligent in their annual licensing of the inns and taverns of Loudoun County.

In the southern colonies, an inn or tavern was referred to as an "Ordinary." The term appears to have had as its root the appellation given to public supper clubs that were in vogue with young gentlemen in England during the reign of James I, in the early 1600s at the time that the Virginia colony was founded. Despite the deprecating representations of some contemporary English travellers, the term was not intended as a description of the accommodations. [Landmarks, pp. 484 and 512].

Traditionally, the Virginia ordinary had one main "public room," where patrons' meals were served in what would today be termed the "family style." Virginia ham, with eggs and coffee, was the standard fare of a "good Hot Diet." Feed and pasturage for horses were essential to the colonial ordinary business and were always available nearby or on the premises. When the rum punch took hold, the conversation waned or the card game ended, the traveller usually made his bed on a pallet equipped with a simple corn husk mattress. A private room would have been a rare exception to the rule, particularly in the more remote areas of the upper Virginia piedmont. Many of the early "Loudoun" ordinaries were maintained by their proprietors as a second or third business, and before the heyday of local grist mills, Loudoun's ordinaries were unquestionably the hubs of social activity in their respective neighborhoods. The more remote ordinaries also served their areas as either a trading place or a store for general merchandise. By the mid-1700s, ordinaries in the more populous areas of the Virginia colony began to take on the customs and appearances of traditional English roadside inns, where the proprietor was engaged in the business full-time and the service of food or drink was given on demand. The "English" approach was probably adopted at West's ordinary and in some of the ordinaries in Leesburg, but "American" service was still considered the norm throughout the Virginia countryside well beyond the era of the American Revolution. [Landmarks, p. 513 ns. 144-148].

Anyone attempting to research the taverns and ordinaries in operation in the piedmont of the colonial Northern Neck must confront and overcome a series of obstacles. The absence of Court Order and Minute Books for Prince William County from

1731-1742, and for Fairfax County from 1742-1749, leaves a two-decade gap in the record that is hard to fill. The loss of these records is particularly troublesome since the ordinaries were primarily documented in the county courts through their annual licensing and the occasional prosecution for an infraction of the license laws. As a consequence, the sum of recorded information for the early ordinaries is found, for the most part, in the occasional mention in a will or deed, infrequent and often confused notations on old maps, or the rare but reliable recitation in the correspondence and diaries of a few colonial men and women. There can be no doubt that a number of ordinaries were operated in "Loudoun" before 1749, but little hard evidence exists upon which we may safely rely. Even when we have all of the Court Orders at hand, for instance, for both Fairfax and Loudoun for 1757, we have human nature taking its turn to add to our confusion. Many Fairfax County ordinary keepers who were in business in "Loudoun" in 1756, perhaps anticipating correctly that the newly formed Loudoun County Court would have more weighty matters in mind during 1757, conveniently forgot to license their businesses in either Fairfax or Loudoun that year.

Pioneer families were moving through "Loudoun" even before the 1722 treaty with the Iroquois opened the piedmont and upper Shenandoah valley to relatively unmolested settlement. By the 1730s, various Indian paths had been given English names. The Carolina Road and further to the west the Philadelphia Wagon Road were significant north-south arteries of migration, and the east-west roads through the gaps where Williams and Vestal had built their cabins were used by white explorers, hunters and settlers alike. There were certainly men in colonial Virginia who were willing to pursue economic opportunities for an honest living, and increased activity along these roads could not have been ignored forever.

The charges allowed to ordinary keepers must have been regulated in Virginia before January of 1639-40, when, in the 14th year of the reign of King Charles I, the Virginia Assembly reduced the prices for "a meale and beer ... because of the great plenty of provisions." In March of 1654-55, the Assembly authorized the various county courts to issue licenses for ordinaries. In March of 1657-58 the Assembly revised the schedule of allowable rates for food and drink in the ordinaries and then, the following March, transferred authority for the regulation of ordinary prices to the county courts. The Assembly specified that the county courts were to "sett [sic] the rates how the drinke shall be sold ... as the prices of tobacco rise or fall from time to time." In the same Act, the Assembly, for the first time, also required ordinary licensees to give "good security." For the next century, the laws of Virginia regulating the inns and ordinaries of the Commonwealth, though increasingly elaborate, remained in essence unchanged. [Hening, I/229, I/287, I/319, I/411, I/446, I/489 and I/521].

In "An Act for regulating Ordinaries and restraint of Tipling Houses," the 1748 Assembly rewrote the laws governing the licensing of ordinaries. At the same time, the Assembly imposed penalties for unlicensed retailers of liquors and prohibited Virginia ordinary keepers from extending credit to sailors. It seems that many of the King's sailors had intentionally run up debts on credit at ordinaries in order to insure detention in jail when their ship sailed. The 1748 Act took effect in 1751 and was still the law in Virginia when Loudoun was formed in 1757. Except for provisions restricting trade on credit, this law was in full force and effect for the duration of the 1757-1766 decade. Prospective license holders were required to petition their county court, where consideration was to be given to "the convenience of the place proposed, and the ability of the petitioner to keep good and sufficient houses, lodging and entertainment for travellers, their servants and horses." When a petitioner was deemed acceptable, the county court would issue a license "for the term of one year next ensuing the date of such license ... upon petition [to be] ... renewed from year to year." Each licensee was required to enter into a bond with security, for £50, certifying that he would:

> *"constantly find and provide, in his said ordinary, good, wholesome and cleanly lodging and diet for travellers ... stableage, fodder, and provender or pasturage and provender ... for their horses ... and shall not suffer or permit any unlawful gaming, in his house, nor on the sabbath day suffer any person to tipple and drink any more than is necessary."*

As a practical matter, it appears that everyone who petitioned for a license to keep ordinary in Loudoun County before 1767 was afforded the opportunity, but we may never know how many men could not find sufficient security for a bond and, as a consequence, did not apply for a license. [Hening, VI/71-76, @/72-73].

The Act of 1748 instructed the respective county courts to "set the rates and prices to be paid at ordinaries for liquors, diet, lodging, provender, stableage and fodder and pasturage" each year in the March court. During Loudoun's first decade, the County Court complied with this provision in every March court except 1765. Ordinary keepers were required to obtain a listing of the new rates from the clerk of the county court, and to openly display each new table of rates in the entertaining room of their ordinary within one month of adoption. An annual ordinary license fee of 35 shillings was paid to the County Clerk who collected on behalf of the Governor. An additional fee of 20 shillings went to the Clerk for recordation of the bond. The penalty for price gouging by an ordinary keeper was set at ten shillings for each offence, but the penalty for not displaying a rate table, or for retailing "any wine, beer, cider, brandy, rum or other spirits" without a license was a rather steep £10. As in the case of Conrad Shanks in 1759 in Loudoun County, the law provided that anyone retailing liquor without a license and then failing to pay the fine within six months was to "receive on his or her bare back, twenty-one lashes, well laid on, at the public whipping post." [Hening, VI/73-74; infra, p. 309; see infra, Rates for "Liquors & Entertainment," p. 316].

Gambling and excessive drinking were fairly common vices in colonial Virginia, and the subject of a good deal of concern. Ordinary licenses could be suspended by any two justices of the peace when they found an ordinary keeper allowing gambling or any "persons to tipple in his house, or drink any more than is necessary." Additionally, in 1748 the Virginia Assembly adopted:

> an *"Act ... to prevent gaming at ordinaries ... which must be often attended with quarrels, disputes, and controversies, the impoverishment of many people and their families, and the ruin of the health, and corruption of the manners of youth, who upon such occasions frequently fall in company with lewd, idle, and dissolute persons, who have no other way of maintaining themselves but by gaming."*

The law provided that an innkeeper who permitted gambling in his house, or any person who gambled "in an ordinary, race field, or any other public place," would be fined £5 "for the use of the poor," and then "be committed to the county gaol there to remain until ... they give sufficient security for ... their good behaviour [sic] for twelve months." Any justice of the peace in the county could render judgment alone, but the convicted gambler could appeal that judgment to the full county court. Loudoun ordinary keepers John Heryford, Benjamin Edwards, John Davis and Richard Coombs were all prosecuted in the county court under this law between 1757 and 1766. Appeals to the General Court were not permitted in the event of a conviction under the gambling laws. The Assembly's 1748 gambling law also specified the games that were permitted at Virginia ordinaries: billiards, bowls, backgammon, chess and draughts (checkers). [Customs, p. 148; Hening, VI/77-79; see infra, The Record, pp. 311 and 313].

In response to the concerns of ordinary keepers arising from irregular practices in the importation of Madeira wines, the 1752 Assembly passed an Act to prevent the importation of Madeira wines in casks with false bottoms. The law, still in effect during Loudoun County's first decade, from 1757 to 1766, established minimum liquid measures required for various cask sizes: 120 gallons in a "pipe"; 60 gallons in a hogshead; and 30 gallons in a quarter-cask. As evidenced by a sampling of the imported goods coming into the Potomac District ports in 1766, rum and Madeira wine, by the cask and hogshead, were the most popular imported liquors in the Northern Neck while apple and peach brandies were distilled and beer was brewed locally in Loudoun County. Lt.Gov. Fauquier apparently served Madeira wines when he entertained during the Virginia Assembly sessions, and the Burgesses showed their gratitude by allowing the good Governor 10 pipes (1,200 gallons!) of duty-free imports every year beginning in 1759. [Hening, VI/235-236 and VII/273; see supra, The Record in Chapter on Agriculture and Economics].

In November of 1762, during a lull in the frontier campaigning of the French (and Indian) War, the law restricting the sale of liquor on credit at Virginia ordinaries was amended to permit ordinary keepers to extend unlimited credit to travelers. The unstated intention of the Burgesses may have been the elimination of impediments to their own access to liquid comforts that the Williamsburg ordinaries provided during their Assembly sessions, because sailors "in actual pay on board any ship" were still not allowed any credit for buying liquor and "inhabitants of the county [and] residents of the town wherein such ordinary shall be kept" were still limited to an annual "tab" of 20 shillings at their local establishments. This later provision in the law explains, in part, the numerous suits brought by Loudoun inn keepers for the collection of relatively small sums. [Hening, VII/595].

Every time the Loudoun County Court reset the schedule of ordinary rates, their Order contained the admonition "that the respective Ordinary keepers in this County do sell according to the above rates in Money (or Tobacco at the rate of 12/6 per hundred) and that they do not presume to demand more of any Person whatsoever." This valuation is in keeping with the 1657-58 authority granted to the county courts and, after February of 1759, confirms the valuation of tobacco established by the Virginia Assembly for the payment of all officer fees, public dues and levies in Loudoun County. The reader, upon review of the Table hereinafter titled "Rates for 'Liquors & Entertainment' in Loudoun Ordinaries," may observe that the prices of many imported liquors increased, steadied and then dropped again, apparently in direct correlation with the military ebb and flow of the French and Indian wars. Some liquors, for example Canary and Rhenish wines and English ale by the bottle, were so infrequently available in Loudoun that their cost was not even rated by the County Court. [Hening, VII/292; Customs, p. 150; and infra, Tables at p. 316].

The first "Loudoun" ordinary business that we can actually prove the existence of was located on the ridge above the Carolina Road crossing of the Potomac River, established by Francis Awbrey Senr.. Awbrey could have had his Potomac ordinary open for business as early as 1735, when he was constructing the Goose Creek Chapel of Ease for Truro parish on the Carolina Road at Big Spring. And cartographer Robert Brooke probably stopped there in 1737, when he hired a canoe and young John Willcoxon Halling as a porter "at Awbrey's" during his mapping expedition on the upper Potomac. Regardless of the exact date of the founding of Awbrey's ordinary, Francis Awbrey Senr. clearly indicated in his Will that his ordinary at the Potomac River ferry was a going concern in the winter of 1741. The subsequent story of Awbrey's Carolina Road ordinary remains shrouded in the mists of a poorly recorded period in Loudoun's history. Richard Awbrey, who inherited the ferry and ordinary from his father, makes no mention of the ordinary business in his Will in 1743, but after Francis

Awbrey's death in 1742 the traffic on the Carolina road was diverted downriver to a new Potomac River ferry at Ebenezer Floyd's landing, and the value of Awbrey's location for an ordinary would have been completely lost with the change. [Ferry, p. 40; PrWmCOWIL, Book C, p. 341; Hening, V/66 and V/189].

The two primary east-west routes into colonial "Loudoun," the Potomac Path and the Bull Run Mountain Road, eventually would prove to be corridors of opportunity for the colonial men and women who kept ordinary. The growth of ordinary businesses along these roads parallelled the development and population growth in Loudoun County as a whole. As early as 1745, until at least 1755 and probably up until the founding of Leesburg in 1758, the more southerly Mountain Road was generally acknowledged as the better, "main road [through Loudoun] west to the Blew ridge Mountains [sic]." The Mountain Road's original terminus was the tobacco warehouse below the falls on the Occoquan. Traffic on the Mountain Road diverted to the port of Colchester, a "town built for the sake of the back country trade," when tobacco warehouses were built there. The exertions of the merchants in Alexandria, the rise of grains to prominence in agricultural production in Loudoun, the opening up of the manor lands along the Potomac and in northwest Loudoun, choice as the route for part of Braddock's army in 1755, and a general "recentering" of the population upon the creation of both Loudoun County and Leesburg, all combined to influence the increased use of the Potomac Path by 1760. [Landmarks, pp. 476-478 and 480-482; Colport, pp. 11 and 14; and, Browne, pp. 310-311; and see infra, Chapter on Bridges, Fords and Ferries].

When we pick up the record trail with the County Court Orders, beginning with 1749 in Fairfax, we learn of a number of ordinaries that were located in the "Loudoun" section of Fairfax County along the Mountain Road. Before 1758, travellers enroute to Winchester considered the Mountain Road a "better Road" than the Potomac Path and, accordingly, most of the earliest ordinaries in western Fairfax were situated along the Mountain Road. The earliest Fairfax ordinary license we have on record below Bull Run Mountain was for an establishment operated by a Quaker named Elisha Hall, who obtained his license in 1749, incidentally, the year before he died. This sad fact, combined with the size of his estate and the proven establishment of no less than three new ordinaries in that section of the Mountain Road within two years of Hall's death, leads us to the inevitable, albeit speculative, conclusion that Hall's business was likely a longstanding one and that he might have entertained, fed and boarded travellers on the Mountain Road as early as 1740. Before its final closing, Hall's ordinary may have been operated briefly but unsuccessfully by Edward Violett, a resident of the Cub Run area who obtained a Fairfax ordinary license only in 1752. [GW Writings, I/6; Browne, p. 310; FXCOCO, 1749 Book; FXCOWIL, Book A, p. 483].

In 1750, the year of Elisha Hall's death, Richard Brown founded an ordinary to the east of Hall's location, below the Mountain Road crossing of little Rocky Run. Brown's ordinary would become a popular establishment and continue in business until at least 1756, but there is no record that Brown ever obtained a Loudoun ordinary license. For several years, from 1761 to 1763, Henry Moore kept an ordinary at his house on the Mountain Road at Rocky Run, near the earlier site of Brown's ordinary. To benefit his business and convenience his customers, Moore went so far as to have the Mountain Road "turned" shortly before he opened his ordinary. Shortly after he opened for business, it appears that Henry Moore had the distinct experience of having to prosecute one of his customers, William McDaniel, for passing forged Treasurer notes in his ordinary. Another resident of Moore's neighborhood, John Hooms, or John Holmes, was cited for retailing without a license by the May grand jury in 1762, and then promptly licensed the informal ordinary at his home in the fork of the Mountain Road below Rocky Run. The unfriendly competition may have doomed both ordinaries, and neither obtained a business license for 1764, but east-west traffic was shifting to the Potomac Path. A few years later, from 1766 to 1768, Sandford Goram operated another ordinary in the Rocky Run section. [FXCOCO, 1749 Book, pp. 185 and 405, 1754 Book, pp. 88, 128 and 453, Book 1756, p. 38; supra, Chapter on Crimes].

It appears that, before 1746, William West operated an ordinary that was situated along the Potomac Ridge road on the grounds of the Fairfax County jail just north of the Fairfax "Springfield" Courthouse (in the area southeast of the feature now known as Freedom Hill at Tyson's Corner). At the same time, while serving as an assistant surveyor for Fairfax County in the 1740s, William West acquired lands around the intersection of the

Carolina Road and the Mountain Road, where he established his residence on "Fruit Hill." In 1751 William West obtained his first ordinary license for the Fruit Hill ordinary (now known as the historic location of first "the" West's, and then Lacey's, ordinary). The opening of West's ordinary that year at the busy crossroads was probably prompted by the closing of Hall's ordinary to his east. By the time Loudoun was formed in 1757, this West's ordinary had propelled William West into a position of stature in the community. West was named as one of the senior Justices of the first Loudoun County Court, and his Mountain Road ordinary may have been the site of the organizational meetings of Loudoun County. [FXCOCO, 1749 Book, pp. 129, 185 and 402, 1754 Book, p. 100, 1756 Book, p. 25; FXCODB, Book B-1, p. 233; Fairfax, p. 53; Landmarks, p. 495; supra, Chapter on the County Court].

Charles Tyler Senr., the future Loudoun County Justice, might have bought out William West at his Fairfax Courthouse location on the Potomac Path before 1750, or Tyler may have operated another ordinary in partnership with John Carlyle at colonial Springfield, but he did not renew his Fairfax County ordinary license in 1753. Tyler subsequently operated the "Colchester Tavern" between 1757 and 1761. Around 1772, his son Charles Tyler Junr. returned to Loudoun County and opened his ordinary at "Newgate" on the Mountain Road. John Peake, a resident of the area above the Mountain Road to the west of the Rocky Run Church in Cameron parish, founded an ordinary at his house in 1752. Peake's ordinary business lasted only two years, probably because of the stiff competition in the area provided by the ordinaries run by Misters Brown and West. [FXCOCO, 1749 Book, p. 305, 1760 Book, p.458; and see generally, Colport].

In 1760, William Owsley opened an ordinary far up the Mountain Road at Bacon Fort, but he did not renew his license in 1761 and the Bacon Fort ordinary site remained dormant for a considerable time. In 1760 George Vandiveer, who initially referred to himself as a Maryland goldsmith, bought land at Mount Hope near the site of the first Broad Run Church, where he opened an ordinary the following year. In 1763 Vandiveer paid Willoughby Newton £45, a rather steep sum, for a three acre site down the Mountain Road near Rocky Cedar Run. At the time, the tract included a "store house built by William Jett." Vandiveer probably reinstituted his jewelry business there, and the location may have served as the final site of his ordinary, but Vandiveer's endeavors as an artificer were successful and he did not renew his ordinary license in 1765. William Dye opened an ordinary on the Mountain Road at Williams Gap in 1764. Dye's ordinary was also short-lived, however, leading us to conclude that, by the mid-1760s, the more northern Potomac Path through Leesburg had eclipsed the Mountain Road as the primary route for transit through Loudoun County to a Blue Ridge crossing. [infra, pp. 309, 313-315; see LDCODB, Book A, p. 363 and Book C, p. 531].

The growth of ordinary businesses along the Potomac Path would follow a more delayed course but would eventually come to dwarf the trade that had been experienced along the Mountain Road. It appears that the first ordinary west of the Fairfax Courthouse on the Potomac Path was opened in 1751 by Thomas Evans at his house on Goose Creek, where he maintained Fairfax County's public ferry. Unfortunately Evans died shortly after obtaining this ordinary license, but the business opportunity was apparent to others living in the area. After Evans' death, Edmund Sands took over both businesses, and when he moved on at the end of 1753, he was followed in turn by Samuel Mead, and in 1754 by Henry Awbrey, who was one of the seven sons of Francis Awbrey Senr. Then, for a two year period beginning in 1756 when John Moss Junr. (another future Loudoun County Justice) took over as keeper of the Goose Creek ferry, the ordinary license at the site was not renewed. John Jenkins, ferry keeper from 1757 to 1759, licensed an ordinary at the site again in 1758, but Jenkins did not renew his ordinary license in 1760. Two more years passed before Loudoun businessman John Hough formed a partnership with Alexandria merchant John Carlyle in 1762. They reestablished both the Goose Creek ferry and the ordinary at the crossing. One can only speculate that the earliest Goose Creek ordinaries were kept on the west side of the Creek, where, at first, there would have been no immediate competition and the convenience would have attracted travellers to detour from the Carolina Road. On the other hand, the Hough-Carlyle ordinary at the ferry was definitely situated "on the lower side" of Goose Creek, but the venture apparently failed along with a proposed mill and the attempted renewal of the ferry. After the late 1750s, the Goose Creek crossing location was not commercially viable. Ordinary business at the Goose Creek crossing was dealt a death blow by the founding of Leesburg, its ordinaries and the growing reputation of their expansive hospitality. [FXCOCO, 1749 Book, p. 208, 1754 Book, pp. 83 and 287; supra, Chapter on Ferries].

When the Fairfax County Courthouse was moved from the Potomac Path at Springfield to the town of Alexandria in May of 1752, the leases for the land at the Springfield site reverted to the Fairfax family. In 1753 Samuel Jenkins, apparently an uncle of the John Jenkins who would situate at Goose Creek, responded to the closing of one or all of the convenient taverns at colonial Springfield by opening his ordinary a little further west on the Potomac Path near Difficult Run. Samuel Jenkins kept ordinary near the Difficult Run bridge until his death in 1756. [FXCOCO, 1749 Book, p. 305, 1754 Book, pp. 60 and 293].

Ezekiel Hickman licensed an ordinary on the Potomac Path in 1756, above Goose Creek where the road was also known as the Shenandoah Road. Hickman probably kept his ordinary (where he was living in 1757) just west of Goose Creek where the Shenandoah Road forked and one road branched off to the north toward Noland's ferry. Or Hickman may have operated his ordinary to the east of this fork in the road, at the Goose Creek ferry where John Moss was the ferryman. But Hickman's venture was short-lived and he did not renew his license in Fairfax in 1757 or in Loudoun in 1758. [FXCOCO, 1754 Book, p. 500].

Richard Coleman (yet another future Loudoun Justice) displayed a shrewd business sense when he licensed his ordinary on March 19, 1755 at the Sugarlands on the Potomac Path, between the Difficult Run bridge and the Goose Creek ferry crossing. His business opening at the end of March coincided nicely with the staged arrival at the Sugarlands, between April 10th and May 1st, of Halkett's 44th regiment of General Braddock's army on its march along the Potomac Path, enroute to their ignominious defeat in the wilderness below Ft. Dusquesne. Coleman must have sold the soldiers of the 44th everything in his pantry because, by the time the regiment's hospital train arrived at Coleman's on June 2nd, they "dined on Salt Gammon [ham they brought with them], nothing better to be had." The Sugarland Ordinary on the Potomac Path was operated continuously by the Coleman family for a decade until Richard Coleman's health failed in the spring of 1762. The Coleman establishment at Sugarland was one of several Loudoun ordinaries that could honestly claim that "Washington slept here !" [FXCOCO, 1754 Book, p. 293 and 501; Browne, p. 311; see The Record infra, p. 309; supra, Chapter on the Sheriffs of Loudoun].

Further up the Potomac Path, beyond the intersection with the Carolina Road, in the vicinity of the crest of the ridge now known as Clarke's Gap, William Dodd licensed his house for an ordinary in 1756. Dodd's financial, and possibly active, partner in this endeavor was none other than James Hamilton, a future Loudoun County Justice who would eventually be elected to represent Loudoun in the Virginia General Assembly for over a dozen years. Hamilton had recently closed his own ordinary in eastern Fairfax County, resigned as a Truro parish vestryman, and moved to Cameron parish in anticipation of the formation of Loudoun County. Mr. Dodd was another keen businessman, and he obtained a prime location lower down on the Potomac Path in Leesburg when it was established in 1758, paying only £4, 6 shillings for Lot #5 on the southeast corner of the intersection of Loudoun and King Streets. He apparently wasted no time building an edifice in Leesburg suitable for his trade, where he kept ordinary from 1759 until 1762 and undoubtedly turned a tidy profit. Catherine Dodd, his wife, was likely the hostess at both establishments. Dodd sold or leased the location of his first ordinary to John Evans, who continued the business there through 1762, when Evans and Dodd appear to have had a falling out. When Craven Peyton was in search of a better location for the ordinary he established early in 1762 with his cousin Micajah Powell, he bought Dodd's Leesburg ordinary on Lot #5, paying the extraordinary sum of £200 in "current money." William Dodd retired to his original homestead west of Leesburg by the spring of 1763. Craven Peyton, whose appointment as a Loudoun Justice in 1762 coincided with his first active involvement in the Leesburg ordinary business, was a son-in-law of William West and appears to have benefitted from West's help in the operation of his Leesburg ordinary. Peyton purchased several other lots in and around Leesburg and mortgaged his Leesburg ordinary heavily to finance various business ventures. By 1765, Peyton had turned the management of the Leesburg ordinary over to John Wilkinson; Peyton continued to license his ordinary at the intersection of King and Loudoun Streets, the in-town crossroads of the Carolina Road and the Potomac Path until at least 1769. [FXCOCO, 1749 Book,

p. 35; FXCOCO, 1754 Book, p. 448; LDCODB, Book C, p. 472 and Book E, p. 10; infra, the Record, pp. 308, 309 and 311].

The first ordinary in Leesburg was licensed in March of 1758 (long before Dodd relocated) by Benjamin Edwards and his wife Jane Edwards - the same day they purchased town lot #15 on Loudoun Street. In time, Edwards probably contracted with Aeneas Campbell and Thomas Pritchard to construct several large structures on his lot, and Benjamin Edwards personally conducted business in Leesburg for a decade. The clientele at Edwards' ordinary may have been of a somewhat more genteel persuasion than your average colonial tavern patron. Unlike Dodd's and most of the other Leesburg ordinaries, Edwards' ordinary was never situated within the various prison bounds that were established in Leesburg for the County jail. Edwards retired in 1766, when he was found to be an "ancient and infirm person," and he probably leased his tavern to Charles Barkley that year. Barkley kept ordinary in Leesburg until 1770, the year Edwards sold all of his town properties to Samuel Canby for the then-outrageous sum of £450. [LDCODB, Book G, p. 301; infra, Chapter on Leesburg].

John Moss Senr. and John Moss Junr. followed Edwards, probably contracting with John and William Trammell for the construction of Leesburg's second ordinary in the summer of 1758. The Moss ordinary was situated advantageously on town lot #21, on the southeast corner of the intersection of King and Market Streets directly across from the new County Courthouse then under construction. In real estate "location is everything" and the Mosses enjoyed a decade of prosperity thanks, in part, to their immediate proximity to the Courthouse lots. In 1763, when the Indians renewed their raiding into Virginia's frontier settlements, militia Captain John Moss Junr. led the Loudoun reinforcements to Winchester for two months of garrison duty. John Moss Senr. took over the ordinary that year, and renewed the license thereafter until his death five years later even though the Leesburg property was sold to the Trammell family in 1765. John Moss Junr., after exchanging properties with William Trammell in 1765, resumed the ordinary business near Difficult Run on the Potomac Path in 1769. [LDCODB, Book B, p. 108, Book D, p. 463 and Book E, p. 220; supra, Chapter on The Militia; see infra, p. 315].

As previously discussed, William Dodd founded Leesburg's third major ordinary in 1759 on town lot #5, which he sold to

Craven Peyton in 1762. A number of other men who owned or operated ordinaries in eastern Fairfax County eventually relocated to Loudoun County and resumed business. The most prominent of these men was John Herryford. His father, John Senr., had owned land on Dogue's Neck in Fairfax and operated a ferry and ordinary on the Potomac River. When his father died before 1750, John Junr. continued operation of the family businesses with the help of his brothers. In 1759, John Herryford (Junr.) sold his holdings on the Potomac and quickly reestablished himself in Loudoun County, acquiring several choice properties in and around Leesburg at bargain prices. Herryford obtained his first Loudoun ordinary license in 1760, opened a tavern on lot #32 across King Street from the Courthouse, and immediately bid on and won the contract to supply the new Courthouse with firewood and water. Herryford's Ordinary, the fourth major ordinary establishment in Leesburg, was destined to obtain the stature of a Leesburg landmark of sorts, open for business continuously for two decades, through the American Revolution. Other Leesburg ordinaries followed. [FXCOCO, 1749 Book, 1756 Book, p. 205].

Between 1752 and 1754, Robert Sanford (aka Robert Sandford) operated the only business, an ordinary, at "Cameron" in eastern Fairfax, the site futilely offered by John Minor as a town below the West family Hunting Creek tobacco warehouses. Both the ordinary and town at Cameron failed, and by 1758 Sanford was Inspector of tobacco at Hunting Creek. But in 1760, Sanford was once more in league with the town-building Minors, this time in Leesburg where he was probably operating an ordinary as a tenant of John Minor's brother, Nicholas Minor. Sanford acquired lands on the Potomac Path at Broad Run in 1762, where William Hancock had opened an ordinary briefly in 1761, but the location must have proven untenable. William Winn's ordinary, which he opened in 1762, may have been located on leased lands along the Potomac Path at Difficult Run, but Winn and Sanford both appear to have left the ordinary business by 1764. [FXCOCO, 1749 Book, p. 320; and, Landmarks, pp. 344 and 414].

One John Davis, a farmer living near Broad Run church, sold liquors without a license sometime in 1759. But a second John Davis, apparently a Leesburg resident, acquired an ordinary license early in 1761 and opened for business on a town lot owned by [his brother ?] Daniel Davis - either #8 or #36, then moved to town lot #7, where he was in business until 1763. The Loudoun Street location gave his ordinary a facing on the in-town route of the Shenandoah Road, but the venture was not a success and Davis left the ordinary business still in debt to his creditors. Richard Coombs, John Maginnis and Daniel Lawrence all opened ordinaries in Leesburg in 1763. Coombs was in business on town lot #36, which he had purchased in the summer of 1762, until just before his death in 1769. The site had been used previously as a blacksmith's shop, so Coombs almost certainly had a stable on the immediate premises of his ordinary. Coombs' was the northern-most tavern in Leesburg situated along the Carolina Road, at the corner of King and Cornwall Streets just outside of the County prison bounds. Meginnis originally identified himself as a tailor by trade and opened his ordinary on either lot #53 or #54 on the west end of Market Street, where he was still in business at the time of the American Revolution. Daniel Lawrence apparently moved from Maryland to Leesburg in the fall of 1763, after previously obtaining backing for his endeavor from Philip Noland, the Loudoun Justice who owned the primary Carolina Road ferry on the Potomac. Lawrence obtained his license in November and the next month, for £50, Noland purchased a prime location - Lot # 29 on the northwest corner of the intersection of King and Market Streets. To finance his business, Lawrence used his belongings as collateral to secure a loan of £32 from a Maryland merchant financier. The business was apparently unable to compete with Moss' ordinary diagonally across the intersection and Herryford's ordinary next door, and Lawrence never renewed his ordinary's business license. The Maryland creditor, Christopher Lownes, eventually took possession of Lawrence's personal property and belongings and he seems to have disappeared from Loudoun County late in 1764. [LDCODB, Book C, pp. 246, 320 and 451, and Book D, p. 705; supra, Chapter on the Grand Jury].

In 1752, as another response to the closing of the Potomac Path ordinaries at the Fairfax Courthouse at colonial Springfield, Thomas Sorrell opened an ordinary on leased property along the Sugarlands rolling road to Little Falls, in the vicinity of the Great Falls. The location on the rolling road proved slow, and despite backing from Alexandria merchant Benjamin Sebastian, Sorrell closed his ordinary in 1753, and removed west along the Potomac Path to the dusty crossroads that would become Leesburg. He was promptly appointed as a Fairfax County Constable for the area above Goose Creek, "up to the mountains," and was named as one of the first "Directors and Managers" of Leesburg in 1758. In 1764, Sorrell opened a new ordinary near the Potomac Path, at his plantation house just east of town near the Tuscarora. In 1762, William Trammell opened another ordinary on the Little Falls rolling road near the Sugarlands, but the venture was abandoned the next year. In 1765, Aeneas Campbell rented his Leesburg town lots #19 and #20, along Market Street and on the southwest corner of the intersection of King and Market Streets across from the Loudoun Courthouse, to John Miller. Miller licensed an ordinary and opened a stables, and they were both identified in the plat of the new prison bounds recorded that year. In 1766 Miller purchased one of the older houses in Leesburg, across Market Street on Lot # 30, where he and his wife Catherine Miller, trading on their own account, no doubt, reopened for business. The same year, 1766, Charles Barkley and his wife Sarah Barkley opened their Leesburg ordinary, either on Lot #15 as tenants of Benjamin Edwards or on Campbell's Lot #20. Miller died in 1769 and Barkley did not renew his license the following year after Edwards sold his Leesburg town properties, but Thomas Sorrell was still keeping ordinary at his house near Leesburg in the 1770s. [FXCOCO, (1749) pp. 180, 297 and 474; and see, LDCODB, Book G, p. 301].

To the west of Leesburg the Shenandoah Road crossed the Short Hill at a feature known as The Gap (Hillsboro), where the north fork of Kitoctin Creek cuts through the hill. The first tavern at The Gap, which became known as the Hickory Ordinary, was probably opened by Samuel Awbrey around 1756. Samuel Awbrey apparently leased land for the site from the Fairfax family, but he did not record the lease and he never obtained a license for his ordinary either. On the other hand, Samuel Awbrey's location at the Gap was a well known area landmark before July of 1757, as evidenced in the first Loudoun County road orders, and the Awbrey family men all had a good deal of experience with the ordinary business. Shortly after they completed indentures as servants for Thomas Awbrey (Samuel Awbrey's brother), Conrad Shanks and his wife Margaret set up for business at the Hickory Ordinary. Unfortunately Conrad Shanks, like his apparent predecessor Samuel Awbrey, overlooked the prerequisite of obtaining an ordinary license. This set the stage for a brief but eventful competition for the traveller's shilling at the Gap in 1759 between ordinary keepers Conrad Shanks and Samuel Butcher. Knowing that Samuel Awbrey had lost interest in his Hickory Ordinary, Samuel Butcher licensed an ordinary at his house in the Short Hill neighborhood. Butcher had no desire to tangle with the well-connected Awbrey family, but he was moved to action when Margaret and Conrad Shanks, fresh from their indentured service, failed to license the Hickory Ordinary. Butcher's unrelenting complaints put an end to the Shanks' budding business venture at the Hickory Ordinary in 1759, even though Shanks obtained an ordinary license after taking over the business. After taking lashes for his offense, Conrad Shanks was noted disabled in the fall of 1760. The Hickory Ordinary remained inactive until Thomas Pursley opened for business in 1762. The scare of the 1763 Indian massacres just over the Blue Ridge may have given Pursley second thoughts about his business location, but he had reopened by 1770. [supra, pp. 290 and 296, and infra, The Record, p. 309 and 309; infra, Chapter on Servants, infra, Chapter on Loudoun Tax Lists].

Inns and taverns flourished along the Carolina Road, but only at the major crossroads. As mentioned, Francis Awbrey's establishment at the Potomac crossing, in operation until around 1742, was the first Carolina Road ordinary in 'Loudoun.' On the basis of circumstance alone we could speculate that Francis Hague kept an ordinary near the Carolina Road crossing of the Secolon branch before 1749. Hague was known to the colonial Governor in Williamsburg as a respected Quaker gentleman, and he owned a large tract between Tuscarora and Secolon that would later be acquired by Loudoun Clerk Charles Binns and added to the Rokeby plantation. But the absence of court records for the period before 1749 leaves us without proof of the theory.

West's Ordinary at "Fruit Hill" was already a well-known resting stop for colonial travellers on the Carolina Road when Loudoun County was formed in 1757, but Loudoun Justice William West did not obtain his first Loudoun ordinary license until May of 1758. As we have already observed, the ordinary William West founded around 1751 at Fruit Hill was his second ordinary business. Fruit Hill stood about a mile due east of the north end of Bull Run Mountain, just northeast of the intersection of the Carolina and Mountain Roads. West's Ordinary at Fruit Hill was the first tavern we can prove to have been established on the Carolina Road after Awbrey's Potomac ordinary had closed a decade before. Between 1751 and Leesburg's founding in 1758, West's Ordinary was also distinguished as the only tavern along the Carolina Road between the Potomac River and the crossroads to the south, in Prince William County, now known as Haymarket. William West kept his Fruit Hill ordinary continuously until 1763, when he appears to have retired from public life and moved to Leesburg. Thereafter, until his death several years later, William West probably devoted his energies to assisting his daughter and her husband Craven Peyton at their Leesburg ordinary at the corner of King Street and Loudoun Street. It is no small coincidence that Craven Peyton's last ordinary license was acquired in 1769, the year William West Senr. died. The Fruit Hill ordinary was still in business, but beginning in 1764 the license was obtained and the ordinary was kept by Charles West, one of William Senr.'s sons. During the 1770s Charles West would consistently fail to obtain his annual license for the Fruit Hill Ordinary, and he was just as consistently cited by the Loudoun County grand juries for selling liquor without a license. In the 1760s, an orphan named Joseph Lacey had been apprenticed or hired to work at West's Fruit Hill ordinary. When Lacey grew up he purchased the business from William West's successors, and the ordinary at Fruit Hill became known as Lacey's Ordinary.

Promptly after the founding of Leesburg in 1758, the town residents successfully petitioned the Loudoun County Court for the diversion of both the Carolina Road and the Potomac Path. The route of the Carolina Road, the north-south highway, was altered to fall into King Street through the town. Thus, the Leesburg ordinaries served the Carolina Road as well as the Potomac Path. For nearly three decades after Francis Awbrey's ordinary had closed early in the 1740s, no one seems to have identified the need for another ordinary at the Carolina Road crossings of the Potomac. But by the 1750s, the absence of an ordinary at the Potomac crossings must have been viewed by residents of the area as a prime business opportunity. In 1758, Edward Harding was the first to respond, licensing an ordinary near Lucketts on the Carolina Road. Harding's venture failed, and it was three years before Hugh Fouch opened another ordinary on the Carolina Road north of Leesburg, probably at the intersection where the

Potomac Path branched off toward the east. When Fouch closed for business at the end of 1763, Samuel Luckett promptly opened his own tavern a little further north along the Carolina road, where today both a school and crossroads bear his family name. Finally, Philip Noland Junr. (actually the 3rd) licensed an inn at his father's ferry on the Potomac in 1768. This series of ordinary openings was indicative of an increase in business opportunities on the Carolina Road beginning in the early 1760s, and implies that the pattern of north-south migratory traffic was redirected, from the Philadelphia Wagon Road leading into the Shenandoah Valley, to the more easterly route over the Carolina Road leading through Loudoun County -- another tangible consequence of the French (and Indian) War. [supra, Chapter on Bridges and Ferries].

Several other ordinaries were established around the County but none of them stayed open very long. William Grant and his young apprentice Squire Boone (apparently one of Daniel Boone's younger brothers) opened for business on the lower section of Kitocton Creek below modern-day Waterford in 1761, but Grant suffered a severely disabling injury that year which spelled the end of the venture, and Squire returned with the rest of the Boone family to their homes in the forks of the Yadkin River in North Carolina. Jacob Lasswell, who had been cited for retailing spirits without a license in 1759 and 1760, finally licensed his informal ordinary in 1761. Lasswell lived about half way between Leesburg and West's ordinary, where an alternate route of the Carolina Road crossed Goose Creek at a fording place below the mouth of the Piney Hill branch. But either Lasswell's ordinary was too close to both Leesburg and West's, or that section of the road not well travelled, and the ordinary at Lasswell's ford on Goose Creek was closed by 1762. [see infra, Chapter on Tithables; and see Boone, p. 52].

The absence of two other Loudoun County men from the licensing records should put an end to speculation that they were operating ordinaries, and indirectly gives us an insight into the nature of the people of colonial Loudoun and their time. Remarkable for their absence from the Fairfax and Loudoun ordinary records were Edward Thompson, that kindly Quaker who lived at The Gap of the Short Hill, and Nicholas Minor, the proprietor of Leesburg, both of whom established themselves along the Shenandoah Road. The records prove that, after 1749, neither

Thompson nor Minor obtained an ordinary license and we are therefore fairly safe in saying that neither was operating an ordinary in 1755. When Halkett's regiment of General Braddock's army marched past their homes in the spring of that year, opening their cellars and pantries to the officers and regimental commissary was merely an extension of the hospitality and colonial sense of "patriotism" that was already a broad tradition in the Virginia colony. A county ordinary license never was a prerequisite to furnishing supplies to a regiment of the King's army. [Landmarks, p. 513 n. 149; and, re Minor see infra, Chapter on Leesburg; but see, Browne, p. 312].

From 1755 to 1757 a man named Jacob Pshaw (aka Jacob Faw or Jacob Pfhow) ran an ordinary in Alexandria "on Benjamin Sebastian's lot," with the financial backing of two of the most reputable men in Fairfax County, Justices Hugh West [Senr.] and John Dalton. Mr. Pshaw never obtained an ordinary license in Loudoun County, but he used the modest earnings from his Alexandria ordinary to purchase Leesburg town lot #25 in 1758 and acreage on the Tuscarora near town in 1760 and 1761. This was the same man who apparently obtained the first deed for town lot #27, where the Loudoun County Courthouse was eventually built. Pshaw had not built a suitable structure on either of his town lots by 1763, when he had to obtain a second deed for lot #25 before selling it and buying town lot #41, in effect exchanging a lot on Market Street for a Cornwall Street location. In Loudoun County, Jacob Faw identified himself as a saddle maker by trade, not an ordinary keeper, and he probably operated a livery stables in Leesburg. John Gladen, an ordinary keeper in eastern Fairfax from 1755 to 1757, purchased Leesburg town lot #14 on Loudoun Street, a promising location next to Benjamin Edwards' ordinary. Gladen never kept an ordinary in Loudoun County but, like Pshaw (Faw), he probably maintained a stables instead. [FXCOCO, 1754 Book, pp. 204, 207 and 450, 1756 Book, pp. 24 and 181; and see LDCODB, Book A, pp. 87-91 and 128].

George West, Loudoun County Justice and Surveyor, was also familiar with the ordinary business, although he never licensed an ordinary in Loudoun. Nephew of ordinary keeper William West and a son of Fairfax Justice and Burgess Hugh West, George licensed an ordinary at his house in Alexandria in 1752, the very year that the Fairfax County Courthouse was moved to that town.

Shortly thereafter, however, when George West was advanced to the position of Surveyor for Fairfax County and inherited lands above Goose Creek, he left the ordinary business and moved to Pea Hill, his new plantation home situated northwest of the Goose Creek crossing at Morris' ford (near the terminus of modern Rte. 648). [FXCOCO, 1749 Book, p. 228; see, Balch/Lewis #53-898; see infra, Chapter on Bridges, Fords and Ferries].

In passing, we mention one other ordinary keeper who was certainly well known to the residents of colonial Loudoun. In the mid-1750s, James Ingo Dozier moved up the Potomac from Richmond County and, backed by Loudoun Justice James Lane, established an ordinary in Fairfax, just east of Rocky Run and the Loudoun line, on the southern fork of the Mountain Road leading to Colchester. Dozier operated his ordinary on the road to Colchester from 1756 to 1760, and he also served as a vestryman for the "Fairfax" section of Cameron parish. Dozier's ordinary was, no doubt, frequented by the churchmen of the Rocky Run area as well as the Loudoun farmers, merchants and traders who hauled their goods and produce to Colchester for sale or shipment.

The reader may have discerned a common thread that is woven throughout our discussion of these early Loudoun taverns and the colonial ordinary keepers: keeping an ordinary seems to have been the colonial equivalent to a modern law degree as a foundation for launching a career in politics. At one time or another there were over a dozen of the early Loudoun County Justices involved in an ordinary business: James Hamilton, Aeneas Campbell, William West, Richard Coleman, George West, Charles Tyler, John Moss Senr., John Moss Junr., Philip Noland, Craven Peyton, Leven Powell, James Coleman, James Lane, John Minor and Charles West each had some experience in keeping or financing an ordinary. This hard evidence gives substance to the contention that an ordinary keeper in colonial Virginia, unlike his counterpart in England, was usually a respected leader in his community, with a reputation gained through honest dealings.

Most of the entries in The Record identify individual applicants and issuance of the annual ordinary licenses. In some instances the exact location of the intended or existing ordinary was indicated. The "George Town" of the record was the initial settlement area around the then-budding community of Leesburg, before the new town name was generally adopted or in use.

July 12, 1757 - In the first session of the new Loudoun County Court, Surveyors of the Highways are appointed. Among them are: John Smarr, "from Mr. William Wests Plantation to broad run Church ..."; Stephen Embry, "from William Dodds to Samuel Awbrey's at the Gap of the Short Hill ..."; Joseph Jones, "from Samuel Awbreys at the Gap of the short Hill to the County line on the blueridge ..."; and, John Thomas, "from the Fork of the Road above Goose Creek at Ezekiel Hickmans to the great Lime Stone." These orders indicate the location of four of the oldest ordinaries in Loudoun. "Embry" and Jones were both tenants living on Col. Tayloe's tract at the Gap of the Short Hill. Book A, p. 3; see FXCODB, Book D-1, p. 280.

August 9, 1757 - "At a Court held for Loudoun County at the Courthouse on Tuesday," with ten Loudoun County Justices in attendance including ordinary owners and financiers William West, Richard Coleman, Charles Tyler and James Hamilton, "[t]he Court proceeded to rate the Liquors for this County," after listing the allowable charges for various items, the Court then "Ordered that the respective Ordinary keepers in this County do sell according to the above rates in Money or Tobacco at the rate of 12/6 per hundred and that they do not presume to demand more of any Person whatsoever." Book A, p. 7; and infra, The Rate Table, p. 316.

August 10, 1757 - James Coleman - license for an ongoing ordinary business "at his House at Sugar Lands ... he with Security having given Bond as the Law directs." Book A, p. 11.

September 13, 1757 - William Dodd - licenses an ordinary "at his House in this County." Book A, p. 17. Dodd's was one of the few ordinaries already in operation when Loudoun County was created. His first ordinary was located near Clarke's Gap where the "Shenando Waggon Road" crested the ridge of the Kitocton Mountain range. In 1759 he relocated to Leesburg.

March 14, 1758 - Benjamin Edwards - license for the first ordinary "at George Town in this County." Book A, p. 66.

March 15, 1758 - "Rates of Liquors for this County are continued for the ensuing Year except the Rum which is rated at ten shillings per Gallon and so in proportion." Book A, p. 71; see infra, The Rate Table, p. 316.

March 15, 1758 - Samuel Butcher obtains a license for an ordinary "at his House at the short Hills," and subsequently is identified in deeds as an "Innholder" although he never obtains another license. Book A, p. 75; and, LDCODB, Book A, p. 148.

May 9, 1758 - John Jenkins - license to reestablish "an Ordinary at the ford of Goose Creek where the Ferry was usually kept." Book A, p. 99.

May 10, 1758 - William West - a license "renewal" for the ordinary "at his House on Fruit Hill." Book A, p. 106.

June 13, 1758 - Edward Harding - his only license for an ordinary "at his House in this County." Book A, p. 113. The site of this ordinary may have been on Kitocton Creek near the later site of Roach's Mill, where Harding had acquired land in 1751 from John Hanby. FXCOCO, 1749 Book, p. 157.

September 12, 1758 - John Moss Junr. obtains a license for a new ordinary at his father's House "at George Town in this County [on Lot #21 in Leesburg]." Book A, p. 158.

March 13, 1759 - "The Court proceeded to Rate the Liquors for the County," listing the charges allowable for the coming year. William West and Richard Coleman were two of the sitting Justices at the time the Loudoun County rates were set. Book A, pp. 207-208; see infra, The Rate Table, p. 316.

March 13, 1759 - Richard Coleman - license renewal for an ordinary "at his House." Book A, p. 208.

March 15, 1759 - William Dodd - license for a new ordinary "his House in the Town of Leesburgh." Book A, p. 219.

April 10, 1759 - Conrad Shanks obtains a License "to keep Ordinary at the Gap of the short Hill commonly called the Hickory Ordinary in this County." Book A, p. 229.

April 10, 1759 - Benjamin Edwards - license renewal for an ordinary "at his House in Leesburgh." Book A, p. 230.

May 8, 1759 - The Grand Jury presents charges against: "John Davis [and] Jacob Lasswell ... for selling of Liquor by retail small measure ... [without a license]." Book A, p. 233.

May 9, 1759 - William West Gent. - license renewal for an ordinary at his "House on Fruit Hill." Book A, p. 237.

June 13, June 14, and August 14, 1759 - Conrad Shanks is convicted by a jury for retailing liquors without a license, on the complaint of Samuel Butcher and with the testimony of Samuel Stillwell and Benjamin Shacklett. Shanks is fined £10, with 1 penny awarded the informant, Butcher, for his damages. The Sheriff is ordered to summon Conrad Shanks to pay his fine. Shanks, failing to pay, is sentenced to receive 21 lashes on his bare back at the "Public Whiping Post." Book A, pp. 255, 262 and 265.

September 12, 1759 - John Moss Junr. - license renewal for "an Ordinary at [Lot #21 in] Leesburgh." Book A, p. 291.

January 28, 1760 - Hugh Guttray keeps an ordinary at his house "in the town of Dumfries." PRWMCOA, vol. 19, p. 224.

March 11, 1760 - "The Court [including Justices William West and Richard Coleman] proceeded to Rate the Liquors & Entertainment for this County." Book A, p. 322; see infra, The Rate Table, p. 316.

March 11, 1760 - William Owsley - obtains a license to establish a new ordinary "at his House at Bacon Fort in this County." Book A, p. 329.

May 9, 1760 - George Washington spent the night at Richard Coleman's Sugarland Ordinary. GW Writings, II/168.

May 13, 1760 - A Grand Jury charges "William Dodd for not having

Rates of Liquors [posted] in his Public Entertaining Room." Book A, p. 343.

May 13, 1760 - Robert Sandford - "an Ordinary at his House." Book A, p. 344. This is an example of an experienced Fairfax ordinary keeper who relocated in Loudoun. Sandford's first ordinary, licensed as early as 1752, was near "Cameron" - the site proposed as an alternative to Alexandria in 1748. FXCOCO, 1749 Book, p. 184; and, FXCOCO, 1756 Book, p. 316.

May 13, 1760 - Benjamin Edwards obtains another license renewal for "an Ordinary at his House in Leesburg." Book A, p. 344; and see, LDCODB, Book B, p. 8.

May 14, 1760 - William Dodd - license renewal for "an Ordinary at his House in Leesburg." Book A, p. 345.

June 10, 1760 - Richard Coleman - license renewal for "an Ordinary at his House." Book A, p. 362.

June 10, 1760 - John Herryford - license for a new "Ordinary at his House in Leesburg." Book A, p. 362.

June 12, 1760 - "John Davis [and] Jacob Lasswell [each of whom is] Presented by the Grand Jury for selling of Liquors by small Measure and Tipling in his House ... Ordered that the Deputy [King's] Attorney file an Information against [each of them]." Book A, p. 368.

June 12, 1760 - "William Dodd who stands Presented [by the Loudoun Grand Jury] ... for not having the Rates of Liquors in his Public Entertaining Room on being heard is Excused." Book A, p. 370.

February 10, 1761 - George Vandiveer - license for an ordinary "at his House ..."; John Davis - license for an ordinary "at his [brother's] House [on either lot #8 or lot #36 in Leesburg]." Vandiveer appears to be living at Mount Hope, near the site of the first Episcopal Broad Run Church. Order Book A, p. 409; LDCODB, Book A, p. 363, Book B, p. 236, and Book C, p. 32.

February 11, 1761 - William Grant licenses an ordinary "at his House on Kittockton Creek." Grant lived on leased lands on the south fork in the Earl of Tankerville's "Catoctian Manour." Later that year, Grant was declared levy-free in Loudoun, due to some as yet undetermined disability. Book A, p. 413; see, LDCODB, Book B, p. 342; see infra, Chapter on Tithables.

February 11, 1761 - Jacob Lasswell - license for an ordinary "at his House." Book A, p. 415.

March 10, 1761 - William Hancocke - his only license for an ordinary "at his House." Book A, p. 427.

March 10, 1761 - "The Court proceeded to Rate the Liquors for this County," listing the allowable charges for Loudoun ordinaries for the coming year. Book A, p. 428; see infra, The Rate Table, p. 316.

March 11, 1761 - Benjamin Edwards - license for an ordinary "at his House in this County." Book A, p. 431.

March 11, 1761 - William West - license for an ordinary "at his House on Fruit Hill." Book A, p. 431.

June 10, 1761 - William Dodd - license for an ordinary "at his House in Leesburgh." Book A, p. 460.

July 14, 1761 - John Heryford - license for an ordinary "at his House." Book A, p. 480.

August 11, 1761 - John Evans - "an Ordinary at his House where William Dodd formerly lived." Book A, p. 481.

August 12, 1761 - On a Petition by Henry Moore dated July 14, 1761, suggesting "that the Mountain Road as it now stands is very Injurious to him," and then after hearing the report of a viewing conducted by Fielding Turner, Charles Tyler and Francis Peyton, the Court Orders Charles Eskridge, the "Surveyor of the old Road [is Ordered] to clear [the new Mountain Road] ... turned as it is now marked." Book A, pp. 481 and 487.

September 30, 1761 - Jacob Frederick Curtiss keeps an ordinary in Prince William at his house at the Occoquan ferry. PRWMCOA, vol. 24, p. 36.

November 10, 1761 - Henry Moore licenses an ordinary "at his House on Rockey Run with Francis Peyton and Charles Binns his Securities having entered into Bond as the Law directs." This is the first entry in Loudoun Court Orders of the Securities on an ordinary license Bond. Book A, p. 531.

February 9, 1762 - John Carlyle, Gent. and John Hough license an ordinary "on the lower side of Goose Creek at [their] Ferry ... they with Hugh West their Security having entered into Bond as the Law directs."; and, Richard Coleman, Gent. licenses an ordinary "at his House in this County" Hugh West is entered as the Security on Coleman's Bond "as the Law directs." Respectively, they each pay £2, 15 shillings to Loudoun County Clerk Charles Binns and obtain their ordinary licenses. Book A, p. 554; Clerk's 1762 Fee Book, last page.

March 10, 1762 - "The Court [including Richard Coleman and Francis Peyton] proceeded to Rate the Liquors for this County," listing the allowable rates for ordinaries for the year. Book A, p. 562; see infra, The Rate Table, p. 317.

March 10, 1762 - Micajah Powell - license "to keep Ordinary at Leesburg ... with Craven Peyton [as] his Security." Powell then pays £2, 15 shillings to Charles Binns, Loudoun County Clerk, and obtains his ordinary license. Book A, p. 564; Clerk's 1762 Fee Book, last page.

March 12, 1762 - Benjamin Edwards - license for an ordinary "at his House in Leesburgh." Book A, p. 579. He pays £2, 15 shillings to Charles Binns and obtains his ordinary license. Clerk's 1762 Fee Book, last page.

May 12, 1762 - Ordinary keeper John Moss Junr. obtains judgments, averaging only £3, 10 shillings, for "Debt due by account" from John Owsley and David Davis, two of the clientele of his ordinary. Book A, p. 590.

May 12, 1762 - Robert Sandford - licenses an ordinary "at his House in this County," pays £2, 15 shillings to Charles Binns, Loudoun Clerk, and his ordinary license is issued. Book A, p. 594; Clerk's 1762 Fee Book, last page.

May 12, 1762 - The Loudoun grand jury presents charges against "William Beevers ... Robert Bland ... John Lewis ... John Hooms ... [and] Daniel Deskins [each] for keeping a Tipling House ... within six months last." Book A, p. 599; and see supra, Chapter on the Grand Jury.

May 12, 1762 - The Loudoun grand jury charges "John Heryford, Tavernkeeper [and] Benjamin Edwards, Tavernkeeper [each] for allowing unlawful Gaming in his House to the knowledge of two of us within six months last past." Book A, p. 600; and see supra, @ p. 291.

June 8, 1762 - Thomas Pursley [sic- Thomas Presley?] obtains a license for an ordinary "at his House [at The Gap of the Short Hill] in this County, with William Janney [as] his Security having entered into and acknowledged Bond as the Law directs." Book A, p. 626.

June 8, 1762 - William Dodd renews his license for an ordinary "at his House in this County with Aneas Campbell ... his Security." Book A, p. 627.

June 8, 1762 - Thomas Pursley and William Dodd each pays £2, 15 shillings to Charles Binns, Clerk of Loudoun County, obtaining his ordinary license. Clerk's 1762 Fee Book, last page.

June 8, 1762 - "John Heryford [sic] [and] John Davis [each is] Convicted of ... permitting unlawful Gaming particularly Cards and Dice ... in his House as an ordinary keeper in the Town of Leesburgh before Nicholas Minor and James Lane Gent. Justices ... from whose judgment [they] appealed to this Court ... [a fine of £5 is affirmed] for the use of the Poor of [Cameron] Parish." It appears that the chief culprit in this gambling was Potomac ferrykeeper Patrick McKenzie. Book A, pp. 627-628; supra, Chapter on Crimes and Punishment.

July 15, 1762 - John Heryford - license for an ordinary "at his House in ... Leesburg." Book B, p. 25. He pays £2, 15 shillings to Charles Binns, Clerk, and obtains his ordinary license. Clerk's 1762 Fee Book, last page.

August 10, 1762 - Hugh Fouch - license for an ordinary at "his House in this County"; and, John Hoomes - license for an ordinary at "his House in this County." Book B, p. 29. Each pays £2, 15 shillings to Charles Binns and obtain ordinary licenses. Clerk's 1762 Fee Book, last page.

August 11, 1762 - John Davis - license for an ordinary at "his House in this County." Book B, p. 35. He pays £2, 15 shillings to Charles Binns, Clerk, and obtains his ordinary license. Clerk's 1762 Fee Book, last page.

August 12, 1762 - "Joseph Pollard who as well for us as himself ... Prosecutes agt. Robert Sandford} In Debt." Sandford insists on a jury trial, and then there is no further record of the case. Book B, p. 17.

September 15, 1762 - William Trammell - license for an ordinary at "his House in this County." Book B, p. 59.

September 15, 1762 - William West - license for an ordinary at "his House in this County." Book B, p. 60.

September 15, 1762 - William Trammell and William West each pays £2, 15 shillings to Charles Binns for his license. Clerk's 1762 Fee Book, last page.

September 15, 1762 - "John Evans who as well for us as himself [as an informer] in This behalf Prosecutes agt. William Dodd} In Debt." Dodd reserves his exceptions to the complaint and has the matter continued to the next Court, but there is no further record of the case. Book B, p. 65; supra, p. 298.

November 10, 1762 - Henry Moore - licensed for an ordinary at "his House." He pays Loudoun Clerk Charles Binns £2, 15 shillings and obtains his ordinary license. Book B, p. 72; Clerk's 1762 Fee Book, last page.

December 14, 1762 - George Vandeveere [sic] - license for an ordinary at "his House." Book B, p. 77. Based on the absence of a reference in the Clerk's 1762 Fee Book, it appears that George Vandiveer omitted the payment of his ordinary license fee in 1762, a rare exception to the rule.

April 13, 1763 - John Maginnis - license for an ordinary "at his House in ... Leesburgh." Book B, p. 105.

April 13, 1763 - "The Court proceeded to Rate the Liquors for this County," listing the allowed charges and ordering "that the several respective ordinary keepers in this County do sell according to [the list] ... in Money or Tobacco @ the rate of 12/6 [shillings and pence] Per Ct. [hundred weight of tobacco] and that they do not presume to demand, ask or receive more of any Person whatsoever." Book B, p. 107; see infra, The Rate Table, p. 317.

April 13, 1763 - Craven Peyton - license for an ordinary "his House in the Town of Leesburg for one year from this time." Book B, p. 108.

April 14, 1763 - Craven Peyton [sic] - license for an ordinary "his House in Leesburg." Book B, p. 110.

May 12, 1763 - James Hamilton, Jacob Janney, Robert Cavens and Israel Thompson are appointed to view the route for a new "Road from William Dodd's [homestead] to Goose Creek through Leesburg." Book B, p. 153.

June 14, 1763 - Richard Coombs - license for an ordinary "at his House in Leesburg." Book B, p. 163.

July 12, 1763 - Thomas Pursley - license for an ordinary at "his House in this County." Book B, p. 192.

July 12, 1763 - Robert Sandford - license for an ordinary at "his House in this County." Book B, p. 193.

September 13, 1763 - John Moss Senr. - license for an ordinary at "his House in this County." Book B, p. 232.

September 13, 1763 - John Evans - license for an ordinary at "his House." Book B, p. 235.

September 14, 1763 - Hugh Fouch - license for an ordinary "at his House in this County." Book B, p. 240.

September 15, 1763 - John Herryford - license "to keep an Ordinary at his House in Leesburg." Book B, p. 256.

November 8, 1763 - Daniel Lawrence - license "to keep an Ordinary at his House in Leesburg." Book B, p. 260.

March 13, 1764 - William Dye - obtains his only license for an ordinary "at his House in this County." Book B, p. 278.

March 14, 1764 - "Richard Coombs ... [was] convicted of unlawful Gaming (on the 17th day of February last past at the House of John Maginnis a Licensed Ordinary) before Nicholas Minor Gent. a Justice of the Peace of this County ... [on appeal, the full County Court rules that the conviction is] affirmed ... [Coombs is fined £5] for the use of the poor of Cameron Parish." The Court then orders Coombs to give Security for his good behavior for the next year. James Abbett entered as his Security on the Peace Bond. Book B, p. 281.

March 16, 1764 - "The Court [consisting of James Hamilton, Aneas Campbell, Nicholas Minor and Philip Noland] proceeded to rate the Liquors for this County," listing the various charges allowed in Loudoun ordinaries for the coming year. Book B, p. 313; see infra, The Rate Table, p. 317.

April 10, 1764 - George Vandiveere [sic] - license for an ordinary "at his House in this County." Book B, p. 315.

April 10, 1764 - Samuel Luckett - license for an ordinary "at his House in this County." Book B, p. 319.

April 10, 1764 - Charles West - license for an ordinary "at his House [at Fruit Hill] in this County." Book B, p. 324.

April 11, 1764 - Benjamin Edwards - license for an ordinary "at his House in Leesburg." Book B, p. 335.

April 12, 1764 - Craven Peyton - license for an ordinary "at his House in Leesburg." Book B, p. 338.

June 12, 1764 - Thomas Sorrell - license for an ordinary "at his House in this County." Book B, p. 358.

June 14, 1764 - Richard Coombs - license for an ordinary "at his House in Leesburg." Book B, p. 381.

September 14, 1764 - John Heryford sues on a number of open accounts for an average of £2, 12 shillings (all apparently customers at his ordinary), naming William Winn, John Trammell, William Bernard Sears, Charles Eskridge, Patrick McKenzy, Sampson Turley, John Owsley, Thomas Kelly, John Pyles and John Urquhart as individual defendants. Book B, pp. 467-468.

November 13, 1764 - William Winn - license for an ordinary "at his House in this County." Book B, p. 492.

November 13, 1764 - John Meginnis - license for an ordinary "at his House in this County." Book B, p. 494.

November 15, 1764 - John Heryford - license for an ordinary "at his House in this County." Book B, p. 506.

March 14, 1765 - Benjamin Edwards - license for an ordinary "at his House in this County." Book B, p. 535. He pays £2 and 15 shillings to Charles Binns and obtains his ordinary license. Clerk's 1765 Fee Book, last page.

April 8, 1765 - The Loudoun Court, consisting of James Hamilton, Aneas Campbell, Nicholas Minor and George West, "Ordered that the Rates of Liquors Settled by the Court in March 1764 at which the Ordinary keepers were allowed to Sell &c. for the Year last past be Continued." Book B, p. 536; see infra, The Rate Table, p. 317.

April 11, 1765 - Adam & Patterson, "Merchants of Leesburg," obtained a judgment against John Davis for debts that totalled £38. This was probably a debt generated by Davis' operation of an ordinary on Loudoun Street that had gone out of business around 1763. Book B, p. 568; see supra, p. 300.

April 11, 1765 - A Loudoun jury awards a verdict, in favor of Fairfax County Justice and Colchester merchant Benjamin Grayson, against Leesburg ordinary keeper John Herryford for debts on an account found to total £157, 14 shillings, 2 pence and a half penny! John Herryford apparently withheld payment on this large debt for some time, which may have been the 'start-up' costs he incurred when he built and opened his Leesburg ordinary. But the Loudoun

County jury (undoubtedly composed of a number of Herryford's regular customers) limited Grayson's claim for "Damages by Occasion of the Detention of the said Debt to one penny besides his Costs." Book B, p. 568.

April 11, 1765 - John Patterson & Fleming Patterson, Leesburg merchants, discontinue their action in debt against William Dye, which was probably for supplies Dye purchased for his ordinary business. Book B, p. 574.

June 11, 1765 - Edward Snickers of Frederick County, both in his own right and as assignee of Joshua Gore, takes two judgments against William Dye totalling £45. "One old hoe" belonging to Dye was attached to satisfy the judgments. Dye's dealings with these men suggests that Dye's unsuccessful ordinary was probably located at Williams (aka Snickers) Gap. Book B, p. 622.

July 8, 1765 - Richard Comes [sic], John Moss Senr. and Thomas Sorrell, each obtains a license for an ordinary "at his House in this County for one year." Book B, pp. 673 and 674.

July 8, 1765 - Richard Coombs, John Moss Senr., and Thomas Sorrell, each pay £2 and 15 shillings to Loudoun County Clerk Charles Binns and obtain their ordinary licenses. Clerk's 1765 Fee Book, last page.

August 12, 1765 - John Miller - license for an ordinary "at his House in this County." Book C, p. 2.

August 12, 1765 - Charles West - license for an ordinary "at his House [at Fruit Hill] in this County." Book C, p. 6.

August 12, 1765 - John Miller and Charles West, each, pay £2 and 15 shillings to Loudoun Clerk Charles Binns and obtain an ordinary license. Clerk's 1765 Fee Book, last page.

May 15, 1766 - Capt. Robert Ashby's ordinary is located southeast of Ashby's Gap on the Blue Ridge, in Fauquier County. MdGaz., p. 3, col. 1.

August 15, 1766 - Richard Coombs - license for an ordinary "at his House in Leesburg." Book C, p. 183.

September 9, 1766 - John Moss Junr., Gentleman Justice - license for an ordinary "at his House," near Difficult Run on the Potomac Path. Book C, p. 190; see LDCODB, Book D, p. 461.

September 19, 1766 - One advertisement in the *Virginia Gazette* suggests the after-tax, wholesale price of rum in the lower Chesapeake: "For sale, by the subscriber at Norfolk. Choice Barbados Rum. @ 2s. [shillings] 9d. [pence] a gallon. [offered by] John Tucker." VaGaz./PD, p. 4, col. 3.

October 13, 1766 - Benjamin Edwards is referred to as an "ancient and infirm person." Book C, p. 207.

October 15, 1766 - John Miller - license for an ordinary "at his House in Leesburg." Book C, p. 213.

Monday, November 10, 1766 - Thomas Sorrell, Charles Bartlet, Sandford Goram, John Herryford and John Moss, is each licensed for "an Ordinary at his House." Book C, p. 218.

"LIQUORS & ENTERTAINMENT" IN LOUDOUN ORDINARIES
(in shillings.pence)

	1757	1758	1759	1760	1761
For a Gallon of Rum ... and so in proportion	8.	8.	12.6	12.6	12.6
Nantz Brandy per Gallon	10.	10.	10.	10.	10.
Peach or Apple Brandy ... per Gallon	6.	6.	6.	8.	8.
New England Rum ... per Gallon	2.6	2.6	2.6	2.6	2.6
Virginia Brandy ... from Grain per Gallon	4.	4.	5.	6.	6.
Arrack the Quart ... made into Punch	8.	8.	10.	10.	10.
For a Quart of White, Red or Madeira Wine	2.6	2.6	3.	3.6	3.6
For Foyall and other low Wines Per Quart	1.6	1.6	1.6	1.6	1.6
English Strong Beer ... the Quart Bottle	1.3	1.3	1.3	1.3	1.3
London Beer ... called Porter Per Quart	1.	1.	1.	1.	1.
Virginia Strong Beer ... Per Quart	.7½	.7½	.7½	.7½	.7½
Cyder the Quart Bottle	.3¾	.3¾	.3¾	.3	.4
English Cyder ... the Quart Bottle	1.3	1.3	1.3	.4	.4
For a Gill of Rum ... made into Punch with Loaf Sugar	.6	.6	.7½	.7½	.7½
"Ditto" with Fruit	.7½	.7½	.9	.9	.9
"Ditto" without Fruit with brown sugar	.3	.3	.5	.5	.5
For a good Hot Diet ...	.9	.9	.9	-	-
with Beer or Cyder	-	-	-	1.	1.
For a Cold Diet	.6	.6	.6	.6	.6
A Gallon of Corn or Oats	.4	.4	.4	.4	.4
Stableage & fodder ... for a Horse 24 Hours or 1 Night	.6	.6	.7½	.7½	.7½
Pasturage for a Horse ... 24 Hours or 1 Night	.4	.4	.4	.4	.4
For lodging one Night ... with Clean Sheets	.6	.6	.6	.6	.6

"ALL SOLDIERS AND EXPRESSES ON HIS MAJESTY'S SERVICE PAYING READY MONEY SHALL HAVE 1/5TH PART DEDUCTED."

"LIQUORS & ENTERTAINMENT" IN LOUDOUN ORDINARIES
(in shillings.pence)

	1762	1763	1764	1765	1766
For a Gallon of Rum ... and so in proportion	10.	10.	10.	10.	10.
Nantz Brandy Per Gallon	10.	10.	10.	10.	10.
Peach and Apple Brandy ... Per Gallon	6.	6.	6.	6.	6.
New England Rum ... Per Gallon	2.6	2.6	2.6	2.6	2.6
Virginia Brandy ... from Grain per Gallon	5.	5.	5.	5.	5.
Arrack the Quart ... made into Punch	10.	10.	10.	10.	10.
For a Quart of White, Red or Madeira Wine	3.6	3.6	4.	4.	4.
Claret Per Bottle or Quart	-	4.	4.	4.	4.
For Foyall and other low Wines Per Quart	1.6	1.6	1.6	1.6	1.6
English Strong Beer ... the Quart Bottle	1.3	1.3	1.3	1.3	1.3
London Beer ... called Porter Per Quart	1.	1.	1.3	1.3	1.3
Virginia Strong Beer ... Per Quart	.6	.6	.6	.6	.6
Cyder the Quart Bottle	.4	.4	.4	.4	.4
English Cyder ... the Quart Bottle	1.3	1.3	1.3	1.3	1.3
For a Gill of Rum ... made into Punch with Loaf Sugar	.7½	.7½	.7½	.7½	.7½
"Ditto" with Fruit	.9	.9	.9	.9	.9
"Ditto" without Fruit with brown sugar	.5	.5	.5	.5	.5
For a good Hot Diet ... with Beer or Cyder	.10	-	-	-	-
without Beer or Cyder	-	1.	1.	1.	1.
For a Cold Diet	.6	.7½	.7½	.7½	.7½
A Gallon of Corn or Oats	.6	.6	.6	.6	.6
Stableage & fodder ... for a Horse 24 Hours or 1 Night	.7½	1.	1.	1.	1.
Pasturage for a Horse ... 24 Hours or 1 Night	.4	.4	.4	.4	.4
For lodging one Night ... with Clean Sheets "(otherwise nothing)"	.6	.6	.6	.6	.6

LICENSED ORDINARIES, OWNERS AND LOCATIONS, 1736-1766

Carolina Road Ordinaries

FRANCIS AWBREY	1737-1742	at first Carolina Road ferry
EDWARD HARDING	1758-1759	north of Leesburg @ Lucketts
JACOB LASSWELL	1759-1762	at a ford of Goose Creek
HUGH FOUCH	1762-1763	north of Leesburg
SAMUEL LUCKETT	1764-1765	north of Leesburg @ Lucketts

"West's Ordinary" Carolina Road - Mountain Road intersection

WILLIAM WEST	1751-1757	(licensed in Fairfax)
WILLIAM WEST	1758-1763	"at Fruit Hill"
CHARLES WEST	1764-1769...	(son of William Senr.)

Mountain Road at or near Little Rocky Run

RICHARD BROWN	1750-1757	(licensed in Fairfax)
HENRY MOORE	1761-1763	
JOHN HOOMES	1762-1763	at fork below Rocky Run
SANDFORD GORAM	1766-1768	(aka Sanford Goreham)
CHARLES TYLER	1772- ...	at "Newgate"

Other Mountain Road Ordinaries

ELISHA HALL	... -1749	'the post' above Cub Run
JOHN PEAKE	1752-1754	west of Cub Run
WILLIAM OWSLEY	1760-1761	at Bacon Fort
WILLIAM DYE	1764-1765	at Williams Gap ?

Potomac Path Ordinary at the Goose Creek Ferry

THOMAS EVANS	1751	(died in Fairfax, 1751)
EDMUND SANDS	1752-1753	(licensed in Fairfax)
SAMUEL MEAD	1754	(licensed in Fairfax)
HENRY AWBREY	1755-1756	(licensed in Fairfax)
JOHN JENKINS	1758-1759	
CARLYLE & HOUGH	1762	

Coleman's Sugarland Ordinary on the Potomac Path

RICHARD COLEMAN	1755-1757	(licensed in Fairfax)
JAMES COLEMAN	1757-1758	
RICHARD COLEMAN	1759-1762	

LICENSED ORDINARIES, OWNERS AND LOCATIONS, 1736-1766

Shenandoah Road/Potomac Path near Clark's Gap

WILLIAM DODD	1756-1759	(Fairfax)/(in Leesburg, 1759)
JOHN EVANS	1761-1762	moved to Little River in 1762

Shenandoah Road/Potomac Path at the Gap of the Short Hill

SAMUEL AWBREY	? ... -1757	(not licensed !)
SAMUEL BUTCHER	1758-1759	
CONRAD SHANKS	1758-1759	Hickory Ordinary @ the Gap
THOMAS PURSLEY	1762-1763; 1770- ...	

Leesburg Ordinaries (Shenandoah Road and Carolina Road)

BENJAMIN EDWARDS	1758-1765	Lot # 15; ("infirm" in 1766)
JOHN MOSS JUNR.	1758-1762;	Lot # 21
JOHN MOSS SENR.	1763-1768	(died, 1768) Lot # 21
WILLIAM DODD	1759-1762	Lot # 5 (Clark's Gap, '56-59)
JOHN DAVIS	1759-1762	(Lot # 8 or 36 ?); Lot # 7
JOHN HERRYFORD	1760-1770 ...	Lot # 32; later Lot # 38 ?
MICAJAH POWELL	1762 only;	(Craven Peyton, as security)
CRAVEN PEYTON	1763-1764; 1767-1770 ...	Lot # 5
RICHARD COOMBS	1763-1768	Lot # 36 (died @ Aug. 1769)
JOHN MAGINNIS	1763-1764; 1767-1770 ...	Lot # 54 ?
DANIEL LAWRENCE	1763-1764	Lot # 29 (w/Philip Noland?)
THOMAS SORRELL	1764-1772 ...	Tuscarora east of Leesburg
JOHN MILLER	1765-1769	Lot # 20; Lot # 30 (died, '69)
CHARLES BARKLEY	1766-1770	(aka Bartlet) Lot # 15 ?

Other Potomac Path Ordinaries

SAMUEL JENKINS	1753-1756	(Fairfax) near Difficult Run
EZEKIEL HICKMAN	1756-1757	(Fairfax) west of Goose Creek
WILLIAM HANCOCKE	1761-1762	near Broad Run bridge
WILLIAM WINN	1762-1763	? near Difficult Run ?
WILLIAM TRAMMELL	1762; 1768	near Sugarlands

Other Loudoun Ordinaries

ROBERT SANDFORD	1760-1763	"at his house" (in Leesburg ?)
WILLIAM GRANT	1761-1762	near Waterford on Kitoctin
GEORGE VANDIVEER	1761-1764	Mt. Hope, Broad Run Church

THE TOWN PLAN OF LEESBURG

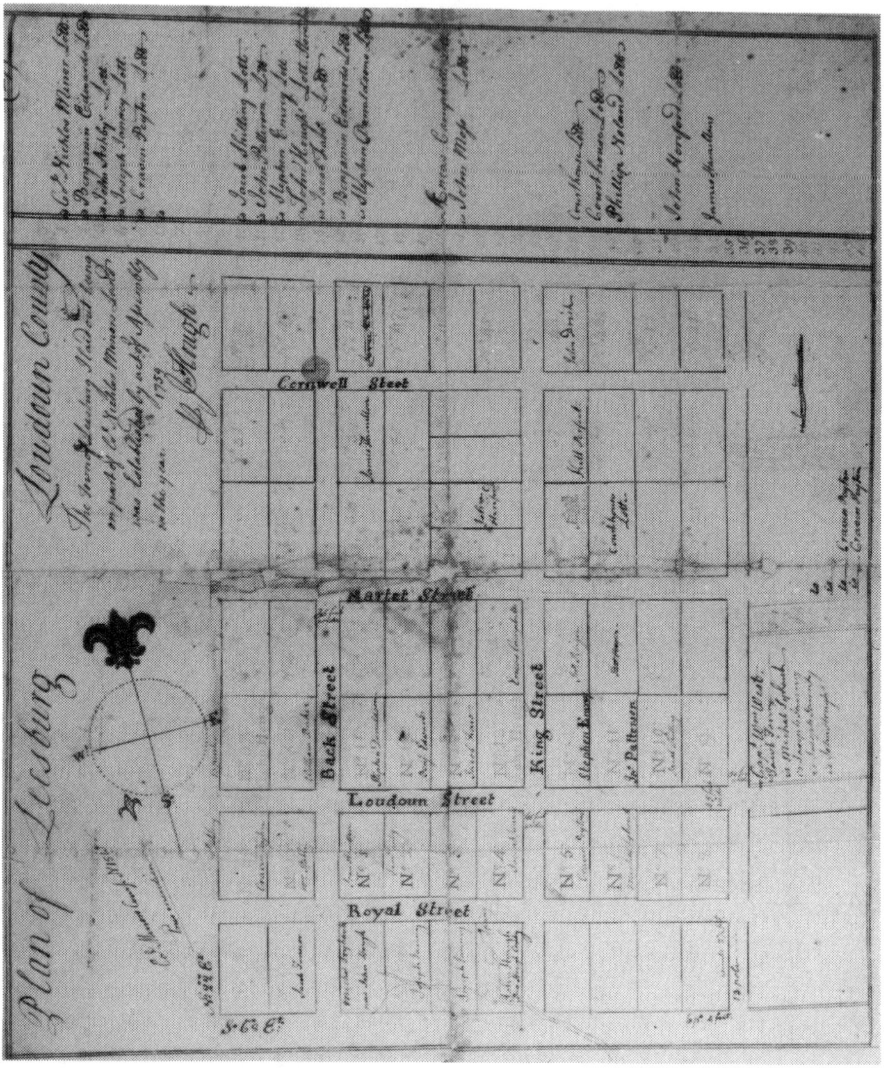

This "Plan of Leesburg, Loudoun County" was probably John Hough's personal copy of the first town survey, conducted in the winter of 1757-58. The Courthouse and gaol are shown on the two public lots, but only a few dozen of the early lot owners are identified, including most of colonial Loudoun's leading citizens: James Hamilton, Aeneas Campbell, William West, John Moss, Benjamin Edwards, Philip Noland, Craven Peyton, John Herryford, Joseph Janney, Stephen Emery, Jacob Shilling, John Patterson and Stephen Donaldson. Some entries were added to this copy of the Plan as late as 1769. *Courtesy of the Loudoun Museum, Leesburg.*

Leesburg is named after Thomas Lee (1690-1750), one of the younger sons of Richard Lee II of Virginia. Thomas parlayed a small inheritance, family connections, a self-imposed classical education, and wise investments in property into a position of prominence in the Virginia colony. In 1722 Thomas Lee married Hannah Harrison Ludwell, increasing both the Lee family holdings and position. Col. Thomas Lee and his wife and young family lived at the Lee ancestral home at Mt. Pleasant in Westmoreland County. Thomas Lee served as a Justice of the Peace, for a time as the resident agent for Lord Fairfax in the Northern Neck, and as a member of the Virginia Assembly of Burgesses. In one famed incident the brick manor house at Mt. Pleasant was burned down by transported English convicts whom Lee had sentenced for additional crimes. Lee's loss came to the attention of George II's Queen Caroline who, with an award of £300 from her Privy Purse, assisted Thomas Lee in the construction a new manor house that he named Stratford. [Lee, pp. 103-127 and 248].

Thomas Lee was elevated to the Virginia Council in 1732, taking the seat vacated upon the death of Robert "King" Carter, the resident agent for Lord Fairfax in the Northern Neck at the time. Lee served on the Governor's Council for the next 17 years. In 1744, Thomas Lee and William Beverley (of Orange County) represented Virginia, negotiating with the Iroquois, at the Treaty of Lancaster. When Lt. Gov. Gooch left for England in 1749, John Custis, the senior member of the Council (and also from the Northern Neck), stepped down. This advanced Thomas Lee to the position of President of the Virginia Council and, as such, the Acting Governor of the colony. Lee was sworn in on September 4, 1749, and served as Governor for just over a year until his death on November 14, 1750. King George II commissioned Thomas Lee as the Lt. Governor (ie., resident Governor), but the King's Commission arrived from England after Lee's death.

During his lifetime, Thomas Lee actively promoted the expansion of trade and commerce beyond the falls, on the upper reaches of the Potomac River. In 1747, Thomas Lee organized the (Virginia) Ohio Company, which rapidly grew to involve and ally nearly all of the most powerful Northern Neck families of the time. Thomas Lee's sixth son, Francis Lightfoot Lee, became the first County Lieutenant (head of militia) for Loudoun County. As a bachelor, Francis Lee lived in Loudoun on land he had inherited from his father. Thomas Lee's other sons, Philip Ludwell, Thomas Ludwell, Richard Henry, William and Arthur Lee, also rose to positions of prominence in colonial and Revolutionary Virginia and then in the United States. Early in the 1700s, Thomas Lee patented a vast acreage along Goose Creek, east of where Louis Michel had depicted a swan on his 1707 map of the Potomac. In keeping with Virginia tradition, as the first patentee on the creek, Thomas Lee named it "Lee Creek" in his deeds but, in order to bolster the cause of Lord Fairfax in a dispute over the boundaries of the Northern Neck, the proprietor's land office insisted on using "Goose Creek." Thomas Ludwell Lee's sons would eventually inherit most of the Lee family lands in Loudoun County.

While many of Virginia's colonial Governors had a County named for them during their lifetime, the honor to Thomas Lee was posthumous, but no less the honor. Less than a decade after Thomas Lee's death, a little crossroads just west of "Lee's Creek" was selected as the seat of government for Loudoun County. Situated at the crossing of the Carolina Road and the Shenandoah road to Winchester (a western extension of the Potomac Ridge Road), the dusty crossroads was centrally located in the new county. In September of 1758, the Assembly passed "An Act for erecting a town on the land ... of Nicholas Minor, in ... Loudoun," which became Virginia law when Governor Francis Fauquier gave his assent on October 12, 1758. The Act provided that:

> *"... Nicholas Minor, of the county of Loudoun ... hath laid off sixty acres of his land adjoining to the court-house of the said county ... with proper streets for a town, many of which lots are sold, and improvements made thereon, and the inhabitants ... have petitioned ... the land so laid off ... is hereby erected and established a town ... by the name of Leesburg; ... freeholders and inhabitants thereof shall forever hereafter enjoy the same privileges which the inhabitants of other towns ... now enjoy."*

The founding Act went on to appoint Trustees:

> *"... to regulate the buildings in ... Leesburg ... honorable Philip Ludwell Lee, esquire, Thomas*

Mason [sic- Thomson Mason], esquire, Francis Lightfoot Lee, James Hamilton, Nicholas Minor, Josias Clapham, AEneas Campbell, John Hugh [sic- John Hough], Francis Hague, and William West, gentlemen ... any five or more of them, are hereby authorized and impowered [sic] ... hereafter, to settle and establish such rules and orders for the more regular and orderly building of the houses in ... Leesburg as to them shall seem best and most convenient ... in case of the death or removal or other legal disability ... the surviving or remaining trustees ... [are] to elect and chose so many other persons ... as shall make up the number of ten; ... trustees so chosen shall to all intents and purposes be vested with the same power as any other."

[Hening, VII/234-236; see infra, The Record, p. 337].

Deeds for town lots subscribed in 1758, prior to Leesburg's formal incorporation, identified Anthony Russell, Loudoun's senior Justice in the original County Commission, and Thomas Sorrell, who had been living nearby for about five years, as two of the original town "Managers." In the incorporating statute the Assembly replaced Russell and Sorrell, adding the Lee brothers, Thomson Mason, Francis Hague and William West as Trustees. Hague, a Quaker preacher in the Fairfax Meeting at Janney's Mill, appears to have avoided an active role in the management of Leesburg until some time in 1762, when town deeds first name him as a Director for the town. William West's placement on the list of Trustees by the Assembly might indicate that his addition was a legislative afterthought, perhaps as a measure of consolation when the crossroads around his Mountain Road ordinary lost the competition for the site of the first Loudoun County Courthouse.

The land where Leesburg was eventually situated was purchased by Francis Awbrey in 1730 as part of a 4,054 acre acquisition from Thomas, Sixth Lord Fairfax. Upon Awbrey's death around 1741, a 326 acre section that included the site of downtown Leesburg passed to John Awbrey, one of Francis' sons who was living there at the time, with his house probably situated on what became town Lot #59. The first identifiable graveyard in the Leesburg tract, a forty foot square area to the southwest of the intersection of Loudoun and Back Streets, gives us a first clue to the likely locale of John Awbrey's 1730s plantation home, and the possible location of the slave "quarters" and "out" buildings on the tract. John Awbrey moved down the Potomac to eastern Fairfax County after his father's death, and when he died around 1744 the tract that would become colonial Leesburg passed to his widow Mary. In 1745, before she took a third husband and moved even further down the Potomac to St. Marys County, Maryland, Mary Awbrey sold the "373 [sic - actually 326] acre" tract "where John Awbrey formerly lived" to John Carlyle, a Fairfax County Justice and merchant in Alexandria. [Grants, Book C, Folio 102; FXCODB, Book A, pp. 400-403; supra, Chapter on Ferries].

References in the Fairfax County Court Orders prove that Nicholas Minor established himself on the piedmont before 1754, possibly as a resident manager for the Carters or under a lease-purchase arrangement with Carlyle. In 1755, Braddock's 44th regiment found Minor ensconced at "Fruitlands," his plantation home near the crossroads. This Nicholas Minor, younger brother of former Fairfax County Justice John Minor and an officer in the Fairfax militia under Carlyle's command, eventually established Leesburg just west of his plantation home. The Awbreys, Carlyle and the Minors were all associated with the tobacco trade, and it seems likely that the initial farm use of the tract would have been for the growth of cash tobacco. The use of traditional tidewater "old field" methods of tobacco production for the twenty years before Leesburg's founding would have severely depleted the soil, and in any event tobacco production appears to have given way to grain crops on the tract by 1765. In anticipation of Loudoun County's creation, John Carlyle and Nicholas Minor engaged the assistance of Minor's neighbor, Josias Clapham, in clearing title to the crossroads site in 1757. Josias Clapham had an interest in talking to the widow Awbrey, on his own account, about some of the old Awbrey-family property near his Potomac ferry. With Clapham's assistance and £46, Carlyle obtained a deed from Mary Awbrey's new husband, James Mills, in May of 1757, confirming Carlyle's title to the "Leesburg" site. Four months later, in September, Carlyle and his wife transferred title to the tract to Nicholas Minor for £64, for a profit of just one shilling per acre after expenses. [infra, Chapter on Militia; supra, Chapter on Bridges and Ferries; FXCODB, Book D, pp. 417-420; LDCODB, Book A, p. 133, and Book E, p. 168; see Landmarks, p. 140].

Heretofore, John Carlyle has been overlooked in the discussion of Leesburg's origins even though, having acquired the tract in 1745, he had owned the Leesburg site for fully a dozen years when the new town was proposed. Carlyle was a Scottish merchant who moved from Quantico to Hunting Creek warehouse around 1740. His acquisitions in the 1740s included property between Difficult Run and Sugarlands on the Potomac Ridge Road, and the "Leesburg" tract. Carlyle associated with Col. Thomas Lee and the Fairfax family, promoting development of the upper Potomac River valley in 1747, and he joined with the Wests, Washingtons and Alexanders as a founder of Alexandria in 1748. In 1749, John Carlyle was appointed as a Fairfax County Justice along with Moses Linton, Francis Hague and Anthony Russell. In 1752, Carlyle was the Fairfax Justice responsible for taking the lists of tithables in upper Cameron parish, above Goose Creek. He was made Colonel of the Fairfax militia late in 1755; and in 1756, when John Colvill died, John Carlyle was advanced to the Quorum on the Fairfax County Court. In 1755, when General Braddock selected John Carlyle's home for his headquarters, the Carlyle House was widely acknowledged to be the finest residence in Alexandria. Carlyle influenced selection of the Potomac Path, instead of the Mountain Road, as the line of march for Braddock's 44th Regiment and that choice of roads, at a critical juncture in the history of the Northern Neck, undoubtedly sped the founding of Leesburg and, ultimately, its selection as the seat for Loudoun County government. When G.W. Fairfax travelled to England in 1760, Carlyle took over as the active manager of properties in the Piedmont and Shannondale manors in western Loudoun County. In February of 1762, at what was then thought to be the end of the French War, Carlyle joined George Mercer, James Hamilton and John Hough at the Fredericktown (Maryland) meetings, intent on furthering development on the upper Potomac; the same theme resounded when Carlyle participated in John Ballendine's Potomac navigation projects in the 1770s. In combination with both Loudoun's John Hough and Alexandria merchant John Dalton, Carlyle maintained an active role in Loudoun affairs, and the Alexandria firm of Carlyle & Dalton was well known in Leesburg trading circles during Loudoun's first two decades. Carlyle's second marriage to Sybil West made him the proprietor of the West family tobacco warehouses at Alexandria, a brother-in-law to

Loudoun Surveyor George West and Loudoun's first Deputy King's Attorney Hugh West, nephew-in-law to Loudoun's William West, and a cousin-in-law to Nicholas Minor of Leesburg. [see Landmarks; Council V, p. 279; FXCOCO (1756), p. 84].

The father of Leesburg's proprietor, Nicholas Minor Senr., served as a Justice in Westmoreland County in the 1740s and as the inspector of tobacco at the Carters' Nomini Hall warehouses in 1745-46. Nicholas Junr.'s older brother, John Minor, had been a Potomac neighbor of the Fairfax, West and Washington families, a Fairfax County Justice in the 1740s and 1750s, and the founder of an erstwhile colonial town in eastern Fairfax that he had named Cameron. When John Minor died in the spring of 1753, Nicholas Junr. took his brother's place as a Captain of the Fairfax militia, in the command of then-Major John Carlyle. Before map maker John Dalrymple travelled down the Shenandoah road in 1754, perhaps as early as the spring of 1752, Nicholas Junr. seated his family above Goose Creek near land that had been cleared and occupied by John Awbrey. Nicholas might have been pursuing his brother's plans - a decade earlier John Minor had patented a tract further up the Shenandoah road where it crossed Kitoctin Creek. We can thank Capt. Dalrymple for the notation on the 1755 Fry & Jefferson map showing Minor's plantation near the piedmont crossroads. An entry in the diary of a Madam Browne (in Braddock's hospital train) on June 3, 1755, that upon her arrival at Minor's plantation she "order'd some Fowls," has led to the mistaken assumption that Minor kept an ordinary at Fruitlands. In the 1920s, Fairfax Harrison misinterpreted the Browne diary entry and, to add to the confusion, Harrison's assertions have been repeated as gospel ever since. Most of the known ordinaries in the Northern Neck are identified as *"Ordy."* on Fry & Jefferson's 1755 map, while Minor's plantation was <u>not</u> so designated. At a time when retailing liquor without a license was stridently prosecuted by the colonial county courts, neither Carlyle nor Minor had obtained a license for an ordinary anywhere in Fairfax County, but neither was prosecuted for improper retailing of liquor either. So the myth of a Minor's ordinary is based solely on the fact that a Captain of the Fairfax militia was assisting a regiment of the King's army with provisions, and a reaching, self-important woman (Browne), who was literally "fresh off the boat," would presume to order about a Virginia gentleman in his own plantation home. Are we surprised in the least that Madam Browne's expectation for fowl was not met on that June day? [Council V, pp. 103, 179 and 330; LDCODB, Book C, p.88; infra, Chapter on Familial Relations; supra, Chapter on Inns and Taverns; NorNeck, E/396; contra, Browne, p. 312; see contra, Landmarks, p. 344; 1755 Fry & Jefferson map, @ Landmarks, verso p. 518].

About the same time that he obtained clear title to the Leesburg site in the fall of 1757, Nicholas Minor commissioned one of Lord Fairfax's surveyors, Loudoun's John Hough, to lay out sixty acres for the proposed town. Hough must have staked out the main streets by November of 1757, when Minor, representing "Inhabitants of George Town" (Leesburg), presented the county court with a petition asking that the Carolina and Shenandoah Roads be turned into King and Loudoun Streets, respectively. The two roads were duly ordered to be turned into the town site, and the new alternate routes were declared public roads in April of 1758. John Hough had been busy in the mean time, and his full, marked survey of the first seventy town lots was probably finished by the first of February in 1758, when Nicholas Minor started issuing deeds to subscribers. By the end of March in 1758, two dozen lots, fully one third of the town, had been snapped up. Not surprisingly, corner lots, lots facing Loudoun Street (Shenandoah Road), and a cluster of lots near the town spring on Lot #66, were the first to go. Loudoun County Surveyor George West does not appear to have been involved in laying out the new town initially, but Minor probably employed him to set off lots on twenty acres adjacent to the original numbered lots, paying him in part with a sweetheart deal on Lot #22, directly across Market Street from the Courthouse. Two other town lots, #13 on the corner of King and Loudoun, and #57 at the west end of Loudoun Street, were reserved for John Hough in consideration for his survey work. Lot #13 contained what was described as a "storehouse," one of two existing structures in the new town, and as a consequence Hough paid nearly triple the going rate for his lot. The other pre-existing structure in town seems to have been on Lot #59, which was purchased by James Hamilton for a premium price. The property, as previously suggested, was the 1730s site of John Awbrey's home, and James Hamilton would have had both eyes fixed on the approaching Loudoun Assembly elections when he purchased the house with a prestigious history. [LDCODB, Book A, pp. 74, 76 and 372, and Book E, p. 168; supra, Town Plan on p. 320].

Initially, most lots on Market Street sold for £2, while lots on Loudoun Street went for £4. After a first rush of sales in 1758, the pace of new purchasing slowed, but Minor had sold half of the seventy Leesburg town lots by September of 1759. At that point, sale prices for vacant lots doubled overnight and the pace of new lot sales slowed to a steady trickle. Nicholas Minor had sold 75% of Leesburg's lots by 1763, as the value of the unimproved ½-acre lots on Market Street tripled to £6 and the cost of a vacant lot on Loudoun Street reached £10. Minor gave three lots to members of his family in 1764, and sold two more, but then made no new sales for two years. In May of 1766, Minor conveyed lot #50 to a "Churchwarden" of the Leesburg Methodist meeting, and then sold the tract surrounding Leesburg, surveyed at 258½ acres, to John Patterson (a land agent for the Earl of Tankerville who was trading on his own account). Between 1766 and 1773, Nicholas Minor disposed of three more town lots, including the townhouse he had lived in, on Lot #1; by 1774 Leesburg's "Proprietor" held only a half dozen vacant town lots. John Patterson died, heavily in debt, and his creditors forced his brother and business partner, Fleming Patterson, to liquidate assets in 1775, with the property surrounding the town going to Pattersons' primary creditor, Alexandria merchant and retired sea captain Henry McCabe Senr.. [LDCODB, Book D, p. 279, Book E, p. 168, Book F, pp. 275 and 334, and Book L, p. 114; supra, Chapter on Surveys and Land].

Deeds that Minor originally issued for Leesburg town lots contained restrictive covenants calling for each purchaser:

> *"To build, erect and finish on said Lott one house of twenty feet long and sixteen feet wide and [roof] nine feet pitched ... a brick or stone chimney, within three years ... agreeable to the orders, rules and Directions of ... Directors of George Town [sic]."*

The three-year deadline for construction of an appropriate structure was not strictly adhered to, but restrictive covenants in the deeds were not toothless either. In Leesburg's first decade, nearly a dozen deeds lapsed when the construction covenants were not met, and Nicholas Minor resold the lots to new purchasers. The first lapsed deed involved Michael Leatherman, one of the earliest subscribers, who re-purchased his Lot #56 in May of 1761 shortly after his first deed lapsed. But perhaps the most significant lapsed deed was arranged for long before Leatherman's re-issuance. In March of 1758, months before the Assembly founded Leesburg or the Council had established the site of Loudoun's County Courthouse, Jacob Pfhaw (aka Jacob Faw) subscribed town Lot #27 for £4. Some serious manoeuvering must have taken place privately between Minor and Faw in the next several months, because on September 12th Faw's lot was one of two lots selected as the site of the first Courthouse-gaol complex, and Faw never exerted his ownership interest in the property. Almost immediately after Faw's original deed for Lot #27 lapsed in the spring of 1761, Nicholas Minor issued a deed for Lots #27 and #28, conveying the Courthouse lots to the other Justices of the Loudoun County Court. [LDCODB, Book A, pp. 60, 89 and 117, and Book B, pp. 149 and 326; supra, Chapter on the Courthouse].

The town "Directors" were first called upon to rule on the conformity of existing structures in 1761. In the fall of 1759, ordinary keeper Benjamin Edwards had purchased town Lot #2 (across Loudoun Street from his ordinary) from the estate of John Poultney. Structures Poultney and Edwards had built must have been inadequate under the covenants, because Edwards obtained a new deed directly from Minor, for the nominal sum of five shillings, three months after Poultney's original deed lapsed. The situation undoubtedly sparked the town Trustees to action, and new purchasers were promptly found for two previously subscribed, vacant, town Lots #17 and #54. Surprisingly, among those who lost their town lots through "lapsed" deeds were two Quakers who had been among the first purchasers: Israel Thompson, the first subscriber of a Leesburg lot (#3), and Mahlon Janney (Lot #16 modern site of the Loudoun Museum, which was resold to colonial silversmith Stephen Donaldson). Minor waited a respectful five years before re-selling both lots in 1763. Israel Thompson's lot must have been improved substantially, since Fauquier carpenter Minor Winn paid £40, the going rate for an improved town lot. Nicholas Minor extended a commensurate courtesy to Dumfries merchant Richard Graham who, for £8, purchased Lot #69 on Royal Street from Loudoun merchant John Westby in 1759. Six years later, Minor re-sold the unimproved lot to Craven Peyton for £7. Greater latitude was extended to Henry Boggess, scion of an old tidewater family and the original subscriber of town Lot #23.

Minor waited seven years before re-selling the lot on Market Street to Leesburg ordinary keeper John Herryford in 1765. And Jacob Faw continued to be mindful of the restrictive covenants on Leesburg lots - in 1763 he paid £2 for a re-issue of his original deed immediately before selling Lot #25 to John Reiger for £10. [LDCODB, Book A, pp. 66-105, 117, 238, 243, 308, 361 and 514, Book B, pp. 118 and 338, Book C, pp. 18, 90, 117, 246 and 567-574, and Book D, pp. 1, 454, 537 and 608; Landmarks, p. 388].

Once the owner of a town lot built any structure on his lot, he enjoyed the privilege of voting in the election of Burgesses, but the right to vote does not appear to have attracted additional residents to town. Town lots and their occupants were accorded special treatment in other respects. With few exceptions, residents of Leesburg were not called upon to work on the maintenance of the roads around the town. Town lots were also afforded status as special property. In November of 1762, a law providing for the maintenance of highways specified that surveyors of the roads through town (as opposed to any other road in the county) could "not take any earth from any of the lots within the limits of the ... town without the permission of the owners thereof." [see supra, Chapter on Loudoun's Burgesses; and Hening, VII/578].

It appears that, at most, a half dozen of the first buildings in Leesburg, including the Courthouse, were made of brick or stone. The resale prices of the various town lots provide vital clues. In 1762 William Dodd sold his ordinary on Lot #5 to Craven Peyton for the then-staggering sum of £200, and four years later the property was so improved that Craven was able to use the buildings on the property as security for perhaps £450 of an £800 mortgage loan. In 1765 John Moss Junr. sold the Moss family ordinary on Lot #21 to William Trammell for £200. In 1766 Jacob Faw paid Fairfax merchant Robert Adams £300 for the warehouses and stores on Lots #65 and #66. When Benjamin Edwards finally retired and sold his ordinary on Lot #15 on Loudoun Street in 1770, the value of the building probably accounted for over £350 of the sale price. The price of each of these properties was comparable only to the cost of brick construction. Brick churches and other brick public buildings that were constructed in Loudoun and Fairfax Counties during the 1750s and 1760s invariably cost between 5 and 7 shillings per square foot. During Leesburg's first decade, the high average price for a town lot, improved by a wooden structure passing muster under the covenants, was only £40. This is a strong suggestion that wooden construction in Leesburg cost, at most, 2 shillings per square foot, one-third the cost of brick construction. In other words, the first buildings that were erected on town Lots #5, #15, #21 and #66 could have been as large as 700 sq.ft. in brick or stone, or relatively massive wooden structures in excess of 2,000 sq.ft.. Regardless, these structures must have been the most impressive privately owned structures in Leesburg during its infancy, and in every likelihood were constructed of a combination of stone, brick and wood. [LDCODB, Book C, p. 248, Book D, p. 463, Book E, pp. 10, 204 and 220, and Book G, pp. 36 and 301; supra, Chapter on the Courthouse; Fairfax, pp. 40 and 69].

The new colonial town of Leesburg, just as other colonial and modern county seats, attracted tradesmen, merchants, yeomen farmers and land speculators alike. In anticipation of the steady stream of business brought to town by the monthly sessions of a county court, several inns and taverns were rapidly constructed - three of the first twenty purchasers of town lots were ordinary keepers. With the arrival of John Herryford in 1760, there were four ordinaries doing business in Leesburg. By 1765 there were at least seven taverns in and around Leesburg, and thereafter the number of competing ordinaries remained fairly steady. In the early years of the American Revolution, Leesburg still boasted of a half dozen ordinaries in the town. The predominant means of travel for colonials was horseback, and ordinary keepers were obliged to provide for the horses of their customers. Accordingly we find that most of the owners of the early Leesburg ordinaries, like Benjamin Edwards, William Dodd, John Herryford, the John Mosses, Craven Peyton and Thomas Sorrell, purchased and fenced in a few acres of meadowland on the edge of town where horses could be let out. A few ordinary keepers, like John Herryford and Richard Coombs on King Street and John Miller on Market, also had stables on their premises. And several merchants, like Joseph Janney, John Patterson and Jacob Faw, maintained stables along with their other businesses. [supra, Chapter on Inns and Taverns; generally, Cresswell; LDCODB, Book D, p. 575].

Town proprietor Nicholas Minor, whether from a desire to set an example for the purchasers of town lots, out of sheer necessity when his house was used for County Court sessions from

1758 to 1760, or probably for a combination of both reasons, constructed a commodious house on town Lot #1 (across Loudoun Street from the modern Loudoun Museum), where he resided during the 1760s cheek-to-jowl with his fellow County Justices James Hamilton, William West and Craven Peyton, and Loudoun's multi-faceted John Hough. [LDCODB, Book G, p. 196].

The restrictive covenants on town lots, an immediate demand for housing and work on Loudoun's public buildings all attracted a number of carpenters and joiners to Leesburg by 1760. The most prominent early Leesburg builder was Loudoun County Justice Aeneas Campbell, who erected the first brick Courthouse before turning his attention to the improvement of town Lots #19 and #20 in 1761. Fairfax County contractor Daniel French [3rd], who in 1767 would build the (surviving) Pohick Church for Truro parish, completed the first Leesburg jail for Loudoun late in 1759. Both Campbell and French probably employed Joseph West, an early Loudoun stonemason, in their public works projects. And John Moss Senr. probably hired John Trammell and William Trammell to hurry the completion of his ordinary in 1758. But the most successful early Leesburg carpenter or joiner was certainly Thomas Pritchard. Pritchard probably assisted in the construction of either Dodd's or Edwards' ordinary in 1758, and then the Adams storehouses in 1759. In 1760 he and his wife Rachel Pritchard sold their small farm below Goose Creek and began purchasing Leesburg town lots. Pritchard moved to Leesburg that winter, beginning a second career that would transform him into Leesburg's foremost resident contractor/developer. Between 1760 and 1767 Thomas Pritchard bought, improved, and then resold a half dozen Leesburg town lots. Pritchard's building credits included Jacob Shilling's blacksmith shop on Loudoun Street, Loudoun County Justice Anthony Russell's town house on Market Street, Dr. John Whitmire's home on one half of Lot #9, and Michael Korts' blacksmith shop across from the Courthouse on Market Street. Business was so good that in 1762 Pritchard became the first sub-divider of a town lot, contracting with James Vestal to improve half of Lot #9. Thomas Pritchard repaired the Leesburg gaol in 1766 and when the gaol burned down in 1767 the Loudoun Court hired him to build the permanent replacement. Before the onset of the American Revolution, Pritchard had built at least one of every ten buildings in Leesburg. Other carpenters followed Pritchard's example. Minor Winn Junr. purchased Lot #3 in 1763 and, with help from his apprentice William Phillips, promptly constructed a massive store and warehouse complex before selling the property to John Ashby of Fauquier County for £160 - at the time the highest price commanded by a structure of predominantly wooden construction. And when the clamor for Pritchard houses reached a peak in 1764, joiner Robert Popkins renewed James Vestal's work on the house on Lot #9 that surgeon Jacob Cautsman would eventually call his home and office. But not every colonial carpenter met with success in Leesburg. Philadelphia joiner William Faulk moved to Loudoun in 1764 and bought Lot #38 next to the Courthouse. His expenses apparently surpassed his progress and Faulk was forced to sell out, at a loss, four years later. [LDCODB, Book A, pp. 379 and 382, Book B, pp. 230, 266 and 335, Book C, pp. 93, 109, 143, 255, 454, 529 and 570, Book D, pp. 106, 294, 300, 463, 494 and 608, Book E, p. 220, Book F, p. 240, and Book G, pp. 204 and 312; also see LDCOCO, Book C, p. 289; supra, Chapter on the Gaol; infra, Chapter on Trades; and Radicalism, p. 64].

Carpenters generated a demand for nails from the smithys' forges, and horses required horseshoes and saddles. A number of blacksmiths and saddlers responded to the opportunity. Saddler Michael Stoker was one of Leesburg's first residents, but he moved to Maryland in 1760 and sold his prime location, across the street from the County Courthouse, to ordinary keeper John Herryford. Blacksmiths Jacob Janney, Stephen Emery, Daniel Davis (who sold his business to Jacob Shilling), and Daniel Miller all situated themselves on Loudoun Street, clustered around Dodd's ordinary on Lot #5. Thomas Pritchard, the builder, apparently developed a business relationship with Jacob Shilling, relying on him for a steady supply of nails and building materials. Jacob Faw set up a successful saddlers shop and stables on Lot #25, on the northwest corner at Market and Church Streets. Faw generated considerable profits, and he bought other town lots and several outlying farm tracts. In 1763 Faw sold his business on Lot #25 to John Reiger and retired to his farm. On King Street (the Carolina Road), John Cargill ran a smithy on town Lot #36 before ordinary keeper Richard Coombs bought the property. Coombs maintained a stables at his ordinary, and he hired saddler Martin Zehorne before 1766 to look after that end of the business.

John Meginnis, identified as a tailor, set up for business on Market Street in 1761, first on Lot #53 and then on Lot #54. That October Leesburg's first resident physician, Dr. John Urquhart moved to town, settling on Lot #49 on Cornwall Street. Dr. Whitmire joined Dr. Urquhart early in 1764, but he must have found the town still too small to support another physician, and Whitmire left Leesburg in 1765. In 1763 John Reiger began supplementing the income from his stables by operating a tannery, locating his tanning vats on the eastern bounds of town. The sights and smells of curing hides must have punctuated the frontier character of the infant town in the eyes of travellers as they entered Leesburg along the Shenandoah Road. With a supply of leather at hand, shoemakers Abraham Moore and Robert Hamilton set up shop in Leesburg in 1763 and 1764, on Lots #8 and #34, respectively. Hamilton won the shoemaking competition and opened an ordinary on the side, and Moore moved on to Frederick Maryland in 1769. By 1770, Hamilton had accumulated sufficient profits to enable the purchase of town Lot #1 where he resumed the ordinary business. Stephen Donaldson, Loudoun's first practicing silversmith, arrived in 1763 and, benefitting from Mahlon Janney's lapsed deed, bought Lot #16. Modern visitors to Leesburg can examine Donaldson's cabin on Loudoun Street, thanks to the efforts of the Loudoun Restoration and Preservation Society. A dozen men who bought Leesburg lots and identified themselves simply as a "farmer" or "yeoman," undoubtedly, were seeking a convenient place to market their goods in town when the County Court was in session. [LDCODB, Book D, p. 667].

Loudoun Quakers Israel Thompson, John Hough, Mahlon Janney and Joseph Janney were the first merchants to subscribe Leesburg town lots in 1758. German merchants and tradesmen with ties to Frederick, Maryland promptly joined them. Both dealt primarily with Philadelphia import houses, using the Carolina Road and Noland's, Clapham's and Payne's Potomac ferries, but their links to the Pennsylvania colony were as much familial as they were mercantile. Interested in claiming their fair share of the Loudoun trade, Scots merchants from Alexandria, Colchester and Dumfries promptly weighed in. The first, early in 1758, was John Westby, identified as a Loudoun merchant but probably acting on behalf of Dumfries tobacco traders, selecting Lots #67 and #69 on Royal Street next to the town branch. John Gladdin from Fairfax established himself on Lot #14 on Loudoun Street, where he continued in business into the 1770s. After the Council had designated Minor's land as the site for the Loudoun Courthouse in June of 1758, Fairfax Justice Robert Adams and his brother Andrew Adams, both identified as merchants, took up over an acre around the town spring on King Street. Robert Adams acquired the storehouse on Lot #13 at the intersection of King and Loudoun in 1759, and then bought Lot #65 in 1760. The Adams brothers maintained a dominant position in Leesburg until the fall of 1766 when they sold out to Jacob Faw, the former saddler, who appears to have grown weary of his comfortable retirement. In 1769 Faw sold off most of his town holdings to the Loudoun County mercantile combination of Hough & Janney, who had apparently developed a convenient working relationship with the Alexandria trading firm of Carlyle & Dalton.

Dumfries merchant Richard Graham purchased Westby's warehouses on Royal Street in 1759, but the tobacco trade was already in decline west of Goose Creek. Graham was a trader, not a builder, and he must have viewed improvement of town Lot #69 as a wasteful investment since he allowed his deed for the property to lapse. In November of 1759, Benjamin Grayson (the Fairfax, not the Loudoun, Justice) and Loudoun King's Attorney Hugh West formed a partnership and bought Lot #33 across King Street from the Courthouse. Grayson had substantial ties with the Colchester trading houses, while West lived amidst merchants in Alexandria, so their activities must have been wide-ranging. John Patterson, the land agent for Charles Bennett, Earl of Tankerville, arrived in Leesburg in the fall of 1761, purchased Michael Stoker's house on town Lot #11 on Loudoun Street and opened the Earl's land office. He had a silent partnership with his brother Fleming Patterson, who had travelled with him from England, and with Fleming acting as the "front" the Pattersons purchased several lots on west Market Street for their own account. Most of the early German town subscribers, notably Peter Creger, Andrew Link and Michael Stoker, sold their holdings to the late-coming tidewater merchants in 1761, extracting modest profits. [LDCODB, Book A, pp. 274, 369 and 374, and Book B, pp. 266 and 335].

It has been suggested that colonial towns "were breeding grounds for aristocrats ... [where the gentry] by more information, better polish and greater intercourse with strangers, insensibly acquired an ascendancy over the farmer." A parallel argument has already been advanced to explain the high proportion of frontier ordinary keepers who became Justices of the Loudoun County Court. While only one of every fifteen Virginia colonists could properly be considered to be a member of the gentry, a large proportion of leading colonists lived in Virginia's towns. Holding colonial Leesburg up as an example, the premise would be true if modified to incorporate the assertion that colonial Leesburg was both a strong magnet and a "breeding ground" for the gentry. In Leesburg's first decade at least two dozen of the most prominent local merchants, doctors, attorneys and magistrates acquired perhaps half of all the town lots, and most of these men eventually made Leesburg their home. [Radicalism, p. 31; supra, Chapter on the County Court, and Chapter on Inns and Taverns].

The Loudoun Record

September 8, 1757 - John Carlyle and his wife Sarah Carlyle transfer title to the 326 acre Leesburg ("George Town") tract to Nicholas Minor. Minor had been residing nearby for four or five years. LDCODB, Book A, p. 133.

November 9, 1757 - "The Petition of the Inhabitants of George Town [sic] praying that the Roads leading from Alexandria [to Winchester] ... and from Noland's Ferry [to the Carolinas] ... may be opened to go through the said Town. James Hamilton and John Moss Gent. [Justices], and Thomas Sorrell [are to] view the most convenient way ... and make Report to the Court." Book A, p. 52.

February 13, 1758 - Israel Thompson, a resident of the Gap at Short Hill, is the first purchaser of a Leesburg town lot, buying Lot #3 with frontage on both Loudoun and Royal Streets. LDCOBD, Book A, p. 66.

February 17, 1758 - After sending notices to the precincts west of his plantation, Nicholas Minor sells eleven more lots on his land at "George Town." Purchasers include County Justice John Moss Senr., tradesmen, and residents of both the Gap and the German settlement. Not surprisingly, they all select either a corner lot or a property adjacent to one of the in-town water sources, the spring head or the town branch of the Tuscarora. Blacksmith Stephen Emery and merchant Joseph Janney both pay a premium for one of the corner lots at the intersection of Loudoun and King Streets. LDCODB, Book A, pp. 60-182.

February of 1758 - Initial deeds for town lots in "George Town" all identify Nicholas Minor, James Hamilton, Anthony Russell, Josias Clapham, Aeneas Campbell, Thomas Sorrell and John Hough as the seven "Directors and

Managers of ... George Town [Leesburg]." LDCODB, Book A, pp. 60- et.seq.

March 14, 1758 - After obtaining subscriptions and issuing deeds for twenty lots in "George Town," Nicholas Minor records his deed to the 326 acre tract that contains 60 acres laid out for Leesburg. Minor purchased the tract from his cousin, Alexandria merchant John Carlyle. LDCODB, Book A, p. 133.

April 11, 1758 - "Ordered that Nicholas Minor, John Moss [Senr.] Gent. [Justices] and Ezekiel Hickman ... view the Road from George Town [sic] to the upper side of the Mouth of Goose Creek and make Report to the Court." This is a road from town to Thorpe's landing on the Potomac. Book A, p. 80.

April 12, 1758 - In response to a "Petition of the Inhabitants of George Town [ie., Leesburg] praying that the Roads leading from Alexandria to Winchester and from Noland's Ferry towards Carolina may be opened to go through said Town," Justices John Moss and James Hamilton, with new town Trustee Thomas Sorrell, "viewed the most convenient ways for the Roads to pass through the Town [finding] them convenient and good with proper clearing." The Court "Ordered that the same be established as public Roads." Book A, p. 92.

July 20, 1758 - Robert Adams, a Fairfax County merchant, buys Lot #66, on the corner of King and Royal Streets. The deed reserves a 10 foot public right-of-way to a spring head on the property, 128 feet south of Royal Street on the west side of the lot. Andrew Adams buys an unnumbered "bottom" lot south of Lot #66 facing King Street, which includes "part of the [Town] branch running through the marsh." The Town Plan clearly shows the location of the spring and the town branch. LDCODB, Book A, pp. 182-189; supra, The Plan at p. 320.

September 23, 1758 - Records of the Virginia Assembly, in session, reflect that: "A Petition of sundry Inhabitants of the County of Loudoun, praying that an Act may pass for establishing a Town on the land of Nicholas Minor ... agreeable to the Plan thereto annexed, was presented." The Petition was favored, and referred to a Committee for drafting of an Act. Assembly, (1758) p. 20.

October 9, 1758 - The Governor's Council transmits a message to the Assembly, indicating their agreement with passage of a Bill to establish the town at Leesburg (promoted as "George Town"), in Loudoun. Assembly, (1758) p. 42.

October 12, 1758 - The Governor transmits a message to the House of Burgesses, giving his assent to the Bill "for erecting a Town on the Lands of Nicholas Minor, in the County of Loudoun." Assembly, (1758) pp. 44-45 and 76.

May 8, 1759 - Thomas Owsley, Nicholas Osborn and Joshua Gore report a new Road "from Williams' Gap to the Town of Leesburgh ... by John Palmers and by Isaac Nichols' ... thence to the [Shenandoah] Road where Samuel Davis formerly lived ... thence to the Town ... Jacob Janney be appointed Overseer from said Nichols' to [the location of Davis' former house on] the [Shenandoah] Road that leads to Leesburgh." The founding of this new road is the origin of modern Rte. 7 west of Clark's Gap. Book A, p. 235.

November 10, 1760 - John Moss Senr. gives his ordinary, across Market Street from the County Courthouse on town Lot #21 at King and Market Streets, to his son John Moss Junr. LDCODB, Book B, p. 108.

August 11, 1761 - Samuel Smith, William Smith and Thomas Stump are appointed to lay out a new "Road [through Piedmont manor] from Thomas Stump's [Potomac] Landing [west of Dutchman's] to Leesburg." Book A, p. 483.

September 7, 1761 - A deed issued from Nicholas Minor for a lot in Leesburg identifies Philip Ludwell Lee, Thomson Mason, Francis Lightfoot Lee, Nicholas Minor, James Hamilton, Josias Clapham, Aeneas Campbell, John Hough and William West as nine of the "directors and Managers of said Leesburg for the time being." LDCODB, Book C, p. 96; DALD, (1761) p. 89.

November 26, 1761 - William West Junr. purchases Lot #36, at the corner of King and Cornwell, from blacksmith John Cargill and wife Catherine Cargill, who purchased the lot from Daniel Davis. LDCODB, Book C, p. 115.

October 14, 1762 - A deed identifies Philip Ludwell Lee, Thomson Mason, Francis Lightfoot Lee, Nicholas Minor, James Hamilton, Josias Clapham, Aeneas Campbell, John Hough, William West and Francis Hague as the ten "Directors of the said Leesburg for the time being." This is the first evidence that Francis Hague is acting as a town Trustee. LDCODB, Book C, p. 448.

May 12, 1763 - "Ordered that James Hamilton Gent., Jacob Janney, Robert Cavens and Israel Thompson ... first sworn before a Justice of this County do view the most convenient way for a Road from William Dodd's [house west of town] to Goose Creek through Leesburg and make Report of the Conveniency and Inconveniency that will attend the same." Book B, p. 153.

November 8, 1763 - A Grand Jury presents Leesburg resident "John Herryford, Overseer of the [Shenandoah] Road from Leesburg to Trenary's [above Clarks Gap] for not keeping the same in lawful repair." Book B, p. 262.

May 3, 1765 - Minor Winn and his wife Margaret Winn, of Fauquier, deed town lot #3 to John Ashby, a Fauquier County merchant, for £160. Book B, p. 619; LDCODB, Book D, p. 494.

June 10, 1765 - Aneas Campbell, Nicholas Minor, John Hough and John Moss, Gent., are appointed to view the route for a "Road from Williams' Gap to ... Leesburg." Book B, p. 626.

May 12, 1766 - William Mead Junr. is appointed as the Surveyor of the road along the Carolina Road, from Leesburg south to the "Siccolon," replacing Francis Elgin. Book C, p. 77.

May 12, 1766 - Christopher Perfect, (aka Kitt Perfect), pays Leven Powell a premium price (£100) for the house on town Lot #37, adjacent to the Courthouse. LDCODB, Book E, p. 84; see supra, Town Plan on p. 320.

August 12, 1766 - Nicholas Grimes is appointed as Surveyor of the Ox road "from Broadrun to the [Potomac Path] Road leading from Sugarland run to Leesburgh [sic]." Book C, p. 154.

Surrounded by abundant natural resources, colonial men in Loudoun County seldom had just one trade.

> *"[W]oods furnished timber and plank for the carpenters and coopers, and charcoal for the blacksmith ... cattle ... supplied skins for the tanners, curriers, and shoemakers ... sheep gave wool ... fields produced ... flax for the weavers and spinners ... orchards fruit for the distiller ... carpenters and sawyers built and kept in repair all the dwelling-houses, barns, stables, ploughs ... coopers made the hogsheads the tobacco was prized in and the tight casks to hold the cider and other liquors [and flour] ... tanners and curriers with the proper vats ... dressed the skins ... spinners, weavers and knitters made all the coarse cloths and stockings."*

Loudoun County merchants, carpenters, farmers and blacksmiths frequently had second careers as millers. Colonial laws encouraged ferry keepers to operate ordinaries. Ordinary keepers usually maintained a stable and pasturage, undertook service as a smithy and worked in leather. Surveyors invariably managed other business ventures, like a mill or an ordinary. Practically every colonist farmed, or at least tried to. Artisans aspired to the title of either "merchant" or "planter," but colonial tradesmen were valued for their skills. In the early years of the colony, tobacco farming was so profitable that the Assembly was forced to require that all gunsmiths, "naylers, brickmakers, carpenters, joyners, sawyers, and turners [sic - lathe operators] ... worke at theire trades and not ... plant tobacco or corne ... [provided] they have good payment ... for theire work [sic]." [Home, pp. 53-54; Chapter on Agriculture, supra @ p. 195; Hening, I/208].

The pattern of Loudoun's development was at variance from the Virginia tidewater in two essential ways. The piedmont, or western, social pattern, which prevailed west of Kitoctin Mountain, reflected a reliance on roads for trade and migration, and promoted the growth of small commercial hubs within inter-dependent communities. The economic inter-twining of piedmont farms and plantations led to increased opportunities for artisans and skilled tradesmen, as well as a heightened sense of community. Key crossroads and prime locations on Loudoun's main roads, like The Gap, Newgate, Sugarland, Waterford and West's ordinary, and later Leesburg, all attracted skilled tradesmen. It should be no surprise to anyone that George Vandiveere, Loudoun's first goldsmith, opened a shop at Newgate shortly after his arrival; Loudoun's first silversmith, Stephen Donaldson, made his home in Leesburg. The eastern plantation system is more familiar to most of us. Centered on the rivers and other major waterways, the prototype tidewater plantation featured a "complete society in miniature, containing within itself almost all the trades and professions necessary for a civilized life." These self-sufficient plantations were dominant east of Goose creek when Loudoun was formed, and stretched up the eastern slopes of Kitoctin Mountain by the end of the 1760s. [Home, p. 52].

Colonial society expected everyone to undertake a skilled trade or profession. Most children, and all orphans, were bound out to learn a trade. Apprenticeship contracts give an indication of the callings of various craftsmen in Loudoun County as well as the level of demand in Loudoun for skilled trades. Of the forty-some apprentices who were bound out in Loudoun between before 1767, we find: 8 carpenters; 7 cordwainers; 6 coopers; 4 joiners; 4 leather dressers or tanners; 4 blacksmiths; 3 weavers; a shoemaker; a tailor; a stone mason; a wheel wright; and a maltster. If the numbers alone are any indication, before 1767, there was a large demand in colonial Loudoun for men who built houses and furniture, and men who manufactured essentials like clothing, shoes, barrels and cloth. [Chapter on Apprentices, infra @ pp. 356-361; for definitions, see Glossary, infra @ pp. 539-543].

"Strolling persons," the idle and the disorderly were unwanted and actively prosecuted. Colonial Virginia had its own system of work permits: in order to obtain employment for more than two days, a tithable individual had to produce a certificate showing that he had paid all colony, county and parish taxes. It was unlawful for any housekeeper to "entertain, employ, or hire" a worker without the certificate. Householders and uncertified workers violating the law were both fined, with the fines going to the informer! Violations of the "work permit" law were decided by a single Justice, not in the county court, so we will never know how frequently the law was enforced. But at least one "strolling" colonial was prosecuted before the full Loudoun County Court. [Hening, VI/29-32; in re Absalom Mullenax, supra @ p. 181; generally, see Chapter on Tithables, infra].

By 1757, it was widely known that there was a strong demand in Virginia for "all sorts of tradesmen except weavers, for carpenters and blacksmiths earned 7 shillings, 6 pence a day, and other artisans received comparable wages." More experienced blacksmiths were known to have received as much as £11 for 25 days of work. Wheelwrights and carpenters were also highly valued, and in times of military stress were rewarded with salaries comparable to a colonel or major. Skilled tradesmen could obtain exceptional guarantees in exchange for relocating to Loudoun County. For example, in 1766, William Carr Lane had to promise Charles Davis, a Dumfries saddler, that he (Lane) would build a "dwelling house and sadlers shop ... near the said Lane's store." This was a prime location along the Mountain road, on two acres at Newgate, and Davis was also allowed his choice of 25 acres of farm land as an appropriate inducement to move his business to Loudoun. [Democracy, pp. 42 and 49; Hening, IV/201; LDCODB, Book E, pp. 274-275].

Numerous Virginia laws put a low value on refractory and runaway servants. Formulas that were used to determine the amount of labor that runaways owed to their masters, clearly, used below-market values. Even so, the labor of these men and women, the most recalcitrant of all colonial workers, was rated at 100 pence, or over 8 shillings, per month. While most servants were mere farm hands or helpers in the ordinaries, there is ample proof that apprentices and servants alike had plenty of opportunities for advancement, and after their time of service either moved south or west to take up cheap lands or stayed, acquired lands and slaves, and prospered. [Democracy, pp. 9 and 25; Chapter on Servants, infra @ pp. 367-369].

Virginia Assemblies did not hesitate to regulate colonial trade and monopoly professions, either for the promotion of public safety or, more usually, to advance the free flow of trade. Colonial doctors, attorneys, surveyors, millers, coopers, blacksmiths, and ferry and tavern keepers all had their charges and fees regulated at one time or another. [for example, see Hening, II/11].

The Assembly began regulating the colony's coopers as early as 1646. As a part of the 18th-century export trade laws, the

Assemblies of 1748 and 1762 imposed regulations controlling the size and finished capacity of barrels; even barrel stave sizes were codified. The 1762 Assembly instructed: "every cooper ... master or owner of every servant or slave who shall set up barrels ... [to] make the same with good strong well seasoned timber, tight and well hooped, with twelve hoops at least." All of the coopers were instructed to have their "name ... at length, stamped or branded upon every barrel" that they made. [Hening, I/330, VI/151 and VII/575; see Chapter on Economics, supra @ pp. 198-204].

In 1666, during the war with the Dutch, the "obstruction of trade and the nakedness of the country" led the Assembly to instruct every county in Virginia to "provide and sett up a loome and [hire a public] weaver," regardless of the number of "private" weavers resident in their county. It was asserted that, "if they would betake themselves to spinning," five women or teenagers could cloathe 30 persons. It has also been suggested that colonial:

> *"families must have spent most of their time working in the fields and a good share of the remainder of it [their time] in spinning and weaving to keep themselves clothed ... a family of four, with no servants, could turn out as much as thirty-nine yards of cloth and four pairs of stockings in a single year."*

If this is an accurate portrayal, it may explain the noted lack of demand for weavers in the 1750s. [Hening, II/238; Home, p. 86].

The exportation of Virginia hides was also regulated and taxed. Richard Abrill, who was active in western Loudoun by 1745, appears to have been the area's first notable resident fellmonger. Beginning in 1762, peddlers of skins were licensed directly by the Governor's Council. Following the defeat of the French and Indians, the 1765 Assembly determined "that the manufacturing of leather hath of late years very greatly increased in this colony, and become a considerable article of commerce." An exemption was carved out that allowed for the duty-free exportation of all hides and skins that had been "imported into this colony." Loudoun County merchants, astride Virginia's primary western trade routes, were ideally situated to take advantage of the abundance of pelts that were packed east from the Ohio and Great Lakes frontier. Several colonial tanneries were in evidence around Leesburg by 1767. [FXCODB, Book B, p. 283; Hening, VIII/142; Chapter on Leesburg, supra @ p. 334; Glossary].

Colonial Virginia had something of an unrequited love for exotic manufactures. As early as 1624, silk production was encouraged through promotion of the planting of mulberry trees. The concern was not with the ornamentation of colonial gardens. Silk worms eat mulberry leaves. In 1656, colonists were ordered to plant 10 mulberry trees on every 100 acres, and "George the Armenian" was offered 4,000 lbs. of tobacco (about £50) if he would "stay in the country to follow the trade of silk." An "Encouragement" in 1658 included an offer of about £125 for the first colonist to produce and export 100 lbs. of silk. Premiums for silk were offered again in the 1700s, as late as 1762, but the manufacture of silk never took hold in colonial Virginia. [Hening, I/126, I/420, I/425, I/469, I/487, I/521 and VII/566].

The domestic Virginia grape vine, still known by an Indian name, scuppernog, renders a large and sweet product, but is ill suited to the manufacture of fine wines. European root stocks were introduced by 1624, when all Virginia colonists were instructed to plant vines. The 1630 Assembly urged colonists "to yielde theire best assistance in setting and raysing [sic]" grape vines, but to no avail. In the 1600s, Virginia's colonists favored Spanish wines, brandy and Portuguese wines over French wines. The expense of imported wines caused concern for decades, with the Assembly repeatedly banning and then lifting their bans on wine. Virginia was so hard-pressed for a domestic vineyard or brewery that the 1652 Assembly attempted to issue exclusive licenses "to distill and brew in wooden vessels." The 1658 Assembly offered a premium of about £125 for the first colonist who would "make two tunne [500 gallons] of wine raised out of a vineyard made in this collonie." The production of hops was also promoted in 1658, but the premium was conditioned upon the exportation of 10 tons. [Hening, I/126, I/151, I/192, I/226, I/287, I/295, I/300, I/350, I/374, I/446, and I/469-470; and see "tun" defined in Glossary, infra @ p. 543].

The French War, with its attendant interruptions of trade, inspired the 1759 Assembly to another initiative for "improving the arts and manufactures." Their plan, offering a mere £20 bounty "for any one discovery or improvement," provided no real incentive for the cultivation of vines. The 1762 Assembly took more serious action, inaugurating a Virginia wine competition after noting that:

"It has been long lamented that this colony should

pay annually a considerable sum ... for foreign wines ... of mean quality ... at an extravagant price, when we have the greatest reason to believe our climate capable of producing as fine wines [sic] as any in the world, were the cultivation of the vineyard properly attended to ... We shall find the planter continue, without deviation, in the beaten track, until ... roused by some great and certain profit."

Thereafter, through 1770, any Virginian making 600 gallons of wine was eligible for the competition. The maker of "the best wine" would win the First prize of £500; Second prize was £100; both were considerable sums. The prize money was collected by subscriptions from prominent men of the colony. Among the promoters were Gov. Fauquier, Landon Carter, Robert Carter, William Ellzey, Henry Lee, Richard Henry Lee, James Mercer, John Tayloe, George Washington and George Wythe. [Hening, VII/288 and VII/563; Chapter on Ordinaries, supra, @ p. 291].

Virginia's general obsession with the procurement of quality beer and wine was unending. In 1769, Frenchman Andrew Estave was awarded £450 to establish a vineyard "convenient to Williamsburg," on the condition that Estave train apprentices and produce 600 gallons of "good and mercantable" wine, annually, before 1775. Numerous accounts list "still worms" among the assets of colonial estates, giving mute evidence of the widespread production of fruit brandies in Loudoun County. Loudoun had at least three dedicated resident maltsters before 1767; Thomas John, William Mead and Jacob Janney must have kept busy filling orders from the numerous local ordinaries. They were followed by Septimus Levering who, with his son-in-law James Lawrason, operated a "malt house, brewery and still" across Market Street from the Leesburg Courthouse. [Hening, VIII/364; LDCOWIL, Book B, p. 395; The Record, infra @ pp. 350 and 361].

Mining operations played a key role in the settlement of the eastern reaches of colonial Loudoun. Colonial law and the Proprietor of the Northern Neck encouraged the development of mineral deposits. By 1729, Robert Carter's family had cleared the original Ox road, opening up the area known as the Frying Pan, in hopes that deposits would justify a copper mine there. The Carter's ore did not "pan out," but other adventuresome capitalists like John Lewis and John Colvill followed, establishing mining operations on the western branches of Difficult Run. Colvill's mill and Lewis' mine, south of Seneca falls, were in full swing by 1731. [Hening, VI/137; Grants, Book I, folio 124; Grants, generally].

Other colonials sought mineral wealth in the Loudoun soil. John Ballendine formed partnerships with the Ewells, Peytons, Tayloes and Thorntons, and had established a forge and grist mill at the falls on the Occoquan by 1755. The "Occoquan works" were said to include an iron furnace, forges, two saw mills and a bolting mill in 1759. Only a few years later, in the mid-1760s, James Ingles, John Linton and Benjamin Sebastian formed a partnership for mining "copper ... or some other mine or mineral ... on the lower side of Broad Run." Ballendine and a new partner, John Semple from Maryland, in search of iron ore and lime to feed their furnaces, bought up large tracts above Great Falls on the Potomac and on the north side of Kitoctin Mountain in Loudoun. Semple eventually took over the Occoquan works and the mining operations. When Semple abandoned the Loudoun mines, he sold out to Josias Clapham. Clapham set up forges and a gun factory north of Leesburg, on what is today known as Furnace Mountain, during the Revolution. John Ballendine turned his attention to the improvement of navigation on the Potomac and James rivers. The American Revolution would find Ballendine near Richmond on the James river, operating Virginia's largest forges with new partners. [Grants, Book E, folio 40; Landmarks, p. 428; LDCODB, Book E, pp. 15 and 207; The Record, infra @ p. 350].

The Assembly initiated the regulation of Virginia's physicians and apothecaries in 1645, in response to unscrupulous practices that were being foisted upon the sick and ailing in the aftermath of an Indian massacre. Doctors were instructed to provide treatment to all colonists regardless of their ability to pay, with penalties imposed on any doctor refusing to treat the sick. County courts were given the authority to regulate the charges that doctors were entitled to, and anyone who provided medicines of any kind could be required to declare, on oath, the true value of the drugs being administered. [Hening, I/316 and I/450].

As the Virginia colony matured, the reliability and professionalism of the resident medical community apparently grew to match. In the half-century before the Revolution, except for two years when the 1736 Assembly imposed an experimental schedule of prices for medical care, the practice of medicine went largely unregulated. Of greater concern, according to the 1748 Assembly, were the "many negroes, under pretence of practising physic, [who] have prepared and exhibited [applied] poisonous medicines, by which many persons have been murdered, and others have languished under long and tedious indispositions." The Assembly imposed the death penalty, with certain narrow exceptions, on any slave who prepared or administered any medicine unless expressly ordered to do so by their master. Sadly, this statute found an application in colonial Loudoun County. After the mysterious death of George Chelton in 1771, two slaves were brought to trial for "preparing poisonous medicines." [Hening, IV/509-510 and VI/105; LDCOCO, Book E, p. 211].

At the time of Loudoun County's formation in 1757, and throughout the French War, doctors, unlike millers or ferrymen, were required to muster alongside their neighbors in the county militia. The 1766 Assembly finally exempted "all persons bred to, and actually practicing physic or surgery ... from appearing or mustering at the private or general [militia] musters of their respective counties." Thereafter, doctors could be called out with the militia only in the event of invasion or insurrection. In lieu of mustering, physicians were required to "provide compleat sets of arms ... for the use of the[ir] county." [Hening, VIII/242].

Dr. John Urquhart became Leesburg's first resident physician when settled in the town in the spring of 1761. By 1764, there were at least three other doctors around Loudoun County and one, John Whitmire, had moved to Leesburg as well. But doctors Samuel Creswell and John Whitmire apparently removed from Loudoun in 1765, and Dr. James Broadbelt died in 1766. The turn of events apparently left Leesburg's "ancient and infirm" Dr. Urquhart as the only physician in the entire county, and when he died the following year Loudoun was without a resident physician. Doctor Jacob Cautsman, a physician in Frederick, Maryland, moved to Leesburg early in 1769, and purchased a house on Loudoun Street the following year, where he established what would become a lucrative practice. [LDCOCO, Book C, p. 263; LDCODB, Book B, p. 266, and Book G, p. 101].

The reader is directed to the several other chapters for studies of the most prominent colonial professions, like lawyering, farming, milling, surveying, operating a ferry and keeping an ordinary. [for example, Chapter on Mills, supra @ pp. 213-232].

July 2, 1757 - Jacob Janney is identified as a blacksmith. LDCODB, Book A, p. 28; and, Order Book A, p. 25.

July 19, 1757 - John Ariss is a "joyner." LDCODB, Book A, p. 3.

September 13, 1757 - William Ramsay is a merchant. Book A, p. 11.

September 13, 1757 - George Norman is a cordwainer. Book A, p. 17.

September 13, 1757 - Samuel Mead is a tanner. Book A, p. 15.

February 17, 1758 - Jacob Pfhow, aka Jacob Faw, is a "saddler"; and, Joseph Janney is a merchant. LDCODB, Book A, pp. 89 and 94.

February 17, 1758 - "Stephen Emrey of Loudoun County, Blacksmith ..." DALD, (1757) p.18; Order Book B, p. 41; LDCODB, Book D, p. 401.

May 1, 1758 - Peter McKean is a schoolmaster living on the upper section of the Mountain Road near John Garrett's lands. McKean leased a farm from Mahlon Janney, a well-known Quaker, so he probably conducted the Quaker meeting school that had been founded in that area. LDCODB, Book A, p. 196.

May 9, 1758 - Andrew Cochran, Esqr., and Company are merchants in Glasgow. Book A, p. 101.

July 20, 1758 - Andrew Adams and Robert Adams are merchants from Fairfax County, who set up for business at the corner of King and Loudoun Streets in Leesburg. LDCODB, Book A, pp. 182-189.

August 8, 1758 - James Shreves agrees to bind himself as an apprentice to Daniel Davis, a blacksmith, for three years. The terms of the agreement permit Shreves to make his own tools during the apprenticeship. Davis keeps his smith's shop on King Street, on Lot #36, in Leesburg. DALD, p. 19; supra, Chapter on Sheriffs and the Gaol and Chapter on Leesburg.

September 13, 1758 - Aneas Campbell is identified as a carpenter. Book A, p. 166.

November of 1758 - On William West's 1758 tithable list, one William Allen is identified as a carpenter. He is also identified as a carpenter on James Hamilton's 1762 ["List No. 2"] and Levin Powell's 1765 list. LDTX/1, pp. 4, 17 and 32; and, see Property Tax Lists, 1757-1799, in undated MS series, at p. 1356.

March 11, 1759 - George Vandiveere is identified as a goldsmith, moving from Prince Georges County, Maryland. LDCODB, Book A, p. 363.

August 16, 1759 - Josias Clapham "of Fairfax," [sic - !] is identified as a merchant. Book A, p. 276.

March 11, 1760 - Michael Stoker, living in Leesburg, is identified on a deed as a "sadler." LDCODB, Book A, p. 374.

May 13, 1760 - The Rev. Charles Green, of Truro Parish and Fairfax, is referred to as "Clerk and M.D." Book A, p. 344.

May 14, 1760 - Leonard Johnston is a carpenter. Book A, p. 346.

August 14, 1760 - Thomas Stigh, merchant, is a plaintiff at Court. Book A, p. 398.

October 16, 1760 - William Hatcher is identified on a deed as a wheelwright. LDCODB, Book B, p. 44.

November of 1760 - On John McIlhaney's tithable list, one Joseph Jones is identified as a carpenter, distinguishing him from a farmer with the same name. LDTX/1, pp. 11 and 12; and see, Order Book B, p. 187.

January 16, 1761 - One John Champe [Senr. ?], a merchant, brings an action for debt against the Estate of John Anderson, merchant, and the Estate of James Power, in the General Court in Williamsburg. VaGaz./H, p. 4, col. 2.

June 16, 1761 - Thomas Pritchard, the first "Builder/Developer"s in Leesburg, is identified in deeds as a "House carpenter and joiner." LDCODB, Book C, p. 93 and Book D, p. 294; see supra, Chapter on Leesburg.

September 8, 1761 - In a deed, mill owner Joseph West identifies himself as a stonemason. LDCODB, Book B, p. 286.

October 13, 1761 - Jonas Potts the blacksmith sells 122 acres on a branch of the north fork of the Kittoctin to Jonas Potts the farmer. LDCODB, Book C, p. 27; see also, LDTX/1, p. 34.

November 12, 1761 - "Thomas Blincoe, Carpenter" is a defendant at Court. Book A, p. 543.

December 8, 1761 - John Cargill is identified as a blacksmith on various deeds. LDCODB, Book C, p. 112, and Book E, p. 197.

January 19, 1762 - Joseph Roberts is identified as a carpenter; James Steer is identified as a cooper. LDCODB, Book C, p. 138.

February 20, 1762 - Thomas Gregg [Junr.] is identified in deeds as a "joiner" and, alternately, as a wheelwright. LDCODB, Book C, p. 152, and Book D, pp. 40 and 353.

May 12, 1762 - Reference is made to one "Samuel Davis of [Loudoun] County, Labourer." Book A, p. 600.

June 14, 1762 - John Griffy is identified as a blacksmith coming from the Pennsylvania colony. LDCODB, Book C, p. 635.

July 14, 1762 - One of the three Benjamin Graysons is identified as a merchant. Book B, pp. 10 and 146.

July 15, 1762 - "John McCarty of Loudoun County, Taylor ..." Book B, p. 25.

August 12, 1762 - John Orr is a merchant. Book B, p. 41.

August 12, 1762 - Thomas Sligh is a merchant. Book B, p. 46.

October of 1762 - On the tithable list of Charles Tyler, Joseph Puller is identified as a weaver; and, on the list of John McIlhaney, one Joseph Jones is again identified as a carpenter and Joseph Burson is identified as a mason. LDTX/1, p. 22.

November of 1762 - On a tithable list, referred to as Loudoun County "List No. 2," compiled by James Hamilton; William Brooks is identified as a

"Schoolmaster." Property Tax Lists, 1757-1799, in undated MS series at p. 1356.

November 18, 1762 - Daniel Neal is identified in a deed as a carpenter. LDCODB, Book C, p. 413.

April 13, 1763 - John Moss Senr. is identified as a house carpenter, alternately as a "tite cooper." Book B, p. 109; FXCOCO, 1756 Book, p. 361.

April 15, 1763 - Peter Wagener, Gent., is Clerk of the Fairfax Court. Book B, pp. 120 and 507.

May 10, 1763 - Jesper Grant is referred to as the Overseer on the plantation of Col. Lee. Book B, p. 122.

May 10, 1763 - John Reiger, purchaser of Faw's lot in Leesburg, is identified as a tanner. Reiger also identifies himself as a shoemaker. He sets up tanning vats on the east side of Leesburg. Book B, p. 122; LDCODB, Book C, p. 574, and Book D, p. 667.

May 12, 1763 - Adam & Patterson are identified as "Merchants of Leesburg." Book B, p. 152.

August 7, 1763 - Robert Rutherford is identified as a merchant in Frederick County, Virginia. LDCODB, Book C, p.681.

September 13, 1763 - "John Hite, Gent.," a Justice from Frederick County, Virginia, is a plaintiff at the Loudoun County Court. Book B, p. 233.

September 14, 1763 - James Rogers gives his blacksmith's tools as security for a debt. LDCODB, Book D, p.1.

September 15, 1763 - Robert Dreghorn & Co. are Glasgow [Scotland] merchants. Book B, p. 244.

September 15, 1763 - Robert Loxham, a plaintiff at the Loudoun County Court, is a merchant. Book B, pp. 247 and 652.

September 15, 1763 - Richard Brooke, Gent., an absentee landlord, is a plaintiff at Court. Book B, p. 253; supra, Chapter on Lands, @ p. 261.

September 15, 1763 - Stephen Donaldson, a silversmith and future Justice of Loudoun, purchases Leesburg Lot # 16. LDCODB, Book D, p. 1.

November 5, 1763 - Stephen Gregg is identified in a deed as a stonemason. LDCODB, Book D, p. 43.

January 24, 1764 - John Frederick Whitmire, a doctor from Frederick Maryland, moves to Loudoun Street in Leesburg. LDCODB, Book D, p. 106.

March 15, 1764 - Jonas Potts is a blacksmith. Book B, p. 288.

April 10, 1764 - James Donaldson is the "Schoolmaster in Loudoun County." Book B, p. 322.

April 11, 1764 - John Keele [John Keene ?] is identified as a "joyner" [sic - joiner]. Book B, pp. 334, 425 and 649.

May 7, 1764 - Thomas John sells his plantation on the upper reaches of Limestone Run, calling himself a "Malster." John reserves the right to live in a "brick apartment" during his life, an annual supply of rye and firewood, and the right to continue his use of the "Malt and Brew houses [on the premises] with all utensils for malting and Brewing." LDCODB, Book D, pp. 178-180.

May 22, 1764 - In a deed, Jacob Janney identifies himself as a

"Malster." LDCODB, Book D, p. 211.

June 15, 1764 - William Ramsay, a plaintiff at the Loudoun County Court, is a merchant from Alexandria. Book B, p. 388.

June 15, 1764 - William Allason is a merchant. Book B, p. 390.

August 15, 1764 - Alexander Parker is a Doctor. Book B, p. 420.

August 16, 1764 - Matthias Gossell [a/k/a Mathias Gossett], a defendant at Court, is a potter. Book B, pp. 426 and 657.

September 13, 1764 - Robert Brent is a merchant. Book B, p. 448.

September 13, 1764 - Samuel Creswell is a Doctor. Book B, p. 448.

September 14, 1764 - "John Walker, [a] Shoemaker." Book B, p. 466.

September 14, 1764 - John Urquhart, who is well known as a "Loudoun Doctor of Phisick," mortgages his house built on town lot # 49 in Leesburg for £37. LDCODB, Book C, p. 21, and Book D, p. 426.

October 10, 1764 - James Butler Brodbelt is a Doctor in Loudoun. Book B, p. 487; Clerk's 1764 Fee Book, p. 73.

November of 1764 - John Bland is now a merchant in Loudoun County. Clerk's 1764 Fee Book, p. 74; and Book C, p. 58.

December 12, 1764 - Samuel Hanson and George Lee are "Merchants and Partners." Book B, p. 514.

April 10, 1765 - "George Johnson, Gent." [sic- George Johnston, an attorney living in Alexandria] is a plaintiff at the Loudoun County Court. Book B, p. 560.

April 19, 1765 - John Hale "mariner" appoints Thomas Awbrey with his power of attorney to collect his debts and monies owed him. DALD, (1765) p. 75; LDCODB, Book D, p. 457.

April 20, 1765 - Frederick Nicholas gives his blacksmith's tools as security for a debt. LDCODB, Book D, p. 453.

April 22, 1765 - Patrick McCarty is identified as a weaver in a mortgage of his business property. LDCODB, Book E, p. 83.

May 13, 1765 - Joseph Cadwallader is identified as a mason. LDCODB, Book D, p. 433.

May 16, 1765 - "William Crawfurd, Thomas Dunmoor & Company, Merchants in Great Britain [actually Glasgow] ..." Book B, pp. 599 and 628.

May 16, 1765 - Edward Trafford, Esqr., sues (the Reverend) John Andrews, Clerk, for a debt. Book B, p. 600.

June 10, 1765 - William Gale is a merchant. Book B, p. 617.

June 11, 1765 - William Lux is a merchant. Book B, p. 628.

June 12, 1765 - "John Urquhart, Doctor," a Leesburg resident, is a defendant at Court. Book B, p. 646.

June 13, 1765 - "The Right Honorable Thomas Lord Fairfax" is a plaintiff. Book B, p. 658.

June 13, 1765 - John Semple, the former partner of John Ballendine in the furnaces at the falls of the Occoquan, purchases land on the northeast end of Kitoctin Mountain along with "all the Iron Ore and ... also what limestone the said Semple may want ..." for his furnaces. LDCODB, Book D, p. 683.

August 13, 1765 - James Lane and William Carr Lane [as partners], are merchants. Book C, p. 12.

August 13, 1765 - Apparently before leaving Loudoun County and the Virginia colony for England, doctor Samuel Creswell sells his horse, trade credits, "books of Phisick [sic] ... also all the said Creswell's medicines" to James Lane and his business partner cousin William Carr Lane. LDCODB, Book D, p. 704.

September 12, 1765 - "Messrs. Adam and Campbell" are "Merchants in Leesburg." Book C, p. 55.

October 28, 1765 - Daniel James, identified as a blacksmith, mortgages his household and business property. LDCODB, Book E, p. 90.

November of 1765 - On Nicholas Minor's tithable list for 1765, Amos Davis is identified as a "waggoner" working at John Ballendine's quarter at the Seneca Falls; on John McIlhaney's list, one Thomas Phillips is also identified as a "waggoner"; and on the tithable list of William Carr Lane, Jeremiah Thomas is identified as a wagoner in the employ of John Carter Esqr. [of Sudley mill]. LDTX/1, pp. 28, 31 and 40; and, LDCODB, Book D, p. 566.

June 6, 1766 - Martin Zehorne, in a mortgage of his business property, is identified as a "saddler." LDCODB, Book E, p. 95; DALD, (1766) p. 12.

June 9, 1766 - John Evans, a blacksmith, is the father of Griffith Evans. Book C, p. 79; LDCODB, Book E, p. 48.

June 10, 1766 - "Messrs." John Patterson and Fleming Patterson, [the brothers, as partners], are identified as merchants. Book C, p. 98.

July 7, 1766 - William Fox is identified in a deed as a Loudoun County merchant. LDCODB, Book E, p. 102.

July 13, 1766 - Daniel Mitinger gives his cooper's tools as security for a debt. LDCODB, Book E, p. 286.

August 2, 1766 - James Boyd of Loudoun County is identified in a deed as a weaver. LDCODB, Book E, p. 174.

August 11, 1766 - John Gibson is identified in the sale of a slave as a merchant in Alexandria. LDCODB, Book E, p. 150.

August 15, 1766 - "Messrs. Hough & Janney" [partners] are merchant millers. Book C, p. 182.

October 17, 1766 - Alexander Henderson, of Colchester, is the resident agent for Glasgow Scotland merchants John Glassford and Archibald Henderson. LDCODB, Book E, p. 344.

November 11, 1766 - The itemization of the County Levy implies that Jacob Shilling is a blacksmith since he fashioned a pair of handcuffs for the Sheriff's use. Book C, p. 220.

November 12, 1766 - Charles Davis, who is from Dumfries in Prince William County and moving to the "Newgate" section of Loudoun, is identified on a lease as a "sadler." LDCODB, Book E, p. 274.

December 4, 1766 - Among the "Letters remaining in the Post Office at Alexandria" is one for "Dr. James Urquart [sic- Dr. John Urquhart], Leesburg." VaGaz./Ri, p. 2, col. 1.

Apprentices and Orphans Bound to Tradesmen

In colonial Virginia the practice of binding young children as apprentices to tradesmen, farmers and merchants took two distinct paths. The first course, the volitional indenture of children to merchants and other professionals, generally involved members of the families of planters and the more well-to-do, and served to cement business connections as well as provide useful business training for second and third sons. Occasionally, a free man, aspiring to advance himself, would voluntarily bind himself into apprenticeship in order to learn a trade. The other course taken, the court ordered bonding of poor, abused and orphaned infants as apprentices to farmers and tradesmen, ultimately proved to be just as valuable to the growing colony. This procedure culled the ranks of impoverished children dependent on the parish for maintenance, and insured the availability of essential artisans and skilled tradesmen. Orphan children were treated differently depending on their station in society, or more particularly the station of their parents. Orphans from wealthy families, bastard and mulatto children, and orphans from reduced circumstances were all distinguished and treated differently under the laws of colonial Virginia. Information regarding the latter group and the voluntary contracts of apprenticeship recorded in Loudoun County is presented in this chapter. Information on the various other types of orphans is presented in the Chapter on Infants and their Guardians and the Chapter on Base Born and Mulatto Children.

Apprentices were introduced into Virginia in 1619 when the City of London sent 100 boys and girls to the colony. There can be no doubt that the English practice of binding local children to tradesmen as apprentices was being followed in the colony in 1642-43, when the Burgesses passed an Act calling for a month imprisonment for anyone who bought from, sold to, or otherwise traded with another man's servant or apprentice without the consent of the master. The first Act of the Virginia Assembly which institutionalized apprenticeships unfortunately took the form of a legal kidnapping. In October of 1646, the Assembly required that two poor children "of eight or seaven [sic] years at the least ... from parents who by reason of their poverty are disabled to maintain and educate them," were to be selected and sent from each county to work in the public flax houses in James City. [ColVa, p. 69; Hening, I/274 and I/336-337].

In December of 1656, the Virginia Assembly codified the longstanding custom and provided that:

> *"... if [an orphan's] estate be so meane [sic] and inconsiderable that it will not reach to a free education ... that orphan [shall] be bound to some manuall trade till one and twenty yeares ... except some friends or relations be willing to keep them."*

Apprentices were fed and clothed by their masters, provided "accomodations fit and necessary," usually lived in their master's household and were generally treated well. The Virginia Assembly instructed "those that are bound apprentices to charge their masters if he [they] use them rigourously [sic] or neglect to teach them his trade." These practices were maintained and refined but not substantially altered by the Virginia Assembly throughout the century preceding the incorporation of Loudoun County. [Hening, I/416-417 and V/452].

In October of 1748 the laws of the Virginia colony were amended to the form that governed the county court rulings ordering the apprenticing of infants throughout Loudoun County's first decade, from 1757 to 1766. Every male child, by the direction of the county court or by the deed [ie., contract] of his father, could be bound as an apprentice "to some merchant, mariner, or other person ... until he shall attain the age of [21] ... and every female to some suitable trade or employment 'til her age of [18]." Apprentices were to be taught to read and write, "and at the expiration of his or her apprenticeship," receive the prevailing "freedom dues" that were paid to servants. The Assembly, citing "the evil consequences attending the neglect or inability of poor people to bring up their children in an honest and orderly course of life," gave vague criteria which enabled the county courts to order the episcopal churchwardens of a parish to bind designated poor children out as apprentices, just "as the law directs for poor orphan children." It may seem odd, by modern standards, but in colonial times a child was considered an "orphan" when his or her father passed away regardless of whether the mother was still living. It was not unusual for a child to be ordered bound out as an orphan apprentice despite the objections of the child's mother. The law also gave the county court authority to act whenever the court determined that a person or persons were "incapable of supporting and bringing up their child or children, in honest courses, or where it shall appear ... that ... they neglect to take due care of the education ... and their instruction in the principles of christianity." The Loudoun County court exercised its authority under this provision in August 1763 when the Watts family children apparently were abandoned by their parents. [Hening, V/452-453 and VI/29-33; see infra, The Record, p. 359].

Shortly before the creation of Loudoun County, in November of 1753, the Assembly enacted a provision whereby an indenture of apprenticeship binding anyone under age 21 in any "trade, art, mystery or occupation," when approved or consented to by any court of record in the colony, would be enforced and legally binding "as if such apprentice were of full age at the time of making the same [contract]." The practical result of this law, as indicated by the Record, was that all indentures involving minors were submitted for the scrutiny and approval of the Loudoun court so as to insure their enforceability. When the presumed master failed to submit the indenture for court approval, the Loudoun Court did not hesitate to void the apprenticeship and set the youth at liberty. In this way David Davis lost his servant Reuben Willard in June of 1758 and the following September Samuel Awbrey's contract with his servant John Parsons was voided. [Hening, VI/356 and VI/368-369; infra, The Record, pp. 357 and 360].

In 1753 the Burgesses also revised the Virginia law concerning servants, establishing £3, 10 shillings as the amount to be paid to every Virginia servant (except convicts) for freedom dues at the expiration of the contract period of servitude. However, since many apprenticeships were voluntary, the agreements often called for the master to provide the apprentice with tools and clothing, a linen wheel, a bed or a cow in addition to the compulsory freedom dues at the end of the apprenticeship. After 1753, the Virginia law governing apprenticeships was not revised again until the Assembly session of November of 1769. [Hening, VI/358-359 and VIII/374-377].

The reader will note that there are various types of information in the orphan orders of apprenticeship that are made available in the Record. Ages and the birthdates of infants are often set out. When a male infant is ordered apprenticed, one of the trades or professions of the master is usually identified. Some parents of apprentices are plainly identified in the Record. By cross-referencing the information presented in this chapter with the dates of death of individuals with the same last name as a given orphan, as given, infra, in the Chapter on Coroners, Deaths and Estates, the reader might determine some family relationships that are not plainly stated. As an example, various entries in the Record reveal that Patrick McKenzie died before October of 1766, shortly after he had lead the first Loudoun County jail-break. Lacking any other information on the McKenzie family, one can readily surmise that orphan John McKenzey, who was bound out as an apprentice in October of 1765, was probably Patrick's son. [see supra and infra, The Record, pp. 152, 361 and 512].

And, as an example of other possible extrapolations using the Record, one could assume, by inference, that John Parsons, upon his change of apprenticeship in September of 1758, was put to work by Aeneas Campbell in the construction of the first Loudoun County Courthouse, which was then underway at Campbell's direction. [supra, Chapter on The Courthouse; see infra, The Record, p. 357].

The format used by the County Clerk in recording most of the orphan orders is illustrated with this sample text:

> *"Ordered that the Church Wardens of Cameron Parish bind out James Buckley an Orphan of three years old last June to William Buckley according to Law ... to learn him the Trade of a Cordwainer."* [see infra, The Record, pp. 361].

The Loudoun Record

August 9, 1757 - John Fryer, "a poor Infant of sixteen years old the 2d day of March next," is bound out to John Ethell, a blacksmith. Book A, p. 6.

August 9, 1757 - William Fryer, "ten years old the 25th day of July Last past [1757]," is bound to Obed. Harris [sic- Obadiah Harris], a house carpenter, who is to "cause him to be taught to Read and Write." Book A, p. 7.

September 13, 1757 - Joseph Green, 6 years old [on June 6, 1757], is bound to Samuel Mobley, to learn the trade of a cordwainer. Book A, p. 17.

December 14, 1757 - John Caruthers, an orphan, is bound to William Brown, to learn the trade of a leather dresser. Book A, p. 57.

April 11, 1758 - Catharine Mecabe, an orphan, is bound to Mary Janey [sic- Mary Janney]. Book A, p. 85.

June 13, 1758 - Diana Sampleton, orphan "four Years of age last March," is bound to William Hatcher. Book A, p. 111.

June 15, 1758 - "David Davis exhibited an Account against his Servant Reuben Willard for Runaway time ... [the Court finds that Willard] became a Servant by Contract in this Colony ... is an Infant ... [and the] Contract is Invalid ... Reuben be discharged from further Service." Book A, p. 124.

July 11, 1758 - "An Indenture of Apprenticeship between Jacob Beeson ... [to] Owen Roberts ... [to learn the trade of a tanner and currier] is Acknowledged by the Parties thereto and ... Recorded." Book A, p. 131; and see, LDCODB, Book A, p. 167.

August 8, 1758 - "An Indenture of Apprenticeship between James Shrives [to] Daniel Davis [to learn the 'Art, trade and mistery' of a blacksmith] was ... executed and ... recorded." Book A, p. 136; LDCODB, Book A, p. 199.

September 13, 1758 - On the "Complaint of Catherine Parsons against Samuel Awbrey for ill usage of her son John Parsons an Orphan ... [the court orders that] John Parsons be discharged from ... his former Master the Indenture ... being void in Law." Book A, p. 143.

September 13, 1758 - John Parsons, age 14 "the 25th of September Instant," is bound out to Aneas Campbell, "to learn the Trade of a carpenter." Book A, p. 143.

September 13, 1758 - Mary Orton, an orphan, is bound to James Hamilton, Gent. Book A, p. 166.

November 14, 1758 - "An Indenture of Apprenticeship between Thomas Gore ... and David Hudson ... acknowledged by the Parties thereto and ... Certified." Book A, p. 178.

December 12, 1758 - Elizabeth Jenkins, orphan, bound to Francis Wilks, who agrees to pay her "a good linen wheell, a cow and a calf" at the expiration of her service. Book A, p. 183.

December 12, 1758 - William Crawford, a 15 year old orphan, is bound to shoemaker Samuel Combs. Book A, p. 188.

February 13, 1759 - John Muschet is bound to William Robinson, a shoemaker. Book A, p. 190.

February 14, 1759 - Amey Bare, and orphan, is bound to John Morris. Book A, p. 192.

February 14, 1759 - William Orton is bound to Josias Clapham, Gent., a carpenter. Book A, p. 194.

May 9, 1759 - Mary Noland, an orphan age nine, is bound to Elizabeth Davis. Book A, p. 238.

June 12, 1759 - An Indenture of Apprenticeship between "Joseph Yates ... and [to] George Crawford ... [is] acknowledged by the Parties and ... Certified [by the Loudoun County Court]." Book A, p. 249.

August 14, 1759 - William Bolton is bound to Andrew Adams as an apprentice "to learn ... the Art and Mystery of a Merchant." Book A, p. 265.

August 14, 1759 - Sarah Preston is bound to Samuel Combs. Book A, p. 265.

August 14, 1759 - Aaron Redmond is bound to Peter Wilson, to learn the trade of a shoemaker. Book A, p. 265.

August 15, 1759 - Daniel Preston, a four (4) year old orphan [born on December 12, 1754], is bound to Thomas Watson, to learn the trade of a carpenter. Book A, p. 271.

September 13, 1759 - James Carr Barrett, an orphan, is bound to James Lane, Gent., to learn the trade of a house carpenter. Book A, p. 295.

November 13, 1759 - Jonathan Hall, orphan age 7, bound to William Smith, cooper. p.301.

March 11, 1760 - Mary Roberts, an orphan, is bound to William Smith. Book A, p. 324.

May 14, 1760 - Margaret Roberts, an orphan, is bound to William Smith. Book A, p. 346.

May 14, 1760 - John Roberts, orphan age 10, is bound to Philip Noland, to be taught the trade of a house carpenter. Book A, p. 347.

May 14, 1760 - Henry George Green, age 2 "on the 16th day of January last past [1760]," is bound to William Noding, who is to teach him the trade of a cooper. Book A, p. 349.

November 11, 1760 - William Fleming, an orphan, is bound to James Whaley, cordwainer. Book A, p. 403.

June 9, 1761 - Henry Franks, an orphan 10 years and 3 months old, is bound out to Thomas Stump, to learn "the Trade of a Cord Winder [sic - cordwainer]." Book A, p. 453.

August 11, 1761 - Jessee McNeal, and orphan, is bound to Thomas Lewelling, "who is to learn him the Trade of a Cordwainer." Book A, p. 484.

September 8, 1761 - John Winn Hays, an orphan 3 years old "on of May last," is bound out to John Hall. Book A, p. 494.

March 10, 1762 - "Nicholas Minor Gent. acknowledged a Counterpart of an Indenture of Apprenticeship for his Son Spence Minor to Robert Adam, Gent.." Book A, p. 563.

March 10, 1762 - John Rawdery, an orphan, is bound to John Trammell, "who is to learn him the Trade of a Cooper." Book A, p. 567.

May 11, 1762 - James Binks, orphan, 9 years old "February last past," and James Prim, aged 5 "in December last past [1761]," are bound to Kitchen Prim, who is "to learn them the Trade of a House Carpenter." Book A, p. 584.

May 12, 1762 - Leonard Dyall, an orphan, is bound to John McGinnis, "till he Arrives to the Age of twenty one Years, who is to learn him the Trade of a Taylor." Book A, p. 594.

June 9, 1762 - Winifred English, "an Orphan eight Years old next July [1762]," is bound to Robert Popkins "according to Law." Book A, p. 633.

April 12, 1763 - James Freeland, an orphan "(of ten years old)," is bound to Thomas Gore, to be taught the trade of a skin dresser. Book B, p. 88.

April 13, 1763 - Thomas Windsor, "of nine Years old in February last past," is bound to Thomas Connell to learn "the Trade of a House Carpenter." Book B, pp. 105-106.

April 13, 1763 - James McCoy, an orphan six years old, is bound to William Fielder, to learn "the Trade of a Stone Mason." Book B, p. 108.

April 13, 1763 - Jesse Hall is ordered to be bound to John Moss Senr. "who is to learn him the Trade of a House Carpenter." Book B, p. 109.

May 10, 1763 - Thomas Mashel is bound to John O'Cain to be taught the trade of a weaver. Book B, p. 121.

May 10, 1763 - Rebecca Craig, "she being Eleven Years of Age," is bound to James Henderson. Book B, p. 124.

June 14, 1763 - "Robert Sinclair ... agreed to serve William Morland two Years after Christmas ... [who] agrees to Learn [ie., teach Sinclair] the Trade of a House Carpenter and Joyner and to give him [meaning Sinclair] £6 at the expiration of his Service." Book B, p. 159.

August 9, 1763 - Frances Rucard, an orphan, is ordered to be bound to William Hoge, "she being six years old in September next." Book B, p. 195.

August 9, 1763 - "James Watts of two years old and Elizabeth Watts of five years old (children of --- Watts who is run away and left them behind in a distressed manner) ..." are bound to "Jacob Schachon who is to learn [James] in the Trade of a Weaver." Book B, p. 196.

August 11, 1763 - An "Indenture of Apprenticeship from John Coats, Labourer, to Christopher Perfect, was with the Consent and Approbation of the Court executed ... and is Ordered to be Recorded." The Indenture included a statement that Perfect "paid Robert Watson the sum of £5 current money on account of aforesaid servant [Coats, formerly] being indented to Robert Watson." Book B, p. 207; and, LDCODB, Book C, p. 687.

September 13, 1763 - It was noted that "Samuel Coombs released William Crawford [from] his Indenture of Apprenticeship ... William agreed to serve John Reiger one year and three months from the date hereof ... Reiger on his part agreed to learn the said William the Trade of a Cordwainer and to pay him his Freedom dues." Book B, p. 232.

February 15, 1764 - "Richard Pascals an Orphan of seventeen years of Age the ninth day of March next [is bound] to James Hamilton, Gent., who is to learn him the Trade of a Cordwainer or [leather] Taylor." Book B, p. 274.

March 10, 1764 - The Will of Andrew Redmond directs that his "sons John Redmond and Andrew Redmond are to be bound to [son-in-law] Edmund Phillips [the shoemaker] until they are twenty-one years of age." WALD, 1757-1771 Book, p. 28; LDCOWIL, Book A, pp. 111-112.

March 13, 1764 - Cruise Mercer, "three Years old in September last," is bound to Richard Mercer to learn "the Trade of a Cooper." Book B, p. 279.

March 13, 1764 - Rebecca Oldridge, "six Years old," is bound out to John Moss Junr., according to Law. Book B, p. 280.

March 14, 1764 - Moren Woodhouse, "of fifteen months old, [is bound out] to Minor Winn." Book B, p. 281.

March 14, 1764 - James Aldridge, "of nine Years old," is bound out to Alexander Wedner, to learn the "Trade of a Wheel Wright." Book B, p. 285.

March 15, 1764 - Charles Secres, an orphan fifteen years old, is bound to Joseph Janney to learn the trade of a cooper. Book B, p. 287.

May 8, 1764 - John Patterson, "of sixteen Years old the 19th day of this Instant [May, 1764]," and Joseph Patterson, "eight years old the 8th day of September next [1764]," are bound out to William Patterson, "who is to learn them the Trade of a Black Smith." Book B, p. 353.

June 13, 1764 - William Phillips of Loudoun County "put himself of his own free will apprentice to Minor Winn Junr. of Loudoun [sic] to learn his art and trade [of carpentry] ... for four years and six months ... [and when free he is] to have 1 ax, 1 adze, 1 hand saw, 2 chisels and 1 suit of clothes worth £3, ten shillings current money." Recorded June 14, 1764. Book B, p. 382; LDCODB, Book D, pp. 233-234; see infra, Glossary.

June 14, 1764 - An "Indenture of Apprenticeship between David Edwards ... [to joiner] Robert Popkins ... acknowledged ... ordered to be recorded." The voluntary indenture is for three years and four months, and calls for "£4 worth of joiners tools properly sorted so that they will be fitting for him to work at his trade." Book B, p. 373; LDCODB, Book D, p. 232.

June 14, 1764 - Mary Conner, "an orphan of Eleven Years old the 26th day of December last [1763]," is bound to William Mead. Book B, p. 373.

September 14, 1764 - Rachel McNab is bound out to Benjamin Edwards. Book B, p. 467.

October 9, 1764 - "Ordered ... the Church Wardens of Cameron Parish bind out James Buckley an Orphan of three years old last June to William Buckley ... who is to learn him the Trade of a Cordwainer." Book B, p. 473.

October 9, 1764 - "Ordered ... Edward Garret take into his Possession Tobias Allan an Orphan Child formerly kept by William Allan and that he produce him here at the next Court." Book B, p. 473.

November 15, 1764 - Jeremiah Fryer, "of fourteen Years old the first of September last," is bound to Thomas Watson, "who is to learn him the Trade of a Carpenter." Book B, p. 506.

March 12, 1765 - Reuben Vines, "of eight Years old the 1st Day of February last," is bound to William Hoge, who is identified as a cordwainer. Book B, p. 523.

March 12, 1765 - "Job Jenkins (son of Harness Jenkins dec'd.) a poor Orphan of twelve Years old in February last, [is bound] to John Morris who is to learn him the Trade of a Tight Cooper." Book B, p. 527.

April 10, 1765 - Valentine Holifield, "a poor orphan of nine Years old [is bound] to Robert Sanford who is to learn him the Trade of a Weaver." Book B, p. 551.

May 13, 1765 - Catharine McKay "of Eleven Years old in August last past [is to be bound] to Margaret Jenkins according to Law." Book B, p. 572.

May 13, 1765 - "Ordered that Joseph Acley by Consent ... be put [apprenticed] to Hezekiah Boone who undertakes ... to perform all the Covenants that Henry Oxley was bound to do by an Indenture of Apprenticeship ... Oxley agreeing [to release his interest]." Book B, p. 574.

June 10, 1765 - Sarah Finass, "four years old the twenty Second Day of December next [is bound] to John Cavins according to Law." Book B, p. 622.

August 12, 1765 - Stephen Cox, age 12 on September 12, 1765, is ordered to be bound to Samuel Smith, "who is to learn him the Trade of a Cord Wainer." Book C, p. 5.

October 15, 1765 - John Talbut, 15 years old last December, is bound to Jason Morlan, to learn the Trade of a Joyner. Book C, p. 63.

October 16, 1765 - John McKenzey, age 11, is bound as an apprentice to John Reiger [of Leesburg], a tanner and cordwainer. Book C, p. 68.

May 12, 1766 - Jane Wells, age 12 last September, is bound to Samuel Arwin. Book C, p. 83.

May 12, 1766 - Isaac Eaton, 16 years 6 months old, is bound to Joshua Jones "who is to learn him the Trade of a Tanner." Book C, p. 83.

June 11, 1766 - James Aldridge, a poor orphan, 11 years old last February, is bound to William Mead to learn the trade of a "Malster" [see infra, Glossary]. Book C, pp. 109-110.

August 11, 1766 - Zachariah Jenkins, 10 years old "last April," and Elizabeth Barrett, 6 years old "next October," are bound to John Goram, a shoemaker. Book C, p. 148.

August 13, 1766 - Nicolle Bevito, a 9 year old orphan, is bound to John Miller. Book C, p. 155.

August 14, 1766 - It is "Ordered that the Churchwardens of Cameron Parish bind out according to Law John Phillips [a] thirteen Years old to William Dickson who is to learn him the Trade of a Blacksmith ---." Book C, p. 175.

September 10, 1766 - "William Cummins & Bridget Cummins his wife" bring a "Petition to remove an Apprentice." The Court sets aside "a Former Order ... binding Isaac Eaton to Joshua Jones as an Apprentice" and Orders Eaton brought in to the next Court. Cummins had been found disabled and was granted an exemption from tithable taxes in 1764. Book C, p. 194.

October 14, 1766 - William Keith is bound to Abraham Warfurd, a blacksmith. Book C, p. 211.

Monday, November 10, 1766 - Stacey Lanham, 13 years old "next January," Jane Lanham, 8 years old "next April," and Henry Lanham, 11 years old "next August," orphans, are bound to John Piles, "who agrees to teach the said Henry the Coopers Trade." Book C, p. 219.

December 8, 1766 - John Stephens, 15 year old orphan, [probably a son of deceased farmer Joseph Stephens; see infra, Chapter on Coroners and Deaths], is bound out to Joseph Parker, "who is to learn him the Trade of a Blacksmith." Book C, p. 231.

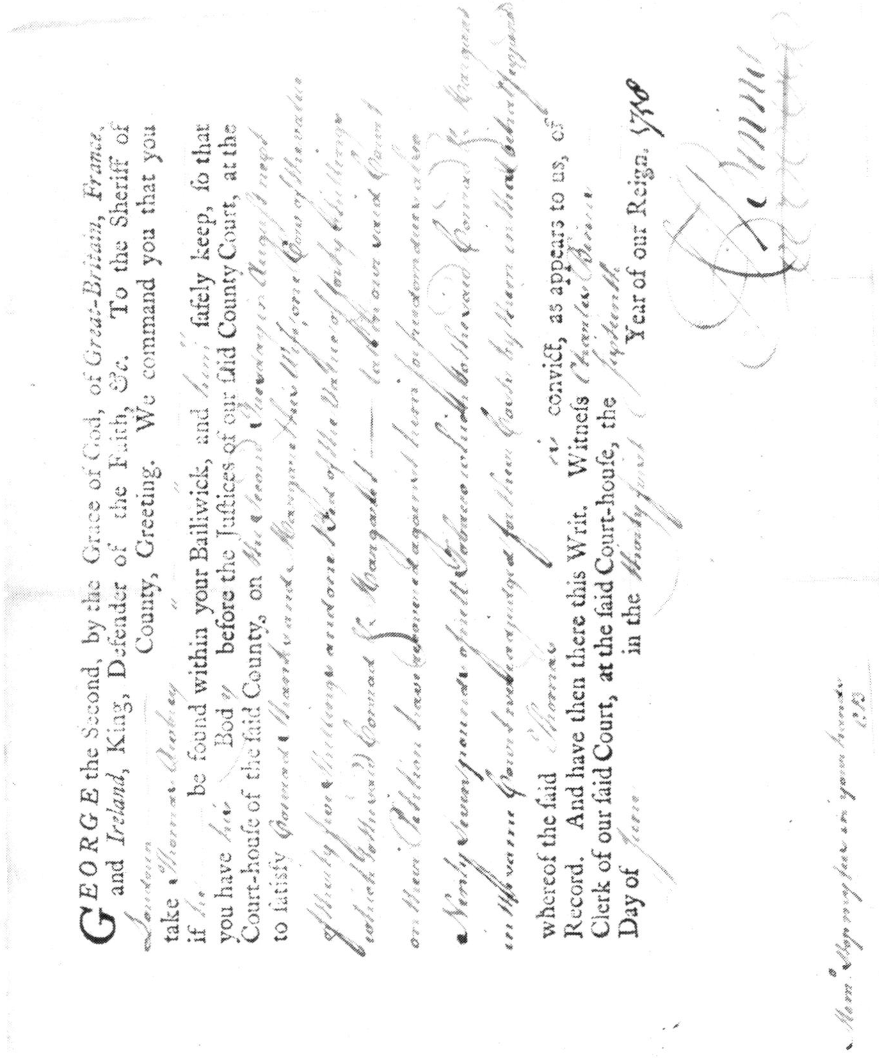

GEORGE the Second, by the Grace of God, of Great-Britain, France, and Ireland, King, Defender of the Faith, &c. To the Sheriff of Loudoun County, Greeting. We command you that you take Thomas Awbrey if he be found within your Bailiwick, and him safely keep, so that you have his Body before the Justices of our said County Court, at the Court-house of the said County, on [illegible] to satisfy [illegible] whereof the said [illegible] convict, as appears to us, of Record. And have then there this Writ. Witness [illegible] Clerk of our said Court, at the said Court-house, the [illegible] Day of June in the [illegible] Year of our Reign. 1758

This Writ of Attachment, issued on June 31, 1758 against Thomas Awbrey, was served by Sheriff Aeneas Campbell, who noted that the attachment was "Executed & Satisfied." The Writ recites the judgment awarded to Conrad Shanks and his wife Margaret Shanks in May of 1758 for recovery of their unpaid servant's freedom dues. Their indenture stipulated that they be paid "one cow ... and one bed." [HDC; infra, The Record, p. 372]

Servants and Indentures of Servitude

During the 1757-1766 decade, servants in Loudoun County and elsewhere in the Virginia colony were bound to their masters under a wide array of legal and contractual standards. Youthful and adult voluntary apprentices, imported indentured servants, contract servants "on wages," convicts from England sold into servitude, poor children and bastard apprentices, mulattos, and slaves, were all given separate and certainly not equal treatment under the colonial laws of Virginia. Experienced workmen, who were able to market their skills "for wages" and transportation expenses, and apprentices obtaining vocational training were accorded the highest status. Ordinary bondsmen, also known as "redemptioners," were accorded lower prestige. Convict-servants were set apart and suffered from a number of legal disabilities. [supra, Chapter on Apprentices, and infra, Chapter on Slaves].

Terms of indenture varied as did the social and economic circumstances from region to region in the British Isles. While it is true that poor children were sometimes kidnapped, transported to America and sold into servitude, the vast majority of indentured servants coming to the colonies were semi-skilled young English, Welsh and Scots tradesmen and farmers who were of limited means and searching for advancement and the opportunity to better themselves. In the early 1700s, the work of servants in Virginia was viewed as "no other than what every common freeman does." Indentured servants worked under contract for four or five years as shopkeepers, farm hands, domestic servants and common laborers. If they were not convicts, servants were rewarded with clothes and/or tools of their trade when their term of service was completed. Skilled artisans could obtain contract wages for their service as well as greater severance pay, and sometimes even an advance on their wages that enabled them to buy property in their own right. Migration within the British Isles was not a novel concept, and indentured service in Virginia must have seemed like an attractive alternative to unemployment in the often-depressed English economy. By the 1690s, there were 15,000 indentured servants under contract in Virginia at any one time, compared with only 3,000 slaves in the colony. [Voyagers, pp. 166-192; Legends, p. 55; ColVa, p. 301; infra, Chapter on Trades].

The policy of transporting English convicts for indentured service in the colonies was instituted by King James I in 1615. Originally, felons condemned to death were reprieved for seven years of service in colonial exile. The practice was extended to include soldiers and political prisoners taken in the numerous British civil wars of the time, who were often exiled for life. This form of populating the Virginia colony met with resistance from the Virginia Assembly and was suspended between 1670 and 1705. In 1705, Parliament extended the "benefit of clergy" to Irish, Welsh and English convicts, even those unable to read, and the flood gates opened in 1717 when Parliament inaugurated a program of subsidizing merchant contractors who transported convicts to the colonies. Seven year terms of servitude for non-capital felons and fourteen year terms for convicts under death sentences were legislated. By the 1720s, the Virginia Assembly was debating the formation of a Virginia county where all newly arriving convicts could be segregated. It has been suggested that, during the 1730s, a majority of the convicts who were transported to the American colonies were either sold or subsequently settled in Virginia's Northern Neck counties. Reliable estimates indicate that, on average, about 330 English, Irish (and in later years Scottish) transported convict servants arrived in the upper Chesapeake annually between 1722 and 1772, when Parliament finally ended the subsidies to transportation contractors. The Maryland colony, and Virginia's Northern Neck counties, were the recipients of a high proportion of the convicts brought into the Chesapeake Bay largely as a matter of fateful timing. The upper Virginia Piedmont and the trans-Allegheny region were opened for settlement with the conclusion of the Indian treaties of 1722, and a shift in colonial agricultural emphasis to the production of grain crops, in response to European market forces, coincided with the renewed availability of inexpensive convict-servant labor. The Record herein seems to support the notion that perhaps 20 or 30 new indentured servants were arriving in Loudoun County annually in the 1757-1766 decade. With the average length of indenture being four years, there might have been 100 or more contract servants in Loudoun County at any given time during this decade. Parliament extended the convict transportation laws to include Scottish convicts in 1766. That year, the Virginia Assembly felt compelled to institute the quarantine of ships "importing convicts or indented servants infected with the goal fever or small-pox." [ColVa, pp. 25-26; Voyagers, pp. 261-263 and 294; Hening, VIII/260].

Shortly before the incorporation of Loudoun County, in November of 1753, the Virginia Assembly recodified the laws of the colony regarding servants and slaves. This law described in detail the relationships of the various parties involved in servitude in the Virginia colony. Because the 1753 Act codified, for the most part, the prevailing law in force during Loudoun County's first decade, from 1757 to 1766, an extensive revisitation is appropriate and is provided hereinafter. [Hening, VI/356-369].

In the March 1642-43 session of the Virginia Assembly, limits were first placed on the duration of contracts of servants who were "brought into the Colony without indentures or covenants ... if they be above twenty year old to serve fowre [4] year; above twelve and under twenty [years old], five years; and under twelve to serve seven years." Subsequently, in 1657-58, these provisions for limits on the duration of servant contracts were changed, with those over sixteen to serve 4 years, under sixteen "to serve till ... one and twenty years of age, and the [county] courts to be judges of their ages." The amendments of the 1753 Act of Assembly provided that:

> *"all servants, except convicts, imported into this colony without indenture, if they be christians ... above nineteen years of age, shall serve but five years; ... under nineteen years of age, 'til they become twenty four years of age and no longer: but every such servant, under nineteen, shall be brought, within six months after ... importation, before the court of the county where the master lives, and his, or her age adjudged by the court, otherwise shall be a servant no longer than the accustomary five years, although under nineteen; ... the age of such servant, so adjudged and recorded shall be accounted his or her true age in respect to the time of service."*

The 1765 Assembly repealed the provisions of the Act of 1753 that applied to the legal duration of contracts of servants who were "imported into this colony without indenture." At the same time, the Virginia Assembly imposed severe penalties on anyone who attempted to sell a servant into slavery. [Hening, I/257, I/441-442, VI/356 and VIII/133-137].

The 1753 Act disabled all Negroes, mulattoes, Indians, Jews, Moors, "Mohometan"s, and "other infidel"s from purchasing or owning a white christian servant in Virginia. However, they were allowed to own christian servants "of their own complexion." If a master of a white christian servant married any individual of "complexion," the servant was, by law, thereby "freed from all service then due to such master or mistress." [Hening, VI/359].

Beginning in the early days of the Virginia colony, and up to the time of the American Revolution, indentured servants with "just cause of complaint [against their master] ... by harsh or unchristianlike usage; or otherways for want of diet or convenient necessaryes," had legal recourse and were urged to bring their cases to the attention of the authorities. In the Act of 1753, the duty of every master to his or her servant was set out: to "provide for them wholesome and competent diet, cloathing [sic] and lodging and shall not give immoderate correction, nor whip any christian white servant naked, without order from a [county] justice of peace." A master whipping a christian servant naked, without a Justice's permission, would owe the servant 50 shillings. Sick, lame and disabled servants who were mistreated by their masters were to be provided for by the parish, with the master to pay the costs, and if necessary, his goods and belongings subject to be sold at distress for the costs of providing care for the servant. The Loudoun County Court displayed its compassion for mistreated servants, as in October of 1764 when the ailing Mary Brane [sic] was removed from the custody of her master, Robert Watson, and placed in an ordinary and under a doctor's care. Masters were fined £10 if, in an attempt to avoid responsibility for their care, they tried to free sick and lame servants prematurely. Servants were obligated to "faithfully and obediently, all the whole time of their service, do all their masters or owners just and lawful commands." Resisting or offering violence to a master or overseer could result in additional service of "one whole year, after the time by act of Parliament, indenture, custom, or former order of the court shall be expired," for each offense. [Hening, I/254, I/440, VI/358 and VI/357-360; see infra, The Record, p. 374].

The county courts had jurisdiction to hear complaints of servants in a summary manner, on the summons of any county justice, without a formal petition from the servant. The full county court had the authority to "make such order as to them shall appear just and necessary." When the order of the court was ignored by a master, and a second complaint brought by the servant, the county court could remove the servant from the master and sell the indenture to a new master. The Loudoun County Court may have mistakenly applied this provision when Jesse Hall was removed from the service of Thomas Awbrey for "ill usage" in 1763. [Hening, VI/358; infra, p. 374].

Masters contracting with servants for service past the term of their indenture were required to submit the contracts for "the approbation of the court of the county wherein the master resides." Servants, even while indentured, could acquire and enjoy the use of any property or assets they obtained on their own account. From the time of Queen Anne's reign (circa 1705), "freedom dues" paid to indentured servants at the expiration of their term of service in Virginia were 10 bushels of corn, 30 shillings and "one well fixed musket." This provision was amended by the Virginia Assembly in 1748 and again in 1753, increasing the freedom dues for "every servant, male or female (except convicts) not having wages" to £3 and 10 shillings. Prior to final enactment of the 1753 amendment, in response to political pressures exerted by the Kings Privy Council, the tidewater-controlled Virginia Assembly reversed itself and rejected a proposal to extend freedom dues to the benefit of transported convicts. Thus, despite the absence of proof of the mode of transportation utilized by a given immigrant servant, the reader can properly conclude that any indentured servant who presented a claim for freedom dues in the Loudoun Court most certainly did not arrive in the Virginia colony as a transported convict. Occasionally, servants were able to negotiate terms for their freedom dues that exceeded the legal minimums. For example, an Order of the Loudoun Court in May of 1758 calls for the payment of a cow and a bed in settlement of a servant's claim for freedom dues. [Landmarks, pp. 165-166; Hening, VI/358-359; supra, p. 362; infra, The Record, p. 372].

An English tradition, the requirement that servants obtain the permission of their masters before marrying, was incorporated into Virginia law in 1753. A servant marrying without permission would owe the master an additional year of labor or £5, and a free person marrying the servant would also owe the servant's master £5 or "one whole year in actual service." Liability was imposed on masters for fines and penalties incurred by servants who violated various colonial laws. This provision, or the avoidance of freedom dues, may have caused Henry Brewer to provide his troublesome servant John Riley with an early release from his indenture at the Loudoun Court in November of 1758. The county courts were authorized to determine the type and method of repayment from the servant to the master. The Assembly restated old law in 1753, to-wit, that "no person whatsoever shall buy, sell, or receive of, to, or from [sic] any servant or slave, any coin or commodity ... without the leave or consent of the master or owner." An offender was liable to the servant's master for four times the value of the transaction and costs, along with a penalty of £5, in an action brought "in any county court of this dominion." If the offender failed or refused to pay, he was to receive 39 lashes on the bare back, "well laid on at the public whipping post" and still be held accountable for the costs of the court action. In instances where a servant was convicted of a criminal offence, "where free persons are punishable by fine, servants shall be punished by whipping after the rate of twenty lashes for every five hundred pounds of tobacco or fifty shillings." The Assembly went on to prohibit the imposition of penalties of more than forty lashes at one time on any servant. [Hening, III/401, VI/83-84, VII/101 and VI/359-360; supra, Chapter on Crimes and Punishment].

The colonial Assembly of Virginia first took note of the problem of runaway servants in March of 1643, in the 18th year of the reign of Charles I, when punishments for runaway servants and slaves were established. Runaways servants were to serve their masters double the time that they had absented themselves from their duties, after the term of their first obligation expired. For a second attempt the runaway servant was to be branded with an 'R' on the cheek, and suffer further punishment under a statute for "incorrigible rogues." Any runaway so forgetful or unfortunate as to leave "either piece [ie., gun], powder and shott ... with the Indians" would be sentenced to death. These penalties were modified in March of 1658 by the Assembly so that "all runnaways [sic] that shall absent themselves from their said master's service [were still] liable to make satisfaction by service at the end of their times of service by indenture - vizt. double the time so neglected," but the second time the servant ran away he or she was to be branded with an 'R' on the shoulder. Fines were imposed on anyone lodging a runaway - set at 30 lbs. of tobacco for every night that sanctuary was given. This amendment was, in turn, modified in March of 1659 when, in order to facilitate the discovery and apprehension of repeat offenders, the Assembly added the provision that "the master of everie such runaway shall cutt the hair of all such runaways close above their ears." After 1753, runaway servants who were captured were still required to serve their masters, "after all other time of service due shall be expired ... double the time of his or her absence," and an additional 1½ months of service for every 100 lbs. of tobacco paid in charges, pursuit and recovery. The terms of this repayment were to be determined at the next county court following the recapture of the servant. [Hening, I/254, I/439-440, I/517-518 and VI/367-368].

The 1753 Act established comprehensive procedures and a series of rewards for the return of all runaways to their masters. A runaway taken over five miles, but less than ten, "from his or her usual place of abode" would entitle the "taker up" to a reward of 100 lbs. of tobacco. When a runaway was taken up more than ten miles from home the reward was doubled. Rewards were paid out of the annual county levy, and then taxed to the master. The "taker up" of a runaway was supposed to appear before a county justice, obtain a certificate entitling him to the appropriate reward, and turn the runaway over to the nearest constable. The constable was then to take the runaway into custody and:

> *"give him ... a number of lashes as the said justice shall think fit to direct, not exceeding [39] and then ... to convey and deliver [him] to the next constable, ... so from constable to constable until the runaway be delivered to his or her owner or overseer."*

Constables and "other officer[s] charged with conducting runaways" were "to impress men and horses, where necessary, for the safe convey[ance]" of the runaway. One proviso was that the corporal punishment meted out by a constable did not deprive a master from his own satisfaction. [Hening, VI/363-364 and VI/367].

In October of 1765, the Virginia Assembly, finding that "the method for apprehending runaway servants and slaves and conveying them to their owners ... [is] very inconvenient to the owners ... burthensome [sic] to the constables and is also attended with great trouble and expense in settling the publick claims of the colony," amended the provisions of the 1753 Act regarding runaways. Thereafter, the "taker up" [capturer] of a runaway would appear before any justice of the peace in the county where the runaway was caught and obtain a certificate which verified, among other things, "the distance of miles ... from the place of residence of the owner or ... the quarter where the runaway was usually kept." The taker up was directed to then:

> *"immediately carry such runaway to his or her owner, or cause the same to be delivered ... upon such delivery ... producing the certificate ... the taker up shall be entitled to a reward of five shillings for taking up, and four pence for every mile mentioned in such certificate, to be paid by the owner."*

If the owner refused or was unable to pay the appropriate reward, the "taker up" was entitled to sue for the reward before either a single justice, where the reward was less than 25 shillings, or in any county court in the colony. [Hening, VIII/135-137].

If a runaway would or could not give the name of their owner the servant was to be "committed to the gaol of the county where taken" and the sheriff or jailer was to post notices describing the servant, "publicly affixed at the door of the court house, and there continued two months." The clerk or reader of every church in the county was similarly instructed to post a copy of the description and notice "in some open and convenient place near his church." Sheriffs were to release runaways to masters claiming them after the master paid 200 lbs. of tobacco, "or 20 shillings for the taking up," and the sheriff's fees. The reader will observe that the Loudoun Court record is replete with entries awarding 160 lbs. of tobacco in recovery costs to masters - the equivalent of the 200 lbs. reward after the 20% discount permitted for all officers fees in Loudoun County. Servants who belonged to an inhabitant of either the Maryland or Carolina colony were to be put in the county jail, advertised for locally, and then "with consent and approbation of his county court," the county sheriff could hire out the runaway to pay the rewards and other charges.

After 1753, when a master failed to claim his servant at a county jail, the runaway was "conveyed from one constable to another" until he arrived at the public jail in Williamsburg. The jailer of the colony then was required to advertise a description of the runaway in the *Virginia Gazette* for three months. Masters claiming a runaway from the Williamsburg jail were required to obtain a certificate from their county court proving ownership, and pay "all charges for taking up, imprisonment, conveying to goal, maintaining, and releasing such runaway. Jailers were allowed 4 shillings or forty lbs. of tobacco for every commitment and release of a runaway, and 6 pence or 5 lbs. of tobacco for every 24 hours a runaway was in jail. The Williamsburg jailer was authorized to hire out servants, with "a strong iron collar, with the letters 'P G' [ie., 'Public Gaol'] stamped thereon, to be put on the neck of every runaway hired out." After the jail charges were paid by their hire, and when no owner appeared to claim, the runaway's indenture was sold, at auction, with the proceeds going to the colonial treasury. The most frequent type of advertising in the *Virginia Gazette* was not, however, from the colony's jailer, but from individual masters who were describing and offering rewards for the return of their absent servants. [Hening, VI/364-367].

The 1753 Assembly also provided that, "to the end poor people may not be destitute of employment ... as well as to prevent servants running away ... every servant, upon expiration of his or her time," was obligated to appear at the county court, prove where he last served, have his freedom recorded and obtain a freedom certificate from the clerk of the county court. Penalties for harboring or entertaining a servant traveling without a freedom certificate were established at 30 lbs. of tobacco "for every natural day." Runaway servants who used or manufactured a forged certificate were to "stand two hours in the pillory, on a court-day" and pay a £10 fine, half to the colony and half to their owner, aside from the other penalties imposed for running away. Runaway servant forgers with unpaid fines six months after sentencing were to be punished with 39 lashes on the bare back at the county whipping post. [Hening, VI/362-363].

Servants in colonial Loudoun County were not reluctant to bring their masters to court when they thought that they were being subjected to "ill usage." The record also reflects the frequent return of runaways servants and identifies a number of masters who were delinquent in paying freedom dues. A review of the entries in the record shows that a majority of the servants with claims against them for runaway time or claiming nonpayment of freedom dues in Loudoun County in the 1757-1766 decade appear to have been either Irish or Scots-Irish.

October 12, 1757 - "John Vilet [a/k/a John Violet] exhibited an Account against William Jones a runaway Servant ... thirty daies Absent time and [480 lbs.] of Tobacco expended in pursuit." Book A, p. 36.

November 8, 1757 - Thomas Jenkins sues James Leith [his former employer] for his freedom dues. Book A, p. 41.

December 14, 1757 - "Phillis Manley [who was probably a minor] ... acknowledged her Indenture for serving Thomas Fields seven Years ... [and it is] Ordered to be Certified." Book A, p. 57.

March 14, 1758 - "Mary Green, a Servant of William Nodding ... agreed to serve her said Master one year and three months above her Indented time ... William paying her fine and Costs to the Churchwardens of Cameron Parish for having a Base Born Child &c." Book A, p. 67.

May 9, 1758 - "John Morris exhibited an Account against Isaac Manuel a runaway Servant, for [160 lbs.] of nett tobacco expended in pursuit of him." Book A, p. 100.

May 9, 1758 - "William Brewer a Servant man belonging to John Bortley [sic- John Berkley] agrees to serve his said Master six Months over and above his Indented time." Book A, p. 103.

May 10, 1758 - On "the Complaint of Conrad Shanks and Margaret Shanks his wife against Thomas Awbrey for not paying them their freedom dues ... the Plaintiffs recover against the Defendant a Cow of the value of thirty five shillings and a Bed of the Value of two Pounds as Covenanted by Indenture." Book A, pp. 76, 94 and 109; see supra, Writ of Attachment on p. 362.

June 14, 1758 - On "the Complaint of Hugh McGuire against George Chelton for his [McGuire's] Freedom Dues ... [it is Ordered] Chelton pay ... Hugh McGuire [£3], ten shillings Current Money." Book A, pp. 105 and 122.

July 21, 1758 - In a Loudoun County Court session for certification of public claims to the Virginia Assembly, Thomas Lewis, John Moss Junr., David Robinson, William Owsely [sic] and Joseph McGeach each produced and proved Certificates for taking up and returning Runaways. Book A, p. 133.

November 14, 1758 - "John Ryley [sic- John Riley] a Servant to Henry Brewer is discharged from any further service to his said Master ... Ryleys [sic] acquitting his said Master from the paiment [sic] of his freedom dues." John Riley was apparently a troublesome servant. Not long after this discharge from his indenture Riley was arrested on assault charges and he then "skipped bail." Book A, p. 178; see supra, Chapter on Crimes and Punishment.

March 13, 1759 - On a "Complaint of Margaret Gibbs against Thomas Fields for unlawfully detaining her in his Service and sundry other ill usuage ... the Indenture is [ruled] void," and Gibbs is freed from service. Book A, p. 209.

March 14, 1759 - The Court Summons Thomas Fields "to answer the Petition of Margaret Gibbs exhibited against him for freedom dues." Book A, p. 211; and see previous entry.

March 16, 1759 - "The Petition of Isaac Manuel against John Morris for Freedom Dues is dismissed being agreed." Book A, pp. 179, 203-204 and 224.

May 8, 1759 - Thomas Connell [apparently an employer violating his servant's indenture] is summoned to "show cause why Jonathan Turner a detained Servant should not be discharged from him." Book A, p. 235.

May 9, 1759 - The "Petition of George Scott against John Westby ... that Westby hath his Son Joseph Scott in his possession by Indenture which is Illegal ... believes he is removing him out of the Colony ... [the Court rules] said Indenture is void ... [and orders that] Joseph Scott be discharged from all further service to ... John Westby." Book A, pp. 211, 237 and 238.

May 9, 1759 - "The Petition of Margaret Gibbs against Thomas Fields for Freedom dues is dismissed being agreed." Book A, pp. 211, 237 and 238.

November 12, 1759 - In a session of Public Claims, "Jeremiah Hutchison, John Lane and Aneas Campbell produced Certificates for taking up Runaways." Book A, p. 296.

September 23, 1760 - In a session "For Proof of Public Claims ... Richard Smith also produced a Certificate for taking up a Runaway Servant belonging to Thomas Baker of Fairfax County ... Certified to the next Session of Assembly." Book A, p. 401.

July 14, 1761 - Cornelius Vaune exhibits his accounts "against Margaret Watson a Runaway Servant ... [and] against Jane McDaniel a Runaway Servant ... [both] for four Daies Absent time and [160 lbs.] of tobacco and [15] shillings and nine pence expended in taking [them] up." Book A, p. 478.

July 14, 1761 - On a "Motion of Susanna Grimes against John Davis for detaining of her as a Servant contrary to an Order of this Court ... [the Court orders that a citation for] Contempt issue against him." Book A, p. 481.

May 14, 1762 - The Loudoun County Court rules that "the Complaint of Jesse Hall against Thomas Awbrey for Ill usuage &c. ... being fully heard ... [is] dismissed." Book A, pp. 568 and 622.

August 10, 1762 - Benjamin Harris is summoned to "Answer a Petition exhibited against him by George Parsons for detaining of him [Parsons] as a Servant without reasonable Cause." Book B, p. 28.

August 11, 1762 - Mary Bruster, the Executrix of the Estate of Thomas Bruster, is summoned "to Answer the Petition of Job Dundass for Freedom Dues." Dundass obtains a judgment for "£2, ten Shillings (the same being the ballance [sic] of his Freedom Dues) and also his Costs." Book A, pp. 591 and 629, and Book B, pp. 13 and 35.

December 14, 1762 - "Christian Woodhouse a Servant belonging to Minor Winn ... having a Base born Child ... declared that Withers Smith is the Father of the said Child ... Winn undertook to pay [her] fine [of 500 lb. of tobacco and cask to the Churchwardens, and] ... Christian [is Ordered to] serve her said Master nine Months over and above her Indented time." Book B, p. 77; see also infra, Chapter on Base Born Children.

April 13, 1763 - Ruling on "the Petition of Barrett Traverse against Robert Watson for ill Usage and detaining of him as a Servant ... fully heard ... dismissed." Book B, pp. 70 and 93.

April 13, 1763 - On "the Petition of Jesse Hall against Thomas Awbrey on a second Complaint for Ill Usage ... the parties being fully heard ... Hall [is to] be removed from the Service of the said Thomas Awbry [sic] ... Thomas prayed an Appeal." Book B, p. 109.

May 12, 1763 - "Alexander Sinclair came into Court and agrees to serve Jacob Janney one whole Year from the Date hereof in Consideration of the said Janney's having paid a Debt due from the said Sinclair to John Glasford." Book B, p. 154.

September 15, 1763 - "Petition of Phillis Styles against John Champ Junr. for Freedom Dues ... fully heard ... [Styles] recovers ... £3 and ten shillings, and her Costs." Book B, p. 251.

December 13, 1763 - On a second "Complaint of Barrett Traverse against Robert Watson for Ill usage ... being heard is Dismissed ... Ordered that the said Robert use the said Barrett better for the future." Book B, p. 269.

March 9, 1764 - John Peter Pickler and his wife Mary Magdalene Pickler, with their passage from Rotterdam paid by John Hough, agree to serve as "apprentices" to John Hough for 4½ years. LDCODB, Book D, p. 666.

August 14, 1764 - John Peake is summoned to Answer the Petition of Joannah Harper. Book B, p. 407.

September 11, 1764 - The Court orders that "Robert Watson be Summoned ... to Answer the Complaint of Mary Braine his servant ... for misusuage and that he ... [must] not Presume to beat or abuse her on this account." Book B, p. 433.

October 10, 1764 - On the "Complaint of Mary Brane against Robert Watson for misusuage ... fully heard ... Mary be Removed for the Ill treatment which she has received ... put under the care of [ordinary keeper] Thomas Sorrell during the Continuance of her disorder ... Robert having refused many times to have proper Medicines administered to her ... Mr. [Dr.] James Butler Brodbelt [sic] [to] attend her as a physician during her Illness." Book B, p. 487.

December 12, 1764 - In open Court, "Joseph Mouren ... informing the Court that Sarah Fletcher his Servant woman hath lately been Delivered of a Bastard Child." Book B, p. 517.

April 9, 1765 - "Simon Triplett exhibited an Account against James Faulkner a Runaway Servant for [397 lbs.] of tobacco expended in taking him up ... Ordered that James do serve his Master ... after his time by Indenture ... shall be fully expired." [Requiring 6 months additional service.] Book B, p. 547.

April 10, 1765 - The "Petition of Henry Loyd against William Mead for detaining him as a Servant ... is Dismissed." Book B, pp. 525 and 554.

May 16, 1765 - The "Petition of Mary Howman against William Mead is Discontinued." Book B, pp. 326 and 615.

June 10, 1765 - "Robert Hamilton exhibited an Account against James Faulkner a Runaway Servant [£6, 16] shillings expended in taking him ... Ordered that the said James do serve his said Master for the same ... further Ordered that the Sherif take ... James to the Publick Whipping post and give him Twenty five lashes on his Bareback well laid on." Robert Hamilton had purchased Faulkner's indenture from Simon Triplett (April 9, 1765 entry), and Faulkner had promptly run away again. The lashes were meted out because the Court considered Faulkner an incorrigible after his second offence, and an example was to be made. Faulkner had at least 25 more months to serve on his indenture as part of the penalties imposed on him in the two Court hearings. Book B, p. 625.

September 12, 1765 - John Carr "exhibited an Account against John Pincher a Runaway Servant" for £3 and 160 lbs. of tobacco "expended in taking him." This required an additional twelve months service. Book C, p. 53.

September 12, 1765 - Thomas Carr "exhibited an Account against Richard Hindmore a Runaway Servant" for £3 and 160 lbs. of tobacco "expended in taking him." [Requiring an additional twelve months service.] Book C, p. 53.

October 14, 1765 - "Peter Peckler [John Peter Pickler] came into Court and Agreed to serve John Hough his present Master [18 additional] Months ... Hough in Consideration thereof agrees to Release Mary Magdaline Peckler the Wife of the said Peter from any further Service." In passing, one wonders how often the children of colonial Loudoun were heard to mockingly intone: "Peter Peckler picked a pipe of pickled peppers ..." Book C, p. 60.

July 26, 1766 - Benjamin Grayson (of Fairfax) sells his contract for William Dunn, a "servant lad," to Edward Snickers. LDCODB, Book E, p. 243.

August 11, 1766 - "Robert Watson exhibited an Account against Mary Brawner a Runaway Servant ... Absent seven Months and twenty six daies." Book C, p. 148.

August 12, 1766 - "George Headen Jr. exhibited an account against Thomas Fitzpatrick a Runaway Servant ... absent thirteen days ... chargeable with £4 in taking." Book C, p. 154.

September 10, 1766 - Ann Moore brings a "Petition for the Nonpayment of her Freedom Dues" against William Cavens and his wife Mary Cavens. She obtains judgment for £2, with John Moore [probably her husband] and Alice Fouch appearing as her witnesses. Book C, pp. 87, 175 and 195.

October 27, 1766 - In a session for Public Claims: "William Mead Junr. exhibited ... a claim for taking up a Runaway Servant Lad named Robert McFarlane belonging to Thomas Carney. John Minor Gent. and Stewart Minor also exhibited Claims for taking up Runaways ... [all were] certified to the next General Assembly." Book C, p. 218.

Slave Ownership in Loudoun, 1757-1765

	1757	# Slaves*	1761	# Slaves*	1765	# Slaves*
Totals:						
Tithables*:		364.e		553		728
Owners**:	90.e		134		186	
Absentee ...	34.e	233.e	36	283	34	278
Resident ...	56.e	131.e	98	270	152	450
Sub-totals:						
Plantation owners, (15+ slaves):						
Absentee ...	6.e	92.e	5	90	5	120
Resident ...	0	0	1	18	2	48
Large owners, (6-14 slaves):						
Absentee ...	12.e	92.e	16	141	15	120
Resident ...	3.e	19.e	8	53	15	113
Medium owners, (3-5 slaves):						
Absentee ...	11.e	40.e	11	44	8	27
Resident ...	25.e	80.e	36	126	46	163
Small owners, (1-2 slaves):						
Absentee ...	5.e	9.e	4	8	6	11
Resident ...	28.e	32.e	53	73	89	126

* - Tithables are used to obtain the most accurate assessment of owner interests; Loudoun's black population is estimated at 1½ times tithables. See infra, Chapter on Population; Glossary.

** - Owners and slaves are grouped on the basis of both the owner's residency status and the number of tithable slaves owned.

".e" - Designates numbers that have been estimated, for 1757.

Actual owner and tithable numbers are used for 1761 and 1765.

Slavery is not an easy subject to discuss with both brevity and accuracy. The history of slavery in the Virginia colony has been explained, restated, analyzed, and too often misunderstood in a wealth of tomes that deal with the subject at great length. The reader is encouraged to explore those volumes. In the limited space available here, the focus will be on the legal development of the institution of slavery and its status as it was practiced in Virginia in the later 1700s, followed by an analysis of racial population trends in Loudoun County from the 1740s to the 1760s.

Tradition has it that Negroes were first introduced into Virginia from a Dutch man-of-war in August of 1619. Initially, Negroes were sold as indentured servants since slavery did not exist, by law or by custom, either in Britain or in Virginia. The practice of slavery was slow to take hold. In 1625, black servants accounted for only 6% of Jamestown's total population. [ColVa, p. 70; contra, Hening, I/146; Jamestown, pp. 51-55 and 120].

A type of slavery was practiced by the native Indian tribes, but the colonial Assembly of Virginia did not recognize and begin to codify the unique institutional forms of black slavery until the mid-1600s. The young colony was careful to avoid offense to its powerful Indian neighbors, and instructed colonists that Indian children were not to be used or treated as slaves. A fairly simple formula evolved to govern the status of every individual born in the colony. The Assembly provided that, with a few exceptions, a child born in Virginia was to be slave, bond or free in accord with the legal status of the mother. [Hening, I/396 and VI/356].

By 1660, the colonial slave trade had become so lucrative that the Virginia Assembly, in its first attempt to restrain the trade, imposed a tariff on Dutch slavers, requiring a payment of two shillings for every hogshead of tobacco that was accepted in payment for imported Negro slaves. Over the course of the next 120 years, the Virginia Assembly would make numerous efforts to slow or stop the import of slaves into the colony. Unfortunately, British Royal policy consistently encouraged colonial production of foodstuffs, tobacco and raw materials useful in maritime operations, and the Crown viewed colonial slavery as an essential expedient. [Hening, I/540, IV/118, V/28-31; see infra, p.472].

The 1710 Assembly imposed a duty of £5 on every slave imported into Virginia, both to lessen the financial burden of quitrents on property owners and to discourage the slave traffic. In 1723 and again in 1728, London merchants successfully lobbied the King and obtained repeal of the Virginia duties on imported slaves. Ultimately, the Virginians were able to prevail by imposing an import duty on the buyer rather than the seller. Duties enacted in Virginia in 1732 were renewed every four years up to the time of the American Revolution, when the Virginia Assembly finally stopped the importation of slaves completely. [ColVa, pp. 491-492 and 522; Hening, IV/317-322, V/92-94 and IX/471-472].

The 1755 Assembly imposed an add-on duty of 10% on the purchase price of all imported slaves, ostensibly "for raising the sum of £20,000 for the protection of his Majesty's subjects against the insults and encroachments of the French." In April of 1757, an additional 10% duty was assessed on the purchase price of every imported slave. In May of 1760 and March of 1761, as the frontier war with the French and Indians appeared to ease, the add-on duties were repealed. When the financial aftermath of the costly campaigns on the frontier became more clear in November of 1766, the Assembly revived the 20% add-on duties, through 1769. [Hening, VI/466, VII/81, VII/363, VII/383 and VIII/190-191].

By the mid-1700s, the purchase price of an exceptionally strong or skilled slave would reach £100; the average field hand cost perhaps only £30 at the time. By 1760, the average price for a slave in Loudoun would reach £50. Putting these prices into some perspective, a partially improved 1,000 acre tract on the Loudoun piedmont might have been purchased for £100 in the mid-1750s. At the same time, a 7-year contract for an unskilled indentured servant could be purchased for as little as £10 or £20. [for example, see infra, The Record, pp. 481 and 484].

In 1705, Virginia's Robert Beverley had written that:

> *"work of the servants and slaves is no other than what every common freeman does ... An overseer ... having served his time [as an indentured servant], has acquired the skill and character of an experienced planter, and is therefore entrusted with direction of the servants and slaves."*

This statement clearly glosses over the harshness of slavery as an institution, but the blurring of the distinction between the toil of servants and slaves leads this commentator, three centuries later, to pause in reflection. Beverley's letter was elemental to an attempt to recruit new servants, not slaves; either Beverley was deluded, or slaves in Virginia were neither abused nor viewed with contempt or derision. Slaves were incorporated as an integral part of the community in their plantations and settlements, partly as a result of British policies opposing the formation of colonial towns. As well as serving as field hands and overseers, slaves were taught the skills of craftsmen and artisans, and some learned "manners" and became domestic servants in homes and ordinaries. Slaves on large plantations in the tidewater were usually allowed to have Sundays to themselves, when they would cultivate small plots dedicated for their personal use or visit and socialize at other slave quarters nearby. [Legends, p. 55; generally, Home, pp. 51-72].

At the end of the 1600s, "the few Negroes [living along the Potomac] were mostly house servants." A slave was considerably more expensive than an indentured servant, and work in the fields on the frontier was still dangerous. Workers were often sent into the fields armed and ready but, by law, slaves were not permitted to carry guns. Thus, slaves on the frontier required escort for their defense as well as management. The simple economics of the situation placed an emphasis on the use of indentured servants. Slaves accounted for only 5% of the population in the upper Chesapeake and Potomac in 1680, but by 1710 slaves constituted nearly 25% of the population. This pattern is similar to the Jamestown experience, but the increase in Virginia's Northern Neck in the early 1700s requires an explanation. The opening of the upper tidewater created new areas of tobacco production, resulting in an exponential increase in the demand for unskilled agricultural laborers. The Royal African Company's monopoly of the slave trade was eliminated in 1697. The flow of indentured servants from the British Isles slowed around the turn of the century. And a number of powerful Virginia families, like the Carters, Fitzhughs, Lees and Byrds, with an accumulated "critical mass" of vast land holdings and combined political influence, had access to British financial markets - allowing them to borrow sufficient venture capital for slave purchases. The Virginia equation had been firmly established: fresh land plus steady labor equals great wealth. [Landmarks, p. 157; generally, see Bailyn, *The Peopling of British North America*, (for background reading)].

The Virginia Assembly revised the provisions regarding the status of slaves in 1706, essentially elevating slaves to the legal equivalent of real property (they had been considered chattels), in order to provide more security against creditor claims for orphans who inherited slaves. Anyone who was over the age of 18 could legally buy or sell black slaves, but free blacks were not permitted to own white slaves. The 1723 Virginia Assembly disqualified all Negroes, both free and slave, from voting in the Virginia colony. The Governor, his Council and the Assembly all asserted as an excuse that many free Negroes and mulattoes had been implicated (falsely, it seems) in an insurrection of slaves that year. The same Assembly also prohibited free Negroes and mulattoes from sitting on a jury, or appearing in any court as a witness, except in the trial of slaves or other free Negroes or mulattoes. [Hening, III/371-376, IV/223, IV/283 and V/232; Democracy, p. 81; and see ColVa, pp. 396-397 and 525-528].

In 1749, Rev. Charles Green, the minister of Truro parish, noted that: "The Country born Negroes [in Loudoun and Fairfax] are chiefly Baptised [sic]." In 1753, shortly before Loudoun's incorporation, the Virginia Assembly revised the laws of the colony regarding all servants and slaves. A previous law had been poorly drafted and one clause, specifying that white Christians could not be held as slaves, was widely misunderstood by baptized black slaves as applicable to their circumstance. The new law defined precisely who could and would not be slaves in Virginia:

> *"all persons ... imported into this colony ... not christians in their native country, <u>except</u> Turks and Moors in amity with his majesty, and such who can prove their being free in England or any other christian country before they were shipped for transportation here ... shall be accounted and be slaves and as such bought and sold, notwithstanding a conversion to christianity after their importation."*

Anyone stealing "any negroe, mulattoe, or Indian slave" would be treated as a felon and subject to the death penalty, without the "benefit of clergy." This may have been the fate of John Maris, who was extradited from Loudoun County to Maryland in 1765 on the charge of stealing a slave. [Green, *"Fairfax County List of Titheables for 1749,"* MS, p. 5; Hening, VI/356-357 and VI/369; Glossary; see Chapter on Crimes, supra, pp. 159 and 171].

In April of 1757, the Assembly required that all gifts of slaves be made in writing, either by will or deed, and required the proof of gifts in a county court. The recording requirement for a deed to a slave was more stringent than that imposed on the conveyance of real estate. County Clerks were allowed to charge only 20 lbs. of "nett tobacco" [the equivalent of 2 shillings, 6 pence] "for the recording of any deed ... conveying ownership of slaves." This recording fee continued in force until the time of the American Revolution. [Hening, VII/118-120 and VII/238-239].

The 1758 Assembly determined that:

> *"frauds have been committed by means of secret gifts made, or pretended ... of slaves, by parents and others, who have notwithstanding remained in possession ... whereby creditors and purchasers have been frequently involved in expensive law suits and often deprived of their just debts & purchases."*

The 1757 law failed to account for several situations involving verbal gifts of slaves made prior to the enactment, so new rules and procedures were enacted. Thereafter, gifts of slaves would not be valid "unless ... by will, duly proved and recorded, or by deed in writing ... proved by two witnesses ... or acknowledged by the owner ... and recorded in ... the court of the county where one of the parties lives, within eight months after the date of such deed." Where a slave had not been delivered pursuant to a gift, a writing or deed from the donor or the donor's heir-at-law could be proven in a county court within two years of the 1758 Act. "Good and effectual ... title" in a slave would vest in anyone who could prove that he had actual possession of the slave for five years by virtue of a prior gift. Where a verbal donor refused to make a deed to confirm a prior gift, "and such slave ... hath not since come into the possession of a bona fide [innocent third party] purchaser," the donee could "summon the ... witnesses present at the making [of] such gift to the court of the county where such donor ... lives." A county court's determination that a gift had been made would have the legal effect of "a deed in writing," conveying the slave to the claimant. The 1758 Assembly filled loopholes by providing that the donee of a prior gift who was an infant, temporarily out of the colony or otherwise legally disabled, could obtain a confirmation of a prior gift "at any time within two years after such disability shall be removed." [Hening, VII/237-239].

From mid-1760 to December of 1762, the Loudoun County Court was embroiled in a family dispute over a verbal gift of slaves. Initially, the County Court ruled that Joseph Brown failed to prove that Thomas Brown, his father, had made him a gift of two slaves. Joseph appealed and won in the General Court of Virginia, which ordered a re-hearing in Loudoun County. Thomas still refused to acknowledge his prior gift, so Joseph brought three witnesses to Leesburg and finally obtained clear title to slaves "Charles and Patt" in the County Court. [infra, pp. 481-483].

The Virginia prohibition barring a slave from giving testimony in court against a free man would ultimately work to disadvantage the prosecution of conspirators in slave rebellions in the 1800s. Nonetheless, men and women "of complexion" were called to testify in colonial courts against others of their own race. Free and slave alike were punished severely for perjury. Any:

> *"negroe, mulattoe or indian ... upon due proof made or pregnant circumstances appearing to any county court ... [found] to have given a false testimony ... without further trial ... [was to] have one ear nailed to the pillory, and there to stand for the space of one hour ... then the said ear to be cut off ... thereafter the other ear nailed ... and cut off at the expiration of one other hour ... [the perjurer was then to] receive thirty nine lashes on his or her bare back, well laid on, at the public whipping post."*

Needless to say, the prosecution of a slave for perjury in Virginia's colonial courts was rare. There were no prosecutions recorded in Loudoun prior to the American Revolution. [Hening, VI/106-107 and VI/359; Egerton, *Gabriel's Rebellion*, (background reading)].

Unlike white colonists, every slave facing criminal charges, regardless of the severity of the crime, was tried without a jury in a county court. If the county Justices were divided in opinion, the accused slave was acquitted. The death penalty was expected in every felony case and when death was the sentence, a pause of "ten days, at least ... [was given before] the day of execution, except in cases of conspiracy, insurrection, or rebellion." Delay in execution was a measure to allow an owner the opportunity to petition the colonial Governor for a Royal pardon or reduction of the sentence under "the benefit of clergy." County courts "put a valuation in money upon [every] slave" that was to be executed, and certified that value "to the next session of Assembly" so the owner could be reimbursed for his loss. On March 2, 1767, three slaves belonging to George West would become the subjects of Loudoun's first slave executions, after they admitted that they had hacked their overseer to pieces with axes and hoes. Even though this act constituted both conspiracy and insurrection, the Loudoun County Court allowed the ten day grace period after trial. There is no indication that the Governor granted a reduction of sentence in the case. [supra, Chapter on County Court, and Chapter on Crimes and Punishment; Glossary; LDCOCO, Book C, p. 237].

It has been suggested that "slaves were 'not worked near so hard, nor so many Hours a Day' as the white farm workers," due to their masters' concern for their investment. Nonetheless, there can be little doubt that slaves occasionally were abused in the hands of rough overseers or heartless masters, and that some slaves found good reason to flee their sad existence. Virginia is known as the mother of the states for good reason. Throughout the 1600s and 1700s, a vast expanse of fertile frontier land was situated just west of Virginia's settled areas - a magnet for venturesome settlers. Runaway slaves often fled to these southern and western frontiers of the colony where a death in relative obscurity awaited them. Sometimes, skilled artisans among the runaway slaves, usually blacksmiths and coopers, were accepted into frontier communities when they successfully passed themselves off as freed men. Black watermen, both bond and runaway, as a group would also find relative autonomy before the American Revolution. The most unfortunate runaway slaves perished under the hatchet of an Indian, or were returned home to be put back to work in chains. In the mid-1600s, Virginia's captured runaway slaves were branded with an "R" on either the face or shoulder. [Jamestown, pp. 52-55; generally, Home, pp. 51-72; Egerton, supra, @ pp. 119-123; supra, Chapter on Servants].

The 1672 Assembly, concerned that many slaves had "too much latitude to walk about," enacted stringent regulations aimed at returning and punishing runaway slaves and indentured servants. Runaways were still subjected to harsh treatment in the 1700s. The 1753 Assembly provided that upon the capture of a runaway slave, the nearest Justice could order an immediate punishment of 39 lashes. More lashes awaited the delinquent at the hand of his overseer when he was returned to his master. Overseers had a great deal of latitude in the punishment that they could mete out to the slaves in their charge. Many overseers were undoubtedly men who had been hardened by years of toil, although a few overseers on larger plantations were sons of the tidewater gentry who were being prepared for their own inheritances. In light of contempt citations handed out by the Loudoun Court, language used by the overseers, collectively, must have been remarkably coarse, even for a farming community like Loudoun County. Because slaves were expensive, the loss of a runaway was never readily accepted. *Virginia Gazette* colonial newspapers were full of the advertisements of owners describing runaway slaves, offering private rewards for the prompt return of their property. [Hening, II/299-300 and VI/363; supra, Chapter on Peace Bonds].

Before 1766, when a runaway slave was detained, the captor was entitled to a "Public Claim" reward, but Virginia's Sheriffs and county constables were responsible for the slave's return to his owner. In 1766, public rewards and incentives for the capture of a runaway slave were revised. Thereafter the individual captor was personally responsible, and rewarded, for the return of a runaway slave. [Hening, VI/109 and VI/417-421; supra, pp. 67 and 110; re rewards for return of runaways, see supra, Chapter on Servants; infra, The Record, pp. 480, 482 and 485].

After the tidewater Indians were reduced during Bacon's Rebellion in 1676, an insurrection of slaves was increasingly viewed as the primary "internal" threat to the colony. In 1730, in response to the third major slave uprising in twenty years, the Assembly formally provided for the response of Virginia's county militias in the event of a slave insurrection. Twenty-five years later, after Braddock's defeat and with all of the frontier settlements in a panic, the specter of a fifth column led Virginia's Governor Dinwiddie to fear "Villany of the Negroes on any [further] Emergency of Government." The Assembly responded to the perceived threat and revised the 1726 slave patrolling laws. Beginning in 1757, patrols of county militiamen were instructed to visit and inspect Negro quarters in order to avert insurrections. Thereafter, small patrols of the county militias were regularly encountered on Virginia's country roads and at slave quarters on the plantations. In their regular patrols, the militia were to:

> *"visit all negroe [slave] quarters, and other places suspected of entertaining unlawful assemblies of*

slaves ... or [arrest] any other [individual] strolling about from one plantation to another without a pass from his or her master, mistress, or overseer."

If one patrol was not sufficient, the County Lieutenant or Colonel of the county militia could "order more companies for the same service." Everyone arrested by a patrol was to be taken directly to the nearest county Justice, who had the discretion to order an immediate punishment of the delinquent with up to twenty lashes "on his or her bare back well laid on." The officer of every patrol was supposed to deliver a written report to the County Lieutenant who subsequently, at the time of the annual county court martial, would certify an allowance to the county court "requiring at the laying of their county levy ... for every one of the patrollers [pay at the rate of] ten pounds of tobacco for every day or night they shall so patrol." Patrollers were also to be "exempt from the payment of public, county, and parish levies ... for the years they shall be employed in that service." In the absence of surviving officers' reports, the annual county levies and entries in the annual tithable lists are the only documents available to enlighten us on the activities of the early patrollers of Loudoun County. According to the tithable list of Justice Nicholas Minor (who was the acting Colonel of the county militia at the time), the Loudoun slave patrol was inaugurated in 1764. [infra, Chronology Appendix; Braddock, p. 127; Hening, VII/104-105; supra, Chapter on the Militia, and supra, Chapter on Servants; see infra, p. 485].

The 1766 Assembly declared that "the appointment of patrollers, their duty and reward, has been found inconvenient," and amended the patrolling law again slightly. Thereafter, patrol officers reported only twice a year instead of monthly, and the chief county officers' reports were no longer submitted to the annual court martial, but were "certified and delivered [directly] to the court of the said county ... before [the] laying [of] the county levy," ie., before November. County courts were instructed "to allow to and levy for every one of the patrollers [pay at the rate of] twenty [20] pounds of tobacco, for every twelve [12] hours they shall so patrol." In a trade-off for the pay raise, patrollers were no longer exempt from annual county and parish levies. When additional patrols were activated, it was specified that they were not to be "continued in office longer than the pressing cause of their appointment shall remain." [Hening, VIII/195-197].

Colonial Virginians' mental image of a fifth column of armed slaves in their midst never faded. On June 29, 1776, when the Assembly adopted the Virginia Declaration of Independence, it was asserted that one of the "detestable and unsupportable" tyrannies of King George III was his "prompting [of] our negroes to rise in arms among us, those very negroes whom ... he hath refused us permission to exclude by Law." Most Virginia planters recognized the political and moral evil in slavery, but were at a loss to find resolution for their own dilemma. Many slave owners, including George Washington and Thomas Jefferson, provided for the manumission of some or all of their slaves upon their deaths. But a majority of colonial slave owners did or could not, and the odious institution would resist the compelling force of freedom for nearly 250 years. [Hening, IX/113; Democracy, p. 72].

Any demographic study of colonial Loudoun County during it's first decade must rely upon the 1761 and 1765 county tithable lists for a proper starting point. Tithable lists for those years identify every slave in Loudoun over the age of 16. The only other document from the early colonial period, a tithable list for Truro parish compiled by Rev. Charles Green in 1749, also includes Cameron parish (later Loudoun County) residents. As a result, Rev. Green's list serves to identify many of the earliest "Loudoun" resident slave owners. But Green's list was nearly a decade old when Loudoun County was created, and did not distinguish the parish of residence for slaves of the largest owners, and is thus limited in value. Analysis of the tithable lists has allowed for a study of the patterns of slave ownership in Loudoun, presented for the reader in both Table form and in the following discussions. [see generally, supra, Green, *"Fairfax County List ..."*, MS; Table summarizing Slave Ownership in Loudoun, 1757-1765, supra @ p. 376; see infra, Chapter on Tithables and Tax Lists; contra, Democracy, pp. 72-74; contra, Fairfax, pp. 32-35].

Previous estimates of the slave population in the colonial Northern Neck have proven erroneous because they followed a formula that had been articulated by Governor Dinwiddie: that the numbers of blacks given in a county tithable list should be doubled to obtain the slave population. This formulation is reliable for tidewater counties where slave-operated plantations were predominant, and would seem to be reliable for the slave plantations around Mt. Vernon by the 1780s, but does not apply in the upper piedmont or valley of Virginia. Inventories of the estates of slave owners on the 1749 parish list reveal that the total number of slaves owned by "Loudoun" and Fairfax residents in Cameron parish is more nearly estimated by accepting the actual number of tithable slaves listed in 1749, rather than by doubling the number. The rate of acquisition of non-tithable (underage) slaves and the absence of identifiable "breeding" populations, evident from County Court Orders and tithable list entries, support the notion that the old tidewater formula simply did not apply in Loudoun County. Regardless, colonial commentators are shown deference herein and a formula has been adopted to estimate Loudoun's total slave population at 150% of tithable slaves. This probably results in an <u>over</u>-estimate of the slave population in colonial Loudoun, but with that forewarning we proceed apace. [contra, Fairfax, pp. 33-34; infra, Chapter on Population].

Analysis of the Loudoun County tithable lists for 1761 and 1765, combined with a general knowledge of the precincts that the various tax lists were compiled for, has given us a picture of where slave populations were concentrated in Loudoun before the Revolution. A Map representing the distribution of slaves in Loudoun in 1765 is presented for the reader herein. [for a Map of Racial Distribution in Loudoun County in 1765, see in seriatim, pp. 478-479; infra, Chapter on Tithables and the Tax Lists].

We can only speculate as to when and where the first slaves were introduced into Loudoun in the 1720s. Perhaps the McCartys were the first to bring their slaves, to work their patent on the Potomac around Sugarland; it could have been Henry Lee or George Turberville around Chantilly; the Carter family when they cleared the Ox Road or for working their copper mine at Frying Pan; or perhaps it was John Tayloe, or Francis Awbrey, or Walter Griffith, or the Newtons or Graysons, on quarters they installed in the Bull Run-Rocky Run area. By the mid-1730s, the Awbrey family had at least one slave quarter in the vicinity of modern Leesburg; John Colvill and John Lewis had begun mining operations west of Difficult Run; Thomas Lee and John Tayloe opened slave quarters in the vicinity of modern Dulles; Abraham Barnes installed a slave quarter near McCarty at the Sugarlands; and John Colvill, Catesby Cocke and members of Lord Fairfax's family were busy opening large tracts between Difficult Run and Clarks Gap on the Potomac Ridge Road. It seems likely that

Loudoun county Justice Francis Awbrey was the "Loudoun" resident with the largest slave holdings during the 1730s, when he was constructing the Chapel of Ease at Big Spring, and building up his ordinary and ferry east of Conoy Island on the Potomac.

Elisha Hall was probably the resident owner with the largest number of slaves for most of the decade before Loudoun's incorporation. As the proprietor of an ordinary on the Mountain Road near Cub Run, Hall was identified on Rev. Green's 1749 list as a Quaker living in the "upper [Cameron] parish" and owning ten tithable slaves. Elisha Hall was an exception to the rule for the members of his faith, but he was not the only Quaker who owned slaves. Francis Hague, an elder of the Fairfax Meeting of Quakers at Waterford, was repeatedly identified on the Loudoun tax rolls as a slave owner. Using Rev. Green's 1749 lists and the 1760s tithable lists as guideposts, it is reasonable to assume that a number of Loudoun residents had "modest" holdings of between a half-dozen and a dozen slaves in 1757. The Linton, Awbrey, Noland and Turley families, Richard Coleman, Anthony Russell, Francis Summers and William West are all likely to have been members of that group. This observation points to one traditional tidewater pattern that was continued on the Loudoun piedmont. Fifteen of the first sixteen Justices appointed to the Loudoun County Court, and all of the first dozen Vestrymen elected for Cameron parish, were slave owners. Even the sole exception, Loudoun County Justice John McIlhaney, was entered on the tithable lists as a slave owner before 1765. Loudoun's ordinary keepers who, as a group, were constantly "serving" the public, were also likely to be found among the Loudoun tithable listings of slave owners. [supra, Chapter on the County Court; supra, Chapter on Ordinaries; see The Record, infra pp. 395-398].

In Fairfax (which included Loudoun) County in 1749, about 17% of the white male population owned slaves. Curiously, when Loudoun was created eight years later, slaves in residence in the new county accounted for 17% of the resident population of about 3,300, but only 8% of Loudoun's adult white males were slave owners. The entire eastern region of Fairfax County in 1756, including the section of 1757 Loudoun situated east of Goose Creek, was dominated by slave-operated plantations. Very few, if any, slaves were held west of the Kitoctin-Bull Run range in 1757. Simply stated, the further away from the tidewater one travelled on the piedmont of colonial Loudoun, the lower the density of the slave population. The slave population in Fairfax County did not suddenly bolt from 29% in 1756 to 41% after the formation of Loudoun, nor was the County "dominated by slave labor." When the predominantly white western precincts were removed from Fairfax to create Loudoun, the population in the eastern, plantation, precincts of Fairfax County was simply easier to focus on. [see Democracy, pp. 72-74; contra, Fairfax, pp. 32-35].

In 1757 there were, altogether, only about 600 households of residents in Loudoun County. Some 30 or 35 of these were small slave plantation "quarter"s, owned by members of the gentry who lived elsewhere, in either Fairfax, Prince William, Richmond, Stafford or Westmoreland County. These plantations were called "quarter"s because the most prominent dwellings on the properties were usually the slave quarters. Each quarter was operated by a resident "overseer" who was either an indentured servant or an employee of the owner. The overseer managed the work of the plantation, was exempt from working on public road projects and was, by law, disqualified from the general musters of the county militia if he was in charge of four or more slaves. Absentee landlords normally kept less than a dozen slaves on their Loudoun County quarters, since a larger slave population required the active management of more than one overseer. [Fairfax, p. 30, contra, p. 35; see also, Chapter on the Militia, supra, @ pp. 69 and 82].

Thirty absentee slave owners accounted for about 65% of the total slaves in Loudoun in 1757. There were also about 60 slave owners residing in Loudoun County in 1757, representing less than 15% of all resident households in the county. Stated another way, over 85% of the white householders of Loudoun County did not own a slave in 1757. In 1766, the same could still be said. During the 1757-1766 decade, the total slave holdings of absentee owners remained essentially unchanged at about 400-425, while the number of slaves owned by Loudoun residents increased from about 200 to over 650. Two-thirds of this population increase was accounted for by Loudoun resident slave owners who had acquired fewer than six slaves, and another 15% by large slave owners who moved their residences to Loudoun. For the first five years, up until 1762, increases in the number of slaves quartered in the county by large absentee owners, small acquisitions by Loudoun residents, and immigration of slave owners with modest holdings, all contributed evenly to the growth of the slave population. This growth pattern changed dramatically around 1761, probably as a result of a lull in the chronic Indian warfare on the western frontier. Thereafter, until at least 1765, increases in Loudoun's slave population were the result of acquisitions by slave owners, both large and small, residing in or moving to Loudoun County. From 1761 to 1765, the total number of slaves owned by Loudoun residents increased from about 400 to roughly 675.

The total slave population, the number of households of Loudoun County residents, and the number of households owning slaves all, in proportion, essentially doubled in Loudoun's first decade - to about 1,150, 1,050 and 180, respectively, in 1766. During that time, the number of absentee-owned slave quarters held constant at less than three dozen. About 30 of the 60 resident slave owners, one-third of all slave owners in 1757, owned just one slave. On the average, resident slave owners had two slaves each, while the average absentee owner kept seven slaves on his quarter. This pattern continued through 1761, despite other population shifts, when the majority of resident owners still held only one or two slaves but non-resident owners quartered an average of eight slaves in Loudoun. By 1765, thirty absentee slave owners, with an average of about fourteen slaves each, accounted for barely 40% of the total slaves in Loudoun County, while 90 Loudoun residents, who held only one or two slaves each, now comprised half of all slave owners. [infra, Chapter on Population; see supra, Table of Loudoun Slave Owners @ p. 462].

Daily life in colonial Loudoun must have changed along with the practice of slavery. Two patterns, reflecting on the "complexion" of Loudoun County society during this first decade, offset each. The first pattern is an increasing diffusion of the slave ownership in Loudoun between 1757 and 1766, exemplified by the three family groups with the largest slave holdings. In 1757, five Lees, three Carters, and two Masons between them owned over 30% of the total number of slaves in Loudoun County. By 1765, the Masons, Lees and Carters (in a new order), together owned less than 20% of the tithable slaves in the county. On the other hand, the number of "large" slave owners, holding between 10 and 20 slaves, doubled in Loudoun's first decade. While the total number of slaves living in Loudoun also doubled between 1757 and 1765, the numbers of both resident owners and, particularly, small resident owners, tripled. As the middle class of yeomanry expanded and their collective purchasing power grew, they weighted in by obtaining a modest work force of field hands.

A second pattern that developed during Loudoun's first decade was the immigration of a number of youthful members of the tidewater gentry into Loudoun County. Francis Lightfoot Lee became the first of many socially and politically prominent slave owners to actually reside in the county. His situation is exemplary of the larger picture. Before Francis Lee moved to Loudoun County in the winter of 1757-58, all but one of the two dozen largest Loudoun slave owners were men who lived in other counties. Members of the Carter, Fairfax, Fitzhugh, Lee, Mason, McCarty and Mercer families, Thomas Blackburn, John Colvill, Daniel French, Willoughby Newton, John Tayloe and Joseph Watkins all owned at least one "quarter" in Loudoun County. These plantations were operated in the traditional tidewater manner, utilizing "old field" tobacco agriculture. During the French and Indian War, landowners from the tidewater seem to have been content, for the most part, to let employees manage their "upland" Loudoun slave quarters. After the urgency of the conflict with the French and Indians dissipated around 1761, the younger generation of several tidewater families followed Francis Lightfoot Lee's example and seated themselves on their Loudoun lands. Prime examples of this trend were Spence Grayson and William Douglass, both promptly appointed as a Justice of the Loudoun County Court, Landon Carter Junr., the son of a Virginia Councilman, and Thomson Mason, who individually would eclipse the entire Lee family in total slave holdings before 1765 and, subsequently, replace Francis Lee as First Justice of the Loudoun County Court after Lee moved back to Richmond County. Others, the best example being John Ballendine of Prince William, utilized slaves in their exploration of mercantile opportunities on the Potomac and along Loudoun's primary roads. [see generally, LDTX/1; infra, The Record, p. 485; Fairfax, p. 32].

The general public's indifference to the institution of slavery may be explained, in part, by the design of colonial tax policy. Slave owners and quarters constituted less than 20% of all Loudoun households between 1757 and 1766, but Loudoun slave owners paid over 50% of all colony, county and parish tithable taxes collected in the County. [infra, Chapter on Colonial Taxes].

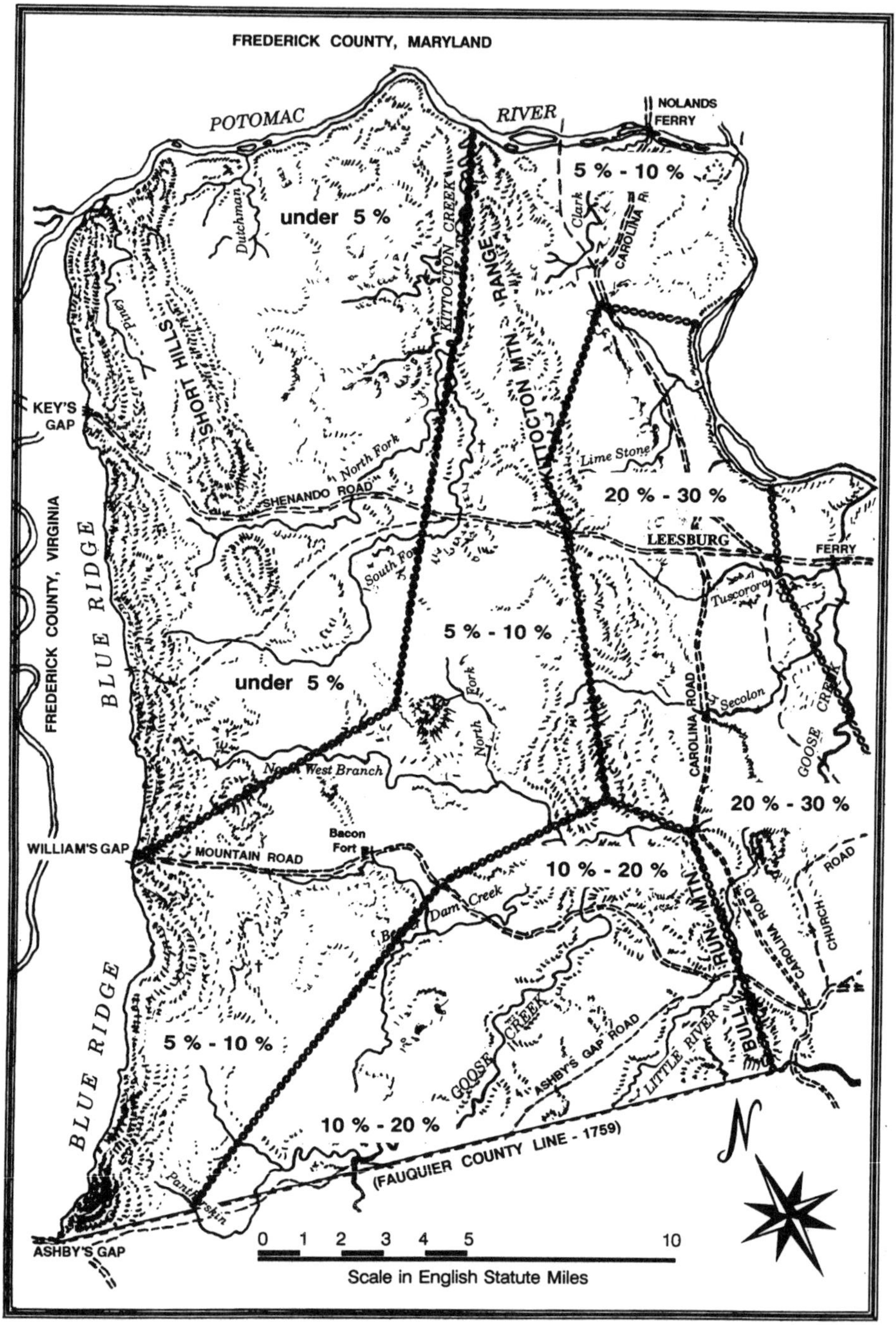
FREDERICK COUNTY, MARYLAND
POTOMAC
RIVER
NOLANDS FERRY
5 % - 10 %
under 5 %
KITTOCTON CREEK
KITTOCTON MTN. RANGE
SHORT HILLS
KEY'S GAP
SHENANDO ROAD
20 % - 30 %
LEESBURG
FERRY
FREDERICK COUNTY, VIRGINIA
BLUE RIDGE
5 % - 10 %
under 5 %
CAROLINA ROAD
GOOSE CREEK
20 % - 30 %
WILLIAM'S GAP
MOUNTAIN ROAD
Bacon Fort
10 % - 20 %
BULL RUN MTN.
CHURCH ROAD
BLUE RIDGE
5 % - 10 %
GOOSE CREEK
ASHBY'S GAP ROAD
LITTLE RIVER
10 % - 20 %
(FAUQUIER COUNTY LINE - 1759)
ASHBY'S GAP
0 1 2 3 4 5 10
Scale in English Statute Miles
N

-LOUDOUN COUNTY - VIRGINIA-

SLAVES
As A Percentage of the TOTAL POPULATION circa 1760

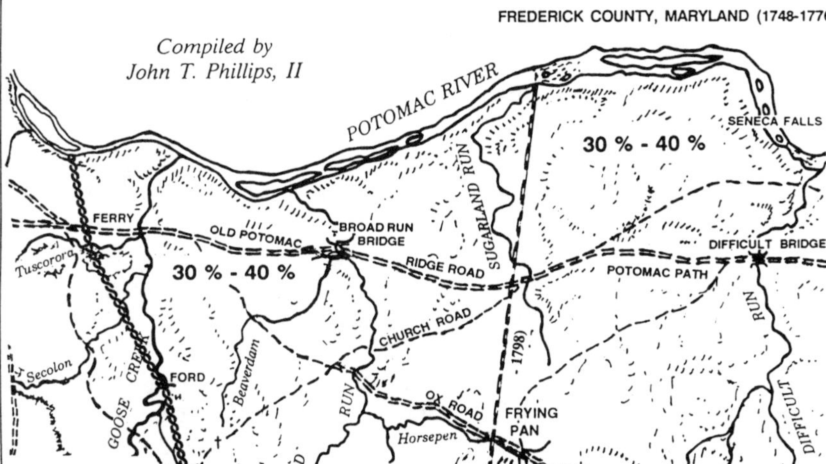

July 30, 1758 - The Loudoun tithable list returned by County Justice Francis Peyton identifies overseers at several of the slave quarters in Loudoun: Smith Johnston is overseer for John Mercer at Little River, Moses Botts is the overseer for Benjamin Grayson's Estate, Henry Parker is overseer for Henry Peyton south of Beaver Dam branch of Goose Creek, Aaron Botts is overseer for Daniel French, William Wadlington [sic- William Wigginton ?] is the overseer at Richard Henry Lee's quarter at the mouth of Goose Creek on the Potomac, and Benjamin Smith is the overseer for Minor Winn. LDTX/1, p. 1.

September 12, 1758 - "Ordered that ... John Ethell and his ... Negro Lonnon ... [and] Francis Hague and his ... Negro Isaac ... be added to the List of Tithables taken for this County this present Year [1758]." Book A, pp. 159-160.

October 22, 1758 - The Virginia Assembly, in session in Williamsburg, receives a Petition from Andrew Hutchison [of Loudoun County] seeking the statutory compensation "for taking up a Runaway". Assembly, (1758) p. 39.

February 24, 1759 - The Virginia Assembly refers the October 1758 Petition of Andrew Hutchison "to the Consideration of the next Session of Assembly", but no further entries appear in the subsequent Assembly records. Assembly, (1758) p. 64.

March 2, 1759 - The Virginia Assembly, acting on the "Claim of ... Richard Coleman, [of Loudoun], for taking up Runaways ... Ordered to allow the said Claim in the [Assembly's] Book of Claims." Assembly, (1758) p. 74.

August 14, 1759 - The ages of various slaves are "adjudged" by the Court: slaves belonging to Vincent Lewis - boys Sam, 12, and Bray, 15, and girls Pat, 13, and Cate, 12; and a slave belonging to John Smarr - Rose, a girl, age 12. Book A, p. 264.

August 15, 1759 - "Ciller, Negro girl belonging to Leven Powell ..." age 11. Book A, p. 270.

September of 1759 - The Loudoun tithable list returned by County Justice Richard Coleman identifies overseers at several slave quarters: Leroy Hughlet is an overseer, probably for Francis Lightfoot Lee between Difficult and Horsepen runs, Joshua Harrison is overseer for Capt. Samuel Oldham, John Elliot is overseer for John Husk, Patrick O'Brien is the overseer for William Adams, John Jenkins is the overseer at Abraham Barnes' quarter on the Potomac Ridge road near Sugarland run, Nicholas Wren is the overseer at Francis Lightfoot Lee's quarter east of Sugarland run near Potomac Ridge road, Steerman Chilton is the overseer for Col. Philip Ludwell Lee north of Belmont ridge, John Stone is the overseer at Col. William Fitzhugh's quarter on Sugarland run, and Thomas Lewis (of Little River) is the overseer at Col. Thomas Ludwell Lee's quarter between Goose Creek and Broad run. LDTX/1, pp. 2-3.

September 11, 1759 - "Ordered that ... Henry Wisheart and his Tithable to-wit Negro Frank ... [and] Benjamin Edwards and his three Tithables, to-wit, Negroes Joan, George and Sarah ... [all] be added to the List of Tithables taken for this County this present Year [1759]." Book A, pp. 283-284.

September 11, 1759 - "Sylvia, Negro girl belonging to George West ..." age 10. Book A, p. 284.

September 11, 1759 - "Chloe, Negro girl belonging to John Herryford ... nine Years old." Book A, p. 285.

September 12, 1759 - "Winney, Negro girl belonging to John Moss ...", age 12. Book A, p. 290.

September 13, 1759 - "Ordered that Thomas Awbrey and his ... Negroes Butcher, Cuffey and Bess be added to the List of Tithables taken for ... [1759]." Book A, p. 294.

November 13, 1759 - The ages of various slaves are "adjudged" by the Court: slaves belonging to Charles Tyler - Isaac, 13, and Jane, 9; and slaves belonging to Anthony Russell - Sylvia, 12, and Delia, 10. Book A, p. 298.

November 13, 1759 - Two slaves in the Estate of Edmund Linton are valued at £75. LDCOWIL, Book A, p. 20.

December 12, 1759 - On the "Petition of Susanna Grimes against John Davis for unjustly detaining of her as a Slave ... [the Court rules that] Susanna ought to be Free ... Ordered that ... John Davis do not detain the said Susanna any longer as a Slave." Book A, p. 321; see supra, Chapter on Servants.

June 10, 1760 - "Leah, a Negro Girl belonging to Aaron Botts is adjudged ... to be fourteen Years of Age." Book A, p. 360.

June 11, 1760 - On the "Motion of Joseph Brown ... [after] Notice to his Father Thomas Brown ... to prove a Verbal Gift of two Slaves Vizt. Charles and Patt ... [the Loudoun Court ruled that the evidence was] not sufficient to Establish the Gift." Joseph Brown appealed the ruling of the County Court to the Virginia General Court in Williamsburg. Book A, p. 366.

August 12, 1760 - "Dinah, a Negro Girl belonging to William Landrum, is ... adjudged to be fourteen Years of Age." Book A, p. 384.

September 23, 1760 - The Loudoun Court, in session "For Proof of Public Claims ... Charles Lewis produced a Certificate for taking up a Runaway Negro belonging to Abraham Farrow of Prince William County ... Certified to the next Session of [the Virginia] Assembly [in Williamsburg]." Book A, p. 401.

September of 1760 - The tithable lists for 1760 name overseers at several slave quarters in Loudoun: on Justice George West's list, John Railey [sic- John Reilly] is the overseer at William Douglass' quarter on Goose Creek; on Justice William West's list, William Bannister is the overseer for William Winn, Arthur Mortimore is the overseer for Benjamin Sebastian on the upper reaches of Broad run, and William Berkeley is the new overseer for John Mercer at Little River; on Justice James Hamilton's list, William Lane and Richard Lightfoot are overseers for Thompson Mason [and the Seldens] north and east of Leesburg; on Justice Fielding Turner's list, William Montgomery is the overseer for the Estate of Richard Blackburn; on Justice Francis Peyton's list,

Joseph Moren is Peyton's overseer and Thomas Gorham is the overseer for William Bronaugh; on Justice Richard Coleman's list, John Elliott is the overseer for John Hurst; and Justice James Lane [Junr.]'s list identifies William VanDevander as his overseer, James Whaley as the new overseer for Col. Henry Lee at his Sully plantation, John Lane as the overseer for Col. John Tayloe [Junr.] on Horsepen run near Frying Pan, Jacob Gardner as overseer for Samuel Winn, and Thomas Cockrill as an overseer for Willoughby Newton near Rocky run. LDTX/1, pp. 3-8; but see infra, Chapter on Crimes re John Riley.

April 25, 1761 - In Williamsburg, the General Court rules that a new trial must be had in the suit between Joseph Brown and his father Thomas Brown for the determination of the ownership of certain slaves. see Book B, p. 68.

June 9, 1761 - "Surry a Negro Boy and Celana a Negro Girl belonging to Charles Binns are adjudged ... Surry to be [12] Years and Celana to [10] Years of Age." Book A, p. 449.

July 14, 1761 - "Bess a Negro Girl belonging to Thomas Owsley adjudged ... to be ten Years of Age." Book A, p. 480.

August 11, 1761 - "Bess a Negro Girl belonging to Roger Wigginton ... adjudged to be twelve Years of Age." Book A, p. 481.

August 12, 1761 - "Nan a Negro Girl belonging to John Lewis is adjudged ... to be twelve Years of Age." Book A, p. 488.

September 8, 1761 - "Cate a Negro Girl belonging to William Noding is adjudged ... to be thirteen Years of Age." Book A, p. 491.

September 8, 1761 - "Ordered that Greenbury Dorsey and his two Tithables to wit Negroes Peter & Phebe be added to the List of Tithables for this County this Present Year [1761]." Book A, p. 496.

September 10, 1761 - "David Davis and his Tithable ... Negro Sampson ... be added to the List of Tithables taken for this County." Book A, p. 517.

September 10, 1761 - John Heryford and his Tithables, to-wit, [three] Negroes Joseph, Moll and Margaret ... be added to the List of Tithables taken for this County." Book A, p. 523; see supra, Chapter on Ordinaries.

October 13, 1761 - "Dick and Tom, Negroes belonging to Jeremiah Hutchison, are adjudged," both to be ten years old; "Chloe a Negro Girl belonging to Walter Williams is adjudged ... to be ten"; "Will a Negro Boy belonging to Thomas Williams, is adjudged ... to be eight"; and, "Sambo a Negro Boy and Esther a Negro Girl belonging to Jeremiah Cockrill are adjudged ... Sambo to be ten & Esther to be twelve." Book A, p. 525.

November 11, 1761 - "Ordered that Thomas Awbrey and his two Tithables, to wit, Negroes Butcher & Bill be added to the List of Tithables taken for this County this present Year [1761]." Book A, p. 532.

March 10, 1762 - It is Ordered that "... Negroes belonging to Patrick O'Bryan are adjudged ... James to be thirteen Years and Jenny to fourteen Years of Age." Book A, p. 566.

June 8, 1762 - "Harry a Negro Boy belonging to James Lane was adjudged ... twelve Years of Age." Book A, p. 627.

June 10, 1762 - In the Loudoun County tithables lists, Aaron Botts is listed as one of the overseers on Thompson Mason's quarter north of Leesburg, with responsibility for thirty-three slaves. LDTX/1, p. 20.

August 10, 1762 - A slave, "Harry ... belonging to Walter Williams is adjudged ... to be ten [10] Years of Age ... [and] Sam ... belonging to James Buckley is adjudged ... to be twelve [12 years old]." Book B, p. 28.

August 10, 1762 - It is "Ordered that ... William Landrum and his ... Negro Bob ... Edward Porter and his Tithable, to-wit, Negro Nan ... George Hancocke and his Tithables, to-wit, Negroes Hagar & Milford ... Samuel Oldham's Tithables ... Negroes Hazard, Philip, Tim, Nan and Judith ... James Shead and his Tithable, to-wit, Negro Harry ... [and] George Ashford and his Tithables to-wit, Negroes Bash and Stacey ... [all] be added to the List of Tithables taken this Year." Book B, p. 30-31.

August 13, 1762 - "Ordered that ... William Hancocke and his ... Negroes Mag and Jone ... David Davis and his Tithable to-wit, Negro Sampson ... [all] be added to the List of Tithables taken for this Year." Book B, p. 55.

September 15, 1762 - "William Trammell and his Tithables to-wit, Negroes Glasgow and Maria, be added to the List of Tithables taken for this Year." Book B, p. 59.

September 16, 1762 - Based on a ruling of the Virginia General Court in Williamsburg issued in the spring session of 1761, the Loudoun County Court Orders "a new Contestation [trial or hearing] of Joseph Brown's right to Slaves in the Possession of Thomas Brown his Father." Book B, p. 68.

September of 1762 - In the Loudoun tithables lists: James Whaley is identified as the overseer on Col. Henry Lee's quarter at Sully, south of Frying Pan, managing nine slaves. LDTX/1, p. 19.

October of 1762 - On Loudoun County "List No. 3," John Violett is identified as the Overseer for Daniel French [of Fairfax County], managing seven slaves. Property Tax Lists, 1757-1799, in undated MS series, at p. 1357.

November 9, 1762 - "Ordered that ... Aaron Lane and his ... Negro Sam ... be added to the List of Tithables taken for this Year." Book B, p. 69.

December 15, 1762 - Joseph Brown established a gift of two Slaves, Charles and Pall, from his father Thomas Brown, in a case of contested ownership, with the testimony of Adam Mitchell, William Landrum and John Goram. Book B, p. 82.

June 14, 1763 - Two "Negroes belonging to John Smarr are adjudged ... Hannah to twelve and Sneber to eight Years of Age." Book B, p. 159.

June 14, 1763 - "Negroes belonging to Thomson Mason Esqr. are adjudged ... Moody to [8] years and Barber [2] Years of Age." Book B, p. 161.

June 15, 1763 - Four slaves in the Estate of Nicholas Seward are valued at £230. LDCOWIL, Book A, p. 86.

June 16, 1763 - Joshua Hickman sues Ezekiel Hickman for possession of a "Negro Boy Sampson", a jury valuing Sampson at £80 and awarding damages against Ezekiel, finding that Joshua had possession at the time of trial only because Sampson "having run away from Richard Coleman's [ordinary] out of the possession of the Deft. [defendant]." Book B, p. 174.

September 13, 1763 - "Ordered that ... John Berkley's Tithables, to-wit, Negroes Frank, Dick and Cesar ... [and] Josias Clapham Gent. and his Tithables, ... Negroes Duke, Tom, Cate, Nan and Jack ... [all] be added to the List [of Tithables] taken for this Year." Book B, p. 233.

September 14, 1763 - "Ordered that ... Sampson Trammell and his Tithables, to-wit, ... Negroes Jamey, Dick, Boson, Rose, Patt and Maria ... William Ellzey's Tithables, to-wit, ... Negroes Will and Tom ... [all] be added to the List [of Tithables] taken for this Year." Book B, p. 237.

September 15, 1763 - "Ordered that ... Charles Bennett Earle of Tankerville and his Tithables, to-wit, Negroes Valentine, Jerry, George, Joe, Jack, Morris, and Pidgeon ... [all] added to the List [of Tithables] ... for [1763]." Book B, p. 251.

September 15, 1763 - "Ordered that ... Richard Stephens and his ... Negro George ... added to the List ... for [1763]." Book B, p. 252.

November 8, 1763 - "Ordered that ... Jonathan Monkhouse and his Tithables to-wit, Negroes Jack, and Harry ... be added to the List taken for this Year." Book B, p. 261.

November 9, 1763 - "Ordered that John Davis and his ... Negro Sue be added to the List of Tithables taken for this Year." Book B, p. 264.

April 10, 1764 - Lucy, a Negro Girl belonging to James Whaley, is adjudged to be twelve years of age. Book B, p. 317.

May 8, 1764 - "... Proceedings against Martin Hollyback for misusing a Negro belonging to Samuel Tillet ... heard ... Dismissed." Book B, p. 355.

June 10, 1764 - The Loudoun tithable list returned by County Justice Nicholas Minor identifies Cornelius Donohue, Samuel Compton, John Lewis and Nicholas Osburn, each as exempt from the county levy due to their service as a "patroler". The officer of the first patrol is not recorded, but may have been Nicholas Minor himself. Minor was then the Lt. Colonel of the Loudoun militia. LDTX/1, pp. 25-27; and see supra, Chapter on Militia, @ pp. 90-91.

August 14, 1764 - "One Negro Girl named Luce", the property of Elisha Reagan, is ordered sold to satisfy judgment debts. Book B, p. 402.

August 13, 1765 - "Ordered that ... George Chelton and his Tithables, to-wit, Negroes Ben and Fander ... be added to the List taken and returned for this Present Year." Book C, p. 11.

September of 1765 - In "Capt. [Aeneas] Campbell's" tithables list for Loudoun County, Francis Hague, a Quaker living near Waterford, is listed as the owner of a slave; and, in "Mr. Noland's" list, Lewis Massey, and "Negro George" are listed as ferrymen. LDTX/1, pp. 35 and 36.

September of 1765 - The Loudoun County tithable lists identify several militiamen who were exempted from the county levy due to their service as "Patroler"s: on Justice Nicholas Minor's list, John Lewis and Thomas Pritchard; and on Justice William Carr Lane's list, Sanford Cockrill, Thomas Cockrill Junr. and Robert Thomas. LDTX/1, pp. 29 and 40-41; infra, Chapter on Militia.

October 16, 1765 - It is "Ordered ... George William Fairfax, Esqr., his Tithables ... Negroes Harry, Frank, Cezar, Clarey, Luner, Betty and Febay ... [are all] added to the List taken & returned for this present Year." Book C, p. 68.

September of 1766 - On the tithable list returned by William Carr Lane, Robert Thomas is identified as a "patroler" and exempt from the county levy. LDTX/1, p.43.

October 14, 1766 - "On the Motion of John Ballendine the following Tithables and Land be Entered on the Lists returned for this present Year vizt. Negroes Frederick, Bess, Nan, Sarah, Will, Frank, Dick, James, Juler and Prince [all] ... At McCarty's Quarter [below the mouth of Sugarland run on the Potomac river]; ... At Barne's Quarter [near Sugarland run and the Potomac Ridge road] ... Negroes Sam, Rhode, Alce, Grace, Winney, Winney [sic], Dick, Bosen, Pompey and Dick. At Seneca Falls, [one of John Ballendine's commercial ventures on the Potomac river; his overseer] John Melaley, Negroes Dick, Chloe, Gray General, Silvia and Jack." Book C, p. 208.

October 27, 1766 - In a Public Claims session for Loudoun County: "Charles West exhibited ... a claim for taking up a Runaway man Slave belonging to Colo. George William Fairfax." Book C, p. 218.

Concerned with the imperfect state of the collection of taxes in the colony, in the February 12, 1762 edition of the *Virginia Gazette* published by Royle, John Robinson, the Treasurer of Virginia, inserted the following notice:

> *"Whereas many Sheriffs, Inspectors and Clerks, have failed to pay the Taxes by Them collected, this is to give Notice that if They do not immediately settle their Accounts, and pay the Taxes due from Them, They will be prosecuted as the Law directs and the several County Court Clerks are desired to send me a List of the Sheriffs, and their Securities, from the Year 1755 to this Time."*

Thurſday December 4th, 1766.

ORDERED,

THAT the Clerks of the ſeveral County Courts in this Colony do tranſmit to the Clerk of the HOUSE of BURGESSES, in the firſt Part of every Meeting of the General Aſſembly, a Liſt of the Tithables in their Counties, containing the Names of ſuch Tithables, and that they tranſmit alſo at the ſame Time a Liſt of the public Charges of their reſpective Counties.

By Order of the Houſe of Burgeſſes,

JOHN RANDOLPH, C. H. B.

The *Virginia Gazette* of December 11, 1766, published by Rind, contained the above Order from the House of Burgesses to "the Clerks of the several County Courts in this Colony." The Clerks were instructed, thereafter, to transmit complete lists of Tithables from their Counties in order to assist the Assembly in more accurately setting the annual levies for the colony.

The British practice of levying parish and county "poll" (ie., per head) taxes, called "tithes," was continued in the Virginia colony. In the fifth year of the reign of King Charles I, the Virginia Assembly of October of 1629 "thought fitt that all those that worke in the ground of what qualitie or condition soever, shall pay tithes [sic]." In March of 1642-43, a tithable was redefined to include "all freemen that are hired servants [who] shall pay their own tithes and duties ... collected per pol [sic - poll, ie., person] for the country service." [Hening, I/144 and I/241]

In 1649, the Virginia Assembly, concerned with a prevalent method of tax fraud "through false & imperfect lists" in the colony, required that "all male servants imported hereafter into the colony," including those under the tithable age of 16, "be brought into the lists and shall be liable to pay country [colony and county] leavyes [sic]," and the tithes to parish ministers as well. This provision did not affect anyone under age 16 who was either a native Virginian or imported as a free person - they were still not held liable for the tithable levies. The Assembly of March 1661-62 redefined tithables as all male and female "imports" into the colony, both white and Negro, and all Indian servants, male and female, over 16 years of age. Christians under age 16, both those imported free and native Virginians, were exempt. In 1662, all women servants "working in the crop" were promoted to tithable status. Difficulties in enforcement of these provisions led the Assembly, in September of 1672, to provide that all Negro and mulatto children and slaves "borne in this country" were to be registered, within 12 months of their birth, in the parish registry, and Negro women over age 16 were included as tithables. [Hening, I/361, II/84, II/170 and II/296].

In 1705 the Assembly revised the definition of a tithable:

> *"all male persons, of the age of sixteen years and upwards and all negro, mulatto, and Indian women, of the age of sixteen years, and upwards, not being free, shall be ... tithable ... for defraying the public, county and parish charges in [Virginia]."*

Every eligible person who reached age 16 before June 10th was considered a tithable in that year. The Governor and his family, all certified ministers, and any colonists that the county court or the parish vestry "in charity ... think fit to excuse," were exempt from tithable levies. In 1748, the 1705 definition of a tithable was continued and amended. Additional exemptions were granted to "Indians tributary to [allied with] this government," but the "wives of free negroes, mulattos and Indians, except as before excepted ... [were now] declared to be tithable." The 1748 law also added several other sets of exemptions from the poll, or tithe, taxes for: "all mariners and seafaring persons, not being freeholders, commonly employed in navigation, and who actually pay towards the support of Greenwich hospital out of their wages;" "domestick servants" of the Governor; "the President, masters, scholars and domestick servants of the college of William and Mary ...[; and] the person of any constable, so long as [while] he continues in his office." This definition of a tithable, along with the full set exemptions, was the law applied in Loudoun County during the 1757-1766 decade. [Hening, III/258-259 and VI/40].

The 1705 and 1748 recodifications of the tithable laws enhanced the provisions "for ascertaining the age of children imported into this colony." Thereafter, every imported servant or slave who was a child, and every newly arriving free male child, was to be brought before the county court of the child's residence so that the child's age could be judged and recorded, no later than the third court session after importation. Otherwise, the child was immediately considered as a tithable to the importer, overseer, owner or parent, regardless of age. This "viewing" provision was the reason for the large number of Loudoun Court Orders that recorded the names, ages and owners of slaves. The absence of recorded entries for free and servant children arriving in Loudoun County leads one to conclude that the penalty provision was very loosely applied or ignored altogether when white children were involved, at least in Loudoun County. [Hening, III/259 and VI/41; supra, Chapter on Slaves; infra, The Record].

The Assembly first provided "for the releife of diverse poore people ... disabled to labor by reason of sicknes, lamenes or age [sic]" in 1642, empowering every parish vestry with the right to grant a certificate "which shall free them from all publique [sic] charges except the ministers & parish duties." In the 1700s, the power to grant a charitable exemption from public tithes was given to the county courts as well as the parish vestries. The Loudoun

Court continued the practice, which was in full use in the Northern Neck in the 1750s. From 1757 to 1766, disabled, aged, sick and lame residents of Loudoun were frequently excused from tithable liability, "for charitable reasons," by the Loudoun County Court. Surprisingly, we find that retiring Loudoun ordinary keepers (Conrad Shanks, Jacob Lasswell, William Grant and John Davis) as a group constituted more than 10% of the exempted disabled in Loudoun's first decade. [Hening, I/242; three dozen examples of charitable exemptions are in The Record, infra, pp. 407-415].

The 1649 Assembly normalized the process of making tithable lists, requiring that every colonist turn in his tithables to the county court by June 25th each year. A penalty was imposed of "trebble [sic] assessments for every person [given] in short." In 1659, the Assembly repealed a provision in the tithable laws calling for "people bringing in the list of their families," restoring the previous practice whereby the county sheriffs were responsible for taking the county tithables lists. In March of 1660-61, the next Assembly addressed the "fraud of sheriffes in bringing in their lists ... [which had] very much augmented the taxes of the country," and directed the county Constables to instruct residents to turn in their lists directly to tithable list commissioners in each county. This law also directed the county courts to divide each county into four precincts for list-making. The Assembly amended the law again in the very next session, in March of 1661-62, instructing the county courts to divide the counties into "several precincts," and to appoint commissioners who were "to take the lists of tythables [sic]," before June 10th each year, with the accounts to be delivered during or before every August county court days. Sitting county court Justices invariably appointed a regionally diverse group, from their own membership, as the annual tithable list commissioners. These procedures, by both custom and colonial law, were maintained in Virginia for the next century. [Hening, I/361, II/19 and II/83].

The tithable laws of 1705 and 1748 detailed procedures that were followed in Loudoun County for the compilation, reporting and verification of tithable lists. Every county court divided their county into "convenient precincts, and annually, before the tenth day of June, appoint[ed] one of the justices for each precinct, to take a list of the tithables therein." In Loudoun, the size and area encompassed by each of these precincts changed from year to year, depending on which Justices were taking the lists. While the law did not specifically say so, the Sheriff was never involved in compiling the lists, probably because he was responsible for collecting the levies. Each Justice would affix a notice to the door of his parish church, "at what place or places he intends to receive the lists" on June 10th, or June 11th if the 10th was a Sunday. There were a large number of religious "dissenters" in Loudoun and it would be reasonable to assume that many of the Loudoun Justices left additional notices with the various Baptist, Methodist, Presbyterian, German Reformed and Quaker meetings all over the county. In practice, Loudoun tithables could and did report to any of the Justices regardless of the precinct that a particular Justice was responsible for. Additional time was allowed, until the end of June, for anyone who was ignorant, sick or absent from the county, "to carry or send their lists to the said justice's house ... and so doing, shall be free and acquit [themselves] from penalty." August Court days were established as the appropriate time for Justices to deliver their lists to the Clerk, although lists were occasionally returned beforehand. Every county Clerk was directed, "on the next court day, [to] set up fair copies of such lists in his court house ... for the inspection of all persons and the better discovery of such as shall be concealed." Penalties for "concealing" a tithable were increased dramatically (by a factor of 10) in 1705, from treble tithes, to proper tithes plus 1,000 lbs. of tobacco. The 1748 law halved the penalty for "concealing," to proper tithes plus 500 lbs. of tobacco (over £3). As with many other types of civil penalties, "one moiety" (half) of the penalty went to the King "for the use of the parish," and one moiety "to the informer." An owner of slaves or master of servants was accountable for the tithable list omissions of his overseer. Despite substantial sanctions provided for "concealers," the Loudoun County Court appears to have adopted the practice of allowing Loudoun residents to clarify their status on the lists without penalty at all times of the year. These additions and deletions, sometimes given in August, were extensive in every September county court session. This leads us to conclude that Charles Binns, the first Loudoun County Clerk, normally posted the Loudoun tithables lists for inspection during the September County Court sessions, "the next court day" after the August term. [Hening, III/259-260 and VI/41-43; Glossary].

The 1738 Assembly had first acted to stop the fraudulent removal of tithables from counties where an annual levy was likely to "run high ... by reason of [the construction of] public buildings, or other emergencies." Virginia law thereafter provided that it would be considered "concealing" to remove any:

> *"tithables, [slaves and servants] from one plantation to another, with intent to avoid the payment of levies in the county or parish ... afterwards caus[ing] the same or other tithables in their room, to return to the plantation from whence they were removed."*

Loudoun County and parish levies were generally lower than those in neighboring counties, but an otherwise inexplicable drop in the number of tithables took place in Loudoun in 1759, the year that the first Courthouse and the Leesburg jail were both under construction. There were no actions against "concealers" in Loudoun in the 1757-1766 decade, perhaps because intent had to be proven as an element of this type of tax fraud. [Hening, V/35 and VI/43; infra, Chapter on County Levy; generally, Fairfax].

Status as a tithable person also determined an individual's responsibility for assisting with the upkeep and maintenance of the public roads and by-ways, under the supervision of surveyors and overseers of the roads (appointees who were replaced annually by the county court). In the 1750s, every tithable resident of Loudoun living within 1½ miles of a dedicated county roadway, along with all of his tithable servants and slaves, would be expected, on occasion, to personally assist in clearing or improving the roads. [see infra, The Record, pp. 407 and 408].

Tithables information in court orders takes a number of different forms. Since many of the tithable lists have been either mislabeled, lost or destroyed, in some circumstances the tithable information contained in a Loudoun County Court Order is the only certain documentation of a given individual. A number of Loudoun Orders, usually based on the motion of the individual, add or delete some or all of his named tithables on the lists for a given year. These individuals were either new arrivals in the county, were omitted by mistake or design, or were double entries. Where an individual failed to correct an omission, the Grand Jury would bring a presentment for the understatement of tithables. Listings of charges on the annual County Levy frequently included line-item entries that identified individuals who were credited for overcharges in a previous year's levy of tithables. The published abstracts of Loudoun County tithable lists, with few exceptions, have not taken these tithable list amendments into account.

The County Levy (in November) would always include a statement of the total number of tithables on the Loudoun lists that year, along with the value of "tobacco" assessed "per Poll." Comparison of the surviving tithable lists with these annual totals, after taking into account additions and exemptions noted by the County Court, discharges for the disabled and obvious duplicate listings, has led to the determination that complete tithable lists for Loudoun County have survived for 1761 and 1765. These provide a basis for detailed demographic studies of Loudoun's population, which are presented elsewhere in this volume. [also see supra, Chapter on Slaves; infra, Chapter on Colonial Taxes; and infra, Chapter on Loudoun Population].

Analysis of surviving Loudoun tithable lists shows clearly that tithables were placed on the lists as they were presented to the Justice taking the list, in no particular geographic order even within a given precinct. Individuals who lived in different sections of a precinct were frequently entered consecutively on the same list. In a few instances individuals appear on the tithable list of a Loudoun Justice who had responsibility for a precinct on the opposite side of the county. Regardless, we can rely on the identification of a Justice's precinct as an indication of the general area of the county where any listed individual was living about 95% of the time. Every year a new court order named the Justices who were responsible for taking the lists that year but, except in 1766, the order did not identify the precinct assigned to each Justice. The Loudoun Justices undoubtedly made their own informal arrangements to achieve full coverage of the county.

A map has been prepared as an aide to additional research, identifying precincts covered in the Loudoun tithable lists. Map labels {A} to {Q} have been arbitrarily assigned to various neighborhoods and then identified with each of the list-making Justices as recited in the annual orders of appointment. Determination of the precinct covered by each Justice has required extensive analysis of the tithable entries, along with a good deal of research to ascertain the residence of various listed individuals. [for the precinct of each list-making Justice, see annual orders of appointment, in seriatim, pp. 407-415; Map, @ pp. 416-417].

August 10, 1757 - "Ordered that the Tithables in this County Work on the [repair of the] several Roads as formerly [assigned by Fairfax County Surveyors before the creation of Loudoun County]." Book A, p. 11.

September 13, 1757 - "On the Petition of John Carr ... that he is aged and infirm ... he be discharged from paying Levy for the future." Book A, p. 16.

September 13, 1757 - "Archibald Campbell is ... discharged from the Payment of Public and County Levies for the future." Book A, p. 17.

December 13, 1757 - "Ordered that the Sherif Collect twenty seven [27] pounds of Tobacco for every Tithable Person in this County according to the Levy this Day laid." Book A, p. 55.

May 9, 1758 - "Ordered that James Hamilton {D-E-G}, Nicholas Minor {B-D-F} and John Mucklehaney {A-C}, Gent., take the List of Tithables for this County [west of] Goose Creek and that Richard Coleman {J-K}, Francis Peyton {G-H-L-P}, James Lane {M-N-P-Q} and Benjamin Grayson {L-M}, Gent., take the same below [east of] the Creek." Book A, p. 99; and for the Map of the various Tithable List areas, see infra, pp. 416-417.

June 13, 1758 - "Robert Hopper on his Motion is ... discharged from the Paiment [sic] of Public and County Levies and Taxes." Book A, p. 110.

August 8, 1758 - "Lists of Tithables taken ... by Nicholas Minor, Francis Peyton, John Mucklehaney, Richard Coleman and Benjamin Grayson, Gent., [are] returned into Court [and ordered recorded]." Book A, p. 138.

August 8, 1758 - Charles Morriss and John Champe [sic], both of whom are on the list of tithables for 1758 enrolled by Francis Peyton, are referred to as "levy free," apparently having been discharged from tithable levies prior to this time due to either old age or an infirmity. LDTX/1, p. 1.

September 12, 1758 - "Ordered ... Joseph Hutchison ... Simon Reedy ... John Coleman ... John Ethell and his three Tithables, to wit, Abraham Ethell, John Fryer and [one] Negro ... George Winn ... James Shead ... Thomas Roden ... [and] ... Francis Hague and his three Tithables, to wit, Joseph Harris, John Hague and [one] Negro ... [all in separate Orders] ... be added to the List of Tithables taken for this County this present Year [1758]." Book A, pp. 159-160.

September 13, 1758 - "Ordered that Daniel Miller be added to the List of Tithables taken for this County this present Year [1758]." Book A, p. 166.

November 14, 1758 - "Ordered that ... Thomas Shepherd ... John Trammell ... Jacob Lasswell ... [and] Charles Russell ... [each is to] be added to the List of Tithables taken for this County this Present Year." Book A, p. 174.

November 14, 1758 - "William Molton on his Motion ... is discharged from the Paiment of Public and County Levies for the future." Book A, p. 174.

November 14, 1758 - In the County Levy, credits are listed for: "John Carlyle, Gent. for 5 Levies overcharged last Year [1757] ... 135 [lbs.t.] ... Francis

Hague for 4 [ditto] ... 180 [lbs.t.] ... William Mead for 2 Ditto ... 54 [lbs.t.] ... Robert Colclough for 3 Ditto ... 81 [lbs.t.] ... Henry Brown for 1 Ditto ... 27 [lbs.t.] ... [and] William Brown for 1 Ditto ... 27 ... William Owsley for 1 Levy overcharged last Year ... 27 ... Thomas Triplett for 1 [ditto] ... 27 ... Thomas Shepard for 1 Ditto ['Levy overcharged Last Year'] ... 27 [lbs.t.]." Book A, p. 176.

November 14, 1758 - "William Lynn on his Motion is ... discharged from the payment of Public and County Levies for the future." Book A, p. 178.

November 15, 1758 - "Ordered that John Buckley and his two Tithables be scratched off of the List taken for this County this present Year they being twice entered." Book A, p. 179.

November 15, 1758 - It is "Ordered that James Goulding be added to the List of Tithables for ... this present Year [1758]." Book A, p. 179.

December 12, 1758 - "Ordered that John Davis and Benjamin Shreeve, pursuant to the last Court's Order, Clear the Roads whereof they are Overseers and that the Tithable persons within one and half Miles of the said Roads on each side Assist in clearing the same." Book A, p. 189.

May 8, 1759 - "Ordered that Fielding Turner {L-M}, William West {H-L-P}, Richard Coleman {D-J-K-M}, George West {D-F-L}, Josias Clapham {B-D}, Francis Peyton {G-H}, John Mucklehaney [aka McIlhaney] {A-C-E} and James Lane {M-N-Q}, Gent. take the List of Tithables." Book A, p. 234; and for the Map of the various Tithable List areas, see infra, pp. 416-417.

June 12, 1759 - "John Mason on his Petition is ... discharged from the paiment [sic] of Public and County Levies &c. ..." Book B, p. 245.

September 11, 1759 - "Ordered that ... Henry Wisheart and [one] Negro ... Joseph Lyles [who is 'added to William Starks List'] ... James Abbett ... Daniel Miller ... Benjamin Edwards and his three ... Negroes ... James Churchill [who is 'added to James Lane's List'] ... John Richard ... [and] James Stephens ... [and] Andrew Adam ... [all] be added to the List of Tithables taken for this County this present Year [1759]." Book A, pp. 283-284.

September 12, 1759 - "Ordered ... John Tramell [sic- John Trammell] be added to the List of Tithables taken ... this present Year." Book A, p. 291.

September 13, 1759 - "Ordered that Thomas Awbrey and his five Tithables, ... Thomas Flemmon [aka Thomas Fleming], Thomas Leggett, [and three] Negroes ... added to the List of Tithables ... for [1759]." Book A, p. 294.

November 13, 1759 - "Ordered that ... Francis Awbrey [Junr.] ... Susanna Burnett [sic - who is 'added to Thomas John's list'] ... Matthias Hersman ... Joseph Bradley ... Richard Self ... Daniel Neale ... [and] William Holmes ... [all] be added to the List of Tithables taken for ... [1759]." Book A, pp. 297-298.

November 13, 1759 - In the itemization of credits in the County Levy are: "John Johnson for 4 Levies overcharged last Year [1758] as Per Acct. sworn to ... 192 [lbs.t.] ... Jacob Remey for 1 Ditto as Per Ditto ... 48 [lbs.t.] ... Elizabeth Lewis for 8 Levies overcharged last Year ... 384 [lbs.t.]." Book A, p. 302.

November 14, 1759 - In the itemization of the County Levy, credits are listed: "Samuel Combs for 1 Levy overcharged last Year [1758] ... 48 [lbs.t.] ... Robert Thomas for 2 [ditto] ... 96 [lbs.t.]." Book A, pp. 303-304.

November 15, 1759 - "... Thomas Fleming be scratched off of Thomas Awbrey's List [sic - Awbrey was no longer liable for Fleming]." Book A, p. 306.

March 11, 1760 - "John McManamy on his Motion is ... discharged from the paiment of Public and County Levies for the future." Book A, p. 324.

May 15, 1760 - It is "Ordered that Fielding Turner {F-L-M}, James Hamilton {A-C-D-E-F), William West {H-L-P}, Richard Coleman {D-J-K-M}, Josias Clapham {B}, George West {B-D-F}, Francis Peyton {G-H}, John Mucklehaney {A-C} and James Lane {L-M-N-P-Q}, Gent., take the List of Tithables." Book A, p. 356; Map of Tithable List areas, infra, pp. 416-417.

June 11, 1760 - "John Groom [aka John Goreham] on his Petition is ... discharged from the payment of Public and County Levies and Taxes for the future." Book A, p. 364; and for his exemption in 1761, see LDTX/1, p. 10.

August 12, 1760 - "Upon the Motion of Conrad Shanks he is discharged from the paiment [sic] of Levies &c. for the future." Book A, p. 386; see supra, Chapter on Inns and Taverns.

August of 1760 - John Carr Senr., who was first exempted from the county levy in 1757, is shown on the tithable list enrolled by James Hamilton, living with his sons John Carr Junr., Peter Carr and Thomas Carr; Edward Thompson is also identified as exempt in the tithable list of James Hamilton, apparently having been declared exempt prior to 1757; and also in Hamilton's list, the levy for William Debell "Senr." is charged to Mary Debell, who would appear to be his son's widow. LDTX/1, pp. 4, 5 and 32.

November 11, 1760 - "Rodolphus Shomaker [sic] on his Petition is by the Court discharged from the Paiment [sic] of Levies and Poll Taxes for the future." Book A, p. 402.

November 12, 1760 - At the itemization of the County Levy, credits are listed for: "Thomas Connell for one Levy overcharged last Year [1759] ... 46 [lbs.t.] ... John Eaton for one Levy [ditto] ... 46 [lbs.t.] ... Joseph Power for one Levy [ditto] ... 46 [lbs.t.]." Book A, pp. 404 and 405.

November 12, 1760 - "Ordered that Silvanus Lay ... [and] ... John St.Clair and William Mason be added to the List of Tithables taken for this County this Present Year [1760]." Book A, p. 405.

November 12, 1760 - "William Metheney on his Motion is ... discharged from the Paiment [sic] of Levies and Poll Tax for the future." Book A, p. 406.

November 12, 1760 - "Jacob Jones on his Motion is ... discharged from the Paiment [sic] of Levies and Poll Tax for the future." Book A, p. 407.

June 9, 1761 - It is "Ordered that Fielding Turner {D-F-L}, James Hamilton {B-C-D-E}, William West {H-L-P}, Richard Coleman {J-K-L-M}, Charles Tyler [who did not turn in a list that year], Josias Clapham {B}, George West {F-L}, Francis Peyton {G-H}, John Mucklehaney {A-C} and James Lane {M-N-Q}, Gentlemen, take the List of Tithables for the County this present Year." Book A, p. 450; and for the Map of the various Tithable List areas, see infra, pp. 416-417.

August 11, 1761 - "John Fielder [aged or infirm] on his Motion is discharged from the paiment [sic] of Levies &c., for the future." Book A, p. 482.

August of 1761 - John Carr Senr., who was exempted from the county levy in 1757, is again identified as "levie free" on the tithable list enrolled by James Hamilton, living with his sons John Carr Junr. and Peter Carr; and, Thomas Moore appears on the tithable list of William West as exempt, probably having been determined levy free before 1757. LDTX/1, pp. 8 and 14.

September 8, 1761 - "Ordered that John Warford ... Thomas Bryan ... Ephriam Dunham ... Nehemiah Garrison & his three Tithables to wit [sic] Moses Garrison, Aaron Garrison and John Garrison ... [and] ... that William Shrieve ... [all] be added to the List of Tithables taken for this County this present Year [1761]." Book A, pp. 491-492.

September 8, 1761 - "William Jones on his Petition is discharged ... from the Paiment [sic] of Levies and Poll Taxes for the future." Book A, p. 493.

September 8, 1761 - "Ordered ... Patrick Molholland be added to the List of Tithables ... for this County this Present Year [1761]." Book A, p. 494.

September 8, 1761 - "Ordered that Greenbury Dorsey and his two ... Negroes ... be added to the List of Tithables for this County this Present Year [1761]." Book A, p. 496.

September 9, 1761 - It is "Ordered that Cornelius Donohoe ... be added to the List of Tithables taken for ... [1761]." Book A, p. 500.

September 9, 1761 - Hugh Caldwell and his two Tithables to-wit, William Caldwell and Hugh Caldwell [Junr.] ... John McCollom and his Tithable to-wit, James Force ... [and also] John Wormsley ... [all] be added to the List of Tithables taken for ... [1761]." Book A, p. 501.

September 10, 1761 - "Christian Hame ... be added to the List of Tithables ... for this County." Book A, p. 509.

September 10, 1761 - "Jacob Lasswell on his Petition is ... discharged from the Paiment [sic] of Levies & Poll Tax for the future." Book A, p. 517; see supra, Chapter on Inns and Taverns.

September 10, 1761 - "David Davis and his ... Negro ... John Yount and his Tithable, to-wit, Michael Burgun ... be added to the List of Tithables taken for this County." Book A, p. 517.

September 10, 1761 - John Heryford and his ... [3] Negroes ... added to the List of Tithables taken for this County ... [in 1761]." Book A, p. 523; see supra, Chapter on Inns and Taverns, and see supra, Chapter on Slaves.

October 13, 1761 - "Ordered that James Goulding ... George Vandiver ... [and] Richard Trenary ... [all] be added to the List of Tithables taken for this County this present Year." Book A, p. 525.

Wednesday, November 11, 1761 - "William Grant on his Motion is ... discharged from the Paiment [sic] of Levies and Poll tax for the future." Book A, p. 531; see supra, Chapter on Inns and Taverns.

November 11, 1761 - "Ordered that Daniel Neale be added to the List of Tithables ... this prest. [present] Year." Book A, p. 531.

November 11, 1761 - "Ordered ... Thomas Awbrey and his ... [Two] Negroes ... added to the List of Tithables ... this present Year." Book A, p. 532.

November 11, 1761 - In the County Levy, credits are listed for: "Benjamin Sebastian for 2 Levies overcharged last Year 6 lb. tobo. each ... is ... 12 [lb. tobacco] ...William Allan for 1 Levy [ditto] ... 6 [lbs.t.] ... George Allan for 2 Ditto ... 12 [lbs.t.] ... John Allan for 1 Ditto ... 6 [lbs.t.]." Book A, p. 533.

May 12, 1762 - It is "Ordered that James Hamilton {C-D-E-G-H}, Nicholas Minor {D-F}, James Lane {M-N-P-Q}, Charles Tyler {L-M ?}, John Moss Junr. {D-J-K}, Lee Massey {B}, John Mucklehaney [sic] {A-C} and George West {F-L-P}, Gent., take the List of Tithables for ... [1762]." Book A, p. 589; for the Map of the various Tithable List areas, see infra, pp. 416-417.

June 8, 1762 - "Robert Homan [sic] on his Petition is by the Court discharged from the Paiment [sic] of Levies & Poll taxes for the future." Book A, p. 627.

June 8, 1762 - "John Davis on his Motion is ... discharged from the Paiment [sic] of Levies & Poll taxes for the future." Book A, p. 628; and see supra, Chapter on Inns and Taverns.

June 8, 1762 - "William Hail [sic] on his Motion is ... discharged from the Paiment [sic] of Levies & Poll taxes for the future." Book A, p. 628.

July 13, 1762 - Lee Massey returns a list of tithables for Loudoun "given in to me since the 9th of June ... as also my own." LDTX/1, p. 25.

August 10, 1762 - "Ordered that ... Jonathan Turner [probably as a hired hand] be added to Jacob Remey Junr. his List ... John Hopewell and his Tithable, to-wit, Smith King ... Jonathan Pike ... William Landrum and his Tithables, to-wit, James McKenney and [his] Negro ... Peter Chapman ... George Winn and his Tithable to-wit Owen Winn ... Edward Porter and his Negro ... [and] John Goddard ... George Hancocke and his [two] Negroes ... [and] John Ellzey ... [and] Jeremiah Thomas ... [all] be added to the List of Tithables ... Samuel Oldham's Tithables be added to the List taken this Year viz Thomas Williams Overseer, [and five] Negroes ... William Suddith and his Tithables, to-wit, Lawrence Suddith and William Suddith Junr. ... James Shead and his Negro ... George Ashford and his [two] Negroes ... [and] Ferdinando O'Neale and his Tithables, to-wit, John Peake and George Awbrey ... be added to the List of Tithables taken this Year [1762]." Book B, p. 30-31.

August 11, 1762 - "Ordered that Thomas Awbrey be added to the List of Tithables for [1762]." Book B, p. 32.

August 11, 1762 - "Paldis Horonimus [sic] a Lunatick Person [sic] be discharged from the Paiment [sic] of Levys and Poll Taxes during his Indisposition [sic] ... Francis Horonimus his Brother take care of him ... [during his incapacity]." Book B, p. 32.

August 12, 1762 - "Ordered that ... Michael Vanbuscark ... [and] Isaac Vanbuscark and his Tithable, to-wit, John Vanbuscark ... [all] be added to the List [of Tithables] Taken for this Year." Book B, p. 47.

August 13, 1762 - "Ordered that ... Christopher Swiger ... William Hancocke and his Tithables to-wit, Ralph McDonald, [and two] Negroes ... [and] David Davis and his ... Negro ... [and] Thomas Clews and his Tithables, to-wit, Joseph Clews and James Cruderus ... Jacob Shilling ... William Beavers and his

Tithables to-wit, James Dorough and Joseph Briggs ... Henry Darflinger ... Jacob Wildman and his Tithable, to-wit, Joseph Wildman ... [and] Daniel Jones and his Tithables, to-wit, George Burson, Jonathan Burson and Benjamin Burson ... [all] be added to the List of Tithables taken for this Year." Book B, pp. 54-55.

August of 1762 - John Carr Senr., exempted from the levy in 1757, is again identified as levy free on the tithable list enrolled by James Hamilton, still living with his sons John Carr Junr. and Peter Carr. LDTX/1, p. 17.

September 15, 1762 - It is "Ordered that ... Thomas Pritchard and his Tithable to-wit, William Mason ... Robert Hamilton ... John Reiger and his Tithable to-wit, Anthony Harvey ... John Markey ... [all] be added to the List of Tithables taken for this Year." Book B, p. 55.

September 15, 1762 - "William Trammell and his [two] Negroes ... be added to the List of Tithables taken for this Year." Book B, p. 59.

November 9, 1762 - "Ordered that ... Aaron Lane and his Tithables, to-wit, William Lane, Daniel Atkins and [one] Negro ... [and] Richard Williams ... [and] James Compton ... be added to the List of Tithables taken for this Year." Book B, p. 69.

November 9, 1762 - It is "Ordered that ... Thomas Williams ... be added to the List of Tithables taken for this Year." Book B, p. 70.

Wednesday, November 10, 1762 - "Ordered that ... John Sinkler and his Tithable to-wit, William Mason ... [and] Jacob Eler ... [all] be added to the List of Tithables taken for this Year." Book B, p. 72.

November 10, 1762 - In the itemization of the County Levy, credits are listed for: "John Palmer Junr. for one Levy overcharged Last Year ... 15 [lbs.t.] ... William McCoy for one Levy [ditto] ... 15 [lbs.t.] ... Andrew Redmond for one Ditto ... 15 [lbs.t.] ... Thomas Wyatt for one Ditto ... 15 [lbs.t.] ... Jonathan Richardson for one Ditto ... 15 [lbs.t.] ... [and] Andrew Hatfield for one Ditto ... 15 [lbs.t.]." Book B, p. 73.

April 14, 1763 - It is "Ordered [that] ... Fielding Turner {F-L-M}, James Hamilton {C-D-E}, Aneas Campbell {D}, Nicholas Minor {D-J-K}, Chas. Tyler [Charles Tyler] {L-M ?}, George West {F}, Francis Peyton {G-H-P}, James Lane {M-N-P-Q}, Lee Massey {B-D} and Philip Noland {B}, Gent., take the Lists of Tithables for the County this present Year." Book B, p. 110; and for the Map of the various Tithable List areas, see infra, pp. 416-417.

April 14, 1763 - "Josias Clapham Gent. Sherif of this County with John Moss Junr. his Security entered into and acknowledged Bond for collecting the Levy which Bond is Ordered to be Recorded." Book B, p. 110.

June 14, 1763 - "On the Petition of John Smith he is ... discharged from the Paiment [sic] of Levies & Poll Taxes for the future." Book B, p. 159.

August 9, 1763 - "Joseph Coombs on his Petition is ... discharged from the Paiment [sic] of Levies & Taxes for the future." Book B, p. 196.

September 13, 1763 - "Ordered that ... John Berkley's Tithables, to-wit, [three] Negroes ... [and] Josias Clapham Gent. and his Tithables, to-wit, Patrick Obryon, [sic] [and five] Negroes ... [all] be added to the List taken for this Year." Book B, p. 233; and supra, Chapter on Slaves.

September 14, 1763 - "Ordered that ... Sampson Trammell and his Tithables, to-wit, James Dial, [and six] Negroes ... Benjamin Shrieve's Tithable ... Isaac Fouch's Tithable ... William Ellzey's Tithables, to-wit, Samuel Henderson, [and two] Negroes ... [and] Conrad Cornelius [individually, a tithable] ... [all] be added to the List taken for this Year." Book B, p. 237.

September 14, 1763 - "Ordered that ... Timothy Howell and Abner Howell his Tithable ... be added to the List taken for this Year." Book B, p. 238.

September 15, 1763 - "Ordered that ... John Patterson and his Tithables to-wit, Fleming Patterson and John Martin be added to the List ... for [1763]." Book B, p. 249.

September 15, 1763 - "Ordered that ... Charles Bennett Earle of Tankerville and his Tithables, ... [seven] Negroes ... [be] added to the List ... for [the tax year 1763]." Book B, p. 251.

September 15, 1763 - "Ordered that ... Richard Stephens and his Tithables, to-wit, Robert Stephens Junr. and [one] Negro ... [all are] added to the List ... for [1763]." Book B, p. 252.

November 8, 1763 - "Ordered that ... Jonathan Monkhouse and his Tithables to-wit, [two] Negroes ... be added to the List taken for this Year." Book B, p. 261; and supra, Chapter on Slaves.

November 9, 1763 - "John Davis and his Tithables, to-wit, Amos Davis, John Davis Junr. & [one] Negro ... be added to the List of Tithables taken for this Year." Book B, p. 264.

November 9, 1763 - Among the itemized credits listed on the County Levy are: "James Mercer for one Levy overcharged last Year [1762] ... 6 [lbs.t.] ... Edward Porter for 2 [ditto] ... 12 [lbs.t.] ... David Davis for 2 Ditto ... 12 [lbs.t.] ... Matthias Gossett for 1 Ditto ... 6 [lbs.t.] ... [and] Benjamin Sebastian for 1 Ditto ... 6 [lbs.t.]." Book B, p. 266.

May 9, 1764 - It is "Ordered that James Hamilton {A-C-D-E-G}, Fielding Turner {F-L-M-P}, Nicholas Minor {D-J-K-L}, George West {F-L}, Charles Tyler {L-M ?}, John McIlhaney {A-C}, William Carr Lane {J-K-M-N-P-Q}, Philip Noland {B}, Leven Powell {G-H} and John Pearce {E}, Gent., take the List of Tithables, Lands and Wheel Carriages for this County this present Year [ie., 1764]." Book B, p. 357; for the Map of the various Tithable List areas, see infra, pp. 416-417.

June 12, 1764 - "John Lewis Senr. on his Petition is discharged from the Paiment [sic] of Levies and Poll Tax for the future." Book B, p. 358.

August 14, 1764 - "James Murray on his Petition is ... discharged from the paiment [sic] of Publick and County Levies for the future." Book B, p. 407.

September 11, 1764 - "Ordered that ... four Tithables returned by George West Gent. belonging to James Mercer be taken from the List of Tithables the same being Twice entered." Book B, p. 432.

September 11, 1764 - "Ordered that ... Henry Lander and Peter Chapman his Tithable be added to the List of Tithables." Book B, p. 433.

September 12, 1764 - "Ordered ... Frederick Cooper be added to the List of Tithables taken and Returned for the Present Year." Book B, p. 436.

September 12, 1764 - "Ordered ... Thomas Gorham be added to the List of Tithables taken and Returned for the Present Year." Book B, p. 437.

November 13, 1764 - "William Cummins on his Petition ... discharged from the Paiment of Publick and County Levies" for the future. Book B, p. 492.

November 13, 1764 - The Loudoun Grand Jury Presents charges against: "Jacob Wildman ... [and] John Hague ... for not giving in [their] Tithables ... [for 1764]." Book B, p. 493.

November 13, 1764 - "Ordered that Francis Clock ... [Doctor] James Butler Brodbelt ... [and] Joshua Yates ... [all] be added to the List of Tithables taken and returned this Present Year." Book B, p. 493.

November 13, 1764 - Credits in the itemized County Levy are listed for: "Henry Lander for one Levy overcharged Last Year [1763] ... 8 [lbs.t.] ... [and] William Metheny ... one [Levy] Ditto ... 8 [lbs.t.]." Book B, p. 495.

Wednesday, November 14, 1764 - "Richard Freeman on his Petition is by the Court discharged from the Paiment [sic] of Public and County Levies for the future." Book B, p. 496.

November 14, 1764 - "Ordered ... four Tithables belonging to Samuel Mead be taken of [off] the List the same being entered twice." Book B, p. 496.

November 14, 1764 - Among credits in the County Levy: "William Winn for two Levies overcharged Last Year [1763] ... 16 [lbs.t.] ... David Smith for one [ditto] ... 8 [lbs.t.]." Book B, p. 497.

November 14, 1764 - It is Ordered that "Thomas Willson on his Petition is ... discharged from the Paiment [sic] of Public & County Levies for the future." Book B, p. 499.

April 10, 1765 - "John Bishop on his Petition is ... discharged from the Paiment [sic] of Publick and County Levies for the future." Book B, p. 553.

May 15, 1765 - It is "Ordered that Fielding Turner {F-L-M}, James Hamilton {A-C-D}, Aneas Campbell [sic - Aeneas Campbell] {A-C-D}, Nicholas Minor {C-D-F-J-K-L}, George West [who did not turn in a list] {F}, Francis Peyton {H-L}, John McIlhaney {A-C}, James Lane [no list turned in] {Q}, Craven Peyton [no list] {D}, Philip Noland {B}, William Carr Lane {K-M-N-Q}, Leven Powell {E-G} & John Pearce {E}, Gent., take the List of Tithables, Lands & Wheel Carriages for this Present Year [1765]." Book B, p. 588; for Map of the various Tithable List areas, see infra, pp. 416-417.

August 12, 1765 - "Hugh Caldwell Junr. on the Petition of his Father is ... discharged from the Paiment [sic] of Parish and County Levies for the future." Confirmed by the entry for the Caldwell family in the 1765 tithable list of Nicholas Minor, showing 4 males and 3 tithes. Book C, p. 2; LDTX/1, p. 28.

August 13, 1765 - "Ordered that George Saunders ... George Chelton and his Tithables, to-wit, [his two] Negroes ... [and] Mark Chelton and Benjamin Hardy his [Chelton's] Tithable ... [all] be added to the List taken and returned for this Present Year." Book C, p. 11.

August 13, 1765 - "Ordered that Richard Williams and his Tithables, to-wit, Jenkin Williams and Joseph Williams ... be added to the List ... this present Year." Book C, p. 18.

August 13, 1765 - "Ordered that ... Garret Cornelius ... be added to the List ... this present Year." Book C, p. 22.

August 14, 1765 - "Ordered that William Davis be added to the List of Tithables ... for this Present Year." Book C, p. 29.

September of 1765 - Richard Freeman, who was first exempted from the county levy in 1764, is identified as "levy free" on the tithable list of Levin Powell; John Smith, identified as exempt from the levy on John Pearce's tithable list {E}, apparently was granted his exemption before 1757; and, John Carr Senr. is once again identified as levy free on the tithable list returned by Justice James Hamilton. LDTX/1, pp. 34 and 35.

September 11, 1765 - "On the Motion of James Goulding, he is discharged from the Paiment [sic] of Levies for the future." Book C, p. 51.

October 14, 1765 - "Ordered that ... George Monroe ... [and] Thomas Triplett and his Tithable, to-wit, Enoch Triplett ... be added to the List ... taken for this present Year." Book C, p. 59.

October 14, 1765 - "John Palmer on his Motion is ... discharged from Paiment of Levies and Poll Tax." Book C, p. 59.

October 16, 1765 - "Ordered that George William Fairfax, Esqr., his Tithables, to-wit, Thomas Violett, [seven] Negroes ... [be] added to the List taken & returned for this present Year." Book C, p. 68.

November and December of 1765 - In protest of the enactment of the Stamp Act, no General Court sessions are held in Loudoun County during these two months. Book C, p. 73.

May 12, 1766 - "Fielding Turner {L-M}, William Carr Lane {M-N-Q}, John Moss Junr. {J-K} and Leven Powell {H-P}, Gent. ... below Goose Creek ... [and] James Hamilton {C-E-G}, Nicholas Minor {D}, John McIlhaney {A-C} & Philip Noland {B-D}, Gent. ... above Goose Creek ... [are appointed to] take the List of Tithables, Lands and Wheel Carriages ... this present Year." Book C, pp. 77-78; for the Map of the various Tithable List areas, infra, pp. 416-417.

September 8, 1766 - "Ordered ... John Davis ... be added to List returned for this present Year." Book C, p. 185.

October 14, 1766 - "On the Motion of John Ballendine the following Tithables and Land be Entered on the Lists returned for this present Year vizt. At Sugar Lands John Moffit; [ten] Negroes ... At McCarty's Quarter [on the Potomac] ...; At Barne's Quarter John Gallahue, [and ten] Negroes ... [and] At Seneca Falls, John Melaley [sic- and five] Negroes." Book C, p. 208.

October 14, 1766 - "On the Motion of Joseph Reid ... [it is ordered that] he be added to the List of Tithables this present Year." Book C, p. 209.

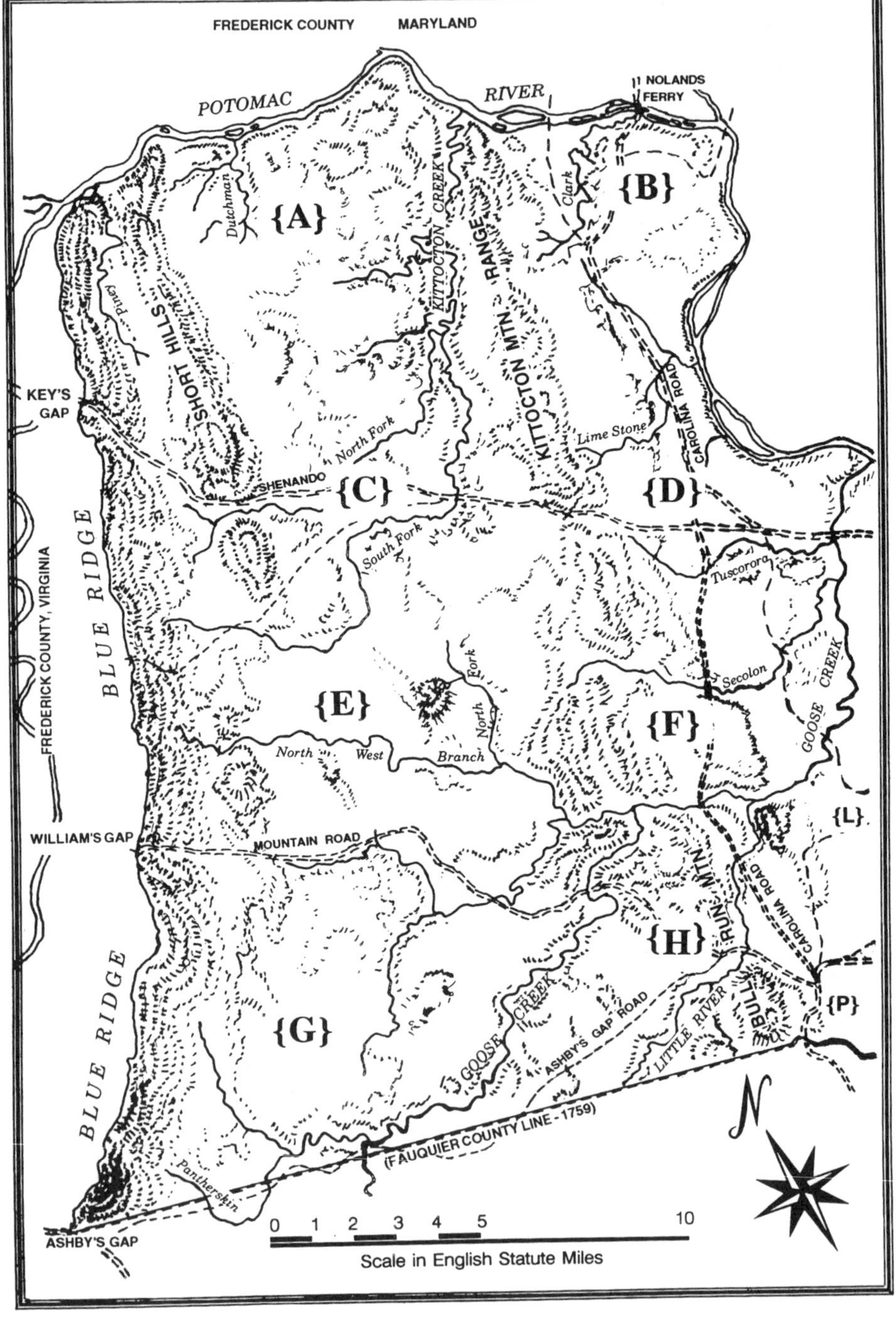
FREDERICK COUNTY MARYLAND
POTOMAC RIVER
NOLANDS FERRY
{A}
{B}
{C}
{D}
{E}
{F}
{G}
{H}
{L}
{P}
Dutchman
Clark
Piney
SHORT HILLS
KITTOCTON CREEK
KITTOCTON MTN. RANGE
CAROLINA ROAD
KEY'S GAP
North Fork
Lime Stone
SHENANDO
South Fork
Tuscorora
Secolon
GOOSE CREEK
BLUE RIDGE
FREDERICK COUNTY, VIRGINIA
North Fork
North West Branch
WILLIAM'S GAP
MOUNTAIN ROAD
BULL RUN MTN
CAROLINA ROAD
GOOSE CREEK
ASHBY'S GAP ROAD
LITTLE RIVER
BLUE RIDGE
(FAUQUIER COUNTY LINE - 1759)
Panthersk[in]
ASHBY'S GAP
0 1 2 3 4 5 10
Scale in English Statute Miles
N

-LOUDOUN COUNTY - VIRGINIA-

TITHABLE LIST AREAS
circa 1757-1766

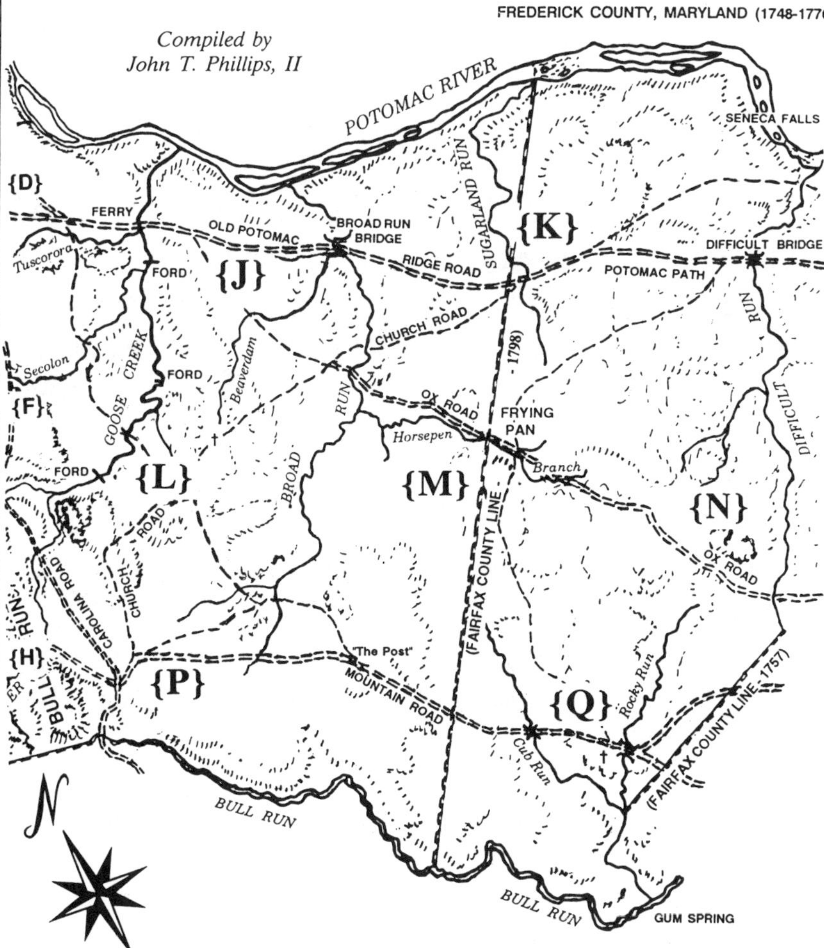

LOUDOUN, *April* 5, 1766.

THE Subſcriber requeſts it as a Favour of all his Acquaintances, That they will never take any LETTER directed to him out of the POST-OFFICE, as he is determined never willingly to pay a Farthing of any TAX laid upon this COUNTRY, in an UNCONSTITUTIONAL MANNER.

FRANCIS LIGHTFOOT LEE.

B O S T O N, *April* 21.

The Merchants in *London* are ſo certain of a Repeal of the Stamp-Act, that they have ſent large Quantities of Goods to their Correſpondents here, tho' contrary to the Counter Orders they received with Reſpect to the ſame.

P H I L A D E L P H I A, *May* 1.

On Tueſday Evening the Gentlemen of the LAW, and other public OFFICERS, met here and unanimouſly determined immediately to proceed to Buſineſs; and the OFFICES are now all open.

Rind's *Virginia Gazette*, published in Williamsburg on May 16, 1766, contained notices from other American cities reflecting both colonial resistance to the Stamp Act and the colonial response to Parliament's repeal of the Act in 1766. Francis Lightfoot Lee's notice, which represented the sentiments of his Loudoun County constituents, was placed before Lee had learned of the repeal.

Colonial Taxes and the County Levy

In the mid-1700s, every tithable individual in Virginia or, in the case of a tithable servant or slave, the master of the tithable regularly paid three different taxes based on the annual "poll" (head count) of tithables. The oldest colonial tithable tax was Virginia's colony-wide levy, used for "defraying and payment of the public charge of the country," meaning the administration of the colonial government. Virginia's poll tax was, technically, the first property tax instituted in colonial America, as slave owners were assessed on the basis of their human property. The second type of tithable tax was the county levy; the parish levy was the third. Colonial taxes and duties were also imposed on a variety of other transactions and types of property. [supra, Chapter on Tithables].

When the Virginia Assembly was in session, it usually assessed the colony levy bi-annually. The county and parish levies were normally assessed annually to cover the costs of the various public functions that each was distinctly responsible for. The county was the larger jurisdictional unit, since many Virginia counties incorporated more than one parish. The county levy accounted for the essentials of the local colonial government - the construction and maintenance of public buildings such as the courthouse and jail, purchase of a standard set of weights and measures, a county Seal and law books for the county court Justices - and various other "public charges" that the Assembly assigned to the county. Parish vestries were responsible for what can best be described as the "social services" of the community, like the provision for all orphans, widows, the sick, and destitute, as well as the construction and maintenance of all Anglican places of worship. [Jamestown, pp. 81-82; Hening, VII/395 and VII/543; infra, Chapter on Cameron Parish, Glossary].

Budgeted expenses of the colony were limited. Most of the administrative functions of government were essentially self-supporting. The costs of inspecting tobacco, flour and other commodities, issuance and retirement of Virginia's Treasury notes and collection of the colonial levy were all paid for by associated fees. Incidental costs of government that were accounted for in the colonial levy, such as the expenses of the Assembly and the cost of missions sent to "treat" with Indians, were of little consequence in times of peace. In the five year period from 1748 to 1753, colony levies totalled only 18 lbs. of tobacco [lbt.] per tithable, under 6 pence per year. [Hening, VI/247 and VI/374].

The costs of administering the colonial system of justice dominated annual Loudoun County budgets, with "public works" running a strong second. Before 1767, the entire annual budget for Loudoun was normally under 20,000 lbs. of tobacco, the equivalent of about £115, or $400. County accounts were kept on a current basis. The only method of "financing" in evidence was when the payments for large public works were spread over the anticipated period of construction. In 1758, 1759 and 1764, years that the levy was significantly higher, Loudoun residents paid for the construction of the first county Courthouse, two county jails and a new bridge across Broad run on the Potomac Ridge road. The salaries of the three "full time" county officials, and the costs of providing for both prisoners and guards at the jail, were also accounted for in the county levy. Loudoun County Clerk Charles Binns and Deputy King's Attorney Hugh West were "permanent" appointees; each retained his office until his death. Loudoun's colonial Sheriffs were all County Court Justices who were rotated into office every or every other year. The salaries of these three officials, combined, totalled 5,500 lbt. per year. In a low-tax year, like 1763 or 1765, salaries of the three "full time" officials constituted over 35% of the County budget. However, Mr. Binns and the Sheriffs derived most of their income from fees they charged to the individuals who utilized their services. These transaction fees were paid directly by the "user" and thus were not budgeted in the county levy. Sheriffs accounted for the jail as one of the incidental expenses of their office before Leesburg ordinary keeper John Herryford took over management of the jail around 1770. Guards at the county jail were paid and accounted for individually. Loudoun's first Burgesses, Francis Lightfoot Lee and James Hamilton, were selective in submitting their expense accounts for the county levy. They deferred a rendering of their first accounting until after the first county Courthouse had been levied and fully paid for. [Chapter on Courthouse, supra @ p. 104; Chapter on Gaol, supra @ p. 148; Chapter on Burgesses, supra @ pp. 35-36; Table of Taxes, infra @ p. 431].

The early Cameron parish levies are still something of a mystery, since the first vestry books have disappeared. Some light is thrown on the subject by a surviving copy of the 1764 parish levy which indicates that the annual budget for Cameron parish would have grown steadily from £150 in 1758 to about £250 in 1764. At 21 lbt., roughly 2 shillings, 7½ pence, per tithable, the average annual Cameron parish levy was nearly double the Loudoun County levy assessment per tithable, but was only half of the levy assessed in neighboring Truro parish, in Fairfax County. With Virginia ministers' salaries set at 16,000 lbt., and the Cameron parish vestry apparently allowing an additional 7% in payment for "cask," the Cameron parish minister's salary, alone, was triple the combined salary of Loudoun County's three primary officers. An additional 6,000 lbt. was allocated for the clerks and sextons at four Episcopal chapels, so salaries of the Cameron parish church functionaries normally exceeded the entire Loudoun County budget. However, the remarkable thing here is not the size of the Cameron parish levy but, in contrast, the frugality evidenced in the colonial administration of Loudoun County government. [Chapter on Cameron Parish, infra @ pp. 462-463].

Even though Loudoun was officially on a "cash" basis, colonial county levies were computed in the manner traditional in tidewater Virginia, with accounts stated in or computed into terms of lbs. of tobacco. Tobacco receipts from "any of the warehouses in Fairfax and Prince William" were designated as legal tender in Loudoun, and passed in payment of all levies, taxes and officer fees. In 1765, notes from the tobacco warehouses at Colchester, Pohick, Hunting creek [Alexandria] and one "on the land of Philip Ludwell Lee Esq. at the [Little] falls of Potowmack [sic]" in Fairfax County, and a warehouse "at Quantico" in Prince William, would have satisfied any tax or fee that was assessed in Loudoun County. But most Loudoun tithables probably paid their levy assessments with Virginia Treasury notes, which were circulating widely from 1757 to 1770. [Hening, VIII/78-79 and VIII/100].

During the 1700s, colonial Assemblies and Governors manipulated tax policy, abating one or all of the public and church levies for a specified period, to encourage the settlement of Virginia's frontiers. When Spotsylvania and Brunswick Counties were created in 1720, residents were exempted from the Virginia levy until 1731. In 1753, settlement in Augusta County, "westward of the ridge of [the Allegheny] mountains that divides the rivers Roanoke, James, and Potowmack, from the Mississippi," was encouraged by exempting pioneers from "public, county and parish levies" through 1768. Thus, residents of West Virginia, Ohio and Kentucky may rightfully attribute the colonial development of their states to their inclusion within one of the original American "enterprise zones." The Virginia Assembly employed a different type of "tax incentive" to promote settlement in Loudoun County, providing for a 20% discount on all off-budget officers' fees. [Hening, IV/77-78 and VI/355-356; for example, see Chapter on the County Clerk, supra @ pp. 96-98].

The Assembly might have voiced the concerns of the Virginia gentry, or may have merely given "lip service" to the mood of the general public, when it took the position that "a poll tax [was] always grievous and burthensome [sic] to the subjects here." Regardless, other taxes, such as duties on imported liquors, were imposed "for the better payment of the public debts, claims and other exigencies of this government." In the mid-1700s Virginia's colonial Assembly regularly imposed taxes on various kinds of goods in trade. Duties were assessed on imported slaves, cattle and horses, and on the purchase of hogsheads of export tobacco and imported rum or wine, with revenues normally applied to the colony's general budget. As French War debts mounted, and with some consideration given to avoiding additional increases in Virginia's tithable and property taxes, the Assembly eventually applied revenues from many of the transaction taxes toward the retirement of Virginia Treasury notes. [Hening, VI/126, VI/355 and VIII/110; Chapter on Colonial Economics, supra @ pp. 193, 205 and 210-212; supra, Chapter on Slavery; infra, @ p. 424].

The inaugural duties on imported non-British liquors and ales were imposed during one of the perennial wars with France. The 1745 Assembly considered "laying a duty upon liquors ... useful and beneficial in lessening the poll tax, by raising a fund for defraying part of the necessary expences [sic] of ... government." Ostensibly intended as a "trading-with-the-enemy" measure, the liquor duties also stimulated domestic production and assisted in stemming the colonial balance-of-payments problem. Ultimately, duties were imposed totalling 4 pence per gallon of rum, wine, brandy or other distilled spirits, and 1 penny on each gallon of "cyder, beer or ale." If the ship manifests from 1766 are any indication, liquor duties in the Potomac district, alone, would have generated about £800 in annual revenues. So as not to offend

British merchants, all "liquors ... [coming] directly from Great Britain [were] exempt ... from any imposition, duty or custom." Another feature of the liquor taxes, designed like the duties on imported slaves to avoid confrontation with the English merchants, required the importer or purchaser to pay the duty. Before 1761, liquor duty revenues were, primarily, applied to the colony's general fund obligations. In the 1750s, one penny of the liquor duty was appropriated "for re-building the Capitol" and then, beginning in 1759, "to the relief of the College of William and Mary ... for the founding of professorships, scholarships, and such other good uses." In mid-1761, the Assembly diverted revenues from three pence of the liquor duties and all of the revenues from the duty on beer and ale, applying the first £10,000 of proceeds to defray the cost of the tax exemptions that had been extended to residents of Augusta County in order to "encourage ... and protect ... the settlers ... on the waters of the Mississippi [meaning in the Ohio river basin]." Ever mindful of the heavy burden borne by their colony's chief executive, the Assembly also allowed Virginia's Lieutenant Governor annual duty-free imports of up to 1,200 gallons of Madeira wines, "for his own use"! Liquor duties were such a popular revenue measure with the Assembly that they would be retained in force for the duration of the American Revolution. [Hening, VI/193, VI/222, VI/354, VI/471, VII/265-273, VIII/38, VIII/190, VIII/529 and VIII/335].

Two other transaction taxes were the duties on imported slaves and exported hides. A duty on exported hides was of long standing, instituted in 1705 as the first constant means of financial support for the colonial College of William and Mary. Duties on furs and hides were expanded in 1744, and continued again with modifications in 1765. Before the Virginia Assembly imposed a duty on "the buyers" of imported slaves in 1752, the British Board of Trade had succeeded in blocking all colonial attempts to tax the slave trade. A 1760 provision "oblige[d] persons bringing slaves into this colony from Maryland, Carolina and the West-Indies for their own use, to pay a duty for the term" the slave was in Virginia. Duties on imported slaves were continued through 1773, with the proceeds normally applied to the colony's general obligations. The Assembly also tinkered with supplemental duties on slaves in their French War debt retirement program. [Hening, VIII/110, VIII/142 and VIII/336; supra, Chapter on Slavery].

Escalating frontier combat with the French and Indians following Washington's defeat at Great Meadows in 1754 led to an extraordinary increase in Virginia's military expenditures. Initially, special colony tithe and land taxes were instituted to cover the cost of "the troops raised for the protection of the frontiers." As the outstanding Virginia Treasury notes mounted rapidly, (issuance of over £500,000 in Virginia notes was authorized during the French War), the Assembly thrashed about in search of additional sources of revenue for the general obligations of the colony. Among the variety of new taxes and duties was an assessment on the issuance of ordinary licenses, writs and petitions. This particular tax may have inspired the British Ministry with the not-so-bright idea for their ill-fated Stamp Act several years later. Duties on export tobacco were increased, nominally, and the Assembly imposed Virginia's first tax on "luxury" vehicles, a tax on the axles of carriages and wheeled chairs (but not wagons). The Assembly resolved that "applying [proceeds of the new taxes] towards securing the final redemption of the treasury-notes, to supply any possible deficiency ... may tend to preserve the credit of our paper money," adding a 5% duty on imported slaves, and extending taxes on carriages and ordinary licenses through 1770, with all of the proceeds applied "for the encouragement and protection of the settlers upon the waters of the Mississippi." But the sheer volume of the French War Treasury note obligations led to considerable increases in the colony tithable and land taxes. There were several reasons for the Assembly's reliance on tithe and land taxes for retirement of the Treasury notes. Virginia's population growth was exponential but predictable during this period, the Virginia tidewater was fully seated, and frontier land was being occupied at a remarkable rate. Thus, both sources provided a broad, reliable base for revenue projection, at a time when the Assembly desperately needed just that. [Hening VII/9, VII/28, VII/77, VII/166-167, VII/259-265, VII/497 and VII/639-641; supra, Chapter on Lands; infra, Chapter on Slaves].

Predictable revenues were essential in the business of Treasury note issues. The 1760 Assembly found itself trying to predict revenues for 1769. Estimates of colonial population that were used by the Virginia Assembly in determining revenues from the Treasury note taxes tend to corroborate the efforts of modern statisticians. In 1757 the Virginia Assembly planned on a total of

90,000 tithables by 1762, representing a Virginia population of 290,000; the 1759 Assembly anticipated a tithable population of 130,000 by 1766, representing a colony-wide population of over 415,000. [Hening, VII/77-79, VII/256-264, VII/349, VII/359 and VII/497; see Chapter on Population, infra @ p. 433].

From 1755 to 1770, Virginia's colony-wide tithable taxes increased dramatically, from a pre-war average of only 6 pence per tithable colonist in 1750 to double that amount by 1757, and ten times that sum, 5 shillings per tithable, by 1765. If one regards the King's quitrents as the equivalent of a land tax, then Virginia's land taxes doubled in the decade from 1755 to 1765. Even though only 300,000 acres were on the Loudoun County tax lists, the 1765 land tax would have generated £300, over triple the sum of the Loudoun County levy that year. Special colony tithable taxes generated another £475 in Loudoun in 1765. Accounting for just the special tithable and land taxes, Loudoun's contributions to Virginia colony revenues increased from the nominal pre-war levels of only £25 a year to triple that sum by 1757, and then rocketed skyward to what must have seemed an incredible £775 by 1765. Loudoun's colonial residents could not have overlooked an increase in the colony's taxes by a multiple of thirty in a single decade. [Hening, VII/77-79, VII/256-264, VII/349, VII/359 and VII/497; supra, Chapter on the Grand Jury, Chapter on the Sheriff; see the List of Loudoun's 101 Largest Landowners, supra @ pp. 260-262; see Table of Taxes, supra @ p. 431].

Sheriffs were responsible for the collection of all special colony tithable and property taxes, as well as the colony and county levies. Parish vestries had the right to designate their own agents for collection of the parish levy and they often did, with mixed results. One failure by Cameron parish's collection agents led to the litigation that "preserved" the 1764 parish levy in the Loudoun Court records. As a practical matter, when they could, Sheriffs and their deputies accepted the payments of all three tithable taxes at the same time, along with any special tithable and property taxes, later rendering separate accounts for their collection activities. Sheriffs were entitled to a 6% collection fee, regardless of the specie tendered, and another 4% commission for making "cask" when collecting tobacco. Other tax collectors, the King's Customs Officers and collectors of Virginia duties on imported livestock were also compensated through 6% collection commissions. Despite the sense of urgency underlying many of the colonial taxes and duties, the Virginia Assembly maintained a healthy respect for what they viewed as the rights of colonial "Englishmen." A warrant issued by a Justice of the Peace, and the presence of a county constable, were both prerequisites to a search and seizure conducted by any tax collector in Virginia. [Chapter on Sheriffs, supra @ p. 139-140; infra, Chapter on Cameron Parish; Hening, VI/126, VII/268-269, VIII/102 and VIII/179].

County and colony levies, and the first special tithe and land taxes during the French War, were all due for payment before April 10th annually. Special procedures were instituted for the collection of Treasury note taxes when the issues became substantial, with lists of land and carriages compiled in every Virginia county. Starting in 1759, landowners were obliged to give an inventory of their lands to the county Clerk before the end of each December. Clerks were to transcribe complete lists for their counties by the end of March, and then "transmit ... true copies of the[ir] list of wheel-carriages, and an account of the quantities of land in their several counties" to the Sheriff and the Treasurer of Virginia. Loudoun Sheriffs were supposed to collect the land taxes by the end of April, the May grand jury would review the tax lists and present charges against any "concealers," and Sheriffs were then obliged to complete their collections and give a full account to Virginia's Treasurer by June 10th. It became readily apparent that enforcement would be difficult in the "Proprietary ... of Lord Fairfax" because the Northern Neck's land lists had been kept in the Proprietor's office and not in the colonial capitol, and delays in compilation of the lists were to be expected. The Assembly acted quickly to adjust the plan. Sheriffs in the Northern Neck were instructed to advertise and publish "the method prescribed for enlisting lands," and an amnesty for penalties was broadcast, under the proviso that Northern Neck taxpayers submit their lists of land to the offices of the county Clerks and pay their taxes before November 1, 1759. [Hening, VII/77-79 and VII/256-264; supra, Chapter on the Grand Jury, and Chapter on the Sheriff].

The 1762 Assembly expressed alarm at "great frauds ... [committed] by the Sheriffs in collecting the taxes imposed on lands, tithables and wheel carriages, for the support of the [French] war." The thrust of the Assembly's adjustment was the unification of county tax lists compilations, which is the event that modern researchers can look to as the ultimate cause for the preservation of so much Loudoun County land tax list information in the decade beginning with 1762. Every Virginia colonist was directed to deliver "an exact list of his or her lands ... [and] a list of every coach, chariot, or ... wheeled carriage ... at the time appointed [for the taking of] the list of tithables." County Clerks were advised to display land and carriage tax lists at the county courthouses along with the tithable lists, between August and October, and then "deliver [all of the lists] to the grand-jury, at every court ... held in the month of November." Presiding Justices of every November county court were directed to "charge the[ir] grand-jury to ... present every concealer." After 1762, "list[s] of the tithables, lands and wheel-carriages" were sent to the Treasurer of Virginia by the end of each November. [Hening, VII/539-543].

The Assembly of 1762 also provided that a landowner who failed to deliver "an exact list of his or her lands ... a concealer ... shall forfeit and pay [20] shillings [ie., £1] for every [100] acres of land so by him or her concealed." Concealers of carriages and chariots were penalized 30 shillings per axle. As civil penalties, fines would be divided between the individual "informer" and the King (meaning the colony), "for the use of the publick." The Grand Jury practice of presenting the concealers of taxable lands and wheeled vehicles was apparently instituted in Loudoun County in May of 1762. Sheriffs were instructed to "levy the arrears of all such taxes upon the persons who ought to pay" through the seizure and auction of the tax debtors' personal property. [Hening, VII/539-543; re land concealers, see Chapter on Lands, supra @ pp. 252-259; re carriage concealers, see infra @ pp. 429 and 430].

When the Assembly imposed a substantial colony levy on tithables in 1764 (generating over £530 in Loudoun County alone), Virginia Sheriffs were instructed to enter an additional bond and security "at the court ... in [their] County in February [1765, or] the next Court." Loudoun's new Sheriff, Charles Tyler, was instructed to sell any tobacco that he collected in payment of the levy "at Dumfries, on the court day of Prince William County ... in July" of 1765. All Sheriffs were to account directly with the Treasurer of Virginia before September 10, 1765. Collection of the 1764 colony levy caused a number of problems, primarily due to the size of the assessment. The 1765 Assembly remarked that, with "the large quantities of transfer tobacco so to be collected, the Sheriffs of several counties exact great prices ... and the inhabitants [are] much injured." The Assembly gave "every person in this colony" the option of paying in cash "so much per poll of their publick levies as is intended [sic] to be sold for the use of the militia" in cash at the (Loudoun!) exchange rate of 12 shillings, 6 pence per 100 lbt. of transfer notes, or, remarkably, in packed but unclean crop (not warehoused) tobacco. Sheriffs were instructed to refrain from exchanging specie for tobacco and vice versa. Loudoun's levy tobacco was again scheduled for sale at Dumfries, along with the Fauquier tobacco, "on the court day [of Prince William County] in ... August" of 1766, with an accounting to the Treasurer expected that October. Following the collection of the 1764 colony levy, the Assembly restored the provision that all levy payments made with tobacco "transfer receipts" were to be paid by April 10th each year. [Hening, VIII/38-41, VIII/103 and VIII/178-181; re Sheriff Tyler's collections, see Chapter on Sheriffs, supra @ pp. 141-142; and see Chapter on Economics, supra, @ p. 191].

The Virginia Assembly's success in retiring colonial Treasury notes brought a set of mixed blessings: Virginia's fiscal responsibility was rewarded with new taxes imposed from London, which in turn, inspired that tax revolt many know today as the American Revolution. As Virginia approaches the year 2000, her fiscal responsibility is maintained in balanced biennial budgets.

The Loudoun Record

December 13, 1757 - The first Loudoun County levy is itemized and laid: 27 lbs. of tobacco is assessed to each of 1,066 Tithables, with total County expenditures of just under 28,782 lbs. of tobacco [about £180]. Book A, p. 55.

December 13, 1757 - In the County levy, a debit is listed for: "The Public Proportion [paid to the Virginia Treasurer] ... @ 10 lb. Tobo. per Poll ... 10,660 [lbs. of tobacco]." This is an unusual inclusion of the Virginia colonial levy (poll tax) in the accounts of the county budget. The colony levy was normally assessed separately. Book A, p. 55; Table of Colonial Taxes, infra @ p. 431.

December 13, 1757 - Also in the itemization of the County levy, a debit is listed for the "Ballance [sic] due to Fairfax [County] from this County ... 5,412 [lbs. of tobacco]." This is Loudoun County's apportioned payment of the Fairfax County levy for the first half of 1757. Book A, p. 55.

December 14, 1757 - Sheriff "Aneas Campbell Gentn. Acknowledged

Bonds for Collecting the levy, Land & Note Tax[es] in this County with Anthony Russell and James Hamilton Gentlemen his Securities." Book A, p. 58.

November 14, 1758 - The County levy is itemized and laid: 48 lbs. of tobacco charged to each of 1,156 Tithables, with total County expenditures of 56,416 lbs. of tobacco. Book A, p. 177.

February 28, 1759 - The Virginia Assembly Resolves "That ... £26,298 ... be raised for the Clothing, Subsistance, Provision, and Recruiting the [1st Virginia] Regiment ... by a Tax of two Shillings on every tithable Person ... in the Years 1765 and 1766; and likewise a Tax of two Shillings on every Hogshead of Tobacco shipped ... in the Years 1765 and 1766." Assembly, (1758) p. 71.

November 14, 1759 - The County levy is itemized and laid: 46 lbs. of tobacco is assessed to each of 1,113 Tithables, with total County expenditures of 51,232 lbs. of tobacco. Book A, p. 304.

November 14, 1759 - "Ordered that George West, Richard Coleman and Aneas Campbell ... [are] appointed Commissioners to meet with the Justices of Fairfax County & to settle the proportion of the Money in the hands of John West, Gent., late Sherif of [Fairfax] County and that Nicholas Minor, Gent., receive the same and Account ..." Book A, p. 305.

December 11, 1759 - "Aneas Campbell ... one of the Commissioners for this County to settle with John West Gent. late [former] Sherif of Fairfax County for the proportion due from that County to this and having done so ... [West had] twenty six pounds [£26,] nine shillings and [2,761] pounds of Tobacco which [West agreed] to account for at twenty five shillings Per Ct. [100 lbs.]," the new Loudoun Sheriff Nicholas Minor is ordered to receive and "account to the Court for the same." Book A, p. 318.

June 11, 1760 - "Ordered that Nicholas Minor, Gent., Sherif ... receive of John West, Gent. late Sherif of Fairfax County ... [2,761 lbs.] of Tobacco and ... sell the same for the best price that can be got." Book A, p. 366.

November 12, 1760 - The County levy is itemized and laid, with 6 lbs. of tobacco charged to each of 1,270 Tithables in the County, and with total County expenditures of 18,307 lbs. of tobacco. Book A, p. 405.

November 12, 1760 - "Ordered that Leven Powell pay unto Nicholas Minor Sherif [£31,] seven Shillings and four pence it being the Money in his hands due from him to this County." Book A, p. 406.

November 11, 1761 - The County levy is itemized and laid, with 15 lbs. of tobacco charged to each of 1,479 Tithables in the County, and with total County expenditures of 17,905 lbs. of tobacco. Book A, p. 533.

May 12, 1762 - The County Grand Jury Presents charges against three Loudoun residents, each, "of this [Loudoun] County for not entering [on the tax lists] in the Clerk's Office a two Wheeled Chair: ... John Peak ... Thomas Brown ... [and] Evan Price." Book A, p. 599.

November 2, 1762 - It is "enacted ... seven pounds of tobacco be paid by every tithable person within this dominion [Virginia] ... being the publick levy from the sixth day of March [1761] ... to [November 2, 1762] ... [to be] paid by the collectors of the several counties to the several persons and counties, respectively, to whom it is proportioned by this General Assembly." Hening, VII/543.

November 10, 1762 - The County levy is itemized and laid: 6 lbs. of Tobacco charged to each of 1,573 Tithables, with Constables not counted. Total County expenditures were 18,716 lbs. of tobacco. Book B, p. 73.

May 11, 1763 - "Ordered that William Ellzey, Gent., receive from the Sheriff of Fairfax County [812 lbs.] of Tobacco for a Proportion due from that County to this ---." Book B, p. 125.

November 9, 1763 - The County levy is itemized and laid: 8 lbs. of tobacco are charged to each of 1,790 Tithables, Constables exempted, with total County expenditures of 14,320 lbs. of tobacco. Book B, p. 266.

October of 1764 - The Virginia Assembly enacts: "That [46 lbs.] of tobacco be paid by every tithable person within this dominion for the defraying and payment of the publick charge of the country, and the pay and expenses of the militia drawn out into actual service." Hening, VIII/38-41.

November 14, 1764 - The County levy is itemized and laid: 22 lbs. of tobacco to each of 1,846 Tithables, with total County expenditures of 40,612 lbs. of tobacco. Book B, p. 497.

November of 1765 - In the various tithable lists returned for the year, the owners of carriages and wheeled carriages are identified: Aeneas Campbell with one two-wheeled chair; Anthony Russell with one "riding chair," John Carter Esqr. [apparently living at Sudley plantation] with "one two-wheeled chair," Capt. James Lane [Junr.] with two two-wheeled chairs, and Simon Triplett with "a two-wheeled chair." The owners of wagons are also identified in the tithable lists. LDTX/1, generally and pp. 34, 39-41; see supra, Chapter on Trades.

December 26, 1765 - The County levy is itemized and laid, with only 2½ lbs. of tobacco assessed to each of 1,901 Tithables, after a large credit carried-over from 1764, and with total of County expenditures of only 15,317 lbs. of tobacco. Book C, p. 73.

November 11, 1766 - The annual Loudoun County levy is itemized and laid: 12 lbs. of tobacco is assessed against each of 1,979 Tithables, with the total County collections of 23,748 lbs. of tobacco. Book C, p. 220.

December 9, 1766 - Loudoun Sheriff Francis Peyton, with his sureties Leven Powell, Stephen Donaldson, Elijah Chinn and Sampson Turley, enters his Bond for the penal sum of 47,496 lbs. of tobacco (double the total annual levy), on the condition that he will "duly collect the levy laid and assessed on the Tithable persons within the County of Loudoun." LDCODB, Book E, p. 282.

Tithables, the County Levy and Colonial Taxes Loudoun County, 1757-1766

	County Budget	Tithables	County levy	Virginia poll*/‡ and land¤ taxes
1757 -	18,122 lbt.	1,066 Ts	27 lbt./T	[incl.: 10 lbt./T*]
	** [total tax/T: 49 lbt., or 6 shillings, 1½ pence]			
1758 -	56,416 lbt.	1,156 Ts	48 lbt./T	3 shillings/T‡
	** [total tax/T: 94 lbt., or 11¾ shillings]			+ 1 shilling¤
1759 -	51,232 lbt.	1,113 Ts.¥	46 lbt./T	6 lbt./T* 3 shillings/T‡
	** [total tax/T: 98 lbt., or 12¼ shillings]			+ 1 shilling¤
1760 -	18,307 lbt.	1,270 Ts	6 lbt./T	3 shillings/T‡
	** [total tax/T: 52 lbt., or 6½ shillings]			+ 1 shilling¤
1761 -	17,905 lbt.	1,479 Ts	15 lbt./T	6 lbt./T* 3 shillings/T‡
	** [total/T: 67 lbt., or 8 shillings, 4½ pence]			+ 1 shilling¤
1762 -	18,716 lbt.	1,573 Ts	6 lbt./T	7 lbt./T* 3 shillings/T‡
	** [total/T: 59 lbt., or 7 shillings, 4½ pence]			+ 1 shilling¤
1763 -	14,320 lbt.	1,790 Ts	8 lbt./T	3 shillings/T‡
	** [total tax/T: 54 lbt., or 6¾ shillings]			+ 1 shilling¤
1764 -	40,612 lbt.	1,846 Ts	22 lbt./T	46 lbt./T* 4 shillings/T‡
	** [total tax/T: 122 lbt., or 15¼ shillings]			+ 1 shilling¤
1765 -	15,317 lbt.	1,901 Ts	2½ lbt./T	5 shillings/T‡
	** [total tax/T: 64½ lbt., or 8. shillings]			+ 2 shillings¤
1766 -	23,748 lbt.	1,979 Ts	12 lbt./T	8 lbt./T* 5 shillings/T‡
	** [total tax/T: 82 lbt., or 10¼ shillings]			+ 2 shillings¤

"lbt." - represents taxes assessed in "pounds of tobacco"
"T" - "Tithable" individual, subject to poll tax; see Glossary
"*" - regular, usually bi-annual, colony-wide poll taxes
"‡" - poll tax imposed to retire "French War" Treasury notes
"¤" - land tax assessed on every 100 acres in Virginia
"¥" - official (probably inaccurate) figure used in 1759 levy
"**" - total tax/T includes estimated avg. 22 lbt./T parish levy

The Population of Colonial Loudoun

Population growth in colonial Virginia was exponential for roughly 125 years before the American Revolution. Between 1650 and 1700, Virginia's resident population doubled and redoubled, from about 16,000 to 65,000. Virginia's population quadrupled again in the first half of the 18th-century, passing the ¼-million mark around 1750. Various estimates put Virginia's population as high as 285,000, about 170,000 whites and 115,000 blacks, by the time Loudoun County was created in 1757. Virginia's last colonial Governor, Lord Dunmore, estimated that the colonial population had doubled yet again since 1750 and was ½-million in 1774, comprised of 300,000 whites and 200,000 blacks. [Democracy, p. 72; Independence, p. 154; generally, ColVa; for estimates by the Assembly, Chapter on Colonial Taxes, supra @ pp. 424-245].

Before the 1720s, population growth in the northwestern reaches of the Northern Neck did not keep pace with the rest of Virginia. In 1700, the population of Stafford County was only about 2,800; in 1725, the entire resident population of Stafford County, which still included a sparsely settled Loudoun piedmont, was under 6,000. On the Potomac river, the Little Falls was considered the extreme upper bounds of white settlement in 1700. Between 1707 and 1722, speculators took out patents on lands in eastern Loudoun, mostly in what is now Fairfax County, up to Cub run from the Occoquan, and to Goose creek on the Potomac. The difficulty of determining the size and location of early Loudoun settlements derives, in part, from the absence of a "seating" requirement in Northern Neck Proprietary patents. But very few if any European settlers had a desire to risk their lives and fortunes on the piedmont before the Iroquois gave up their claim to the Loudoun "hunting grounds" in 1722 in the Treaty of Albany. During the following decade, Loudoun experienced its first major surge of permanent settlers. By 1735, the resident population was sufficient to constitute several small congregations for worship, on both sides of Kitoctin Mountain. [Landmarks, p. 117].

The most significant population growth in Loudoun, at least before the Revolution, took place in the 1740s after Lord Fairfax surveyed his Proprietary boundaries and Virginia manors, and then reopened his land office in 1739. The population literally burst upon the Loudoun piedmont in the 1740s. At the end of that decade, the resident population of Loudoun, particularly in settlements between Rocky run and Goose creek, from the Tuscarora north to Clarks run, and from Rock Hill north along Kitoctin creek to the Potomac, was sufficient to justify the creation of Cameron parish. Between 1735 and 1750, the resident population in Loudoun increased five-fold. A clear focus on Loudoun's colonial population growth now allows for the debunking of one myth here. "Seating of the upper Potomac" was not "delayed by the creation of the 'manors'" as Fairfax Harrison once suggested. To the contrary, erection of the manors in the 1730s signalled the Fairfax family's confidence in the future of the piedmont lands, and encouraged settlement in Loudoun. The emigrations of Loudoun residents to the Carolinas, Kentucky, Ohio and Tennessee in the 1770s and 1780s are another matter. During the decade following the creation of the Fairfax manors in Loudoun and on the Blue Ridge, Loudoun's resident population tripled. [contra, Landmarks, p. 147; contra, Fairfax, p. 25].

A third period of dramatic population growth began around 1755, shortly before Loudoun County was created. Steady growth in Loudoun continued unabated for over a decade, until at least 1766, and seems to have been caused, at least in part, by an eastwardly diversion of settlers from Virginia's frontiers during the French and Indian War. During this entire decade, the growth rate in neighboring Fairfax County was under 5% per year - about half of Loudoun's rate of growth. In ten years, Fairfax County's population had grown by barely half, while Loudoun County's population almost doubled. As a consequence, Loudoun and Fairfax were equal in total population by 1766 - each with about 6,000 residents. [both citing and contra, Fairfax, p. 33; contra, Democracy, p. 15; see supra, Chapter on Slaves].

In 1761, three years after Leesburg had been founded, 35% of the Loudoun population was still living west of Kitoctin Mountain and Little River, while another 25% was situated between the Kitoctin range and Goose creek. Due to a difference in racial composition, by 1761 Loudoun County's white population surpassed that of her tidewater parent, Fairfax County. The growing conditions and racial composition of the population east of Goose creek were similar to the Fairfax tidewater, and during the mid-1760s a surprising retrograde took place. Some of

Loudoun's prominent tidewater families moved eastward and promptly began to militate for either a return of some eastern Loudoun lands to Fairfax or the creation of a new trans-piedmont county centered on the fall line. Prime examples of this trend were Loudoun Justices John Moss Junr., who moved to the Long glade of Difficult run in 1765, and Col. Nicholas Minor, the proprietor of Leesburg, who moved to the Belmont Ridge area.

Demographic information for colonial Virginia is most readily extracted from the annual county and Episcopal parish tithable lists. In this respect Loudoun County has mixed blessings. The county tithable lists from the 1750s for Fairfax County, which would have contained every "Loudoun" resident, have disappeared. Only one pre-1770 parish tithable list for Loudoun has survived. It was compiled by Rev. Charles Green for Truro and Cameron parishes in 1749, the year that Cameron parish was created. Rev. Green listed many of the early residents of the Loudoun piedmont, but his parish list was nearly a decade old when Loudoun County was created and did not distinguish the parish of residence for many individuals. Of the early records of Cameron parish, which was essentially coterminous with Loudoun from 1749 to 1770, only the 1764 parish levy has been found. On the other hand, the Truro Parish vestry minute book and Fairfax County Court Orders give us the total number of tithables in Fairfax (which included Loudoun) County prior to 1757. Partial or complete originals of Loudoun's colonial tithable lists, and annual levies, giving the total number of tithables in the county, are available for every year from 1757 up to the time of the Revolution. Fortunately, the complete tithable lists from 1761 and 1765 for Loudoun have survived for over two centuries. They provide two detailed "annual" portraits of the entire adult population of Loudoun County, identifying every slave and every white man over the age of sixteen. [Green, *"Fairfax County List of Titheables for 1749,"* MS, pp. 1-5; Slave Ownership, 1757-1765, Table, supra, @ p. 376; supra, Chapter on Slaves, Chapter on Tithables and Tax Lists].

The population study of colonial Loudoun, presented here, relies heavily upon the following assumptions for the years before 1757. European settlement of Loudoun began around 1720 and was sporadic before 1725. For Loudoun's population prior to 1730, one "guesstimate" is nearly as good as another. Rev. Green's assertion that there were 621 tithables in Truro parish in 1738 was reliable. Green's 1749 list was essentially complete. The "back-country" settlers were no more than 40% of the total population in 1738, the same percentage they constituted in 1749. Rates of population growth, from 1729 to 1749, and from 1749 to 1757, were fairly constant. The pre-1757 growth patterns of Loudoun, for both white and black populations, were reflected in post-1757 patterns. The slave population of Loudoun is best estimated as 150% of the number of black tithables. The percentage of slaves in Loudoun gradually increased from about 15% of tithables in 1727 to 35% in 1757, as Loudoun made the transition from a "frontier" to "settled" area. And, previous estimates regarding the pre-Revolutionary population of Fairfax County are unreliable and can be applied only indirectly to Loudoun. [see supra, Green, *"Fairfax County List ..."*, p. 5; contra, Fairfax, pp. 32-35].

Additional assumptions have been made for the study of Loudoun's colonial population in the years after 1760. The 1761 and 1765 Loudoun tithable lists, both individually and together, provide a reliable basis for the projection of population numbers in other years. Growth in the white and slave populations mirrored the growth of the number of tithables as a whole over the decade. Rates of population growth, from 1757 to 1761, and from 1761 to 1765, were fairly constant; growth of Loudoun's slave population from 1757 to 1761 was similar to the growth found between 1761 and 1765. And, patterns of population growth exhibited by large sub-sets of the Loudoun population between 1757 and 1761 are representative of county-wide population trends.

Colonial administrators had a formula that was used to calculate the total population of Virginia: the white population was equal to four times the number of white tithables, and the slave population was double the number of black tithables. For various reasons that have been discussed earlier, the slave population of colonial Loudoun is over-estimated by multiplying black tithables by 1½, the formula that has been adopted here. [see Chapter on Slaves, supra, @ pp. 386-387].

POPULATION OF LOUDOUN COUNTY, 1720-1766

Year	Total Tithes	Slave Tithes	White Tithes	Slave Pop.*	White Pop.**	Total Pop.
1720 ...	10.e	1.e	9.e	1.‡	19.‡	20
1725 ...	40.e	5.e	35.e	5.‡	75.‡	80
1730 ...	80.e	15.e	65.e	25.‡	195.‡	220
1735 ...	150.e	30.e	120.e	45	480	525
1738 ...	245.e	55.e	190.e	83	760	843
1740 ...	320.e	75.e	245.e	113	980	1,093
1745 ...	605.e	151.e	454.e	227	1,816	2,043
1749 ...	828	233.e	595.e	350	2,380	2,730
1750 ...	860.e	248.e	612.e	372	2,448	2,820
1755 ...	1015.e	331.e	684.e	497	2,736	3,233
1757 ...	1066	364.e	702.e	546	2,808	3,354
1758 ...	1156	403.e	753.e	605	3,012	3,617
1759 ...	1195.¥	428.e	767.e	642	3,068	3,710
1760 ...	1270	465.e	805.e	698	3,220	3,918
1761 ...	1479	553	926	830	3,704	4,534
1762 ...	1573	597.e	976.e	896	3,904	4,800
1763 ...	1790	667.e	1,123.e	1,001	4,492	5,493
1764 ...	1846.#	695.e	1,151.e	1,043	4,604	5,647
1765 ...	1901	728	1,173	1,092	4,692	5,784
1766 ...	1979	770.e	1,209.e	1,155	4,836	5,991

"e" - Designates an estimated number of tithable individuals.
Population estimates are projected using the following formulas:

* * - The total resident "Slave population" is arrived at by multiplying the number of tithable slaves by 1½.
* ** - The total resident "White population" is arrived at by multiplying the number of tithable white males by 4.
* ‡ - Assumptions were varied for Loudoun's "frontier" years.
* ¥ - Estimated; tithables in the 1759 levy appear incorrect.
* # - Also in parish levy; infra, Chapter on Cameron Parish.

The Virginia colony was never made a part of any diocese in the English church. After 1690, the Anglican Bishop of London exerted his authority in the Virginia colony through a personal emissary who was given the title of "Commissary." The Virginia Commissary, until 1752, had ecclesiastical jurisdiction over the Episcopal clergy of the colony and by tradition served as president of the College of William and Mary. Since there was no Bishop in Virginia and the King was the temporal head of the Church, Governors, as the King's representatives, had authority in Virginia equivalent to church functionaries with extra-ecclesiastical rights. The Governor of Virginia nominally had the authority to fill parish vacancies and induct new ministers into their rectories, to regulate the ministers in their activities and, with the King's consent, to grant pardons based on pleas of the "benefit of clergy." The latter practice was the colonial equivalent of the power of reprieve and pardon that has been reserved to Governors in every Virginia Constitution since 1776. In colonial Virginia, other civil powers that were exercised by the church in England - the license of marriages without banns and the probate of wills - were legally delegated to the county clerks and the county courts. Improper conduct of ministers was brought to the attention of the Governor and his Council first and then, upon cause, turned over to the Commissary for further action. [ColVa, p. 466; Hening, IX/115].

Beginning in 1732, the Virginia Assembly initiated the practice of dividing counties in the Northern Neck into multiple parishes, and subsequently creating new counties along the lines of the parish boundaries. That year, Truro parish was formed, incorporating all of modern Fairfax and Loudoun Counties:

> *"... from [November 1, 1732] ... Prince William ... [is to] be divided into two distinct parishes; by the river Ockoquan [sic], and Bull Run (a branch thereof) ... from thence to the Indian Thoroughfare [Ashby's Gap] of the Blue Ridge of Mountains; ... below the said bounds, shall ... retain the name of Hamilton: ... all that other part ... which lies above those bounds, shall thereafter be called ... Truro."*

The language in this act was the first designation of the dividing line that ultimately separated Fairfax and then Loudoun County from Prince William and Fauquier Counties. When Fairfax County was formed in May of 1742, it was described simply as "consisting of the Parish of Truro." [Hening, IV/367 and V/208].

In an act that presaged the creation of Loudoun County, Cameron parish was created out of western Truro parish in October of 1748 in a Private Act of the Assembly, but the Assembly inserted a delaying clause which set June 11, 1749 as the effective date for the creation of Cameron parish. The new parish was named in honor of Thomas Lord Fairfax, Baron of Cameron, and, incidentally, was also the name given to the Truro parish glebe. The language of the 1748 act, describing the dividing line between Truro parish and Cameron parish, was recited in Hening's Statutes in "An act to impower the Vestry of the parish of Truro ... to sell their Glebe" enacted in February of 1752:

> *"... Truro should be divided by Difficult Run, and its meanders from the mouth to the head thereof ... thence by a line to the head of Pope's head-run, and down the said run, its several courses and meanders to the mouth thereof ... the said parish, situate on the lower side should ... retain the name of Truro, and all that other part thereof, situate on the upper side of the said runs and line, should be ... called ... Cameron."* [Hening, VI/271].

Eight years after Cameron parish was created, Loudoun County was created as its political alter ego. Only a segment of the eastern boundaries differed - the Cameron parish line along Pope's Head Run was not followed for part of the eastern county line, but rather, from the headwaters of Difficult Run, a more westerly county line was designated, southwest to the head of Rocky Run. Thus, after Loudoun was created in 1757, Cameron parish still contained a small portion of western Fairfax County, between Pope's Head Run and Rocky Run. This explains the situation when Churchwardens of Cameron parish brought morals charges in Loudoun County against Ann Nelson, a resident of Fairfax County, in 1757. It also gives geographic specificity to the otherwise surprisingly small tithable lists "for Cameron Parish" that were occasionally brought in for Loudoun County before 1763. The 1762 Assembly adjusted the southern boundary of Cameron parish, restoring to Truro parish the section of Cameron parish that was situated in Fairfax County, between Rocky Run and Popes Head Run. As a consequence, Cameron parish Vestryman Leonard Dozier was "moved" into Truro parish and his place on the vestry was taken by William Carr Lane. [infra, Chapter on Non-Residents; Hening, VII/612; infra, The Record, p. 461].

The vestry of each parish in colonial Virginia had a wide variety of duties. Sometimes, through their Churchwardens, they acted like a super grand jury - presenting moral violations (in Loudoun County particularly, bastard births) for prosecution in the county court. Each vestry budgeted for and set the annual parish levy, which included the cost of providing for the poor and infirm. Up until shortly before the Revolution, the levy continued to include the minister's salary, the purchase of the church "plate," the land and construction costs of the churches, chapels and parish glebe, the costs of maintaining parish records, salaries for church clerks and Sextons, and every other expense of Episcopal worship. The vestry supervised the apprenticing of bastard, orphaned, and impoverished children. The Vestrymen managed the quadrennial processionings of the boundaries of the parish landowners. It was a Virginia custom for the Governor to suggest a candidate for a vacant parish rectory, but the parish vestry would then consider any and all candidates and make their own choice of a minister. The new parish rector, who may have been recruited from another parish or imported from England, often consulted with neither the Commissary nor the Governor before assuming his duties. The Virginia Assembly codified the procedure in 1748, providing that each vestry had the "sole right" of selection of a minister during the first twelve months of a vacant parish ministry. In so doing, the Assembly doubled the customary six month period for presentation that then prevailed in England, in an effort to account for the difficulties in transport and correspondence that existed between the colony and London.

In the 1643 session the Virginia Assembly repealed all existing laws except one: the law governing the Episcopal Church in Virginia. The reenacted law provided for the continued use of the liturgy and the Church of England's Book of Common Prayer. The law also retained provisions for the vestries' annual election of two Churchwardens as their legal representatives in every parish as well as the requirements for the maintenance of parish registers of weddings, christenings and burials in every parish of the colony. The Churchwardens and ministers were required to "visit" with their respective county courts once a year, and reminded to take the opportunity at those visitations to present charges against drunkards, swearers, fornicators, whores and adulterers. Churchwardens were not to be "discharged [by their county court] until they have given upp [sic] their presentments." The Record herein, in the Chapters on Crimes and Punishment, the Grand Jury, Apprentices and Orphans, and Base Born Children, gives ample testimony that these Episcopal church practices were still in active use in Loudoun County during the 1757-1766 decade. [Hening, I/240-243; and see the other Chapters mentioned].

The 1642-43 Assembly also provided "for the releife of diverse poore people ... disabled to labor by reason of sicknes, lamenes or age [sic]," empowering each parish vestry with the right to grant a certificate "which shall free them from all publique [sic] charges except the ministers & parish duties." By the 1700s, this power had been granted to the county courts as well. The vestry and Churchwardens were legally responsible for the care and clothing of the poor inhabitants of their parish. Churchwardens were also responsible for the maintenance and cure of all of the sick and disabled poor in their parish, regardless of their parish of residence. In the instances where poor persons were found outside of their home parish, they were provided for by the host parish and then returned to their parish of residence, with the charges ultimately paid by "the parish where such poor person was last legally settled." Housekeepers "entertaining" the poor were legally obliged to notify their Churchwardens, presumably so that church officials would have adequate opportunity to monitor the status and the expenditures for the care of the poor in their parish. Starting around 1751, Churchwardens and parish levy collectors were involved in the certification of the individuals moving out of their parish. The certification was proof that the last parish levy had been paid, so that an individual leaving the parish with a certification in hand was not treated as an idler or a disorderly person in other parishes in Virginia. The law specifically defined the impoverished who were to be "provided for at the parish charge ... [and] accounted an inhabitant, so as to have gained a legal settlement in any parish." The primary requirement was that "such person shall have been actually resident in such parish, one whole year." One could properly assume that this provision amounted to a residency requirement when the householders in Cameron parish were summoned for rare vestry elections in 1759 and 1771. [Hening, I/242, III/259 and VI/29-33].

A number of amendments to the laws governing church vestries were enacted between 1645 and 1665. One provision specified a plurality vote, with a majority of the parishioners voting as they "think fitt," to elect the parish vestry. The vestry of each parish was set at twelve in number. Oaths of office required of Vestrymen were specified as the oaths of allegiance and supremacy. Each Vestryman was also required to declare his comfort with the doctrine and discipline of the Church of England. Parish vestries were authorized to adopt by-laws to address any local concerns not covered specifically in Virginia statutes. Vestries were instructed to elect new Churchwardens annually, and with their minister, to elect replacements for any disqualified or deceased Vestrymen. Bacon's rebels attempted to eliminate the self-perpetuating nature of the colonial vestries in 1676, but their statutes were repealed the following year. Unfortunately, colonial law providing for the election of replacement Vestrymen resulted in numerous abuses. The Assembly was frequently drawn into disputes similar to the one affecting the vestry of Truro parish (which then included Loudoun) in 1744. The Assembly dissolved the Truro vestry that year because "divers of the inhabitants have acted as vestrymen ... altho' many of them were never lawfully chosen or qualified." The freeholders and house-keepers of Truro were then instructed to elect a new vestry of "twelve of the most able and discreet persons" before February 1, 1745. In February of 1745, the parishioners of Truro petitioned the Assembly again, this time with a request that the Truro vestry election returns be declared valid. [Hening, I/290, II/25, II/44, II/171, II/362, II/380, V/274, and, V/380].

The instances of abuse and mismanagement of parish affairs in the Northern Neck did not end with the creation of Cameron parish. In 1758, Vincent Lewis resigned from the vestry and shortly thereafter the "inhabitants" of Cameron parish petitioned the Virginia Assembly, alleging that the parish vestry was guilty of "arbitrary and illegal practices to the great oppression of the inhabitants." The Assembly legally dissolved the Cameron parish vestry and "the freeholders and house-keepers" of the parish were instructed to meet and elect a new vestry of "twelve of the most able & discreet persons of [Loudoun County]" on or before August 1, 1759. Entries in The Record dated on and shortly after August 14, 1759 confirm the seating of eleven new Vestrymen for Cameron parish. Among the new Vestrymen elected in 1759 were six County Justices, and another was Charles Binns, the Loudoun Clerk, while two Justices on the original vestry were not reelected. The twelfth Vestryman was Leonard Dozier, the only member of the original vestry reelected that year, and he renewed his oaths and rejoined the vestry late in 1760. It seems safe to assume that the complaints raised against the Cameron vestry in 1758 were not, per se, anti-Establishment. The legislative petition, if it still exists, is buried somewhere in the Archives at the State Library in Richmond. But a wealth of circumstantial evidence is at hand that allows us to suggest the likely origins of the complaints. As one might suspect, the Episcopal Vestrymen in Cameron parish in the 1749-1759 decade were all representatives of old "Tidewater" families. So, too, were the dozen Vestrymen elected in 1759. But where only one member of the first group lived above Goose Creek, two-thirds of the Vestrymen elected in 1759 lived above the Goose Creek-Little River demarcation that, in 1771, would separate Shelburne parish from Cameron parish. The Record from the spring of 1759 refers to James Lane and Thomas Awbrey as Churchwardens "for the time being." It seems curious that the old Cameron vestry would have chosen their only member living above Goose Creek (Awbrey) as a Churchwarden at a time that the vestry was operating under a cloud of alleged abuses. An "old" decision also might have come back to haunt the vestry - their choice of a site east of Goose Creek, near Gum Spring, for the first parish glebe. The petition of complaint corresponds in time to the founding of Leesburg, construction of the first County Courthouse, and a re-centering of the Loudoun community's focus on that crossroads, west of Goose Creek. One could speculate that, when Leesburg was founded, the old vestry announced plans to construct a new church instead of using the new Courthouse for services, which would have provoked the non-Episcopals in western Loudoun. Use of a County Courthouse as a place of Episcopal worship was a widely accepted practice in Virginia's frontier counties. Many religious dissenters encouraged the practice, since every tithable in a parish was legally obligated to share the cost of constructing the Episcopal houses of worship and the multiple use of the Courthouse directly reduced the cost of their personal support for the King's church. The election in 1759 advanced four men to the vestry who lived in the area west of Little River, suggesting that the interests of the "Middleburg" community had been ignored by the old vestry. Shortly after the 1759 election, we find that the Courthouse and a new Mountain Chapel west of Little River were both in use for worship services. We must also note that the three replacement Vestrymen elected in 1752 and 1755, William Ellzey, Edward Payne and James Ingoe Dozier, apparently were not residents of the parish - at various times each of them was referred to as residing in either Prince William or Fairfax County, not Loudoun. Election of even one non-resident to the Cameron vestry would have been improper. In all likelihood, several of the foregoing elements weighed-in, together, to force the election of a new vestry. The replacement of the Cameron parish vestry by election in 1759 is probably the best evidence one could hope to find to support the proposition that the provisions for local government in colonial Virginia were generally acceptable to the populous and, at least in Loudoun County, promoted the careers of leaders who could appreciate the power inherent in democratic actions undertaken by a unified community of modest yeomen. [Hening, VII/301-302; infra, The Record, p. 458; supra, Chapter on the County Court].

The laws providing for the election of Virginia vestry were next amended in April of 1757, shortly before the creation of Loudoun County. At that time the Assembly determined that thereafter the remaining Vestrymen of a parish, alone, would elect the replacement of any Vestryman who resigned. This provision was first applied when Charles Binns, the first Loudoun County Clerk of Court, resigned from the Cameron parish vestry in 1763. In the Act of 1757, the oaths for new Vestrymen were changed to: "the oaths appointed by act of Parliament ... the oath ... for the further security of his majesty's person and government ... and for extinguishing the hopes of the pretended Prince of Wales and his open and secret abettors." New Vestrymen were also required to subscribe to "the Test" and to "subscribe in vestry to be comfortable to the doctrine and discipline of the Church of England." The Loudoun Court apparently misunderstood this law and universally required the later subscription in open Court from all new Vestrymen. In the same law, the Assembly adopted: procedures for the disqualification and divestiture of any Vestryman who became a dissenter from the church (ie., a non-Episcopalian) after assuming office; the requirement of a quorum of at least seven Vestrymen for conducting church affairs; and, a prohibition barring ministers and Vestrymen from serving as the clerk of their own parish vestry. [see The Record, infra, p. 462; Hening, VII/132 and VII/302-303; and see infra, Glossary].

Processioning, the regular re-marking of the boundaries of land holdings, was another English custom that was maintained in the Virginia colony. The 1662 Assembly codified the practice in an attempt to quell:

> *"... many contentious suites [that] are dayly incited and stirred up about the bounds of land ... surveighors being for the most part careles of seeing the trees marked ... owners never renewing them ... chopps being growne up, or the trees fallen, the bounds become as uncertaine as at first [sic]."*

The law instructed every county court to order their parish vestries to divide each parish into precincts "for the neighbors to joyne and see each others markes renewed, and to appoint certaine dayes betweene Easter and Whitsunday to goe the said processions [sic]." The law further directed that inhabitants "of every neck and tract of land adjoining shall goe in procession and see the marked trees of every mans land in those precincts to be renewed," with the processioning to take place thereafter every four years. Boundaries thus established or confirmed "by the consent of the present proprietors" were to be deemed the legal property boundaries thereafter. Provision was made for the resolution of differences "that cannot be by the neighbors themselves decided:"

> *"two honest and able surveyors ... in presence of the neighbor-hood [to] lay out the land in controversie and the bounds then laid out to be the certaine bounds ... it tending ... to the preservation of friendship among neighbors to have a present and final decision of their differences, while men yet live that are acquainted with the first surveys [sic]."*

Processioning was conducted this way in Virginia up to the time of the American Revolution, with only minor changes in 1733,

1748 and 1752. The Truro parish records confirm that land processionings were undertaken in "Loudoun" in 1743 and again in 1747, but the lands west of the south fork of Kitoctin Creek and west of the northeast fork of the Beaverdam branch of Goose Creek were said to contain "no freeholder," and accordingly were not processioned. [Hening, II/101-102; Truro, p. 39].

The processioning law was recodified and revised during the 1748 "Lawyer's Session" of the Assembly in an "Act for settling the Titles and Bounds of Lands, and for preventing unlawful Hunting and Ranging." This law called for processioning to resume everywhere in the colony every fourth year beginning in 1751. New procedures called for the county courts to issue instructions to the various parish vestries between June 1st and September 1st, with the vestries to select "two or more intelligent honest freeholders of every precinct to see such processioning performed ... between the last day of September and the last day of March then next coming." The days selected for processioning in the precincts were to be advertised in the parish churches on the three Sundays "next before the same is to be performed." The 1748 law provided that when boundaries were processioned three times, they "settle[d] such bounds, so as the same may never afterwards be altered," except in rare instances when an heir, "in reversion," resumed tenure on property after the death of a life tenant. The Fairfax County Court ordered the full processioning of Cameron parish in 1751 and again in 1755 but, with the loss of the Cameron parish vestry records, we can only assume that these processionings were conducted since there was no prosecution of the vestry for their failure to comply with the county court Order. In Loudoun County, processionings were ordered for Cameron parish by the county court, right on schedule, in 1759 and 1763. [Hening, V/426-429; infra, The Record, pp. 458 and 461].

The 1643 Assembly redefined a tithable, established the ministers' annual salaries, and how they were to be paid:

> *"tenn [10] pounds of tob'o. [tobacco] per poll [person] & a bushell of corne per poll paid to the ministers ... for all tithable persons ... [ie.] all youths of sixteen years of age upwards, as also for all negro women at the age of sixteen years; ... upon the [20th] of November ... the parishioners shall bring in the duties ... of tob'o. ... for the ministers ... [and]*

corne to be brought in upon the 19th of December ... unto a place appointed by the churchwardens ... The payment to be made by two bushells of ears for one bushell of shelled corne [sic]."

Additionally, the law set:

"... the ministers petty duties ... [in:]	*lb.tob.*
For solemnization of matrimony without a lycense	*40*
... If with a license	*100*
... for burialls	*10*
... for churching [baptism]	*10*

... ffor breaking ground in the church the pay is left to the churchwardens & vestrie; ffor breaking ground in the chancell att the discretion of the ministers [sic]." [Hening, I/242-243].

By the mid-1700s, the Assembly had increased a minister's fees to 20 shillings (or 160 lbs. of tobacco) for each marriage performed with a license, but maintained the fee of 5 shillings (or 40 lbs. of tobacco) for a marriage when the parties published their banns. Each publication of the marriage banns, as well as the issuance of a certification, cost another shilling and 6 pence. Every minister was entitled to the "benefit of the fees arising within his parish for marriages and also for funeral sermons" in supplement of his fixed salary. Ministers were permitted to charge as much as 40 shillings [£2] for a funeral sermon. The 1748 Assembly established the annual salary of every minister in Virginia at 16,000 lbs. of tobacco "and cask" along with an allowance of an additional 4% "for shrinkage," the total equivalent to about £110 per year, not counting income derived from resident industries or rental of the parish glebe lands. To "further prevention of that abominable mixture and spurious issue," [ie., mulatto children], the 1753 Assembly amended the Act regulating servants and slaves to strictly prohibit a "minister of the Church of England, or other minister or person whatsoever" from performing a marriage joining any white person to any negro or mulatto." Any offending minister would be subject to a fine of 10,000 lbs. of tobacco, with one moiety of the fine to go to the treasurer of the colony and "the other half to the informer, to be recovered with costs." [Hening, VI/84 and VI/362; see, Glossary].

The 1748 act of Assembly also set out the parish vestry's right of presentation of new ministers, codified the procedures for the vestry to lay and collect the annual parish levy, and provided specific requirements for every parish glebe in the Virginia colony. Glebes were to be situated on "a good and convenient tract of land, to contain two hundred acres at the least ... for the use of the minister of such parish." The habitation of each minister, "erected and built on such glebe, [was to include] one convenient mansion house, kitchen, barn, stable, dairy, meat house, corn house, and garden well pailed [fenced], or inclosed with mud walls ... and other convenient out-houses." The ministers were instructed to maintain and keep their glebe buildings in good repair, and the expense of repair was accounted for in the annual parish levy. Vestries were to meet annually before the first of December and "lay," meaning account for and set, the annual parish levy, and to:

> *"assess, upon the tithable persons in their respective parishes ... the minister's salary ... as all other the parish charges, and also the legal allowances for cask, where the tobacco due to any parish creditor shall be contracted for to be paid with cask ... with the allowance of six per centum for collecting."*

Each vestry was "impowered [sic] to nominate and appoint such person as they shall think fit to collect and receive their parish levy." Quaker elders Francis Hague and Edward Thompson probably led a brief "tax revolt" in Fairfax County in 1753 when they failed to pay the parish levy. The parish levy that year almost certainly included the costs of construction of the new church at Broad Run, and the parish assessment would have been offensive to the dissenters living in the western reaches of the county. But the prompt prosecution of Hague and Thompson in the Fairfax Court ended with the payment of their parish assessments, and then no further objections to the parish levy are noted. [Hening, VI/88-90; see supra, p. 441; infra, The Record, p. 456].

Shortly after the "new parish took place" Truro's Rev. Charles Green sold a 600 acre tract to the new vestry for the Cameron parish glebe. The first Cameron glebe was situated on the north fork and the Piney Branch of Broad Run, west of modern Arcola, then known as Gum Spring. Rev. Green also owned substantial properties above Little River that he surely would have offered to the new parish as an alternate site. That the vestry would have chosen the land situated east of Goose Creek for the first glebe is indicative of their "tidewater" orientation as a group, which, undoubtedly contributed some ammunition to the allegations of "arbitrary and illegal practices" that ultimately resulted in the election of a new Cameron parish vestry in 1759. The original glebe was retained in use by Cameron parish even after Shelburne parish was created in 1771, but was sold around 1774. [NorNeck, E/145; Truro, p. 56; see infra, The Record, p. 459; and see supra, p. 452].

The Assembly of 1752 noted that no provision had been made for the inhabitants of Cameron parish to be reimbursed "for the purchasing and building on the [Truro] glebe, before the said parish of Truro was divided, it being just that they should have some satisfaction for the same." The Truro parish vestry was instructed to divide the purchase money derived from the sale of the Truro parish glebe with the vestry of Cameron parish, "as their proportion thereof would have amounted to at the time of the said division, [as] if such sale had been then made," but the Assembly forgot or ignored the need to apportion the Truro church plate. Fifteen years after the creation of Cameron parish, Truro parish was on the verge of splitting once again to form Fairfax parish in northern Fairfax County. The situation forced the Cameron parish vestry to rush a Petition to the General Assembly in order to obtain Loudoun's share of the Church Plate of old Truro parish, the original plate having been conveniently retained for Truro's use the entire time by Truro's able Rev. Charles Green. [Hening, VI/214, and, VI/270-271; see infra, The Record, p. 464].

The early Rectors of Cameron parish, John Andrews (1749-1768), Archibald Avens (1768-1771) and Spence Grayson (1771-1776) are discussed with some detail in *Cameron parish in Colonial Virginia,* by Margaret Hopkins, and the avid reader is encouraged to visit that work. Suffice it to say that Cameron parish was poorly served by John Andrews who, as his time in service progressed, gained a widening reputation as a profane drunkard. When Rev. Charles Green, minister of Truro parish, died in 1764, Andrews was invited to act as an interim visiting minister. After hearing Rev. Andrews deliver only two sermons late in 1764, the parishioners of Truro had experienced enough. Thereafter, Truro parish sent to Dettingen parish for the Rev. James Scott to supply their needs. In 1765, the Truro vestry accounted for a payment to "the Revd. Mr. John Andrews for 2 sermons [in 1764] ... 664 [lbs. of tobacco]," but in the two years following Rev. Green's death Truro happily paid Dettingen's Rev. Scott for over 35 sermons. The periods of service of the Reverends Avens and Grayson are beyond the parameters of the present undertaking, but a remark in passing is appropriate. Spence Grayson was one of three Episcopal ministers serving between Goose Creek and Occoquan (ie., lower old Truro parish) at the onset of the American Revolution who, prior to taking the cloth, served as a Justice on his county court. Another was Lee Massey, a Justice in both Fairfax and Loudoun Counties in the 1750s and 1760s, and subsequently the minister of Truro parish in the 1770s. [Truro, pp. 91, 100 and 107; see Browne, p. 312].

The first Episcopal church in "Loudoun" was called the Goose Creek Chapel of Ease, a log and wooden structure built by Francis Awbrey Senr. around 1733. Before the Chapel of Ease was built, the Episcopal residents living west of Goose Creek had to travel along the Potomac Path to worship at a chapel at Michael Regan's crossroads, 35 miles to the east, at a site now known as Falls Church. Awbrey situated the Goose Creek chapel on a hillside above the Carolina Road, at a spring where the Potomac Path turned north and joined the Carolina Road, two miles north of a dusty crossroads that is now known as Leesburg. The Goose Creek chapel was still actively used for worship in 1755, but fell into disuse shortly thereafter. The then-new Loudoun County Courthouse appears to have replaced the Goose Creek chapel as the Episcopal place of worship in the Leesburg area by 1759. [Landmarks, p. 287; infra, pp. 452 and 456].

In 1747, the second Episcopal chapel in "Loudoun," the Rocky Run church, was constructed by the Truro parish vestry. This chapel, also made of wood, was situated just east of the Salisbury Plain along the Mountain Road, in the center of an area that had developed rapidly during the previous decade. In 1749, at the direction of the Truro vestry, Jacob Remey repaired the "new church" at Rocky Run by fencing in the church yard, tarring the church for weatherproofing, and building horse blocks for the convenience of the worshipers. Significantly, similar improvements were ordered for the Goose Creek chapel in 1749 but there is no record that they were ever undertaken. The church at Rocky Run on the Mountain Road was maintained as an active place of worship, and one of the primary churches in Cameron parish, continuously through at least 1764. [Landmarks, p. 287; Truro, pp. 52 and 55; see infra, The Record, pp. 454 and 462].

It seems likely that, after their election in 1749, one of the first official acts of the Cameron parish vestry was to arrange for the construction of a church situated closer to the center of the new parish. They selected a site in the upper reaches of the Beaver Dam Run of Broad Run, just east of Goose Creek and about equidistant from the Potomac Path and the Mountain Road on land owned by the Sturman family. By September of 1751 the Church west of Broad Run was referred to as already in existence, and between 1751 and 1753 the Fairfax County Court was busy administering the situation and clearing of roads to the Broad Run chapel. This chapel, the third Episcopal church in "Loudoun," was also widely known as the Beaver Dam church. The importance of the Broad Run church was evidenced by the preoccupation that the county courts had with the maintenance and improvement of the roads that led both to the church and the nearby Cameron parish glebe, but the parish vestry apparently never obtained title to the land where the church was built. The 1750s was the decade of eminence of the Broad Run church within the Cameron parish community. Population growth throughout the 1750s in southwest Loudoun and around the county seat of Leesburg resulted in changes in the parish schedule of worship services. The Broad Run Church was the least-used of the four parish Churches by 1764. The Broad Run Church seems to have fallen into disuse during the Revolution, but the tract where it had been built was still identified with the old Episcopal church site in the 1800s. [see infra, The Record, pp. 455 and 462; see Cameron, pp. 39-41].

Perhaps as early as 1759, but most certainly before 1764, probably at the instigation of the vestry elected in 1759, the new Leesburg Courthouse replaced the original Goose Creek chapel as the place of Episcopal worship services in that area of Loudoun. Along with the use of the Courthouse as a chapel came its elevation to the status of the primary "church" in Cameron parish. The vestry accounts for 1764, showing the largest of the payments for the various parish church Clerks going to Thomas Lewis for his service as the parish Clerk "at Leesburg & [Roszel's] Mt. Church," gives credence to both notions. Additional circumstantial evidence is at hand. We are hard pressed to find any contemporary reference, official or otherwise, to the Goose Creek Chapel of

Ease after 1755. The 1764 parish accounts list Loudoun County Justice John Moss Junr., who lived just across Market Street from the Courthouse, as the parish Sexton "at Leesburg" that year. And in 1763 the Truro parish vestry determined to build a new brick Church at the site of the Falls Church. The original Falls Church was a wooden structure that had been built about two years before the first Goose Creek Chapel of Ease, and its state of disrepair by the late 1750s was notorious. The Goose Creek Chapel of Ease at Big Spring was likely to have been in a similar state of disrepair at a time when the beautiful new brick Courthouse was under construction at Leesburg. The urge to relocate worship services to the Courthouse must have been overwhelming.

Population growth in the section west of Little River in the 1750s, reflected in the election of four new Vestrymen from that area in 1759, led to the construction of a new chapel of ease along the Mountain Road. Planning and construction by the vestry may have started as early as 1760, and by the summer of 1763 the Mountain chapel, ie., Roszells chapel on the Mountain Road, was completed. This chapel was occasionally referred to as the Goose Creek church, and as a consequence has sometimes been confused with the original Goose Creek Chapel of Ease, which was, by then, no longer in use. The 1764 parish budget identifies the four churches then in use in Cameron parish. The 1764 budgeting also serves as an indication that the new Mountain chapel promptly surpassed the Broad Run church in importance to the Cameron parish community. [see infra, The Record, @ p. 462].

Shelburne parish was created out of the western half of Cameron parish in 1771. The reconstituted Cameron parish vestry constructed two more churches before the Revolution - the church at Sugarland Run around 1773 and a church at Cub Run in 1775. Discussion of these subjects is reserved for a later time.

As other researchers and writers have noted, the first Cameron parish vestry book and registers of the parish are missing, either lost or destroyed. This sad fact puts additional emphasis on the court records, in both Loudoun and Fairfax, as rare extant sources of information on the inhabitants and workings of Cameron parish in colonial Loudoun County. Accordingly, The Record herein includes a number of documentary references obtained for the years preceding the formation of Loudoun. [Landmarks, pp. 289 and 681; and see generally, Cameron].

October 10, 1748 - The Truro parish vestry, in the last accounting for the annual parish budget before the formation of Cameron parish, lists payments to: *"lbs.tobacco*

...	*Thomas Evans, Clerk at Goose Creek*	*1200*
	William Champneys, Clerk at the new Church	*800*
...	*Alexander Jennings, Sexton at Goose Creek*	*400*
	William Grove, Sexton, the new [Rocky Run] Church	*400*
...	*the widow Richeson [Richardson] for her support*	*600*
[and]	*Thomas Evans for burying Ralph Frankland*	*300*

..." It would be a fair assumption that the men who were identified as the Clerks and Sextons at the Goose Creek and Rocky Run churches were continued in their offices in 1749 and during the first years of Cameron parish. Thomas Evans died in Fairfax in 1751; Jennings is believed to have died in Fairfax in the early 1750s; William Grove died in Loudoun in the 1780s; the fate of Champneys is unknown to the author. A number of Richardson families were settled in the "Cameron parish/Loudoun" section of Truro parish at this time. Truro, p. 53; see supra, Chapter on Ferries and Chapter on Ordinaries.

September 26, 1749 - At the Fairfax County Courthouse at "Springfield," aka Freedom Hill, now known as Tyson's Corner: "The [newly elected] Gentlemen of the Vestry of the Parish of Cameron took the Oaths appointed by Act of Parliament to be taken and Subscribed the Test and to be conformable to the Doctrine and Discipline of the Church of England and Ordered to be Certifyed [sic]." FXCOCO, 1749 Book, p. 34.

October 9, 1749 - The Truro parish vestry, in the accounting for the annual parish budget, lists the Truro parish proportion of a payment for "Jacob Remey ... for pailing in [sic- paling, ie., making a picket fence at] the new Church [at Rocky Run] making horse blocks & tarring the Church & pails [sic] ... 1950 [lbs. tobacco]." Truro, p. 55.

October 8, 1750 - The Truro parish vestry, in the accounting for the annual parish budget, lists a payment "To Cameron Parish for their proportion of the Clerks & Sextons Salaries [at Goose Creek chapel and Rocky Run church ... 527 [lbs. tobacco]." Truro, p. 60.

March 27, 1751 - Fairfax ["Loudoun"] Justices Moses Linton and Anthony Russell are to take tithables lists in Cameron parish. FXCOCO, 1749 Book, p. 134.

September 24, 1751 - Vincent Lewis and Francis Summers take the Oaths of Vestrymen for Cameron parish at the Fairfax County Court. FXCOCO, 1749 Book, p. 162.

September 25, 1751 - The Fairfax County Court orders that a new road be "cleared from the Mountain Road by Martha Hall's [the widow of Elisha Hall, near 'The Post'] to the Church." The same day Vincent Lewis is appointed Surveyor of the road from Berryman's quarter "to the Church." These appear to be the first official references to the new Broad Run church, built that year on the upper reaches of the Beaver Dam Run of Broad Run. FXCOCO, 1749 Book, p. 164; see supra, Chapter on Ordinaries.

September 27, 1751 - For the first time, the Fairfax County Court orders the Cameron parish vestry to procession the lands in their parish between "September and the last of March ... and to appoint two honest intelligent freeholders of every precinct ..." for that purpose. FXCOCO, 1749 Book, p. 171.

March 31, 1752 - Fairfax Justice Anthony Russell is appointed to take the tithables lists for Cameron parish. FXCOCO, 1749 Book, p. 187.

April 1, 1752 - The Fairfax County Court orders the opening of a new road from the Sugarlands on the Potomac Path to the "Chappel on Beaver Dam [branch of Broad Run, east of Goose Creek]." FXCOCO, 1749 Book, p. 192.

May 22, 1752 - Fairfax Justice John Carlyle, Gent., is appointed to take the tithables lists for Cameron parish. FXCOCO, 1749 Book, p. 201.

July 21, 1752 - William Ellzey takes the Oath and is enrolled as a Vestryman for Cameron parish, replacing Francis Ellzey, who has died. FXCOCO, 1749 Book, p. 212.

October of 1752 - Administration of the Estate of Cameron parish Vestryman Moses Linton is granted to his relict and widow, Susanna Linton. FXCOCO, 1749 Book, p. 242.

November 22, 1752 - Edward Payne takes the Oath and is enrolled as a Vestryman for Cameron parish, replacing Moses Linton, who has died. FXCOCO, 1749 Book, p. 255.

March 21, 1753 - The Fairfax County Court orders the clearing of several new roads, from Sugarlands on the Potomac Path and Broad Run near the Mountain Road to the "new Church" at Beaverdam run of Broad Run. FXCOCO, 1749 Book, p. 309.

March 22, 1753 - Fielding Turner and William Ellzey are identified as two Churchwardens for Cameron parish. FXCOCO, 1749 Book, p. 317.

May 15, 1753 - Fairfax Justices Anthony Russell and Fielding Turner are appointed to make the lists of tithables in Cameron parish. Both live east of Goose Creek. FXCOCO, 1749 Book, p. 341.

January 16, 1754 - Edward Payne takes the Oaths of Churchwarden for Cameron parish. FXCOCO, 1749 Book, p. 499.

January 16, 1754 - Edward Payne and Francis Summers are identified in litigation as the Cameron parish Churchwardens; Moses Linton and Richard Coleman are referred to as [apparently the old] Churchwardens. FXCOCO, 1749 Book, pp. 499, 500-502.

January 16, 1754 - Francis Hague, a Quaker, is identified as a defendant cited by the Cameron parish Churchwardens; he agrees to pay costs of the litigation and settles the claim. FXCOCO, 1749 Book, p. 501.

February 21, 1754, and July 17, 1754 - Edward Thompson, a Quaker, is a defendant cited by the Cameron Churchwardens; he agrees to pay costs of the litigation and settles the claim. FXCOCO, 1754 Book, pp. 52 and 138.

May 21, 1754 - Francis Summers is identified as a Churchwarden for Cameron parish. FXCOCO, 1754 Book, p. 93.

June 18, 1754 - In the process of establishing Constable precincts, the Fairfax County Court designates "the Road which leads to Broad Run Chappel [from either the future site of Leesburg or West's ordinary] from thence, to Vestals [sic - Keys'] Gap," with the great road as a long boundary line, for the precinct assigned to Constable Thomas Owsley. FXCOCO, 1754 Book, p. 101.

January 22, 1755 - A road is proposed from the Cameron parish glebe, on the Lenah branch of Broad Run near Arcola, to the "Goose Creek Chappel." The Fairfax County Court instructs Hugh Caldwell, William Barry and Jacob Morris to view the most convenient way for the new road. This Court Order is official evidence that the old Chapel of Ease at Big Spring, built around 1733 by Francis Awbrey, was still in use as late as 1755. The road designated that year was a predecessor to the modern Evergreen Mills road below Goose Creek. FXCOCO, 1754 Book, p. 205.

May 20, 1755 - Administration of the Estate of Cameron parish Vestryman Burgess Berkley is granted to his widow, Statia Berkley, in Fairfax County. FXCOCO, 1754 Book, p. 299.

June 17, 1755 - Fairfax Justices Fielding Turner and Anthony Russell are to take the tithables lists in Cameron parish. FXCOCO, 1754 Book, p. 303.

July 15, 1755 - The Fairfax County Court orders the Cameron vestry to divide the parish into "so many precincts ... for processioning every persons land." FXCOCO, 1754 Book, p. 371; see text, supra @ p. 446.

February 19, 1756 - In litigation in Fairfax County, Anthony Russell and Leonard Dozier are identified as the Cameron parish Churchwardens for 1755. It appears that they were involved in some disagreement with three other Vestrymen, James Ingoe Dozier, Vincent Lewis and Francis Summers, possibly over the performance of contracts undertaken for the renovation of the new church at Broad Run. FXCOCO, 1754 Book, p.471.

May 18, 1756 - Fairfax Justices Anthony Russell, James Hamilton, Fielding Turner and Aeneas Campbell are appointed to list tithables in Cameron parish. FXCOCO, 1754 Book, p. 501.

November 17, 1756 - James Lane takes the Oaths of a Vestryman for Cameron parish. FXCOCO, 1756 Book, p. 37.

March 16, 1757 - The Churchwardens of Cameron parish bring an action against Mary Hague, charging her with having a base born child. FXCOCO, 1756 Book, p. 50.

July 12, 1757 - The various Surveyors of the Highways in Loudoun are appointed: ... Vincent Lewis, "from the Post to Broad Run Church," Franklin Perry, "from the Sugar Land run to broad run Church," and John Smarr, "from Mr. William Wests Plantation to broad run Church." Book A, p. 2.

September 14, 1757 - Anthony Russell is Ordered to allot Hands to work "on the Road leading from the Post [on the Mountain Road] to broad run Church where Vincent Lewis is Surveyor," and Richard Coleman is to allot Hands to work "on the Road leading from the Sugar Land run to broad run Church whereof Franklin Perry is Surveyor." Book A, p. 23.

April 11, 1758 - "Vincent Lewis acknowledges in open Court his Deed of Renunciation of the Office of Vestryman which on his Motion is Ordered to be Certified." Book A, p. 80.

April 11, 1758 - James Lane and Thomas Awbrey are referred to as the Churchwardens of Cameron parish "for the time being." Book A, p. 80.

May 9, 1758 - The Grand Jury Presents "The Surveyor of the Road from Broad run Church to little River for not having a Sign Post up at the fork of the Road." Book A, p. 98.

May 9, 1758 - A Grand Jury Presents charges against "The Surveyor of the Road from Broad run Church to William Wests for not keeping up a Sign Post." Book A, p. 99.

June 14, 1758 - Overseers of several Loudoun County Roads are appointed: George Juring replacing Vincent Lewis, with "Fielding Turner [to] allot the hands," and Jacob Morris, "from Morris' ford to broad run Chappel ... George West [to] allot the hands." Book A, pp. 118, 119 and 122.

July 11, 1758 - Silvester Gardner is appointed Surveyor of the road from Keen's Spring to West's plantation, and Richard Keen, is appointed Surveyor of the road "from John Keen's Spring to broad run Church," both replacing John Smarr. Book A, pp. 129-130.

November of 1758 - The Cameron parish vestry lays the levy for the year, assessing 20 lbs. of tobacco for each tithable in the parish. Infra, p. 463.

February 14, 1759 - James Spurr is appointed as the new Overseer of the Road from Sugar Land Run to Broad Run Church, replacing Franklin Perry. Book A, p. 191.

March 1, 1759 - Meeting in Williamsburg, the Virginia Assembly hears "a Petition of sundry Inhabitants of the Parish of Cameron ... complaining of several illegal and oppressive Proceedings of the Vestry ... praying that the same may be dissolved," and refer the Petition to the Committee on Propositions and Grievances. Assembly, (1758) p. 75.

March 14, 1759 - The Virginia Assembly determines that the "Petition of the Inhabitants of the Parish of Cameron in the County of Loudoun, praying that the vestry of that Parish be dissolved, is reasonable," and a new vestry election is ordered. Assembly, (1758) pp. xviii and 92.

May 9, 1759 - The jury verdict against James Whaley, for fathering the child of his wife's sister, based on an information brought by former Cameron parish Churchwardens James Lane and Thomas Awbrey, is objected to since "the Suit abated before the Jury were Impannelled to try the said Issue joined by the Dissolution of the late Vestry." Book A, pp. 244 and 314.

August 14, 1759 - Francis Peyton, Charles Binns, Benjamin Grayson, James Hamilton, Nicholas Minor, Thomas Owsley, James Lane Junr., Charles Tyler and Elijah Chinn take the Oaths as new Vestrymen of Cameron parish; and the Court orders the Cameron parish vestry to "divide the Parish ... for Processioning every Particular Persons land ... between the last day of December and the last day of March ensuing." Book A, p. 266.

September 13, 1759 - John Owsley takes the Oaths of a Cameron parish Vestryman. Book A, p. 295.

November 13, 1759 - John Lewis replaces George Juren and William Hancocke replaces James Spurr as Overseers of the roads to Broad Run Church. Book A, p. 301.

November 14, 1759 - Sampson Turley takes the Oaths of a Cameron parish Vestryman. Book A, p. 305.

November 16, 1759 - James Lane Senr. and Thomas Awbrey make their last appearance in Court as Churchwardens, in their action against James Whaley. Book A, p. 314.

March 10, 1760 - On Monday of the second week of a reconvened session, the Virginia Assembly receives "a Petition of Sundry Inhabitants of the Parish of Cameron, setting forth, that the late Election of Vestrymen for the said Parish was illegal and praying that the same may be dissolved," but refers the Petition to the next [1761] session of the General Assembly for consideration. Assembly, (1758) p. 164.

March 14, 1760 - Francis Peyton and Nicholas Minor are Cameron parish Churchwardens. Book A, p. 339.

June 11, 1760 - "James Lane, Gent. Late Churchwarden of Cameron Parish against Anthony Russell and Richard Coleman Gent. Lately [former] Churchwardens of Cameron Parish. This suit is Dismissed being agreed by the Parties." Book A, p. 376.

November 11, 1760 - George West is named "Surveyor of the Highwaies" for the road from Morris' ford on Goose Creek to Broad Run Church, replacing Jacob Morris. Book A, p. 402.

November 11, 1760 - Anthony Russell replaces John Lewis as a Surveyor of the Highwaies for the road from The Post on the Mountain Road to Broad Run Church. Book A, p. 403.

November 11, 1760 - Leonard Dozer takes the Oaths of a Vestryman. Book A, p. 403.

February 12, 1761 - Nicholas Minor and Francis Peyton are identified as the Churchwardens of Cameron parish "for the time being [as former Churchwardens]." Book A, pp. 419 and 424.

March 10, 1761 - Greenbury Dorsey is appointed as the new Surveyor of Road from Sugar Land Run to the Broad Run Church, replacing William Hancocke. Book A, p. 428.

March 10, 1761 - In session, the Virginia Assembly refers the 1760 Petition for dissolution of the Cameron vestry to the Committee of Privileges and Elections. Assembly, (1758) p.206.

March 26, 1761 - The Virginia Assembly resolves "That the Petition of sundry Inhabitants of the Parish of Cameron ... praying that the Vestry of the said Parish may be dissolved, be rejected." Assembly, (1758) p. 231.

May 19, 1761 - Several Petitions are presented in the Fairfax County Court at Alexandria, one "... signed by sundry Inhabitants of Loudoun praying that the part of Cameron parish Lying in the County of Fairfax [between Popes Head Run and Rocky Run] may be added to the parish of Truro parish," and a similar Petition "... by sundry Inhabitants of Truro parish" requesting the same remedy. FXCOCO, 1756 Book, p. 582.

June 9, 1761 - Road hands are identified and ordered to "work on the Road [from Morris' ford to Broad Run Church] whereof ... George West is Surveyor." Book A, p. 450.

June 9, 1761 - "Ordered that Fielding Turner Gent. Allot the hands to Work on the Road [to Broad Run Church] whereof Anthony Russell Gent. is Surveyor." Book A, p. 454.

June 12, 1761 - Archibald Campbell, Clerk, brings an action against "John Andrews of the Parish of Cameron and County of Fairfax, Clerk," for debts. Book A, p. 472.

September 8, 1761 - "John Andrews of the Parish of Cameron and the County of Fairfax, Clerk." Book A, p. 502.

September 8, 1761 - Rev. Charles Green "Clerk, Minister of Truro Parish in Fairfax County and Margaret [Green] his wife" deed 800 acres to William Ellzey of Prince William County. The Ellzey tract was originally part of a larger 1,400 acre tract that also contained the glebe of Cameron parish. The deed also refers to a previous conveyance of the Cameron parish glebe from the Greens to the Cameron parish vestry, and mentions that Loudoun Justice William West surveyed the glebe, around 1749. This William Ellzey became a Justice for Fairfax County in 1764 and later served on the Loudoun County Committee of Correspondence during the American Revolution. LDCODB, Book B, p. 273; and see infra, Chapter on Surveys, Lands and Leases.

September 10, 1761 - Nicholas Minor and James Lane [Junr.], Churchwardens of Cameron parish, vs. Catharine Stewart, spinster, is "Dismissed (the Fine being paid)." Book A, p. 508.

September 10, 1761 - "Ordered ... Sherif summon James Coleman and Jane Coleman his wife ... to Answer an Information [of Churchwardens Nicholas Minor and James Lane] exhibited against them for Incestuous Copulation." Book A, p. 517.

November 12, 1761 - The Information of Churchwardens Nicholas Minor and James Lane against "James Coleman and Jane Coleman his wife [for incest] is Discontinued the Plts. not further Prosecuting." Book A, p. 539.

December 5, 1761 - A deed for 625 acres in the Green-Ellzey tract "on the north side of [modern Beaverdam Reservoir] of Goose Creek," purchased by Anthony Russell, makes reference to the "Church Road" to Broad Run Church on the east of the tract and the Cameron parish glebe lands south of the tract. DALD, (1761) p. 95; see LDCODB, Book C, pp. 166-172.

May 11, 1762 - John Sasser is appointed Surveyor of the road from Keen's Spring to Broad Run Church, replacing Richard Keen. Book A, p. 583.

July 15, 1762 - Nicholas Minor and Francis Peyton are identified as the Churchwardens for Cameron parish in a case that was initiated in 1760. Book B, p. 17.

August 10, 1762 - John Connillie [sic] is appointed "Surveyor of the Highwaies from the Sugar Land Run to Broad Run Church [replacing Greenbury Dorsey]." Book B, p. 30.

August 12, 1762 - Francis Peyton and Charles Tyler are first identified as the newly elected Churchwardens for Cameron parish in a complaint brought against Ann Griffin. Book B, p. 37.

November 27, 1762 - The Virginia Assembly resolves "That the two Petitions of sundry Inhabitants of the Parishes of Cameron and Truro ... praying that so much of the said Parish of Cameron as lies below the Line dividing [Fairfax and Loudoun] may be added to the Parish of Truro are reasonable," and instructs the Committee on Propositions and Grievances to "bring in a Bill" to effect the change. Assembly, (1761) p. 116.

April 15, 1763 - "George West, Gent. produced a Certificate from the Vestry of Cameron Parish ... it appears that he was chosen by the Minister and a Majority of the Vestry to be a Vestryman in the room of Benjamin Grayson who is removed out of the said Parish and thereupon [West] took the Oaths ... and subscribed to be conformable to the Doctrine and Dicipline [sic] of the Church of England." Book B, p. 119; and see, Glossary.

May 10, 1763 - The Loudoun County Court names and allots the road hands to assist "John Connellie Surveyor of the Road from Sugar Land run to broad run Chappel." Book B, p. 122.

May 11, 1763 - "John Lewis is appointed Surveyor of the Road from the South Fork of Broad run [at Gum Spring, south] to the Mountain Road and ... Anthony Russell [is to] continue [as] Surveyor of the said Road [from Gum Spring] to Beaver Dam Chapel [ie., Broad Run Church]." Book B, pp. 126-127.

May 11, 1763 - The Grand Jury presents charges against the "Overseer of the Road leading from John Keen's Spring to broadrun Church for not keeping the same in lawful repair within one Month last past." At the time, John Sasser was the Overseer of that stretch of road. Book B, p. 131.

June 14, 1763 - Elijah Chinn, Henry Downs and Thomas Dawson, "... the persons appointed to view the most convenient way from the Road leading from Ashby's Gap to Alexandria from Leven Powell's Plantation to Goose Creek Church," reported to the Loudoun Court, and the new road is ordered. "Leven Powell be appointed Surveyor thereof and that Francis Peyton Gent. allot the hands to work thereon." This is a reference to the new chapel at Roszel's on the Mountain Road. Book B, pp. 106 and 161.

July 12, 1763 - "Ordered that Nicholas Minor, Gent., allot hands to work on the Road [Sugarland to Broad Run Church] whereof ... John Connellie [is] Overseer." Book B, p. 193.

August 10, 1763 - "In Pursuance to an Act of Assembly for Settling the bounds and Title of Lands and preventing unlawful Shooting and ranging ... this Court doth Order and direct that the Vestry of Cameron Parish do divide the said Parish into so many Precincts as to them shall seem most convenient for Processioning every particular Person's Land within the same that they do appoint the particular times between the last Day of September and the last Day of March next ... when such Processioning shall be made in every such Precinct ... that they do appoint two intelligent honest Freeholders in every respective Precinct to see such Processioning performed and to take and return to the said Vestry an Account of every Persons Lands they shall Procession ... the Persons present at the same and what Lands in their respective Precincts they shall fail to Procession and the particular reasons of such failure." Book B, p. 197.

August 12, 1763 - Leonard Dozier and Nicholas Minor are identified as the Cameron parish Churchwardens "for the time being" in a case brought against Sarah Pritchard, shortly before Dozier is referred to as living in Truro parish. Book B, p. 37.

September 14, 1763 - Charles Binns, the Clerk of the Loudoun County Court, sues Nicholas Minor and Leonard Dozer, Cameron parish Churchwardens, "by Account for Clerk's fees ... [370 lbs.] of Nett Tobacco." Book B, p. 235.

September 15, 1763 - Churchwardens of Cameron parish "for the time being," Fielding Turner and Sampson Turley, bring a complaint against William Owsley, Vestryman John Owsley, George Chelton, William Norris and Benjamin Edwards, possibly for gambling in Leesburg at Edwards' Loudoun Street ordinary. Vestryman Thomas Owsley represents the Estate of William Owsley, who has died since the offence. This could be a foreshadowing of an incident, several months later, that ends in the death of John Owsley. Book B, p. 246; see infra, p. 463; see supra, Chapter on Crimes and Punishment.

November 8, 1763 - The Grand Jury presents charges against "Charles Eskridge, Overseer of the Road from Cub run down by Rockey run Church for not keeping the same in lawful repair." Book B, p. 263.

November of 1763 - The Cameron parish vestry lays the levy for the year, assessing 22 lbs. of tobacco per tithable in the parish. See infra, The Record, p. 463.

November 9, 1763 - "William Carr Lane, Gent., presented a Certificate from the Vestry of Cameron parish whereupon it appears that he was Chosen by the Minister and a Majority of the Vestry to be a Vestryman in the room of Leonard Dozer who lives in Truro Parish and thereupon he took the Oaths to his Majesty's Person and Government and subscribed to be

Conformable to the Doctrine and Dicipline [sic] of the Church of England." This was six months after Lane served as Foreman of a very thorough County Grand Jury. Book B, p. 264; and see infra, Chapter on Grand Juries.

November 9, 1763 - Clerk of the Loudoun County Court "Charles Binns, in open Court, acknowledged his Deed of Resignation of the Office of Vestryman" of Cameron parish. Book B, p. 267.

February 15, 1764 - Anthony Russell, Gent., and John Pyles, [aka John Piles, sans co-appointee Vincent Lewis] report the best route for a new Road "to John Hough's Mill on Goose Creek ... from Broad run Church ... as it is now Marked out ..." John Pyles is appointed Surveyor, with Charles Tyler, Gent., to "allot the hands to clear the same." Book B, pp. 265 and 274.

March 14, 1764 - The Court grants the "Motion of Bryan Phinican against Nicholas Minor Gent. late Churchwarden of Cameron for not paying him his claim of [400 lbs.] of Tobacco levied by the Vestry of the said Parish in the Year 1762," apparently for his support as an infirm or pauper. Book B, p. 283; see infra, 1764 parish levy, payment to Edward Thompson.

March 16, 1764 - The complaint of the Churchwardens against George Chelton and William Norris is continued. It appears that Benjamin Edwards and the Owsleys voluntarily paid their fines and were dismissed. Book B, p. 295.

May 8, 1764 - A Grand Jury charges "Rev. John Andrews for Neglecting his Duty in Cameron parish." Book B, p. 354.

October 10, 1764 - "John Moss [Senr.] produced a Certificate from the Vestry of Cameron Parish wherein it appears that he was Chosen by the Minister and a Majority of the Vestry to be a Vestryman in the room of Charles Binns who Resigned and thereupon he took the Oaths to his Majesties Person and Government and Subscribed to be Conformable to the Doctrine & Discipline of the Church of England." Book B, p. 488.

November 13, 1764 - The Grand Jury presents charges against "... Reverend John Andrews for Neglecting his Duty in Cameron Parish within Six Months last past to the knowledge of two of us." Book B, p. 493.

November 13, 1764 - William Perry is appointed "Surveyor of the Road from Sugarland Run to Broad Run Church [replacing] John Connilee." Book B, p. 494.

November 16, 1764 - The Cameron parish vestry lays the levy for the year, assessing 21 lbs. of tobacco per tithable in the parish. *"At a [meeting of the] Vestry held for Cameron Parish ... This Vestry proceeded this day to Lay the Levy [for the parish] as followeth vizt. ...*

		Dr.lb.tobacco
pd.To	*The Revd. John Andrews, his [Salary]*	*17120*
"	*Henry Willson, Clerk at Rocky Run Church*	*1200*
To	*John Lewis, [Clerk] at Broad Run [church]*	*800*
"	*Thos. Lewis, [Clerk] at Leesburg & Mt. Church*	*2600*
pd.To	*Charles Eskeridge, Sexton at Rocky Run Church*	*400*
"	*John Piles, [Sexton] at Broad Run [church]*	*400*
"	*John Moss Junr., [Sexton] at Leesburg*	*400*
"	*John Harris, [Sexton] at Mt. Church*	*400*

[Cameron parish levy for 1764, con't.]:		*Dr.lb.tobacco*
pd.To	*Levin Powell, Clerk of the Vestry*	*500*
"	*Josias Clapham, per ...[entry illegible- account, supplies?]*	*400*
To	*The Revd. John Andrews, by Do. [ditto- supplies?]*	*84*
pd.To	*Adam & Campbell [merchants], by [ditto]*	*41*
"	*John Carlyle by [account allowed] William Ross*	*1136*
"	*John Moss Esqr. [Senr.] by [account]*	*300*
"	*[Fleming] Patterson by [account]*	*748*
"	*William Mead, 4 Levys overchd.in 1758 @ 20 ...*	*80*
To	*Benjamin Sebastian, [3 levies overcharged] last year*	*66*
pd.To	*Charles Binns, by [account]*	*219*
"	*William Winn, 2 Levys [overcharged] last year*	*44*
"	*Charles Binns, his ledger vs. Churchwardens*	*422*
To	*Robert Hamilton, by [account]*	*80*
pd.To	*John Queen for the support of Eliz. Powderall*	*1500*
"	*Doctor John Urquhart, by [account]*	*240*
pd.To	*Craven Peyton Esqr., by [account]*	*480*
"	*Elenor Coleman, by [account]*	*1200*
"	*William Metheny for the support of a child*	*800*
To	*William Carr Lane Esqr., by [account]*	*210*
"	*Edwd. Thompson ... the support of Bryan Fennikan*	*800*
"	*Tobacco levied for the use of the Parish*	*4000*
"	*Henry Landis, 1 levy [overcharged] last year*	*22*
pd.To	*William Metheny, 1 [ditto - levy last year]*	*22*
...	*[and a charge of] 6 [percent] for Collecting:*	*2190*
...	*[paid] By Mr. George West as per [account]*	*(1139)*
	[paid] By 21 [lbs.] tobacco on 1846 Titheables ...	*(38766)*

..." Transcribed from original in Cameron, p. 34. This is the only record of a Cameron parish levy known to survive from the colonial period.

December 12, 1764 - The Cameron parish vestry certify that Craven Peyton is elected as a Vestryman to replace John Owsley, (who was murdered by Francis Kennedy). Craven Peyton takes the appropriate Oaths. Book B, p. 516; supra, Chapter on Crimes and Punishment; see, LDCOCO, Chancery #M-2491.

May 13, 1765 - The Grand Jury presents charges against the "Overseer of the [Mountain] Road from Williams' Gap to the new Church [Stephen Roszell's Mountain Chapel] for not keeping the same in Repair ... [and] Reverend John Andrews [of Cameron parish] for getting Drunk within Two Months last past by the knowledge of two of us." Book B, p. 570.

May 13, 1765 - James Whaley, perhaps still smarting from a prosecution by Churchwardens for immoral activity, informed on a number of men "for unlawful Gaming on the Sabbath." The defendants included Charles West and John Tyler, sons of two Loudoun County Justices. Book B, p. 570.

August 14, 1765 - In the suit of The Reverend Doctor Hugh Deane against The Reverend John Andrews, the defendant was returned not found in the County. Book C, pp. 24 and 38.

February of 1766 - Former Loudoun County Justice Lee Massey, who is once again residing in Truro parish in Fairfax County, is recommended to the Truro parish vestry for investiture as their new minister. Truro, p. 95.

May 10, 1766 - Kitchen Prim, in a deed conveying land from to John Pyles, identifies the location of Broad Run church on his land and mentions the Broad Run Church Road as a boundary on the property. DALD, (1766) p. 9; LDCODB, Book E, p. 72.

May 12, 1766 - Jonathan Davis is appointed Surveyor of the Road "from Keen's Spring to Broad Run Church," replacing John Sasser. William Carr Lane is ordered to allot the hands to work on the road. Book C, p. 77.

June 9, 1766 - William Musgrove is appointed Surveyor on a new Road "from the Carolina Road near little River to Capt. West's Church Road at John Keen's Spring ... Francis Peyton [to] allot the hands." Book C, p. 79.

August 12, 1766 - William Muirhead is appointed the new Surveyor of the Road "from Broad run Church to Broadrun." James Lane is to allot hands on the Road. Book C, p. 154.

September 8, 1766 - Francis Elgin, Benjamin Shreive and John Peake report the route for a new Road "from Dawson's Ford on Goose Creek into the [Broad Run] Church Road by Thomas Beaver's ... from the foot of the Hill ... running up the [a] Branch till you come near a Cabbin on the left ... to Daniel's old Field where you meet with the Church Road." Book C, p. 186.

November 13, 1766 - Absolom Fox is named Overseer of the road "from [the south fork of] Broadrun to [broad run] Beaver dam Church," replacing Anthony Russell. Book C, p. 229.

November 22, 1766 - The Virginia Assembly refers "a Petition of the Vestry of the Parish of Cameron, in the County of Loudoun, setting forth that before the Division of the said Parish from the Parish of Truro there was a Considerable Quantity of Church Plate belonging to ... Truro, no part of which they have ever received, and praying that they may have their Proportion of the said Plate, or an Equivalent in Money" to Committee for further action. Assembly, (1766) p. 35.

November 25, 1766 - The Virginia Assembly resolves "That the petition of the Vestry of the parish of Cameron, in the County of Loudoun ... [for] an equal Proportion of the Church Plate belonging to the said Parish, before the Division of the same from the parish of Truro ... is reasonable." Another Petition, from "the Vestrymen, Freeholders and Inhabitants" of Truro parish, seeking the authority to sell the Church Plate and Glebe lands of their parish, (in order to divide the proceeds) is also deemed "reasonable." The Assembly instructs its Committee of Propositions and Grievances to prepare a Bill to accomplish the objects of the petitions. Assembly, (1766) p. 38.

Cameron Parish Vestry and Churchwardens, 1749-1766

Rev. John Andrews, Rector (1749-1768) died @ 1770

Thomas Awbrey, *, V (1749-1759); CW (1757-1759)
Burgess Berkeley, *, V (1749-1755, died) [died in Fairfax]
Richard Coleman, *, V (1749-1759); CW (1750-52; 1754-1757)
Leonard Dozier, *, V (1749-1759; ** !1760-); CW (1754-1755)
Francis Ellzey, *, V (1749-1751, died) [died in Fairfax]
Edward Hughes, *, V (1749-@1754?) [disappears @ 1754 ?]
Vincent Lewis, *, V (!1749-1758, resigned)
Moses Linton, *, V (1749-1752, died); CW (@ 1750-1752)
Anthony Russell, *, V (1749-1759; ** !1771-); CW (1755-1757)
Francis Summers, *, V (!1749-1759; ** !1771-); CW (1753-1754)
Fielding Turner, *, V (1749-1759; ** !1771-79); CW (1752-59?)
Joseph Watkins, *, V (1749-1759)

William Ellzey, V (!1752-1759); CW (@ 1753-54) [Ellzey]
Edward Payne, V (!1752-1759); CW (1753-1755) [Linton]
James Ingoe Dozier, V (?1755-1759?) [Hughes/Berkeley ?]
James Lane Senr., V (!1756-1759; ** !1771-); CW (1757-59)

------- [Full New Vestry Elected in 1759] -------

Francis Peyton, V (!1759-1771; ** SP !1771-); CW (1759-1763)
Charles Binns, V (!1759-1763, resigned)
Benjamin Grayson, V (!1759-1763, either moved or died)
James Hamilton, V (!1759-1771; ** SP !1771-)
Nicholas Minor, V (!1759-1771); CW (1759-1762)
Thomas Owsley, V (!1759-1771; ** SP !1771-)
James Lane Junr., V (!1759-1771; ** !1771-); CW (1761-1762)
Charles Tyler, V (!1759-1767, died); CW (1762-1763)
Elijah Chinn, V (!1759-1771, died)
John Owsley, V (!1759-1764, murdered) [see Crimes Chapter]
Sampson Turley, V (!1759-1771); CW (1763-1764)
Archibald Campbell, Clerk, of the Vestry ? (1759-1763 ?)
Leonard Dozier, *,**, V (!1760-1763, in Truro); CW (1763)

----

* - "original" ; V - "Vestryman"; CW - "Churchwarden"
** - reelected; ! - Oath on record;
? - date uncertain; SP - Shelburne parish

CAMERON PARISH VESTRY AND CHURCHWARDENS, 1749-1766

GEORGE WEST, V (1763-1771); CW (1763-1765) [Grayson]
WILLIAM CARR LANE, V (1763-1771, d.); CW (1764-65) [Dozier]

LEVIN POWELL, Clerk of Vestry (1764-...1771?) [Campbell?]
HENRY WILLSON, Clerk for Rocky Run church (1764-...?
JOHN LEWIS, Clerk for Broad Run church (1764-...?
THOMAS LEWIS [of "Little River"], Clerk, (1764-... 1770?
@ Leesburg Church and Mountain church
CHARLES ESKERIDGE, Sexton, Rocky Run church (1764-...?
JOHN PILES, Sexton, Broad Run church (1764-...?
JOHN MOSS JUNR., Sexton, Leesburg church (1764-... 1768?
JOHN HARRIS, Sexton, Mountain church (1764-...?

JOHN MOSS SENR., V (1764-1768, d.); CW (@ 1765-66) [Binns]
CRAVEN PEYTON, V (1764-1771; ** SP !1771-); [John Owsley]
ARCHIBALD AVENS, Rector (1768-1771)
JOHN MINOR, V (!1768-1771) [Tyler]; *** CP; [in SP, 1771]
WILLIAM SMITH, V (!1769-1771;** SP !71-); CW (1770-71)[Moss]
THOMAS LEWIS "Ltl.River," V (!1770-1771;** SP !1771-) [Turley?]

---------- [Full New Vestry Elected in 1771] ----------
JAMES COLEMAN, V (!1771-...? [Richard Coleman's son, * V]
JEREMIAH HUTCHISON, V (!1771-...?
JAMES LANE SENR., **, V (1756-1759; !1771-...?
JAMES LANE JUNR., **, V (1759-1771; !1771-...?
BENJAMIN MASON, V (!1771- ...?
JOHN MOSS [JUNR.], V (!1771- ...?
JACOB REMEY JUNR., V (!1771- ...?
ANTHONY RUSSELL, *, **, V (1749-1759; !1771- ...?
FRANCIS SUMMERS, *, **, V (!1749-1759; !1771- ...?
GEORGE SUMMERS, V (!1771- ...?
FIELDING TURNER, *, **, V (1749-1759; !1771-1779; resigned)
CHARLES WEST, V (!1771- ...? [Justice William West's son]
SPENCE GRAYSON, Rector (1771-1776)

----

* - "original" ; V - "Vestryman"; CW - "Churchwarden"
** - reelected; ! - Oath on record; ? - date uncertain
SP - Shelburne parish; *** - contested election of 1771

In October of 1748, the Virginia Assembly recodified the Virginia marriage laws of the colony, which had been in effect since 1705. The marriage laws adopted in 1748 then remained essentially unchanged for the next twenty years and Loudoun County's first decade, from 1757 to 1766. Ministers were subject to one year of imprisonment, "without bail or mainprise," and a huge £500 fine if they celebrated "the rites of matrimony" for parties who had not obtained a license or published banns. The law of 1748 codified "the rubric in the book of common prayer," requiring the publication of banns, where the parties stated their intent to marry, in the parish church of each of the parties three times prior to a marriage. When no objection was made against the parties joining together, the minister of the second parish was to issue a certificate to that effect for the benefit and information of the minister performing the ceremony. The certificate for a prospective bride would certify that the woman had been an inhabitant of the parish for one full month prior to the issuance of a certificate. A parish clerk or reader could issue the necessary certificate, certified by a justice of the peace, in any parish that did not have a minister. The issuance of a false certificate would be punished by imprisonment without bail and prosecution for forgery. [Hening, VI/81-85; see Glossary].

When the intended couple obtained a license from the clerk of a county court instead of publishing banns, they were required to obtain their license in the county where the woman resided. The county clerk was directed to "take bond with good surety for the sum of fifty pounds current money ... with condition that there is no lawful cause to obstruct the marriage." When either party was under age 21, the law provided that the clerk was to certify to the consent of the father or guardian of each infant. As discussed previously, a servant was not allowed to marry without the express permission of his or her master. The "first justice sworn in commission" for the county, "or in his absence ... the next justice sworn," was then to sign and direct the license to the attention of a minister of the parish. Information from the Loudoun County Clerk's Fee Books of the 1760s is provided in the Record, confirming the Loudoun County residency and adult status of a number of women. [Hening, VI/82-84; see supra, Chapter on Servants; see infra, the Record, at pp. 474, 477, 478, 479-481].

The marriage license fee was set at 20 shillings [£1], collected by the clerk for the Governor. Every October, all county clerks were to give the Governor a list of the licenses issued in their county that year. Ministers were allowed to charge 20 shillings for performing a marriage with a license, but could only charge 5 shillings if the parties had published banns. Also, the minister was authorized to charge a shilling and 6 pence for each publication of the banns as well as for the issuance of a certificate. Each minister was also entitled to the "benefit of the fees arising within his parish for marriages and also for funeral sermons."

The Record gives us an indication that the colonials in Loudoun County were not altogether unsophisticated. We have as one example the Premarital Agreement between Hester Linton and Wayman Sinkler proven at Court in March of 1761. Another example is the way Andrew Hutchison avoided probate of his estate. At the time of his death in 1763 there appears to have been no Will, but there was no need for one. The Record reveals how, from 1757 to 1760, Hutchison gave all of his property to his sons by deeds of gift.

The Loudoun Court Record contains a large number of incidental references - to wives, widows, sons, daughters, stepmothers, half-brothers, heirs-at-law, grandmothers and sons-in-law. The reader may be pleased to know that every effort has been made to include every such reference within the Record that follows. Deeds of Gift and recorded marriage agreements (contractually establishing dowry and other inheritance rights) often provide solid proof of a family connection between parties, without stating an exact relationship. Accordingly, when found, they have been identified in the Record of this chapter, along with the incidental familial references.

Unfortunately, the Cameron Parish registers for the decade from 1757 to 1766 have been either lost or destroyed. Thus, the information provided in The Loudoun Record may in some instances provide the only proof of a marriage or a clue to understanding some family relationships. The reader should use caution in casting assumptions when finding individuals in the Record named "Senr.," "Junr.," or "younger" - these designations usually imply a father-son relationship between the named parties, but on occasion a uncle-nephew or cousin status can be proven.

Additional information regarding family relationships in colonial Loudoun is presented elsewhere herein in The Record of these Chapters: Apprentices and Orphans Bound; Tithables and Tax Lists; Infants and their Guardians; Base Born and Mulatto Children; and, Coroners, Deaths and Estates.

The Loudoun Record

July 15, 1757 - Sarah Ball McCarty Barnes, mother of colonial Ensign Dennis McCarty and a cousin to George Washington, had remarried Abraham Barnes and was noted as living at Sugar Land run. GW Papers, IV, p. 309.

August 9, 1757 - Andrew Hutchison records Deeds of Gift to his sons, John Hutchison and Daniel Hutchison. Book A, p. 5; LDCODB, Book A, p. 2.

August 9, 1757 - Samuel Awbrey enters his appearance as a personal bond for his brother Thomas Awbrey in the suit brought by Henry Boggess. Book A, p. 8.

August 9, 1757 - Samuel Awbrey, Francis Awbrey [Junr.], Thomas Awbrey and Peter Noland witness a deed of lease from Philip Noland to John Wells. LDCODB, Book A, pp. 17-18.

September 13, 1757 - Rachel Gore, the wife of Thomas Gore of Frederick County Maryland, is a sister of Margaret Neighbors and Sarah Neighbors. They are daughters of Nathan Neighbors and his wife Mary Neighbors, and granddaughters of Samuel Thacker. LDCODB, Book A, p. 19, Book D, p. 257; and see, Order Book B, p. 406.

October 10, 1757 - John Abrell is a son and the heir at law of Richard Abrell. LDCODB, Book A, pp. 20-23.

October 28, 1757 - Robert Stukesbury, who died before Loudoun County was formed, had a son who was called Robert Stukesbury Senr., and a grandson named Robert Stukesbury [Junr.]. LDCODB, Book A, pp. 28-34.

March 14, 1758 - Abel Janney records a Deed of Gift to Joseph Janney. Book A, p. 66.

April 12, 1758 - Thomas Awbrey's wife is named Jamima Awbrey. Book A, p. 93.

April 12, 1758 - In what seems to be Loudoun County's first case of a divorce action in the County Court: a suit in Chancery brought by Sarah Colclough against Robert Colclough, abates on Robert's death. (Robert's death was probably occasioned by his execution in Williamsburg as a criminal). Book A, p. 94; see supra, Chapter on Crimes and Punishment.

May 1, 1758 - Matthew Adams, with his wife Elizabeth Adams and their son Luke Adams, lease a farm on a hill near Francis Sanders. LDCODB, Book A, p. 192.

May 1, 1758 - A three-life lease identifies Edward McKean, William McKean, and Charles McKean as the sons of a "schoolmaster," Peter McKean. LDCODB, Book A, p. 196.

June 13, 1758 - Robert Thomas Junr. is a defendant in a case. Book A, p. 112.

June 13, 1758 - Charles Graham of Prince William County is married to Mary Graham and Edward Graham's son. LDCODB, Book A, pp. 115-200.

July 14, 1758 - It appears William Ellzey, an attorney from Prince William County, is the son of Prince William Justice Lewis Ellzey, and that Elizabeth Hancock, the wife of William Hancock, is one of Lewis' daughters. LDCODB, Book A, p. 246.

July 20, 1758 - Samuel Mobley, with wife Mary Mobley and daughter Mary Mobley, lives on the Potomac River east of Kittockton Mountain, between Awbrey's Spring branch and Indian Cabin branch. LDCODB, Book A, p. 190.

August 8, 1758 - James Whaley brings an action in Trover against Jacob Ramey [the father or brother of 'Barbary' Ramey ?]. Book A, p. 136; and see infra, Glossary.

August 9, 1758 - John Champ and John Champ Junr. are indebted to the Estate of Benjamin Grayson, [the Prince William County Justice], deceased. Book A, p. 140.

August 10, 1758 - Stacy Grayson is the wife of another Benjamin Grayson [probably the Fairfax County Justice]. "Stacey" is a daughter of Lewis Ellzey (who was a Justice in Prince William and Fairfax Counties from the 1730s to 1770), widow of Cameron parish Vestryman Burgess Berkeley, and mother to the William Berkeley who lived in the Fairfax County section of Cameron parish. Order Book A, p. 148; LDTX/1, pp. 8-10; WAFX, p. 47.

September 12, 1758 - Andrew Hutchison records Deeds of Gift to three of his sons, Jeremiah Hutchison, Joseph Hutchison and Benjamin Hutchison. Book A, p. 159; and see, LDCODB, Book A, pp. 203-207.

October 5, 1758 - Phebe Hollingsworth, Ann Hollingsworth, Jonah Hollinsworth and Lydia Hollingsworth are children of Isaac Hollingsworth and his wife Rachel Hollingsworth. LDCOWB, Book A, pp. 21-23.

March 3, 1759 - Anthony Poultney, Sarah Poultney and Mary Poultney are the children of John Poultney and his wife Eleanor Poultney. LDCOWB, Book A, pp. 12-14.

March 15, 1759 - Robert Stukesbury Junr. [the 3rd?] and Elizabeth Ponderell, his Step-mother, deed land to Jacob Janney. LDCODB, Book A, p. 258; and, Order Book A, p. 229.

May 8, 1759 - Rachel Prichard [Rachel Pritchard], formerly Rachel Davis, is the new bride of Thomas Prichard [Thomas Pritchard], a niece of Sarah Davis, Mary Wright and Elizabeth Thomas and probably the daughter of John Davis. LDCOWB, Book A, p. 15; see, LDCODB, Book A, p. 363; and see supra, Chapter on Leesburg.

May 9, 1759 - Spence Grayson is an orphan of Benjamin Grayson of Prince William County. LDCODB, Book A, p. 292.

June 12, 1759 - David Potts acknowledges a Deed to his half-brother Jonas Potts, the blacksmith, for 270 acres southwest of the Short Hill adjacent to Samuel Potts and "another Jonas Potts." Book A, p. 245; and see, LDCODB, Book A, pp. 293-298.

June 14, 1759 - Holland Middleton Junr. is a defendant in a suit. Book A, p. 257.

August 14, 1759 - "Mary Ball of this County made Oath that James Cannady [a/k/a James Kannaday], a Married Man is the Father of the Child she now goes with ..." Book A, p. 266.

September 29, 1759 - Ann Mason and Thomson Mason lease 100 acres to David Smith, his wife Ann Smith, and their sons Alexander Smith and David Smith Junr. LDCODB, Book B, p. 39.

November 13, 1759 - William Shrieve and his wife Catherine Shrieve deed 245 acres in the branches of Secolon to William's brother Benjamin Shrieve. LDCODB, Book A, p. 336.

November 19, 1759 - George William Fairfax leases 125 acres to Thomas Wyatt, his wife Margaret Wyatt and their son John Wyatt. LDCODB, Book A, p. 355; DALD, (1759) p. 32.

November of 1759 - The 1759 and 1761 tithable lists returned by Richard Coleman indicate that at least three men named Thomas Lewis live in Loudoun County, Senr. and his son, a Junr., living "on Difficult" run, and another Thomas Lewis from or living near "Little River." LDTX/1, pp. 2 and 16.

March 14, 1760 - Simon Pearson and his wife Milkey Pearson, William Starke and his wife Susanna Starke, Ezekiel Hickman and his wife Elizabeth Hickman, and William Trammell bring a Chancery action against John Trammell and Sampson Trammell. Apparently the women are the sisters of William, John and Sampson Trammell, and they are all the children of John Trammell Senr., deceased. Book A, p. 336; and, Book B, p. 454.

May 13, 1760 - Elizabeth Hanby has remarried and is now the wife of George Gregg. LDCODB, Book A, p. 392.

June 10, 1760 - Sarah Fairfax is the wife of George William Fairfax, Esqr.; and, Elizabeth Fairfax is the wife of Bryan Fairfax, Esqr., the son of George William. Book A, p. 361.

June 11, 1760 - In a deed of release, Loudoun Justice Nicholas Minor reveals his family tree: his father was Nicholas Minor of Westmoreland County, his brothers William Stewart Minor, John Minor [formerly a Captain and Justice in Fairfax] and Stewart Minor, widow of his brother John was Jemima Minor, and her children were Nicholas Minor, Elizabeth Minor, John Minor [Junr.], Penelope Minor, Daniel Minor, Ann Minor and George Minor. LDCODB, Book B, p. 6; see contra, Landmarks, p. 344.

June 12, 1760 - On a deed of sale, Mary Ansley, formerly known as Mary Foster, is identified as the wife of Henry Ansley. LDCODB, Book B, p. 8. See also, infra, p. 474.

June 24, 1760 - John Patterson, agent for Charles Bennett the Earl of Tankerville, grants leases in Catoctin Manor: 113 acres to William Grant "aged [32], his wife aged [26] and son John Grant aged [1]"; and, 150 acres to Samuel Combs "aged [32], his wife Mary Combs aged [27] and son Samuel [Combs Junr.] aged [1]." LDCODB, Book B, pp. 342-350; DALD, (1761) p. 79.

August 12, 1760 - Andrew Hutchison records Gifts to his sons Joseph Hutchison, Jeremiah Hutchison, John Hutchison, Benjamin Hutchison and Daniel Hutchison. Book A, pp. 385-386.

August 12, 1760 - On deeds of sale, Mary Potts is identified as the wife of Jonas Potts the blacksmith. LDCODB, Book B, p. 36 and Book D, p. 215; and, Order Book A, p. 451.

August 16, 1760 - Esable Merick [sic] is the wife of Griffith Merick. Book A, p. 386.

August 16, 1760 - Margaret Swain is the wife of Charles Swain. Book A, p. 392.

August 16, 1760 - Defendant "Samuel Davis the Younger" is reported not found. Book A, p. 393.

November 11, 1760 - "A Deed Poll of Gift from John Alexander the Eldest Gent. [a County Justice of Stafford County] to [his daughter] Ann Binns, wife of Charles Binns ... Recorded." Book A, p. 402; LDCODB, Book B, p. 49.

November 12, 1760 - Sarah Janney is the wife of Mahlon Janney. Book A, p. 405; and, LDCODB, Book C, p. 185.

November 20, 1760 - John Patterson, agent for Charles Bennett the Earl of Tankerville, leases 100 acres in Catoctin Manor, adjacent to Ralph Braddock, to William Braddock aged 25, "his wife Mary Braddock aged [30] and their daughter Prudence Braddock aged [1]." The same day, the adjacent lease for 100 acres is let to Ralph Braddock aged 65, and his sons Francis Braddock, 16, and Joshua Braddock, 11. LDCODB, Book B, p. 350; DALD, (1761) p. 79.

December 9, 1760 - Amos Janney was the father of Mahlon Janney. LDCODB, Book B, p. 110.

March 10, 1761 - A Deed from William Hatcher to "James Hatcher his son ..." is recorded. Book A, p. 427.

March 11, 1761 - Articles of a Premarital Agreement "between Wayman Sinkler of Prince William County and David Flynt [as "next friend"] and Hester Linton, widow, of Loudoun County [were presented,] proved ... and Ordered to be Recorded." Wayman and Hester agree that, despite their marriage, their property and estates will remain separate and under their individual control. Book A, p. 431; LDCODB, Book B, p. 92.

March 31, 1761 - Rebecca Elgin is the wife of Francis Elgin, Gent.. LDCODB, Book B, p. 140.

April 24, 1761 - John Patterson, agent for Charles Bennett the Earl of Tankerville, leases 100 acres in Catoctan Manor to "James Ferguson aged [32], his wife Margaret Ferguson aged [28] and daughter Auzabah Ferguson aged [7]." LDCODB, Book C, p. 355; and, DALD, (1760) p. 79.

April 24, 1761 - Other deeds in Tankerville's Catoctin Manor indicate that Dorothy Schooley [nee Dorothy Albertson ?] is the wife of Samuel Schooley (aged 32), and their children are William Schooley, Garrett Schooley and Nicholas Schooley. LDCODB, Book C, pp. 5-14; DALD, (1761) pp. 80-81.

May 1, 1761 - John Carlyle, agent for George William Fairfax, leases 100 acres to William Hurley, his son Stephen Hurley, and his brother Philip Hurley. LDCODB, Book B, p. 289.

May 1, 1761 - One Thomas Gore is the son of Joshua Gore [Senr. ?]. LDCODB, Book B, p. 306.

May 13, 1761 - John Carlyle, agent for George William Fairfax, leases 150 acres to William Wildman and his sons John Wildman and William Wildman [Junr.]. LDCODB, Book B, p.178.

May 23, 1761 - John Newton of Westmoreland County, the son of Capt. Willoughby Newton, sells 660 acres on Rocky Run along the Mountain Road to "William Carr Lane of the Parish of St. Stephens and the County of Northumberland, Planter." LDCODB, Book C, p. 329; DALD, (1761) p. 109.

June 9, 1761 - "A Deed Poll of Gift from Moses Botts ... to Joshua Botts" is recorded. Book A, p. 452.

June 9, 1761 - Elizabeth Gore is the wife of Joshua Gore Junr.. Book A, p. 453.

June 10, 1761 - A Deed of Gift is recorded for three cows and a bull yearling, from Ann Murphey to grand-daughters Sarah Collins and Kezia Collins, two daughters of Thomas Collins and his wife Winifred Collins. Book A, p. 456.

June 12, 1761 - Several entries indicate that Elizabeth Lewis, the widow of former Fairfax County Justice Stephen Lewis, has recently married William Douglass. Book A, p. 471.

July 14, 1761 - Mary Boyle is identified as the wife of William Boyle. Book A, p. 480.

August 10, 1761 - Ellen Plummer, now the wife of Thomas Plummer of Frederick County Maryland, was formerly known as Eleanor Poultney, the widow of John Poultney. LDCODB, Book B, p. 238.

August 10, 1761 - Thomson Mason leases 150 acres, "including the dwelling plantation therein," to James Sanders, his wife Sarah Sanders and their two sons Presley Sanders and Henry Sanders. LDCODB, Book C, p. 77.

August 11, 1761 - Martha Wilks is the wife of Francis Wilks. LDCODB, Book B, p. 228.

August 11, 1761 - Elizabeth Davis is the wife of Daniel Davis. LDCODB, Book B, p. 236.

September 8, 1761 - "An Indenture of Gift between William West Gent ... and Craven Peyton Mecht. [merchant] son in Law of the said William West" is recorded. Book A, p. 492.

September 8, 1761 - Margaret Green is the wife of Charles Green, Clerk, who is a Doctor and the Minister of Truro Parish. Book A, p. 493.

September 8, 1761 - On a deed, Rebecca Berry is identified as the wife of William Berry. LDCODB, Book C, p. 15.

November 10, 1761 - Charles LittleJohn, Samuel LittleJohn and Henry LittleJohn, probably brothers, deed land to Samuel Iden. Book A, p. 528.

November 10, 1761 - Richard Roberts records a Deed of Gift for 65 acres on the north side of Clarks Run to his son Joseph Roberts. Book A, p. 529; and, LDCODB, Book C, p. 57.

November 11, 1761 - On the Motion of William Adams [apparently heir-at-law], appraisers are appointed to allot the dower interest of Elizabeth Adams in the Estate of Gabriel Adams, her late husband. Book A, p. 531.

December 5, 1761 - Alice Ellzey is the wife of William Ellzey. LDCODB, Book C, p. 166.

January 19, 1762 - Agness Roberts is identified on a deed as the wife of Joseph Roberts. LDCODB, Book C, p. 138.

March 10, 1762 - Mary Monkhouse, formerly Mary Ansley, nee Mary Foster, and most recently the wife of Jonathan Monkhouse, is Administering the Estate of her late husband, Henry Ansley. She and Henry owned land on the southeast side of Leesburg. Book A, p. 568, and, LDCODB, Book B, p. 8.

March 10, 1762 - Elizabeth Morris is the wife of Charles Morris; Mary Morris is the wife of John Morris; John is the son of Charles and Elizabeth; Nimrod Morris appears to be the son of John and Mary. Book A, p. 569; and, Middleburg, p. 11.

March 11, 1762 - Ann Vandiveere is the wife of George Vandiveere. Book A, p. 574; see supra, Chapter on Inns and Taverns.

March 12, 1762 - Sarah Clapham is the recent wife of Josias Clapham, and still serving as the Administratrix of the Estate of Rodolphus Ellinger [of Maryland], deceased. Book A, p. 577, and Book B, p. 103.

May 10, 1762 - Sarah Hough is identified as the wife of John Hough. LDCODB, Book C, p. 180.

May 14, 1762 - Rebecca McManimy is identified as the wife of William McManimy. Book A, p. 607.

May 14, 1762 - Benjamin Grayson of Fairfax sues Benjamin Grayson of Loudoun for a debt. Book A, p. 613.

May 14, 1762 - Anne McDowell is the new bride of James Abit [aka James Abbett]. Book A, p. 617.

May 20, 1762 - Simon Pearson of Fairfax County is the son and heir-at-law of Thomas Pearson, Gent. [ie., former Justice] of Fairfax County. LDCODB, Book C, p. 338.

May 24, 1762 - John Patterson, agent for the Earl of Tankerville, leases 109 acres and 13 perches to "James Hamilton Gent. [Justice for Loudoun County] Farmer, aged [42], his wife Priscilla Hamilton aged [49] and the life of Aeneas Campbell Junr. aged [4]." LDCODB, Book C, p. 277; see Glossary.

May 25, 1762 - Nicholas Seward and Ann Sorrell [probably the] "spinster" [sister of Thomas Sorrell], pay Charles Binns, Loudoun Clerk, the £1 fee and obtain their marriage license. Clerk's 1762 Fee Book, last page.

June 9, 1762 - A case brought by Mary Jordan "abates by [her] Marriage." Book A, p. 631.

June 10, 1762 - "Richard Stephenson the Elder" is a defendant at Court. Book A, p. 645.

June 11, 1762 - Jane McDowell is the new bride of John Dodd. Book A, p. 655.

July 10, 1762 - A deed for 140 acres on the Potomac at the Sugarlands reveals the family tree of William Harrison Junr., dec'd: his parents were William Harrison Senr. and Sarah Harrison [she is now Sarah Lewis], and his four daughters are "Margaret Blackburn the wife of Edward Blackburn, Sarah Monroe the wife of John Monroe, Susanna Slaughter the wife of Robert Slaughter, and Mary Waler [nee Mary Harrison] now wife of John Waler." LDCODB, Book C, p. 355, and Book D, p. 397.

July 13, 1762 - It is "... Ordered that the Executors of Wayman Sinckler Dec'd. [sic- Wayman Sinclair] deliver the Testators' Children to Mary Shirley their Grand Mother who engages to Maintain and bring them up without any burden to their Estates." Book B, p. 3.

July 14, 1762 - Susanna Cooper is identified as the wife of George Cooper. Book B, p. 8.

August 10, 1762 - A Deed from Abel Janney to his son-in-law Joseph Hutton, and a Deed from widow Mary Janney to Jacob Janney, blacksmith, are recorded. Book B, pp. 28 and 29.

August 10, 1762 - Catherine Jett is the widow of William Jett Junr.. Ann Jett and William Eskridge Jett are the orphans of William Jett Junr.. Book B, p. 31; LDCODB, Book C, p. 372.

September 3, 1762 - John Squires and Elizabeth Taylor, "spinster," pay Loudoun Clerk Charles Binns the £1 fee and obtain their marriage license. Clerk's 1762 Fee Book, last page.

September 13, 1762 - John Johnson and Mary Debell, "widow," pay the £1 fee and obtain their marriage license from Charles Binns. Clerk's 1762 Fee Book, last page.

September 16, 1762 - Hannah Spencer is identified as the wife of Nathan Spencer. Book B, p. 64.

November 10, 1762 - Bryan Fairfax Gent. [Justice of the Peace] of Fairfax County [a cousin of, and ultimately a successor to, the 6th Lord Fairfax], leases 150 acres to Henry Downs, his brother Benjamin Downs, and their sister Mary Clarke. LDCODB, Book C, p. 481; and, DALD, (1762) p. 11.

December 14, 1762 - Henry Oxley deeds land to his sons Henry Oxley Junr., Everitt Oxley and John Oxley. Book B, p. 76.

March 8, 1763 - The Right Honorable Thomas Lord Fairfax, living in Frederick County Virginia, leases 109 acres in his Manor of Leeds to Casper Sybold and his sons Robert Sybold and Jesse Sybold. LDCODB, Book C, p. 509; and, DALD, (1763) p.13.

April 11, 1763 - Hannah Janney is identified as the wife of Jacob Janney. LDCODB, Book C, pp. 491 and 495.

April 12, 1763 - Henry Settle records a Deed of Gift to his son Reuben Settle. Book B, p. 85.

April 12, 1763 - Jacob Remey the Eldest records a Deed of Gift to his Daughter Frances Thomas, the wife of Robert Thomas. Book B, p. 86.

April 13, 1763 - "William Cummings and Bridgett Cummings his Wife." Book B, p. 98.

April 13, 1763 - Nicholas Minor records a Deed of Gift to his daughter Elizabeth Minor. Book B, p. 105.

April 13, 1763 - "Jane Walker, the new wife of Benjamin Walker in her Administration of her late [former] husband Robert Stukesberry, deceased ..." Book B, p. 108.

April 14, 1763 - Catharine Lane, the wife of John Lane, is the "late widow" of William Jett Junr. [is she nee Catharine Eskridge ?] Book B, p. 111; see Record infra, August 10, 1762.

May 1, 1763 - John Patterson, agent for Charles Bennett the Earl of Tankerville, leases 175 acres in "Colvills Difficult tract" to "William Trammell aged [36] ... his son Sampson Trammell aged [10] and daughter Amelia Trammell aged [5]." LDCODB, Book C, 660; and, DALD, (1763) p. 25.

May 10, 1763 - It appears that Martha Sorrell is the wife of Thomas Sorrell. Book B, p. 123.

May 10, 1763 - Deeds identify three daughters of Francis Wright, deceased: Elizabeth Striplin the wife of Toliver Striplin [sic- Elizabeth Stephen and Toliver Stephen] of Frederick County Virginia, Frances Ashby the wife of Nimrod Ashby of Fauquier County, and Dorothy Winn the wife of John Winn of Loudoun. Book B, p. 192; LDCODB, Book D, p. 185, and Book E, p. 248.

May 11, 1763 - Margaret Peyton is identified as the wife of Henry Peyton [Senr.], Gent. [a Justice in Prince William County]. Book B, p. 140.

May 12, 1763 - Sarah Bullett is the wife of Benjamin Bullett. Book B, p. 153.

May 12, 1763 - Mary Ellzey is identified as the wife of Lewis Ellzey of Fairfax County. Book B, p. 153; LDCODB, Book C, p. 601.

June 16, 1763 - Sarah Berkley [aka Sarah Barkley] is identified as the wife of Charles Berkley [aka Charles Barkley]. Book B, p. 176, Book C, p. 199.

June 17, 1763 - Elizabeth Carroll is identified as the wife of Demsy Carroll. Book B, p. 187.

August 9, 1763 - John Mattux records a Deed of Gift to his son John Mattux [Junr.]. Book B, p. 195.

August 12, 1763 - Isabella Galloway is identified as the wife of John Galloway. Book B, p. 219.

August 27, 1763 - A deed confirms that Elizabeth Garrett was the widow of Edward Garrett Senr., that she subsequently married Richard Nelson, and was probably the mother of Edward Garrett Junr. and John Garrett. LDCODB, Book D, p. 140.

September 13, 1763 - John Oliver acknowledges and records a Deed of Gift to his son Reason Oliver. Book B, p. 230.

September 15, 1763 - William Sadd Junr. is a plaintiff at Court. Book B, p. 248.

September 15, 1763 - Martha Green is identified as the wife of Shadrick Green. Book B, p. 253.

September 23, 1763 - George Forster [sic- George Foster] is referred to as the son [and apparently heir] of Robert Forster [sic- Robert Foster], deceased. LDCODB, Book D, p. 12.

November 8, 1763 - A Deed of Gift from Jacob Remey to Jabe Fryer, the first son of John Fryer, is proved and recorded. This implies that Remey is Jabe's grandfather. Book B, p. 261.

November 8, 1763 - James Fergo [sic- James Fargo] is the son of Alexander Forgoe [sic] and Margaret Forgoe [sic]. LDCODB, Book D, p. 20.

November 8, 1763 - Lettice Langfitt is identified as the wife of Philip Langfitt. Book B, p. 262.

February 14, 1764 - Christopher Hopwood and Martha Coombs pay Charles Binns, Loudoun Clerk, the £1 fee, and another 30 shillings for the marriage bond, and obtain their marriage license. Clerk's 1764 Fee Book, p. 4 and last page.

February 14, 1764 - Joseph Gardiner [sic- Joseph Gardner Senr.] records a Deed of Gift to his son Joseph Gardiner Junr. Book B, p. 272; Clerk's 1764 Fee Book, p. 9.

February 15, 1764 - Francis Summers, John Lane, James Hardige Lane, William Lane and George Summers, all of Loudoun County, record a Deed of Gift "in consideration of the affection we have and bear unto Amy Lane." Book B, p. 273.

February 15, 1764 - Edward Bland records a Deed of Gift to Robert Bland; and, Susanna Johnson is identified as the wife of John Johnson. Book B, p. 274.

March 12, 1764 - Thomas Gregg sold 332 acres of land to John Gregg for £50. LDCODB, Book D, p. 180.

March 14, 1764 - An Indenture of Feoffment from Nicholas Minor Gent. to Margaret Naper, the infant daughter of Jane Hamilton, was proved and recorded. Book B, p. 285.

March 15, 1764 - Jane O'Neal is the wife of Ferdinando O'Neale. Book B, p. 289.

March 16, 1764 - Ann Watson, [formerly Ann Seward, nee Ann Sorrell] now the wife of Robert Watson, is Executrix of the Estate of Nicholas Seward, deceased. Book B, pp. 299, 393 and 617; see supra, the Record, p. 474, 477, 478, 479.

April 11, 1764 - Eleanor Gardner is identified as the wife of Silvester Gardner. Book B, p. 335.

April 12, 1764 - "... Rachel Tayler late [nee] Rachel Carruthers ..." Book B, p. 348.

April 20, 1764 - Simon Triplett and Martha Lane "spinster" pay Charles Binns, Loudoun Clerk, the £1 fee, 30 shillings for the marriage bond, and obtain their marriage license. Clerk's 1764 Fee Book, pp. 40 and last page.

May 3, 1764 - Mary Lacewell [sic- Mary Lasswell] is the daughter and heir of John Lacewell [sic- John Lasswell]. She married Thomas Cordery, and they moved to the Halifax District in Georgia and opened an inn. LDCODB, Book D, p. 286.

May 9, 1764 - Richard Stephenson Junr. and Elizabeth Summers "spinster," pay Charles Binns, Loudoun Clerk, the £1 fee, and another 30 shillings for the marriage bond, and obtain their marriage license. Clerk's 1764 Fee Book, p. 47 and last page.

May 12, 1764 - On a deed of sale, Elizabeth Ariss is identified as the wife of John Ariss. LDCODB, Book D, p. 448.

June 12, 1764 - Richard Eskridge and Elizabeth Reed "spinster" [either the recent widow or the orphan of Joseph Reed], pay Charles Binns, Loudoun Clerk, the £1 fee, and another 30 shillings for the marriage bond, and obtain their marriage license. Clerk's 1764 Fee Book, p. 49 and last page.

June 14, 1764 - In the suit of Thomas Beavers vs. Mary McGeach [the widow of Joseph McGeach] "since Suit [was] brought [Mary McGeach] Intermarried with William Cavins." Book B, p. 377; infra, August 15, 1764 entry.

June 14, 1764 - "Catherine Palmer wife of John Palmer Senr. an Evidence for John Palmer Junr. ..." against Edward Snickers. Book B, p. 379.

August 14, 1764 - A Deed is recorded with John Miller and Mary Miller as witnesses. Book B, p. 406.

August 14, 1764 - Samuel Willson [sic- Samuel Wilson] records a Deed of Gift "in consideration of natural love and affection which I have and bear unto Isabel Wilson my wife." One witness, Rachel Wilson, appears to be their daughter. Book B, p. 406; LDCODB, Book D, p. 260; DALD, (1764) p. 54.

August 15, 1764 - A Petition of Simon Pearson against Greenbury Dorsey and his wife Catharine Dorsey, late [formerly or nee] Catharine Grymes, and against Stacey Grymes, is discontinued. Book B, p. 411.

August 15, 1764 - Deeds of Gift from Mary McGeach to her sons Thomas McGeach and James McGeach are recorded. Book B, p. 412; see also, infra, March 12, 1765 entry.

August 16, 1764 - A deed of Gift from Nicholas Minor to his son John Minor, for two town lots in Leesburg [#45 and #46 ?], is recorded. Book B, p. 414; LDCODB, Book D, p. 279.

August 16, 1764 - Phebe Stewart is identified as the wife of Robert Stewart. Book B, p. 415.

September 12, 1764 - On a deed of sale, Catharine Popkins is identified as the wife of Robert Popkins. LDCODB, Book D, p. 292.

September 13, 1764 - Martha Jones is identified as the wife of John Jones. Book B, pp. 445 and 566; Clerk's 1764 Fee Book, p. 65.

October of 1764 - Robert Stephens Senr. and Thomas Phillips Senr. are two plaintiffs at the Loudoun County Court. Clerk's 1764 Fee Book, p. 68.

October 6, 1764 - In a grant from the Proprietor's land office for a tract on Difficult run, William Saunders Junr. is said to be the heir-at-law of Daniel Saunders, deceased, of Loudoun County. Apparently, William Junr. is either the nephew or the eldest surviving brother of Daniel. NorNeck, p. 97; Grants, Book I, folio 122.

October 10, 1764 - John McKenny is also known as John McKenzy. Book B, p. 477.

October 10, 1764 - Elenor Hopper [sic- Eleanor Hopper], formerly

Eleanor Smallwood, is now the wife of William Hopper. Book B, p. 478; and see, LDCODB, Book E, p. 344.

October 10, 1764 - "John Talbut Senr." is a defendant at Court. Book B, p. 481.

October 10, 1764 - Mary Caudrey is identified as the wife of Thomas Caudrey. Book B, p. 484.

November of 1764 - Thomas Middleton Senr. is a plaintiff at the Loudoun Court. Clerk's 1764 Fee Book, p. 72.

November 13, 1764 - "Jonas Potts Junr." obtains land in Loudoun County. Book B, p. 492.

November 14, 1764 - Jonathan Palmer and his wife Margaret Palmer deed property to Harmon Cox and his wife Jane Cox, who, in turn, deed lands to William Fowler. LDCODB, Book D, pp. 485-491.

December 15, 1764 - Robert Cavins and Ann Todd pay Charles Binns, Loudoun Clerk, the £1 fee, and another 30 shillings for the marriage bond, and obtain their marriage license. Clerk's 1764 Fee Book, p. 76 and last page.

December 18, 1764 - Jonathan Davis and Betty Keen [widow of Richard Keen], pay Charles Binns the £1 fee, 30 shillings for the marriage bond, and obtain their marriage license. Clerk's 1764 Fee Book, last page.

February 1765 - John Smith and Mary West, widow, pay £1 to Charles Binns, Clerk of Loudoun County, and obtain their marriage license. Clerk's 1765 Fee Book, last page.

March 12, 1765 - Thomas McGeach is identified as the heir of Joseph McGeach, deceased, and Mary Cavins, now married to William Cavins, is his mother. LDCODB, Book D, p. 406.

April 8, 1765 - "Deeds to Uses" were recorded, from John Keen the Elder and his wife Sarah Keen, and from Vincent Lewis, to "John Lewis, Benjamin Mason, Anthony Keen, Betty Keen, widow of Richard Keen, deceased (who was the Reputed son of the said John Keen), and John Keen the Younger and Anna Keen (Children of the said Richard Keen by the said Betty Keen his wife) ..." Betty Keen is the daughter of Vincent Lewis. In December of 1764 she remarried, to Jonathan Davis. Book B, p. 538; LDCODB, Book D, pp. 415-421.

April 10, 1765 - Henry Taylor and his wife Susanna Taylor [formerly Susanna Whitely], and William Whitely, record a Deed of Gift of 4 slaves to Margaret Whitely, the "daughter to said Susanna and sister to said William." Book B, p. 549; and, LDCODB, Book D, p. 432.

April 11, 1765 - Martha Berryman is the wife of John Berryman. Book B, p. 569.

April 11, 1765 - William Berkley Junr. and William King Junr. are both defendants at Court. Book B, pp. 573 and 574.

April 17, 1765 - William Smith and Margaret Whiteley pay £1 to Charles Binns, Clerk of Loudoun County, and obtain their marriage license. Clerk's 1765 Fee Book, last page.

May 13, 1765 - Mary Cadwallader is identified as the wife of Joseph Cadwallader. Order Book B, p. 571; LDCODB, Book D, p. 433.

May 13, 1765 - Rachel Carr is identified as the wife of Peter Carr. Book B, p. 577.

May 13, 1765 - George William Fairfax leases 100 acres in the Piedmont manor, on the beaver dam branch of Kitoctin Creek, to George Nixon, his wife Ann Nixon and their son William Nixon. LDCODB, Book D, p. 457.

May 14, 1765 - Mary Moss is the wife of Loudoun Justice John Moss Junr.. LDCODB, Book D, p. 463.

May 14, 1765 - George William Fairfax leases 172 acres to Moses Cadwallader [Senr.], his wife Elizabeth Cadwallader, and their son Moses Cadwallader [Junr.]. LDCODB, Book D, p. 623.

May 16, 1765 - Elizabeth Dye is identified as the wife of William Dye. Book B, p. 604.

May 16, 1765 - "John White, the son of Timothy White, Planter, in Frederick County ... Maryland" is a defendant at Court. Book B, p. 606.

May 16, 1765 - "Jonathan Davis and Betty Davis his wife, late [nee] Betty Keen ..." Book B, p. 609.

May 30, 1765 - Enoch McKenzey and Eliza. West, spinster, pay £1 to Charles Binns, Clerk of Loudoun County, and obtain their marriage license. Clerk's 1765 Fee Book, last page.

June 10, 1765 - Susanna Redmon is identified as the wife of William Redmon [sic- William Redmond]. Book B, p. 618.

June 10, 1765 - Thomas Tipten is the son of Silvester Tipten. LDCODB, Book D, p. 492.

June 12, 1765 - William Hudson is "an Evidence for Joseph Jones and Martha Jones his Wife at the Suit of Joseph Gardner ..." Book B, p. 650.

June 13, 1765 - "John Lewis and Elizabeth Lewis his wife, late [nee] Elizabeth Davis." Book B, p. 657.

August 6, 1765 - Sanford Payne and Abigail Lay pay £1 to Charles Binns, Clerk of Loudoun County, and obtain their marriage license. Clerk's 1765 Fee Book, last page.

August 8, 1765 - Margaret Mead is identified on a deed as the wife of Samuel Mead. LDCODB, Book D, p. 548.

August 12, 1765 - Indentures of Gift were recorded from Mahlon Janney and wife Sarah Janney to "Mary Janney (the Younger) his sister" and "Ruth Janney his sister ..." Book C, p. 1.

August 12, 1765 - James Wheelock, his wife Frances Wheelock, and his "natural son" John Hulls alias John Wheelock [sic- the base born son of Rachel Hall ?], lease 150 acres on the side north of Goose Creek "whereon Thomas Owsley now lives including the plantation whereon William Patterson lived." LDCODB, Book D, p. 541; and see infra, Chapter on Base Born.

August 14, 1765 - John Bast Junr. is a witness for John Griffith. Book C, p. 30.

September 9, 1765 - William King Senr. and William King Junr. are both defendants in Court. Book C, pp. 32 and 41.

September 10, 1765 - Nicholas Minor leases 56 acres, just northwest of Leesburg, to John Pyott, his wife Hester Pyott and their son John Pyott Junr..

LDCODB, Book D, p. 611; and, DALD, (1765) p. 94.

September 11, 1765 - "Jacob Ashburn & Sarah Ashburn his Wife late [nee] Sarah Penmill." Book C, p. 43.

September 11, 1765 - Ann Middleton is the wife of Thomas Middleton Junr. Book C, p. 48.

September 11, 1765 - George William Fairfax leases 140 acres on south side of Quarter Branch [east of modern Lovettsville] to Simon Shoemaker, his wife Elizabeth Shoemaker and their son Martin Shoemaker. LDCODB, Book D, p. 636.

September 12, 1765 - John Tayloe of Richmond County, a member of the Governor's Council, leases lot #18 of his tract at the Gap of Short Hill to Thomas Purcell, and his sons John Purcell and Benjamin Purcell. LDCODB, Book D, p. 639.

September 12, 1765 - George William Fairfax leases 100 acres under a life lease to three brothers, John Jackson, William Jackson and Richard Jackson. LDCODB, Book D, p. 673.

September 12, 1765 - George William Fairfax leases a 175 acre tract to William Jackson, his sons James Jackson and Richard Jackson [Junr.], and his daughter Sarah Jackson. LDCODB, Book D, p. 691; DALD, (1765) p. 103.

September 12, 1765 - George William Fairfax leases a 100 acre tract to Hannah Cadwallader and her sons John Cadwallader and David Cadwallader. LDCODB, Book D, p. 697.

September 12, 1765 - John Tayloe of Richmond County leases lot #10 of his tract at the Gap of Short Hill to Loudoun County Justice John McIlhaney [Senr.] and his sons James McIlhaney and John McIlhaney [Junr.]. LDCODB, Book D, p. 707.

September 23, 1765 - William Colton Junr. and Frances Taylor, spinster, pay £1 to Loudoun Clerk Charles Binns and obtain their marriage license. Clerk's 1765 Fee Book, last page.

October 14, 1765 - John Williams of Loudoun County is the eldest son and heir of Owen Williams of Frederick County, Virginia. NorNeck WS, IV/77.

October 15, 1765 - James Lane records a Deed of Gift to Simon Triplett and his wife Martha Triplett, James Lane's daughter. Book C, p. 63; LDCODB, Book D, p. 676.

December 13, 1765 - Bryan Fairfax leases 126 acres to Jeremiah McCarty, "his now wife" Elizabeth McCarty, and his son Daniel McCarty. LDCODB, Book E, p. 91.

February 16, 1766 - John Tayloe of Richmond County leases lot #25 of his tract at the Gap of Short Hill to Joshua Gore Junr., his wife Elizabeth Gore and their daughter Hannah Gore. LDCODB, Book E, p. 138; for the illustration of Tayloe's tract, see Chapter on Lands, supra @ p. 248.

June 12, 1766 - Millisant Piper is identified as the wife of John Piper. Book C, p. 113.

June 12, 1766 - Hanah Spencer is the wife of Nathan Spencer. Book C, p. 126.

August 13, 1766 - George Hardy Senr. and George Hardy Junr. are both defendants at Court. Book C, p. 159.

August 14, 1766 - "Harrison Manley and Margaret Manley his wife" bring a complaint In Chancery against "Samuel Tillet and Anne Tillet his wife, John Herryford and James Herryford, infant." Book C, p. 173.

August 15, 1766 - Sarah Maginniss is identified as the wife of John Maginniss. Book C, p. 183; and see supra, Chapter on Inns and Taverns.

September 9, 1766 - Catherine Cargill is identified on a deed as the wife of John Cargill. LDCODB, Book E, p. 197.

September 10, 1766 - Alice Fouch is identified as the wife of Jacob Fouch. Book C, p. 195.

September 10, 1766 - On a deed of sale, Magdalina Phaw, aka Mary Phaw, [or Mary Pshaw or Mary Faw], is identified as the wife of Jacob Phaw, [or Jacob Pshaw or Jacob Faw]. LDCODB, Book E, p. 238.

September 11, 1766 - "Thomas Jenkins, son of Samuel Jenkins" is a defendant. His father, Samuel Jenkins Senr., died in 1759. Book C, p. 197; and see infra, Chapter on Deaths.

October 4, 1766 - In his Will, John Evans, a blacksmith in Loudoun County, names his wife Elizabeth Evans, sons William Evans, David Evans, Joshua Evans, Griffith Evans and Richard Evans, and his daughters Amy Thomas and Elizabeth Evans. He apparently signed his name Thomas Evans [sic]. NorNeck WS, IV/153.

November 12, 1766 - William Carr Lane leases 27 acres, for a "Sadlers shop," to Charles Davis, his wife Ann Davis and their son Charles Burgess Davis. LDCODB, Book E, p. 274.

An "infant" in colonial Virginia was specifically defined by statute as anyone under the age of 21 years, although various legal disabilities were lifted and tithables taxes were imposed on free whites when they reached age 16. Orphan children in Virginia were treated differently depending on their station in colonial society, or more particularly the station of their parents. As previously discussed, infant orphans of reduced circumstance were bound out as apprentices to tradesmen, and bastard and mulatto children were born into lives of extended servitude. The children of the landed and merchant classes fell into a different category altogether, and were treated with regard for their property rights and station. They are the subject of this chapter. [Hening, VI/223 and VII/519; see supra, Chapters on Tithables and Apprentices; and infra, Chapter on Base Born and Mulattos].

Guardians of all orphans were required to preserve and keep the estate of their infant wards, and render an accounting once a year. Land belonging to an orphan could not be disposed of until three years after the orphan came of age. Virginia's colonial laws of 1642-43 also "injoyned [sic] [guardians] ... to educate and instruct [the infant orphans] according to their best endeavours [sic] in Christian religion and in rudiments of learning and to provide for them necessaries ..." [Hening, I/260-261].

The Assembly Acts of December of 1656 revised these requirements slightly, providing that "orphans be kept and maintained and educated according as their estates will beare," also allowing for orphans who were not bound as apprentices to obtain the produce of their own labors [ie., their earnings] after they reached age 17. "Apprizers" of an orphan's estate were to be allowed 30 lbs. of tobacco in payment for each day they served. Provisions that the lands of orphans could not be sold or considered deserted until three years after the orphan reached "full age" [ie., age 21], were continued by the Assembly Acts of March of 1657-58, with the added proviso that timber on an orphan's lands was not to be "wasted," or cut and sold without account. [Hening, I/416-417 and I/443].

These rules of law prevailed for over a century with minor amendments and little elaboration. All of the laws of the Virginia colony regarding the management and security of orphans were recodified by the 1748 Assembly, and thereafter the guardianship laws of Virginia were not revised again until after the American Revolution. As previously discussed, colonial children were considered orphans when their father died. The 1748 Act provided that a father, even if the father was under 21 years of age, had the right to "dispose of the custody and tuition" of his unmarried children under the age of 21, either "by his deed executed in his life time" or in his last will. Thus, for over thirty years, this act was the legal basis for the validity of all contracts of apprenticeship arranged by Virginia fathers and the propriety of testamentary directions concerning the guardianship, apprenticing and education of surviving children. [Hening, V/449].

"Popish recusants," ie., proselytizing catholics, were prohibited from serving as legal guardians in Virginia. Guardians were instructed to take custody "to the use of such child ... the profits of all lands, tenements, and hereditaments ... the slaves, goods, chattels and personal estate of such child," and to "maintain an action of ravishment of ward or trespass against any person ... who shall wrongfully take away or detain such child." Guardians were required to give "good and sufficient security" in the county court when they qualified, and then render an accounting at the county court "in the month of August in every year or ... the next succeeding court held for that county." If an accounting proved questionable or unusual, a guardian's security had the right to have the county court compel the guardian to give financial "counter security." During the first decade of Loudoun County, from 1757 to 1766, Henry Wisheart is the only Guardian prosecuted by the Kings Attorney for apparent mismanagement of a ward's estate. [Hening, V/449-451 and V/453; infra, The Record, p. 488].

The county court, as with less fortunate children, had the authority to "take cognizance of all matters concerning orphans and their estates and appoint [or replace] guardians in such cases" as the court determined circumstances to warrant. Guardians could be removed by a county court:

> *"upon a complaint ... of such guardian abusing the trust reposed in him, by misusing the child ... or neglecting the care of their education suitable to their estate, or [for] wasting, converting to his own use, or otherways mismanaging such estate."*

A guardian was authorized "to charge in his account all reasonable disbursements and expences ... suitable to the degree and circumstances of the estate of such orphan," up to the amount of the annual "profits," ie., income, of the estate. When actual expenditures for education and maintenance of the orphan were shown to exceed the annual income, a guardian was entitled to take reimbursement in another year's account of the estate. Upon the death of an infant's guardian, "so much as shall appear due to the estate of such orphan" was given legal priority "before any other or proper debt whatsoever of such testator or intestate." As with the masters of apprentices and servants, the guardian of an infant orphan was held legally responsible for any civil fines or penalties incurred by an infant in his custody. [Hening, V/450-454 and VII/100-101].

Instances of infant litigants, and their personal representatives at court, have been included in this chapter as well. The reader may also note that The Record is replete with evidence of a custom maintained in the Loudoun County Court - allowing children, presumably of suitable age and discretion, to choose their own Guardians in the absence of some directive from the deceased father.

The Loudoun Record

June 13, 1758 - "Mary Janings is appointed Guardian to her daughter Rebecca Janings to receive the Legacy left said Rebecca by Thomas Davis [Senr.], deceased." Book A, p. 110.

July 11, 1758 - William Grayson, infant orphan of Benjamin Grayson Gent., deceased, chooses Benjamin Grayson [either a brother or a cousin] for his Guardian. Book A, p. 130.

July 11, 1758 - Loudoun Justice Benjamin Grayson, with fellow Justices Anthony Russell and Charles Tyler and County Clerk Charles Binns as his Securities, enters a bond to preserve the estate of William Grayson, the orphan son of Benjamin Grayson, a Prince William Justice. DALD (1758) p. 17.

December 12, 1758 - Henry Herryford, an infant orphan of James Herryford, deceased, and the nephew of John Herryford Junr., chooses Charles Tyler, Gent., as his Guardian. Book A, p. 184.

December 12, 1758 - Charles Tyler, Francis Peyton and William Ellzey enter into a bond to preserve the estate of Henry Herryford, an orphan son of

James Herryford and nephew of John Herryford, the future Leesburg ordinary keeper. DALD (1758) p. 23.

March 16, 1759 - At Court, plaintiff "John Fryer Buckley [is represented] by William Buckley his Father & next Friend ..." Book A, p. 228.

May 8, 1759 - Henry Wisheart qualifies as Guardian to Jemima Neale, who is the orphan of Presly Neale, deceased. Book A, p. 235.

May 8, 1759 - Henry Wisheart, with Hugh West as his Security, enter a bond to preserve the estate of Jemima Neale, the orphan of Presley Neale. DALD, (1759) p. 27.

May 9, 1759 - Spence Grayson, an infant orphan of Benjamin Grayson [the Prince William County Justice], deceased, chooses William Ellzey Gent. [Attorney of Prince William] for his Guardian. Book A, p. 237.

May 9, 1759 - Robert Stephens is represented at Court by Richard Stephens, his Guardian. Book A, pp. 240 and 441.

November 13, 1759 - William Shores, an infant orphan of Richard Shores, deceased, chooses Francis Hague for his Guardian. Book A, p. 299.

November 13, 1759 - Francis Hague, with Aeneas Campbell as his Security, entered a bond to preserve the estate of William Shores, orphan of Richard Shores. DALD, (1759) p. 31.

March 14, 1760 - John Shackliff, an infant, is represented at Court by Benjamin Shackliff, "his Father and next Friend ..." Book A, pp. 340 and 514; and Book B, p. 43.

May 13, 1760 - John Garrett, orphan of Edward Garrett [Senr.], dec'd., chooses Edward Garrett [probably his brother] for his Guardian. Book A, pp. 344 and 527.

May 13, 1760 - Edward Garrett, with William Ellzey as his Security, enters a bond to preserve the estate of his brother John Garrett, the orphan of Edward Garrett [Senr.]. LDCODB, Book A, p. 405.

May 14, 1760 - Mary Hall and Susanna Hall, orphans of William Hall, deceased, both choose John Hall as their Guardian. John Hall, with William West as his Security, enters a bond to preserve the estates of the two orphans. The Hall family were William West's neighbors. Book A, p. 348; LDCODB, Book A, p. 458-459; and see, DALD, (1760) p. 40.

August 13, 1760 - Rebecca Eades, an infant, is represented at Court by Thomas Hamilton, her Guardian. Book A, p. 396.

February 11, 1761 - John Minor and wife Elizabeth Minor [formerly Elizabeth Ellzey], both under the age of 21, are represented at Court by Nicholas Minor, "their next Friend." Book A, pp. 415, 420 and 523.

September 10, 1761 - Robert Peyton, an infant, is represented by John Peyton, his Guardian. Book A, p. 509.

November 11, 1761 - William Floyd, orphan of John Floyd, deceased, chooses William Ellzey as his Guardian who, with Lee Massey his Security, enters a bond to preserve the estate. Book A, p. 531; and, LDCODB, Book C, p. 92.

May 11, 1762 - Clater Smith is appointed Guardian of Temple Smith, who is identified as an orphan of Nathaniel Smith, deceased. Book A, p. 584.

May 11, 1762 - Clater Smith, with Charles Tyler and John Peak as his Securities, enters a bond to preserve the estate of Temple Smith, the orphan of Nathaniel Smith. LDCODB, Book C, p. 213; and see, DALD, (1762) p. 98.

May 14, 1762 - Emanuel Lay and Silvenus Lay, infant plaintiffs against James Whaley, are represented at Court by their Guardian Nicholas Grimes Junr. Book A, p. 609.

July 15, 1762 - Rebecca Eades, an infant under age 21 is represented at court by her Guardian and next friend, Thomas Hamilton, in case of trespass, assault and battery against John Lackey and Jacob Gardner. Book B, p. 15.

July 15, 1762 - Robert Peyton, infant under age 21 is represented by his Guardian, John Peyton, in a suit against James Leith. Book B, p. 20.

August 11, 1762 - James Lane is appointed as the Guardian of Ann Jett and William Eskridge Jett, the orphans of William Jett Junr., deceased. Book B, pp. 4 and 33.

August 12, 1762 - Joseph Shackliff, an infant, is represented by Benjamin Shackliff, his Father. Book B, p. 43.

August 13, 1762 - Claytor Smith is the Guardian of Temple Smith. Book B, p. 51.

August 13, 1762 - Alexander Colclough, orphan of Robert Colclough, chooses Josias Clapham as his Guardian. Book B, p. 51.

May 12, 1763 - Benjamin Steward, an infant plaintiff, is represented at Court by "Craven Peyton, his Guardian and next Friend." Book B, p. 147.

June 14, 1763 - Benjamin Grayson renders accounts for the Estate of William Grayson, an orphan and his ward, and is discharged from the Guardianship. Book B, p. 160.

August 12, 1763 - Silvanus Lay and Emanuel Lay, infant plaintiffs, are represented at Court by Nicholas Grimes Junr., their "Guardian and next Friend." Book B, p. 227.

August 12, 1763 - "Ordered that Process issue against the several Guardians of orphans who ought to have rendered their Accounts to this Court and have failed ..." Book B, p. 229.

June 12, 1764 - Benjamin Berkley is appointed the Guardian of Elizabeth Read. Book B, p. 359.

June 12, 1764 - Benjamin Berkley, with Richard Eskridge as his Security, enters a bond to preserve the estate of Elizabeth Reed, the orphan of Joseph Reed. LDCODB, Book D, p. 224.

June 12, 1764 - Jacob Smith [Junr.], an infant orphan and Heir of Jacob Smith, deceased, chooses Enoch Grigsby for his Guardian, with Robert Sandford as Security. Book B, p. 361.

June 12, 1764 - Enoch Grigsby, with Robert Sanford as his Security, enters a bond to preserve the estate of Jacob Smith [sic- James Smith], orphan of Jacob Smith [Senr.]. LDCODB, Book D, p. 231; Clerk's 1764 Fee Book, p. 51.

June 12, 1764 - The dower interest in the Estate of Jacob Smith, deceased, of Hester Wells [nee widow Smith], now wife of Thomas Williams Wells is ordered to be surveyed and allotted. Book B, p. 361.

June 15, 1764 - Rennes Sadd, an infant under age 21, is a plaintiff at Court represented by William Sadd, her father and next friend. Book B, p. 387.

June 15, 1764 - Lettice Mocavoy, an infant, is represented by William Ellzey, "her next Friend." Book B, p. 390.

August 14, 1764 - John Willcoxon Halling, orphan of William Halling, with consent of Court chooses John Willcoxon for his Guardian. Book B, p. 405.

August 14, 1764 - John Wilcoxon, with Philip Noland as his Security, enters a bond to preserve the estate of John Wilcoxon Halling, orphan of William Halling. LDCODB, Book D, p. 256.

August 13, 1765 - John Willcoxon Halling, orphan of William Halling, makes the "... Choice of William Lucket for his Guardian." Book C, p. 8.

September 11, 1765 - Alice Butcher and Mary Butcher, under age 21, are represented at Court by their "Guardian and next friend" [usually the father] Samuel Butcher. Book C, p. 46.

September 11, 1765 - James Muir, an infant, is represented by his Guardian Robert Adam. Book C, p. 47.

October 14, 1765 - John Roberts, the orphan of Richard Roberts, dec'd., chooses Thomas Green for his Guardian, with Josias Clapham as Security for the Estate. Book C, p. 59.

October 14, 1765 - Thomas Green, with Josias Clapham his Security, enters a bond to preserve the estate of John Roberts, orphan of Richard Roberts. LDCODB, Book D, p. 635.

October 16, 1765 - Hugh West is granted leave to prosecute the Bond given by Henry Wisheart, Guardian of Jemima Neale, for his failure to settle her Estate. Book C, p. 70.

June 12, 1766 - Susannah Hill, infant [under age 21], is represented by Samuel Hill her "Guardian and next friend" in a suit against Sarah Laycock. Book C, p. 121.

June 13, 1766 - Robert Peyton, infant [under age 21], is represented at Court by John Peyton his "Guardian and next friend." Book C, p. 128.

August 14, 1766 - John Herryford is named Guardian of his son James Herryford. Book C, p. 173.

August 14, 1766 - Sarah Lyles, an infant, is represented at Court by William Berry, her Guardian. Book C, p. 173.

October 13, 1766 - Thomas Currey, orphan of Barnaby Currey, chooses Kitchin Prim for his Guardian. Book C, p. 207.

October 13, 1766 - Kitchen Prim, with Benjamin Mason as his Security, enters a bond to preserve the estate of Thomson Curry, orphan of Barnaby Curry. LDCODB, Book E, p. 219.

Dirty Laundry
Base Born and Mulatto Children

In the parlance of colonial Virginia, "base born" was the term used when one spoke of a bastard, ie., an out-of-wedlock child. Mulatto children, at least in the first generation, were the product of an illegal union since interracial marriages were prohibited in colonial Virginia. Accordingly, the Virginia General Assembly subjected mulatto children to legal disabilities that often resulted in a perpetual cycle of indented servitude. By the time Loudoun County was established, base born children of all-white unions were generally treated as if they were orphans and bound out by the parish churchwardens as apprentices to tradesmen. These apprenticeships were for a limited period of years, and it was provided that the base born child would be taught to read and write. However, as we have mentioned elsewhere, all children born in Virginia were to be considered bond or free in accord with the mother's legal status. [see supra, Chapter on Apprentices and Orphans; and, Hening, VI/357].

In March of 1657-58, fornication and the bastard children of servants were subjects of several Acts of the Virginia Assembly. The father of a bastard born to a servant woman was required to give security to the parish to defray any charges incurred in keeping and raising the child, and, if the father was a free man, pay 1500 lbs. of tobacco to the master of the servant woman in compensation. Servant mothers and fathers were each to serve the master of the servant mother for one additional year after the expiration of their existing indentures. Fornication was a crime whether or not the result was a bastard child, and the penalty imposed was a fine of 500 lbs. of tobacco payable to the parish, "or be whipt." These penalties were still in effect with some minor modification and actively enforced in Loudoun County in the 1760s, as evidenced by the many entries noted in the Record herein. Perhaps the best example is provided by the prosecution of Sarah Fletcher in December of 1764, who, upon refusing to pay her fine, was sentenced to "receive on her bare Back twenty five Lashes well laid on at the common whipping Post." In the Assembly session of March of 1661-62, the penalty for servant women "haveing [sic] a bastard ... [was increased to] serve two years after her time by indenture." Penalties for the unwed fathers remained unchanged. [Hening, I/438-439 and II/114-115; see infra, the Record, pp. 493 and 496].

The Assembly recodification of the laws relating to servants and slaves in November of 1753 provided that a woman servant who delivered a bastard child during her time of service, "in recompence [sic] of the loss and trouble occasioned her master," was required "for every such offence, [to] serve her said master or owner one whole year after her time by indenture ..." or pay her master 1,000 lbs. of tobacco. If the father of the child was a free man, he was required to give security to the churchwardens of the child's parish to indemnify them for the maintenance and care of the child. Fathers who were indentured servants were required to "make satisfaction to the parish for keeping the said child, after [completing] his time by indenture." When the master fathered a bastard child by one of his female servants, the Assembly provided that the woman would not be bound to that master for any additional service, but rather that, after she completed her indenture with the father/master, the churchwardens of the parish were to sell the extra year of the woman's services and apply the proceeds "to be employed by the vestry to the use of the said parish." [Hening, VI/360-361].

The Act of 1753 also provided that any woman, free or servant, who delivered a bastard mulatto child was to pay a £15 fine to the churchwardens of the parish within one month of delivering the child, or the mother was to be sold into servitude for five years with the proceeds to be applied to the use of the parish. Servant women were to serve an additional year for their current masters before being sold for the additional five years. All mulatto children were to be bound out by the churchwardens of the parish, presumably to the mother's master, until they reached age 31. The Loudoun County Court may have misapplied this provision in the law in September of 1761 when the mulatto sons of Patricia Locklan were bound out to John Gest. "And for a further prevention of that abominable mixture, and spurious issue ... by English and other white men and women intermarrying with negroes or mulattoes, as by their unlawful coition with them," the Assembly provided that any free white marrying any negro or mulatto was to be sentenced to six months in jail "without bail or mainprize" and pay a £10 fine to their parish. [Hening, VI/361; see infra, The Record, p. 494].

Special provisions were made for the children of female Indians and mulattoes when the mother was already bound to serve until the age of 31. In those cases, when the servant "delivered of any child during the time of her servitude," the child was obliged to serve the master of the mother until the child also reached the age of 31. In October of 1765 the Assembly noted that this provision presented an "unreasonable severity towards such children" and amended it so that children born to the bound-to-age-31 mulatto servants would be subject to lesser periods of indentured servitude. Thereafter, male children were to be bound to serve to age 21 and female children to serve "only" to age 18. [Hening, VI/357 and VIII/135].

The 1765 Assembly, also finding:

> *"that divers ill disposed persons have of late years been guilty of selling and disposing of mulattoes and others as slaves, who ... are subject to a service only of thirty one years, after which they become free,"*

placed civil penalties totalling £35 on anyone attempting such a sale. For a second violation, an offending party forfeited "the residue of the time of service due from such servant" in addition to the monetary penalties. Just as with other types of civil penalties, the Assembly provided that an "informer" would receive a portion of the fines. When he could not pay the penalties, a violator would be "obliged to serve the person to whom such servant was sold as a slave the full time ... due by law from such servant[!]" [Hening, VIII/133-134].

While not quite as dramatic a circumstance as the sale of mulattoes apprentices into slavery, Loudoun County had its own case involving a contest over rights to the apprenticeship of a base born child. For three years in the 1760s, Thomas Middleton Junr., a cordwainer, and Moses Botts, a cooper, fought a running battle in the Loudoun County Court over the apprenticeship of a youth named Tobias Allan. At one point, Botts falsely represented that Middleton, who had originally been awarded custody of Allan, had moved from Loudoun County. The truth prevailed and Thomas Middleton eventually recovered the custody of his apprentice. [see The Record, pp. 494-496].

The Loudoun Record also reveals details of the story of James Whaley, who apparently fathered a child by his sister-in-law Barbara Remey and then fought conviction all the way to the

General Court in Williamsburg. Unfortunately, the records of the colonial General Court were burned by the British, and no record of James Whaley's appeal bond has been found among the Loudoun County records. But the entry of a second, improper Information against Whaley, in June of 1760, nearly four years after the child's birth, suggests that Whaley's attorney successfully exploited a technical flaw in the initial Grand Jury Presentment and Whaley thereby avoided the lawful penalties that were his due. His paramour Barbara Remey was not so fortunate and in April of 1764, fully seven years after their tryst, was finally convicted and fined for her offence. [supra, Chapter on the Grand Jury titled Maintaining Morality; and see infra, The Record, pp. 493, 495 and 496].

The Loudoun Record

August 10, 1757 - Sarah Proctor, a "base born child [who was 8] years old [last] March [is bound to] Thomas Owsley ... to be taught to Read & Write." Book A, p. 8.

August 10, 1757 - Peter Jennings, "a base born child three years old next October," is bound out to William Dodd, a shoemaker. Book A, p. 11.

September 13, 1757 - Jane Russell, "a Mulatto daughter of Anne Russell likewise Henry Magiss son of Elizabeth Magiss, also a Mulatto [are bound] to Thomas Awbrey"; Rebecca Macon "alias Rinah," a Mulatto, is bound to John Gibson. Book A, p. 17.

May 9, 1758 - The Grand Jury presents "Barbary Ramey for having a base Born Child within six Months last past." Book A, p. 98.

May 10, 1758 - Anthony Parker and Margaret Parker, "his wife, petition to set aside an Order ... binding Rebecca Rian ... bound by the Name of Rebecca Macon alias Rebecca Rinah to John Gibson ... without notice to the Mother [Margaret] nor Proof of the said Rebecca's being a Mulatto ... Gibson [since dead] ... sold the said Rebecca to Philip Noland ... [the Loudoun Court Orders that:] Anthony Parker and Margaret ... should have the said Child ... bringing her up in the Principles of Christianity ... Philip Noland ... prays an Appeal." Book A, pp. 36, 63 and 106-107.

June 13, 1758 - In an action brought by the Churchwardens of Cameron Parish "Ann Hays ... having a Base born child ... declared that John Winn is the Father of the said child." Book A, pp. 98 and 113.

November 15, 1758 - Margaret Redmond is "Summoned ... to Answer the Information of the Churchwardens of Cameron Parish for having a Base born Child." Book A, p. 180.

March 14, 1759 - Churchwardens bring an Information against Sarah Jones, probably on morals charges, shortly after she is released from jail as Loudoun's first insolvent debtor. Book A, p. 214; infra, Chapter on Debtors.

May 8, 1759 - The Grand Jury charges "Mary Proctor for having a Mulatto Base born ... [and] Thomas Kelly for encouraging and Detaining a certain Mary Proctor to cohabit with a certain Negro named Peter and when ready to be delivered conveys said Mary out of the County." Book A, p. 233.

May 9, 1759 - A jury tries James Whaley for cohabiting with his sister-in-law Barbary Ramey and fathering her child. The verdict is suspended for consideration of procedural objections. Book A, p. 244; see also supra, Chapter on the County Court, and Chapter on the Grand Jury Presentments.

November 16, 1759 - In the now celebrated case of James Whaley: The "jury finds him Guilty ... the Plea of the Deft. in Arrest of Judgment being argued and Overruled ... Deft. shall make [pay] a fine [of £10] ... for the use of the Poor of the said Parish of Cameron ... Deft. prayed an Appeal to the next General Court which is granted him on his giving Bond in the Clerk's Office." Whaley's attorney, William Ellzey, then attacked the May 1758 Grand Jury Presentments and succeeded in having them Quashed, setting up another legal grounds for Whaley's appeal. Book A, pp. 314-315; see supra, Chapter on the Grand Jury Presentments; and see The Record, supra, p. 492 and infra, p. 495.

June 10, 1760 - A complaint of the Churchwardens against Elizabeth Grantham [sic- aka Elizabeth Grant], on morals charges, "By Agreement of the Parties ... Dismissed ... the Deft. [to] pay ... Plts. their Costs." Book A, p. 360.

June 12, 1760 - Mary English, Rachel Duncan and Mary Franks, each being "Presented ... for having a base Born Child ... [is fined, to] pay the Churchwardens of Cameron Parish ... [500 lbs.] of Tobacco ... or 50 Shillings." Presentments against Lydia Dodd and Chloe Poor are dismissed; the case against Elizabeth Tapman is continued when the Sheriff's return indicates that she is "not found." Book A, pp. 367-369.

June 12, 1760 - John Barrett, "Presented for Cohabiting with Mary Franks [is fined 500 lbs.] of Tobacco ... to the use of the Poor of [Cameron] Parish"; a similar Information is read to defendant James Whaley [Junr.], renewing the charges against him for fathering a child by his sister-in-law. Book A, pp. 370 and 379; see supra, Chapter on the County Court.

June 12, 1760 - The "Information of the Churchwardens of Cameron Parish agt. [against] Margaret Redmond for having a Base born child is Discontinued" by the Court. Book A, p. 376.

February 12, 1761 - The complaint of Cameron parish Churchwardens Francis Peyton and Nicholas Minor vs. Sarah Owsley, (presented by the Grand Jury in 1760 for having a base born child), is "Discontinued the Plts. not further prosecuting." Book A, p. 419.

February 12, 1761 - Complaints brought by the Cameron Churchwardens against Mary Martin and Elizabeth Grantham, probably morals charges, are continued. Book A, p. 424.

September 8, 1761 - Joseph Locklan, 10 years old, and Henry Locklan, 12 years old, Mulatto children of Priscilla Locklan, are bound to John Gest, "until they Arrive to the Age of [21] and that he learn them the Art of a Cord Wainer." Book A, p. 493.

September 10, 1761 - A suit brought by Churchwardens against Catharine Stewart, spinster, probably for morals charges, is "Dismissed (the Fine being paid)." Book A, p. 508.

September 10, 1761 - Mary Winsor, on an Information brought by the Churchwardens of Cameron Parish for having a base born child, is fined 50 shillings or 500 lbs. of tobacco, and 82 lbs. of tobacco and 15 shillings or 150 lbs. of tobacco for costs, all "for the use of the said Parish." Book A, p. 521.

November 11, 1761 - Mary McNab, base born child age 2 "the 13th of this instant November [1761]," is bound out to John Carr. Book A, p. 532.

February 9, 1762 - John Proctor, who is a Mulatto base born child [apparently son of Mary Proctor], is bound to Thomas Kelly. Book A, p. 554.

March 11, 1762 - Charles Tyler and Francis Peyton, as Churchwardens, bring Informations against Ann Griffin and Elizabeth Black each "for having a Base born Child." Book A, pp. 572 and 608.

May 14, 1762 - Ann Hays is fined 500 lbs. of tobacco and cask or 50 shillings for the use of the Parish, for not answering the complaint on her base born child, originally brought by the Churchwardens in 1758. Book A, p. 615.

June 9, 1762 - Penegrin Allan, "a Base born child of eight years old," is bound out to Craven Peyton, "who is to learn him the Trade of a House Carpenter." Book A, p. 630.

June 11, 1762 - Ann Griffin "the Deft. not appearing ... [is fined 500 lbs.] of Tobacco and Cask or [50] shillings Current Money ... and costs" for the use of the poor of the Parish, based on the complaint of her having base born child. Book A, p. 653.

July 15, 1762 - Mary Winsor did not answer the summons of the Churchwardens of Cameron Parish when charged with having a base born child, and there is judgment against her, for 500 lbs. of tobacco with cask, or 50 shillings. Book B, p. 17.

July 15, 1762 - The Churchwardens of Cameron Parish bring Informations against Sarah Owsley, Ruth Harle and Jemima Harle, for "having Base born Children." Book B, pp. 25-26.

August 10, 1762 - Mary Jackson, a Base Born child, is bound out to Abel Janney; and, Tobias Allan, base born child, is bound to Thomas Middleton Junr., "who is to learn him the Trade of a Cordwainer." Book B, p. 29.

August 12, 1762 - Elizabeth Black did not answer the summons of the Cameron Parish Churchwardens when charged with having a base born child. There is judgment entered against her for 500 lbs. of tobacco with cask or 50 shillings. Book B, p. 37.

August 12, 1762 - "Josiah Miles ... on the Oath of Lydia Dodd ... [charged with] begetting her with Child (since born) ... with Craven Peyton his Security ... acknowledged themselves Indebted ... Upon condition ... Josiah shall keep the ... Parish from all costs charges and Troubles ... by reason of the Birth Maintenence [sic] and bringing up the said Child." Book B, p. 48.

September 16, 1762 - Cameron Parish Churchwardens renew their summons on Barbary Remey for having a base born child early in 1758. Book B, p. 67; and see infra, p. 492.

September 16, 1762 - Rachel Hall is summoned to answer for the Information of the Cameron Parish Churchwardens, "for having a Base born Child." Book B, p. 68.

December 14, 1762 - "Christian Woodside a servant belonging [sic] to Minor Winn was brought before the Court by her said Master for having a Base born Child ... Christian being sworn declared that Withers Smith is the father," and judgment is entered against her for 500 lbs. of tobacco with cask or 50 shillings, to be paid to the Churchwardens of Cameron Parish for use of the poor of the parish. Book B, p. 77.

June 17, 1763 - Sarah Owsley did not answer the summons of the Churchwardens of Cameron Parish when charged with having a base born child, and there is judgment against her for 500 lbs. of tobacco with cask or 50 shillings. Book B, p. 37.

August 11, 1763 - An Information of the Churchwardens of Cameron Parish against Elizabeth Grantham, originally brought in June of 1760, is deemed "not good and sufficient in Law for the Plts. to have & maintain their Action," and the morals charges against Grantham are dismissed. Book B, p. 212.

August 11, 1763 - On hearing an Information of the Churchwardens of Cameron Parish against Mary Martin, first brought in 1761, the Court rules: the "Declaration and the matters therein contained are not sufficient in Law ... the Plts. take nothing by their Bill but for their false Clamour [sic] [Martin recovers] her Costs by her about her defence in this behalf expended." Book B, p. 213.

August 12, 1763 - The complaint of the Churchwardens against Rachel Hall is "Discontinued the plaintiffs not further Prosecuting." Book B, p. 215.

August 12, 1763 - A complaint of the Churchwardens against Sarah Pritchard is "Discontinued the plaintiffs not further Prosecuting." Book B, p. 222.

February 15, 1764 - James Carr Barrot, "a base born Child of seven Years old," is bound to John Goddard to learn "the Trade of a Joiner -- James Lane Gent. to whom [he] was formerly bound relinquished in Court his right in favor of the said Goddard." Book B, p. 275.

March 15, 1764 - The judgment and fines originally entered against Mary Windsor in 1761, for having a base born child, are confirmed: first another 64 lbs. of tobacco and costs; a second time with an additional 72 lbs. of tobacco, 15 shillings and costs, "for the use of Cameron Parish." Book B, pp. 290-291.

March 15, 1764 - The judgment and fines originally entered against Ann Hays in 1762 for having a base born child are confirmed, with costs, "for the use of the Parish." Book B, p. 291.

April 11, 1764 - In a case arising from a Grand Jury presentment first brought in May of 1758, Barbary Remey, "not appearing tho' again solemnly called," is fined 500 lbs. of tobacco and cask or 50 shillings for the use of Cameron Parish, for having a base born child. Book A, p. 98; Book B, p. 327.

November 13, 1764 - The Grand Jury presents charges against "Elizabeth Finican for having a Base born Child within two months last past." Book B, p. 493.

November 13, 1764 - "Tobias Allan (who was formerly bound to Thomas Middleton Junr. who is since runaway) [is to be bound] to Moses Botts ... who is to learn him the Trade of a Cooper." Book B, p. 495.

December 12, 1764 - Based on the Complaint of the Churchwardens against Sarah Fletcher for having a base born child, she is fined 50 Shillings or 500 lbs. of tobacco for the use of the Parish. "Sarah Fletcher refusing to pay the fine ... Ordered that she receive on her bare Back twenty five Lashes well laid on at the common whipping Post." Book B, p. 517.

April 11, 1765 - "Ordered that Moses Botts Deliver up to Thomas Middleton [Junr.] Tobias Allan who was Ordered to be Bound to [Botts] on a Suspicion that the said Thomas Middleton his former Master was gone away and that the said Thomas hold him by his former Indenture." Book B, p. 569.

May 13, 1765 - "Thomas Martin a Base born Child [probably the son of Mary Martin] of eight Years old the 25th day of December last past [is bound out] to Ralph Martin according to Law who is to learn him the Trade of a Weaver." Book B, p. 571; and see infra, February 12, 1761 entries.

May 13, 1765 - The Court again orders "that Moses Botts Deliver up, to Thomas Middleton, Tobias Allan ... the said Thomas [to] hold him by his former Indenture." Book B, p. 572.

August 12, 1765 - William Douglass, a base born child age 15 "March last past [of 1765]," is ordered to be bound to John Trammell, a cooper. Book C, p. 5.

September 10, 1765 - Hezekiah Butler Windsor, a base Born child "nine years old the Seventh of July last" is bound to Benjamin Shreive, as a carpenter apprentice. Book C, p. 36.

May 12, 1766 - Jane Melven, a base born Mulatto age 2 "the 19th of next November" bound to Fielding Turner, Gent. Book C, p. 83.

August 11, 1766 - Mary Brawner, a base born Mulatto, bound to Robert Watson. Book C, p. 148.

The responsibilities of the office of coroner in colonial Virginia were somewhat different than what the modern reader might imagine. As expected, when an official inquiry was appropriate, it was the role of the coroner to undertake the review and make a determination of the cause of an individual's death. What may surprise the reader is the status of the colonial county coroner as a sort of sheriff-in-waiting, empowered to fulfill the responsibilities of the sheriff and entitled to identical payment for those services when rendered. Study of the Loudoun Record reveals that three of the first six Sheriffs, Nicholas Minor, Josias Clapham, and Charles Tyler, each served as the Loudoun County coroner prior to their appointment to the office of Sheriff. [see supra, the Chapter on The Gaol and the Sheriffs].

The first county coroners of record in the Virginia colony were simply described in 1674 and 1676 as the "next justice of the peace [listed after the Sheriff] ..." in a given county commission. In October of 1677, the Virginia Assembly established the fee for a coroner's inquest at 13 shillings, 4 pence, or the equivalent of 133 lbs. of tobacco. Early in the 1700's the Assembly extended the applicability of the fee schedule for Sheriff's services, to apply when those services were performed by the county coroners. The fee schedule for county officers, enacted in February of 1745, was still in force during the first decade of Loudoun County, from 1757 to 1766, and specified:

"... *To the Coroner.* *[lb. tobacco]*
For taking an inquisition on a dead body;
to be paid out of the deceased's estate,
if the same be sufficient, if not by the county, *133*
... *For all other business, done by him, the same fees*
as are allowed the Sheriff for the same services."
[Hening, II/325, II/355, IV/73, IV/503 and V/340].

Coroners in Loudoun County were only paid 107 lbs. of tobacco for performing an inquest, however, since the Assembly abated 20% of all officers fees in Loudoun when the county was established in 1757. In October of 1765, the Assembly instituted penal liability similar to that of the county sheriffs for a coroner's "neglect or breach of duty when employed in the execution of civil process to him directed." [Hening, VII/149 and VIII/119-120; and see infra, The Record, pp. 504, 506, and 511].

The British law of inheritance, including primogeniture, was in force throughout the Virginia colony and in Loudoun County from 1757 to 1766. Under primogeniture, in the case of intestacy, the eldest surviving son of a deceased was exclusively entitled to inherit the lands of his ancestor. Unless a will provided otherwise, the widow was only entitled to a "dower" estate - a lifetime interest in one-third of the real property (interests in land) of her husband. The widow of anyone dying intestate was entitled to live in the mansion house, without rent, until her dower interest was assigned. This provision in the law may have been the cause for several Loudoun County heirs at law to petition for and obtain a recordation of the dower interests of their mothers. [Hening, V/448; and see infra, The Record, pp. 505, 507 and 511].

The Virginia Assembly, in 1748, recodified the laws of inheritance and the rules and procedures applicable to all wills and estates probated in the Virginia colony. The probate laws and court procedures adopted and reenacted in 1748, which went into effect in 1751, remained in force, without further amendment, until after the onset of the American Revolution. Perhaps not surprisingly, the colonial laws of probate and inheritance bear a strong resemblance to the probate law of Virginia in use today, near the close of the Twentieth century. Many of the terms remain unchanged: a "testator" is the author of a Will; an "intestate" is any individual who dies without leaving a valid Will; a "codicil" is a document changing the terms of a will; an "Executor" is the individual named in a Will to settle an estate; and an "Administrator" is an individual appointed by the county court to act in cases of intestacy or where no Executor qualifies. Each county court was given:

> *"jurisdiction and authority to hear and determine all causes, matters, suits and controversies testamentary ... examine and take the proof of wills ... hear and determine the right of administration of the estates of persons dying intestate, and to grant certificates thereof."* [Hening, V/454-467].

In Virginia, a "holographic" will, "wholly writ [written] by the said devisors own hand," was and still is legally binding.

Otherwise, devises and bequests were required to "be in writing, and signed by the party devising the same, or by some other person in his presence, and by his express direction," and attested by two or more credible witnesses. "Nuncupative" [ie., "verbal"] wills were allowed if proven by the oaths of two or more witnesses who had been present at the making of the will, and made during the last illness of the deceased at his residence or when the last illness was a "surprise." Courts were required to wait two weeks before issuing administration based on a verbal will, and unless a nuncupative will was reduced to writing within six days "after the making," testimony to prove the will would only be allowed in court within six months of the death. A written will could be revoked either with a formal, witnessed, written statement or by being intentionally "burnt, cancelled, torn or obliterated" by the testator. Verbal codicils were allowed only when reduced to writing in the presence of the terminally ill testator and proven by two witnesses then in attendance. Regardless, soldiers and seamen were able to "dispose of ... moveables, wages and personal estate" as allowed by the traditions of their service. [Hening, V/456-457].

With regard to the probate of wills, the Act of 1748 provided that:

> *"... if any person having a mansion house or other place of known residence and abode ... shall depart this life and dispose of his or her estate ... by will ... such will shall be proved in the court of the county"*

where the decedent lived, or in any county where the testator died or owned lands if he or she was not a Virginia resident. If an Executor refused to serve, or refused to give a bond when required, the county court had authority to appoint an Administrator. The estate of an intestate was to be administered in the county court where the decedent had resided, or, if he was not a Virginia resident, where he died. When a will was presented to a county court, the proof offered by witnesses could be taken immediately and the court was instructed to then appoint at least three appraisers. Court appointed appraisers of estates were entitled to compensation of 30 lbs. of tobacco for every day that they served. Where no Executor had qualified or a decedent was intestate, the priorities established for the administration of the estate were nearly identical to those in modern-day Virginia: first, the spouse; second, the children; third, the parents; fourth, siblings; fifth, "the next of kindred to the deceased"; and last, over 30 days after the death, "any creditor ... suing for the same." The county court was required "to proceed immediately to grant certificate for ... administration," or replace any administrator, when circumstances threatened the waste or embezzlement of an estate. Executors and administrators were allowed "all reasonable charges and disbursements" in their accounts "for selling any estate and receiving the money upon such sale ... and also for collecting and receiving the outstanding debts of their testator or intestate; and no other allowance whatsoever." [Hening, V/454-458, V/461-462 and V/466].

Every Executor and Administrator was required to "give bond, in a sufficient sum, proportionable to the full value of the estate ... with such sufficient security of persons residing in the same ... county." Executors gave the following oath:

> *"'I' swear that this writing contains the true last will of the within named A.B., deceased, as far as I know or believe, and that I will well and truly perform the same, by paying, first, his debts, and then the legacies, contained in the said will, as far as his goods, chattels, and credits, will thereunto extend, and the law charge me, and that I will make a true and perfect inventory of all the said goods, chattels, and credits. So help me God."*

Administrators gave the following oath:

> *"'I' swear that A.B. deceased, died without any will, as far as I know or believe, and I will well and truly administer all and singular the goods, chattels, and credits of the said deceased, and pay his debts, as far as his goods, chattels and credits will thereunto extend, and the law require[s] ... and that [I] will make a true and perfect inventory of all the said goods, chattels, and credits, as also a just account when thereunto required. So help me God."*

[Hening, V/459].

Bonds of executors and administrators commanded that inventories and accountings be presented to the county courts, that legacies were to be paid and delivered, and in the event of intestacy, that the administrator "pay unto such person ... as the said justices [of the county court] by their order or judgment shall direct." Bonds given for faithful and proper administration were subject to prosecution by injured parties up to the whole sum of the penalty amount. When any of the securities on a bond were suspected of insolvency, the county court had equity jurisdiction, "to make such order and decree ... as to them shall seem just and equitable, for relief and indemnifying [any] petitioner, by counter security or otherwise." Any testator had the power to direct, by will, that no bond or security would be required of his executor, or that the estate be preserved in specie, or that no appraisal of the estate be required by a court. [Hening, V/459-461 and V/464].

When a testator, by will, devised away any part of lands that otherwise would have gone to an heir at law, the heir had special standing to contest the validity of the will. Notice to heirs at law was to be served in person, or when the heir was unknown, notice was posted on the courthouse door and at every church in the parish. Disinherited heirs who were legally "infant," mentally incompetent, out of the colony temporarily, in prison, or "feme covert" were allowed ten years after the removal of their disability within which to contest the proof of any such will. [Hening, V/455; infra, The Record, at p. 505, 507; see Glossary].

The probate law of 1748 instructed all executors and administrators to dispose of estate goods that "may be liable to perish, consume, or be the worse for using or keeping ... by public sale or auction," so long as the goods were not part of a specific legacy. Special classes of property were recognized and treated differently under the law. Slaves, treated as a special form of real property, could only be sold by an executor or administrator if the Will specifically directed or if necessary for the payment and satisfaction of debts of the estate. When the death of the master occurred between March 1st and Christmas day, slaves and servants were to "be continued and employed upon the plantation ... for making and finishing a crop of tobacco, corn, or other grain," and only after Christmas day, "delivered up to the ... parties having legal right to demand the same." Servants and slaves over age 10 were to "be delivered, well cloathed, at the charge of such decedent's estate." Where an intestate left property sufficient to satisfy his debts without the sale of either slaves or cattle, and the heir at law was an "infant," the guardian or administrator was directed by law to maintain the "neat cattle ... with their increase," on the plantation of the heir until the orphan came of age.

Another law enacted in 1748 provided that there should be no distribution of the goods of intestates for nine months after death, to allow creditors an opportunity to present their claims. [Hening, V/448 and V/463-465].

Twice each year, in April and again in October, the clerk of each county court in Virginia was obligated to provide the Secretary of the Virginia colony with lists of all probates and administrations granted in their respective county court. When any testator or intestate left an estate valued in excess of £100, the general court in Williamsburg had jurisdiction, concurrently with the county courts, over probate of the estate. This may explain the absence of estate proceedings in the Loudoun County Court for some of the county's larger landowners. [Hening, V/466].

The Record in this chapter will assist the reader in resolving, either directly or by inference, a wide assortment of questions of concern in the study of family histories. The Record includes references to the deaths of individuals involved in litigation, often in the form of dismissal of the case as "abated" [ie., legally void]. The reader may find these references relevant for fixing the date of death of an individual who was a non-resident, or who left neither a Last Will nor an estate large enough to warrant the formality of an administration. Accordingly, the first such reference for each individual is included in the record. The Record also includes references to Executors and Administrators of estates from outside of Loudoun County who were parties of record in Loudoun litigation, so care should be taken when making assumptions regarding the residency of individuals and decedents based merely on the existence of an entry in the Record.

One of the oldest surviving legible tombstones in Loudoun County marks the grave of John Herryford, a Leesburg ordinary keeper and a town notable both during the 1757-1766 decade and afterwards in the American Revolution. Among other commercial activities, for a number of years Mr. Herryford supplied the county courthouse with candles, firewood and water. [see supra, Chapter on the Courthouse]. His tombstone, rendered above, can be found in the northeast corner of the Old Methodist Church graveyard in Leesburg. *Artwork courtesy of Caroline Phelps Phillips.*

August 9, 1757 - Richard Self and his wife Ann Self are Executors of George Plummer, deceased. Book A, p. 6.

August 9, 1757 - Adam Davis and his wife Catherine Davis are Executors of William Thomas, deceased. Book A, p. 6.

September 13, 1757 - Abraham Adams is granted Letters of Administration for the Estate of Elizabeth Adams, deceased. Book A, p. 16.

September 14, 1757 - Cases brought by Richard Moxley abate on his death; and, Ann Neale is Administratrix of the Estate of Christopher Neale, deceased. Book A, p. 21.

October 12, 1757 - Joshua Hickman is Executor of Joshua Hickman, deceased; Jane Hall is the widow of John Hall; Thomas Awbrey is Administrator of William Hale, deceased; and, Josias Clapham Administrator of Josias Clapham, deceased. Book A, pp. 30 and 33.

November 8, 1757 - Benjamin Burson and Sarah Burson, Quakers, prove the Will of Evan Thomas. Book A, p. 41.

November 9, 1757 - John Poultney is the Executor of Thomas Davis, deceased. Book A, p. 45.

December 13, 1757 - In itemizing the County Levy, a debit is listed for "Nicholas Minor Gent. as Coroner for taking an Inquisition ... 107 [lbs. tobacco, and] ... for Summoning a Jury [of inquest] ... 40 [lb.t.]." Book A, p. 55.

March 15, 1758 - Cases involving both Benjamin Grayson, and John Gibson the husband of Elizabeth Gibson, abate upon their respective deaths. Book A, pp. 69 and 77.

March 14, 1759 - William Hall is the Executor of the Estate of Moses Pimit, deceased. Book A, p. 214.

April 11, 1758 - Margaret Davis is named Administratrix of the Estate of Thomas Davis [Senr.], deceased. Book A, p. 89.

April 12, 1758 - An action brought by Sarah Colclough against Robert Colclough, abates on Robert's death. Order Book A, p. 94. [Also see supra, Chapter on Crimes and Punishment and Chapter on Familial Relations; and see infra, The Record herein, p. 507].

April 12, 1758 - Rose Bronaugh is one of the Administrators of the Estate of Jeremiah Bronaugh, Gent. (a former Fairfax County Justice of the Peace), deceased. Book A, p. 96.

May 9, 1758 - Elizabeth Davis is the widow of Thomas Davis [Junr.]. Book A, p. 103.

June 14, 1758 - "William West, Richard Coleman, Josias Clapham and James Lane Junr. Gent. are by the Court recommended to the Honble. [Governor] Francis Fauquier Esqr. as proper Persons to execute the Office of Coroner for this County." Book A, p. 120.

August 8, 1758 - Mary Bruster, the widow, [aka Mary Brewster] qualifies as the Administratrix of the Estate of Thomas Bruester, dec'd. Book A, p. 136; and, LDTX/1, pp. 2 and 6.

August 9, 1758 - William Williamson and his wife Jane Williamson, the Administratrix of John Hall, deceased, sue Cornelius Vaughan on a "Note of Hand." Book A, p. 138.

September 12, 1758 - Elizabeth Davis is granted Administration of the Estate of Thomas Davis Junr., deceased. Book A, p. 162.

September 13, 1758 - Sarah Raughton is Executrix of Hezekiah Raughton, dec'd.; and, Sampson Turley and Jane Turley are Executors of John Turley, dec'd. Book A, pp. 164 and 165.

October 11, 1758 - Benjamin Mason is Executor of the Estate of George Mason, [of Stafford], deceased. Book A, p. 173.

November 14, 1758 - In the itemization of the County Levy, a debit is listed for "Nicholas Minor Gent. for taking 2 Coroners Inquests ... 213 [lbs. tobacco]." Book A, p. 176.

December 12, 1758 - Josias Clapham receives his Commission and takes the required Oaths "to be Coroner of this County." Book A, p. 189.

February 13, 1759 - Susanna Ratcliff is granted Letters of Administration for the Estate of John Ratcliff, deceased. Book A, p. 191.

March 14, 1759 - William Shreive [Junr.], Heir at Law of William Shreive, dec'd., motions to have the dower interests of widow Freelove Shreive apportioned. Book A, pp. 217 and 234.

April 10, 1759 - Eleanor Poultney obtains probate of the Will of John Poultney, deceased. Book A, p. 230. See also, LDCOWIL, Book A, pp. 12-14, and, LDCODB, Book A, pp. 320.

May 8, 1759 - The Will of Sarah Davis, deceased, is exhibited "by Thomas Pritchard and Rachel Pritchard his Wife, late [formerly] Rachel Davis." Book A, p. 234.

May 9, 1759 - John King is Executor of Richard Osborn, deceased. Book A, p. 240.

May 9, 1759 - Sarah Lewis is the widow of Thomas Lewis, deceased. Book A, p. 242.

May 9, 1759 - John Davis and his [new] wife Margaret Davis, late ... Administratrix of Thomas Davis the Elder, deceased, sue Elizabeth Davis, Administratrix of Thomas Davis the Younger, deceased. Book A, p. 242.

May 9, 1759 - John Trammell [Junr.] and Sampson Trammell are Executors and Legatees of John Trammell, deceased, "late of Fairfax County." Book A, p. 242.

June 12, 1759 - Charges against John Johnson abate on his death. Book A, p. 246.

August 14, 1759 - Esther Linton is granted Administration of the Estate of Edmund Linton. Book A, p. 265.

September 13, 1759 - James Layton is the Administrator of the Estate of William Layton, deceased. Book A, p. 294.

November 13, 1759 - The Will of Isaac Hollingsworth is proved, and Rachel Hollingsworth qualifies as Executrix of the Estate. Book A, p. 301.

November 14, 1759 - In itemizing the County Levy, a debit is listed for "Josias Clapham, Gent. for taking a Coroners Inquest on Henry Owen ... 147 [lbs. tobacco]." This appears to include fees for summoning a jury of inquest. Book A, p. 302.

March 11, 1760 - Margaret Jenkins, the widow, qualifies as the Administratrix of the Estate of Samuel Jenkins [Senr.], with Richard Coleman and Thomas Jenkins as her Securities. Thomas Jenkins, Samuel Jenkins Junr. and a John Jenkins are three surviving sons. Book A, p. 326; LDTX/1, pp. 2 and 7.

May 14, 1760 - Charles Carter, Esqr., is Executor of the Will and Estate of Henry Fitzhugh, deceased. Book A, p. 348.

June 11, 1760 - "A Deed Poll ... from Nicholas Minor Gent. ... to Nicholas Minor [the 2nd, his nephew] (if living), Elizabeth Minor, John Minor, Penelope Minor, Daniel Minor, Ann Minor and George Minor, Children of [his brother] John Minor, deceased ... is ... Recorded." Book A, p. 366.

June 12, 1760 - Cornelius Donohue and his wife Margaret Donohue, John Sinkler and his wife Sarah Sinkler, and Isaac Fouch and his wife Mary Fouch bring a Complaint in Chancery against Jane McDowell and Ann McDowell, Executors of the Will of Mary Jennings, deceased. Book A, p. 371.

July 17, 1760 - A warrant for the arrest of Sampson Turley, in the case brought by Samuel Moxley as the Administrator of the Estate of Richard Moxley, deceased, for a judgment debt in amount of £3, 8 shillings and 10 pence, is returned as "not found" by John Minor, Sub-Sheriff. [HDC]

August 11, 1760 - On a Writ of Fifae [attachment] issued from the Loudoun County Court against Ezekiel Jenkins and John Jenkins, Administrators of the Estate of Ezekiel Jenkins, deceased, for a judgment debt owed to Thomas Awbrey as the Administrator of the Estate of Walter English, deceased, the Sheriff of Fairfax County, John Rhodes, notes that "Nothing [was] found to Execute [ie., attach]." [HDC]

August 12, 1760 - Richard Spurr is the Executor of the Will and Estate of his father James Spurr, deceased. The widow is Judah Spurr. Book A, p. 384; and, LDTX/1, pp. 2 and 7.

August 13, 1760 - A case against Rodolphus Ellinger abates on his death. Book A, p. 387.

November 11, 1760 - Mary Smith obtains Administration of the Estate of John Smith, deceased. Book A, p. 403; and see, Clerk's 1764 Fee Book, p. 12.

February 11, 1761 - John Craig is Administrator of the Estate of David Craig, deceased. Book A, p. 426.

March 11, 1761 - Jane Ashton qualifies as the Administratrix of the Estate of Henry Ashton. Book A, p. 430.

March 11, 1761 - Elizabeth Hudson's case abates on her death. Book A, p. 432.

March 12, 1761 - Samuel Moxley obtains Administration in Loudoun County of the Estate of "Richard Moxley, late of Fairfax County, deceased." Book A, p. 441.

June 9, 1761 - Mary Inste [sic], the widow, qualifies as Executrix of the Will and Estate of Henry Inste [sic], deceased. Book A, p. 450.

June 9, 1761 - William Adams qualifies as Executor of the Will and Estate of Gabriel Adams, deceased; and, Mary MeGeach qualifies as the Executrix of the Will and Estate of Joseph MeGeach, deceased. Book A, p. 451.

June 10, 1761 - William Colclough is granted Letters of Administration for the Estate of Robert Colclough, deceased. Book A, p. 460.

July 14, 1761 - Elizabeth Awbrey is the widow of Henry Awbrey, deceased. Book A, p. 478; LDCODB, Book B, p. 203.

August 12, 1761 - "Thomas Hale [the eldest] son and Heir at Law of William Hale, deceased, late of Virginia," is summoned to contest the will of his father. Book A, p. 486.

August 12, 1761 - Franklin Perry takes judgment against the Estate of Samuel Jenkins, Margaret Jenkins, Admrx., on an account for 800 lbs. of tobacco. Book A, pp. 461 and 488.

September 10, 1761 - A case against Henry Ansley abates upon his death. Book A, p. 515.

September 10, 1761 - A case abates on the death of "Zachariah Ward of Frederick County, carpenter." Book A, p. 519.

November of 1761 - Mary Sherridine is identified as a widow on the tithable list of by William West, but her deceased husband is undetermined. [sic-Mary Sheridan ?] LDTX/1, p. 14.

November 10, 1761 - Alice Yates and Israel Thompson qualify as Executors of the Will and Estate of Joseph Yates, deceased. Book A, p. 529.

March 9, 1762 - Sarah George is granted Letters of Administration for the Estate of Travers George, deceased. Book A, p. 561.

May 14, 1762 - A case brought by Joseph Yeates abates on his death. Book A, p. 616.

May 14, 1762 - A case brought by Gerard Alexander, Gent., abates on his death. Book A, p. 620.

June 11, 1762 - A case against William Berkley abates on his death. Book A, p. 652.

June 11, 1762 - Sarah Hicks qualifies as Executrix of the Will and Estate of William Hicks, Esqr.. Book A, p. 654.

July 13, 1762 - Eleanor Holyfield, the wife of Valentine Holyfield, dec'd., relinquished her right of Administration in favor of James Lane, Gent.. Book B, p. 3.

July 14, 1762 - Nicholas Minor, Charles Tyler and Philip Noland are recommended to the Governor for appointment as the County Coroners. Book B, p. 11.

August 13, 1762 - Thomas Stump, as Executor of the Estate of Robert Booth, deceased, appears at Court to defend a case brought by William Murphey.

Book B, p. 48.

September 15, 1762 - Mary Patterson, the widow of Samuel Patterson, deceased, relinquishes her Right of Administration in favor of Hezekiah Boone, with Philip Noland and Robert Popkins as his Securities. Book B, p. 56.

September 16, 1762 - A case brought by William Owsley abates on his death. Book B, p. 62.

September 16, 1762 - John Lewis and Elizabeth Lewis his Wife, "late Eliza. Davis," are defendants in the suit brought by Campbell & Co. Merchants. Book B, p. 66.

October 1763 - An accounting of Mary Patterson's estate, who dies shortly after her husband, indicates that she stayed with William Kirk during her last illness, which lasted three weeks. The accounts also show that Kirk hired Ruth Tarton and Jemima Robbins to care for Mary, and that he dispatched a horse and rider to Leesburg to bring a doctor. LDCOWIL, Book A, p. 74.

Wednesday, November 10, 1762 - "Nicholas Minor and Philip Noland, Gent., Produced Commissions from the Honble. the Lieut. Governor appointing them Coroners of this County & thereupon they took and Subscribed the usual Oaths to his Majesty's Person and Government and subscribed the Test and also took the Oath of a Coroner." Book B, p. 72; see, Glossary.

November 10, 1762 - Jane Owsley, the widow of William Owsley, deceased, relinquishes her right of Administration in favor of Thomas Owsley, who pays the Court fees. Book B, p. 75; and, Clerk's Fee Book for 1762.

December 14, 1762 - Jane Stretchberry is granted Letters of Administration for the Estate of Robert Stretchberry, deceased. Book B, p. 77.

April 12, 1763 - Mary West, the widow of William West Junr., qualifies as Administratrix of the estate after William's brother-in-law Craven Peyton and brother Charles West, Executors named in his Will, refuse to qualify. In a deed dated March 24, 1763, William West Junr., in his capacity as an assistant Loudoun surveyor, was still referred to as living. Book B, p. 88; LDCOWIL, Book A, p. 73; and see, LDCODB, Book C, p. 584.

April 13, 1763 - "Thomas Bealy [is the] Surviving Executor &c. of Edward Bealy, deceased." Book B, p. 97.

April 13, 1763 - Catharine Shrieve is qualified as the Executrix of the Will and Estate of William Shrieve, deceased. Book B, p. 104.

April 13, 1763 - Alexander Sinkler is the Heir at Law of Wayman Sinkler, deceased. Book B, p. 105.

May 10, 1763 - Ann Seward qualifies as Executrix of the Will and Estate of Nicholas Seward, deceased. Book B, p. 123.

May, 1763 - Thomas Harrison, James Nesbett, Benjamin Grayson and Spence Grayson are the Executors of the Will and Estate of Benjamin Grayson, deceased. Book B, pp. 140-141.

June 15, 1763 - When an accounting for the estate of John Poultney (who died in 1759) is finally submitted, it gives some indication of the way that estate auctions were conducted: a barrel of liquor is provided for the bidders at one auction, and two quarts of liquor at a second auction, sale of the plantation and mill, and a town lot in Leesburg, are advertised in the Virginia Gazette (published in Williamsburg), and Joseph McGeach and Thomas Gregg were hired for auctioneering duty ("crying") at the sales. LDCOWIL, Book A, pp. 87-88.

August 12, 1763 - Brigar Haney, Thomas Williams Wells and his wife Hester Wells are Executors of the Will and Estate of Wayman Sinclair, deceased. Book B, p. 222.

August 12, 1763 - "The Right Honble. Thomas Lord Fairfax" brings an action "In Case" against Ann Seward, who is apparently the recent widow of Nicholas Seward. Book B, p. 222.

August 12, 1763 - John Dodd and his wife Jane Dodd, and James Abbett and his wife Ann Abbett, are Executors of the Will and Estate of Mary Jenings, deceased. Book B, p. 223.

August 12, 1763 - William Cummyns and his wife Bridget Cummyns, are Executors of the Estate of John Eaton, deceased. Book B, p. 228.

September 13, 1763 - William Remey qualifies as the named Executor of the Will and Estate of Ann Omehundro, deceased. Book B, p. 230.

September 14, 1763 - Charles Tyler produces the "Commission appointing him ... [he takes] the Oath of a Coroner." Book B, p. 238.

September 14, 1763 - The suit of Bogle & Co. vs. John Champe [Senr.] "abates by the Death of the Defendant." Book B, pp. 239-240.

September 15, 1763 - Jacob Hite, John O'Banion and William O'Banion are Executors of the Will and Estate of Bryan O'Banion, deceased. Book B, p. 256.

September 23, 1763 - Andrew Hutchison [Senr.] is referred to as having recently died. LDCODB, Book D, p. 12.

October 11, 1763 - Ann Roberts is the widow of Richard Roberts, deceased. Book B, p. 259.

November 8, 1763 - John Champ [Junr.] and Thomas Champ qualify as the Executors of the Will and Estate of John Champ [Senr.], deceased. Book B, p. 261.

February 14, 1764 - Eleanor Coleman and James Coleman qualify as the Executors of the Will and Estate of Loudoun County Justice of the Peace Richard Coleman, Gent., deceased. Book B, p. 271.

February 14, 1764 - William Jones, Executor of the Estate of Richard Roberts, dec'd., returns an Account of the Administration. Book B, p. 272.

February 15, 1764 - Administration of the Estate of Edward Conner is granted to Robert Conner. Book B, p. 274.

March 14, 1764 - The Last Will and Testament of Samuel Harris deceased, is proved "by Oaths of William West and Ann Peyton late Ann West." Book B, p. 286.

March 15, 1764 - Sarah Lewis, the widow of Thomas Lewis, deceased, brings an action In Chancery against William Douglass and his wife Elizabeth Douglass, "late Elizabeth Lewis," and Thomas Lewis and Sarah Lewis, children and Legatees of Stephen Lewis, deceased. Book B, p. 287.

March 16, 1764 - A suit against John Hurst Junr. abates on his death. Book B, p. 297.

March 16, 1764 - A case brought by Robert Jackson abates on his death. Book B, p. 299.

March 16, 1764 - Elizabeth Snowden, Thomas Snowden, Samuel Snowden and John Snowden are the Executors of the Estate of Richard Snowden, deceased. Book B, p. 310; and see, Clerk's 1764 Fee Book, p. 30.

April 10, 1764 - A case against Thomas Leggett abates on his death. Book B, p. 314.

April 10, 1764 - A suit brought by John Bell "abates by the Death of the Plt. [Plaintiff]." Book B, p. 319.

April 11, 1764 - Elizabeth Keen is granted Letters of Administration for the Estate of Richard Keen, deceased. Book B, p. 335.

May 8, 1764 - Edmond Phillips and Elizabeth Redmond qualify as the Executors of the Will and Estate of Andrew Redmond, deceased. Book B, pp. 354-355.

May 9, 1764 - A case brought by William Baylis abates on his death. Book B, p. 356.

Wednesday, June 13, 1764 - "On the Petition of Israel Thompson and Thomas Arnett Securities for the Administration of the Estate of Andrew Redmond dec'd. It is Ordered that Edmund Phillips and Elizabeth Redmond the Executors deliver up the Estate of the said Decedent to the Petitioner or give them sufficient Counter Security for the same.-" Book B, p. 367.

June 14, 1764 - Francis Piles qualifies as Administrator of the Estate of Josias Piles, deceased. Book B, p. 378.

August 16, 1764 - John McKenny and his wife, Susannah McKenny, "late [formerly] Susanna Ratcliff Administrators of John Ratcliff, deceased." Book B, p. 421.

September 11, 1764 - John Sinclair qualifies as the Executor of the Will and Estate of Margaret Sinclair, deceased. Book B, p. 432; see also, LDCODB, Book D, p. 529.

September 13, 1764 - Henry Ellison is the Executor of the Will and Estate of Sarah Hicks of Whitehaven, deceased. Book B, p. 446.

September 13, 1764 - George William Fairfax, Esqr., and John Carlyle, Esqr., are Executors of Lawrence Washington, dec'd. Book B, p. 447.

October 9, 1764 - Ann Vandiveer, widow, relinquishes her right to Administration for the Estate of her husband George Vandiveer, deceased, to James Lane. Book B, p. 474; Clerk's 1764 Fee Book, p. 70.

October 10, 1764 - Sarah Mortimore, widow, is granted Letters of Administration for the Estate of her husband Arthur Mortimore, dec'd. Book B, p. 488; Clerk's 1764 Fee Book, p. 71.

November 13, 1764 - John Lewis is granted Letters of Administration for the Estate of Vincent Lewis, deceased. Book B, p. 492.

November 13, 1764 - "Ann McCoy, widow and relict of William McCoy Deceased" is granted Administration of the Estate. Book B, p. 494; Clerk's 1764 Fee Book, p. 73.

November 14, 1764 - The "Slaves and Personal Estate of Jacob Smith, Deceased, ... [are allotted to] Jacob Smith [Junr.] the Heir ... [and] Hester Wells Wife of Thomas Williams Wells, [formerly Hester Smith is allotted], her Dower." Book B, p. 496.

March 12, 1765 - Ann Owsley is the widow of John Owsley, deceased; Sarah Lewis is the widow of William Harrison, Gent., deceased. Book B, p. 526; LDCODB, Book D, p. 392.

April 9, 1765 - Ann Davis is Administering the Estate of David Davis, deceased. Book B, p. 547.

April 10, 1765 - "Thomas Beatty, Surviving Executor ... of Edward Beatty, deceased.." is a plaintiff. Book B, p. 553.

April 10, 1765 - A case against Richard Allan "abates ... [upon the] Death of the Deft. [Defendant]." Book B, p. 555.

May 14, 1765 - A case against "John Willcoxon, Farmer of Loudoun County ... abates by [his] Death." Book B, p. 584.

May 16, 1765 - Several cases involving "Arthur Mortimore & Sarah Mortimore his Wife" abate by their death. Book B, pp. 600 and 602.

June 10, 1765 - James Williamson is granted Letters of Administration for the Estate of Benjamin Williamson, deceased. Book B, p. 627.

June 11, 1765 - The Will of "John Willcoxon alias John Winser" is presented at Court for admission to probate. Book B, p. 630.

September 9, 1765 - Mary Alexander, Robert Alexander and Philip Alexander are admitted as the Executors of the Estate of Gerard Alexander, deceased. Book C, p. 34.

September 12, 1765 - Mary Monkhouse, who is now the wife of Jonathan Monkhouse, represents the Estate of her former husband, Henry Ansley, deceased. Book C, p. 53.

September 12, 1765 - A suit against John Baylis abates on his death. Book C, p. 58.

October 15, 1765 - The Will of Charles Megrew, deceased, of Berks County, Pa. is admitted to probate in Loudoun County. Book C, p. 66.

November 11, 1765 - In itemizing the County Levy, a debit: "To ... Charles Tyler, late [former] Coroner, for taking an Inquest on [the body of] John Owsley dec'd. ... 107 [lbs. of tobacco]." Book C, p. 73.

May 12, 1766 - Winifred Ethell qualifies as Executrix of the Estate of John Ethall, deceased [one of the Loudoun Constables]. Book C, p. 76.

May 12, 1766 - The Will of William Dyet [William Dye or William Dyer ?], deceased, is Probated. Book C, p. 77.

May 12, 1766 - Joseph Stephens is appointed Surveyor of the road from Broadrun to Frying Pan, replacing John Hopewell, dec'd.. Book C, p. 77.

June 9, 1766 - Nicholas Grimes [Junr.?] and Philip Grimes are admitted as Executors of the Estate of Nicholas Grimes, dec'd.. Book C, p. 81.

June 9, 1766 - Joshua Gore [Junr.?] qualifies as Administrator of the Estate of Joshua Gore. Book C, p. 82.

June 9, 1766 - Hannah Hopewell qualifies as Executrix of the Estate of John Hopewell, deceased. Book C, p. 84.

June 10, 1766 - A suit brought by John Gladen "abates by the Plt's. [plaintiff's] death." Book C, p. 87.

June 12, 1766 - A law suit against John Athell abates on his death. Book C, p. 113.

June 12, 1766 - A law suit against Robert Conner abates on his death. Book C, p. 114.

June 13, 1766 - A law suit against George Tavener "abates by the death of the Deft. [defendant]." Book C, p. 129.

June 13, 1766 - "Cornelius Donohue and Margaret Donohue his wife, John Sinkler and Sarah Sinkler his wife, and Isaac Fouch and Mary Fouch his wife [sue James Abbitt [sic] and Ann Abbitt his wife and John Dodd and Jane Dodd his wife, Executors of [the Estate of] Mary Jennings." Book C, p. 130.

June 13, 1766 - A suit against David Davis "abates by the Death of the Deft." Book C, p. 131.

August 12, 1766 - Sarah Wigginton qualifies as the Executrix of the Estate of James Wigginton, deceased, with the extensive family holdings in Stafford County ordered to be appraised. Book C, p. 153.

August 14, 1766 - Case involving Micajah Powell and Joseph Stephens abate on their respective deaths. Book C, p. 167.

August 14, 1766 - A case involving Robert Conner abates on his death. Book C, p. 170.

August 14, 1766 - Ann Massey is qualified as the Administratrix of the Estate of Lewis Massey. Book C, p. 177.

September 8, 1766 - John Baker [Junr.?] is granted Letters of Administration of the Estate of John Baker, deceased. Book C, p. 186.

September 9, 1766 - A suit brought against Dr. James Butler Broadbelt abates by his death. Book C, p. 188.

September 9, 1766 - Barbary Berkley is granted Letters of Administration for the Estate of Benjamin Berkley, deceased. Book C, p. 191.

October 13, 1766 - Mary Ellis and Elias Ellis are the Executors of the Estate of Robert Ellis. Book C, p. 206.

October 15, 1766 - A law suit against Patrick McKenzy [sic] abates upon his death. Book C, p. 214.

November 10, 1766 - Hannah Harris is the widow of William Harris, dec'd. Book C, p. 219.

November 13, 1766 - A suit against Philip Peill [aka Philip Peale ?] abates upon his death. Book C, p. 228.

"Non-Residents" of Loudoun County

The Loudoun Court Orders contain different types of references that give us information about colonists who were either non-residents of Loudoun County, or Loudoun residents who were about to leave the Virginia colony. Any party to a case who felt that his witness was "going out of this colony" before trial could obtain a special Dedimus of deposition, directed to several of the Justices of the county courts, whereby the testimony of the witness would be taken out of court and then reported at the time of trial. Since these entries are usually found in the context of an Order authorizing the deposition of a non-party witness in a case, they are seldom or never listed in the Index of the Order Books by the name of the witness; hence the merit of their inclusion here. A large number of entries in the Loudoun Court Orders award costs and fees to witnesses who travel from another county, or in some instances from Maryland, to appear as a witness in the Loudoun County Court. After 1736, every witness was allowed a fee of 25 lbs. of tobacco for each day of attendance. Non-resident witnesses were entitled to claim ferriage charges and a mileage allowance for each mile they travelled to reach the Courthouse. Mileage charges for non-resident witnesses were standardized in Virginia in 1705 (during the reign of Queen Anne), and thereafter a fee of 1½ lbs. of tobacco was awarded for each mile travelled, along with any ferriage charges proven. The County Court was responsible for rating the distance in miles that a non-resident witness travelled from his home to the Loudoun Courthouse at Leesburg; these distances may be of value to the historian or family researcher and for that reason are included in The Record herein. For example an entry in June of 1758, showing that Marylander Rodolphus Ellinger travelled only 4 miles to appear as a witness at the Loudoun Court, gives us the first evidence that Loudoun County Court sessions were held at a site near Leesburg at that time. [Hening, III/299, IV/523, V/480 and V/505; infra, The Record, p. 515, and generally, pp. 514-521; supra, Chapter on the Courthouse; for more information regarding witness fees see supra, Chapter on the Sheriffs].

Occasionally, incidental references appear in the court Orders giving the occupation, and/or the county or colony of origin of a non-resident who was involved in litigation in the Loudoun County Court. The reader will also note the inclusion of rare information regarding non-residents of Loudoun County that was obtained from the Loudoun County Deed Books and various issues of the *Virginia Gazette*, presented in The Loudoun Record herein in an effort to enhance the amount of general background information available to the reader.

The Loudoun Record

1757 to 1766 - Gersham Keys, the owner of a ferry on the Shenandoah River below Keys' (later known as Vestal's) Gap, is a Justice of the Peace and member of the County Court in Frederick County, Virginia. Council, V/391.

July 19, 1757 - Peter Rust, Gent., is from Westmoreland County. LDCODB, Book A, p. 3.

August of 1757 - George Beall [a proprietor of the Maryland port of Georgetown] is identified as a storekeeper at Rock Creek on the Potomac River, near the port town that he had helped found. GW Papers, IV, pp. 324-325.

August 9, 1757 - John Hopkins is a witness "coming thirty six [36] miles from Fairfax County and returning." Book A, p. 6.

September 14, 1757 - Alexander Southerland is "of Fairfax County, Planter." Book A, p. 18.

September 14, 1757 - James Leith is "of Frederick County" Virginia. Book A, p. 21.

September 14, 1757 - One Thomas Davis is "of Fairfax County." Book A, p. 22.

September 14, 1757 - "John Davis of Frederick County [Virginia] Farmer." He apparently settles near the Broad Run church and is prosecuted for retailing liquor without a license in 1759. Book A, pp. 50 and 300.

September 14, 1757 - "Thomas Awbrey, otherwise called Thomas Avery, of Fairfax County, Farmer." Book A, p. 51.

October 11, 1757 - Samuel Smith is "of Fairfax County, Planter." Book A, p. 26.

October 11, 1757 - John Stephens is a witness "coming Forty [40] miles from Fairfax County" to attend the Loudoun County Court. Book A, p. 29.

October 11, 1757 - Thomas Gore is living in Frederick County, Maryland. LDCODB, Book A, p. 18.

October 12, 1757 - William Harbin is known to be "living in Fairfax County." Book A, p. 30.

October 12, 1757 - Thomas Sorrell and John West Junr. are both referred to as "of Fairfax County." Book A, p. 34.

November 9, 1757 - A case brought by "The ... Churchwardens of Cameron Parish against Ann Nelson is discontinued the Deft. [defendant] being an Inhabitant of Fairfax County." Book A, pp. 37 and 47.

November 9, 1757 - William Hicks, Esqr., a merchant in Whitehaven [Great Britain] sues "Samuel Jenkins of Fairfax County, Planter" Book A, p. 51.

December 13, 1757 - David Zwilling "of the Borough of Lancaster in the County of Lancaster ... in Pennsylvania, Doctor" is named defendant at the Loudoun County Court. Book A, p. 56.

December 14, 1757 - Howsing Hoor travelled "thirty [30] miles from Prince William County" to attend the Loudoun County Court. Book A, p. 60.

February 13, 1758 - A Writ of "Fifae" [an attachment] issued by the Loudoun Court against Stephen Lee, for a judgment debt of £2, 8 shillings, 10 pence and a half penny owed to George Shelton, is returned by John Washington, the Sheriff of Stafford County, Virginia, with the note that he "[has] the sums within mentioned redy [sic] to Render as this Writ requires." [HDC]

February 31, 1758 - On a "Casa" [warrant] issued by the Loudoun County Court for the arrest of Isaac Murphey, for a judgment debt owed to George Shelton, the Sheriff of Stafford County, Virginia, John Washington, notes on his return that "the within Isaac Murphey so conscales [sic - conceals] himselfe ty [thusly] I can't execute this writ as I am within commanded." [HDC]

March 15, 1758 - William Perkins is "of Frederick County Virginia, Planter." Book A, p. 68.

March 15, 1758 - Thomas William Wells is known to be a resident "of Fairfax County." Book A, p. 70.

March 15, 1758 - A Commission "de bene esse" is issued for the examination of John Robinson, a witness who is "going to depart this Colony." Book A, p. 71; and, see "de bene esse" in Glossary, infra @ p. 540.

April 11, 1758 - Frederick Cryder is from Frederick County, Virginia. Book A, p. 82.

June 14, 1758 - John Owsley and Thomas Field are both "of Fairfax County." Book A, pp. 116-117.

June 14, 1758 - Rodolphus Ellinger, a witness, is "travelling four [4] miles [sic] from Maryland." Book A, p. 120.

June 14, 1758 - William Cocke, a witness, is "travelling forty [40] Miles from Fairfax County," Book A, p. 123.

July 11, 1758 - Notley Williams is identified as "of Fairfax County, Planter." Book A, p. 130.

August 9, 1758 - Peter Wagener, witness, travelled "forty four [44] Miles from Fairfax" (where he is Clerk of the County Court); Edward Washington is noted as a witness who travelled "thirty six [36] Miles from Fairfax [County]"; and, James Goulding is noted as being from Fairfax County. Book A, p. 139.

August 9, 1758 - John Graham is identified as a resident of Prince William County. Book A, p. 141.

October 11, 1758 - Morgan Williams is identified as "an Inhabitant of Prince William County." Book A, p. 170.

October 11, 1758 - "Robert Mundell of Frederick County, Merchant" is a plaintiff in the Loudoun County Court. Book A, p. 173.

November 15, 1758 - Robert Thomas and William Talbot, witnesses, are "travelling [37 and 35] Miles [respectively] from Fairfax County." Book A, p. 181.

November 15, 1758 - Richard Halbert is identified as a witness "travelling [36] Miles from Fairfax County." Book A, p. 182/1.

March 28, 1759 - In London, John Patterson "of Westminster in County Middlesex" agrees to leave England within six weeks and travel to Virginia to act as the property manager for the Earl of Tankerville. LDCODB, Book C, p. 109.

April 10, 1759 - Cases brought by William Hicks, Esqr., a merchant in Great Britain, abate upon his death. Book A, pp. 232 and 311.

June 11, 1759 - William Mathews is a schoolmaster in Frederick County Maryland. LDCODB, Book A, p. 303.

June 13, 1759 - Benjamin Robinson and Elizabeth Harrison, witnesses, each travelled "fifty five [55] Miles from Stafford County." Book A, pp. 249-250.

June 13, 1759 - John Hopkins is a witness "travelling twenty two [22] Miles from the Providence of Maryland." Book A, p. 252.

June 14, 1759 - Abraham Raw, Benjamin Hambrick, William Beard and David Kinshelow, witnesses, are each noted as having "travelled ... thirty [30] Miles from Prince William County" to Leesburg. Book A, pp. 258-259.

August 15, 1759 - One man named Benjamin Grayson is referred to as "lately ... of [meaning, from] Spotsylvania County." Book A, p. 273.

September 12, 1759 - "Franklin Perry ... [is] living in Fairfax County." Book A, p. 289; and, see entry in The Record for June 12, 1765, infra @ p. 520.

November 16, 1759 - Henry Garrett is identified as "an Inhabitant of Fairfax County." Book A, p. 312.

November 16, 1759 - John Neavill Junr. is identified as a resident "of Prince William County." Book A, p. 312.

February 23, 1760 - Daniel Carroll Junr., is identified as a merchant from "Malbron" [could this be modern Upper Marlboro?], in Prince Georges County, Maryland. LDCODB, Book A, p. 448.

March 12, 1760 - Pierce Bayley, Bennett Hill and Bennett Atchison are witnesses in Leesburg, noted to be "travelling [44, 47 and 43] Miles [respectively] from Fairfax County." Book A, p. 330.

March 14, 1760 - One Joshua Hickman was known to have "lived and died in Maryland." Book A, p. 334.

April 3, 1760 - Col. John Champe is identified as a merchant doing business at Dumfries, in Prince William County, who regularly imports slaves. MdGaz., No. 778, p. 3, col. 1.

April 3, 1760 - Benjamin Grayson [Junr.] is a merchant in business at the port of Colchester in Fairfax County. MdGaz., No. 778, p. 3, col. 2.

May 15, 1760 - John Goram is referred to as "of Fairfax County." Book A, p. 354.

June 11, 1760 - William Winn, a witness, is "travelling seventeen [17]

Miles from Prince William County" to Leesburg. Book A, p. 364.

June 11, 1760 - Thomas Graffort, [aka Thomas Gaffort], is a witness "travelling thirty [30] Miles from Fairfax County." Book A, pp. 365 and 399.

August 8, 1760 - Based on a warrant issued from the Loudoun County Court for the arrest of Samuel Hammond, a judgment debtor, Samuel Williams, a Sub-Sheriff of Richmond County, Virginia, notes on his return to the Loudoun Court that: "By virtue of this writ ... I have taken [arrested] the within named Saml. [Samuel] Hammond ... [and I am] ready to satisfy [the judgment creditor in Loudoun, ie.,] Henry Awbrey, of the debt and damages." [HDC]

August 13, 1760 - William Hickman is identified as a witness "travelling ten [10] Miles from the Province of Maryland." Book A, p. 387.

August 13, 1760 - "John Ballendine [is identified as a resident] of Prince William County [Virginia], Merchant." Book A, p. 394.

August 13, 1760 - "Benjamin Musgrove of Ann Arundell County," is a Maryland defendant at the Loudoun County Court. Book A, p. 395.

August 13, 1760 - "William Artherbury of Prince Georges County, a Sawyer," is a Maryland defendant at Court in Loudoun County. Book A, p. 395.

August 14, 1760 - Zachariah Ward is a resident "of Frederick County [whether Maryland, or Virginia, is not indicated], carpenter." Book A, p. 397.

August 14, 1760 - Ralph Broadax, "of Baltimore County, [Maryland] Planter." Book A, p. 398; and, also in Book B, p. 46.

February 11, 1761 - The Loudoun County Clerk of Court identifies "Charles Morris of Prince William County, Planter." Book A, p. 419.

March 12, 1761 - "Joseph Claypoole of Fairfax County [is identified as a] ... Farmer." Book A, p. 437.

March 12, 1761 - William Murphy is a witness "travelling thirty four [34] Miles from Prince William County" to Leesburg. Book A, p. 448.

June 10, 1761 - Ezekiel Hickman, a witness, is "... travelling thirty [30] Miles from Frederick County." Book A, p. 456.

June 12, 1761 - "John Ross Dewitt [is identified as a resident] of Fairfax County." Book A, pp. 467 and 524.

June 12, 1761 - James Dozer [sic] is a witness "travelling thirty [30] Miles from Fairfax." Book A, p. 489.

September 9, 1761 - John Robinson is a witness "travelling thirty five [35] Miles from Fairfax County." Book A, p. 500.

September 9, 1761 - Benjamin Berkley is a witness "travelling twenty seven [27] Miles from Fairfax County." Book A, p. 500.

September 9, 1761 - George Chelton is a witness "travelling thirty [30] Miles from Prince William County." Book A, p. 501.

September 9, 1761 - Leven Powell and William Speakman, witnesses, are "travelling thirty [30] Miles from Prince William County." Book A, p. 502.

September 10, 1761 - One "William Owsley [is a resident] of Fairfax County." Book A, p. 516.

September 10, 1761 - "Jesper Grant [is identified as a resident] of Prince William County." Book A, p. 517.

September 10, 1761 - Thomas Roden, a witness, is "travelling sixty [60] Miles from Frederick County, Virginia" to Leesburg. Book A, p. 519.

October 12, 1761 - Thomas Clemson and his wife Elizabeth Clemson are living in Lancaster, Pennsylvania. LDCODB, Book C, p. 23.

March 26, 1762 - Harmon Cox, of Orange County, North Carolina, deeds Loudoun lands to William Davis of Fauquier County. Book A, p. 583; and, see LDCODB, Book C, p. 177.

May 13, 1762 - George Hardy is a witness "travelling thirty [30] Miles ... from the Province of Maryland" to Leesburg. Book A, p. 605.

May 13, 1762 - Absolem Remy [sic] is a witness "travelling forty five [45] Miles from Fauquier County." Book A, p. 605.

June 9, 1762 - A Power of Attorney from Jeremiah Warder is certified before Jacob Ducke, Esqr., Mayor of the City of Philadelphia. Book A, p. 632.

July 14, 1762 - George Russell is referred to as a resident "of Fairfax County, Planter." Book B, p. 10.

August 10, 1762 - William Linton is a witness "travelling forty five [45] Miles from Fairfax County." Book B, p. 29.

August 12, 1762 - "William Fielder [is identified as a resident] of Prince William County," Virginia. Book B, p. 36.

August 12, 1762 - "Thomas Sligh [is identified as] of Baltimore County [Maryland] ... merchant." Book B, pp. 46 and 64.

September 15, 1762 - Richard Recksey Senr. and Richard Recksey Junr. [sic], witnesses at Court in Leesburg, twice "travelling thirty nine [39] Miles from Prince William County," and attending the Court for 6 days, were each awarded 384 lbs. of tobacco (valued at 48 shillings) for their witness fees. Book B, p. 57.

September 16, 1762 - Leonard Dozer is a witness "travelling thirty [30] Miles from Fairfax County." Book B, p. 69.

March 21, 1763 - Willoughby Newton, Gent., is a County Justice in Westmoreland County, Virginia. LDCODB, Book C, p. 531.

April 13, 1763 - "William Perry and Daniel Mills [are both identified as residents] of the County of Fairfax, in Virg.a. [sic]." Book B, p. 100.

April 13, 1763 - "John Kent [is identified as a resident] of the County of Fairfax." Book B, pp. 102 and 144.

May 12, 1763 - "James Hunter & Co., [are identified as] Merchants in Great Britain." Book B, pp. 146 and 170.

May 12, 1763 - "Samuel Harris Junr. [is identified as a resident] of Fairfax County." Book B, pp. 149 and 648.

May 12, 1763 - "John Glasford in Glasgow [Scotland] ..." is named as a plaintiff at the Loudoun County Court in Leesburg. Book B, p. 151.

May 12, 1763 - A Bond for Performance of Covenants, from "Thomas, Lord Fairfax, Baron of Cameron in that part of Great Britain called Scotland," (who was already living at Greenway Court), is proven at Court. Book B, p. 153.

June 15, 1763 - William Fitzgerald is identified as a witness "travelling thirty five [35] Miles from Fauquier County." Book B, p. 166.

July 17, 1763 - Henry Gunnell is a identified as a witness "travelling twenty three [23] Miles from Fairfax County" to Leesburg. Book B, p. 193.

August 10, 1763 - Fairfax County Court Justice Marmaduke Beckwith is a witness at the Loudoun County Court for Joseph Pollard, "travelling twenty eight [28] Miles from Fairfax County." Book B, p. 197.

September 15, 1763 - Daniel Thomas, a defendant at the Loudoun County Court, is identified as "an Inhabitant of Fairfax County." Book B, p. 246.

September 15, 1763 - "Peter Smith of Charles County, [Maryland, is identified as a] Taylor." Book B, p. 256.

November 9, 1763 - The Loudoun County annual Levy lists a payment "To ... Anthony Buckner ... [who apparently had appeared in Leesburg as a witness in a criminal case, for] travelling once from Fairfax County thirty [30] Miles and once from Prince William County Forty five [45] Miles as a Witness ... [payment of] 323 [lbs. of tobacco]," or about 40 shillings. Book B, p. 266.

December 13, 1763 - Christopher Lownes is identified as a merchant from Maryland, (probably Frederick County). LDCODB, Book D, p. 705.

January 12, 1764 - John Ballendine, of Prince William County, is identified as an "ironmonger." LDCODB, Book D, p. 268.

March 16, 1764 - Francis Eaton is identified as a witness "travelling thirty five [35] Miles from Fairfax County" to Leesburg; while witnesses Thomas Gaffort, Joseph Moxley and John Hurst were each noted as "travelling thirty [30] Miles from Fairfax County" to the Loudoun County Courthouse. Book B, p. 312.

April 10, 1764 - Samuel Conner is identified as a witness "travelling thirty seven [37] Miles from Fairfax County." Book B, p. 322.

April 11, 1764 - "Samuel Burton of Frederick County, [Virginia, is referred to as a] Planter." Book B, p. 337.

April 11, 1764 - Samuel Mead and Francis Wilks, who seem to have moved, are referred to as "of Fairfax County." Book B, p. 339.

April 11, 1764 - Catesby Cocke, the first Clerk of the Fairfax County Court (from 1742 to 1746, which then included all of modern Loudoun County), is referred to as "now in England." LDCODB, Book D, p. 177.

April 12, 1764 - James Ingoe Dozer [sic] is identified as a witness "travelling thirty four [34] Miles from Prince William County." Book B, p. 340.

May 12, 1764 - John Ariss and his wife Elizabeth Ariss have moved to Fauquier County. LDCODB, Book D, p. 448.

May 29, 1764 - One William West, a Philadelphia cooper (who apparently was unrelated to the prominent West family of the Northern Neck that was already well-established in Loudoun County at the time), purchased acreage on the Northwest fork of Goose Creek. LDCODB, Book D, p. 512.

June 8, 1764 - In one deed, John Semple is identified as a merchant from Charles County, Maryland. LDCODB, Book D, p. 225.

August 16, 1764 - Thomas Palmer is identified as a witness "travelling forty [40] Miles from Fairfax County." Book B, p. 414.

August 16, 1764 - Thomas Wadlington is identified as a witness "travelling twenty seven [27] Miles from Frederick County." Book B, p. 430.

September of 1764 - James Nisbett [sic] is identified as a doctor practicing in Prince William County. Clerk's Fee Book for 1764, p. 67.

October 10, 1764 - A summons for Thomas Eaton goes unserved, with Eaton referred to as "not being an Inhabitant of this County." Book B, p. 477.

October 10, 1764 - Elizabeth Waters is identified as a witness "travelling thirty [30] Miles from Fairfax County ... [and later, apparently after having moved,] travelling fifty [50] Miles from Fauquier County." Book B, p. 491.

November 13, 1764 - A special Power of Attorney from the Earl of Tankerville, under the Seal of "Sir Richard Glyn Knight Lord Mayor" of London, is finally recorded by Leesburg's John Patterson. LDCODB, Book C, p. 108.

November 14, 1764 - "Joseph Coombs [who was a witness in] Evidence for Leven Powell, in the Suit of Josias Myles [sic] ... travelling thirty [30] Miles from Frederick County," Virginia, to Leesburg. Book B, p. 500.

November 15, 1764 - "John Bland [is referred to as a resident] of the City of London, Merchant." Book B, p. 504.

November 15, 1764 - James McCarty is identified as a witness who is "travelling twenty four [24] Miles from Fairfax County." Book B, p. 506.

December 12, 1764 - "John Frederick Whitmire of Frederick [County] in Maryland" is a defendant at the Loudoun County Court. Book B, p. 514.

December 12, 1764 - "Peter Hudson of Charles County [Maryland] ..." is a defendant at the Loudoun County Court. Book B, p. 514.

March 12, 1765 - Peter Wagener, Esqr., the Clerk of the Fairfax County Court, is a witness at the Loudoun County Court referred to as "travelling forty five [45] Miles from [his home near Colchester in] Fairfax County" to Leesburg. Book B, p. 524.

March 13, 1765 - Samuel Marbury is referred to as "being no Inhabitant" of Loudoun County. Book B, p. 529.

March 13, 1765 - James Jenkins is identified as a witness "travelling twenty five [25] Miles from Fairfax County" to Leesburg. Book B, p. 534.

March 14, 1765 - Charles Rigney is identified as a witness "travelling thirty three [33] Miles from Frederick County." Book B, p. 535.

April 8, 1765 - "John Haddox of Culpepper County ... " is a defendant at the Loudoun County Court. Book B, p. 543.

April 9, 1765 - William Buchanan is identified as a witness "travelling twenty two [22] Miles from Prince William County." Book B, p. 547.

May 15, 1765 - Thomas Boydstone is identified as a witness "travelling thirty eight [38] Miles from Frederick County." Book B, p. 592.

June 10, 1765 - John Sasser is a defendant at Court in Leesburg, noted as "being no Inhabitant" of Loudoun County. Book B, p. 622.

June 12, 1765 - "John Johnson of Frederick County ... Maryland" is a defendant at Court. Book B, p. 648.

June 12, 1765 - James Buckley is a witness at the Loudoun County Court, "travelling twenty five [25] Miles from Fairfax County." Book B, p. 650.

June 12, 1765 - Franklin Perry is identified as a witness "travelling twenty five [25] Miles from Fairfax County." Book B, p. 650.

June 13, 1765 - Abednego Adams is identified as a witness "travelling twenty six [26] Miles from Prince William County" to Leesburg. Book B, p. 672.

October 25, 1765 - Francis Moore and William Coppedge are farmers living in Fairfax County. VaGaz./R, Supplement, p. 3.

April 18, 1766 - William Russell is a farmer from, or living in, Frederick County, Virginia. VaGaz./P, p. 4.

June 10, 1766 - Defendants "John Connelley and John James ... [are noted as having] removed out of this County." Book C, p. 89.

June 12, 1766 - "Daniel Stephenson of Bladensburg, [Maryland, is identified as a] Merchant." Book C, p. 122.

August 11, 1766 - A Power of Attorney from Ann Hopkins to Thomas Young is Certified under the Seal of John Dickson Esqr. the Provost of Dumfries, Scotland. Book C, p. 143.

September 5, 1766 - William Carr is identified as a merchant at Dumfries, in Fairfax County. VaGaz./PD, Supplement, p. 2, col. 2.

September 9-10, 1766 - Robert Adam, Gent., a Justice on the Fairfax County Court who identifies himself as a merchant, loans substantial mortgage monies to Loudoun County landowners. LDCODB, Book E, pp. 197 and 238.

September 12, 1766 - John Corneilson and Elizabeth Cashalt, witnesses, are noted as "about to depart this Colony." Book C, p. 204.

September 22, 1766 - In an auction at the Fauquier County Courthouse, Burgess Smith causes 7,750 acres of his lands in Fauquier, "on or near Goose Creek," to be sold. VaGaz./PD, August 22, 1766, p. 3.

October 15, 1766 - " --- Williams," [first name not given], is noted as having left Loudoun County and "removed to Carolina." Book C, p. 212.

October 16, 1766 - Joseph Richardson is referred to as "about to depart the [Virginia] Colony." Book C, p. 217.

November 13, 1766 - James Russell is identified as a farmer living in Fairfax County "near the Potowmack river," between the Rock Creek ferry and Four Mile Run. VaGaz./PD, p. 3, col. 1.

December 4, 1766 - Among "Letters remaining in the Post Office at Alexandria" is one for "Doctor Richard Peile, near Shepherd's in Frederick [County], Virginia." VaGaz./Ri, p. 2, col. 1.

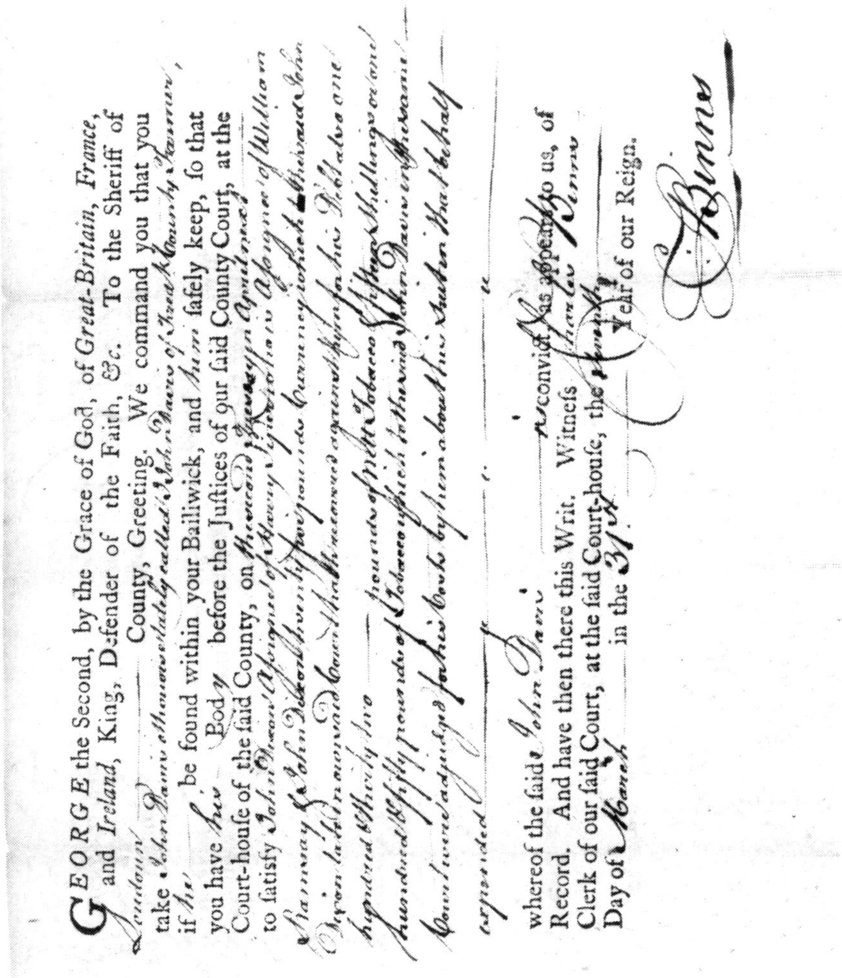

GEORGE the Second, by the Grace of God, of *Great-Britain, France,* and *Ireland,* King, Defender of the Faith, &c. To the Sheriff of Loudoun County, Greeting. We command you that you take John Davis [illegible] if he be found within your Bailiwick, and him safely keep, so that you have his Body before the Justices of our said County Court, at the Court-house of the said County, on [illegible] to satisfy [illegible] whereof the said John Davis is convict, as appears to us, of Record. And have then there this Writ. Witness Charles Binns Clerk of our said Court, at the said Court-house, the [illegible] Day of March in the 31st Year of our Reign.

Binns

The above Warrant, for the arrest of judgment debtor John Davis, a farmer "of" Frederick County, Virginia, was issued March 7th, 1758, and returned "Executed & body in custody. Leven Powell." At the time, Powell was an Under Sheriff of Loudoun. The case, involving a debt of £25 currency, 132 lbs. of "nett Tobacco," and 15 shillings, owed to John Dixon as the assignee of William Ramsay & John Dixon, had been in the Loudoun Court since September of 1757. The return on this document suggests that Davis may have originally been "from" Frederick County, but was living in Loudoun County by 1758.

[HDC; and see infra, The Record herein, p. 514].

Various and Sundry and the Unusual

A number of different types of entries in The Record are presented here. Some of these entries are included because they provide interesting information, some because the individuals involved are noteworthy, and others because the parties are obscure and not mentioned elsewhere.

Quakers were a comfortable minority in colonial Loudoun County. As previously mentioned, one of Loudoun's early Quaker residents, Francis Hague, had been appointed by the Governor to serve as a Justice on the Fairfax County Court in the 1740s, but apparently refused to take the Test Oath required of Justices and never joined the bench of the Court. Otherwise, in matters relating to the everyday business affairs of the colonists, Virginia laws of the 1700's took into account the Quaker objections to swearing and bearing arms. Practicing Quakers were allowed to give an "affirmation" in lieu of an oath when voting, witnessing and proving documents, or giving testimony in court, and Quakers were permitted to hire substitutes to replace them in the county militias. The Record reflects the almost offhand, occasional mention of the fact when a Quaker was a witness or an interested party at the Loudoun Court and gave an affirmation rather than oath. The reader may be interested in William Hatcher's sale and Samuel Mead's donation of lands for new Quaker meeting sites, in 1757 and 1764, wherein they name many of the Quaker elders of their meetings. [see infra, The Record, pp. 524 and 526].

Aged and infirm persons who were witnesses appeared with some frequency in The Record, when a special "Dedimus" for their out-of-court deposition was ordered. In several instances, these entries inform of us the last illness of prominent Loudoun residents - John Champe Senr. in 1760 and Dr. John Urquhart in 1766. [infra, The Record, pp. 525 and 527].

In the category of an unusual entry, one would have to include the provisions made in 1761 for "Paldos Heronimous a Lunitick Person." The reader will note that the dimensions of the house to be built for Paldos, given by the court with specificity, would disable him from qualifying as a freeholder or voter, effectively disenfranchising him for the duration of his incapacity. [supra, Chapter on Burgesses; infra, The Record, p. 525].

We sometimes come across information that can only be noted and left for further investigation. On August 17, 1756, the Fairfax County Court concerned itself with the mountain road above the Beaver Dam Branch of Goose Creek, appointing a surveyor to maintain that road "to the school above Anderson's." Thus, one school was operating in the upper reaches of Loudoun County when it was formed. [FXCOCO, 1756-II Book, p. 14a].

Also presented in this section are entries that provide background information on a number of Loudoun residents. Colonists and Loudoun residents who probably participated in the public boycotts organized to demonstrate against the Stamp Act (by refusing to claim letters held for them at the post office in Alexandria) are identified in a list originally published in the *Virginia Gazette* on December 4, 1766. We have also repeated the contemporary *Maryland Gazette* report on the travels of George William Fairfax, Esqr., (a Fairfax County Justice and owner of significant acreage in Loudoun County) and his family in 1760. [see infra, The Record, pp. 525 and 527].

The Loudoun Record

August 31, 1757 - Isaac Nichols, Jacob Janney and Thomas Clews, as Trustees, purchase 10 acres from William Hatcher, the site of what later became known as the Goose Creek Quaker Meeting, "to ... permit such of the people called Quakers inhabiting ... Loudoun to erect and build ... meeting houses, school houses and ... places of burial." LDCODB, Book A, p. 24.

October 11, 1757 - Thomas Kelley [claimed] "... a Castor Hat which he had lost and found in the Possession of ... Walter Burwell ..." Book A, p. 26.

November 9, 1757 - Joseph Dixon, William Ross, and Else Moore each sue Lilly Ann Russell. Book A, p. 44.

April 11, 1758 - Abraham Hite, assignee of Benjamin Shoemaker, Daniel DeSue's assignee, claims "In Debt" against Samuel Stillwell "of Smithfield, Bucks County Pa., mason." Samuel Butcher gives personal bail and William Ellzey is entered as the defense attorney. Book A, p. 82.

June 13, 1758 - On the "Petition of Jacob Fare against Joseph Claypoole for a Debt due by Account ... the Deft. came not ... the Plt. recover ... one pound seventeen shillings ... and his Costs." Book A, p. 110.

March 31, 1759 - An accounting of the estate of John Poultney reveals that at the time of his death he had pledged a subscription for the maintenance and/or improvement of the Quaker meeting house at Waterford. LDCOWIL, Book A, p. 89.

April 10, 1759 - John Steere and James Steere are identified as Quakers, probably members at Waterford Meeting. Book A, p. 231.

November 13, 1759 - Edward Norton and Abel Janney, witnesses to a Will, are Quakers. LDCOWIL, Book A, p.23.

May 15, 1760 - John Champ, a witness, is determined to be "an aged and infirm person." Book A, p. 351. This would appear to be the same John Champe who moved from King George County to "Loudoun" early in the 1730s. FXCODB, Book C, p. 370.

May 15, 1760 - In James Ingoe Dozier vs. James McKinney, Robert Wood enters special bail for the Defendant and obtains "leave to impart till the next Court ..." Book A, p. 352.

June 10, 1760 - Franklin Perry obtains a judgment against James Donaldson for 630 lbs. of tobacco and 8 shillings and 6 pence. His attorney is Francis Dade. Book A, p. 363.

June 12, 1760 - George William Fairfax, Esqr., sues Bartholomy Shoemaker and George Shoemaker. Book A, p. 372; and see the illustration of the Warrant of Arrest in this case, in the Chapter on Lands, supra @ p. 262.

August 28, 1760 - "Last week sailed from Patuxent [River] for London, the ship *'Wilson'*, Capt. Judson Coolidge, with whom went passengers George William Fairfax, Esq., of Virginia, his Lady, and Family." MdGaz., No. 799, p. 3, col. 2.

November 11, 1760 - Nathan Spencer, James Hatcher and Thomas Clowes are Quakers. Book A, p. 401.

March 11, 1761 - Josias Clapham sues Patrick McKenzie on an Attachment. Book A, p. 430.

March 11, 1761 - "The Petition of Lewis Ellzey Gent. [a senior Justice of the Peace in Fairfax County] against William Chelton & Thomas Green is Dismissed being agreed by the Parties." Book A, p. 430.

August 11, 1761 - "Ordered that Francis Heronimous build a House ten Feet square to secure Paldos Heronimous a Lunitick Person until he recover his reason [sic] that he be confined therein ... Thomas Owsley and William Owsley [are to] go there weekly and see that he is found with all necessaries by the said Francis for his support." Book A, p. 483.

September 10, 1761 - "Charles Chinn alias Charles Doleman [!]." Book A, p. 521.

March 10, 1762 - On the same day, John McCarty is sued by Craven Peyton, Joseph Janney, John Davis, James Vessells, Andrew Adam and Fleming Patterson, and Benjamin Edwards, all on separate attachments. The plaintiffs are all merchants, tradesmen and ordinary keepers in Leesburg! Book A, p. 565.

May 11, 1762 - Witnesses Jacob Janney and Joseph Parker are Quakers. Book A, p. 583.

May 12, 1762 - There are apparently two men named John Davis, one living on the "Blue Ridge" or above the "Short Hill," and two men named John Morris, one from or living at a "Mountain." Book A, p. 599; and, see Loudoun County Property Tax Lists, 1757-1799, in undated MS series, at p. 1356.

July 15, 1762 - Samuel Patterson brings charges against Patrick McKinzey, who pleads not guilty and demands a Jury trial. Book B, p. 23.

August 10, 1762 - Thomas Dodd, John Hough and Joseph Janney are identified as Quakers. Book B, p. 29.

March 29, 1763 - Nicholas Osborn [sic] and his wife Mary Osborn convey a 2 acre tract "where now the Meeting House is built," in the valley now known as "Between the Hills" east of Loudoun Heights near the Potomac, to the use of the Baptist Church. Peter Romine of Loudoun and Henry Lloyd of Frederick County are identified as the Trustees for the Baptist meeting. LDCODB, Book C, pp. 630-633; DALD, (1763) p. 23.

April 13, 1763 - William Payne Baylis is a plaintiff. Book B, p. 91.

April 13, 1763 - Thomas Awbrey and John Wells bring suits against Patrick McKenzey. Book B, pp. 99 and 101.

April 13, 1763 - An accounting of Mary Patterson's estate includes an entry for the digging of her grave in the burial yard of the Quaker meeting at Waterford. LDCOWIL, Book A, p. 74.

May 11, 1763 - One "James Murray [is identified as living] below Goose Creek." Book B, p. 137.

June 17, 1763 - In the suit of Benjamin Sebastian vs. Samuel Harris, Thomas John enters as security and special bail for Harris. Book B, p. 179.

August 9, 1763 - Henry Terflinger sues Casper Quick on a Note of Hand, and recovers judgment for £3 Virginia money, with William Ellzey as his Attorney. Book B, p. 199.

September 13, 1763 - The out-of-Court deposition of "Lettice Lankfit, an infirm witness," is approved and ordered to be taken. Book B, p. 231.

December 13, 1763 - James Phillips, Solomon Doxon and John Brown are all identified at Court as Quakers when they appear and prove a deed with their Affirmations. Book B, p. 268.

February 14, 1764 - Samuel Mead acknowledges a Deed of Trust, wherein he conveys lands to the use of a Quaker meeting, with Francis Wilks, Jacob Janney, Thomas Clews, Thomas Gore, Solomon Hoge, William Morlan, Samuel Combs, Richard White, William Holmes and Jeremiah Fairhurst as the Trustees of the property. Book B, p. 271.

April 12, 1764 - "Henry Brown, Quaker" is a defendant at Court. Book B, p. 348.

August 14, 1764 - On a Deed from William Tate to William McKnight, witnesses John Gregg and John Brown, are identified as Quakers. Book B, pp. 403-404.

September 12, 1764 - William Baker (Loudoun's Inspector of Flour), in proving a deed, is identified as a Quaker. LDCODB, Book D, p. 309.

October 10, 1764 - John McIlhaney obtains judgment vs. Samuel Stillwell on a "note of hand" for £3. Book B, p. 490.

May 16, 1765 - Thomas Green enters himself as Security for Edward Hardin in defense of a case. Book B, p. 610.

May 16, 1765 - Joseph Janney, an assignee of William Jackson vs. Thomas Bryan, "for trial putteth themselves upon the Country" [ask for jury trial]. Book B, p. 611.

June 10, 1765 - Two cases brought by "Doctr. James Butler Brodbelt agt. Jacob Remey" are "agreed." Book B, p. 617.

October 14, 1765 - Mahlon Janney, William Williams, Joseph Myers and Moses Cadwallader are Quakers. Book C, p.59.

June 11, 1766 - Joseph Janney, an assignee of William Jackson, obtains a judgment against Thomas Bryan for a debt of £16. Book C, p. 107.

August 14, 1766 - "An Instrument of Writing from John Patterson to Ezekiel Jenkins [is] acknowledged by the said John & is Ordered to be Recorded." Book C, p. 177.

October 13, 1766 - [Doctor] John Urquhart of Leesburg is referred to as an "ancient and infirm person." Book C, p. 207.

October 15, 1766 - Thomas McIlhaney is a witness for Philip Slack. Book C, p. 214.

December 4, 1766 - Among the "Letters remaining in the Post Office at Alexandria," apparently in continued protest against the Stamp Act, are letters for: "... Martin Armstrong, Loudon [sic - Loudoun] Virginia ... Alexander Campbell, Loudon [sic - Loudoun] ... Stephen Donaldson, Leesburg ... Mr. Grayson, Potowmack [is this the recently deceased Benjamin Grayson ?] ... Samuel Harrison, Loudon [sic] ... Mr. M'Cauly [sic - probably James McCall who had been living near], Clapham's Ferry." VaGaz/Ri, p. 2, col. 1.

A Chronology for Colonial Virginia

1561 Opechancanough, Powhatan's older brother, leaves the Chesapeake with Spanish explorer Pedro Menendez, travelling to Spain, Mexico and Cuba.
1570 Spanish Jesuits found a mission on the York River in "Ajacan" (Virginia).
1571 Pamunkey Indians massacre the Jesuits and raze the York River mission.
1572 Spanish troops from Florida retaliate against Ajacan's tidewater Indians, inspiring the Algonquian tribes to strengthen the Powhatan confederacy.
1578 England's Queen Elizabeth authorizes Sir Humphrey Gilbert to discover and occupy the "barbarous lands, countries and territories" of America.
1586 Englishman John White maps the lower reaches of the Potomac River.
1587 The English found a settlement on Roanoke Island in the Outer Banks.
1588 The Spanish Armada diverts English attention from the resupply of the colony. The Roanoke settlers disappear and "The Colony, Lost."
1606 King James I charters the Virginia Company, authorizing settlement.
1607 April. Powhatan's braves slaughter the Chesapeake tribe at Lynnhaven. April 26th. A Virginia Company scouting party lands at Cape Henry. May 14th. 105 English settlers and explorers found "James Cittie."
1608 June 16th. After two weeks on the Chesapeake, Capt. John Smith begins exploration of the Potomac River, naming it after the Potowomek Indian village (near modern Stafford), and charting up to the Little Falls. The Algonquian name meant "where something is brought" or "trading place."
1609 400 new colonists arrive, late in the year and without adequate supplies.
+ - and 1610, winter ... "The Starving Time" in the Virginia colony. Indian attacks, famine and disease take their toll. Only 65 colonists survive.
1610 June 10th. The Virginia Company's new Governor, Thomas West, the Baron De La Warr, arrives with supply ships, in time to save the colony.
1612 Assisted by a Potowomek chief, Capt. Samuel Argall kidnaps Pocahontas.
1614 Warfare with the Powhatans ends in a temporary truce. John Rolfe marries Pocahontas; Rolfe ships the first Virginia tobacco to England.
1618 The "Great Charter" ends military government in the Virginia colony.
+ A colonial "College" is authorized on Farrar's Island in the James River.
+ Virginia colonists export over 20 tons of tobacco to England.
1619 July 30th. The Virginia General Assembly, the first elected legislative body in the Americas, meets in the choir loft of the Jamestown church.
+ summer ... Dutch sell "23 and odd Negroes" as servants at Jamestown.
+ Potowomek Indians notify Jamestown of their bumper crop of corn.
+ December 4th. New settlers celebrate the first American Thanksgiving when the ship *Margaret* arrives at Berkeley Hundred on the James River.
1620 Pilgrims found the Plymouth colony in New England.
1622 March 22nd. Warriors of the Powhatan confederacy attempt to eliminate Britain's Virginia colony. Overnight, 350 English colonists are killed. A thousand more die later that year from disease, famine and warfare.
+ Jamestown sends troops to assist Potowomeks make war on Anacostians.
1623 Capt. Henry Spelman, trading up the Potomac, is ambushed and killed.

1624 May 24th. King James I revokes the Charter of the Virginia Company.
1625 Charles I succeeds James I on the British throne.
1627 Capt. William Claiborne dominates fur trading on the Potomac River.
1630 Puritans found their Massachusetts Bay colony settlement at Boston.
1631 Capt. Henry Fleet establishes a trading post on the Potomac River.
1632 Capt. John Utey of the Virginia Council arrests Capt. Fleet for trading on the Potomac River without a license from the Virginia colony.
1634 The first Maryland colony settlers found St. Marys on the Potomac.
\+ The Virginia colony forms the first 8 "shires", leading to creation of the county courts and institution of the offices of Sheriff and County Clerk.
1641 - until 1647, John Campbell, the first Earl of Loudoun, is a leader of the Scottish Covenanters, serving as the Scottish Chancellor. He supports his cousin, the Earl of Argyll, while opposing the policies of King Charles I.
1642 English Civil War: Parliament's "Roundheads" battle the King's Cavaliers.
1643 The Virginia Council, as the "General Court," begins to function as the colony's supreme judicial body; the Assembly of Burgesses begin meeting separately from the Council; the established county courts now total 15.
1644 April 17th. The Powhatan Confederacy massacres 500 colonists. English campaign of total war eliminates hostile Indian tribes from the tidewater.
1646 Survivors of the "Powhatan" Confederacy are forced onto reservations.
1648 Northumberland County is formed on the Northern Neck of Virginia.
1649 Parliament beheads King Charles I at the end of the English Civil War.
\+ September. Charles II issues the first Northern Neck Proprietary grant, to Sir John Culpeper and six other loyal, Royalist councilors.
\+ - until 1655. Iroquoian Beaver Wars rage in New York and Pennsylvania. Using Dutch weaponry, the Iroquois defeat the Huron and Erie tribes and extend their hegemony over an expanse of lands east of the lakes. Susquehannocks in Pennsylvania block Iroquois expansion southeastward.
1651 Adopting the Navigation Act, Parliament tries to eliminate Dutch trading in Virginia by requiring shipment of Virginia produce in English ships.
1652 April. Parliament dispatches a fleet and a siege army, finally forcing the Virginia Assembly to renounce allegiance to Charles II, the exiled King.
1653 Westmoreland County is created, incorporating the upper Potomac.
1658 September 23rd. Oliver Cromwell dies. Parliament's power wanes.
1659 The Virginia Assembly restores Royalist Governor William Berkeley.
1660 May. King Charles II is restored to the British throne.
\+ October. The Virginia Assembly happily restores all references to the supremacy of the British Crown in Virginia's colonial laws.
1664 England seizes Dutch New Amsterdam, renaming the colony New York.
1666 Tobacco prices hit rock bottom during an economic depression.
1670 William Fitzhugh (the 1st) founds Bedford plantation on Chotank Creek.
1675 July. Hog stealing escalates to open Indian warfare on the Potomac.
1676 Virginia Councilman Nathaniel Bacon Junr. leads a "Rebellion" against colonial Indian policy. Bacon heads an army of militia indiscriminately against several tribes, burns Jamestown and then dies from fever before Gov. Berkeley returns from the Eastern Shore to restore Royal authority.

1677 May 29th. In a final peace treaty, survivors of the tidewater tribes become "tributary" to the Pamunkey chief and the King of England.

1688 Before he is driven from the throne, James II extends boundaries of the Northern Neck to the "first heads or springs." His protestant daughter Mary and her husband, William of Hanover, take the British throne.

1689 "Foreign indians" fortify themselves at the falls of the Potomac.

1690 April 1st. The first intercolonial council is convened in New York, but Virginia and Maryland do not send representatives.

1691 To cover debts of £50,000., costs of a military campaign against Quebec, Massachusetts Bay issues the first paper money in the British Empire.

\+ April 23rd. The first American "Olympic Games" are held at Jamestown.

1693 February. The French and lake Indians attack the Mohawks (Iroquois).

\+ A Royal charter is issued, founding the College of William and Mary.

1697 summer ... Piscataway Indians migrate, settle west of Bull Run mountain.

\+ September 30th. The Treaty of Ryswick ends King William's War.

1698 October 21st. Virginia's third statehouse in Jamestown burns down, prompting relocation of the colony's capitol to "Middle Plantation."

\+ The Piscataway Indians migrate again, to Conoy Island on the Potomac.

1699 April. A Virginia delegation visits the Piscataways on Conoy Island.

1700 May. The Assembly and General Court begin meeting in Williamsburg.

\+ June. Seneca Indians raid into Stafford County, killing a family of eight.

1701 The Iroquois League "deeds" the lands in western Ohio to the British.

1702 The Carolina colony uses paper money to finance an invasion of Florida.

1703 Robert Carter becomes the resident manager of the Northern Neck.

1704 February. French and Indians lay waste to Deerfield Massachusetts.

1707 The English and Scottish crowns are united under the "Act of Union."

\+ Prospector Louis Michel starts a temporary settlement at Harpers Ferry.

1709 American expeditions against both Montreal and Quebec fail for lack of British military assistance, causing substantial colonial resentment.

\+ Daniel McCarty patents a tract near Sugarland Island on the Potomac.

1711 June. Governors of the northern colonies meet to coordinate actions.

\+ Thomas Lee is appointed Virginia agent for the Fairfax Proprietary.

1712 Baron de Graffenried surveys the Potomac River between Monocacy and the Shenandoah, noticing a choice tract of land below Point of Rocks.

1713 April 11th. With the Treaty of Utrecht, Spain cedes Gibraltar to Britain and, thereafter, the Iroquois are considered British subjects.

\+ December. North Carolinians crush an uprising of Tuscarora Indians, killing 800 warriors and prompting the survivors to flee to Iroquois lands.

1715 Highland Scots revolt against imposition of the reign of King George I.

\+ Thomas, 6th Lord Fairfax, Baron of Cameron, is appointed to the Court of King George I as assistant to the Treasurer of the King's Household.

1716 Gov. Alexander Spotswood and his "Knights of the Golden Horseshoe" cross Virginia's Blue Ridge and explore the central Shenandoah valley.

1717 Thomas Lee patents thousands of acres along "Lee [aka Goose] Creek."

1718 French found a settlement on the Mississippi River at New Orleans.

1719 Thomas, Lord Fairfax inherits the Culpepers' Northern Neck Proprietary.

1721 Thomas Lord Fairfax purchases a commission as a Coronet in the Royal Regiment of House Guards under Col. Charles, Marquess of Winchester.
+ October 19th. Iroquois deputies meet Gov. Spotswood in Williamsburg; the Iroquois agree not to cross the Potomac east of the Blue Ridge.
1722 September. Spotswood ratifies the Iroquois Treaty in Albany (N.Y.).
+ Piscataways vacate Conoy Island, migrate to Maryland and Pennsylvania.
1724 England's new policy of "salutory neglect" expands "local" colonial rule.
+ Philip Noland Senr. patents lands at Broad Run on the Potomac River.
+ There is an influx of Palatinate Germans into the Pennsylvania colony.
1726 Lord Fairfax leases the Northern Neck to Robert Carter for £450/year.
1727 - until 1735. Gov. Gooch, attempting to limit the Fairfax Proprietary, issues improper land grants for over 300,000 acres in the Northern Neck.
+ Fredericksburg Virginia, named for the new Prince of Wales, is founded.
1731 Joist Hite and 20 German families settle in the northern Shenandoah.
1732 Robert Carter dies. The Northern Neck land office closes for two years.
1733 Amos Janney settles "Janney's Mill" (aka Waterford) on Kittoctin Creek.
+ Thomas Lee advances to a seat on the Virginia Governor's Council.
+ Worship services are begun at Truro's "Chappell above Goose Creek."
1736 fall ... The boundaries of the Northern Neck Proprietary are surveyed.
+ Delaware tribes of Pa. and Ohio adopt the Iroquois Covenant Chain.
+ - to 1741. William Fairfax constructs his Potomac manor home at Belvoir.
1737 Thomas Lord Fairfax returns to England, to resolve his boundaries.
1738 The Goose Creek Friends begin monthly worship services near Lincoln.
+ Iroquois warriors commit minor outrages in the Shenandoah valley.
+ Robert Dinwiddie is named Surveyor General of Customs for the south.
+ Former Gov. Spotswood is buried at Yorktown at Temple Farm estate.
+ November. Francis Awbrey licenses his Potomac ferry below Conoy Isl.
1739 May. Spain does not renew Britain's slave-trade franchise (the Asiento).
+ - until 1748. The War of Austrian Succession, aka "King George's War."
+ William Fairfax re-opens the land office of the Fairfax Proprietary.
1741 April. British Generals mismanage an expedition against Cartagena. Only 600 of 3,500 American colonial soldiers survive. One survivor, Virginia Capt. Lawrence Washington, gratefully names his Potomac River plantation in honor of the campaign's Admiral, Edward Vernon.
+ Ireland undergoes a severe potato famine, prompting colonial emigration.
1742 Ebenezer Floyd licenses his Potomac River ferry near Clarks Run.
+ Fairfax County (including "Loudoun") is formed, in Truro parish bounds.
1743 June. King George II is the last monarch to lead a British army in battle when the English army escapes a French trap at Dettingen in Holland.
+ Lawrence Washington is named adjutant general of the Virginia militia.
+ The Fairfax Meeting Friends construct a house of worship at Waterford.
1744 March 15th. Britain and France finally declare war on each other.
+ Lord Fairfax approves founding of Frederick Town (now Winchester).
+ July 7th. At the Treaty of Lancaster (Pa.), Iroquois, Delaware and Shawnee enter an "alliance" with Virginia, Maryland and Pennsylvania; Virginia's claim to land west to the Mississippi River is acknowledged.

1745 French-allied Shawnee plunder British trading posts on the Ohio.
+ Lord Fairfax returns to Virginia, resuming personal control of his lands.
+ June. Massachusetts colonial militia capture the fortress at Louisbourg.
+ August 5th. With a wee French support, Prince Charles Edward Stuart lands in the highlands, reclaims the Scottish throne and leads the Rising.
+ September 20th. At Prestonpans, Hanoverian supporter John Campbell, 4th Earl of Loudoun and a chief of Clan Campbell, loses his regiment.
1746 winter ... The Earl of Loudoun loses another battle at Inverury. Later, in the "rout of Moy," Loudoun is bluffed by "a blacksmith and other four" and loses a second regiment, and Inverness, to the McDonalds and Royal Stuarts. Lord Loudoun escapes to a remote castle on the Isle of Skye.
+ Presbyterians found the College of New Jersey at Princeton.
+ April 16th. Prince Charles Stuart's Highland Clans are decimated at Culloden. The Duke of Cumberland, aka "The Butcher," orders total destruction in the highlands, touching off a wave of Scottish emigration.
+ John Russell, Duke of Bedford, becomes Secretary for colonial affairs, embarking on an ill-advised increased exercise of the "royal prerogative."
1747 Virginia Councilman Thomas Lee and eleven associates petition King George II for a grant of 200,000 acres southeast of the Ohio River.
+ May. German Reformed church services are inaugurated at Lovettsville.
+ Robert Harper "buys" a Potomac ferry at the mouth of the Shenandoah.
+ October. Thomas Lee and prominent Northern Neck planters, in league with several London merchants, form the Ohio Company of Virginia.
1748 October 18th. The Treaty of Aix-la-Chapelle fails to resolve the dispute between Britain and France over frontier lands in the Ohio River basin.
1749 The French send a "pacifying" expedition into Ohio, but gain little.
+ Scottish merchants found Alexandria, on the Potomac River at Belhaven.
+ Ohio Company (VA) builds trading post at Wills Creek on the Potomac.
+ September 4th. Thomas Lee becomes acting Governor of Virginia.
1750 March. The Ohio Company (Virginia) begins trading at Wills Creek.
+ Christopher Gist is hired to explore and "survey" Ohio Company lands.
+ November 14th. Acting Governor Thomas Lee dies while in office.
1751 June 8th. Maryland Assembly authorizes the founding of Georgetown.
+ July 4th. Robert Dinwiddie is appointed (Lt.) Governor of Virginia.
1752 May. Fairfax Courthouse is relocated from "Springfield" to Alexandria.
+ June 21st. Iroquois and Ohio Indians conclude a treaty at Logstown (now Ambridge Pa.) authorizing Virginia settlements on the Ohio.
1753 French and Indians drive British traders and merchants out of Ohio.
+ September. Delaware and Shawnee Indians meet Virginia Commissioner William Fairfax at Winchester, where they confirm the Logstown treaty.
+ October 31st. Virginia sends George Washington (a 22 year-old Major) to Ohio to seek out the French garrisons and demand their withdrawal.
+ November. Washington returns to Alexandria, then by the Potomac Path via the Short Hills and Keys' Gap to Winchester, to "the forks" of the Monongahela before reaching French garrisons near the Great Lakes.
+ December. George Washington delivers an ultimatum to the French.

1754 January. The Virginia Assembly funds a militia expedition into Ohio.
+ January. British troops and Virginia militia begin construction of a small fort at Pittsburgh landing - later renamed Ft. Duquesne by the French.
+ February 19th. Virginia Lt. Governor Dinwiddie issues a Proclamation granting bounty lands in the Ohio territory for recruits, to encourage "men to Enlist and enter into his Majesty's Service" against the French.
+ March 4th. Newcastle becomes First Lord, and erringly attempts to bluff the French into compromise in America with threats of a general war.
+ April 6th. Washington's militia encamps at the Gap of the Short Hill.
+ April 17th. Ensign Ward, with a small Virginia work party, surrenders the incomplete fort at Pittsburgh to a large French and Indian force.
+ May 28th. George Washington (now Lt.Col. of militia), with the support of the Delaware Indians, surprises and wipes out a French scouting party.
+ Twenty-three representatives from the seven northern colonies attend a congress at Albany New York to further coordination of mutual defense.
+ June 17th. New England militia seize French forts in Nova Scotia.
+ June 26th. The British Cabinet authorizes the expenditure of £10,000 in Virginia for "gifts" to increase Indian pressure on the French in Ohio.
+ July 4th. Washington's force of 300 Virginia militia and 300 regulars from South Carolina and New York is surrounded at Great Meadows Pa. Washington surrenders Ft. Necessity, obtaining only the "honors of war."
+ September 8th. News of the defeat at Great Meadows reaches London.
+ October. King George II accepts a Board of Trade plan requiring the colonies to pay for all troops and defenses erected on the American frontiers, but with military command to remain directly under the King.
1755 January. Britain dispatches Gen. Edward Braddock to Virginia with the task of retaking the fort at Pittsburg Landing, sending two undermanned regiments from Ireland, the 44th Foot and 48th Foot, to serve under him.
+ February 23rd. General Braddock arrives in Williamsburg.
+ February 28th. Gen. Braddock threatens to quarter his troops in private homes in Pennsylvania unless colonists pay for his army's supplies.
+ April 14th. At Alexandria, Braddock meets with mid-Atlantic Governors and demands funding for his expedition under the Board of Trade's plan.
+ May 6th. Construction begins on a military road for Gen. Braddock's army, from Ft. Cumberland on the Potomac northwest into Pennsylvania.
+ May. The French and their Indian allies begin raids into the Virginia backwoods settlements, attempting to distract Braddock from Pittsburgh.
+ May 20th. Gen. Braddock rejects assistance offered by allied Indians.
+ June 13th. Sir John St. Clair, quartermaster of Braddock's expedition, fumes that *"no Magistrate in Virginia or I believe in Maryland gave themselves the least trouble to assist in collecting the Country People to work upon the Roads, and to provide us with Carriages ... on the Contrary every body laid themselves out to put what money they cou'd in their Pockets, without forwarding our Expedition."* [Jennings, *Empire,* p. 149].
+ July 4th. 1,100 Acadians in Nova Scotia, acting on bad advice from their priests, reject a British oath of loyalty and are ordered to be deported.

1755 July 9th. Gen. Braddock is surprised by the French and their Indians. Nearly 1,100 soldiers in the army's advance units are killed or wounded. Of the 400+ Virginia militia in the battle, less than 80 survive.

\+ Col. Dunbar destroys Braddock's ammunition and "leads" 1,500 surviving British regulars to Philadelphia, leaving the Virginia frontier unprotected.

\+ October 17th. French-led Delaware Indians initiate hostilities against the outlying British settlements in the Virginia and Pennsylvania colonies.

\+ October 31st. Gov. Dinwiddie reports that Indians have "murdered and taken off about eighty of our frontier Settlers." [ibid., Jennings, p. 192].

\+ November. Pennsylvania backwoods settlers take refuge in Philadelphia.

\+ winter ... French Indians commit innumerable depredations everywhere on the British frontier, from North Carolina to New England. Virginia, Maryland and Pennsylvania settlements bear the brunt of the onslaught.

1756 March 8th. Lord Loudoun is named British military commander in chief for the American colonies and the new Governor of Virginia.

\+ April 27th. George Washington advises Lt. Gov. Dinwiddie that *"the Bleu-Ridge is now our Frontier ... [unless we act] there will not be a living creature left in Frederick County; how soon Fairfax [Loudoun] and Prince William may share its fate, is easily conceived."* [ibid., Jennings, p. 191].

\+ May 18th. Britain finally declares war on France again, beginning the Seven Years War, in the American colonies aka "The French War."

\+ May 20th. Lord Loudoun, with a mistress and large entourage in tow, finally embarks from London to assume his positions in the colonies.

\+ June. Quaker pacifists withdraw from the Pennsylvania Assembly, and Benjamin Franklin assumes leadership of the anti-Penn faction.

\+ June 8th. A French officer in Canada writes: "I apply myself particularly to sending parties of Indians into the English Colonies ... the English have lost one hundred men for our one." [ibid., Jennings, p. 164].

\+ summer ... Virginia's Ft. Loudoun is built and garrisoned at Winchester.

\+ A second Ft. Loudoun is built, in Cherokee country, near Vonore, Tenn.

\+ 3 am, July 23rd. John Campbell, Lord Loudoun, lands at New York city.

\+ August 14th. Ft. Oswego on Lake Ontario falls to the French.

\+ December. Lord Loudoun quarters British troops in New York homes despite strong and outspoken opposition. The General then threatens Philadelphia with the same treatment, but the taverns provide bedspace.

\+ December. William Pitt takes control of the British government.

1757 March 10th. Lord Loudoun reports to the King that he *"had disputes to Settle, all over this Continent, in settling the Winter Quarters for the Troops; ... the manner of Quartering in England as in time of Peace, on Publick Houses only, will in no shape answer the intent in this Country; for here, there are few Publick Houses, and the most of them ... possess only one room ... where Men cannot be Quartered."* [ibid., Jennings, p. 298].

\+ May. Pitt orders Lord Loudoun to take Louisbourg before attacking Quebec. Loudoun outrages colonists by ordering an over-night dragnet wherein 800 New Yorkers are impressed as seamen for the British fleet.

\+ June. Benjamin Franklin, as Pennsylvania's emissary, travels to England.

1757 July 12th. The first Loudoun County Court convenes [at West's ordinary?] and begins organization of the new County government.

\+ August 4th. Lord Loudoun withdraws his invasion fleet from Louisbourg without attempting an attack, further infuriating colonials.

\+ September 8th. After mismanaging his European military campaign against the French, the Duke of Cumberland signs the Convention of Kloster-Zeven. In disgrace, Cumberland is forced into early retirement.

\+ November. Lord Loudoun threatens to quarter his troops in Boston.

\+ December 30th. William Pitt recalls Lord Loudoun. The Pitt Cabinet obtains a temporary reversal of the Crown's policy on use of the royal prerogative, offering greater cooperation with the colonial assemblies.

1758 January. Upon Lt. Gov. Robert Dinwiddie's departure for England, Virginia Council President John Blair takes over as the acting Governor.

\+ George Mason's plantation home in Fairfax, Gunston Hall, is completed.

\+ April. British General Forbes organizes an attack on Ft. Duquesne. Virginia supplies Forbes with 2,000 troops and musters county militia to provide the troops needed for garrison duty in the Virginia frontier forts.

\+ May. Over 700 southern Indians join General Forbes in Pennsylvania.

\+ June 7th. More than 500 southern Indians abandon General Forbes.

\+ July. General Amherst's expeditionary force retakes Louisbourg.

\+ September. Col. Washington marches Virginia's militia regiment north; they join Gen. Forbes at Ft. Ligonier, 40 miles east of Ft. Duquesne.

\+ October 26th. The Delaware and Iroquois Indians conclude a peace treaty with the Pennsylvania and New Jersey governments at Easton, Pa.

\+ November 25th. Virginia militia under General Forbes occupy Ft. Duquesne at "the forks" of the Monongahela, renaming it "Pittsburgh."

\+ winter ... The Senecas (northern Iroquois) turn against the French.

\+ December 9th. Col. George Washington, after retaking Ft. Pitt, marches his Virginia troops to Winchester, resigns and returns to Mount Vernon.

1759 summer ... For the first time some southern Cherokee, who had always allied themselves with the English colonists, turn against the British.

\+ July. The French surrender both Ft. Niagara and Ft. Ticonderoga.

\+ August. Senecas begin planning the eviction of the British from Niagara.

\+ September 18th. The French surrender Quebec to Gen. James Wolfe.

1760 spring ... Cherokees initiate a siege of Ft. Loudoun in Tennessee.

\+ July. A Virginia Regiment under Col. William Byrd begins a 300-mile march to relieve Ft. Loudoun (in the Tennessee territory).

\+ August 10th. Cherokee massacre the surrendering garrison troops and their families at Ft. Loudoun. Over 100 colonials are taken hostage.

\+ September 7th. The French surrender Canada to the British.

\+ October 25th. King George II dies; grandson George III is crowned.

1761 February 22nd. General Amherst blunders, insulting allied Indian tribes.

\+ summer ... Carolinians waste Cherokee territory, revenging Ft. Loudoun.

\+ September 22nd. Princess Charlotte of Mecklenburg marries George III.

\+ November 3rd. John Stuart, 3rd Earl of Bute, becomes Prime Minister.

\+ December 17th. Treaty terms are dictated to the Cherokee Indians.

1762 January. The British Prime Minister, Lord Bute, declares war on Spain.
+ summer ... Goaded by the French, Ohio and lakes Indians circulate war belts in preparation for total war against the British on the frontiers.
+ July. Lord Loudoun's army stops a Spanish advance, saving Lisbon.
+ November. Charlottesville, in Albemarle County in Virginia's central piedmont, is incorporated as a town "for the reception of traders."
1763 George Grenville succeeds Lord Bute as British Prime Minister.
+ February 10th. In the Treaty of Paris, France is evicted from America. Britain obtains Canada and eastern Louisiana from France and Florida from Spain, and Spain obtains western Louisiana from France.
+ A British Proclamation forbids settlements west of the Alleghenies. This reversal of colonial policy is deeply resented by most Virginians.
+ April 19th. Arsonists burn the Delaware Indians' homes at Wyoming Pa.
+ May 9th. Pontiac and his allied tribes lay siege to Fort Detroit.
+ summer ... English traders and settlers across the frontier are massacred. The Ohio and lake Indians destroy British forts on the great lakes and in the Ohio valley, but Pittsburgh, Niagara and Detroit hold out.
+ July. The garrison at Pittsburgh infects attacking Indians with smallpox.
+ August 1st. The Indians withdraw from their siege of Pittsburgh.
+ September 29th. Senecas sue for peace, rejoining the Covenant Chain.
+ Patrick Henry argues the "Parson's Cause" in Hanover County Court.
+ December 14th. Scots-Irish from Paxton, Pa. massacre (lynch) six friendly Indians, the last of the Susquehannock tribe, at Conestoga, Pa.
1764 April. Iroquois attack the Delaware tribes and recover white captives.
+ August. The Delaware and Shawnee tribes in Ohio sue for peace.
+ September. The Detroit tribes, sans Pontiac, sue for peace.
1765 "Fairfax" Friends in Loudoun build a stone meeting house at Waterford.
+ To raise revenue and retire French War debts, Parliament imposes the Stamp Tax on the colonies. Many American cities erupt in violence.
+ May 29th. The Virginia Assembly adopts resolutions, propounded by Patrick Henry, protesting against the Stamp Act as an illegal direct tax. County courts refuse to take the bench; merchants boycott British goods.
1766 In Williamsburg, John Pinkney begins printing his *Virginia Gazette (Rind)* declaring his publication "open to all parties but influenced by none."
+ February 27th. Northern Neck leaders adopt the Leedstown Resolutions.
+ Parliament repeals Stamp Act but reaffirms its sovereignty over colonies.
+ Leesburg Methodists organize and begin construction of a stone church.
1767 Fairfax Episcopals begin construction of Christ Church and Falls Church.
+ Townshend Act duties are imposed on glass, lead, paper, paint and tea.
+ William Petty, the Earl of Shelburne, a moderate British Secretary for Colonial Affairs, advocates accommodation of colonial trading interests.
1768 March 3rd. (Lt.) Governor Fauquier dies while in office.
+ March 4th to October 26th. John Blair again serves as acting Governor.
+ October 26th. Norborne Berkeley, Baron de Botetourt, the first resident Governor of Virginia since Edward Nott (who died in 1706), takes office.
1769 September. A major hurricane destroys much of Virginia's tobacco crop.

1770 October 15th. Virginia Gov. Botetourt dies in office. William Nelson, the new President of the Virginia Council, takes over as acting Governor.

1771 September 25th. Governor John Murray, Earl of Dunmore, takes office.

1772 To the west of the Loudoun Blue Ridge, Frederick County Virginia is divided into thirds; Berkeley County and Dunmore County are created.

1773 Virginia grants Ohio bounty lands for the 1754 Proclamation recruits in the French War. Officers and speculators obtain most of the land.

\+ December 16th. British East India Co. tea goes overboard in Boston.

1774 Britain closes Boston harbor and annuls the Massachusetts charter.

\+ May. The Virginia Assembly orders a colony-wide day of fasting and prayer in protest against Parliament's "Intolerable Acts."

\+ June 14th. The Loudoun Resolves are adopted at Leesburg.

\+ July 18th. The Fairfax Resolves are adopted at Alexandria.

\+ September 5th. A Colonial Congress meets in Philadelphia; the Speaker of Virginia's Assembly, Peyton Randolph is elected to preside.

1775 The Continental Congress meets continuously in Philadelphia.

\+ March. Virginia's second revolutionary convention meets in Richmond. Patrick Henry declares "There is no peace ... the war is actually begun!"

\+ April 19th. Paul Revere rides. Massachusetts militiamen inflict 244 casualties on British regulars between Lexington, Concord and Boston.

\+ June 8th. Gov. Dunmore flees Williamsburg aboard a British warship.

\+ August 19th. The executive functions of the Virginia government are assumed by the Committee of Safety, chaired by Edmund Pendleton.

\+ Royal Gov. Dunmore proposes the use of Indian raiders into Virginia's frontier settlements and British occupation of the Potomac River valley.

\+ December 9th. At Great Bridge, Virginia and Carolina militia repel an advance of British regulars in the first land battle in the southern colonies. Lord Dunmore abandons his military headquarters in Norfolk.

1776 January 1st. Dunmore sets fire to Norfolk. Some Colonial troops assist.

\+ February. Britain contracts with Hesse-Cassel for 12,000 German troops.

\+ May 15th. Virginia's revolutionary convention, meeting in Williamsburg, unanimously adopts a resolution calling for independence from England.

\+ June 12th. Virginia adopts George Mason's Declaration of Rights.

\+ June 29th. The Commonwealth of Virginia is formally constituted. Virginia recognizes Maryland's sovereignty over the Potomac River.

\+ July 4th. The Declaration of Independence is signed in Philadelphia.

\+ July 6th. Patrick Henry becomes the Commonwealths' first Governor.

\+ July 9th. Revolutionaries on the Bowling Green in New York pull down the 2-ton lead statute of George III, which is melted down for bullets.

\+ July 23rd. British raiders on the Potomac burn the Occoquan flour mills.

\+ + During the Revolution, Israel Pemberton and other Quaker leaders from Pennsylvania are banished into internal exile in western Virginia for refusing to take a Loyalty Oath. Virginia adopts similar measures.

Glossary of Terms

Abjuration Oath - Oath taken by any person holding office in England or her Colonies, binding the office holder not to acknowledge any right in the Pretender to the throne; an Oath renouncing certain doctrines of the Roman church.

Adze - A carpentry or woodworking tool with a handle and a curved blade, used to carve and shape wood surfaces.

Arrack - An alcoholic drink, originally made in the Orient and derived from either rice or molasses. In colonial Virginia the drink was an exceptionally strong liquor, made from molasses.

Auger - A tool for boring holes, usually through or into wood; alternately, a tool for making holes in the ground.

Banns - In the episcopal churches of colonial Virginia, a public announcement of a proposed marriage.

Base born - An individual of illegitimate birth.

Benefit of Clergy - A privilege of exemption from capital punishment in felony cases allowed to Clergymen, subordinate Church officers, and in colonial times also extended to "Clerks," in other words, anyone who could read and write.

Capital Crime - Any offence where a conviction calls for the loss of life or limb.

Cask - An allowance for the cost of making barrels necessary to hold a given quantity of an item. Generally, the standard "cask" assessment was an additional 4% supplement of an official charge for either fees or a salary.

Castor Hat - A hat made of beaver fur.

Clerk - Variant spelling of cleric, meaning clergyman. In colonial usage, the term applies to anyone who can read and write, whether a layman or ecclesiastic.

Colewort - Any cole or cabbage with leaves that do not form a compact head.

Colter - The edged blade on a plow, for making vertical cuts.

Cooper - A tradesman who makes or repairs barrels and casks.

Covenant - A binding and solemn agreement entered into by two or more persons. A compact or contract.

Cordwainer - A tradesman who makes clothing and apparel from cordovan leather. After the colonial period, also meaning a shoemaker.

Currier - Tradesman who prepares tanned leather by soaking, scraping, cleaning, beating and softening the leather.

De bene esse - In law, an action taken provisionally, anticipating a future need.

Dedimus - A variant form of the term "Dedimus Potestatem," a writ whereby the King empowers official appointees with authority to conduct specific functions.

Defalcation - In modern usage, embezzlement; but in colonial Virginia it was used exclusively to mean a "set-off" whereby tobacco owed for officer's fees or in a levy on tithables was partially offset by a lesser amount of credit on account.

Disorderly House - A house of prostitution or a gambling house.

Dower - In colonial law, the provision made for a widow, from the lands or tenements of her husband, for her support.

Draughts - An English name for the game of checkers.

Ejectment - In colonial and modern Courts alike, the action seeking the recovery of possession of land. Commonly used for trying the title to land, the parties are often given fictitious names.

Ell - A measure of length, primarily for cloth. In English colonies, 45 inches.

Esquire - A title below the station of knight and above that of gentleman. In colonial usage the term is applied to Sheriffs, Justices of the Peace and Attorneys.

Feme covert - In colonial Virginia, underage women who married without permission were legally disabled from possessing or selling their property.

Feoffment - For centuries, the English form of a deed used to convey the outright ownership of land in ones possession. This type of deed of transfer has now been almost entirely replaced by land conveyances founded on statutory law.

Freeholder - The essential status prerequisite for a Virginia colonist to be entitled to vote for delegates in the House of Burgesses. In the 1750s, 1760s and 1770s, Virginia's voting laws defined a "freehold" as ownership of at least a life interest in: 100 acres of undeveloped land; 25 acres that contained a plantation house; or, a lot with any size house in any city or town in Virginia.

Gaming - The activity of two or more persons playing together at any illegal game of chance, to win a stake or wager to which all the players contributed.

Gaol - A chiefly British variant for the word "jail," pronounced the same. Often misspelled "goal." **Gaol bounds** - Prison bounds. **Gaol fever** - Typhus.

General Court - In colonial Virginia, the Governor and his Councilors, sitting as the General Court, had exclusive authority to hear and try felony and treason cases, and acted as an appeals court over the various county courts.

Gent., or Gentleman - Originally applied to a man attending a person of rank; in colonial usage, referring to any man of good social standing, and all Justices.

Gill - A liquid quantity of four fluid ounces; one-fourth of a pint.

Glebe - The land belonging to the parish church, traditionally for the use of and yielding income to the rector or minister of the parish.

Habere facias Possessionem - The legal writ commanding a Sheriff to put the owner in actual possession of an identified property.

Heir at Law - Under the law of primogeniture as applied in colonial Virginia, in the event of intestacy, the eldest surviving son was the "heir at law," entitled to inherit the lands of his ancestor.

Hogshead - In colonial Virginia, a term generally applied to a large barrel used for transporting compressed tobacco, containing about 1,000 pounds in weight. By Virginia law, a hogshead had to contain at least 60 gallons in liquid measure.

Indenture - In colonial usage, a contract binding one person to work as a servant or an apprentice for a specific period of time.

Infant - The status of legal infancy; a minor. In the Virginia Colony, an infant is any person under the age of twenty-one years.

"in the room of ..." - A widely used colonial phrase, applied to situations where one individual <u>replaces</u> another in office, responsibility or title.

Joyner - A variant spelling of "Joiner"; a tradesman who constructs articles by joining pieces of wood. In colonial usage, this could mean either a furniture maker or a "finishing" carpenter.

King's Attorney - A prosecuting attorney. The Deputy King's Attorney was the colonial Virginia equivalent of the modern County Commonwealth Attorney. An appointee of the Crown who was responsible for filing criminal charges on behalf of private subjects and the King, usually by direction of the Court.

Lance - A long-shafted wooden spear usually carried by cavalry soldiers; alternately, an instrument used as a fishing spear.

Lease for lives - A lease in property for the life of one or more renters. Large estates in Virginia's Northern Neck were often partitioned and sections rented for the longest life of three named individuals, with the right to name substitutes, perpetually renewing the lease. The lease qualified the tenant as a "freeholder."

Malster - Also spelled "Maltster"; a maker of malt or liquor. In colonial usage, the term is meant to designate a brewer of beer.

Messuage - Now synonymous with "dwelling house," in colonial usage the term referred to a tract of land containing a dwelling.

Moiety - Generally meaning one-half of anything; Moiety Acts of the colonial Virginia Assembly allowed one-half of a fine or fee to be paid to an informer.

Necessary house - An outhouse. One absolutely indispensable requirement for every Courthouse in colonial Virginia.

Oyer and Terminer - The name for a colonial court empowered to try a felony criminal case, where the offence was punishable by death or dismemberment.

Perch - In surveying, a measurement equal to a rod, ie., 16.5 feet or 5.5 yards.

Petit larceny - Minor, or petty, theft.

Pillory - A colonial punishment device; erected on a wooden frame with movable boards in which the head and hands of the criminal are locked in place.

Pipe - Another term for a large cask, or barrel, of 120 gallons. Hening, VI/236.

Plantation - In Virginia and other southern colonies, the term designated not only large planted estates, but also farms occupied by the owners and cultivated in annual crops. The broader legal definition is still in use in North Carolina.

Prison bounds - A district around, and considered to be a part of, a jail. It is defined by limits within which prisoners are allowed to go at large after they have given the proper security to remain inside the bounds.

Processioning - The colonial practice of remarking land boundaries every four years, performed by the parish vestry with the participation of the neighborhood landowners. Analogous to the English custom of a rogation week perambulation.

Prorogue - The procedure whereby the Governor of Virginia proclaims an end, suspension or adjournment of a session of the Virginia Assembly of Burgesses.

"Put upon the Country" - The phrase used by a defendant to formally request a jury trial in a colonial court in Virginia.

Recusant - An English subject who absented himself from his episcopal parish church; Catholic recusants were prosecuted under laws written in the 1600s.

Relict - Survivor of a pair of married people, whether the husband or the wife; intending to mean the survivor of a united pair, not the survivor of the deceased.

Sadler - Variant of "saddler"; tradesman who makes and repairs riding saddles.

Skin dresser - A tradesman who prepares furs and pelts for use.

Squire - A contraction of "Esquire," used as a title.

Stocks - A colonial punishment device. Two pieces of lumber, constructed so that when fastened together they hold the legs or ankles of the offender.

Tanner - A tradesman who makes leather by tanning hides.

Tar Pitch - A sticky resin derived from some types of evergreen, used in sealing, protecting, waterproofing and preserving surfaces. Often used in roofing.

Test Oath - In colonial times, an Oath of fidelity and allegiance to the established government of the British King.

Tight Cooper - The skilled tradesman who can make or repair watertight or airtight barrels and casks. Hence, an expert cooper.

Tipling House - Or "tippling house"; where men resort and intoxicating drinks are sold in small quantities. In colonial times, usually an unlicensed ordinary.

Tithable - A term with peculiar significance in colonial Virginia, meaning the individual persons counted "per poll," (per head), and accordingly subject to colonial tax assessments and annual levies for both the County and the parish.

Trover - The legal action one brings to remedy a wrongful interference with or detention of ones goods or personal property.

Tun - A large cask containing about 250 gallons; used primarily for wine or ale.

Verge - Mace, commissioned by Charles I, that precedes the Lord High Admiral into battle. Also, in heraldry, an edge or boundary. In colonial usage in Virginia, "in the verge of Court" meant within the presence of a Court in session.

Vizt. - Variant of "viz"; abbreviation of "videlicet"; "that is to say" or "namely."

Yeoman - Of a class of English freeholders ranked below the Gentry. A small landed farmer who works his own property.

Assembly - *Journals of the House of Burgesses of Virginia,* 13 volumes in series, edited by H.R. McIlwaine & J.P. Kennedy, Richmond, Virginia (1905-1915).

Balch/Lewis - "Notes on Loudoun County Virginia," the files of John G. Lewis, Thomas Balch Library, Leesburg, Virginia (undated MS collection).

Baron - *Virginia Baron, The Story of Thomas 6th Lord Fairfax,* Stuart E. Brown, Jr., Chesapeake Book Company, Berryville, Virginia (1965).

Black - *Black's Law Dictionary,* Henry Campbell Black, West Publishing Co., St. Paul, Minnesota (1968).

Boone - *Daniel Boone,* John Mack Faragher, Henry Holt and Company Inc., New York (1992).

Braddock - *Braddock at the Monongahela,* Paul E. Kopperman, University of Pittsburgh Press, Pittsburgh and London (1977). [This tome includes a full transcript of Francis Peyton's eyewitness account of the battle.]

Browne - "With Braddock's Army; Mrs. Browne's Diary in Virginia and Maryland," Fairfax Harrison, *The Virginia Magazine of History and Biography,* Vol. XXXII, No. 4, Richmond, Virginia (1924).

C & O - *The Chesapeake & Ohio Canal: Pathway to the Nation's Capital,* Thomas F. Hahn, Scarecrow Press, Inc., Metuchen, N.J. (1984).

Calendar - *Calendar of Virginia State Papers,* edited by H.W. Flournoy, Richmond, Virginia (1890).

Cameron - *Cameron Parish in Colonial Virginia,* Margaret Lail Hopkins, Lynchburg, Virginia (1988).

Cartography - *The Cartography of Northern Virginia,* Richard W. Stephenson, Fairfax County Office of Comprehensive Planning, Fairfax, Virginia (revised second printing, 1983).

Church - *The Colonial Church in Virginia,* Rev. Edward Lewis Goodwin, Morehouse Publishing Co., Milwaukee, Wisconsin (1924).

Colport - *Colchester, Colonial Port on the Potomac,* Edith Moore Sprouse, Fairfax Board of Supervisors, Fairfax, Virginia (1975).

ColVa - *Colonial Virginia,* Richard L. Morton, 2 vols., University of North Carolina Press, Chapel Hill, North Carolina (1960).

Council - *Executive Journals, Council of Colonial Virginia,* Wilmer L. Hall, editor, Virginia State Library, Richmond, Virginia (1945).

Courthouse - "A History of Loudoun County Courthouses," C. O. Vandevanter, *The Loudoun-Fauquier Magazine,* Vol. 3, # 1, pp. 7-8 (winter, 1931).

Cresswell - *The Journal of Nicholas Cresswell, 1774-1777,* Nicholas Cresswell, The Dial Press, New York, New York (1924).

Customs - *Colonial Virginia; Its People and Customs,* Mary Newton Stanard, J.B. Lippincott Company, Philadelphia, Pennsylvania (1917).

DALD - *Deed Abstracts of Loudoun County, 1757-1789,* Ruth and Sam Sparacio, The Antient Press, McLean, Virginia (1986-90).

Democracy - *Virginia 1705-1786; Democracy or Aristocracy?,* Robert E. and B. Katherine Brown, Michigan State University Press, East Lansing (1964).

Fairfax - *Fairfax County, Virginia, A History,* Nan Netherton, Donald Sweig, Janice Artemel, Patricia Hickin and Patrick Reed, published by Fairfax County Board of Supervisors, Fairfax, Virginia (1978).

Fauquier Papers - *The Official Papers of Francis Fauquier,* in three volumes edited by George Reese, The University Press of Virginia, Charlottesville (1980).

Ferry - "A Phantom Ferry," by C.B. Rose, Jr., *The Arlington Historical Magazine,* Vol. 5, No. 4, pp. 39-45, Arlington Historical Society, Arlington, Virginia (October 1976).

Frontier - *From Frontier To Suburbia,* Charles Preston Poland, Jr., Walsworth Publishing Company, Marceline, Missouri (1976).

FXCOCO; FXCODB; FXCOWIL - Fairfax County Court Order Books; Deed Books; Will Books; Archives, Fairfax Courthouse, Fairfax, Virginia (MS).

FXCOSUR - Fairfax County Court Surveys, Archives, Fairfax Courthouse, Fairfax, Virginia (MS).

Grants - *The Land Grant Books of the Proprietor of the Northern Neck (1692-1780),* [microfiche series] Virginia State Library, Richmond, Virginia (1954).

GW Papers - *The Papers of George Washington,* W. W. Abbot, editor, University Press of Virginia, Charlottesville, Virginia (1983-88).

GW Writings - *The Writings of George Washington,* ed. John C. Fitzpatrick, (39 vols.) vol. 2, 1757-1769, U.S. Govt. Printing Office, Washington, D.C. (1931).

HDC - Hambleton Document Collection, the private collection of Robert Hambleton of Springfield, Virginia. Some original warrants and writs issued between 1757 and 1760 by Charles Binns, first Loudoun County Clerk (MS).

Hening - *Hening's Statutes [of Virginia] at Large,* ed. William Waller Hening, 13 vols. (1820), reprinted for the Jamestown Foundation, University of Virginia Press, Charlottesville, Virginia (1969).

Heritage - *Northern Virginia Heritage,* Eleanor Lee Templeman and Nan Netherton, Arlington, Virginia (1966).

Home - *Virginians at Home; Family Life in the Eighteenth Century,* Edmund S. Morgan, The William Byrd Press of Colonial Williamsburg, Williamsburg, Virginia (3rd printing, 1962).

Hornbook - *A Hornbook of Virginia History,* Virginia State Library, edited by Emily J. Salmon, Richmond, Virginia (1983).

Independence - *The War of American Independence,* Don Higginbotham, The Easton Press, Norwalk, Connecticut (Collector's Edition, 1993).

Indian - *The Conspiracy of Pontiac and the Indian War,* Francis Parkman, The Library of America, New York, New York (sixth reprint, 1991).

Jamestown - *Jamestown, 1544-1699,* Carl Bridenbaugh, Oxford University Press, New York and Oxford (1980).

Justice - *Justice in Colonial Virginia,* Oliver Perry Chitwood, John Hopkins Press, Baltimore, Maryland (1905).

Land - *Land Records of Long Standing, Fairfax County Virginia (1742-1770),* Sam and Ruth Sparacio, The Antient Press, McLean, Virginia (1988).

Landmarks - *Landmarks of Old Prince William,* Fairfax Harrison, Prince William County Historical Commission, Gateway Press, Inc., Baltimore, Maryland (reprint, 1987).

LDCH - *Loudoun County Chancery Suits, 1754-1874,* compiled by P.L. Preston and Louisa Hutchison, Leesburg, Virginia (1982).

LDCOCO; LDCODB; LDCOWIL - Loudoun County Court Order Books; Deed Books; Will Books; Archives, Loudoun County Courthouse, Leesburg, Virginia (MS).

LDTX/# - *Tithables, Loudoun County Virginia, 1758-1781,* in series, [identified by #], Ruth & Sam Sparacio, The Antient Press, McLean, Virginia (1991).

Lee - *Lee of Virginia,* Edmund Jennings Lee, M.D., Philadelphia (1895), reprinted by Genealogical Publishing Co., Inc., Baltimore, Maryland (1983).

Legends - *Legends of Loudoun,* Harrison Williams, Garrett and Massie, Incorporated, Richmond, Virginia (1938).

Letterbook - *The Letter Book of James Abercromby; Colonial Agent 1751-1773,* John C. VanHorne and George Reese, editors, Virginia State Library and Archives, Richmond, Virginia (1991).

Lord Loudoun - "Campbell, John, fourth Earl of Loudoun," *Dictionary of [British] National Biography,* eds. Leslie Stephen and Sidney Lee, vol. 8, London (1885-1903). [Library of Congress]

Maps - *A Description of the Country, Virginia's Cartographers and Their Maps, 1607-1881,* E.M. Sanchez-Saavedra, Virginia State Library, Richmond (1975).

MdGaz. - *Maryland Gazette,* (1727-) Annapolis, Maryland. A colonial newspaper published by Green and Rind, 1757-1766.

Middleburg - *The History of Middleburg and Vicinity,* Eugene M. Scheel, Piedmont Press, Warrenton, Virginia (1987).

Mills - "Loudoun County Water Mills," Helen Hirst Marsh, manuscript series, Thomas Balch Library, Leesburg, Virginia (1950-1973).

MRLD - *Marriages of Loudoun County, Virginia, 1757-1853,* Mary Alice Wertz, Genealogy Pub. Co. Inc., Baltimore, Maryland (1985).

MRLD1 - *Loudoun County Virginia Marriage Records to 1891,* compiled by Aurelia M. Jewell, Virginia Book Company, Berryville, Virginia (1975).

NorNeck - *Virginia, Northern Neck Land Grants, (1694-1770),* [abstracts], Gertrude E. Gray, Genealogical Publishing Company, Inc., Baltimore (1987).

NorNeck WS - *Abstracts of Northern Neck Warrants & Surveys, 1710-1780, Vols. III-IV,* abstracts compiled by Peggy Shomo Joyner, Portsmouth, Virginia (1986).

Patents - Map entitled "Patents and Northern Neck Grants of Fairfax County, Virginia," Fairfax County Office of Comprehensive Planning, Fairfax (1977).

PRWMCOA - "Prince William County, Virginia; Order Book 1759-1761," *The Virginia Genealogist,* Vol. 19, John Frederick Dorman, editor, Washington, D.C.

Proprietary - *The Fairfax Proprietary,* Josiah Look Dickinson, Warren Press, Front Royal, Virginia (1959).

Potomac - *The Potomac,* Frederick Gutheim, Rinehart & Company, Inc., New York, New York (1949).

Radicalism - *The Radicalism of the American Revolution,* Gordon S. Wood, Alfred A. Knopf, New York, New York (1992).

Soldiers - *Virginia's Colonial Soldiers,* Lloyd DeWitt Bockstruck, Genealogical Publishing Co., Inc., Baltimore, Maryland (1988).

Truro - *Minutes of the Vestry, Truro Parish Virginia, 1732-1785,* Pohick Church, Lorton, Virginia (1974).

VaGaz. - *Virginia Gazette,* Colonial newspapers, Williamsburg, Virginia. Published by several colonial publishers: /H - Hunter; /P - Purdie; /PD - Purdie & Dixon; /Ri - Rind; /R - Royle.

Virginia - *Virginia; A Bicentennial History,* Louis D. Rubin, Jr., W. W. Norton & Company, Inc., New York, New York (1977).

WAFX - *Abstracts of Wills & Inventories, Fairfax County, Virginia, 1742-1801,* J. Estelle Stewart King, Genealogical Publishing Company, Inc., Baltimore (1983).

WALD - *Abstracts of Wills and Administrations in Loudoun County, 1757-1793,* abstracted and published by Ruth and Sam Sparacio, McLean, (1988-1990).

WAPRWM - *Prince William County, Virginia Will Book C, 1734-1744,* abstracted and compiled by John Frederick Dorman, Washington, D.C. (1956).

Waters - *Legal Rights in Potomac Waters,* edited by Garrett Power, Interstate Commission on the Potomac River Basin, Bethesda, Maryland (1976).

White Oak - *Beginning at a White Oak ...,* Beth Mitchell, McGregor and Werner, Fairfax, Virginia (1977).

Colonial and Virginia History, Generally:

Bailyn, Bernard, *The Peopling of British North America; An Introduction,* Alfred A. Knopf, New York (1986).

Bailyn, Bernard, *Voyagers to the West; A Passage in the Peopling of America on the Eve of the Revolution,* Alfred A. Knopf, New York (1986).

Ballach, James Curtis, *White Servitude in the Colony of Virginia,* Baltimore, Maryland (1895).

Boogher, William Fletcher, *Gleanings of Virginia History,* Genealogical Publishing Co. Inc., Baltimore, Maryland (1976).

Brock, R.A., editor, *The Official Records of Robert Dinwiddie,* Virginia Historical Society, Richmond (1884).

Churchill, Sir Winston S., *A History of the English Speaking Peoples,* Dorset Press, New York (1956, reprinted 1990).

Dabney, Virginius, *Virginia, The New Dominion,* Doubleday & Company Inc., Garden City, New York (1971).

Egerton, Douglas R., *Gabriel's Rebellion; The Virginia Slave Conspiracies of 1800 & 1802,* The University of North Carolina Press, Chapel Hill, N.C. (1993).

Ferguson, E. James, "Currency Finance: Interpretation of Colonial Monetary Practices," *William & Mary Quarterly,* 3d ser./no. 10 (1953).

Fischer, David Hackett, *Albion's Seed; Four British Folkways in America,* Oxford University Press, New York (1989).

Hiden, Martha W., *How Justice Grew,* The University Press of Virginia, Charlottesville, Virginia (1957).

Hutson, James H., *Pennsylvania Politics, 1746-1770; The Movement for Royal Government and Its Consequences,* Princeton University Press, Princeton (1972).

Isaac, Rhys, *The Transformation of Virginia, 1740-1790,* University of North Carolina Press, Chapel Hill, N.C. (1982). [An Australian writer's skewed interpretation of the American experience.]

Johnston, F., compiler, *Memorials of Old Virginia Clerks,* J.P. Bell Company, Lynchburg, Virginia (1888).

Jones, Rev. Hugh, *The Present State of Virginia,* (1724), reprinted by the Virginia Historical Society, Williamsburg (1956).

Malone, Dumas and Thomas, William H.B., *A Miracle of Virginia,* Charlottesville, Virginia (1984).

Osgood, Herbert L., *The American Colonies in the Eighteenth Century,* 4 vols. (1924), reprinted by Peter Smith, Gloucester, Mass. (1958).

Robinson, W. Stitt, Jr., *Mother Earth - Land Grants in Virginia, 1607-1699,* The University Press of Virginia, Charlottesville, Virginia.

Smith, Capt. John, *The Generall Historie of Virginia, New-England, and the Summer Isles,* printed by I.D. and I.H. for Michael Sparkes, London (1624); facsimile reprinted by University Microfilms, Inc., Ann Arbor, Michigan (1966).

Wertenbaker, Thomas J., *The Shaping of Colonial Virginia,* Russell & Russell, New York (1958).

<u>Lord Fairfax's Northern Neck Proprietary:</u>

Conner, E.R., III, *Water Milling on Catharpin Run, Prince William County, Virginia,* Virginia Book Company, Berryville, Virginia.

Green, Rev. Charles, Fairfax County List of Titheables for 1749, MS.

Harrison, Fairfax, "Proprietors of the Northern Neck," *Virginia Magazine of History and Biography,* Vol. 33, No. 2, et.seq. (1925).

Head, James W., *History and Comprehensive Description of Loudoun County, Virginia,* (1908), reprint, Clearfield Company, Inc., Baltimore, Maryland (1989).

Jones, Ray, *Harpers Ferry,* Pelican Publishing Co., Gretna, Louisiana (1992).

Kilmer, Kenton, and Sweig, Donald, *The Fairfax Family in Fairfax County,* Fairfax, Virginia (1975).

Netherton, Nan, *The Story of Theodore Roosevelt Island,* MS, unpublished draft for the National Park Service (March 1980). [Copy on deposit at the Virginiana Room, Central Library, Arlington County Virginia].

Nichols, Joseph V., *Legends of Loudoun Valley,* Potomac Press, Leesburg, Virginia (1961).

Virginia W.P.A. Writer's Program, *Prince William; The Story of Its People and Its Places,* American Guide Series (1941).

"Report of Col. A.W. McDonald Relative to Boundary Lines," *Virginia Senate Journal,* Special Session (1861). [MS - VSL, Richmond, # J87/V7/1861b].

Colonial Wars, Military Affairs and Empire Building:

Abernethy, Thomas P., *Western Lands and the American Revolution,* (1937) reprinted by Russell and Russell, New York, New York (1959).

Baker-Crothers, Hayes, *Virginia and the French and Indian War,* University of Chicago Press, Chicago (1928).

Bond, Beverly W., Jr., editor, "The Captivity of Charles Stuart, 1755-1757," *Mississippi Valley Historical Review,* No. 13 (1926-27).

Fitzpatrick, John C., editor, *The Diaries of George Washington, 1748-1794,* Houghton Mifflin Co., Boston (1925).

Jennings, Francis, *Empire of Fortune; Crowns, Colonies & Tribes in the Seven Years War in America,* W.W. Norton & Company, Inc., New York (1988).

Kegley, F.B., *Kegley's Virginia Frontier,* The Southwest Virginia Historical Society, Roanoke, Virginia (1938).

Knollenberg, Bernhard, *Origins of the American Revolution: 1759-1766,* (1960), revised edition, Collier Books, New York (1961).

Lord, Walter, *The Dawn's Early Light,* W. W. Norton & Company, Inc., New York (1972).

Lowry, H. Graham, *How the Nation was Won; America's Untold Story, 1630-1754,* Executive Intelligence Review, Washington, D.C. (1987).

McCardell, Lee, *Ill-Starred General: Braddock of the Coldstream Guards,* (1958) University of Pittsburgh Press, Pittsburgh (1986).

Pargellis, Stanley McCrory, *Lord Loudoun in North America,* Yale University Press, New Haven (1933) reprinted by Archon Books, Hamden, Conn. (1968).

Pargellis, Stanley, editor, *Military Affairs in North America, 1748-1765; Selected Documents from the Cumberland Papers in Windsor Castle,* (1936) reprinted by Archon Books, Hamden, Conn. (1969).

Peckham, Howard H., *The Colonial Wars, 1689-1762,* The University of Chicago Press, Chicago and London (1964).

Rutman, Darrett B., "A Militant New World, 1607-40: America's First Generation, Its Martial Spirit, Its Tradition of Arms, Its Militia Organization, Its Wars," Ph.D. diss., Univ. of Virginia (1959).

Shy, John W., "A New Look at Colonial Militia," *Wm. and Mary Qtrly.,* 3d series/number 20, (1963).

Sydnor, Charles S., *American Revolutionaries in the Making,* The Free Press, New York (1952).

VanDevanter, Willis, *The Virginia Soldiers' Claim to Western Lands Adjacent to Fort Pitt,* printed privately at Spiral Press, New York (1966).

Washington, George, *The Journal of Major George Washington,* (1754), reprinted by Colonial Williamsburg Foundation, Williamsburg, Virginia (1959).

Wedgwood, C.V., *The King's War; 1641-1647,* (1958) reprinted by Book of the Month Club, New York (1991).

Manuscripts, The Loudoun Papers, Huntington Library, San Marino, California.

"Some Accounts of the Encroachments made by the French on the British Settlements in America," *The Gentleman's Magazine,* Number 24, (July 1754).

History of the British Isles, Generally:

Blaikie, Walter Biggar, editor, *Origins of the 'Forty-Five,* T. and A. Constable, Edinburgh, Scotland (1916).

Colley, Linda, *Britons,* Yale University Press, New Haven (1992).

Daiches, David, *The Last Stuart: The Life and Times of Bonnie Prince Charlie,* G.P. Putnam's Sons, New York (1973).

Douglas, David C., *William the Conqueror: The Norman Impact Upon England,* The University of California Press, Berkeley, California (1964).

Lenman, Bruce, *The Jacobite Risings in Britain, 1689-1746,* Eyre Methuen, London (1980).

Mattingly, Garrett, *The Armada,* Houghton Mifflin Company, Boston (1959).

Philip, James, *The Grameid,* (1691), ed. Alexander D. Murdoch, Scottish History Society, Edinburgh, Scotland (1888). [Library of Congress]

Skene, William F., *Celtic Scotland,* (1876) reprinted by Select Bibliographer Reprints, Ayer, Scotland. [Library of Congress #72-153002]

Stewart, John H. I., and Stewart, Lt. Col. Duncan, *The Stewarts of Appin,* Machlachlan & Stewart, Edinburgh, Scotland (1880).

Woodcock, Thomas, and Robinson, John Martin, *The Oxford Guide to Heraldry,* Oxford University Press, New York (1988).

INDEX OF NAMES

Index of Places and Subjects